A History of American Foreign Policy

THIRD EDITION

Volume I: Growth to World Power (1700–1914)

A History of
American
Foreign Policy

THIRD EDITION

Volume I

Growth to World Power (1700–1914)

ALEXANDER DECONDE

University of California, Santa Barbara

CHARLES SCRIBNER'S SONS / NEW YORK

Copyright © 1978, 1971, 1963 Charles Scribner's Sons

Library of Congress Cataloging in Publication Data

DeConde, Alexander.
A history of American foreign policy.

Includes bibliographical references and index.
CONTENTS: v. 1. Growth to world power.
1. United States—Foreign relations. I. Title.
E183.7.D4 1978   327.73   78-7264
ISBN 0-684-15219-7
ISBN 0-684-15280-0 pbk.

The eight lines from "The White Man's Burden" by Rudyard Kipling on p. 352 are from
The Five Nations and are reprinted with the permission of Mrs. George Bambridge, the Mac-
millan Company of Canada Ltd., and Messrs. Methuen & Co. Ltd.

The eight lines quoted from "An Ode in Time of Hesitation" on p. 354 and the two lines
from "The Quarry" on p. 365 are from *Selected Poems of William Vaughn Moody* edited by
Robert M. Lovett and are reprinted with the permission of Houghton Mifflin Company.

1 3 5 7 9 11 13 15 17 19 V/C 20 18 16 14 12 10 8 6 4 2

PRINTED IN THE UNITED STATES OF AMERICA

Maps from first edition by Edward A. Schmitz

Maps from second edition by Robert Sugar

CONTENTS

MAPS

PREFACE

In this book I attempt a coherent introduction to the history of American foreign policy that accurately embodies latest scholarship. I strive for analysis within factual development. Where pertinent I include references to political, economic, social, and cultural developments which influenced the shaping of policy. In brief, I attempt to explain how and why foreign policy developed as it did and arrived where it is. I analyze main forces and ideas that shaped policy and trace their courses. Even though at times analysis may be detailed, emphasis is on broad policy. I have not hesitated to advance interpretations in the light of my own ideas, and I hope I have done so judiciously.

Max Beloff, the British historian, in the conclusion of his book *Foreign Policy and the Democratic Process,* said that "an historian of foreign policy who merely writes down what everyone knows and is agreed upon, and differentiates himself from the ordinary practical man only by the number and complexity of his footnotes, performs quite inadequately the function for which society supports him." Since I agree with those sentiments, explanation for my notes are in order. I use notes primarily to acknowledge sources of most quotations. The supplementary reading lists for each chapter serve as bibliographic guides for those who may wish a fuller exploration of topics discussed.

Like others who have written historical syntheses, I have built on the writings of many scholars. I am pleased, through the notes and bibliography, to acknowledge my debt to some of them. To others whose names do not appear and to those who have helped in this project in more personal ways, I offer gratitude and thanks.

Alexander DeConde

University of California
Santa Barbara

I

Theory and Practice

Although scholars differ over the implications of national self-interest, most agree that the United States conducts its affairs with other nations to serve its own interests. The means it uses to advance those interests constitute its foreign policy. Since self-interest motivates the policies of all nations, the general objectives of American foreign policy do not differ markedly from those of other countries. Various national interests are often in conflict. We cannot, therefore, consider American policy apart from the foreign policies of other nations.

The interaction of those foreign policies of sovereign, or independent, states comprises the realm of international relations. To regulate international relations, to lessen conflicts between competing foreign policies, and to limit the actions of individual states, most nations recognize a body of vague rules, frequently ineffective, called international law. In concept and practice international law is European in origin. Its philosophy and principles are generally alien to the cultural traditions of non-Western societies, as in Asia, the Middle East, and Africa. Despite its Western bias and various weaknesses, international law forms the basis of modern world order. Without it even the simplest diplomacy, such as negotiations between states, would be arduous.

From its birth the United States, as a product of Western culture, accepted international law in the conduct of its foreign relations. Yet on its own, or through reliance in international law, it could not achieve the immediate goals it had set for itself in world politics. As it grew in size and strength, it acquired not only the capability of attaining the objectives of its foreign policy but also power to influence the foreign policies of other nations, particularly weaker ones. This pattern of growth illustrates a reality of international relations—that the policies of the great powers take precedence over those of the lesser nations, and that power usually determines relations between states. As a result, scholars have traditionally viewed international politics as a struggle for power.

All strong nations have been conscious of their power and have dominated weaker countries. Although it has differed from other great nations, from Russia for example, in the exercise of power, the United States has not been an exception to that general rule. It acquired three-quarters of its territory through use of power in one form or another.

The use the United States has made of power and the motives behind that use have led scholars to speculate on what the basic philosophy of American foreign policy has been and should be. Most recognize that isolationism, essentially abstention from the international politics of Europe, was never absolute, even during the nineteenth century when it had general acceptance as a motivating force in foreign policy. Although much speculation has dealt with isolationism, scholars have also had to contend with opposing theories of idealism and realism. Supporters of both theories usually agreed that in comparison with that of most other nations, the diplomacy of the United States has been marked by streaks of moralism. Beyond this there is disagreement.

Idealist philosophy deprecates power politics as evil. It holds that international struggles have centered in clashes between incompatible ideals and principles, not in rivalries for power and influence. Its adherents seek, among other goals, enduring peace, justice between and among nations, advancement of the welfare of all mankind, and cooperation in international organizations to eliminate war and power politics.

Realism, on the other hand, accepts power politics, or some form of strife between nations, as normal in international relations. Realists maintain that in all social groups, whether in nations or small communities, the struggle for power never ceases. Since rivalries between nations, unlike those within communities, are not controlled by effective law, the task of diplomacy, they argue, is to limit struggles for power. They also perceive the aim of foreign policy as the pursuit of new balances of power. Rough equilibriums may be achieved through compromise and adjustment based on recognition by rival nations that an equilibrium exists.

Theorists realize, however, that national leaders cannot formulate foreign policy solely in terms of power, as if they were playing a game. Domestic politics, ethnic pressures, economic forces, ideology, religious and racial emotions may carry as much weight in the making of foreign policy as does power politics. No other great nation has been more influenced by popular ideas, moods, issues in domestic politics, sectional sentiments, and ethnicity in the conduct of its foreign policy than has the United States. The most important reason for this appears to be the theory of democratic government wherein broad foreign policy, like sovereignty, comes from the people even though the actual conduct of policy is in the hands of an elite. Another reason for the pervasiveness of ethnic influence is the immigrant and racial origins of the American people. Even the ruling elite that shapes policy represents, or has until recently, an ethnic influence. It has been white, mainly British or northern European in origins, and Protestant. This contradiction between policy rooted in the will of the people and conducted, or manipulated, by an elitist establishment may account for the lack of a generally accepted theory that offers a key to understanding the history of American foreign policy.

The Constitution and the President

The men who drafted the Constitution, now the oldest written governmental charter in the world, were steeped in political theory, national and international. They were also practical men who understood the realities of foreign policy. They sought to build a secure and prosperous nation with a national government that exercised full authority over foreign affairs. While they wanted that government to speak for the whole nation and use the strength of all the people in dealing with other nations, they were also elitists who placed the management of foreign policy in the hands of a few indirectly elected and appointed officials.

Among the powers the Constitution specifically assigns to the federal government, as the instrument of all the people, are the negotiation of treaties, the right to declare war, and the authority to appoint and receive ambassadors and to regulate foreign commerce. It expressly prohibits the states from entering "any treaty, alliance, or confederation" or from making "any agreement or compact" with a foreign power.

On other questions concerning foreign relations the Constitution is vague. It does not, for example, say that the national government has broader authority over foreign than over domestic affairs. The courts, however, have ruled that the federal government does have a greater control over foreign relations. Their decisions on this and related points have become part of the constitutional foundation that supports the conduct of foreign policy.

Under the Constitution the president has assumed primacy in the conduct of foreign policy. He has attained greater power over foreign than over domestic affairs, and has made the formulation and conduct of foreign policy the most important part of his job. The Constitution, however, is mute as to the extent of the president's power over foreign relations. Nonetheless, even though the authority granted the president has been only slightly modified since the framing of the Constitution in 1787, his power over foreign policy, as the nation has grown, has steadily increased.

In 1835 the perceptive French writer Alexis de Tocqueville in his classic study *Democracy in America* foresaw the growth of presidential power based on its original constitutional source. "It is generally in its relations with foreign powers," he said, "that the executive power of a nation has a chance to display skill and strength." In foreign affairs, de Tocqueville wrote, the president "possesses almost royal prerogatives."[1] At times, when the president extended those prerogatives into uncharted areas, the Supreme Court reviewed his actions. Generally, the Court upheld the doctrine of the strong executive in foreign affairs.

The effectiveness with which the president employs his constitutional powers in foreign policy depends on many factors, particularly on his own interpretation of prerogatives. Frequently, the power he exerts through politics and public opinion has a greater influence on the course of policy than do his constitutionally derived powers. Practice, precedent, and court decisions, more than the Constitution, have given the president predominance in the conduct of foreign policy.

After the Second World War presidents expanded this predominance more boldly than in the past, taking upon themselves full authority to send troops abroad and to wage war without express constitutional sanction by Congress. Lyndon B. Johnson and Richard M. Nixon claimed that with or without congressional support they had the right to take whatever measures they deemed necessary to carry out foreign policy. Scholars and others disputed this claim, maintaining that without constitutional foundation "presidential primacy . . . has turned into presidential supremacy. The constitutional presidency has become the imperial presidency," mainly through enhancement of power in foreign affairs.[2] Finally, in November 1973, Congress passed legislation, over the president's veto, designed to limit, but not curb, presidential war-making power.

Congress

This slight effort to restrain the imperial executive, stemming from abuses of power during the Vietnam War, reflects constitutional theory that the president shares his power over foreign affairs with Congress. This division, which is neither equal nor clear, has produced conflict between the executive and legislative branches in the conduct of foreign relations, a rivalry inherent in the American system of checks and balances. Thus, the separation of powers tends in foreign affairs to emphasize competition. It has at times, as in the case of Woodrow Wilson's fight with the Senate over the League of Nations in 1919 and the presidential waging of war in Vietnam, been a barrier to cooperation.

Congress, notably the Senate, has never fully accepted the role of subordinate partner to the president in the conduct of foreign policy, though it has been that most of the time. Even so, its part in the making of foreign policy has frequently been significant. The Senate's role in particular has at times been decisive: it can reject a treaty or refuse to approve a diplomatic appointment. But Congress as a whole does not possess the authority to initiate and carry through foreign policy. Most of Congress's authority in foreign affairs, except for its power to declare war, is negative. Even that power may be severely restricted by the president's actions, as in the Korean and Vietnam wars.

Since Wilson's time, when it suited their purposes, presidents have been sensitive to the power of Congress and its desire to participate in the making of foreign policy. Harry S. Truman, for example, tried to include Congress in the formulating of major policies. In seeking its cooperation, the president, or his secretary of state, usually has to work through committees, for the committee system forms the core of congressional procedure. The standing committees responsible for matters pertaining to foreign affairs are among the most important in both houses and normally determine congressional reaction to policy.

Until the end of the Second World War, when foreign economic aid became an important part of foreign policy, the Foreign Affairs Committee of the House of Representatives had been relatively unimportant. Since that time its influence has expanded. The House committee, however, is overshadowed by the Senate Committee on Foreign Relations, one of the most powerful committees in the government. This committee has generally regarded itself as a virtually independent guardian of foreign policy. Its senior members, ordinarily men of considerable political stature who have served in Congress much longer than the president has held office, usually concede little to the president or his secretary of state. They seldom merely approve presidential policies. Ordinarily, they assess each policy, each problem, from their own point of view. If their viewpoint differs from that of the president, as in the case of the neutrality legislation of the 1930s and the Vietnam War in the 1960s, they believe that they and the president, as partners, should compromise.

Chairmanship of the Senate committee probably carries more prestige than any other position in Congress. Under the tradition of seniority, men attain that post only after years of service. The president, therefore, seldom directly influences the selection of committee chairmen. So powerful have some chairmen been, such as Henry Cabot Lodge of Massachusetts and William E. Borah of Idaho, that they have considered themselves *de facto* secretaries of state. This power of the chairman, in addition to the general independence of the committee, has been the source of friction between the executive branch and the committee, even when the same political party has controlled both Congress and the presidency. Astute presidents have often managed to neutralize chairmen they could not remove or influence. Congress seldom retaliated. It is usually reluctant to use its ultimate power, that of the purse, in confrontations with presidents.

The Department of State

One of the significant reasons for the weakness of Congress in the making of foreign policy is that the executive branch controls the machinery that carries out policy. The president is most directly responsible to the people for the conduct of foreign policy. He decides what methods to use—ordinarily the essentials of diplomacy, negotiation and compromise.

Although some presidents, such as Franklin D. Roosevelt and John F. Kennedy, distrusted the Department of State, carried on independent high-level diplomacy, and often bypassed the department in making major decisions, under the president it is the main agency charged by law with the formation and conduct of foreign policy. It normally advises the president on matters of policy and directs official relations with other countries. When George Washington persuaded Thomas Jefferson to become the nation's first secretary of state, he said that the Department of State "involves many of the most interesting objects of the Executive Authority."[3] That observation is still true.

At the head of the State Department stands what is generally recognized as the nation's highest nonelected official, the secretary of state. Appointed by the president with the Senate's approval, the secretary of state is the ranking member of the cabinet and customarily serves as the president's chief adviser in matters of foreign policy. Under the president, the secretary is responsible for the work, the policies, and the administration of the Department of State.

All the secretary's important powers, and hence those of his department, derive from the president. The power and importance of the secretary of state, therefore, depend on his relations with the president. Strong presidents dominate the conduct of foreign policy; some have treated their secretaries of state virtually as figureheads. In the case of James K. Polk and Secretary of State James Buchanan, one contemporary observer remarked that "Buchanan is treated as no gentleman would treat a sensible hireling."[4] Other presidents, such as Warren G. Harding and Dwight D. Eisenhower, have relied heavily on their secretaries of state for the conduct of foreign policy and delegated vast powers to them.

Some secretaries, on the other hand, have considered themselves almost prime ministers. William H. Seward, for instance, told friends that Abraham Lincoln wanted him for his "prime minister." When he accepted the post, Seward told his wife, "It is inevitable. I will try to save freedom and my country."[5]

Most secretaries of state have come from the higher ranks of professional and political life. Often they knew little of world affairs or diplomacy before taking office. Many have been political appointees—men who held high status in the party controlling the executive branch, or who had lost out in the scramble for the presidency and received the secretaryship as a consolation prize. This was true of Seward and also of James G. Blaine and William Jennings Bryan.

In the decades following the Second World War the office of secretary of state has fluctuated in stature. Most of the men who have held it have been experienced in world affairs, though not professional diplomats. When former secretary John Foster Dulles died in May 1959, peoples throughout the world looked upon the secretary of state as the official spokesman for American foreign policy. This status changed under John F. Kennedy and especially in the first administration of Richard M. Nixon. Then Henry A. Kissinger, as assistant to the president for national security affairs, exerted more influence on the making of foreign policy than did Secretary of State William P. Rogers.

To aid the secretary of state in carrying out policy, the United States maintains diplomatic and consular establishments abroad. At the head of its diplomatic posts, known collectively as *diplomatic mission* or *foreign mission,* it has ministers and ambassadors, diplomats who are appointed by the president, with the approval of the Senate, to serve at his pleasure. Ministers rank below ambassadors, but both, as chiefs of mission, are stationed in the capitals of foreign countries. The offices, residences, and staffs of ministers are called legations, and those of ambassadors are known as embassies. Unless a country is under American military government, the chief of mission assigned to it is responsible for all American officials within its borders. The United States exchanges ministers or ambassadors with all independent foreign countries with whom it maintains diplomatic relations and normally deals with foreign governments through them. Until 1893 the highest ranking American diplomatic official was the minister, but now most chiefs of mission are ambassadors.

In important cities throughout the world, primarily seaports, commercial and communication centers, the United States maintains consulates general, consulates, and lesser consular offices, all of them known collectively as *consular station.* Among other important duties, officers at the head of the consular posts are responsible for the commercial and travel interests of the United States and for American citizens, particularly seamen, in their areas. Although consular officers come under the general jurisdiction of the chief of mission in the country in which they serve, the United States normally maintains a supervising consul-general in each major foreign country to coordinate the functions of consular officers stationed there.

The diplomatic missions and consular stations are staffed by members of a professional corps called the foreign service. Formerly, the diplomatic and consular services were separate and most of their posts went to inexperienced political appointees. Not until the demands of the First World War had exposed a need for trained diplomats did the United States consider seriously a professional diplomatic service.

Ultimately, with the Rogers Act of 1924, Congress consolidated diplomatic and consular personnel and created the foreign service as a career corps. The Foreign Service Act of 1946 strengthened the career concept by giving foreign service officers commissions from the president with consent of the Senate, and statutory protection against political manipulation. In 1954 a commission headed by Henry Wriston, a scholar and educational administrator, brought about integration of Department of State civil service personnel with foreign service officers. This career concept and accompanying insulation against politics did not extend to chiefs of major missions. Those who received ambassadorial appointments in places such as London, Paris, or Rome continued to be political appointees, usually persons of wealth who could afford the costly entertaining and other private expenditures required by the positions. The ordinary foreign service officer who lives on his salary cannot meet the unreimbursed expenses of those posts. He usually can expect to go no higher than chief of mission in a smaller country, counselor, the second ranking post in an embassy, or consul-general.

Ironically, as America's involvement in world affairs spread and deepened and its diplomats became more professionally competent, their influence on policy diminished. They could influence policy only in small ways. Instantaneous communication with policymakers in Washington makes the elite, carefully selected and trained foreign service officer corps an instrument, not a shaper, of policy.

Military, Intelligence, and Other Influences

Numerous other agencies within the executive branch also carry out foreign policy or have a hand in shaping it. Of the major agencies, one of the most important is the military establishment consisting of the Department of Defense and its three service units controlling the army, navy, and air force. All the armed forces have intelligence staffs that send agents abroad to gain information on potential enemies. Many embassies have military, naval, and air *attachés* who gather technical data. Their duties reflect the role of power in a world where war has been a legitimate and ultimate test of a nation's ability to attain international objectives. Military power, regardless of efforts to curb it, remains an essential element of foreign policy.

When a policy decision involves the possibility of war or a military operation, leaders of the armed forces and their civilian superiors ordinarily share in reaching that decision. They assess proposed action for its effect on America's military position and that of her allies, as in the case of Secretary of State Cordell Hull's negotiations with the Japanese in 1941 when military leaders said they were unprepared for war. Since they needed time, they asked President Franklin D. Roosevelt to prolong the talks and to soften policy toward Japan so as to postpone the impending war.

This partnership of foreign and military policy is logical, for both theoretically have the same objective, national security or self-interest. Foreign policy should determine the nation's military needs but frequently does not. Policymakers often gear foreign policy to military calculations, meaning that they take into account the force necessary to carry out a policy if force is necessary. Thus, military power is often a main index of a nation's strength and prestige in international affairs.

Like control of foreign relations, management of the military establishment belongs exclusively to the federal government. Congress maintains the army, navy, and air force and can declare war. Under the Constitution, as commander in chief of the armed forces the president has responsibility for military policy. During the Second World War Franklin D. Roosevelt mixed foreign and military policy and emphasized his military powers. In meshing foreign and military affairs, even though the two had always been close, he departed from tradition. In the past Americans had usually thought of the two as functioning in separate worlds. Not until after the Second World War did Americans come to appreciate their intimate relationship. In creating the National Security Council in 1947, Congress reflected the new awareness of military policy. The president, the secretary of state, and secretary of defense have the most important roles in the agency, but at first it was predominantly military in character.

As established by law, the National Security Council has two basic tasks: to assess foreign policy in the light of the nation's military power, and to advise the president on the integration of domestic, military, and foreign policies as they pertain to national defense. Through it, the president attempts to deal with one of society's most perplexing problems, how to make proper use of the vast military power foreign affairs has come to involve. Many students of foreign policy feel that the performance of the National Security Council, particularly in helping to resolve the power problem, has been disappointing.

The persistence of that problem has given the military establishment enormous influence in shaping foreign policy. The secretary of defense is second only to the secretary of state in helping to formulate such policy; and, as the president's principal military advisers, the Joint Chiefs of Staff of the three armed forces have direct access to him on matters of policy. This spreading military influence, especially as wedded to industry and technology, alarmed President Dwight D. Eisenhower. In his farewell in January 1961 he warned of the "conjunction of an immense military establishment and a large arms industry, new in the American experience." It exercised a "total influence . . . felt in every city, every State house, every office of the Federal government." The nation, he warned, "must guard against the acquisition of unwarranted influence, whether sought or unsought, by the military-industrial complex."[6]

This concern with military power stimulated secrecy in government, for military preparations require information about potential enemies, usually called intelligence, and enhanced the use of espionage and undercover intrigue. To carry on such activities the government built, within the executive branch, intelligence organizations that operated in secret all over the world. The most important of the intelligence organizations in the shaping of foreign policy is the Central Intelligence Agency, created in 1947 as an adjunct of the National Security Council. The CIA coordinates federal espionage activities, or the work of what is known as the intelligence community, and advises the National Security Council on secret matters affecting military and foreign policy.

From the beginning the CIA operated virtually on its own terms, with minimum public exposure and freedom from congressional scrutiny. In 1949 its budget and functions, by law, were held secret. Operating silently and secretly, with a great deal of money, it meddled in the affairs of foreign governments, bribed foreign leaders, launched covert military operations, and spied on American citizens. In effect, it acted as a third force within the executive branch in the making of foreign policy. Its activities, made public only after some scandal or blunder in policy, demonstrated the incongruity between theory and practice. In theory American foreign policy is subject to democratic controls, but in practice it is carried out by an elite establishment that often makes decisions in secret on information obtained secretly.

Public Opinion, Politics, and Pressure Groups

Ironically, while foreign policy was subject to intensified secrecy, military policy found itself exposed to greater publicity than in the past. One reason for this is historic. In the United States important foreign policies have often been debated publicly or have been issues in political contests. Because of the partnership of military and foreign policy this tradition of public participation rubbed off onto the making of military policy. The pervasiveness of this tradition has led some students of foreign affairs, and government officials too, to give considerable weight to the influence of public opinion in the making of foreign policy, a concern seemingly incompatible with the secrecy that also persists.

Scholars disagree in defining public opinion and in evaluating what influence it may have on foreign policy. Some question whether public opinion, however defined, can influence policymakers in any meaningful way. Critics say that in most matters of foreign policy public opinion is obscure or ambiguous. They also argue that the man in the street has little opportunity to influence foreign policy and even less to participate in making it. Moreover, he usually evades whatever slight chance comes his way to exert influence. Yet on large issues public sentiment can make itself felt. As perceived by President William McKinley and his advisers, it influenced events leading to the Spanish-American War. Franklin D. Roosevelt acted with sensitivity to public reactions to his policies, and he also tried to manipulate public sentiment. So have most presidents. When Lyndon B. Johnson and Richard M. Nixon, for example, perceived that public opinion, as during the Vietnam War, ran counter to their own views, they ignored it, tried to neutralize it, or discounted it. The mass media— newspapers, radio, televison, particularly the newspapers—have at times been credited with shaping public opinion. Usually journalists offer the people information, and frequently some interpretation of the news on foreign affairs. They also provide a means for the governing elite to reach the people, and occasionally they serve as instruments of the people by disseminating data essential to those who wish to have a sense of participation in the making of democratic foreign policies

Although valuable in indicating the trend of public sentiment on some matters, public opinion polls are unreliable on complex issues of foreign policy. At best, according to one critic, polls can reveal "the extent of public ignorance and knowledge."[7] Most Americans know much less about foreign policy than they do about domestic affairs. Logically, the truest barometer of public opinion should be the ballot box, but Americans seldom have a chance to vote specifically on foreign policy issues, though foreign policy has been prominent in most national elections since the Second World War. Usually voters have to consider foreign questions within a pattern of domestic concerns. Moreover, policymakers often do not tell the people what they should know to make intelligent choices.

Those in high office have not infrequently found it expedient to deceive the public. They have lied on the theory that the public, in the complicated process of conducting foreign policy, has at times to be deceived for its own good.

Political parties also deceive, and try to manipulate foreign policy issues to gain power or other advantages. The emotional rhetoric of their campaign platforms is intended to exploit those foreign policy concerns that may win votes. In several instances presidents have tried to keep politics out of foreign policy with a program designed to elicit bipartisan support. The periods of successful bipartisanship have been brief. Bipartisanship fails usually because it in effect calls for abandonment of party opposition and criticism inherent in the American democratic system. Bipartisanship, in the long run, defies the principle that domestic political considerations influence foreign policy and may even shape it.

Pressure groups, or people and institutions that seek definite objectives from government, operate on this principle. They attempt to influence foreign policy to further the interests of a particular segment of the population, or sometimes of a foreign power. Pressure groups thrive in America's pluralistic society. In a sense, national interest may be the sum of special interests, such as those of ethnic, religious, racial, labor, economic, and other blocs, promoted by pressure politics. Political parties frequently do the work of pressure groups or cooperate with them to affect foreign policy. For years industries interested in tariff protection, for instance, leaned toward the Republican party, believing that it would give their desires special consideration. Pluralism, or the diversity of American loyalties, makes it difficult for policymakers to differentiate between national and special interests. All know, however, that in the conduct of foreign policy as in the working domestic political system, pressure makes the wheels turn.

The Economic Factor

Some historians, noting that economic interests have spawned particularly powerful pressure groups, argue that capitalism lies at the root of international conflict. They say that war results from the schemes and pressures of capitalists who manipulate foreign policy to assure profit for themselves. These historians, and economists too, insist that economics, more than anything else, motivates foreign policy. In the 1960s and 1970s variations of this economic interpretation aroused considerable academic controversy. A group of historians gained prominence by challenging the conventional wisdom and by attempting to explain the development of American foreign policy in terms of a broad theory based on economics. Instead of viewing policy as essentially a product of international power politics, these theorists depicted it as springing mainly from domestic political struggles shaped by a capitalist economy. According to this theory, American policymakers, as guardians of the nation's commercial interests, sought to resolve chronic problems of overproduction, unemployment, depression, and social tensions with aggressive policies abroad. Using diplomacy, and force if necessary, they searched for markets for American goods and money. In their hands foreign policy functioned as a lever to keep open a door to American enterprise in much of the world.

This open door interpretation has characteristics similar to communist or Marxist theory, according to which mature capitalist economies produce surpluses of commodities, population, and capital. In the international struggle to export those surpluses, war results. Controversy revolves around these theories because most American historians do not accept them as adequate explanations for war or for basic motivation in foreign policy. Most scholars agree, nonetheless, that the economic factor and capitalism, however defined, have consistently been of foremost importance in the development of American foreign policy.

One reason for the prominence of the economic factor is the position of the United States as one of the world's major trading nations. From the beginning notable principles in foreign policy have been promotion and protection of trade, and later, of investment and industry abroad. Memorable phrases that stud the nation's history, such as freedom of the seas, the Open Door, and Dollar Diplomacy, attest to the continuous concern of policymakers over economic matters. The secretary of the treasury, as a result, has usually had considerable influence in the making of foreign policy. Indeed, the first secretary, Alexander Hamilton, had a larger voice in formulating broad policy than did Secretary of State Thomas Jefferson. In recent decades foreign affairs, especially economic and military aid programs, consumed such a large share of the annual budget that the secretary of the treasury and his financial experts had to play key roles in decisions on foreign policy.

Usually the Treasury Department concerns itself primarily with economic foreign policy, meaning the pattern formed by economic objectives abroad and the means used to attain them. Difficulty in discerning whether a given policy is political or economic in intent has led to jurisdictional conflicts within the government, as between Hamilton and Jefferson. Early interest in China, for example, was economic, but as American traders expanded their activities they sought government protection. This involved political action, a function of the Department of State. Some presidents tried to lessen the friction, even eliminate it, by resorting to interdepartmental cooperation in formulating foreign economic policy.

At times, as during the administration of William H. Taft, the State Department has taken the initiative in promoting penetration of foreign markets. Regardless of the motivation of the government, its open, as well as its undercover, economic activity has led to harsh criticism of the United States. Critics have accused the United States of economic imperialism whenever the government supported American traders or investors in foreign ventures.

There is considerable truth in another criticism, that the United States used economic pressure as a diplomatic weapon. Thomas Jefferson did so against Great Britain with an embargo in 1807; Franklin D. Roosevelt did so by freezing trade with Japan in 1941; John Foster Dulles did so against Egypt in 1956 by withdrawing aid for the building of a dam on the Nile River; and Henry A. Kissinger did so in 1976 by threatening to cut off economic aid to Italy if communists gained power in national elections that year. The United States has also used economic pressure to force reluctant friends and allies to support a special part of its foreign policy. In the Battle Act of 1951 Congress threatened to cut off military and economic assistance to any country trading with Communist nations.

America's great internal economic strength, based on its growth from a debtor nation to one with the world's wealthiest economy and largest customer market, made possible such pressure. Shifts in United States economic policy could cause riots in Latin America, misery in Africa and the Middle East, or political crises in Europe. As in the case of the Marshall Plan in 1948, American economic power could save nations from chaos and bring hope and livelihood to millions of people. In the twentieth century the foreign policy establishment often tried to use this power to manipulate the world economy to promote American commercial and industrial interests.

Whatever one's focus—economic interpretation, public opinion, pressure groups, idealism, realism, psychological persuasion, or any other theory of motivation—it is clear that foreign policy is complex. Yet neither its theory nor its practice is wrapped in mystery, for it has left a pattern of ideas, decisions, and deeds. We can understand that pattern through history, or the study of policies toward other nations. We shall see that American foreign policy, regardless of changes in the international environment or in the domestic terrain, has continuity. It comprises a record wherein national interest undergoes constant assessment and policymakers search for security in peace, victory in war, and power at all times. What follows is a history of that search.

II

Colonies to Nation

American diplomatic history has European roots. Originally, Spain and Portugal, by right of discovery, the authority of four Papal Bulls in 1493, and their Treaty of Tordesillas of 1494, claimed exclusive dominion over the New World. They tried to protect that claim by controlling the seas and by keeping other nations from gaining a foothold in the Americas. France, England, and then Holland soon challenged their control by asserting that the seas were open to all. "The sun shines for me as for the others," Francis I of France said in 1541. "I should like to see the clause of Adam's will which excludes me from a share of the world."[1]

Since Portugal did not have the strength to fight off the French and British and in 1580 was conquered by Spain who controlled her empire for sixty years, Spain assumed the task of guarding the Iberian claim to monopoly in the New World. After England defeated the Great Armada in 1588, Spain's power also declined, and she could not keep the other countries out of the Western Hemisphere. France, England, and Holland, all hungry for loot, built up their holdings at the expense of Indians—dispossessed from their homelands—and of Spain. Then England, Holland, and France clashed.

After the three powers had forced Spain to recognize their American colonies in the seventeenth century, England fought two naval wars with Holland. By 1667 she had succeeded in forcing the Dutch out of North America. Then, between 1688 and 1763, England and France fought four great wars, each one of them in part a contest for North America.

In the first three wars France and England followed different strategies. France turned her main efforts toward expansion in Europe, making the gain of colonial lands a secondary goal. England, with the help of one ally or another, met France's challenge in Europe and with her powerful navy acquired new colonies, generally at the expense of France and declining Spain.

In the duel for empire all the maritime powers, but England most successfully, followed principles of mercantilism. According to mercantilist theory, the way to power lay in acquiring colonies. Through a monopoly of her colonists' commerce, a country would try to sell more than she bought and thus would achieve a favorable balance of trade and grow wealthy. Colonial trade, moreover, would nurture sea power, for with both wealth and sea power a nation had two keys to greatness. At the same time, the powers accepted the principle that no one colonial empire should be allowed to become so great as to upset the balance of power in Europe. In practice, therefore, mercantilist theory and the principle of the colonial balance of power were bound to lead to conflict.[2]

Yet for two centuries European statesmen had tried to isolate America from Europe's quarrels and Europe from America's under the doctrine of two spheres. According to that doctrine, America was a separate sphere "beyond the line" of European laws and treaties. In the Treaty of Whitehall of 1686, for example, France and England agreed that even though they should go to war in Europe a "true and firm peace and neutrality shall continue in America" between their colonies. The doctrine never really worked, mainly because the rivalries among the colonists were often as intense as they were in Europe. The foreign policies of the European powers, therefore, ultimately decided whether the colonists would be at peace or war.

Colonial Rivalries

Those colonists, transplanted Europeans who had carried their Old World hates with them, lived on the frontiers of their new lands in fear and insecurity. Englishmen, Frenchmen, and Spaniards in America often detested each other and fought when their mother countries fought, and sometimes when the homelands were at peace. Europe's diplomacy was their diplomacy.

Usually the English colonists in America accepted the bloodshed of the European wars as a matter of course and fought loyally for the mother country, even though they might not have grasped the reasons for those wars. They did, however, understand their own parts in the conflicts and sometimes identified their local interests and welfare with the waging of the wars. Many colonists realized that they were fighting the battles of Europe on American soil.

Even before England and France fought the first of their imperial wars, the English colonists in North America gave evidence of fear in relations with their neighboring European colonists. Four of the northern English colonies, Massachusetts, New Haven, New Plymouth, and Connecticut, in 1643 organized the Confederation of New England, "a firm and perpetual league of friendship and amity for offense and defense, mutual advice and succor upon all just occasions."[3] Concerning itself with local diplomacy and relations with its foreign neighbors, this first federation of colonies in North America assumed the right to make war and treaties and sought security against the French and Dutch settlers and the Indians. It even made a treaty with the French of Nova Scotia at Boston in 1644 and another with the Dutch of New York at Hartford in 1650. After 1665, for internal reasons, the influence of the confederation declined.

The next effort at colonial union, the Dominion of New England of 1686 that brought New York and the New England colonies under one head, originated in England. Although James II and his advisers created the dominion for reasons of administrative control, they also had in mind the growing power of France in North America and defense of their colonies through firmer control. Unpopular with the colonists, the experiment collapsed within three years.

As the dominion expired, what was to be the first imperial conflict between England and France, known as the War of the League of Augsburg, broke out in Europe in 1688. Within a year it spread to America where the colonists called it King William's War. The French and their Indian allies invaded Maine, New Hampshire, and New York and in February 1690 destroyed Schenectady. To counter the French, Jacob Leisler, temporarily at the head of New York's government, in April called all the colonies to a congress. Four of the colonies—Massachusetts, Plymouth, Connecticut, and New York—sent commissioners, who planned a land and sea attack upon Canada. Three other colonies—Rhode Island, Maryland, and Virginia—were not present at the New York congress, but apparently pledged cooperation. Although an expedition of New Englanders in May captured Port Royal in French Acadia, the larger plan of conquest failed. The Treaty of Ryswick in 1697 restored all conquests, so that the first Anglo-French war ended indecisively in America.

The colonists did their own fighting. Neither England nor France contributed much to the American campaigns. By their limited joint action, moreover, the English colonists showed that they were, to a considerable extent, capable of defending themselves and of handling their own relations with hostile foreign neighbors.

Four years later, when Louis XIV of France tried to place his grandson on the Spanish throne, England and France renewed their fighting in the War of the Spanish Succession. Again, within a year, English settlers in North America, who named their part of the conflict Queen Anne's War, were fighting Frenchmen and Spaniards. Again, French and Indian allies swooped across New England's frontier and in 1704 massacred or enslaved the villagers of Deerfield, Massachusetts. Again, to eliminate the French menace, the northern colonies wanted to conquer Canada and asked for British help. The southern colonies, particularly South Carolina, urged an advance against French and Spanish lands west to the Mississippi River.

NORTH AMERICA AFTER THE PEACE OF UTRECHT, 1713

The English colonists, in other words, had objectives of their own and tried to influence Britain's policy in attaining them.

In the Peace of Utrecht of 1713, victorious England forced France to surrender the region around Hudson Bay, as well as Acadia, or Nova Scotia, captured mainly by colonial troops, and Newfoundland. English control of that strategic region later contributed to France's complete defeat in North America. After Utrecht, because of England's overseas expansion, France and Spain drew together in defense of the colonial balance of power then established.

True peace, however, did not prevail in North America. The English and French built fortifications against each other, raided each other's frontier settlements, and negotiated alliances with Indian tribes. That skirmishing led England's advisory body on colonial policy, the Board of Trade, to frame a report, called the "State of British Plantations in America, in 1721," on how to provide better government and security for the colonies. It suggested that by unifying its colonies the British government would be "taking the necessary precautions to prevent the encroachment of the French, or any other European Nation" on English possessions. Although the plan never went into effect, it emphasized the old idea that union was the best way to protect the American colonies against foreign danger.

English expansionists were not satisfied with mere defense; some believed that destiny had marked their colonies for expansion beyond the Allegheny Mountains. Seeking more Spanish territory and concessions in the Americas, the British touched off the War of Jenkins' Ear in 1739. The alleged cause was the hysteria created by the tales of a certain Captain Robert Jenkins who claimed that the Spaniards had lopped off one of his ears and had inflicted other cruelties, but agitation in the English colonies over the boundaries of Florida and Georgia was also a cause.

A year later another general conflict, the War of the Austrian Succession, 1740–1748, broke out in Europe. When France allied herself with Spain in 1743, England declared war on her in the following year. The two wars merged and the result was another world-wide struggle, with an American phase known as King George's War, 1744–1748.

Again colonists in America attacked each other. A large British and colonial expedition in June, 1745, captured the French fortress of Louisbourg on Cape Breton Island, but the general war ended in stalemate. By the Treaty of Aix-la-Chapelle in 1748, Britain, to the disgust of the New Englanders, exchanged Louisbourg for French evacuation of captured territory in the Netherlands. England thus used her colonists' victory to stabilize the political balance in Europe. America's concerns were secondary to the European interests of the mother country.

Peace was a mere interlude, for British and French rivalry in North America never slackened. Each appeared determined to destroy the power of the other. English advances into the Ohio Valley threatened France's control of the continent's interior. The French retaliated by sending military expeditions against English posts in the Ohio country and by building a chain of log forts across the frontier to close off the interior. When a force of Virginia militia under a young lieutenant colonel, George Washington, clashed with the French at the forks of the Ohio River in the summer of 1754, the French and Indian War began.

To unify the English colonies "for their mutual security and Defense against the encroachment of their foreign neighbours," and to win Indian allies, the Board of Trade meanwhile called a general colonial congress to meet in Albany, New York, in June 1754.[4] Seven colonies sent representatives who adopted a plan drafted by Benjamin Franklin for a federal union of the colonies. This Albany Plan of Union would have permitted the colonies to make peace or war, the most important power in foreign relations. Jealous of their individual powers, none of the colonies accepted either the plan or the general recommendations of the congress.

The Albany plan was important as a forerunner of later congresses because it dealt with foreign relations. As in the earlier plans, fear of foreign danger spurred the movement toward union. Once the fighting began, however, the British, who had put aside their own plans for colonial union, sent troops to America. After the French and English had fought for two years in America, the conflict spread to Europe where it became the Seven Years' War, 1756–1763.

Significance of the Seven Years' War

Unlike the other imperial conflicts, the Seven Years' War originated in the colonial rivalries of America. England, France, and Spain viewed it as a struggle to determine who would become master of North America. English colonists, however, perceived it as a national war in which the whole Anglo-American nation was "directly and fundamentally concerned."[5]

In that conflict, because of the importance of the colonial stakes, France reversed her traditional policy of seeking dominance in Europe and instead tried to surpass England in America. Nonetheless, France still wasted her armies in Europe fighting England's Prussian ally while England herself threw her main strength against French possessions overseas. In the war at sea and in America, England crushed France.

By the Treaty of Paris of 1763, France ceded Canada and all of her territory on the North American continent east of the Mississippi River, except for New Orleans, to England. France kept only a few small islands in the Gulf of St. Lawrence and in the Caribbean. Spain surrendered Florida and all her possessions east of the Mississippi to England. A few hours after signing the Treaty of Paris, France gave New Orleans and all her territory

NORTH AMERICA AFTER THE PEACE OF PARIS, 1763

west of the Mississippi, the land called Louisiana, to Spain. France parted with Louisiana ostensibly to compensate Spain for her losses, but in fact to keep it out of England's hands.

Since the Seven Years' War destroyed French power in North America and cleared the way for it to become a continent of English-speaking peoples and contributed to the later independence of the United States, it was one of the world's decisive conflicts. France's defeat freed English colonists from fear of invasion by a powerful enemy on their borders. With Spain on the decline, no power in the Western Hemisphere was now capable of containing the expanding English colonies. This new security fed a growing spirit of independence among the colonists.

Even though the colonial experience shows that America was never truly isolated from Europe's quarrels, some historians have claimed that the colonial era gave birth to certain of the nation's foreign policies that were at one time considered basic, such as nonentanglement and isolationism. This colonial experience ostensibly convinced later leaders that the United States should avoid European entanglements, that America's destiny lay in carving a nation from a continent now shared mainly with Indians and Spaniards.

In the decade preceding the American Revolution, for example, writers in America urged their fellow colonists "to keep clear of the quarrels among other states." In 1770, Benajmin Franklin while in England said that the colonies paid more than their share for imperial defense, "for the sake of continental connections in which they were separately unconcerned."[6]

Six years later, Thomas Paine in his pamphlet *Common Sense* apparently convinced many colonists that the issues of foreign policy vital across the sea were of no immediate concern to them. ". . . any submission to, or dependence on, Great Britain," he wrote, "tends directly to involve this Continent in European wars and quarrels, and set us at variance with nations who would otherwise seek our friendship, and against whom we have neither anger nor complaint. . . . It is the true interest of America to steer clear of European contentions."[7] Thus, with the removal of French antagonists English colonists, who were soon to become Americans, lost their sense of identity with the European policies of English kings.

France Seeks To Regain Power

Having emerged from the Seven Years' War as the world's foremost colonial and maritime power, Great Britain would no longer offer concessions to her colonists, as she had previously done, to assure their support against foreign foes. She attempted, instead, to consolidate her enlarged empire and to strengthen the colonial system she had neglected during the imperial wars. To give relief to taxpayers at home, whose national debt had been doubled by the war, she required her American colonies to share not only the cost of the French war but also the expense of administering Canada and the eastern Mississippi Valley. This assertion of imperial authority, coupled with new taxes, provoked the colonists to unrest and resistance.

Humiliated and eager to recover her former greatness by humbling England, France saw in the colonial unrest the flaw in Britain's empire. Étienne François Duc de Choiseul, the foreign minister under Louis XV, told his king that England "is, and will ever be, the declared enemy of our power and your state," and made the separation of the American colonies from Britain a part of French policy. From 1764 until his retirement six years later, Choiseul sent secret agents to America to foment trouble and to report on dissatisfactions there. His successor in 1774, the resourceful Charles Gravier Comte de Vergennes, who also declared that "England is the natural enemy of France," continued the policy of trying to regain prestige. As the American crisis approached, William Pitt, one of England's greatest sons, warned that France was like a "vulture hovering over the British empire, and hungrily watching the prey that she is only waiting for the right moment to pounce upon." [8]

When an angry Parliament, beginning in March 1774, passed a series of laws known as the Coercive Acts, the crisis came. Those five acts (among them the Boston Port Bill that closed the port to all shipping until the townspeople paid for the English tea they had destroyed a few months earlier, and the Massachusetts Government Act which practically nullified Massachusetts's charter) in one way or another denied colonists rights they had been demanding for over ten years. Those acts led to bloodshed a year later at Lexington and Concord, where Massachusetts farmers fired on British troops and started the American Revolution.

Although delighted by trouble in America, Vergennes moved cautiously, unwilling to intervene until he knew the colonists were determined to fight for independence. For, despite the bloodletting, the colonists still insisted they were defending their rights as Englishmen and sought merely to settle their grievances within the empire. Vergennes wanted to mangle the British empire, not mend it.

By spurning compromise and resorting to force, Britain smothered the colonial desire for reconciliation, forcing the colonists to seek French help. Inferior to the British in wealth, manpower, and arms, the American colonists desperately needed outside assistance. For example, they had virtually no gunpowder and no powder mills for its manufacture. "We have no arms, we have no powder, we have no blankets," the New York Committee of Safety wrote the Continental Congress in July 1775. "For God's sake, send us money, send us arms, send us ammunition." France could fill those needs.

Beaumarchais and Secret Aid

That same summer a daring Frenchman, Pierre Augustin Caron de Beaumarchais, learned from Americans in London that the trouble in America had burst into a serious insurrection. In September he returned to Paris and urged Vergennes to assist the colonists. Known to posterity primarily as the author of the comedies, *The Barber of Seville* and the *Marriage of Figaro,* the talented Beaumarchais was an incredible man. In addition to being a poet, playwright, skilled musician, inventor, and politician, he was a wizard at intrigue who took up the American cause virtually as his own, pointing out in one of his memorials to Louis XVI that aid to the Americans "will diminish the power of England and proportionally raise that of France."

Following Beaumarchais's urging, Vergennes that September sent a secret agent, posing as a merchant from Antwerp, to America to sound out the colonists and to tell them that France favored their independence and would aid them in achieving it with no strings attached to her help, but he made no commitments. After talking to the Americans, the "merchant" reported that the colonists were determined to assert their independence.

Vergennes received the report in February 1776 but still did not dare aid the Americans openly and risk war with England. At that point Beaumarchais stepped in. "If it be replied that we cannot assist the Americans without wounding England, and without drawing upon us the storm which I wish to keep off," he told the king and Vergennes, "I reply in my turn that this danger will not be incurred if the plan I have so many times proposed be followed, that of secretly assisting the Americans without compromising ourselves."[9] Despite the objections of the minister of finance, Anne Robert Jacques Baron Turgot, who argued that aid to the American colonies and the resulting war with England would bankrupt France, Vergennes persuaded the king to adopt a policy of limited secret assistance.

When Louis XVI, on May 2, set aside one million *livres* (about $200,000) worth of munitions from the royal arsenals for American use, secret aid became official. Spain, also anxious to cripple England, contributed a like amount. The French and Spainards sent their guns, powder, and other supplies to America in a steady stream through Roderique Hortalez and Company, a dummy firm set up by Beaumarchais. Some 90 percent of the gunpowder used by the American rebels in the first two years of the war came from European arsenals. In effect, two months before the colonists declared themselves free of England and before any American agent went to France to solicit aid, France had committed herself to a limited undercover support of the rebellion. She also rushed preparations for a possible war with England and urged Spain to do the same.

The Second Continental Congress

The Second Continental Congress, meanwhile, had begun a foreign policy of independence. In November 1775, it had created one of its most important standing committees, the Committee of Secret Correspondence, to maintain contact with friends abroad. Consisting of five members, with Benjamin Franklin as its first chairman, this State Department in embryo had little real power. Congress, either through other special committees or the Committee of the Whole, controlled foreign policy even in minute details.

To ascertain the attitudes of foreign powers toward the revolting colonies, Congress at first corresponded with several agents abroad, among them Arthur Lee, a turbulent young Virginian then in London as a commercial agent for Massachusetts, who was in close touch with Beaumarchais. After conferring with Vergennes' undercover "merchant," Congress decided on March 3, 1776, to send a secret agent of its own to France to purchase arms and to sound out the French about an alliance. For the dual commercial and diplomatic mission it chose Silas Deane, a politician from Connecticut.

Overplaying his role, Deane arrived in Paris in July ostensibly disguised as a rich Bermuda merchant. Lacking discretion, he delivered himself into the hands of Edward Bancroft, an old friend who had become a British spy. Secret information on French actions poured through Deane like a sieve to the British. Bancroft, for instance, acted as an interpreter between Deane and Beaumarchais when those two agreed on executing the Frenchman's plan for furnishing supplies to the American forces. George III even complained of the sheer bulk of the information his spies were reporting from sources such as Deane.[10]

Congress, meanwhile, made the final break with Britain. To attract foreign trade and aid, it opened American ports on April 6, 1776, to all countries, on July 2 voted independence, and two days later adopted the Declaration of Independence, making possible the establishment of formal diplomatic relations and the negotiation of treaties. That declaration, in fact, was issued mainly to assure potential allies that the war was real and not a mere family quarrel that could be easily patched by parental leniency.

At about the same time Congress appointed a committee to bring together guiding principles for the use of American diplomats in making treaties. On July 18 that committee offered its report, adopted on September 24, embodying a model set of articles for commercial treaties that came to be known as the Treaty Plan of 1776. It included specific articles for a treaty with France and such principles as free ships make free goods, meaning that enemy materials of a peaceful nature should be immune from capture when transported on neutral ships. This model treaty, the basic document in American maritime practice, marked the beginning of the policy of freedom of the seas.

"Poor Richard" in Paris

Two days later, on September 26, Congress appointed an official diplomatic mission, consisting of Deane, Thomas Jefferson, who declined and was replaced by Arthur Lee, and Benjamin Franklin, to secure French recognition of independence. Deane and Lee might well be called the first of the "militia diplomats," men who were as innocent of diplomatic experience as were the militia men of military training. Yet Congress, without knowing whether or not they would be received, hastily pressed the militia diplomats into service and sent them abroad seeking recognition, a policy disliked by Franklin. ". . . a virgin state," he said, "should preserve the virgin character, and should not go about suitoring for alliances, but wait with decent dignity for the application of others."[11]

Unlike his colleagues who were abroad gaining experience under fire, Franklin himself was not a militia diplomat. Having spent sixteen years in England as the agent of Pennsylvania, New Jersey, Georgia, and Massachusetts, he had come to know the European diplomats accredited to the Court of St. James's. His inventions had won him a worldwide reputation, his *Poor Richard's Almanac* had run through several French editions, and his investigations in natural philosophy had brought him membership in the French Academy. Now in his seventieth year, Franklin was the American the French knew best and admired most and the man the British called the "chief of the American rebels."

When Franklin in plain dress and wearing a comfortable fur cap arrived in Paris in December 1776, he set off a wave of public excitement. In his charm and pleasant manner the French saw the natural man that their Rousseau had taught them to admire. He became the embodiment of the American cause, the symbol of a yet unspoiled land.

The shrewd Franklin took full advantage of his popularity. "It is my intention while I stay here," he said, "to procure what advantages I can for our country by endeavoring to please the court."

Franklin quickly played his trump, telling Vergennes of a possible *rapprochement* with England "unless some powerful aid is given us or some strong diversion be made in our favor."[12] Although he won increased support, Franklin was unable to gain French recognition of independence until the Americans gave concrete evidence that they could wage war successfully. America's arms showed the desired strength in October 1777 at the Battle of Saratoga, where they forced General John Burgoyne to surrender his army of more than five thousand men. When news of the victory reached Paris in December, it assured the French recognition that

Vergennes already favored. The Battle of Saratoga, therefore, ranks as one of the more important battles of American history.

The disaster at Saratoga forced the British to reconsider their position. Early in December they rushed Paul Wentworth, a secret service agent, to Paris to forestall French recognition by offering Franklin and Deane liberal terms if only the colonies would lay down their arms and return to the empire. Since French police shadowed Wentworth from the moment of his arrival and Franklin made no effort to conceal his supposedly secret conversations with him, Vergennes knew of the British feelers and became uneasy lest they might lead to an Anglo-American reconciliation. In a bold move on December 17, therefore, he promised the United States formal recognition only if it insisted on maintaining independence from England.

Wentworth continued his conversations, and on January 6, 1778, told the American commissioners that Britain would fight for another ten years rather than grant Americans independence. "America," Franklin answered, "is ready to fight fifty years to win it." [13] Two days later an agent from Vergennes asked Franklin and Deane what they wanted for terminating their talks with Wentworth. A treaty and an alliance, they said. Vergennes agreed.

The French Alliance

Bound to Spain by a defensive dynastic alliance of 1761 called the Family Compact, France had to consult the Spanish court before making a treaty with the Americans. Although Spain disliked England, she was opposed to American independence. She had secretly aided the colonists in the hope that they and the English would exhaust themselves, but she would not openly sanction the rebellion of colonies, for that would set a terrifying precedent for her own possessions in the New World. Despite the urgings of Vergennes, Spain refused to enter a triple alliance with the United States. France and the United States alone, therefore, on February 6, 1778, signed two treaties.

By the terms of the first, the Treaty of Amity and Commerce, both nations granted each other most-favored-nation treatment, meaning that any commercial favors one party gave to another country would automatically accrue to the other signatory, and other liberal trading privileges. More important, with that treaty France recognized the United States as an independent nation.

The second, the Treaty of Alliance, provided that if war broke out between France and Britain as a result of the first treaty, France and the United States would fight together until American independence was assured. Neither party was to "conclude either Truce or Peace with Great Britain, without the formal consent of the other first obtain'd." France guaranteed American independence and territory "forever" and renounced designs on any portion of the North American mainland held by Britain in 1763. The United States guaranteed French possessions in America against all powers "forever." At Valley Forge, General George Washington later greeted the news of the alliance with heartfelt joy, saying it must "chalk out a plain and easy road to independence."

Within two days after the French treaties were signed, the American commissioners' confidential secretary, Edward Bancroft, sent copies to London. At first the British took no hostile action against the French, though in March 1778, after France announced the alliance, they broke off diplomatic relations. At the same time, through the offer of concessions, they continued to try to bring the colonies back into the empire. In March, Parliament passed laws offering the Americans virtual home rule. In April, hoping to prevent ratification of the French alliance, it sent a formal commission under Lord Carlisle, armed with money to bribe members of Congress, to America to propose the new terms, but Britain had acted too late. Since the French treaties offered everything that England did and independence as well, the Americans refused what once they might have accepted. Without even conferring with the Carlisle commission, Congress ratified the treaties on May 4, 1778.

A month later English and French warships clashed and the War of the American Revolution spread to Europe. In July, a French naval squadron, sent to "destroy the English forces upon the shores of North America," arrived at Philadelphia. With it came a minister plenipotentiary, Conrad Alexandre Gérard, the first accredited diplomatic official in the United States. Next, Vergennes tried to bring Spain into the war.

The Spanish Connection

Both France and the United States wanted Spain as an active ally, and their own alliance had secretly provided for her adherence. For Spain, next to France, had what the United States needed most: money, arms, and sea power. "If the Spaniards," General Washington said, "would but join their Fleets to those of France, and commence hostilities, my doubts would all subside. Without it, I fear the British Navy has too much in its power to counteract the Schemes of France." [14] Spain, however, resented the Franco-American alliance and would not go to war against England unless she could gain objectives of her own, the most coveted of those being Gibraltar, taken from her in 1704 by Britain.

After France and the United States had concluded their alliance, Don José Moniño, Count Florida Blanca, Spain's foreign minister, attempted to force England to give up Gibraltar as the price for Spanish neutrality and even suggested mediation of the American rebellion on terms that would probably have killed independence, but England would not surrender Gibraltar or anything else to the Spaniards. Florida Blanca then bargained with Vergennes who offered the concessions necessary to lure Spain into the war. Using the pretense that England had slighted her in rejecting an unacceptable offer of mediation, Spain, on April 12, 1779, signed a secret treaty of alliance with France, the Convention of Aranjuez.

That treaty, ostensibly in execution of the Family Compact, pledged France and Spain not to lay down their arms until Spain recovered Gibraltar. Without becoming an ally of the United States and without recognizing its independence, Spain thus committed France to fight for her European objectives. Two months later, Spain declared war on England. Since by treaty the United States could not make peace without France and France could not do so without recovering Gibraltar, American independence, if all the treaties were observed, might now come to depend on the fate of "that pile of stones" at the entrance to the Mediterranean.

Encouraged by Spain's entry into the war but unaware of the secret commitment of Aranjuez, Congress in October 1779 sent John Jay, recently its president, to Spain as minister plenipotentiary to seek recognition, Spanish adherence to the Franco-American alliance, and a loan of five million dollars. Jay's instructions also directed him to obtain the right of navigation down the Mississippi River through Spanish territory to the Gulf of Mexico. Arriving in Spain in January 1780, he met constant evasion. At one point he became so exasperated by the refusal of Spanish officials to see him that he blurted out to the French ambassador "that the object of my coming to Spain was to make *propositions,* not *supplications,* and that I should forbear troubling the minister with further letters till he should be more disposed to attend to them. That I consider America as being, and to continue, independent in *fact.*" [15]

Nonetheless, the Spaniards refused to receive Jay officially and would not yield the right of navigation. Even when, as directed by Congress, he offered to waive American pretensions to navigation of the Mississippi, Spain would not recognize the new republic. Although Jay stayed in Spain for over two years, he won no concessions of any consequence, only a small loan of some $150,000.

Armed Neutrality of 1780

England's naval practices, meanwhile, had aroused the ire of neutral nations such as Denmark and Russia, who in 1778 had considered an alliance to protect their shipping. Nothing came of it, but Catherine II of Russia in February 1780 proclaimed a code of maritime principles for the protection of neutral shipping against all belligerents and invited the other maritime neutrals to join her in what came to be known as the Armed Neutrality of 1780. Those principles, most of them already included in the Treaty Plan of 1776 and the Franco-American commercial treaty, stated that neutral ships had the right to enter belligerent ports, that free ships make free goods, and that to be binding a blockade had to be effective.

France and Spain accepted the Russian code, making it part of their maritime practice, but England would not, since she was the dominant naval power and those principles threatened that dominance. Ultimately, Denmark-Norway, Sweden, the Holy Roman Empire, Prussia, Portugal, and The Two Sicilies joined the league of armed neutrality, and for a while members succeeded in closing the Baltic Sea to all belligerent operations.

Although Catherine had not invited the United States to join the league, Congress quickly adopted its principles and tried to gain admittance as a means of winning recognition of American independence from the member nations, particularly from Russia. To obtain that recognition and a commercial treaty with Russia as well, Congress in the spring of 1781 sent one of its former members from Massachusetts, Francis Dana, to St. Petersburg as minister plenipotentiary. But Russia, like the other nations of Europe except France, had little interest in the American Revolution and would not recognize American independence. Since Catherine refused to receive Dana, his mission, like Jay's, ended in failure. As for the Armed Neutrality, even though Catherine at one time called it an armed nullity, it proved fairly effective in protecting neutral rights and did what Vergennes hoped it would. It served French policy by helping to isolate Britain from possible allies on the continent.

Holland's adherence to the Armed Neutrality, moreover, had the effect of spreading the war. The Dutch had two treaties with the British, a commercial agreement of 1674 and an alliance of 1678, later renewed. Three times the British demanded that the Dutch honor their alliance and aid them in the war, but the Dutch refused, arguing speciously that the war had originated in America and hence the alliance did not obligate them to act because it applied only to a European war involving England. The Dutch really wanted to remain neutral to profit from trade with France and other belligerents. Rather than have Holland join the Armed Neutrality and make her ships and goods available to France and Spain, the British preferred war, which would give them freedom to capture Dutch ships. Unwilling, however, to declare war on that basis, the British found another pretext.

In the autumn of 1778 William Lee, a militia diplomat from Virginia, and a minor Dutch official drew up the draft of an unauthorized commercial treaty for their two countries based on the Treaty Plan of 1776. Lee sent the draft treaty to Congress. Later, Congress appointed Henry Laurens of South Carolina, another of its former presidents, as minister to Holland. Members of the Lee family gave him William's draft treaty to use as a guide. While Laurens was on his way to Europe a British frigate captured his ship, and he hastily dumped a bag of documents overboard, but without sufficient weights. The British captain had the bag fished from the sea. In it was the draft treaty.

The British then accused the Dutch of making a secret treaty with the American rebels and declared war on Holland in December 1780. The true cause for war was Holland's decision to join the Armed Neutrality, but the armed neutrals, taking the view that Holland had gotten herself into trouble by meddling in British colonial affairs, did nothing to aid her. Britain quickly swooped down on Dutch shipping and cut off an important source of supplies for France and indirectly for the United States.

For Americans, the most stunning blow was Britain's capture of St. Eustatius, a Dutch island six miles long and three miles wide in the Caribbean, which had been the center of a huge trade between Europeans and Americans, much of it in contraband, or forbidden implements of war. Early in February 1781 before the Dutch inhabitants had heard their country was at war, Admiral George B. Rodney, in command of fifteen ships of the line, fell on the island, plundering it and capturing some two thousand American merchants and seamen. Rodney lingered in the Dutch free port for three fateful months garnering his loot. While he did so, a French fleet under Admiral François J. P. de Grasse slipped by him to join other French ships which later gained a decisive control of the sea in the siege of Yorktown, Virginia.

Probing for Peace

Even though the Dutch were now cobelligerents, they still refused to recognize American independence. Finally, in April 1782 with French assistance, John Adams, who had succeeded Laurens as minister to Holland, was received. Later he secured a loan from the Dutch and on October 8 signed a treaty of commerce with them. Thus, a second European state recognized the United States.

Although now engaged in a war of world-wide dimensions, with most of Europe against her, England refused two opportunities to end the conflict on terms short of American independence. The first came through the secret negotiations from November 1779 to March 1781 between Thomas Hussey, an Irish priest working for the Spanish intelligence service, and Richard Cumberland, an English agent, who attempted to arrange a truce that would have brought Spain out of the war and would have left Britain in control of large parts of her rebelling colonies. The other involved an offer of mediation from Austria and Russia in 1780–1781 that included a similar fate for the United States. Efforts at mediation failed because France in July 1780 had sent an army to the United States and the British insisted that in any truce or mediation the French must withdraw their forces from North America.

The war in America, however, went badly for the British. Even Spanish forces, who fought mainly for their own ends, contributed to Britain's defeat. They launched an offensive against the British in West Florida and by February 1781 were in control of that territory. Eight months later, at Yorktown on October 19, 1781, General Charles Cornwallis, hemmed in by de Grasse's fleet and by French and American armies, surrendered a British army of some seven thousand men. That capitulation virtually ended hostilities in America.

"It is all over!" Lord North, Britain's prime minister, said after the defeat at Yorktown. Many people of influence in England, never happy with the war in America, clamored for peace; the House of Commons passed a motion demanding an end to the war; and George III talked of abdicating. In March 1782 Lord North resigned, and a Whig, Lord Rockingham, before replacing him as prime minister demanded and received the king's assurance that he would agree to recognize the United States as independent. Rockingham's Whig government, however, was divided into two rival factions, the liberals headed by Charles James Fox, the foreign secretary, who had always opposed the war in America and favored independence, and the conservatives led by Lord Shelburne, the minister responsible for colonial affairs, who hoped he could patch up some kind of a peace without losing the American colonies.

Unable to agree over their respective functions and powers, particularly over peace negotiations with England's enemies, where Fox was responsible for peace with France and Shelburne for negotiations with the Americans, the two men quarreled. The split in the British cabinet became known to the French and Americans who used their knowledge to advantage, but in July 1782 Rockingham died. Shelburne succeeded him as prime minister and Fox resigned. Shelburne, an unusually resourceful and capable man, therefore had responsibility for making peace with the Americans and with all of Britain's enemies.

Terms of Negotiation

Informal peace talks began before Shelburne had become prime minister. In April 1782 he had sent Richard Oswald, a philosophical old Scot who had been an army contractor and slave trader and had lived in Virginia, to Paris to talk with Franklin. Although Franklin accepted Oswald's advances, he and Vergennes made it clear that Britain could not expect an independent peace from either France or the United States. In July, while Shelburne was forming his new government, Franklin unofficially told Oswald what the United States expected in the peace.

Franklin divided American aims into "necessary" and "advisable" terms, foremost among the necessary ones being recognition of independence and the evacuation of all British troops from the United States. They also included generous boundaries for the new nation and fishing privileges for Americans in Newfoundland and Canadian waters.

Among the advisable terms Franklin listed a large indemnity, free trade for American ships in British ports, acknowledgement by Britain that she had erred in warring on Americans, and her withdrawal from "every part of Canada." If she gave up Canada and withdrew from North America, Franklin said, Britain and the United States would never again have reason to fight. Impressed by Franklin's arguments, Oswald reported the terms to his government, urging acceptance of most of them. In any event, Oswald's report that the United States and France were willing to make peace led to the opening of formal negotiations.

Shelburne accepted Franklin's necessary terms as a basis of discussion, but would not recognize American independence before negotiating a treaty. Since Oswald's formal commission allowed him to treat only with representatives of England's "colonies," Franklin said Oswald's powers were inadequate and stopped the negotiations. At this point, John Jay, who had arrived in Paris in June to help with the peace negotiations and who, along with Franklin, John Adams, and Henry Laurens, had been designated a member of the peace commission by Congress, took a decisive part in the peacemaking.

When Franklin and Jay discussed Oswald's commission with Vergennes in August 1782, the French minister suggested continuing the negotiations, arguing that the form of the commission was unimportant as long as England recognized American independence in the final peace treaty. Franklin accepted Vergennes's advice, but Jay would not. With good reason as subsequent revelations were to show, Jay suspected that Vergennes wanted to delay American independence until he achieved his goals in Europe, such as Gibraltar. Since Vergennes could not deliver Gibraltar to Spain, he supported Spain's claim to the western territory in America between the Appalachian Mountains and the Mississippi, land desired by the Americans. Besides, American territorial aspirations struck Vergennes as exaggerated. France wanted an independent United States but also a weak one that would still need her.

Then on September 6, Joseph Rayneval, Vergennes's secretary, gave Jay a proposal that Franklin said looked as if Spain wanted "to coop us up within the Allegheny Mountains." Three days later, Jay learned that Rayneval had left for a secret trip to London, apparently to advance Spain's desires. Jay, therefore, became willing to violate Congress's instructions that the peace commissioners follow French guidance and do nothing without French "knowledge and concurrence." Furthermore, Jay believed correctly that Congress was under the thumb of French agents and that its instructions did not represent the nation's true interests.

Earlier Jay had told Franklin, "Let us be grateful to the French for what they have done for us, but let us think for ourselves. And, if need be, let us act for ourselves!"[16] Jay did just that. Without consulting the French or Franklin, he told Shelburne he was now willing to forego prior recognition of American independence if it came in the first article of a peace treaty and that he would discuss terms independently of France if the British agreed to prompt negotiations.

Seeing Jay's overture as an opportunity to break up the Franco-American alliance, Shelburne was delighted. He revised Oswald's commission, and Oswald and Jay proceeded in covert negotiations to draw up a draft treaty. When informed of these negotiations, Franklin at first protested mildly and then agreed with Jay, but sickness kept him from participating in the discussions at this time. British demands stiffened after news reached London late in September that their forces at Gibraltar, under siege by Spain and France for three years, had won a great victory. A month later John Adams arrived in Paris from Holland and joined the negotiations. He enthusiastically approved what Jay had done. Finally, on November 30, 1782, the American commissioners signed a preliminary peace treaty with England that was not to go into effect until France also made peace.

After negotiations had been completed, Franklin immediately told Vergennes of the preliminary treaty. Vergennes, who had originally consented to concurrent American negotiations with the British but not to the secret ones and who probably knew all along of Jay's clandestine actions, expressed no surprise. The Americans, he said, had "managed well." Two weeks later he reproved Franklin, who admitted some "impropriety" in the American action, but, the alert Dr. Franklin quickly added, he hoped that the slight indiscretion would not destoy the alliance with France. *"The English, I just now learn,"* he said, *"flatter themselves they have already divided us. I hope this little misunderstanding will therefore be kept secret, and that they will find themselves totally mistaken."*[17]

Although the Americans had violated their own instructions and the spirit if not the letter of the French alliance, their treaty served French interest as well as their own. Vergennes wanted peace but was hamstrung by obligations to Spain he could not fulfill. By telling the Spaniards that with the American peace, continuation of the war would be useless, he could persuade them to settle for less and extricate himself from his impossible commitment to deliver Gibraltar to Spain. Therefore, he accepted the American treaty without undue protest.

Treaty of Paris

Great Britain made peace with France and Spain at Versailles on September 3, 1783, and the United States signed the definitive Treaty of Paris on the same day. Except for a contingent secret article dealing with West Florida, an article no longer applicable and hence dropped because Britain gave the Floridas to Spain, the terms of the final treaty were those of the

THE UNITED STATES IN 1783

preliminary agreement. Those terms, by confirming independence, allowing Americans the "liberty" to fish off the coasts of Newfoundland and Canada, and ceding them extensive boundaries, gave the United States its three primary objectives. Since Britain gave up her territory between the Appalachian Mountains and the Mississippi River south of the Great Lakes to the Floridas at the thirty-first parallel, the terms were generous.

The Treaty of Paris also appeared to meet Britain's two main objectives in the peace: the United States promised British creditors that they would "meet no lawful impediment" in trying to recover their prewar debts and agreed to "recommend" to state legislatures that they restore or pay for property confiscated from Loyalists, or American colonists who had retained their allegiance to England. Those provisions, plus the vague definition of boundary lines, were to cause trouble later.

When the war ended, the trans-Appalachian West was not in American hands, so that Americans could not claim it by right of conquest. George Rogers Clark, the Revolution's hero of the West, had taken and held only a small part of it. Why, then, did the British give it up? They did so because the American treaty was only part of a general peace settlement England made with the powers. Surrender of the Northwest seemed a negligible sacrifice if it could help in splitting the Franco-American alliance. British statesmen and merchants, furthermore, wanted to buy the goodwill of the United States and lay the basis for a proftable future trade.

The United States, therefore, became an independent nation with a considerable domain, but jealous European neighbors still surrounded it. To the north, England held Canada; to the south and west, Spain controlled the Floridas and Louisiana. Yet those problems and the treaty's troublesome clauses were concerns for the future and minor in comparison to what the peace of Paris bestowed.

In summary, through independent negotiations designed to advance her own objective of driving a wedge between France and the United States, Great Britain consented to a liberal peace out of proportion to American military achievements. With her generous grant of western territory, she conceded to the new nation room for future expansion and a good chance for survival as an independent state.

III

Federalist Policies

"American glory begins to dawn at a favourable period, and under flattering circumstances," publicist Noah Webster wrote in the preface of his spelling book in 1783. "We have the experience of the whole world before our eyes."[1] On the surface, what Webster said was true enough. The new nation had inherent strength. It was big, sprawling over a million square miles of land and water and stretching from the Atlantic Ocean on the east to the Mississippi River on the west. Beyond the frontiers lay room for expansion at the expense of Indian occupants. The Old Northwest, for example, contained some 220,000,000 acres of wilderness, more than a third of the national domain. Over three million people were strung out along the coast between the sea and mountains. The whites, mostly of English stock, were relatively homogeneous and ruled the country. About a half-million black slaves and Indians made up the remainder of the population.

America also had weaknesses. Even though the Revolution had produced interests transcending state boundaries and had created a central government, the bond uniting the thirteen states, the Articles of Confederation and Perpetual Union, was tenuous. That constitution circumscribed the powers of the national government, placing the levying of taxes, for example, in the hands of the states. The Continental Congress, the central organ of government, had declared independence, raised armies, and made an alliance with France through what were later called "implied war powers." After the war those powers collapsed, and for a while so did Congress, a logical result of the exhausting conflict.

Despite its limited authority, the new government had entered the world of independent nations and, to take part in international politics and trade, had created a Department of Foreign Affairs. Congress had the basic powers to carry on foreign relations, but not much more. It had the sole right, under the first constitution, of making peace or war, of sending and receiving ambassadors, of entering into treaties and alliances and of adjudicating all disputes between states, but could not make commercial treaties with the assurance that all the states would comply with them.

Europeans were aware of the weakness of the American union. Many of them, even friendly sovereigns, had believed that the end of the war would remove the pressure for national cooperation and that the union itself would collapse. After all, they pointed out, no republic had ever before existed on so large a scale. "As to the future grandeur of America, and its being a rising empire under one head, whether republican or monarchical," a well-known Englishman, Josiah Tucker, Dean of Gloucester, said, "it is one of the idlest and most visionary notions that ever was conceived even by writers of romance. The mutual antipathies and clashing interests of the Americans, their difference of governments, habitudes, and manners, indicate they will have no centre of union and no common interest." [2]

Nonetheless, the new nation immediately after independence sought a place in world trade and enlisted some of its ablest leaders, men like John Adams, John Jay, and Thomas Jefferson, in its diplomatic service. They attempted, without great success at first, to show the skeptics of Europe that America merited respect. When John Jay returned from Europe in 1784, for instance, and Congress appointed him to succeed Robert R. Livingston as secretary for foreign affairs, the secretary of the Congress offered the advice "that it is not only time but highly necessary for us to think and act like a sovereign as well as a free people." [3]

Commerce with Britain

Jay's most serious diplomatic problems were with Great Britain, and most pressing was that of trade. Americans, ironically, wanted both the advantages of independence and the commercial benefits they had enjoyed as members of the British empire. For a time, during the peace negotiations, it had seemed as if those twin desires would be met. Lord Shelburne and the merchants whose chief business before the war had been trade with America favored the idea of allowing Americans to resume their commerce within the British empire free of the restrictions of mercantilist laws, but the preliminary peace treaty, because of its generosity to Americans, was unpopular in England. Shelburne's government therefore fell in February 1783 before the signing of the definitive treaty, and with it tumbled the policy he had fostered of trying to win American goodwill with trade concessions.

Various opposition groups in Parliament, among them shipowners and certain merchants who saw in the United States a future commercial rival, demanded rigorous treatment of the former colonies. "By asserting their independence, the Americans have at once renounced the privileges, as well as the duties of British subjects," Lord Sheffield wrote in a widely circulated book; "they are become foreign States."[4] In July, Shelburne's successors issued an order in council shutting Americans out of the lucrative carrying trade in the British West Indies, and then in the definitive peace treaty all commercial articles were dropped.

Later, the British placed other restrictions on American traders, causing bitter outcries in the shipbuilding and trading communities of New England. British discriminations made commerce with the United States one-sided. England would buy only raw materials, such as tobacco, furs, and lumber from the United States, but no manufactured goods. She admitted American ships carrying American products to her home ports on liberal terms, but excluded them, as she did other foreign ships, from trade in her colonies. Legally, American goods for England's colonies traveled in English ships. Resourceful New Englanders partially overcame these restrictions through smuggling, particularly in the British West Indies where they built up a large illicit trade.

Despite the restrictions, commerce between the United States and Britain flourished. At the end of the Confederation period about 75 percent of all American exports went to England and about 90 percent of America's imports, mostly manufactured goods, came from there. Many Americans, nonetheless, felt that England was levying commercial war against them. One of them expressed the view of many when he complained that Britain was apparently "aiming to bring about a general bankruptcy in America after finding our trade had returned to its former channel, and that our importations were as great as formerly."[5]

In spite of their grievances, Americans persisted in trading with England because they needed manufactures, such as textiles and household items, and England offered them an established market for their products, such as naval stores and cotton, and was the only country where they could obtain long-term credits. They preferred English goods, moreover, and were familiar with British business methods. Besides, even traders would not ignore the ties of language, blood, and culture to the mother country. Economic dependence on England in the era of the Confederation, therefore, was almost as great as it had been before the Revolution.

Yet Americans protested Britain's discriminations and threatened retaliation. In 1785 New York, for instance, laid a double tax on all goods imported from England. But the United States could force no change in British policy, mainly because the various states would not act in concert and even discriminated against each other. Having nothing to fear in reprisal, England saw no reason to extend generous trading privileges to Americans. "It will not be an easy matter to bring the American states to act as a nation," Lord Sheffield said; "they are not to be feared as such by us."[6]

The American government hoped to overcome some of the British restrictions, particularly in the West Indies, in a commercial treaty. To seek such a treaty, Congress sent John Adams in May 1785 to Great Britain. When Adams announced himself as the minister from the United States, the British asked, according to legend, where were the other twelve? They received him with glacial courtesy and would make no treaty.

Adams wrote to Jefferson urging retaliation. "If we cannot obtain reciprocal liberality," he said, "we must adopt reciprocal prohibitions, exclusions, monopolies, and imposts."[7] Such "means of preserving ourselves," he later admitted, however, "can never be secured until Congress shall be made supreme in foreign commerce."

After spending three fruitless years in London, Adams saw that reconciliation and cooperation with the British were impossible. Still believing that the new republic would break apart, England treated it with contempt. Even though, for commercial reasons, she sent consuls to the United States, she refused to appoint a minister. In April 1788, therefore, at his own request, Adams came home.

When he left London the British were cold. "Mr. Adams," the king told him on his departure, "you may, with great truth, assure the United States that, whenever they shall fulfill the treaty on their part, I, on my part will fulfill it in all its particulars."[8] So, in 1789, at the end of the Confederation, an understanding with Great Britain seemed as remote as it had been in 1783.

Slaves, Debts, and Loyalists

Adams also had instructions to obtain redress for British violations of the peace treaty. That treaty said that in evacuating American soil, British troops should not carry away slaves or other American property, but the soldiers had taken hundreds of—perhaps several thousand—Negroes, apparently allowing some to gain freedom and selling others to planters in the West Indies. Americans, mainly Southerners, demanded compensation for the lost slaves, but the British refused. Americans, therefore, used this violation to justify their own infractions of the treaty.

Before the war, British merchants in Glasgow and elsewhere had loaned Americans, primarily southern planters, millions of dollars in goods. American lawyers argued that the Revolution had dissolved all laws under which the debts had been contracted. The British creditors insisted that the debts had been incurred in time of peace and were justly due. Their pressure on Shelburne had resulted in a provision in the peace treaty saying that creditors should meet no lawful impediment in recovering their debts.

Southerners, however, defied the terms of the treaty. Maryland, Virginia, and other states passed laws prohibiting the use of state courts for the collection of the prewar British debts. Virginia's House of Delegates, by unanimous vote, even demanded that Congress should make no treaty in conflict with the state laws. In some cities people rioted against attempts to recover the debts and threatened to assassinate collectors. Although Congress insisted that the peace treaty had become the law of the land binding on the states and that their legislatures had no right to pass laws in conflict with it, Congress could not open the state courts or force payment of the debts.

Congress was equally helpless in trying to carry out two articles pertaining to Loyalists. The treaty said that Congress should recommend to the states the restitution of Loyalist property and that there should be no further persecution of Loyalists or confiscation of their property. Americans greeted those recommendations with a storm of protest, for feeling between Loyalists and Patriots during the Revolution had been deep and bitter.

About a third of the colonists, according to rough estimates, had been Loyalists. Some had fled to Britain, some to Canada and Florida, and others had stayed behind the British lines. After the peace, many wanted to return to their old homes, but every state had persecuted Loyalists and had passed laws that either confiscated their property or heavily taxed it. Returning Loyalists were often tarred and feathered, mobbed, and even hanged. Those "leeches," angry Americans said, should not be allowed to remain among a free people. "It is the command of God that in cursing we curse them," a leading preacher of Salem, Massachusetts, advised.[9] Finally, by the end of the Confederation era, many of the Loyalists had regained their estates, but the confiscation laws were not repealed.

The Northern Posts

The unpaid debts and the persecuted Loyalists, meanwhile, gave the British an excuse for retaining a chain of military and trading posts in the Northwest strung out along the southern shores of the Great Lakes, in territory that belonged to the United States. In the peace treaty England had promised to evacuate those Northwest posts with all convenient speed and Americans expected a quick transfer, but as soon as powerful Canadian fur traders and merchants in Britain heard of the terms, they protested and demanded retention of the forts. The fur traders who had built up a lucrative business in the region said they needed time to sell their holdings and wind up their business south of the Great Lakes and appealed to the British government to support them.

Some Englishmen, moreover, believed that Lord Shelburne had made a mistake in ceding the Old Northwest to the United States. Others argued that he had violated obligations to Britain's Indian allies who lived there. British commanders in the region, fearing an uprising if the Indians were turned over to the United States, wanted to keep the posts indefinitely and to retain the goodwill of the Indians.

The day before George III proclaimed the peace treaty, therefore, the British government instructed the governor general of Canada not to deliver the posts to the Americans. The British thus decided to retain the posts before the United States itself had clearly violated the treaty. New instructions in 1786 directed the governor general also to recapture those forts that Americans might seize. The presence of British troops on American soil angered many Americans, especially Westerners who wanted to open up the Northwest to settlement. They were convinced, moreover, that British agents from the posts were supplying the Indians with rifles, ball and powder, knives, and other goods, and were encouraging the raids on frontier settlements.

At the same time, from two posts on Lake Champlain and one on the south shore of the St. Lawrence River, the British dabbled in troubles in Vermont. Plagued by boundary disputes with New Hampshire and New York, Vermont had not been granted statehood. The Vermonters, therefore, had a weak attachment to the Union and behaved as though they were autonomous. The fact that their normal trade outlet, via the St. Lawrence to the sea, passed through Canada made union with Canada seem attractive. Aware of this sentiment, the British appeared to encourage a separatist movement in Vermont. Prominent Vermonters—Ethan, Ira, and Levi Allen—talked to British officials about a commerical treaty and a new connection with England. In 1789 Ira went to London to advance the secessionist scheme. At the end of the Confederation period, therefore, the fate of Vermont was uncertain.

Relations with France

From France, ally of the Revolution, the United States expected and received better treatment than from England. "Commercial privileges granted to us by France, at this season of British ill-humour," John Jay wrote to the Marquis de Lafayette, "would be particularly grateful."[10] In August 1784 France relaxed mercantilist restrictions and granted American ships a limited right to trade in her Caribbean ports, but Americans were disappointed. They had expected broader concessions, such as freedom to trade in France's home ports.

Thomas Jefferson, who became minister to France in 1785, was a fitting successor to Dr. Franklin. Although, as the representative of a republic in the day of monarchy, Jefferson found his post "an excellent school of humility," he tried to cultivate and strengthen French friendship through commerce. He believed that trade should thrive because the United States could exchange primary products such as cotton for French manufactures such as textiles, and both countries would benefit. That commerce would, moreover, cement the political bond between the two countries. While recognizing that French policy was based on self-interest, he considered

France's friendship essential to American foreign policy. "I cannot," he wrote, "pretend to affirm that this country will stand by us on every just occasion, but I am sure, if this will not, there is no other that will."[11]

Jefferson's hope for a bustling trade with France was not illusory. The French already had a commercial treaty with the United States, and a foremost aim of their aid during the Revolution had been to break America's economic dependence on England. Yet the policy of the French government in cutting away mercantilist restrictions to attract trade was audacious. It alienated merchants who resented American competition and who objected to having former British subjects trading freely in French Caribbean ports. The merchants' protests caused minor readjustments in their favor, but the commercial concessions to the United States continued as policy, and the French government sent special consuls to America to drum up trade.

American commerce did well under liberal French decrees, but the concessions were gratuitous, were subject to local exceptions, and could be withdrawn at any time. The thirteen states vied with each other for French trade, violated the commercial treaty of 1778, and manipulated tariff and tonnage duties to the annoyance of French merchants. Congress could do little to enforce uniform treatment of French commerce. The French commercial treaty, moreover, while providing for consuls, said nothing about their privileges and immunities. In the summer of 1784, therefore, Franklin and Vergennes had agreed to a consular convention that called for French consuls to deliver their credentials to state authorities rather than to Congress and thus stressed the sovereignty of the thirteen separate states.

When the convention reached the United States, Jay urged Congress not to ratify and recommended negotiation of a new agreement that recognized the sovereignty of "The United States of America." Jefferson renegotiated and in November 1788 signed a revised convention. The new agreement appeared technically reciprocal but in fact was not. It permitted consular courts to exercise civil jurisdiction over their own nationals and thus impinged on American sovereignty. Although the United States was allowed the same privileges in France, the agreement favored France because the United States lacked uniform laws. Under the convention, French consuls could and did meddle in American politics.

Despite the efforts of the French consuls and Jefferson to stimulate commerce, American trade, as Jefferson pointed out, did not find its way to France. Americans profited from the newly opened channels of trade by selling more to France than they bought. They preferred British manufactures. French commercial policy, therefore, failed.

The United States also defaulted on repayment of money France had loaned it during the Revolution. Congress could not meet installments on the principal or even keep up interest payments. It tried to pay, but could raise money only by requisitioning the states. No longer faced with an immediate foreign danger, the states ignored congressional demands. Yet the French government applied no great pressure for payment, even when faced with bankruptcy, taking the view that the debt was a bad one and must be written off as such.

This state of American affairs did not displease French statesmen. A nation unable to raise enough money to maintain a strong government, they realized, would be more amenable to their control than would a financially stable one. They wished to keep the United States dependent. When, for example, after the peace treaty the United States tried to wriggle out of its alliance, the French insisted that it was still binding. "Those who have once been the allies of France," Vergennes said, "are her allies always." [12]

Although relations between the two governments had cooled since the courtship of the Revolution, difficulties with France during the Confederation were minor in comparison with America's other foreign troubles. A bond of some warmth still existed between the people of France and Americans. "I am egregiously deceived if the people of this Country are not in general extremely well affected to France . . . ," Washington told the French minister; "no prejudice has been revived, no jealousy excited, no interest adduced, and, in short, no cause has existed (to my knowledge) which could have wrought a revolution unfriendly to your nation." [13]

Friction with Spain

No lesser term than unfriendly, however, could describe relations with Spain, who had refused to recognize the United States until after the peace of 1783. That recognition did not allay the bitterness between the two countries, which stemmed from three main issues: the navigation of the Mississippi, the new nation's southwestern boundary, and commercial affairs.

The question of the Mississippi grew out of the peace treaty at the end of the Seven Years' War. In that treaty France had given the British the right to navigate the river to the sea, and Spain, who gained control of both banks of its lower reaches, had accepted that obligation when she took over Louisiana from France. In the final Treaty of Paris of 1783, to which Spain was not a party, England said she would share the right with the United States. Arguing that the British privilege had ended in 1779 when she and England had gone to war, Spain refused to recognize any American right to navigate the Mississippi through Spanish territory. England, she said, had no authority to transfer her navigation privilege, particularly since it no longer existed, to a third party. During the war, as a favor, the Spaniards had allowed Americans free use of the river, but in 1784 a royal order closed it to the Americans, touching off a crisis in the Southwest.

Friction over the southwestern boundary arose from the final treaty of peace of 1783. It had fixed the boundary between Spain's West Florida and the United States at the thirty-first parallel, but in the preliminary treaty of 1782, England had inserted a secret article saying that if West Florida remained in British hands, its boundary would be over a hundred miles farther north to the latitude of the mouth of the Yazoo River, about 32° 25′, the line that had formed the boundary of West Florida in the twenty years the British had held it.

When the Spaniards heard of the secret article, they were furious. In the War of the American Revolution, the Spaniards had conquered the Floridas and territory to the north of the thirty-first parallel, and England in her treaty of peace with them in 1783 had ceded the Floridas with indefinite boundaries. The Spaniards contended rightly, therefore, that they were not bound by the terms of the final Anglo-American treaty. Their extreme claim went far beyond the thirty-first parallel, as far north as the Tennessee and Ohio rivers, covering parts of Georgia, Tennessee, and Kentucky, and most of Alabama and Mississippi.

Spain attempted to enforce her claims to the Old Southwest through occupation, by holding military posts in Alabama, Mississippi, and Tennessee, and through intrigue with the Indians there, by supplying them with weapons and encouraging them to use the arms against American settlers, some fifty thousand of whom had swarmed into lower Ohio. Spain also signed treaties with several tribes, offering them protectorates in the hope they would serve as a shield against advancing American frontiersmen. At the same time, American agents roamed the region, pledging the Indians to alliances with the United States. In 1785, therefore, when the Spanish order closing the Mississippi became known in the Southwest, part of that region, like the Northwest, lay under a foreign flag and seethed with international intrigue and Indian warfare.

Insisting that their livelihood depended on unrestricted navigation of the Mississippi, the men of the western waters protested the Spanish closure. They found it easier and less expensive to get their produce, such as tobacco and wheat, to eastern markets via the river and the sea than to attempt to haul it over backbreaking mountain trails. Those impatient frontiersmen, supported by the southern states, demanded that Congress force Spain to reopen the river.

Delegates from the Northeast, representing merchant and shipowning interests, however, were not greatly concerned about the problems of the western settlers. What they wanted most from Spain was a commercial treaty that would allow them to trade in her ports, particularly in the New World, a trade they had enjoyed briefly during the war but that Spain had stopped after the peace.

Fearing that the frontiersmen might try to settle by force what Congress could not solve by diplomacy, the Spainards appeared more concerned about the angry Westerners than did the American government. There was always the danger that they might try to sweep aside Spain's lamentable frontier defenses, occupy the disputed borderlands, force open the Mississippi, gain control of New Orleans, and impose an illicit commerce on Spain's wealthier domains to the south. To forestall that, Spain attempted to foster a separatist movement in the Southwest, particularly in the Kentucky area. With the bait of special trading privileges on the Mississippi she hoped to wean the settlers from their American ties and perhaps win them to Spanish allegiance.

Unlike England, moreover, Spain was willing to negotiate with the new republic over its grievances and make limited concessions, but not without some equivalent. In return for recognition of her exclusive right to control the lower reaches of the Mississippi, Spain was willing to modify her most extensive boundary claims and agree to a commercial treaty granting trading privileges in certain of her homeland ports to Americans. In its essentials, this was the position taken by Don Diego de Gardoqui, the envoy Spain sent to the United States in 1785 to negotiate over the unsettled issues.

The Jay-Gardoqui Treaty

Gardoqui, who knew Jay and spoke English well, was clever in diplomacy and accomplished in the drawing room. Jay, he reported, was "a very self-centered man, which passion his wife augments, because, in addition to considering herself meritoriously and being rather vain, she likes to be catered to and even more to receive presents."[14] Through Mrs. Jay, he believed, he would gain her and her husband's friendship. Gardoqui apparently did not find it difficult to shower attention on attractive Mrs. Jay, giving her presents and escorting her to dances and other festivities.

Jay's original instructions bound him to insist on free navigation of the Mississippi and a boundary settlement at the thirty-first parallel, but Gardoqui could not yield on both points. When the Spaniards offered commercial concessions, eagerly desired by seaboard merchants, for a temporary closing of the Mississippi, Jay, a New Yorker, considered the terms good. After extended discussions, Jay and Gardoqui in 1786 agreed to a treaty in which the United States in return for trading concessions, would "forbear" use of the Spanish portion of the Mississippi for thirty years, but would not yield on the "right" of navigation.

In August, Jay asked Congress for a change of instructions so that he could complete the negotiation on the proposed terms, arguing that the immediate navigation of the Mississippi could be obtained only by a war for which the United States was unprepared. "Why, therefore," he asked, "should we not (for a valuable consideration, too) consent to forbear to use what we know is not in our power to use?" By a simple majority of seven to five Jay won a change of instructions, but had split Congress along sectional lines. All the southern states voted against him.

To Southerners it appeared that Jay was willing to sacrifice the Southwest to the interest of the Northeast. Virginian James Monroe, for example, condemned the proposal as one "of the most extraordinary transactions I have ever known, a minister negotiating expressly for the purpose of defeating the object of his instructions, and by a long train of intrigue & management seducing the representatives of the states to concur in it." [15] Furious Westerners talked of rebelling, even of seeking British protection if the treaty were ratified. "To sell us and make us vassals to the merciless Spaniards is a grievance not to be borne," one of them said. "Should we tamely submit to such manacles we should be unworthy of the name of Americans."

Since the approval of nine states was necessary for ratification and the southern states would not yield, Jay and Gardoqui never completed their treaty. Southern distrust of the North, nonetheless, lingered. In Virginia it almost blocked ratification of the new federal Constitution, and was largely responsible for the constitutional rule requiring a two-thirds vote of the Senate for approval of treaties.

Seeking to take advantage of the Southwest's suspicions of the Northeast and the central government, Gardoqui, after the failure of his treaty, turned to intrigue with the idea of creating an independent state in the Southwest amenable to Spanish policy. A murky figure in Spain's plans to detach the Southwest from the Union was General James Wilkinson, veteran of the American Revolution. While holding a commission from his own government, Wilkinson accepted bribes and swore a secret oath of allegiance to Spain. To facilitate their plans of winning over frontiersmen, the Spaniards in December 1788 opened the Mississippi to American use under a special licensing system and even allowed Westerners to land their cargoes at New Orleans. Despite this toll use of the river, the basic difficulties between Spain and the United States, as the Confederation expired, remained unsettled.

The Nootka Sound Crisis

Under the Articles of Confederation American diplomacy lacked effectiveness. Keenly aware of their country's impotence, some of America's leading statesmen argued that a respected foreign policy could be based only on a stronger national government. John Jay, for instance, summed up the problems of foreign relations by saying that "to be respectable abroad, it is necessary to be so at home: and that will not be the case until our public faith acquires more strength." [16] The new nation gained that confidence in 1789, when the federal Constitution gave the central government power over trade and commerce and exclusive control over foreign affairs.

George Washington, therefore, became president in April 1789 with a government capable of acting decisively in foreign affairs for the whole nation. Since the Constitution did not provide for a foreign office, Congress created the Department of Foreign Affairs in July, but six weeks later changed the name to the Department of State. Although Washington appointed Thomas Jefferson the first secretary of state, he did not wait for Jefferson's return from France before attempting to improve relations with England, the most pressing of the problems in foreign relations that he had inherited from the Confederation government.

In this, his first diplomatic venture, Washington made use of an old friend, Gouverneur Morris, then on private business in Paris, as a special executive agent. He asked Morris to go to London to try to open formal diplomatic relations with England, seek a commercial treaty, and begin negotiations for a settlement of American grievances. Morris went, but attained none of his objectives. Not until a crisis with Spain in North America threatened war did the British even consider exchanging ministers with the United States.

The crisis originated on remote Nootka Sound, on the west coast of Vancouver Island in what is now British Columbia. Spain claimed that territory and declared it closed to all foreigners. When some British traders attempted to establish a post on the sound in 1789, Spanish authorities attacked them, seized several of their ships, and drove them out. Both England and Spain then alerted their allies and prepared for war.

During the crisis, Washington turned to his department heads for advice in shaping a policy in case England should try to strike at the Spaniards in Louisiana, Florida, and New Orleans by cutting across the United States from Canada and thus make American soil a battleground. Alexander Hamilton, the secretary of the treasury, favored granting England permission to move troops across American territory, but Jefferson, who feared British encirclement, opposed this view. Fortunately no war came, and the president did not have to act on the conflicting advice he received.

Spain had counted on France for help, but since France was in the throes of revolution, she turned down her ally's plea. Realizing that alone she could not cope with England, Spain bowed before an ultimatum. In the Nootka Sound Convention of 1790, she agreed to restore English property and recognized the right of Englishmen to trade and settle in territory she had formerly claimed as exclusively Spanish.

Of special significance for the United States was the fact that the crisis had caused concern in London over the American reaction. British officials feared that if war had broken out with Spain, the United States might have attempted to settle some of its grievances by force, mainly by taking the Northwest posts. As a result, British policy toward the United States changed. American friendship now acquired a new importance and for the first time since independence the British government was ready to make limited concessions.

Commerce, Politics, and British Policy

More important than the Nootka Sound crisis in stimulating a change in British policy was the threat of economic retaliation. The new federal government, the British realized, was strong enough to carry out discriminatory commercial legislation against them. Arguing that Englishmen were "mounting their navigation on the ruin of ours," Secretary Jefferson, for instance, urged a policy of retaliation against British trade and shipping. It might, he explained to the president, induce England to agree to a commercial treaty, end her violations of the peace treaty, and establish formal diplomatic relations. With his support, friends in Congress early in 1791 proposed several bills that would have imposed discriminatory duties on British goods and threatened Britain's most valued commerce.

Since Hamilton had anchored his financial system on revenues from British trade, commercial foreign policy now became a national political issue. If the anti-British bills became law, they would ruin Hamilton's system and, as Hamilton himself saw it, the strong central government he desired. Through his followers in Congress, therefore, he managed to block the Jeffersonian legislation. Nonetheless, the threat of retaliatory tariffs and tonnage duties alarmed British traders, who feared the growing strength of the Jeffersonian coalition in the American government.

These factors contributed to the shift in British policy that was most evident in the decision to open normal diplomatic relations with the United States. The first British minister, George Hammond, a young man of twenty-seven years, arrived in Philadelphia in October 1791 with instructions to combat anti-British trade legislation, but otherwise with limited powers. As a result, Hammond's discussions with Jefferson of differences between their countries solved nothing. England had not yet become sufficiently interested in a settlement to offer Americans the concessions they desired.

Hamilton also contributed to Jefferson's failure to make headway. Opposed to anything that might injure relations with England, Hamilton secretly informed British officials that the secretary of state's views did not represent administration policy and hence implied that they could be disregarded with impunity.

Such meddling in foreign affairs was possible because, next to Washington, Hamilton was the most powerful man in government. At this point he had more influence over foreign policy than did the secretary of state. Hamilton's power came from his ability to influence the president. Washington found his ideas congenial, hence they usually became the basis for administration foreign policy.

So angry did Jefferson become over Hamilton's interference in his department that on the last day of 1793 the Virginian resigned his post to share the leadership with James Madison of a political movement against the administration. That opposition crystallized into the Republican party. Hamilton, on the other hand, ruled as leader of administration forces and of those who supported administration policies. His followers became the core of the Federalist party.

The formation of these first national political parties reflected practical and philosophical differences over foreign policy, over the best means to advance the national interest. Hamilton based his thinking on the conviction that America's welfare was tied closely to England and that the French alliance should be terminated. Jefferson, who considered the French alliance the "sheet anchor" of American foreign policy, distrusted England and believed that friendship with France would serve America best.

Before resigning, Jefferson had tried also to resolve differences with Spain, but here as with his English policy, he made no progress. Yet foreign policy made headway in one direction. Under Hamilton's skillful guidance the government from 1790 to 1795 paid off its war debts to Spain and France. Events in France, meanwhile, created tensions in world affairs and new problems for Americans.

Revolutionary France and Nonentanglement

Shortly after Washington's inauguration the French Revolution began. Its expansion so divided emerging political parties that foreign policy in the United States became perhaps the foremost national issue. The international wars stemming from that Revolution preoccupied the European powers and allowed the United States finally to settle its frontier problems advantageously with both Britain and Spain. These conflicts also gave hothouse growth to a number of long-lasting principles, such as neutrality and nonentanglement.

American statesmen realized they would need guiding principles when they received news that on February 1, 1793, France had declared war on England, Holland, and Spain. As a result of bitter maritime controversies what had been a war confined to continental Europe now spread to American shores. By the terms of the French alliance, the United States in time of war, if called upon, was committed to defend France's West Indies. Washington, therefore, turned to his advisers. Would the United States, he asked, have to go to war to honor its treaty obligations to France? In effect, the president had to decide on the nation's official attitude toward the belligerents.

The advisers agreed on a policy of neutrality, but disagreed on its definition. Hamilton and his supporters urged an "impartial" neutrality favorable to England that called for a narrow interpretation of American obligations under the French treaties of 1778. Jefferson desired a "benevolent" neutrality beneficial to France, one based on a broad interpretation of obligations under the French treaties.

Both sides were able to cite authorities in support of their own views, mainly because the idea of neutrality in international relations was changing. By definition, neutrality implies impartiality, meaning that a non-belligerent should not favor one belligerent over another. In the past, however, most "neutral" powers had not been officially impartial. Without taking part in hostilities, they had usually favored one belligerent over another and had aided their favorite with special concessions. Hugo Grotius, the seventeenth-century Dutch jurist and "father of international law," had supported such a theory of neutrality. He expected neutrals to take sides.

In the eighteenth century, Emmerich de Vattel, a Swiss diplomat and publicist, propounded a new theory. Unless obligated by treaty to a belligerent, he said, a neutral could not give to one belligerent what it refused to another. A neutral nation, in other words, must be impartial.

In contrast to Jefferson, Hamilton urged the newer theory, and Washington accepted it. Most nations in the nineteenth century, in fact, came to adopt the idea of impartial neutrality in theory, but rarely in practice. Even in Hamilton's case, the new theory did not mean impartiality. It favored England because, unlike France, she had no special treaty rights with the United States and hence nothing to lose.

Washington made the new idea official policy in a proclamation of neutrality issued on April 22, 1793. It declared the United States at peace with both England and France and warned Americans against committing hostile acts against either belligerent. Disappointed, Jefferson maintained that only the "ardent spirit" of the political opposition could prevent the new policy from becoming a "mere English neutrality."

Next, Washington turned to his department heads for advice on general treaty obligations. Now that France had overthrown the monarchy, he wondered if the treaties of 1778 were still in effect and if he should receive a minister from France's republican government. Hamilton and Jefferson again differed. The secretary of the treasury argued that the president should suspend the treaties until the French Revolution clarified itself and should receive the new minister with a carefully worded reservation on recognition of the republican regime. Hamilton, in other words, wished to use the French Revolution as an excuse for cutting loose from the French treaties and steering the United States closer to England.

Jefferson contended that the treaties were in force, for they were not between particular governments but between nations and hence the United States could not unilaterally abrogate them because the contracting government, the French monarchy, no longer existed. He also urged that Washington receive the new minister without qualification. In this instance the president followed the secretary of state's advice. He recognized the French Republic, accepted the treaties as continuing in force, and decided to receive the republican minister.

Dilemmas of Neutrality

The French alliance, as some feared it might, did not drag the United States into the war. Since Americans had no navy and could contribute little in direct aid to the winning of the war, France did not invoke the alliance by asking them to defend her West Indies. The French believed that American neutrality, if interpreted in their favor, would be more useful to them than would belligerency.

As provided in the treaties of 1778, France expected the United States to give her naval vessels and privateers special privileges, not available to the British, in American ports. With her shipping virtually swept from the seas by the British fleet, France also planned to use American merchantmen to bring needed supplies to her home and colonial ports. To stimulate this trade previously closed to foreigners, she opened it to neutral, meaning American, shipping.

Eager for profit, Americans flocked into French Caribbean ports and immediately built up a flourishing commerce. Since it aided her enemy and strengthened a maritime rival, Britain resented this bloated trade and beginning in June 1793 took steps to throttle it. By three orders in council, essentially executive decrees, of June and November 1793 and January 1794, the British government enforced the dictum that commerce prohibited in time of peace would not be allowed during war. Known as the Rule of 1756, from its application by England in the Seven Years' War, it destroyed American commerce with and between the French colonies.

Enforcing the orders in council, British warships in the Caribbean swooped down on American merchantmen, and their officers confiscated ships and cargoes and impressed seamen. In seizing ships running between American and French colonial ports, a trade France had permitted in time of peace, moreover, the British went beyond the Rule of 1756.

American newspapers played up the Caribbean indignities, whipping up anti-British sentiment. Demands for action against England became so insistent as to endanger the administration's policy of neutrality. Washington, as a result, now found himself in a dilemma. In the commercial treaty of 1778 with France, the United States had committed itself to the practice of maritime principles which Britain had not recognized and consistently ignored, but without a navy the United States could not insist that the British respect those principles.

It seemed that an attempt to enforce the "small navy" principles, such as free ships make free goods, in the French treaty against British naval power would mean war, a war with England that Federalists wished at almost all costs to avoid. Not to try to enforce them, in the view of the Republicans, would violate the French treaty and might lead to war with France.

News of the Caribbean captures reached Philadelphia, the capital, together with evidence of renewed British hostility in the Northwest. The troubles in the Northwest had grown out of Washington's efforts to subdue Indians there with federal arms in 1790 and 1791. Although those two expeditions had failed, they had appeared to threaten British control over the Indians south of the treaty line of 1783. The British, therefore, had offered to mediate the conflict between the Americans and the Indians, hoping to profit from the mediation. They urged Americans to accept a "neutral, Indian barrier state" in the Northwest, one that would protect Canada against American advances and at the same time save the fur trade. Not even Hamiltonians, however, could accept the idea of carving a buffer state out of American soil.

Washington then tried for the third time to crush Indian resistance by placing General "Mad Anthony" Wayne in command of frontier forces on the Ohio. In the winter of 1793 Wayne marched his army into the Indian country of the Northwest, a move that British frontier officials considered a threat to Canada. They believed his true objectives were the posts they occupied.

In February 1794 Lord Dorchester, Sir Guy Carleton, governor general of Canada, told a delegation of Indians, among them representatives of the ones Wayne was preparing to punish, that American settlements in the Northwest were unauthorized. Soon, he said, the Indians would be able to recover the settled lands because within the year Britain and the United States would be at war.

Dorchester's intemperate words, seemingly spoken to stiffen Indian resistance, as well as an order given to his troops at about the same time to occupy Fort Miami, sixty miles southwest of Detroit in territory clearly American, enraged Americans. Talk of war became common. Thus, early in 1794 grievances of the peace treaty, failure of Americans to obtain a commercial treaty, Caribbean spoliations, and frontier troubles all combined with anti-British propaganda to produce an Anglo-American crisis.

Responding to the public anger, Congress pressed anti-British legislation. In March it laid a one-month embargo against foreign shipping, an act directed against Britain, and later extended it another month. It also passed various defense measures, among them a bill to fortify harbors, another calling out eighty thousand militia, and one for obtaining additional military stores. In the Senate a Non-Intercourse bill against England met defeat only by the vote of Vice President John Adams.

Catching the war spirit, Americans rushed their preparations for defense and even began drilling in volunteer companies. Mobs attacked British sailors and in such places as Norfolk and Baltimore tarred and feathered

Americans alleged to sympathize with the British. "Even the Monocrat [Federalist] papers," Jefferson reported, "are obliged to publish the most furious Philippics against England." [17]

Several factors, however, prevented the country from immediately plunging into war. The French, for instance, believed that Americans were obligated to resist British seizure of goods on their ships bound for French ports. Angered by Federalist refusal to defend the treaty principle of free ships, free goods, they retaliated by seizing American ships carrying goods to England. They thus violated their treaty obligations to the United States and alienated American shipping interests.

England, moreover, relaxed her orders in council and allowed a temporary resumption of American trade in the Caribbean, and even paid for many of the cargoes her navy seized, whereas France offered no compensation for her seizures. Furthermore, wartime trade with England was more lucrative than that with France. In England, too, there were statesmen who realized that Washington's administration was basically friendly, and they sought to avert hostilities. At the height of the war hysteria, Hammond was even instructed to encourage the American government to maintain its congenial policy. Most important of all as a deterrent to immediate war was the fact that Federalists friendly to England controlled the Senate and the executive branch of the government.

Jay's Treaty

Federalist control of the government made it possible for the president to send a special mission to London to seek an agreement with the British and thus avert war. At first Federalist leaders agreed upon Hamilton to undertake the task, but he was too unpopular. At Hamilton's suggestion, therefore, Washington chose John Jay, then chief justice.

On the basis of diplomatic experience, Jay was admirably qualified for the mission, but politically he was not. As a staunch Federalist and an Anglophile, he was resented by Republicans. From the outset, therefore, his mission became a party issue. Federalists supported it and Republicans did not.

Jay's instructions, drawn up by Hamilton, gave him wide discretion, but told him to do nothing contrary to treaty obligations to France. He was to adjust the grievances arising from the peace treaty of 1783, gain recognition of American principles of neutrality, obtain compensation for seizures of American ships and property, and, if possible, negotiate a commercial treaty. Edmund Randolph, a lukewarm Republican who had succeeded Jefferson as secretary of state, had managed to add that if the British should prove intractable, Jay should consult with Danish and Swedish ministers in London on the possibility of joining a new armed neutrality then being formed to resist British maritime practices. Concern that such a league of neutrals might form, in fact, had been a factor in inducing the British to negotiate at this time.

Fearing any action that might endanger relations with the British, Hamilton blunted the only coercive weapon Jay possessed. He told the British minister in Philadelphia that American policy was predicated on the principle of avoiding entanglement in European affairs and hence the United States would not join the new armed neutrality. Hamilton thus weakened Jay's already shaky bargaining position.

By ignoring most of his instructions, Jay obtained a commercial treaty signed on November 19, 1794. The treaty itself was Britain's most important concession. Others were promises to evacuate the Northwest posts and to pay for the Caribbean spoliations. Britain did not, however, repudiate the spoliations.

Trading privileges were limited. Jay obtained few commercial concessions the United States had not enjoyed before the treaty. A privilege allowing trade with the British West Indies was so restrictive that later not even a Federalist Senate would accept it. The treaty said nothing about the impressment of American seamen, nothing about abducted slaves, nothing about Britain's tampering with the Indians. Furthermore, contrary to the spirit of the French commercial treaty of 1778, Jay acquiesced in the Rule of 1756 and agreed that the British could seize enemy property and food on American ships if they paid for them. Other problems, namely definition of a disputed boundary between Maine and Canada and to the west of Lake Superior, payment of prewar debts to the British, and the amount of British compensation for maritime spoliations, were to be referred to mixed arbitral commissions.

When news of the treaty reached America the public reaction was hostile. Republicans condemned it as a sellout to England. One of them said, "YES, Sir, you have bitched it; you have indeed put your foot in it, Mr. Jay—for shame, Sir." Another expressed his resentment in rhyme:

> Is it again the patriot's fate,
> To mourn his country's fallen state,
> To weep her honour lost;
> To see her bend at Britain's throne,
> No wrongs redress'd, her freedom gone,
> Her independence an empty boast? [18]

Although crowds burned Jay in effigy and even stoned Hamilton when he spoke in defense of Jay's Treaty, Federalists gave it solid support. In the Senate they blocked Republican efforts to defeat the treaty by approving it twenty to ten on June 24, 1795, with not a single vote to spare. After some hesitation President Washington ratified it. Ratifications were exchanged in London on October 28, and on February 29, 1796, Washington proclaimed the treaty as law. Still the Republicans refused to give up the struggle, carrying it to the House of Representatives where they tried to withhold funds necessary to carry out the treaty. Again, this time by the narrow margin of three votes, they failed. It was Washington's support that saved the treaty and hence probably averted war with England.

In spite of its obvious flaws and the harsh controversy it had aroused, Jay's Treaty served American foreign policy well. At a time when the country was unprepared for war and partisan feeling over foreign policy was so strong that a war with England might have split the Union, it kept the peace. It also finally brought Britain's full execution of the peace treaty of 1783 and stripped the Indians of the Northwest of British support. Thus those Indians, a year after General Wayne's victory in the Battle of Fallen Timbers, came to terms in the Treaty of Fort Greenville on August 3, 1795, when they ceded most of the Ohio country. The United States had finally won full control of the Northwest.

By easing old grievances, Jay's Treaty became the first major step since the American Revolution toward an Anglo-American *rapprochement*. This *rapprochement*, however, brought trouble elsewhere. The treaty's concessions to England on neutral trade, particularly its acceptance of the seizure of noncontraband goods if payment were made for them, gave France grounds for claiming violation of her treaties of 1778. Many Americans, moreover, agreed with the view that Jay's Treaty was incompatible with obligations to France.

Pinckney's Treaty

While Jay was negotiating in England, events in Europe caused a change in Spanish diplomacy favorable to the United States. Spain had been ready for peace with France and even an alliance, but in withdrawing from the war as England's ally and thus reversing her foreign policy, she feared English reprisals. The fact that Spain had decided to break relations with England just as the American government was drawing closer to England influenced Spain's policy toward the United States. Spain feared an attack, perhaps by American frontiersmen, perhaps by Anglo-American forces, on her North American colonies while she was still involved in the European war and helpless to protect them. Her ministers, therefore, decided to forestall such an attack by buying American friendship.

In the summer of 1794 Spain asked the United States to renew disrupted negotiations by assigning a new envoy to Madrid. Washington complied by sending Thomas Pinckney, the minister to Britain. Pinckney's instructions required that Americans be given the right to navigate the Mississippi River "in its whole length and breadth, from its source to the sea." [19]

For her goodwill and willingness to make concessions, Spain at first tried to induce the United States to join her and France in a triple alliance

THE BOUNDARY DISPUTE
WITH SPAIN, 1783–1795

for the common preservation of Spanish and American territory in North America. When that plan failed she offered a boundary settlement and free navigation of the Mississippi for an alliance between herself and the United States. Pinckney refused both offers. Finally, in August 1795 he wrote home that the Spanish king was ready "to sacrifice something of what he considered as his right, to testify to his goodwill to us."

A few months later, on October 27, the Spaniards signed the Treaty of San Lorenzo, usually called Pinckney's Treaty, which gave virtually all that Pinckney's instructions asked. In addition to unrestricted navigation of the Mississippi, the United States secured a three-year right, subject to renewal, to deposit goods at New Orleans for trans-shipment, a boundary settlement in the Southwest at the thirty-first parallel, and a promise that Spain would not incite the Indians on her frontier to attack Americans. The United States, in turn, said it would prevent Indians in its territory from striking at Spanish lands. Both countries also agreed on the following: free ships, free goods; a liberal noncontraband list; and a plan for settlement of claims.

Pinckney's Treaty was as welcome to most Americans as Jay's Treaty was unwelcome. One senator remarked, "the Spanish treaty was so favorable, that if the Spanish Government had asked the American Minister to dictate his own terms, he could scarcely have asked for better." Yet it apparently was Jay's Treaty, which the Spaniards feared as the beginning of an Anglo-American alliance, as well as American frontier pressure, that spurred them into negotiating Pinckney's Treaty.[20] The Senate approved Pinckney's Treaty unanimously in March 1796.

Federalist diplomacy thus achieved noteworthy objectives, but, it should be remembered, if England had not been at war with France, she might have conceded nothing, not even Jay's Treaty. If Spain had not faced war with England, she might not have yielded Pinckney's Treaty. Both countries made concessions because they were more concerned with their European policies than with those in America. Nonetheless, with the Jay and Pinckney treaties, the United States for the first time since achieving independence reached agreements that would in fact free its soil of foreign troops and extend its sovereignty to the limits of its boundaries as established in the peace of 1783.

Citizen Genêt

Federalist policy toward France, however, did not lead to similarly fortunate results. Jay's Treaty, looked upon by the French as a betrayal of their alliance of 1778, brought France and the United States to a state of undeclared war between 1797 and 1800. Yet it was not Jay's Treaty alone that touched off hostilities, for relations with France had begun to deteriorate even before Washington had ratified it. The mission of "Citizen" Edmond C. Genêt, the French republic's first emissary to the United States, brought underlying differences with France to the surface.

Young Genêt was not instructed to invoke the alliance of 1778, but was directed to obtain a liberal interpretation favorable to France of certain articles in the commercial treaty of that year. He also had plans for French conquest, with American assistance, of Spanish America and Canada, for it should be remembered that at this time England and Spain were allied against France. To carry out that part of his mission, Genêt brought blank military commissions to be given to Americans willing to fight France's enemies. In addition, he was secretly instructed to shower Americans with pro-French propaganda.

Genêt's mission could not succeed without American aid which would probably have led to British countermeasures and might have drawn the United States into the war. Genêt's objectives, moreover, conflicted with Washington's policy of allegedly impartial neutrality.

Landing in Charleston in April 1793 amid cheers reflecting a French frenzy then sweeping the land, Genêt immediately began challenging American neutrality. Aided by South Carolina's governor, he set up prize courts and outfitted privateers to cruise against British shipping. He also commissioned George Rogers Clark to lead an army of frontiersmen against New Orleans.

The French emissary then proceeded overland to Philadelphia, besieged on the way by welcoming crowds. At Richmond, Virginia, in the midst of such acclaim, he received his first jolt when he heard of the proclamation of neutrality. The next one came in Philadelphia where Washington, who was already upset by his antics, greeted him coolly.

Then Genêt and the Hamiltonians clashed over differing interpretations of the commercial treaty of 1778. Seeking to use American ports and seamen for French privateers, Genêt argued that the treaty "expressly" authorized France to use those ports for equipping privateers and for condemning and selling prizes. Actually, as Hamiltonians insisted, the treaty obligated the United States merely to close its ports to the outfitting of British privateers and to their prizes. While the United States could allow French privateers and their prizes to use its ports, the treaty did not, as Genêt contended, automatically give France what was denied to Britain.

As a mark of friendship, Jeffersonians at first believed that the government should grant France the privileges denied Britain, but the Hamiltonians did not. Such a gesture, they argued, would violate the policy of impartial neutrality and might lead to war with England. Despite his French sympathies, even Jefferson finally agreed that to remain neutral the United States had to prevent the French from using American ports as bases for hostile forays.

The Hamiltonians and Genêt also clashed over money. To finance his military expeditions and to pay for food he purchased and sent to France, Genêt requested advance payment on America's debt to France. Hamilton opposed such payment, and Washington then refused to make it. Furthermore, Washington asked the French minister to order French privateers that offended neutrality from American ports.

Bitterly disappointed by the lack of sympathy within the government for France's cause, Genêt defied Washington, flagrantly so, when he outfitted a captured British ship, *The Little Sarah,* in Philadelphia and sent her to sea as a French privateer. Popular sympathy for the French Revolution led Genêt to believe that Washington and his policies lacked public support and that he himself could obtain the backing he needed from the people. Allegedly, he threatened to appeal over the head of the president directly to the people, an accusation that Genêt insisted was false. Whether or not Genêt uttered such a threat, Washington decided to get rid of him, a decision endorsed by Hamilton.

Even Jefferson, who had at first praised Genêt, expressed disgust. "Never in my opinion," he said, "was so calamitous an appointment made, as that of the present Minister of F[rance] here. Hot headed, all imagination, no judgment, passionate, disrespectful & even indecent towards the P[resident] in his written as well as verbal communications, talking of appeals from him to Congress, from them to the people, urging the most unreasonable & groundless propositions. . . ."[21]

When Washington demanded Genêt's recall, a new revolutionary government in France obliged. It ordered the new minister, Joseph Fauchet, to arrest Genêt and send him back for trial and probable execution, an order Washington would not allow Fauchet to carry out. Genêt later married an American and remained in the United States for the rest of his life.

Although headstrong and intemperate, Genêt was not a wild-eyed revolutionary. He was an intelligent, though rash, young man of thirty who tried to carry out an almost impossible mission. Any French minister with his instructions would probably have run into difficulties.

British complaints against Genêt's activities, meanwhile, led the government to define neutral obligations. On June 5, 1794, Congress passed a Neutrality Act that made Washington's principles of impartial neutrality the law of the land by prohibiting foreign recruiting in the United States and belligerent activity in coastal waters and ports.

Morris and Monroe in Paris

In Paris at this time, Gouverneur Morris, the American minister, was alienating the French government as effectively as Genêt had outraged Washington. As a confirmed aristocrat, a counterrevolutionary, and a dabbler in royalist intrigue, Morris had irked French governments from the beginning of his mission. Favoring a constitutional monarchy over a republic, he did his best to save Louis XVI from the guillotine, going so far as to draft a plan for Louis's rescue from virtual imprisonment in the Tuileries. During the height of the French Revolution, Morris even used the American legation and his own home as asylums for French nobles fleeing Republican authorities. Such activity, while in some instances humanitarian to a laudable degree, violated French laws and provided cause for official resentment.

Morris's hostility to the French Revolution showed in the reports he sent home. Since he was a close friend of the president, he often went over the secretary of state's head to correspond directly with Washington. Morris's reports, in fact, increased Washington's fears of happenings in France. Jefferson, for instance, had complained that Morris "kept the president's mind constantly poisoned with his forebodings." [22]

The French foreign office believed that Morris's reports were gradually destroying Franco-American friendship. One of the objectives of Genêt's mission, in fact, had been to offset Morris's "malevolent" influence on Franco-American relations. Finally, when Washington asked for Genêt's recall, the Jacobin government insisted that in return he must recall Morris and send an envoy who sympathized with the revolution. Washington reluctantly complied.

Since at this time Jay was headed for England and the French suspected that his mission might endanger the alliance of 1778, the French request fell in with Federalist plans. Federalist statesmen wanted to calm distrust of the Jay mission and assure France of American friendship. In the spring of 1794, therefore, Washington appointed James Monroe, an ardent

Jeffersonian, to succeed Morris. Monroe was instructed to assure the French that Jay could do nothing that would weaken America's attachment to France.

Ironically, Monroe overplayed his part, at least from the Federalist point of view, and from the beginning incurred Federalist displeasure. In an anti-British speech before the National Convention, the French governing body that received him, Monroe praised French-American friendship and voiced sympathy for France in her war. Washington and other Federalists felt that Monroe had "stepped over the true line" of neutrality. After Jay's Treaty was signed, Monroe found himself in an impossible position. When the French asked him if it were an alliance, he denied that it was. "I cannot believe," he said, "that an American minister would ever forget the connections between the United States and France, which every day's experience demonstrate to be in the interest of both Republics still further to cement."[23]

Later, when Monroe learned the contents of Jay's Treaty, he feared it would destroy Franco-American amity. Yet the new secretary of state, Timothy Pickering, an uncompromising Federalist, sent him instructions to defend the treaty. "In our new engagements," Pickering said, "we violate no prior obligations."[24]

Nonetheless, the French threatened to abrogate the alliance of 1778 and other reprisals because of Jay's Treaty, and they even talked of war. In March 1796, when the French presented him with a list of their grievances against the American government, Monroe, it seemed to Federalists, made a tepid defense of administration policy. Washington, therefore, recalled him in disgrace.

The Directory, France's new executive body, meanwhile, began reprisals short of war. In October it recalled its minister to the United States without appointing a successor. At the same time it announced a decree that authorized French warships to deal with American vessels "as these suffer the English to treat them."

Before Monroe left Paris, the Directory said that it would "no longer recognize nor receive a minister plenipotentiary from the United States, until a reparation of the grievances demanded of the American government."[25] In an effort to overcome the French crisis, Washington, however, had already appointed Charles Cotesworth Pinckney, a Federalist, to succeed Monroe. The Directory not only refused to receive Pinckney, but also forced him to leave France under humiliating circumstances.

In the United States, meanwhile, Genêt's successors tried to defeat Jay's Treaty by tampering with Congress and meddling in domestic politics. This meddling infuriated Washington who threw his prestige behind the treaty and against the French. It also prompted him to carry out a decision he had made earlier.

Washington's Farewell Address

Tired by the strain and abuse of politics and upset by the tensions of foreign policy, Washington decided to announce his retirement. French intrigues "in the internal concerns of our country" convinced him, moreover, that a warning to the nation was needed. Following Hamilton's advice, he withheld the farewell warning until three months before the electors gathered to vote for a president. Then, on September 19, 1796, he offered it to the people through newspapers.

Washington had planned a valedictory to the nation in 1792 and James Madison had drafted one, but Hamilton wrote most of the new version and made it a campaign document designed to assure a Federalist victory in the nation's first contested presidential election. Washington told Hamilton that were it not for the status of "party disputes" and foreign affairs he would not have considered it necessary to revise his valedictory. Yet the bulk of the message, one of the most influential statements on American foreign policy ever made, dealt with domestic affairs.

Washington opened the Farewell Address by announcing he would not be a candidate for a third term. Then he stressed the evils of party spirit which "opens the door to foreign influence and corruption." Through party passions, he said, "the policy and the will of one country, are subjected to the policy and will of another." Having in mind, undoubtedly, the French republic, he advised against "a passionate attachment of one Nation for another." Such "sympathy for the favourite nation," he said, leads to wars and quarrels "without adequate inducement and justification."

A free people, Washington continued, ought to be "constantly awake" to "the insidious wiles of foreign influence." Then in the oft-quoted "Great rule of conduct" he advised that with Europe we should have "as little *political* connection as possible." While stressing fidelity to "existing engagements," he said, " 'tis our true policy to steer clear of permanent alliances with any portion of the foreign world." But, he added, "we may safely trust to temporary alliances for extraordinary emergencies."

In summary, the president defended his policies, particularly neutrality, struck at French meddling in American politics, and denounced dangerous implications drawn from the French alliance.

Federalists praised the address, Republicans denounced it as political propaganda, and the French disliked it. A few days later Pierre A. Adet, the French minister who had not yet been recalled, threw himself openly into the presidential campaign to see to it that Washington's words would not have their intended effect. By electioneering against John Adams, the Federalist candidate, and in favor of Thomas Jefferson, the Republican standard bearer, Adet made himself a main issue in the election. Only Jefferson's victory he warned, would eliminate the possibility of war with France.

Adet's interference apparently did Jefferson more harm than good. Federalists campaigned as the party of patriotism, pitting Washington and Adams against Adet and the Republicans, who appeared to be in league with a foreign power. Beware of foreign influence, Federalists told the voters; "decide between the address of the President and the [French]."[26] Adet's activities seemed to confirm the warnings in Washington's Farewell Address. Adams narrowly won the presidency.

Then in the last weeks of Washington's administration, relations with France deteriorated so badly that war seemed imminent. In the Caribbean, French decrees struck at American shipping. On March 2, 1797, two days before Washington left office, the Directory announced renewed seizures of American ships and warned that Americans found serving the British would be treated as pirates. Charging that Jay's Treaty vitiated the commercial treaty of 1778, France again said she would no longer recognize the principle of free ships, free goods. In effect, she announced a limited maritime war against American commerce.

The XYZ Affair

When John Adams took over the presidency, therefore, his most pressing problem was the crisis with France. To deal with it, he immediately called a special session of Congress. He asked for enactment of defense measures so that the country would be prepared in case of war. Contrary to the desires of the war hawks within his own party, he also requested approval for a special mission to France to resolve the crisis. Congress did not enact all the legislation he desired, but it did approve the mission.

Adams's mission consisted of Pinckney, then in Holland, John Marshall, a prominent Virginia Federalist, and Elbridge Gerry, a personal friend and lukewarm Federalist soon to become a Republican. Those commissioners were to offer concessions on neutral rights similar to those in Jay's Treaty. In return, France was expected to restore normal diplomatic relations, respect American rights at sea, consent to release the United States from its obligations under the treaties of 1778 and the later consular convention, particularly from the guarantee of the French West Indies.

The commissioners met in Paris in October 1797, but Charles Maurice de Talleyrand-Périgord, the Directory's minister of foreign affairs, refused to receive them officially. Through intermediaries, including a seductive woman, he demanded a bribe of $250,000, a "loan," but in fact a gift, of several million dollars, and an apology for unfriendly remarks about France that Adams had made in his message to Congress.

Bribery itself did not shock the Americans, but they had no money for a bribe and no instructions to negotiate a loan. Besides, the so-called loan would have violated American neutrality. Nor did they have assurances they could obtain what they desired if they paid. The bribe would pay only for the privilege of presenting their case, not for negotiation. Declaring that they would not make such an "absolute surrender of the independence of the United States," the commissioners rejected Talleyrand's proposals.

Nonetheless, the urbane Talleyrand, though never directly, persisted in his demands, for the French mistakenly believed that most Americans were still pro-French and would not tolerate failure of the mission and a complete rupture. Adams would not, they were convinced, risk war with France and civil war in the United States.

Thus, when one of Talleyrand's excitable agents threatened war, Marshall answered that America would then protect herself. "You do not speak to the point," the agent cried out, "it is expected that you will offer money. . . . What is your answer?"

"It is no; no;" Pinckney blurted out, "not a sixpence!" Legend later transformed this into the slogan, "Millions for defense, but not one cent for tribute."[27]

Finally, after months of waiting to be received, Marshall and Pinckney left Paris. Believing that he could prevent war, Gerry stayed a while longer. A few months later, in July 1798, he sailed for home empty-handed, except for a message from Talleyrand saying that France desired a reconciliation, peace not war.

The first of the commissioners' dispatches telling of their treatment, meanwhile, had arrived in Philadelphia. That story shocked Adams. He consulted his cabinet and for a while thought of asking Congress for a declaration of war. On March 19, 1798, when he went before Congress, he explained the failure of his peace mission, announced limited hostilities with France, and asked for power to arm merchant ships and take other defensive measures.

Unwilling to believe the president's charges, Republicans accused him of sabre-rattling, opposed his war measures, and on April 2 rammed a demand for the dispatches through the House of Representatives. Adams then sent the dispatches to the House and Senate, but substituted the letters X, Y, and Z for the names of Talleyrand's agents. Astounded by what they read, Republicans in the House voted against publication, but in the Senate the Federalists had the upper hand and secured publication.

The dispatches sent a tremor through the country. Sea spoliations and other indignities had enraged Americans. Now the humiliation of Pinckney, Marshall, and Gerry appalled them. France's stock, even among Republicans, fell. Federalists now talked openly of war, and Adams, for the first time, became popular. He was publicly toasted as the nation's foremost patriot and his name was praised in song and poetry. Extreme Federalists desired full-scale war. At this point Adams, influenced by his sudden popularity and the public hysteria, also favored such a war.

On June 21 Adams sent a trenchant message to Congress announcing that he would "never send another minister to France without assurances that he will be received, respected, and honored as the representative of a great, free, powerful, and independent nation."[28] Congress responded by authorizing naval retaliation against French sea marauders and other defensive measures previously refused. It created a navy department, voted appropriations for new warships, authorized increases in the regular army, and in July abrogated the French treaties and consular convention. Washington agreed to come out of retirement to lead the new army, an army to be organized by Hamilton, the second in command. Americans, in other words, readied themselves for war.

The Quasi-War

So far the conflict with France was limited to half-measures, hence the name Quasi-War. Neither country declared war and neither authorized offensive hostilities or the capture of private property by warships. The American navy, whose ships, such as the frigate *Constellation,* won some notable victories, attacked only French warships and privateers and fought primarily to protect commerce.

Extreme Federalists wanted an enlarged war as an excuse for crushing the opposition party, expanding the nation's frontiers, and collaborating with England. They gained enactment of alien and sedition acts, which were directed against French and Irish aliens in the United States, and helped muzzle Republican editors and politicians. They supported Hamilton's scheme to send his army into Louisiana and Mexico and expand at the expense of France's weak ally, Spain. They wished to extend naval cooperation with England, such as the exchange of naval recognition signals and the use of British convoys, into an alliance.

Even though war fever made Federalists popular and gave them majorities in the congressional elections of 1789–99, most Americans apparently did not want a full-scale conflict. Those Federalists who desired war, moreover, were unable to command a majority even within their own party. Most importantly, the president, because of his feud with Hamilton over who should actually command the army, lost his enthusiasm for war.

The stepped-up tempo of naval hostilities and news of anti-French nationalism in the United States also alarmed key Frenchmen such as Talleyrand. They were shocked to find that they had overestimated America's pro-French sentiment. An enlarged war offered France no advantage, and hence they wanted none of it. Furthermore, such a war might ruin their plans to reacquire Louisiana, details of which were nearly completed.

These considerations and the fact that France no longer had direct diplomatic relations with the United States led Talleyrand to make peaceful overtures to William Vans Murray, the American minister at The Hague. Finally, at the insistence of Murray, Talleyrand agreed to meet Adams's conditions for the resumption of diplomatic negotiations. In a letter of September 1798 he said that any envoy the United States would send to France to reconcile differences between the two countries "would be undoubtedly received with the respect due to the representative of a free, independent, and powerful nation."[29] At the same time the French repealed decrees against American shipping, restrained their privateers in the West Indies, and respected America's neutral rights as they had not done previously. They had also told various Americans, such as George Logan, a Pennsylvania Quaker who had gone to Paris on his own to try to end the Quasi-War, that they wanted peace.

At first Adams spurned Talleyrand's overtures, but the president's change of heart toward full-scale war caused him to reconsider. With Talleyrand's letter, moreover, he now felt he had the necessary assurances for a peace with honor. In defiance of his cabinet, which was dominated by extreme Federalists, he sent Congress a message in February 1799 proposing another negotiation with the French. He nominated Murray to carry out the mission, thereby causing a deeper split in the Federalist party. Extremists insisted that the French overtures were meaningless and urged their rejection.

Although the extreme Federalists were unable to defeat Murray's nomination, they forced Adams to expand the peace mission to a commission of three. The new commissioners were reliable Federalists, Chief Justice Oliver Ellsworth and William R. Davie, a former governor of North Carolina.

When the three envoys met in Paris in March 1800, Talleyrand, who had become minister of foreign affairs for the Consulate, France's new government controlled by Napoleon Bonaparte, received them promptly. Negotiations began immediately with a French commission of three headed by Napoleon's brother, Joseph.

As directed by their instructions, the Americans asked the French to pay nearly $20 million in reparations for spoliations against American shipping going back to 1793 and to accept as legal Congress's unilateral abrogation of the treaties of 1778 and 1788. The French argued that the Americans could not have both an indemnity and an annulment of the treaties. The treaties, they said, were either in effect or they were not. If they were dead, then the abrogation was an act that recognized a state of war. The spoliations, therefore, were acts of war and gave no grounds for claims against France. If the treaties were still in force, then France and the United States were still allies, and France could claim American support against her enemies.

Since the French had the better of the argument, when Talleyrand offered a compromise, the American commissioners went beyond their instructions to accept it. The agreement that formally ended the Quasi-War was the Treaty of Mortefontaine, but known also as the Convention of

1800. It was signed on September 30, 1800. As finally ratified, it suspended the treaties of 1778 and 1788 and dropped the spoliation claims.

In effect, the American government, which eventually had to assume
the claims of its own citizens, paid a bargain price for getting rid of the old
French treaties, for the Treaty of Mortefontaine marked an important point
in the nation's development. It paved the way for Napoleon to carry out
schemes for the acquisition of Louisiana and the building of a French empire in North America, and by securing his goodwill it laid the ground-
work for ceding that province to the United States. The convention also
freed the United States from its first alliance, an entanglement that contributed to a wariness toward all alliances for a hundred and fifty years.

In negotiating the convention and achieving peace, John Adams
helped cripple his party and perhaps contributed to his own defeat in the
election of 1800, for the extreme Federalists deserted him. Yet Adams
never regretted his peace missions. "They were," he wrote in later years,
"the most disinterested and meritorious actions of my life." [30]

Although Adams bowed out of office in defeat and his administration
marked the end of the Federalist era, Federalist statesmen in retrospect
could take satisfaction in considerable achievement in foreign policy. They
had successfully guided the young nation through a period of international
turmoil and danger. They left the center of the national stage with the nation's major grievances in foreign affairs settled, its flag flying over all its
lands, and most important, its people at peace and not threatened by a
major enemy.

I V

Jeffersonian Diplomacy

From the moment of independence, the future of Louisiana, the vast domain west of the Mississippi River, had been a prime topic of speculation among Americans. Ceded to Spain by France at the close of the Seven Years' War, Louisiana touched the interests of four nations: Spain, the United States, France, and Great Britain. Not having reconciled themselves to permanent loss of Louisiana, Frenchmen looked forward to the day when they would reverse the decision of 1763 and once again control the heart of the American continent. Although convulsed by revolution and involved in great international conflicts, successive French governments in the 1790s cast covetous eyes on Louisiana, and French statesmen prepared various plans for repossession.

Bringing Spain to her knees, France, in the Treaty of Basel of July 1795, tried to persuade Spain to cede Louisiana, but failed. She did succeed, however, in acquiring the Spanish half of the island of Santo Domingo.

Rumors of French efforts to regain Louisiana in peace negotiations with Spain at Basel in 1795 reached the United States during the election campaign of 1796, when party animosities were at high pitch. Federalists seized upon the rumors, along with known border intrigues, as evidence of French efforts in collusion with Republicans, not only to take Louisiana but also to dismember the Union by incorporating the trans-Appalachian states into Louisiana. Such reasoning, while not unjustified, stemmed from partisan political thinking and from Federalist distrust of France.

Secretary of State Pickering expressed well the Federalist viewpoint. "We have often heard," he said, "that the French Government contemplated repossession of Louisiana; and it has been conjectured that in their negotiations with Spain the cession of Louisiana & the Floridas may have been agreed on. You will see all the mischief to be apprehended from such an event. The Spaniards will certainly be more safe, quiet and useful neighbors."[1]

Napoleon's Plans

Three years later Pickering's fears became fact. On October 1, 1800, the day after Joseph Bonaparte signed the Treaty of Mortefontaine, another of Napoleon's ministers concluded a secret agreement with Spain, the second Treaty of San Ildefonso. For the promise of a kingdom in Italy, Spain gave France six warships and Louisiana, but would not, as Napoleon desired, include the Floridas, territory the British had called East and West Florida, in the cession.

Napoleon wanted Louisiana as a base and source of raw materials and food for a new French empire in North America. The commercial foundation of that empire would be France's "sugar islands" in the Caribbean, particularly rich Santo Domingo. After slaves had rebelled and destroyed white rule in 1795, Santo Domingo had been virtually independent of France. Before Napoleon could build his balanced empire in the New World, therefore, he had to reconquer that island.

If Napoleon succeeded and occupied Louisiana, the United States would lose the advantage of rapid growth of its western settlements, a growth that had alarmed the Spaniards. "Their method of spreading themselves," the Spanish governor of Louisiana had written as early as 1794 of Americans, "and their policy are so much to be feared by Spain as are their arms. Every new settlement, when it reaches thirty thousand [sic] souls, forms a state, which is united to the United States, so far as regards mutual protection, but which governs itself and imposes its own laws."

While it was true that England might intervene if France became too powerful in North America, her intervention would not help the United States. The British, who would then encircle the United States, would be as powerful and as unpalatable as neighbors as the French. Besides, Britain's attitude after preliminary peace negotiations with the French in October 1801 appeared to offer encouragement to Napoleon's dreams of a New World empire. She seemed willing to allow Napoleon to occupy himself with North American colonies so as to divert his attention from projects nearer home, as in the Mediterranean and on the continent.

Spain's attitude toward Louisiana also made Napoleon's task easier. After Pinckney's Treaty, Spain no longer considered Louisiana worth its annual cost. Expensive to govern and difficult to defend, especially against aggressive American frontiersmen, the province had never been profitable. "Frankly," Spain's chief minister confessed to his ambassador in France in June 1800, "it [Louisiana] costs us more than it is worth."[2]

Talleyrand persuaded Spain that France could check the Americans. "The French Republic," he said, "will be a wall of brass forever impenetrable to the combined efforts of England and America." Spain's statesmen liked the idea of placing France between their American lands and the United States.

When Napoleon finally offered the Spanish king the newly created Kingdom of Etruria, comprising Tuscany and Piombino, for his son-in-law, Spain gave up Louisiana. Since the Treaty of San Ildefonso had not defined the Italian kingdom, France, on March 21, 1801, signed a second treaty which did, the Convention of Aranjuez. Still, Napoleon experienced difficulty in obtaining physical possession of Louisiana.

Insisting that Napoleon had not installed the Spanish sovereign in Etruria as he had promised, Spain refused to make delivery of Louisiana. Finally, she offered to surrender the province with conditions. France would have to gain international recognition for the king of Etruria, agree to restore Louisiana to Spain if the new king should lose his Italian throne, and promise "not to sell or alienate" any part of Louisiana. "In the name of the First Consul," France agreed.[3]

Jefferson's Attitude

In the United States, meanwhile, the Republicans had won control of the government. When Thomas Jefferson became President in March 1801 he did not know that France had regained Louisiana. Within six months of the Treaty of San Ildefonso he heard rumors of it, and all during the year more undercover information of Louisiana's transfer drifted into the United States, but Jefferson did not appear as alarmed as the Federalists had been.

Nonetheless, the transfer of coveted Louisiana from weak Spain to strong France could not fail to disturb any government in the United States, even an ostensibly pro-French Republican administration. Despite his French predilections and initial appearance of calmness over the rumors of retrocession, Jefferson became alarmed over the fate of the Mississippi Valley. "There is considerable reason to apprehend that Spain cedes Louisiana and the Floridas to France," he wrote. "It is a policy very unwise to both, and very ominous to us."[4]

Without England's help it appeared that Jefferson could not, without bloodshed, prevent the French from regaining Louisiana. He seemed at first able to do little more than temporize, particularly since he did not know the details of Spain's agreement with France. He was not idle, however, for he quietly increased military strength along the Mississippi to prepare the country for whatever might happen to Louisiana. Westerners and others urged the president to conquer Louisiana before the French could take possession. "I am afraid they may strike at Louisiana," the French chargé in Washington reported, "before we can take it over."[5]

To prevent the occupation, Jefferson worked through influential Frenchmen who sympathized with the position of the United States, and through one of them, Pierre Samuel du Pont de Nemours, an old friend who had spent three years in the United States, he made clear his determination to oppose Napoleon. He gave du Pont two letters to take with him when he returned to France in April 1802. In one of them, to the American minister in France, Robert R. Livingston, he wrote an often quoted passage. "There is on the globe one single spot," he said, "the possessor of which is our natural and habitual enemy. It is New Orleans, through which the produce of three-eighths of our territory must pass to market. . . . France, placing herself in that door, assumes to us the attitude of defiance. Spain might have retained it quietly for years. . . . The day that France takes possession of New Orleans, fixes the sentence which is to restrain her forever within her low water mark. It seals the union of two countries, who, in conjunction, can maintain exclusive possession of the ocean. From that moment, we must marry ourselves to the British fleet and nation."[6]

Du Pont advised against using threats with Napoleon, who would be more "offended than moved." Du Pont said that Jefferson showed "an ambition of conquest," and explained that a British alliance would bring greater dangers than would France in Louisiana. If the United States would not be satisfied with assurance of free navigation of the Mississippi, he suggested, then it should try to buy what it desired. Secretary of State James Madison immediately took up the idea of purchase. On May 1, 1802, he instructed Livingston to find out how much France would take for Louisiana and the Floridas.[7] Americans assumed that Spain had surrendered the Floridas as well as Louisiana to France.

As time passed, Jefferson's fears of early 1802 increased. That summer he said publicly, according to a British diplomat, that if the United States could not expel the French from Louisiana "they must have recourse to the assistance of other powers, meaning unquestionably Great Britain."

Then in the fall the Spaniards delivered an alarming blow. On October 16, the day after the Spanish king gave the final order transferring Louisiana to France, his acting intendant of Louisiana at New Orleans, in violation of Pinckney's Treaty, withdrew the American "right of deposit"—that is, the privilege of leaving goods in New Orleans to await shipment in seagoing vessels.

Although the order did not affect freedom of navigation, it caused inconvenience and aroused talk of war in the West. "Scarcely any Thing has happened since the Revolution," a British observer wrote in January 1803, "which has so much agitated the minds of all Descriptions of People in the United States as this Decree."[8] Assuming that the order came from Napoleon and that he would close the Mississippi once he took over, Westerners demanded that Jefferson do something about this blow to their economic well-being.

The Spaniards, in fact, had suspended the right of deposit on their own initiative, and later, when the United States protested, they revoked the suspension, but not until April 1803. Not knowing of Spain's independent action and thinking that France had the Floridas as well as Louisiana, Westerners feared that when Napoleon took possession he would exclude them from the entire gulf coast.

Jefferson was confronted with a dilemma. Strong measures against France and Spain would lead to war, but to do nothing would play into the hands of his political opponents and perhaps disrupt the Union. For political reasons Federalists backed Western demands for forcible seizure of New Orleans. These fears finally induced Jefferson to go beyond indirect threats in the crisis. "The measures we have been pursuing being invisible, do not satisfy" Westerners and Federalist war hawks, he told Monroe. "Something sensible, therefore, has become necessary." [9]

So, while Livingston in Paris argued that France could not gain from driving America into Britain's arms and that she did not need all of Louisiana, but desired New Orleans and the Floridas, Jefferson had to act. In spite of Federalist support of the Western demands for strong measures, most Westerners still trusted Jefferson and the Republicans more than they did the Federalists.

At this juncture du Pont extricated Jefferson from his predicament. In a letter from Paris, which arrived in Washington on December 31, 1802, he made his earlier suggestion more specific. He advised Jefferson to offer to buy New Orleans and the Floridas for $6 million. He too thought France had gained the Floridas.

Less than two weeks later Congress appropriated $2 million for the use of a special mission to France, and Jefferson authorized Livingston to purchase New Orleans and the Floridas. At the same time, to aid Livingston in the negotiations and to placate Western fears, he appointed James Monroe a special envoy to France. Monroe, the ardent Republican, owned land in the West and for twenty years had championed free navigation of the Mississippi. Understandably, he was popular in the West.

Although Monroe's appointment removed the threat of an immediate explosion in the West, it did not end all danger of war. Shortly before he sailed, the Republican members of Congress gave him a public dinner, where among the many toasts one revealed the temper of Americans. It went, "peace if peace is honorable, war if war is necessary." Yet, Westerners calmed down while awaiting news from France.

Jefferson, moreover, did not abandon plans for a British alliance. "According to all I can gather," the French *chargé* in Washington wrote, "I see that Mr. Monroe has *carte blanche* and that he will go to London if he is badly received at Paris." The *chargé* was partially correct. Only as a last resort, if France refused all overtures and the American envoys learned that she planned to seal the Mississippi were they to go to England and seek an alliance. Basic in Jefferson's policy toward Louisiana was the idea that it was destined to become American and that negotiations and purchase were cheaper than fighting for New Orleans and less dangerous than an alliance with England.

When Monroe sailed for France early in March 1803, American statesmen had little reason to believe his mission would be easy, but when he arrived in Paris on April 13 the whole situation concerning Louisiana had changed. Napoleon had already offered to sell not merely New Orleans, but all of Louisiana.

Jefferson and Secretary of State Madison had not thought they could acquire all of Louisiana at this time. Their immediate objective had been New Orleans and the Floridas. For that territory, all of it east of the Mississippi, they had been willing to pay as much as $10 million and guarantee France free navigation of the river and special commercial privileges in the surrendered ports. If Livingston and Monroe made a good bargain, the president and his secretary of state had even been willing, for a while at least, to guarantee France's possession of Louisiana west of the Mississippi.

Acquisition of Louisiana

Napoleon could have retained Louisiana as well as American goodwill by making minor concessions to the United States. His reasons for offering to sell the entire province, therefore, are important. Since he never directly revealed his motives, they have been the basis of much scholarly conjecture. Yet the circumstantial evidence on motivation is reasonably clear.

The First Consul's colonial venture in the New World had turned out badly, particularly on Santo Domingo, the key to his plans of empire. Pouring men and money into the island, he had made a determined effort to conquer it. An army of veterans under the command of his brother-in-law, General Charles Leclerc, had slashed at the rebels, but behind the leadership of a talented former slave, Toussaint L'Ouverture, the blacks had fought back savagely. Even though the French captured Toussaint within three months, the fierce resistance and the ravages of yellow fever proved too much even for Napoleon's veterans.

When Leclerc himself, as well as thousands of French soldiers, died of yellow fever in 1802, Napoleon's dreams of empire received a blow from which they never recovered. In one year Santo Domingo had swallowed fifty thousand French troops he could not spare. Fighting there had also delayed occupation of Louisiana.

During the fall and winter of 1802–1803, Napoleon had assembled an expedition in Helvoët Sluys, a small port near Rotterdam, to reinforce Santo Domingo and to occupy New Orleans. He gave General Claude Victor, in command of the expedition, secret orders to take and hold a strong position in Louisiana. "The intention of the First Consul," the instructions read, "is to give Louisiana a degree of strength which will permit him to abandon it without fear in time of war, so that its enemies may be forced to the greatest sacrifices merely in attempting an attack on it." [10]

Again Napoleon's plans failed. Various impediments held up provisioning, and in January and February a severe cold gripped the French ships fast in a vise of ice. When spring came, storms and events in Europe kept the transports from sailing.

By the spring of 1803, in fact, Napoleon was ready to admit that the Peace of Amiens of March 1802, which had ended the war between France and England, was merely a truce. Relations with England were now so bad that a new war appeared certain. Even if he wanted to try to defend Louisiana against England, he believed he could not hold it without the Floridas. Since Spain would not give up the Floridas, he felt that without them Louisiana lost much of its value. With England in control of the seas and with no troops in Louisiana, he knew that American or English forces would probably seize New Orleans as soon as war started. Great Britain might even make a firm alliance with the United States as the price for ousting France. Thus, the failure to acquire the Floridas, conquer Santo

THE LOUISIANA PURCHASE

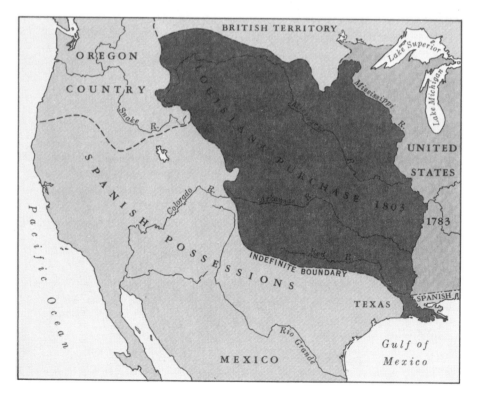

Domingo, and occupy Louisiana combined with pressure and threats of seizure by Americans, and events in Europe, apparently led the Corsican to abandon his New World empire.

To keep Louisiana out of British hands and to prevent an Anglo-American combination against him, Napoleon offered the whole province to the United States. He could, moreover, use the money in his military preparations, though money was not a prime consideration in his action. He had to work quickly, however, while the nominal peace with England continued. He authorized Talleyrand, his foreign minister, and François Barbé Marbois, his minister of finance, to act. What, Talleyrand had asked Livingston the day before Monroe reached Paris, would the United States give for the whole of Louisiana? In the ensuing negotiations Livingston and Monroe overcame their jealousy of each other and were wise enough to recognize a bargain and to go beyond their instructions to clinch it.

As France originally wanted about $25 million the Americans haggled with Barbé-Marbois over the price. "We shall do all we can to cheapen the purchase," Livingston wrote to Madison on April 13, "but my present sentiment is that we shall buy." They did buy, signing a treaty and two conventions which provided for the cession of and payment for Louisiana. These agreements, all dated April 30, 1803, bound the United States to pay $15 million in cash and claims. For some 828,000 square miles of land this amounted to roughly three cents an acre. Livingston and Monroe had bought an empire to get a city. "We have lived long," Livingston said, "but this is the noblest work of our whole lives." [11]

France had acted just in time. On May 9 the American envoys heard that if war broke out, England would send an expedition to Louisiana. Within a week England and France ended their truce and went to war. This did not, however, stand in the way of completing the Louisiana transactions. Since Napoleon wanted cash, not American securities, and French banks would not float a loan, the United States turned to English and Dutch bankers for the money. The firm of Baring Brothers & Company of London loaned the United States over ten million dollars. Alexander Baring, the future Lord Ashburton, even traveled to Paris and the United States to finance the purchase. With the approval of the British government, the money finally reached Napoleon, England's enemy.

Constitutional Problems

Seemingly, the purchase fulfilled the desire of American expansionists and extricated Jefferson from his delicate fix. Yet, acquisition of the vast territory posed serious problems of conscience, principle, and politics. Being a strict constructionist, Jefferson believed he did not have the constitutional power to buy Louisiana and to incorporate its inhabitants into the Union. He thought he could take advantage of the bargain only through a constitutional amendment. By overcoming conscience and overturning princple, Jefferson accepted the purchase, which at no time did he consider rejecting. He did not allow what he called "metaphysical subtleties" to stand in his way.

A few New England Federalists also did violence to alleged principles. Reversing their previous demands for forcible acquisition and challenging the legality of title and constitutionality of the transaction, they now opposed the purchase. Yet most Federalist leaders were also expansionists, and like Alexander Hamilton they favored it but gave Jefferson no credit for consummating it. Although not responsible for planning the purchase, Jefferson deserved credit for quickly taking advantage of a propitious moment.

In addition to raising grave constitutional questions, the circumstances of Napoleon's sale created other problems. One was the legality of the transfer. Napoleon had never fulfilled his obligations to Spain under the Convention of Aranjuez. He had not secured adequate international recognition of Etruria, and French troops had never left the kingdom.

Napoleon also broke his promise to the Spanish king. "The King, my master," the Spanish ambassador in Paris, protested, "decided to deliver the aforesaid Colony only on condition that it should at no time, under no pretext, and in no manner be alienated or ceded to any other power." Using the same argument, Spain protested many times to the United States that France lacked "the power to alienate the said province without the approbation of Spain." Nonetheless, Spain was powerless to block the transfer. She did not have the force to prevent American occupation of Louisiana, and only force could now keep Americans out.

If Napoleon had acted constitutionally, France probably would have rejected the Louisiana treaties. According to France's constitution of December 1799 he could not legally alienate the national domain without consent of the legislative chambers. In addition, he antagonized a substantial body of French public opinion. His brothers, Joseph and Lucien, protested the sale but were unable to stop the negotiations. These were, however, matters of French domestic politics and did not affect the American title.

In giving up Louisiana, the French framed the boundaries so ambiguously that they were bound to lead to trouble between the United States and its neighbors. Napoleon and the American negotiators wanted it that way. "If an obscurity did not already exist, it would perhaps be good policy to put one there," the First Consul told one of his ministers.[12] When Livingston questioned the vague boundaries, Talleyrand said, "I can give you no direction; you have made a noble bargain for yourselves, and I suppose you will make the most of it."[13] Americans did make the most of it. They assumed, on evidence they knew to be dubious, that they had purchased West Florida also.

Through fortuitous developments in Europe and Santo Domingo, Jefferson had avoided possible war with France and an unwanted alliance with England. Pressure on the French, such as threats of seizure, as well as other causes, gave him a province that he and other expansionists had long coveted and which more than doubled the national domain. By placating the West, moreover, the purchase of Louisiana averted the danger of disunion. It also set a precedent for acquiring territory and people by threat and treaty.

Livingston and Monroe, and then Jefferson, did not let a questionable title and vague boundaries keep them from making a "noble bargain." Neither did Congress let ethical obstacles stand in the way of the purchase. The Senate, by a substantial majority, on October 20, 1803, approved the three treaties covering the transfer of Louisiana. Delighted Westerners greeted news of the purchase with wild celebrations.

After taking possession of Louisiana for only twenty days, France turned the province over to the United States on December 20. Some Frenchmen considered the transfer a tragedy. The prefect in New Orleans spoke for them when he said, "What a magnificent New France have we lost."

Commerce and the Tripolitan War

After the acquisition of Louisiana, Jefferson's main problem in foreign relations was the protection of American commerce in a hostile world, for during the remainder of his presidency Europe was at war. This obligation, when force appeared necessary to defend maritime rights, placed him in another predicament. Although not a pacifist, he had talked of peace as the cornerstone of his foreign policy. Peace, he once explained, is "the most important of all things for us, except the preserving [of] an erect and independent attitude." [14]

Jefferson was also economy-minded. As president his money-saving measures affected the conduct of foreign relations. Believing that large armies were the hotbeds of dictatorship, he cut down the army by one-third. "We keep in service no more than enough men to garrison the small posts dispersed at great distances on our frontiers," he said.

Although Jefferson believed that navies were less to be feared than armies, because they could "never endanger our liberties," he disliked them also. "I am . . . for such a naval force as may protect our coasts and harbors from such depredations as we have experienced," he wrote, not "for a navy, which by its own expenses and the eternal wars in which it will implicate us, will grind us with public burthens, and sink us under them." [15] As soon as he took office, therefore, he reduced the active navy to six ships with small crews.

Practical statecraft forced Jefferson to reverse his stand on war, peace, and navies. He was not, however, necessarily inconsistent. He was willing to fight when the cost of peace was high and victory appeared cheap. In war, he believed, American commitments and objectives should be limited, the chances of success good, and the cost relatively low. His war with Tripoli from 1801 to 1805 met those conditions.

Almost from the day the United States had become independent, American shipping in the Mediterranean had suffered blackmail, plunder, capture, and enslavement of crews by the pirates of North Africa's Barbary shore. Spread over two thousand miles of coastline from the Atlantic to the Mediterranean, the four Barbary states of Morocco, Algiers, Tunis, and Tripoli preyed on shipping going to and from the Mediterranean. Their rulers styled themselves the "sovereigns of the Mediterranean" and relied on piracy, their main industry, as a primary source of revenue.

Morocco was virtually independent. The other states owed a nominal allegiance to Turkey. None respected the usual Western amenities of international law. European governments escaped the depredations of the pirate states only by paying tribute.

Since the sea and military power of the Barbary states even by contemporary standards was insignificant, the great powers of Europe, such as Britain or France, could easily have destroyed the pirate nests. They preferred not to, so Americans, according to one poet, considered them,

> Great fall'n powers, whose gems and golden bribes
> Buy paltry passports from these savage tribes—[16]

The European states bought protection because it was cheaper than war and offered them a convenient means of gaining political and commercial advantages over less powerful rivals, such as the United States. "Bribery and corruption," an American consul in Algiers explained, "answers their purpose better, and is attended with less expense, than a noble retaliation."

Before the Revolution, American colonists had profited from the protection England bought, and had developed a lucrative Mediterranean trade. After they gained independence, Americans lost their immunity to capture and robbery. At first, the newly independent United States sought help from England and France against the corsairs. France gave only promises, and Britain would do nothing. Therefore, the American government had to make its own terms with the Barbary states. Since the pirates exacted higher tributes from weak states, such as the United States, than from the strong, the terms were never satisfactory.

The United States purchased its first treaty, a fairly liberal one, in 1786 from the ruler of Morocco. Although the initial cost seemed high, the treaty did not call for continuing payments of tribute, but Morocco did exact tribute in other ways, such as in bribes and ransoms.

Algiers, the most formidable of the Barbary states, in the late 1780s and early 1790s captured more than a dozen American ships and held well over a hundred Americans as slaves. Those humiliating conditions led Congress in March 1794 to authorize construction of six frigates, the nucleus of the navy, to protect American commerce and lives. In September 1795, before the frigates were launched, the Dey of Algiers made a treaty with the United States. For peace, the United States paid a heavy price, ransom money, presents, and large commissions. In addition, it promised to furnish an annual tribute in naval stores amounting to $21,600.

In the following year, the United States paid for a treaty with Tripoli and in 1797 for a more expensive one with Tunis. Although neither treaty called for additional tribute, Americans paid it in one form or another. This was the Mediterranean policy of the Federalist government which gloried in the slogan "millions for defense but not one cent for tribute."

The treaties with the Barbary states proved worthless. All the rulers, when the opportunity arose, were anxious to break them and to prey on American commerce. The first state to repudiate its treaty and to launch large-scale hostilities against the United States was Tripoli. In May 1801, less than three weeks after Jefferson had taken office, its Pasha declared war.

That declaration persuaded Jefferson to meet force with force. First he authorized only defensive measures against the corsairs, then offensive action, and finally he increased the navy. The navy fought for four years, but because Jefferson insisted on a war without expense, it fought with true energy for only one year. In June 1805, after winning a limited victory, the United States signed a peace treaty that forced some valuable concessions from the Pasha but was still humiliating. It recognized the right of the pirates to obtain ransom for imprisoned Americans and did not end the plundering. Jefferson withdrew his naval squadron in 1807, and for the next eight years American shipping in the Mediterranean was virtually defenseless.

Finally, in March 1815 Congress authorized hostilities against the Dey of Algiers, who had declared war against the United States. That summer Commodore Stephen Decatur, commander of the naval squadron sent to the Mediterranean, dictated peace to Algiers, and then to Tunis and Tripoli. His guns ended the Barbary blackmail. Within the year, after European warships had joined in destroying the pirate nests, the payment of tribute ended and with it America's troubles with the Barbary states.

Trade and the European War

Jefferson had bought peace with Tripoli in 1805 and had withdrawn warships from the Mediterranean in 1807 because he faced greater dangers than those posed by petty rulers in North Africa. The war between Britain and France threatened to stifle American trade.

Since the president could not chastise those powerful states as he might those of North Africa, he followed a policy of "peaceable coercion" in dealing with them, meaning that he would threaten them with the loss of trade if they persisted in violating American rights. "Our commerce," he once explained, "is so valuable to them that they will be glad to purchase it when the only price we ask is to do us justice. I believe we have in our own hands the means of peaceable coercion; and that the moment they see our government so united as that they can make use of it, they will for their own interest be disposed to do us justice."[17]

In keeping with this policy and other ideas, Jefferson relied for defense mainly on small gunboats, used with some success in Tripoli. They would patrol the American coastline. "I believe," he had written years earlier, "that gunboats are the only *water* defence which can be useful to us, and protect us from the ruinous folly of a navy." Despite Federalist jeers, he built large numbers of those small one-gun ships.

When trouble with Britain and France mounted, Jefferson's policy of practicing economy with national defense seemingly backfired as the whole swarm of gunboats was useless against warships. Actually, even the frigates would not have been able to challenge British, or French, sea power in distant waters. The United States in those years was not yet strong enough to fight overseas against any major power.

Yet when Jefferson ended his first term he was satisfied with his foreign policy. He told his friends that "peace is smoothing our path at home and abroad . . . with England we are in a cordial friendship; with France in most perfect understanding; with Spain we shall always be bickering, but never at war till we seek it. Other nations view our course with respect and friendly anxiety." Those words were true enough for the years 1803 and 1804.

Even after May 1803, when England and France ended the Peace of Amiens and renewed their long war, American peace and prosperity continued. For two years, in fact, American traders enjoyed a rich commerce and war-swollen profits, as in the earlier years of the Anglo-French conflict. All this led to a phenomenal growth of the American merchant marine. Indeed, the United States had become the world's foremost neutral trader.

American shippers enjoyed a particularly lucrative trade, denied them in time of peace, in carrying goods between French and Spanish ports and between them and French and Spanish colonies in the Caribbean. Since such direct trade violated Britain's Rule of 1756, the Americans took their cargoes from French or Spanish Caribbean ports to an American port where they would go through certain formalities, such as payment of duties which might later be refunded, and thus would convert the cargoes to American property, making them "free goods." Then the ships with their "neutralized" cargoes might proceed to France or Spain.

England herself recognized the legality of that commerce in 1800 in a decision handed down by the High Court of Admiralty in the case of the American ship *Polly*. That kind of trade, which circumvented the Rule of 1756, was known as "broken voyage."

In 1805 that trade and America's good fortune ended. After long protest by British shippers and others against the leniency shown to neutral trade, particularly to Americans, the Lords Commissioners of Appeals in London, in the case of the American brig *Essex*, upheld a reversal of the *Polly* decision. The *Essex* verdict destroyed the principle of broken voyage. Goods could not be neutralized merely by bringing them into a neutral country, it said. The shipper had to pay a *bona fide* import duty. To refund the duty upon re-exporting the goods was a subterfuge and constituted a "continuous voyage" from enemy homeland to enemy colony. Broken voyage, the British decreed, violated the Rule of 1756 and under the doctrine of continuous voyage they would no longer allow such trade.

Without advance warning and before the *Essex* decision was publicized, British cruisers seized scores of American ships carrying French or Spanish goods, especially in the Caribbean. British cruisers hovered off American harbors in such numbers that they practically blockaded the ports. Few American ships going to sea escaped "visit and search" by vigilant British cruisers. The seizures and "the sudden and peremptory manner of enforcing" the *Essex* decision, actually a new principle, infuriated Americans.

Several months later, at the Battle of Trafalgar of October 21, 1805, Admiral Horatio Nelson, at the cost of his own life, smashed the combined French and Spanish fleets, thereby reinforcing England's maritime supremacy and making possible an even tighter control of neutral shipping. On the same day there appeared in London a pamphlet entitled *War in Disguise; Or, the Frauds of the Neutral Flags*. Written by an admiralty lawyer named James Stephen, it expanded the principles of the *Essex* decision.

Neutral shipping, Stephen said, should be regulated and taxed for the benefit of Britain's war effort. Allowing neutrals, particularly Americans, to trade unhampered with the enemy, he maintained, "sustains the ambition of France, and prolongs the miseries of Europe." At the same time, he argued, England denies herself the advantage of her command of the seas. Since she controlled the seas, he said in effect, neutrals had no rights. Nelson's victory at Trafalgar made it possible for England to carry out Stephen's plan, for his cogent arguments had considerable appeal. His pamphlet went through three editions in three months in England. Later, through a series of orders in council, English naval practice toward American shipping practically followed the pattern he had outlined.

Then, in little more than a month after Trafalgar, Napoleon won a tremendous victory at the Battle of Austerlitz which crushed the armies of Russia and Austria, destroyed the third coalition against France, and strengthened his mastery of Europe. Now the efforts of Napoleon and England to get at each other resembled a fight between the tiger and the shark. Each ruled its own sphere but could not directly injure the other. In this desperate battle neutral rights virtually disappeared and the United States suffered whenever it would not submit to the will of either belligerent, lord in its own domain.

England blockaded territory under French control and Napoleon retaliated by throwing a "paper" blockade, a blockade by proclamation, around the British Isles. Caught in the middle of sweeping decrees, the United States insisted that the blockades of both belligerents were illegal. It held that a blockade was legal only when applied to "ports which may be actually invested."

Orders in Council and Napoleonic Decrees

An order in council of May 16, 1806, known as "Fox's blockade," touched off the battle of paper blockades. It established a partial blockade of Europe's coast. Under it the Royal Navy would seize American ships carrying contraband, or enemy goods, anywhere outside the three-mile limit of the United States. Americans could trade with Europe, therefore, only as England allowed.

In November, Napoleon retaliated with his Berlin Decree, declaring the British Isles under blockade. He would seize and condemn any ship coming under his control that had previously touched a British port, but made an exception for American ships. This decree launched his "continental system," a scheme designed to exclude British shipping from Europe and, if possible, from ports throughout the world. With it he hoped to destroy England's commerce. If that commerce died, he reasoned, England's finances would collapse and then she would not have the power to support a navy and make war.

England struck back at the continental system with new orders in council in January and November 1807, prohibiting all trade with ports under France's control except that going through her own system of controls. England designed her plan to push goods through Napoleon's self-imposed blockade and, when neutral shipping carried those goods, to profit from that trade by imposing a tax on it. All trade with Europe, in other words, had to pay tribute to Britain in one way or another.

Napoleon countered the British system with his Milan Decree of December 1807. Any ship that submitted to visit and search by Britain, that visited a British port, or paid taxes to the British, he would treat as a British ship. If it came to a French port or fell into French hands, he would seize it. Since Napoleon could not enforce his decrees as effectively as the British, his continental system cut off American trade with Europe but not with England.

If American traders tried to follow the French system, they were almost certain to be stopped by British cruisers and lose ship and cargo. If they conformed to the British decrees and avoided ports under French control, however, they were usually safe because France's navy had been driven from the seas. Under the British licensing system, therefore, though Americans hated it, their commerce continued to prosper because of the wartime demand for American products in England. Yet, some Americans suspected England of playing the familiar game of using the war to crush commercial rivals, the foremost of which was now the United States.

The Impressment Issue

The licensing system and ship seizures were not the only grievances Americans had against England. The rock-ribbed issue that embittered Anglo-American relations for many years was impressment, or naval recruiting by force.

One reason for the bitterness of the impressment issue was that England and the United States held conflicting views on neutral rights. Except for military personnel, Secretary of State James Madison said, "we consider a neutral flag on the high seas as a safeguard to those sailing under it. Great Britain on the contrary asserts a right to search for and seize her own subjects." Lord Harrowby, Britain's foreign secretary, expressed his country's view quite clearly. "The pretension advanced by Mr. Madison that the American Flag should protect every Individual sailing under it on board of a Merchant Ship," he said, "is too extravagant to require any serious Refutation."

Another reason for difficulties was that England and the United States followed differing theories of citizenship. England insisted that once an Englishman always an Englishman. This was the doctrine of "inalienable allegiance." The United States, a nation of immigrants, upheld the right of "expatriation," that a person could of his own choice renounce allegiance to one country and become the citizen of another. "I hold the right of expatriation," Jefferson said, "to be inherent in every man by the laws of nature."

A more important reason for the emotionalism in the impressment dispute was England's desperate need for seamen. For centuries England had recruited her seamen through press gangs. Her statesmen held that impressment was "a prerogative inherent in the crown, founded upon common law and recognized by many acts of Parliament."

Conditions aboard English warships during the Napoleonic wars were so harsh that few British subjects would enlist, and when impressed they often deserted. So the Royal Navy stepped up recruiting by force. By using press gangs in British seaports, or by boarding its own merchantmen on the high seas and impressing seamen, it filled crews, but it never claimed the right to impress other than British subjects. To escape impressment thousands of Englishmen, particularly seamen, took service in the rapidly expanding American merchant marine. There the berths were safer, the pay higher, and the treatment more humane.

To secure immunity from the press gangs, many Englishmen became American citizens, or secured naturalization papers illegally or forged them. Some fled merchant berths; others deserted naval service. According to one estimate made by an American in 1807, English ships of all kinds in the war years lost about twenty-five hundred men a year to American ships. Since England's major weapon against Napoleon was sea power, this loss appeared to her statesmen a matter of life and death.

To keep its ships staffed, the Royal Navy insisted on, and enforced, its right to examine neutral ships in British ports and at sea for deserters and British subjects fleeing naval service. Since the United States was the most important neutral carrier and many Americans had been born in England, this practice led to trouble with the American government. English searching parties would not recognize the right of Englishmen to become American citizens, though they never insisted on the right to impress natural-born Americans.

Yet the press gangs often impressed even native Americans. They made frequent and convenient mistakes, usually in ratio to their captain's immediate need for seamen. Besides, the British officers argued, it was often almost impossible to distinguish Americans from Englishmen.

In theory, England made a concession to American objections. If the impressed seamen could prove that they were natural-born Americans, the Royal Navy would release them. This placed the burden of proof on the Americans. Getting the proof often took months, even years. Then, after long service, the admiralty would release them without redressing the suffering it had caused. Too often, however, impressed Americans were killed or died in service, leaving their friends and relatives with a deep hatred of England.

In a partial effort to meet the impressment problem, the American government furnished seamen with official statements of citizenship, but would concede nothing on the right of expatriation. The statements did not distinguish between natural-born and naturalized Americans. In addition, sailors often sold the "protections" to British subjects. The British, therefore, would not recognize those documents as evidence of citizenship.

Britain considered the impressment issue as non-negotiable because in time of war impressment provided her with essential manpower. Englishmen defended it as a matter of national survival. The United States considered it a standing insult and a threat to national sovereignty. Americans believed that their flag flying at the mast of a ship should protect the crew. More important than any violation of a theoretical right, however, was the fact that impressment struck Americans as a vicious waste of lives.

From the beginning of the Anglo-French wars, the United States had tried many times to settle the impressment question but had always failed. After suffering under the impact of the *Essex* decision, Jefferson decided on retaliatory legislation. In April 1806 Congress passed a Non-Importation Act, which would exclude certain British manufactures from the United States after November 1 unless England settled American grievances.

At the same time, as it had in past crises, the American government decided to send a special mission to London to negotiate the grievances. This time Jefferson chose William Pinkney, a Baltimore lawyer, to assist James Monroe, who was then the regular minister to England. Monroe and Pinkney were "to settle all matters of difference" with Great Britain. They had the power to make a new treaty defining neutral rights, such as on matters of contraband and blockade, and to resolve the impressment controversy. They were, moreover, to replace the parts of Jay's Treaty that were due to expire in October 1807.

On the issue of impressment, Monroe and Pinkney's instructions were firm. Any agreement had to forbid impressments from American ships at sea. Meanwhile, Jefferson postponed execution of the Non-Importation Act.

The British were willing to make only an informal written pledge that naval officers would exercise "the greatest caution" in impressing British seamen, but refused to incorporate even this limited concession into a treaty. Since Monroe and Pinkney could do no better and were reasonably satisfied with other concessions, on December 31, 1806, they signed an agreement similar to Jay's Treaty.

In the Monroe-Pinkney Treaty the United States gave up the principle that free ships make free goods, as it had done in Jay's Treaty, and England modified its Rule of 1756. This was not enough to please Jefferson. Since he had taken a strong stand on impressment, he withheld the treaty from the Senate. Secretary Madison, meanwhile, instructed Monroe and Pinkney to reopen negotiations on the basis of their original instructions, but the British would not again negotiate on those terms.

Even though Jefferson considered retaliation and even talked of war, he did not invoke the Non-Importation Act. As long as England acted in the spirit of the informal understanding on neutral trade and impressment, he said, he would recommend that Congress continue the suspension.

The Chesapeake *Affair*

Then the *Chesapeake* affair made impressment a burning national issue. On June 22, 1807, the forty-gun American naval frigate *Chesapeake,* Commodore James Barron senior officer aboard, left Norfolk for African waters. On board were four seamen who had escaped from British warships in Hampton Roads and had enlisted in the United States Navy. Since the

Chesapeake did not anticipate hostilities, her gun deck was cluttered with lumber, sails, and cables to be stowed away while at sea. Her guns were virtually unworkable.

In this condition, not far beyond the three-mile limit, she met the fifty-gun British frigate *Leopard.* The *Leopard* hailed her and demanded that she submit to search for the deserters. When Barron refused, the *Leopard* poured several broadsides into the *Chesapeake,* killing three and wounding eighteen men. Within thirty minutes, after firing only one shot, the *Chesapeake* struck colors. Then a British search party climbed aboard, lined up the crew, and took off the four alleged deserters. Thoroughly humiliated, Barron brought the wrecked and bloody ship back to port.

Only one of the four seamen was a real British deserter. The British hanged him from the yardarm of his own ship. The other three were natural-born Americans, two of them Negroes. After recapturing these seamen, the British imprisoned them and did not surrender two of them until 1812. The third died in prison.

Nothing the British had done before aroused the public to such fury as did the *Chesapeake* impressment. In Norfolk a mob ran wild, attacked British sailors, and clamored for war. Jefferson himself told friends that the British had "their foot on the threshold of war" and that the United States "has never been in such a state of excitement since the battle of Lexington."

This time the British had fired on a warship and killed sailors of the United States Navy, something they had not done previously. Although her naval officers had done it more than once, Britain had never claimed the right to seize men from a foreign naval vessel. Such conduct insulted the American flag and trampled national honor. The United States, the British minister in Washington reported, "will engage in war rather than submit to their national armed ships being forcibly searched on the high seas."

If Jefferson had wanted it, he apparently could have had war. The country, according to contemporary evidence, would have supported him, but to go to war against England virtually without a navy and with an exposed seacoast seemed foolhardy. Instead, he tried to use the *Chesapeake* affair as a weapon of peaceable coercion. With it and with economic pressure, he thought, he could force the British to give up impressment.

Under a provision in Jay's Treaty, British warships had been using American territorial waters and ports for provisioning. After calling an emergency session of the cabinet, Jefferson issued a proclamation on July 2, 1807, forbidding such usage. A few days later he asked the state governors for 100,000 militia, made plans for war, readied coastal defenses, and called Congress to meet in special session late in October.

In subsequent negotiations over the *Chesapeake* affair, the British admitted that in this instance they had been wrong, disavowed the *Leopard*'s violence, and offered amends, but would not abandon impressment. The war spirit of 1807 melted away in the extended negotiations. Yet the bitterness of the *Chesapeake* affair rankled for five years. To numerous Americans it, and continued impressments, marked the depth of national disgrace.

The Embargo

In spite of the failure of his efforts to use the *Chesapeake* incident to force a settlement of grievances with Britain, Jefferson did not lose faith in the idea that economic coercion was enough to force respect for American rights. On December 14, 1807, the Non-Importation Act, which had been suspended several times, finally went into effect. It proved not strong enough to make Jefferson's policy of economic coercion effective. Basically, the president wanted to shut off all trade with England and France. If the United States completely cut off exports of raw materials and foodstuffs the belligerents needed, he reasoned, they would come to terms.

Therefore, on December 21, at Jefferson's urging the Congress he had called into special session passed the Embargo Act. That law forbade all American ships to leave for foreign countries and required shipowners engaged in coastal trade to post heavy bonds assuring compliance. Later, Congress tried to remedy defects in the embargo law with supplementary legislation and by giving government agents almost inquisitorial powers in enforcing it. This was indeed a rigorous self-blockade.

In theory, the embargo was impartial. Madison, for instance, said that Britain would "feel it in her manufactures, in the loss of naval stores, and above all in the supplies essential to her colonies." France would feel it in the loss of colonial luxuries. Since England controlled the seas, however, it had the effect of shutting off trade with her only. In practice, therefore, it complemented Napoleon's continental system. "Mr. Jefferson," a Bostonian Federalist exclaimed, "has imposed an embargo to please France and to beggar us!"

Although the embargo inflicted considerable injury on Britain, and even more on her West Indies, Jefferson's plan misfired. The embargo hit the United States harder than it did England. Depression fell on the seaports and elsewhere. A British traveler described New York in this period. "The port indeed was full of shipping, but they were dismantled and laid up; their decks were cleared, their hatches fastened down, and scarcely a sailor was to be found on board." Then he added, "The coffee-houses were almost empty; the streets, near the water-side, were almost deserted; the grass had begun to grow upon the wharves."

Federalists denounced the embargo, and many Republicans joined them. Smuggling, often in open defiance of federal officers, flourished along the Canadian border and traders abused the privilege of coastal shipping. New Englanders revolted against the law and talked of separation from the Union. More than one New Englander damned the embargo in doggerel similar to this:

> O Jefferson! with deep amaze,
> Thou'st overset our cargo;
> We've nought to do but stand and gaze
> At thy own curst embargo.[18]

New England's resistance to the embargo, in fact, drove Jefferson to enforce it by federal action. In so using the federal government, he overturned his own political creed of states' rights and the principles of his own party. Again foreign policy had forced Jefferson, the strict constructionist, to reverse himself. He had interpreted the constitutional authority to "regulate" commerce so loosely that he stopped all foreign trade. His inquisitors even endangered the personal liberties he held dear. The embargo and supporting laws clamped controls, restrictions, and regulations on Americans and their property in time of peace, which the Constitution could hardly justify.

Napoleon shrewdly took advantage of the embargo to serve his own ends. Since American ships could not legally leave port, he said, those in European harbors must be English ships. Under his Bayonne Decree of April 1808, therefore, he seized them. After all, he said, he was merely helping the American government enforce its own embargo law.

In spite of the pressure against it, Jefferson strove to the last to preserve the embargo. He consoled himself for its diplomatic failure by stressing its protective effects. It has, he wrote to a friend, "produced one very happy & permanent effect. It has set us all on domestic manufacture, & will I verily believe reduce our future demands on England fully one half."[19]

Finally, the political pressure became too great for Congress to withstand. Federalist victories in state elections showed the tide of opinion running against Republicans. Fear of war, threats of secession from New England, and election losses, drove Congress on March 1, 1809, just three days before Jefferson left office, to repeal the embargo for all countries except England and France. It did not, however, repeal the principle of peaceable coercion. In place of the embargo, Congress substituted the Non-Intercourse Act.

Jefferson's peaceable coercion had failed. Yet historians have differed as to the effectiveness of the embargo. Even though it caused England considerable hardship, it alone apparently was not a weapon capable of forcing her to capitulate to American demands, such as giving up impressment. Smuggling, internal resistance, and the opening of Spanish America to British trade after the outbreak of the war in Spain in August 1808—as a compensation for lost American trade—all worked against the embargo's effectiveness. Perhaps the most important factor in the failure of the embargo lay in the existence of the American merchant fleet. Jefferson underestimated the determination of the shippers and merchants to fight for wartime wealth. So great was the chance for profit, even under the British and French restrictions, that they would not submit to any law which prevented it.

The Non-Intercourse Act of March 1 excluded American ships from French and British ports and closed American ports to both countries after May 20, 1809. If either France or England relaxed maritime restrictions against the United States, the president was empowered to reopen trade with the cooperative nation while continuing Non-Intercourse against the other. In effect, the law did three things: it invited concessions from England and France while continuing pressure against them, permitted trade with the few remaining neutral countries, and thus gave Americans a back-door access to belligerent markets.

Although supposedly impartial, Non-Intercourse, unlike the embargo, favored Britain. She could gain more from concessions than could blockaded France. Non-Intercourse ended Jefferson's efforts to uphold American neutral rights through peaceable coercion. The next steps came under his successor, James Madison.

V

The War of 1812

As secretary of state, James Madison had believed in, and had carried
out, Jefferson's policy of economic pressure, but even before he became
president, Madison knew it had failed. Several months before entering the
White House, therefore, he explained what his own policy would be in
dealing with the maritime crisis. As president, he said, he would quickly
call a special session of Congress "with an understanding that War will
then be the proper course, if no immediate change abroad shall render it
unnecessary."[1] Thus, in March 1809 when he took his inaugural oath and
told the people that "the present situation of the world is indeed without
parallel and that of our own country full of difficulties," he was prepared to
face war with England.

Yet for several years Madison searched for alternatives. He made Jefferson's basic idea of economic coercion the heart of his own policy and
sought to obtain redress for grievances without resorting to war. This
course appeared logical in view of the actions of David M. Erskine, the
British minister in Washington.

The Erskine Agreement

Believing war imminent, Erskine had talked to Madison and his
friends following the presidential election about the crisis in Anglo-
American relations and had concluded that if Britain were conciliatory, a
settlement could be worked out. He even believed that the focus of American foreign policy might shift and become favorable to England, and hence
suggested to Foreign Minister George Canning that he sacrifice the orders
in council in order to win American goodwill.

Canning accepted the suggestion and in April 1809 instructed Erskine to negotiate a settlement and explore the possibility of a new commer-

cial treaty with the United States. Seemingly, the Non-Intercourse Act had been successful in forcing the British to come to some kind of terms.

Erskine's instructions, however, had serious limitations. They said that if the United States accepted the Rule of 1756, again opened its waters to British warships, and immediately placed the Non-Intercourse Act into effect against France, England would not apply her orders in council against American shipping. Canning also expressed willingness to settle the *Chesapeake* affair with an "honorable reparation for the aggression." The stickler, as far as Americans were concerned, was Canning's insistence that England must enforce the Non-Intercourse Act against France, meaning that the Royal Navy would be allowed to seize American ships caught violating it.

Anxious for a settlement and realizing he could not obtain America's formal agreement to all of Canning's conditions, Erskine departed from his instructions. On April 19, 1809, he and Secretary of State Robert Smith exchanged notes for what has come to be known as the Erskine Agreement, in which nothing was said about the Royal Navy enforcing American law and American acceptance of the Rule of 1756.

On that same day, Madison issued a proclamation saying that on June 10, when the orders in council would cease to apply to the United States as agreed to by Erskine, the Non-Intercourse Act would no longer be in effect against Britain. Joyous traders praised Madison's statesmanship and when the proper day in June arrived some six hundred ships swarmed out of American ports loaded with cargoes for England. Madison's new popularity lasted only a few months, for he had acted prematurely.

Canning not only repudiated the Erskine Agreement almost as soon as he had glanced at it, but also immediately recalled that "damned Scotch flunkey" who had signed it. Since Englishmen hungered for the raw materials the American ships were carrying, Canning magnanimously allowed those ships already at sea to proceed to English ports.

On August 9, a humiliated Madison again placed Non-Intercourse into effect against England. The collapse of the Erskine Agreement thus ended the efforts to settle the *Chesapeake* incident and added new bitterness to Anglo-American relations. In fact, it proved to be the beginning of a fatal rupture between England and the United States.

Macon's Bill No. 2

Early in September, Francis J. Jackson, Erskine's successor, arrived in the United States. Called "Copenhagen" Jackson for browbeating the Danes two years earlier when a British fleet had smashed Copenhagen, he soon showed himself as arrogant and tactless as his nickname suggested. He quickly charged Madison with knowing beforehand that Erskine was violating his instructions and in effect called the president a liar. Madison, therefore, refused to have anything to do with him. Jackson then left Washington but lingered in the United States until the following September consorting with Federalists and denouncing Madison's government. Madison demanded his recall and the British government finally summoned him home, but with honor, and sent no replacement for two years. Diplomatic relations with England thus became partially suspended.

Meanwhile, Napoleon, who had been pleased with the embargo, protested the Non-Intercourse Act, saying it favored England. In ostensible retaliation, he issued two decrees, one from Vienna in August 1809 and another from Rambouillet the following March, which gave him the excuse to seize scores of American ships in French ports. Under the Rambouillet decree alone he seized about $10 million in American property, but even worse, he imprisoned hundreds of crewmen from captured ships.

Since Non-Intercourse now obviously had failed to bring the expected results from either Napoleon or England, and, like the embargo, placed an almost unbearable strain on American commerce, it was droppped. Congress replaced it on May 1, 1810, with Macon's Bill No. 2, a law that reopened American trade to all the world but excluded British and French warships from American waters. The critical feature of that law said that if either England or France agreed to respect American maritime rights before March 3, 1811, the president could again apply Non-Intercourse against the recalcitrant nation, but only after an interval of three months had elapsed that gave that nation an opportunity to follow its rival's example.

Regardless of its theoretical impartiality, Macon's Bill No. 2 from Napoleon's point of view was virtually a surrender to British maritime policy. Since the Royal Navy dominated the seas, whatever trade the new law permitted would in fact be subject to British control. He tried, therefore, to persuade Madison that he had withdrawn his own decrees against American shipping.

In an ambiguous letter of August 5, 1810, Napoleon's foreign minister, the Duc de Cadore, told the American minister in Paris "that the decrees of Berlin and Milan are revoked, and that after the 1st of November they will cease to have effect."[2] This was followed, however, by a nullifying qualification that said that the revocation would apply only if the English rescinded their orders in council or if the United States under its new law forced the English to respect its rights.

Even though Napoleon had not truly lifted his decrees, Madison, who was aware of the equivocal nature of the Corsican's act, accepted his conditional repeal as meeting the terms of Macon's Bill No. 2. Therefore, on November 2, after the British logically refused to repeal their orders in council because of the Cadore letter, the president issued a proclamation saying he would apply Non-Intercourse against Britain, which the American government did on February 11, 1811.

Madison and his advisers were now apparently convinced that war with England was only a matter of time. The secretary of state even told the French minister in Washington that the measures the president would take to protect American maritime rights against England "will necessarily lead to war."[3]

The Little Belt Incident

A cluster of other developments now also contributed to the war crisis. In late February of 1811 William Pinkney, who had become the American minister in London, withdrew from the legation and left it in the hands of a *chargé d'affaires*. Pinkney's announcement of his departure jarred the British government and prompted it to make a belated effort to improve the rapidly deteriorating relations with the United States. It finally decided to send another minister to Washington. Before that minister arrived, a chance encounter between an American and a British warship revealed the raw temper of the American public over the question of neutral rights and underscored the critical need for conciliatory measures.

On May 16 a forty-four-gun American frigate, the *President,* caught the twenty-gun British sloop-of-war *Little Belt* off the Virginia capes. American and British versions differ as to who fired the first shot, but in the battle that followed the frigate almost blasted the sloop out of the water, killing nine and wounding three of her crew. The *President* suffered little damage and only one crew member was injured. Disregarding the heavy odds the *Little Belt* had faced, the American public greeted the news of the encounter with joy, believing that the navy had at last avenged the five-year-old disgrace of the *Chesapeake*.

Many Englishmen considered the attack on their ship unprovoked. "The blood of our murdered countrymen," one London newspaper said, "must be revenged, and war must ensue."[4]

Thus, when the new British minister, Augustus John Foster, arrived in Washington at the end of June, the American people were in an ugly mood, bitterly anti-British, and seemingly ready for war. Since he was himself hostile to the United States and had only limited powers, Foster faced an almost impossible task in trying to reach a settlement on the maritime issues that might prevent war. The harsh realities of his difficulties became even clearer when the Twelfth Congress convened in special session early in November.

War Hawks and Frontier Problems

The leadership of that Congress was made up of a new generation of statesmen who had replaced the old Revolutionary leaders who had guided the government since its founding. These new chieftains, men such as Henry Clay of Kentucky, John C. Calhoun of South Carolina, and William

H. Crawford of Georgia, were young, between thirty and forty years old, from the West and lower South.

Ardent nationalists, they considered impressment and British maritime restrictions a national humiliation. They were also partisan politicians who brought with them anti-British grievances from their own parts of the country. Some of their constituents, as in South Carolina, for instance, were suffering from an economic distress they blamed on the British. They resented the orders in council which they believed ruined their overseas markets. Some of these congressmen represented agrarian expansionists who had steadily pushed the Indian westward and had taken over his lands. Led by these Republicans, the new Congress represented a cross section of anti-British grievances. These young nationalists, who felt strongly about insults to the flag and national honor, controlled most of the important committees and were in a position to make their will felt. One of the first things they did to consolidate their power was to elect Henry Clay, then thirty-four years old, Speaker of the House. Then they demanded war with Britain. These war hawks of 1812 were the men who led the Republican party.

One of the most striking of the nonmaritime grievances stemmed from British relations with Indians. As they had done in the 1790s Westerners of the following decade acquired Indian lands for settlement piecemeal in treaties with individual tribes. Unlike the earlier period, however, the British were no longer occupying American soil in the Northwest and did not openly support Indian resistance to the advancing frontiersmen. Nonetheless, after 1807, when Anglo-American relations grew tense, Westerners believed rumors that the British in Canada were inciting the Indians against settlers.

Indian hostility stemmed from the land policies of the Westerners themselves. In September 1809 William Henry Harrison, governor of the Indiana Territory, had made treaties at Fort Wayne with several tribes, opening three million acres of splendid farm land to settlement. As a result the Indians were forced back to the Wabash River. Many Indians resented the surrender of their lands and two of them, a far-sighted Shawnee chieftain named Tecumseh and his brother, the Prophet, organized a movement to unite all the tribes against further white encroachments. They proposed no additional surrender of land to the whites, questioned the legality of the Fort Wayne treaties, and threatened to resist white occupation.

Westerners believed that the British were behind Tecumseh's confederation and his resistance to their advance. They were convinced that the British were supplying the Indians with arms from settlements near Detroit. The British officials, in fact, did not want Indian hostilities with the United States at this time, but they did try to win Indian friendship with presents and arms so that they could use those Indians as allies when war came.

On November 7, 1811, three days after the Twelfth Congress had convened, Westerners uncovered what they considered evidence of British intrigue with the Indians. On that day Tecumseh's warriors clashed with about a thousand troops under the command of General Harrison at an Indian village on Tippecanoe Creek, a tributary of the Wabash in present-day Indiana, inflicting nearly two hundred casualties before Harrison defeated them. Among the weapons the Indians left behind, Harrison found some made in Britain. The Battle of Tippecanoe, but especially the evidence of British aid to the Indians, aroused the West to an anti-British frenzy and helped crystallize war sentiment in Congress. Although some believed that Harrison's blundering had caused the high loss of life at Tippecanoe, most Westerners blamed the British.

In the following months those Westerners who wanted war argued that the only sure way to end the Indian troubles on the Northwest frontier was to conquer Canada. This argument appealed to other war hawks who pointed out that the United States lacked a strong navy and that an attack on Canada offered the only effective way of striking at the British.

Southern war hawks, too, combined the desire to strike at Britain with sectional expansion. They wanted to invade Spanish Florida. When war came, they feared, the British would occupy Florida and use it as a base against them. Since Spain was once again Britain's ally, moreover, the Southerners had a good excuse for attacking Florida if war should break out with Britain.

A war to acquire Canada and Florida, according to this war hawk interpretation, seemingly had other virtues. The sectional balance between North and South was already a problem in American politics. Neither section, it seemed, wished to promote an increase in territory, population, or influence for the other. The acquisition of both Canada and Florida would retain that balance and would rid the country of dangerous neighbors.

Decision for War

Both the president and his new secretary of state, James Monroe, sided with those who favored war. Monroe had come into office after the Battle of Tippecanoe as an advocate of peace with England, but in a month he came to accept the idea of war. "Gentlemen," he told the war hawks, "*we must fight*. We are forever disgraced if we do not." [5]

Yet the war partisans were unable to bring about an immediate declaration of hostilities against the British. Federalists and moderate Republicans resisted the war hawks, and were sufficiently strong in Congress to prevent immediate action. New England Federalists in particular believed that war against England would be a national tragedy, seeing in Napoleon, whom they considered a tyrant, the real foe. Timothy Pickering summed up their views in a toast, "The world's last hope—Britain's fast-anchored Isle."

Nonetheless, anti-British sentiment continued to gain strength, particularly from such incidents as the president's publication of the letters of John Henry, a British secret agent, in March 1812. Bought by Madison for the exorbitant price of $50,000, those letters hinted at but did not prove British dealings with allegedly treasonable New England Federalists.

Thus, by the spring of 1812, the demands of West and South for war and the anger of Republican politicians over maritime grievances brought the nation to the razor edge of decision. Then on April 1 Madison took decisive action. He confidentially recommended that "a general embargo be laid on all vessels now in port or hereafter arriving for the period of sixty days." Instead, Congress voted a ninety-day embargo to save American shipping from wholesale seizure when war came.

In England, meanwhile, merchants and manufacturers had been urging the government to seek an accommodation with the United States. The Jeffersonian policy of economic coercion, especially when coupled with Napoleon's continental system, had hit them hard. Despite the fact that the opening of new markets in Latin America had given them some relief from the embargo and Non-Intercourse, they suffered from economic depression and desperately needed American markets and raw materials. For some time, moreover, English public opinion had been turning against the orders in council and pressing for their repeal against the United States.

Information from the United States, furthermore, indicated new and serious preparations for war. Although the British considered American military power trifling, the acquisition of another enemy would be a serious blow to a public that had long been carrying the burden of the French wars. In April 1812, therefore, the British government, fearing a permanent loss of the American market, said it was willing to repeal the orders in council. Before it could do so, however, it needed a pretext, an authentic act by the French, such as the repeal of the Berlin and Milan decrees, that would make its own repeal appear a graceful countermeasure. In the following month the French, by coincidence, provided the necessary pretext.

Late in 1811, Joel Barlow, the American minister in France, had complained to the foreign minister, at that time the Duc de Bassano, of France's continuing seizures of American ships. Finally, in May 1812 Barlow asked for evidence of Napoleon's repeal of the Berlin and Milan decrees as they applied to the United States. A few days later, Bassano showed him a decree dated St. Cloud, April 28, 1811, which met the American desires by stating that the Berlin and Milan decrees had not existed for American ships for over a year and a half. Apparently the French had hastily drafted the heretofore unknown paper to meet the American request and had moved the date back a year.

Barlow, who considered the French decree a forgery but potentially useful to his government, immediately sent a copy to the American *chargé* in London, who showed it to the British foreign minister, now Lord Castlereagh, and asked for a repeal of the orders in council. Castlereagh then took advantage of the dubious St. Cloud decree to meet the pressures of domestic politics by announcing to Parliament on June 16 that the government would suspend the orders in council as they applied to the United States. Britain did so on June 23.

That repeal was five days too late. On June 18, 1812, Madison had signed a declaration of war against England. If, as most Americans apparently believed at the time, the major cause for war was maritime rights, "its principal Cause and Justification was removed precisely at the moment when it occurred." [6]

In his war message Madison had stressed that the United States must defend itself against England's flagrant violation of its neutral rights. He placed impressment at the head of his list of British injustices and devoted only a few sentences to the Indian troubles. British cruisers, he said, were "in the continued practice of violating the American flag on the great highway of nations, and of seizing and carrying off persons sailing under it."

Yet, in spite of Madison's message and the depth of public feeling over violated neutral rights, many representatives from maritime states most injured by impressments and ship seizures voted against war. The New England and Middle Atlantic states also profited most from the wartime trade. That commerce, even with the humiliation of impressment, seemed to some too valuable to be destroyed by war. Those states were also the strongholds of French-hating Federalists who could not approve hostilities against England that made the United States a virtual ally of Napoleon.

In the House of Representatives the vote on June 4 on the declaration of war was seventy-nine to forty-nine. The large dissenting minority represented mainly Federalists from the Northern maritime states. The West, according to an interpretation based on geographical blocs, voted most solidly for war. The deep South followed a similar pattern, while the upper South showed some division. Since all Federalists voted against war and most Republicans for it, party loyalty seems more important than geography.

In the Senate, where the war hawks were not as strong as in the House, Federalists debated the declaration for two weeks. Finally, on June 17, the Senate, also along partisan lines, voted nineteen to thirteen for war. Since the United States had good cause for war against France also, the Senate debated for days on whether or not to include France in the declaration. A proposal to that effect lost by only four votes.

On the basis of the vote in Congress, some scholars have concluded that neutral rights and impressment served as righteous pretexts for those who desired war for other reasons. Others have argued that if Congress had known that England would repeal the orders in council, there would have been no war, despite the influence of the war hawks. Still others have stressed the desire to vindicate national honor and to preserve Republican party unity as bringing the war declaration to a decision. Despite the theories, what seems clear is that many voted for war reluctantly and that the causes were not only complex but also rooted in years of controversy, mainly the question of neutral rights.

Ironically, on the day that Madison proclaimed the war, New Englanders, those most concerned with maritime rights, lamented the government's action in fast and prayer. William Cullen Bryant, then seventeen years old, expressed New England's feeling in these words:

> The same ennobling spirit
> That kindles valor's flame,
> That nerves us to a war of right,
> Forbids a war of *shame*.[7]

As if bothered by inner feelings of guilt for allowing themselves to drift into an unnecessary war, both sides made efforts to stop it as soon as it began. On June 26, in the same message that carried the news of the war declaration, Secretary of State Monroe asked the American *chargé* in London to arrange an immediate armistice if England would give up impressment. On that question, Lord Castlereagh would not yield. That was "a right upon which the naval strength of the empire mainly depends," he said.[8]

In America, the new British minister several times urged an armistice, and in September an English admiral under direct instructions from London did the same. The United States rejected those efforts to stop the war before it was truly launched because Britain refused to yield on the question of impressments.

An Unpopular War

Dwarfed by the conflict in Europe, the War of 1812 seemed a squabble fought on the fringes of Britain's empire. It was also a peculiar conflict. Usually a nation at war seeks allies and tries to injure the enemy in any way it can, but the United States, having grievances against Napoleon as well as England, made no effort to form an alliance with France or to cooperate with her against England. For reasons of its own the United States entered the war alone, fought alone, and made peace alone. Yet when Napoleon invaded Russia in the summer of 1812, President Madison believed that he carried the fortunes of the United States with him.

Napoleon failed in Russia, and Americans realized none of their objectives in their own war. Their war ended in a stalemate, almost in defeat.

Militarily and politically, they were unprepared for war. Party feeling was intense, and sectional loyalties seriously divided the people.

New England Federalists offered the greatest opposition to the war. They considered it the Republican party's struggle, and derisively called it "Mr. Madison's War." Some talked of secession and were even disloyal. One New England clergyman, for instance, explained to his congregation that Moses had dissolved the union with Egypt. Then he called on "a resolute, a pious people" to follow the Biblical example. During the war New Englanders supplied invading British troops with food and other provisions, and some did not hesitate to take an oath of allegiance to King George. So strong was Federalist and antiwar opposition that in his bid for reelection in 1812, Madison lost all but two of the states north of the Potomac River. The South and West reelected him.

England realized that the northern maritime states opposed the war, so she cultivated secessionist sentiment in those states. England's commander in chief in Canada made it his policy, he said, "to avoid committing any act which may even by a strained construction tend to unite the eastern and southern states." From the beginning, Britain's most powerful weapon was her blockade of the American coast, but she exempted northern New England from its rigors until the spring of 1814. New Englanders, therefore, traded with Canada and England during almost the entire war and even withheld money from the federal government and invested it in British treasury notes.

Other sections of the country also lagged in support of the government. Some Republicans, even in Madison's Virginia, disliked the war, but usually Federalists outside New England suffered at the hands of aroused pro-war Republicans. In Baltimore in July 1812 a pro-administration mob killed and mutilated Federalists and other prominent citizens who had publicly opposed the war. The opposition claimed that "Mr. Madison's Mobs" crushed honest criticism and free speech.

The Military Struggle

Aware of the divisions within the country and of the nation's unpreparedness, Madison and his advisers wanted an early peace and tried to get one, but the war hawks clamored for a swift victory in Canada first. Therefore, even though it had an inadequate army, the United States in the summer of 1812 launched a three-pronged attack against Canada. Under the leadership of an able British general, Isaac Brock, the Canadians repelled the attack and later invaded American territory. This happened when Britain was so involved in the European war that she could give scant attention to the defense of Canada.

Many Americans did not favor the expedition against Canada. Southerners, for instance, refused full support. Angry Northerners argued that Madison and Monroe as Southerners were unenthusiastic about conquering Canada. The North, however, blocked Southern efforts to take Florida. In July 1812 and in February 1813 Northern opposition in Congress killed legislation which would have empowered the president to take and occupy Florida.

Poor preparations and incompetent leadership, more than sectional friction, accounted for American failures in 1812 and 1813. The notable victory of this period belonged to Lieutenant Oliver Hazard Perry of the navy. In September 1813, with an improvised fleet made of green timbers, he defeated the British forces on Lake Erie.

In 1814 the war took a new turn because of events in Europe. The United States had gone to war, by "coincidence" according to Madison, just as Napoleon invaded Russia. By the end of the year that invasion turned to disaster, and by April 1814 the defeated Napoleon was on his way to exile on Elba. The fall of Napoleon left the United States alone to face the full might of Britain. In the summer of 1814 Britain tightened her blockade and sent thousands of veteran troops released from European service to Canada.

Then British forces invaded the area of Chesapeake Bay, captured Washington, and burned the White House and the Capitol, but failed to take Baltimore. They also attempted an invasion of New England and New York by way of Lake Champlain, but Lieutenant Thomas Macdonough saved that part of the country, and the nation from possible disunion by winning an important naval battle near Plattsburgh in September.

The outstanding American victory on land, fought independently of naval power, was the Battle of New Orleans of January 8, 1815. Andrew Jackson inflicted this defeat on the British after the peace treaty was signed. It did not, therefore, affect the outcome of the war.

Since the United States went to war with a small navy, it could barely challenge Britain's maritime supremacy. American sloops-of-war and super-frigates, such as the *Constitution,* won a number of individual naval duels. "Our little naval triumphs" Madison called them, but before the end of the war the Royal Navy swept the American navy and merchant fleet from the seas.

American privateers inflicted greater damage on the British than did the regular navy. They roamed the seas and preyed on shipping, even in the English Channel itself. Altogether they captured or destroyed almost 1,350 British merchant ships, but Britain strangled even privateering with a convoy system and with an ever-tightening blockade.

Thus, when the war ended, the United States had no navy, its coast was tightly blockaded, and the British held considerable American territory. They occupied part of Maine, and in the Northwest they, or their Indian allies, controlled the upper Mississippi Valley and even portions of northern Illinois and northern Iowa.

The Diplomatic Problems

The diplomacy that brought peace was another of the unusual features of the War of 1812. Since the United States and Britain maintained diplomatic relations while they fought, peace negotiations began almost as soon as hostilities started. Throughout the negotiations the results of the fighting and developments in Europe influenced the demands of both sides. The first efforts, English and American, to make an armistice failed, as we have seen, because neither side would retreat on the issue of impressment.

After those failures, Russia offered to mediate between her British ally and the United States. The tsar, Alexander I, was anxious to relieve England of the responsibilities of the American war which diverted energy from the European conflict. Moreover, Russia wanted to revive the American trade that England now kept from her ports.

Although the tsar made his offer in September 1812, it did not reach Madison until March, nine months after the war began. With the war unpopular, the fighting going badly, the British blockade becoming increasingly severe, and with Napoleon's defeat in Russia now a fact, Madison knew he had to grasp the offer. So anxious was he to quiet the clamor of the peace party and to end the embarrassing war that he even acted without finding out how Britain would respond to the tsar's offer.

Madison immediately appointed two special envoys, Albert Gallatin, his secretary of the treasury and one of his most trusted advisers, and James A. Bayard, a Federalist senator from Delaware, to join John Quincy Adams, the American minister in St. Petersburg, to negotiate peace with British envoys under the tsar's mediation. With polite expressions of regret, Castlereagh, however, refused the tsar's offer, but did say that England was willing to negotiate directly with the United States. For reasons of his own, the tsar ignored Castlereagh's counteroffer and continued to press his own mediation plan on the British.

Finally, in November 1813 Castlereagh wrote directly to Secretary of State Monroe offering to negotiate a peace without intermediaries. Madison jumped at the proposal and appointed a peace commission of five men to meet with the British in Ghent. It included Adams, Gallatin, and Bayard, and two new envoys, Henry Clay and Jonathan Russell, formerly the American *chargé* in London. Gallatin was the outstanding figure, but the commission as a whole was exceedingly able. Since it took many weeks for the exchange of dispatches and instructions between Washington and the negotiators, the commission had wide discretionary powers.

The British commission, composed of three men, was undistinguished. Since it had no power of initiative, it referred almost every-thing to superiors in London. According to Gallatin, its members were little more than puppets of Castlereagh. One reason for this was that the American negotiations were a mere sideshow in comparison to the more important negotiations at the Congress of Vienna. England sent her finest statesmen there.

The contrast between Vienna and Ghent, the Flemish town garrisoned by British troops where the American envoys met the British peace-makers, was striking. In Vienna the diplomats could enjoy the rhythm of dancing, but in Ghent the American commissioners had to negotiate to the cadence of marching boots. After keeping the American envoys waiting over a month, the British commissioners arrived on August 6, 1814. Negotiations began two days later.

Originally the American instructions had called for an end to "illegal blockades," a recognition of American neutral rights, and a settlement of other controversial matters. The one indispensable condition dealt with impressment. If Britain will not abolish impressment, Secretary of State Monroe wrote, "the United States will have appealed to arms in vain." If you fail on the question of impressment, he said, "all further negotiations will cease, and you will return home without delay." [9]

Those instructions would have placed the American commissioners in a weak negotiating position. The status of their government did not help them either. It was almost bankrupt, without friends, and its military future appeared bleak. With England's armed forces no longer tied down in Europe, they could not expect her to make concessions, particularly on the issue of impressment. Even though impressment now became an academic question, because the Royal Navy stopped the practice with the end of the European war, England would not give up her right to impress.

In June, therefore, Madison had asked his cabinet, "Shall a treaty of peace, silent on the subject of impressment, be authorized?" In effect, the advisers answered "Aye." [10] Then Monroe instructed the envoys to put aside the impressment question. This abandonment of the one indispensable condition reached the commissioners on the evening of August 8 and placed them in a stronger bargaining position than they had anticipated. It allowed them to insist, as they did throughout the negotiations, that the settlement must be based on the *status quo ante bellum,* meaning a mutual restoration of territory. This, of course, differed markedly from the objectives Americans had held when they started the war, but it reflected a realistic appraisal of America's position in the negotiations. The fate of Canada or Florida was not mentioned.

The British demands were sweeping. "Their terms," Bayard complained, "were those of a Conqueror to a conquered People." Yet those terms appeared to reflect important opinion in Britain. When the negotiators had prepared to leave for Ghent, for example, *The Times* of London offered its instructions. "Our demands may be couched in a single word," it said, "Submission!" [11]

From the first the British said they would make no concessions on impressment or neutral rights. They demanded initially that Americans place no forts or armed ships on the Great Lakes and cede territory in Maine, northern New York, and between Lake Superior and navigable water on the Mississippi River. The British commissioners also advanced as an indispensable condition the twenty-year-old idea of a nominally independent Indian buffer state between Canada and the aggressive Americans, seeking to carve that state out of American territory in the Northwest.

The Americans flatly rejected the British terms. They would not, they said, "surrender both the rights of sovereignty and of soil over nearly one-third of the territorial dominions of the United States to Indians." The British demands, they felt, "were above all dishonorable." Bayard warned the British that their terms would prolong the war.

At this point so hopeless did the Americans consider their position that they prepared to break off the negotiations. Fortunately, Castlereagh himself did not insist upon the Indian buffer state as an indispensable condition to peace. "The substance of the question is," he wrote to the prime minister, "are we prepared to continue the war for territorial arrangements?" [12] The British cabinet was unwilling to do so and the two commissions, therefore, continued their negotiations.

In the place of the Indian buffer state and exclusive control of the Great Lakes, the British were willing to accept a general amnesty for the Indians which would restore them to the lands they held before the war. In place of the boundary revisions they had demanded originally, they now proposed peace on the basis of *uti possidetis,* meaning that each nation would retain the territory it had won.

The Americans were discouraged. Early in October they heard news of the capture and burning of Washington. "Let them feast on Washington," Britain's prime minister said. The British terms appeared now as demands for American territory which might be enforced by arms. Later in the month, however, the Americans received news of Macdonough's victory on Lake Champlain. Therefore, they again refused the British terms and prepared to leave Ghent. The only acceptable principle, they insisted, now as before, was the *status quo ante bellum.*

After Macdonough's victory the British proposal for territorial settlement was not as sweeping as it could have been. The British did not demand the upper Mississippi Valley still held by their troops and Indian allies. Under the principle of *uti possidetis,* as they advanced it, their main acquisition would have been northern Maine.

After the Americans had rejected their revised demands, the British sought some means of breaking the deadlock. First they asked the American commissioners to present a draft of a treaty acceptable to the United States. Then they tried to find a means of ending the American war through force, for the negotiations at Vienna were going badly and the strain of the war was weakening Britain's foreign policy in Europe.

The government, and the public, wanted the Duke of Wellington to take command of British forces in America. He was willing, but warned that "you could not spare me out of Europe" this year, and that his going would give Europe an exaggerated notion of British defeats in America. He also said his trip might be futile, for "that which appears to me to be wanting in America is not a General, or a General officer and troops, but a Naval superiority on the Lakes." In regard to negotiations at Ghent, he added, "I confess that I think you have no right, from the state of war to demand any concession of territory from America . . . why stipulate for the *uti possidetis?*" [13]

Wellington's advice settled the outcome of the negotiations. Although the British cabinet had at first intended to use the treaty the American commissioners had drafted on November 10 merely as a basis for further negotiation, it now accepted that draft as the foundation for a peace settlement.

The Treaty of Ghent

After another month of steady negotiations, the American and British envoys signed the Treaty of Ghent on Christmas Eve, 1814. "I hoped," John Quincy Adams said, "it would be the last treaty of peace between Great Britain and the United States." [14]

The president accepted the treaty without question the day it arrived. "Peace, at all times a blessing," he told the Senate, "is peculiarly welcome. . . ." [15] The Senate approved on February 16, 1815, by a unanimous vote. Within two more days Madison exchanged ratifications, proclaimed the treaty, and published it.

By restoring all territory occupied by the forces of both nations, the treaty embodied the American principle of the *status quo ante bellum*. It assured an amnesty for the Indians who had fought on either side and provided for several joint commissions to settle boundary controversies, but did not mention impressment, neutral rights, Canada or Florida, or any of the issues that had led to war. The United States was fortunate in not losing any of its own territory. Moreover, that treaty was followed by a lasting peace, and unlike many peace treaties it did nothing that had to be undone.

The reasons for Britain's leniency in her second peace with the United States were the pressure of foreign policy in Europe and politics at home. After twenty years of war, the English government wisely preferred a satisfactory peace in Europe to a complete victory in America.

British nationalists, nonetheless, were disappointed with the treaty. The negotiators, one London newspaper said, "had humbled themselves in the dust and thereby brought discredit on the country." The masses and others who were sick of war, on the other hand, welcomed the return of peace. They were unwilling to fight except in a war of self-defense, and the war in America in 1814 was not that. Manufacturers, shippers, and merchants were also pleased. They wanted to end an unpopular property tax the government had long levied to finance the war in Europe. More important, perhaps, they desired and needed renewed access to American markets. News of Jackson's victory at New Orleans and of Napoleon's return to Paris from his exile on Elba reached London simultaneously in March. After that, even the nationalists and other critics of the peace accepted it without further grumbling.

Americans were delighted with the treaty. Most of them, even Westerners, recognized that under the circumstances the terms were as good as they had any reason to expect. Even though the Federalist press criticized it, the treaty was one of the most popular Americans have ever negotiated. Terms of the settlement reached Washington in February, about a week after the people had learned that Jackson had saved New Orleans. In New York, where the news arrived first, church bells rang in every spire and people filled the streets shouting joyfully, "A peace! A peace!" As the news traveled, other cities responded with similar demonstrations.

The unthinking, while rejoicing in Jackson's victory, assumed as a result that the United States had beaten Britain into submission. "In the fulness of our glory," one naïve American wrote, "we grant peace to a worsted enemy." How else, some Americans reasoned, could the United States with large portions of its territory still occupied, have won such a favorable peace?

Canadians, who had fought hard and well in defense of their homes, were disappointed. The treaty, they felt, left them exposed to future American aggression.

Since the Treaty of Ghent gave the United States none of its original war objectives, some writers, with considerable justification, have called the War of 1812 a useless war. It was not entirely that. Although Westerners had failed to conquer Canada, they realized one objective: the war ended the Indian menace on the Northwest frontier. Since the British surrendered the regions of the American Northwest that they had occupied, they lost prestige and influence with the Indians there. Tecumseh had died in 1813 fighting for the British, and with the peace his plan for an Indian confederation collapsed.

In the South, even though Americans did not obtain all of Florida as quickly as they had desired, they had removed a powerful Indian barrier to expansion and settlement. Andrew Jackson, in the Battle of Horseshoe Bend of March 27, 1814, in present-day Alabama, defeated the most powerful group of southern Indians, the Creek confederacy. In the peace treaty that followed, Jackson compelled the Creeks to surrender half their lands, comprising southern Georgia and two-thirds of Alabama.

More important in the long run were the larger results. By holding sectionalism in check the war enhanced nationalism and tightened the Union. The Treaty of Ghent marked the beginning of what would ultimately be a new Anglo-American friendship, but these developments might have come later without a war.

Other Anglo-American Settlements

The peace at Ghent also led to a larger Anglo-American settlement. The American commissioners had been instructed to make a commercial treaty that would replace provisions of the expired Jay's Treaty. Three of them, John Quincy Adams, who became the minister in London, Clay, and Gallatin, tried to win acceptance of the maritime principles that England had rejected at Ghent. Finally, on July 3, 1815, they signed a convention that freed American and British trade from discriminatory duties and in other essentials renewed commercial relations as they had been before the war. Britain, however, refused to renew certain fishing privileges and to admit American ships to her West Indies. The commercial convention, considered a stopgap at the time, was limited to four years. The next agreement, dealing with disarmament, proved more satisfactory.

After failing to exclude Americans from the Great Lakes and Lake Champlain, England, according to John Quincy Adams, decided "not only to maintain, but to increase the British naval armament upon the lakes." As control of the lakes had been critically important in the war, the United States would not allow England to gain naval ascendancy there. To prevent such supremacy, the United States had either to embark on a costly naval race or work out an agreement for mutual disarmament on the lakes. Therefore, the American government instructed John Quincy Adams in November 1815 to propose mutual disarmament to the British government.

When Adams first advanced the idea in January 1816, Castlereagh agreed that "everything beyond what is necessary to guard against smuggling is calculated only to produce mischief." [16] The British foreign minister, however, did not fully accept the suggestion until April.

Since Adams did not have full powers to conclude a definite agreement, Castlereagh transferred the conversations to Washington. There, Secretary of State Monroe and the British minister, Charles Bagot, discussed the disarmament problem and reached an agreement. Final consent from London did not arrive until Monroe became president. Then, Acting Secretary of State Richard Rush exchanged notes with Bagot on April 28 and 29, 1817. Thus, the agreement that naval forces on the Great Lakes and

Lake Champlain should be limited to a few light naval vessels, a force sufficient only for police and customs service, became the Rush-Bagot Agreement.

Wanting the arrangement to be permanently binding, Bagot suggested that the president send it to the Senate for approval. After considerable delay, Monroe did so. The Senate approved it on April 16, 1818. Monroe than ratified and proclaimed it, thus giving it the status of a treaty.

That agreement, which either government could terminate after giving a notice of six months, applied only to naval armaments on the lakes. It did not extend to the land frontier.[17] The Rush-Bagot Agreement, the first example of reciprocal reduction of naval armaments, though modified, is still in force.

The Rush-Bagot Agreement settled only one of the lesser problems in Anglo-American relations. American statesmen had long wanted to bring all of them together in one general negotiation. Since the commercial convention of 1815 would expire in July 1819, President Monroe appointed Rush, Adams's successor, as minister to England, and Albert Gallatin, then minister to France, special commissioners in 1818 to negotiate a new commercial treaty and to settle all issues with Great Britain.

One of the most important of those controversies concerned the northwest boundary between Canada and the United States. It stemmed from the geographical ignorance of the peace negotiators of 1783. The treaty of that year read that the boundary ran from the northwest corner of the Lake of the Woods, located in present-day Minnesota, on "a due west course to the River Mississippi," but the source of the Mississippi was far south of such a line. Beyond the Lake of the Woods, therefore, the boundary between Canada and the United States was undetermined.

After the United States had acquired Louisiana, Secretary of State Madison had tried to settle the controversy by fixing the boundary at the

THE BOUNDARY AGREEMENT OF 1818 WITH GREAT BRITAIN

forty-ninth parallel. Britain had agreed to that line in the abortive Monroe-Pinkney Treaty of 1806, but that solution died with the treaty. During the negotiations at Ghent the Americans again suggested a boundary settlement at the forty-ninth parallel, only to drop the proposal when the British insisted on access to the source of the Mississippi with the right of free navigation.

When Rush and Gallatin took up the question in 1818, they also proposed a boundary that ran westward from the Lake of the Woods on the forty-ninth parallel to the Pacific Ocean. They refused any change which would give the British a claim to the headwaters of the Mississippi. The British negotiators then gave up their efforts to reach the Mississippi and agreed to a compromise boundary that ran west from the Lake of the Woods on the forty-ninth parallel, but only to the Rocky Mountains.

The Convention of 1818, which was signed on October 20, provided that territory west of the Rockies claimed by either side would be free and open for ten years to Englishmen and Americans without injury to the claims of either country. This clause was the basis for what has been commonly called the "joint occupation" of the Oregon country.

Besides the boundary issue, the negotiators settled a controversy over slaves that the British had carried away after the War of 1812, renewed the stopgap commercial convention for ten years, and resolved a dispute over the fisheries off the coast of British North America.

At Ghent the American commissioners had been unable to secure a renewal of the "liberty" to fish along the coast of British North America as allowed in the peace treaty of 1783. American statesmen had always contended that the "liberty" to fish in those waters was an inalienable "natural" right, but the British argued that Americans had lost their fishing rights under the rule that mutual declarations of war abrogate treaties between the warring powers. The British refused, therefore, to renew the old fishing "liberty" and insisted that the whole fisheries question had to be considered anew.

Without a renewal of their right to navigate the length of the Mississippi, which also stemmed from the treaty of 1783 and which the war had also nullified, the British said, they would not give Americans the "liberty" to fish in their waters. Finally both sides compromised. The British gave up their demand for free navigation of the Mississippi, and the Americans accepted restricted fishing "liberties." Nonetheless, the Convention of 1818 granted enough privileges to make fishing off Newfoundland and Labrador profitable for Americans and made those privileges perpetual.

"It settles at best but a few of the many disputed points between the two nations," Rush said of the convention.[18] Yet with it the United States resolved most of the major conflicts of 1812. It, along with the other settlements, constituted another important step toward a lasting peace with Great Britain.

V I

Florida and the Monroe Doctrine

Expansionists had long been as eager to acquire West and East Florida from Spain as they had been to conquer Canada. Those provinces, Americans said, were like a pistol held by an alien hand pointed at the heart of the nation. The analogy of the pistol, according to the geography of the provinces, was true enough, but fundamentally Americans wanted land and rivers flowing into the Gulf of Mexico. The United States eventually obtained the Floridas, but not all at one time.

The United States began nibbling at the Floridas immediately after it had achieved independence. When Spain reacquired the Floridas in 1783, she had claimed all the territory formerly known as British East and West Florida. Under the British, West Florida ran north from the Gulf of Mexico to the line of thirty-two degrees and twenty-eight minutes between the Mississippi and Apalachicola Rivers. East Florida extended east and south of the Apalachicola. The United States contested Spain's claim to all of West Florida by setting its southern boundary at the thirty-first parallel. Faced with the growing power of the United States and with war in Europe, Spain finally yielded in Pinckney's Treaty of 1795 and accepted the thirty-first parallel as the northern boundary of West Florida. Americans thus took the first step toward acquiring the Floridas.

After Spain ceded Louisiana to France in 1800, the United States mistakenly believed that the Louisiana grant included the Floridas. Jefferson, therefore, tried to buy them along with New Orleans, but when he purchased all of Louisiana in 1803 he did not get the Floridas. This disappointed both the expansionists and the two negotiators, James Monroe and Robert R. Livingston, who were at first convinced that the United States had no claim to West Florida. Less than two weeks after signing the Louisiana treaties, however, Livingston interpreted the vague eastern boundary of the Louisiana Territory to include West Florida to the Perdido

River. Monroe supported that claim, thinking it "too clear to admit of a doubt." Both men urged Jefferson and his secretary of state to claim West Florida as part of the Louisiana Territory. The president did that, but did not occupy the territory to the Perdido. Instead, he made the claim a "subject of negotiation with Spain" to be brought up when Spain was at war and helpless to resist American advances. "We shall certainly obtain the Floridas," he said, "and all in good time."

The Mobile Act

Congress supported Jefferson's efforts to acquire West Florida by passing the Mobile Act of February 24, 1804, which gave him authority to annex and to establish a new customs district at Mobile Bay, clearly Spanish territory. When Spain protested, Jefferson did not push the annexation. Instead he proclaimed the revenue district to include territory lying within the boundaries of the United States and placed the port of entry on the Mobile River a few miles above the thirty-first parallel in American territory. Although that plan of "aggression" failed, Jefferson did not give up.

In Madrid, meanwhile, Charles Pinckney, the American minister, urged Spain to surrender the Floridas, but the Spaniards would not yield. Therefore, in April 1804 the president ordered Monroe to Madrid to assist Pinckney. Spain was now Napoleon's ally in the war against England. This, thought Jefferson, was a good time to take advantage of Spain's weakness in America.

Monroe and Pinckney's instructions directed them to insist upon Spain's recognizing that Louisiana included West Florida to the Perdido and to try to buy East Florida. The United States offered cash, withdrawal of certain financial claims against Spain, and concessions on the southwestern boundary of the Louisiana Territory. Spain, supported by France, still refused to concede territory or sell. When the Madrid negotiations collapsed in May 1805, Monroe and Pinckney wrote to Secretary of State James Madison recommending seizure of West and East Florida. Then, they said, the United States could bargain on retaining the provinces as payment for the claims against Spain.

Although previously he would not support American efforts to acquire the Floridas, Napoleon, who needed money, now changed his mind. In 1805, he offered indirectly to force Spain to yield those provinces for $7 million. While paid to Spain, most of the money would really go to Napoleon, and Jefferson knew it. Even though John Randolph, chairman of the House Ways and Means Committee, considered it "a base prostration of the national character to excite one nation by money to bully another nation out of its property," Jefferson persuaded Congress in February 1806 to appropriate secretly $2 million to start the negotiation.[1] When revealed, this maneuver became notorious as the "Two Million Act."

Before negotiations started, Napoleon's situation in Europe changed to his advantage, so he reversed his stand on aiding the United States in its bid for the Floridas. Jefferson's devious plans then collapsed, but later might have revived. Napoleon wanted American support for his continental system, and in January 1808 tried in vain to induce Jefferson to enter the war against England by offering him the Floridas.

Later that same year, Napoleon took over Spain and then decided against giving the Floridas to the United States. He deposed the king and placed his brother Joseph on the throne. Civil war in Spain and revolution in Spain's colonies in America followed. The United States, meanwhile, suspended diplomatic relations with any Spanish government. When Jefferson left office in March 1809, therefore, his expansionist plans had failed. The United States had no official relations with Spain and had failed to acquire the Floridas.

Nonetheless the American desire for the Floridas did not slacken. President Madison shared Jefferson's views and was himself eager to obtain those provinces. "The acquisition of the Floridas," a French minister in Washington had noted, "is the object of all of Mr. Madison's prayers."

Madison believed that Americans living in West Florida would help bring that territory into the United States. His views were sound. Unlike Spain's other colonies, West Florida had a population that was largely American, in part because Spanish authorities had unwisely encouraged Americans to settle there. In 1810, Spain's authority in the populated districts declined to almost nothing. Secretary of State Robert Smith sent agents into West Florida who spread the word among the settlers "that in the event of a political separation from the parent country, their incorporation into our Union would coincide with the sentiments and policy of the United States." In September, while revolution rocked Spain's other colonies, American settlers encouraged by Madison's agents captured Baton Rouge, declared West Florida "free and independent," adopted a blue flag with a lone star, and asked the United States to annex them.

Needing no urging, Madison acted two days after the declaration of independence reached him. Claiming that West Florida to the Perdido River belonged to the United States by right of the Louisiana Purchase, Madison proclaimed American control over that territory on October 27, 1810, and authorized the governor of the Louisiana Territory to occupy the land, or as much of it as he could without using force against Spanish troops. American troops took possession in December, but only as far east as the Pearl River. They avoided Spanish soldiers at Mobile. Shortly after, while still skirting the Mobile area, American forces took control to the Perdido. This was the second step in acquiring the Floridas. "One keeps on growing bit by bit in this world," the tsar of Russia smilingly told the American minister there on hearing of the Florida acquisition.[2]

Other foreign powers, particularly France and England, protested the

American occupation. Secretary of State Smith said the United States acted to forestall English seizure of the territory, but the British *chargé d'affaires* in Washington asked an embarrassing question. "Would it not have been more worthy of the generosity of a free nation like this" and more in keeping with existing ties of friendship between the United States and Spain, he said, "to have simply offered its assistance to crush the common enemy of both, rather than to have made such interference the pretext for wresting a province from a friendly power, and that at the time of her adversity?"[3]

Although embarrassing, the foreign protests did not decrease Madison's appetite for the Floridas. Already war with England seemed probable and expansionists wanted the rest of the Floridas. If the nation went to war against England, Florida might become an English base. The Spanish governor at Pensacola, moreover, had indicated that he would be willing to surrender the Floridas to the United States. Madison, therefore, threw the influence of his administration behind an effort to obtain congressional approval for the occupation of West Florida beyond the Perdido and of East Florida.

Congress gave that approval on January 15, 1811, in a secret resolution and an act. The resolution said that the United States "cannot, without serious inquietude, see any part of the said territory [Florida] pass into the hands of any foreign power."[4] This "no-transfer resolution" expressed an idea that was to become fundamental in United States policy in the Western Hemisphere. From this time the United States opposed the transfer of territory in the Americas to outside nations.

The act empowered Madison to take Florida east of the Perdido if local authorities gave it up, or if necessary to prevent seizure by a foreign power. It also gave him the authority to spend up to $100,000 and to use the army and navy in seizing the territory.

Revolution in East Florida

Now strengthened by the support of Congress, Madison employed General George Mathews, a Revolutionary soldier and a former governor of Georgia, now in his seventies, as a special agent to acquire the Floridas and gave orders to the army and navy to support Mathews. The general thought he would have no trouble in taking what Spain still held of West Florida. "But East Florida," he told the president, "will be a harder nut to crack than West."

Madison then said that "English occupation of East Florida must be prevented, General Mathews, whatever the cost. For a weak and decadent power such as Spain to control so lengthy an area on our southern border is embarrassing; to have Great Britain in possession would be impossible. The United States must have the Floridas."

"I'll do my best, sar," Mathews answered.

"A revolution," Madison went on, "would create possibilities. As my special agent our army and navy will be at your command. But hide your hand and mine, general."

"Sar," Mathews said, "you can count on my discreetness."

"Remember that this is not West Florida," Madison warned. "There the revolution gave excuse for intervention, but our reiterated claim to the province was justification for the occupation. Except for geography and the indebtedness of bankrupt Spain to our citizens, we have no claim on East Florida." [5]

Mathews found that the Spanish governors of West and East Florida would not deliver their provinces peacefully to the United States. He decided, therefore, to employ the same tactics the lone-star rebels had used at Baton Rouge, of which Madison had approved. He would foment rebellion, supported by Georgia volunteers and American troops, and establish a new government in East Florida. Then he would accept the territory, as the president desired, from the new "local authority."

With an army of "patriots" Mathews launched his revolution in March 1812. Supported by American gunboats, he captured Fernandina on Amelia Island. Then he attacked the fortress of San Marcos near St. Augustine but failed to take it. Yet the "patriots" organized a government, chose a governor, and ceded East Florida to the United States.

The first reports of the "patriot" revolution in East Florida reached Secretary of State James Monroe and the president when they were exploiting the letters of John Henry for war propaganda against Britain. The British, through Henry, had merely sought information among New England Federalists, but Mathews had incited revolution and had used American naval forces against a peaceful Spanish colony. Since Madison had denounced the British for meddling in New England, he knew he could not logically defend Mathews's armed intervention in East Florida. He therefore disavowed Mathews and the "patriot" revolution.

"I am sorry to have to state," Monroe wrote to Mathews, on April 4, 1813, "that the measures which you appear to have adopted for obtaining possession of Amelia Island and other parts of East Florida, are not authorized by the law of the United States, or the instructions founded on it, under which you have acted." A few weeks later he told Jefferson that Mathews's "extravagances place us in a most distressing dilemma."

At first Madison promised to return the occupied half of East Florida, but since war with England now seemed certain, he retained the territory ceded by the revolutionists. When war came, he used American military forces to support the "patriots," even against the will of Congress.

"The East Florida Revolution has been extremely embarrassing," the secretary of state later told Mathews's secretary. "In all my years of service, the government has never before been placed in such a distressing dilemma." Then he added, "But the province of East Florida must never go back to Spain."[6]

While some Americans occupied a part of East Florida during the War of 1812, others completed the conquest of West Florida. General Andrew Jackson left Nashville, Tennessee, in January 1813 with frontier troops who hated the Spaniards and were eager to raise the American flag over Mobile and Pensacola, still held by Spanish soldiers, but they did not achieve their goal. The government ordered Jackson to dismiss his troops before they could launch their attack. General James Wilkinson then occupied the Mobile area bloodlessly in April 1813 and completed the third step in acquiring the Floridas.

Jackson returned to Mobile in 1814 and defended it against the British, who used the neutral Spanish port at Pensacola as a base for their attack. After throwing back the invaders, Jackson, on his own authority, marched on Pensacola, stormed it, destroyed its protecting fort, and withdrew his forces to Mobile. From there he went to New Orleans to win his greatest victory.

Since Spain had not joined England in the war against the United States, she had no part in the peace treaty, though she tried in vain to have her interests considered in the negotiations. The War of 1812 thus ended with the United States in full possession of West Florida to the Perdido River, and with Spain, after the United States had returned the occupied regions, still in control of East Florida.

During and after the peacemaking following the Napoleonic wars, Spain tried to save Florida from the aggressive Americans but knew she could not do so alone. She turned to the European powers at the Congress of Vienna for help and repeatedly sought England's assistance against the United States. "If all Europe or its principal governments," the Spanish minister in Washington warned, for instance, "do not take steps in time against the scandalous ambition of this Republic when they perceive the need of doing so and of obstructing the well-established scheme of conquest which she has set for herself it may well be too late; and she may be master of Cuba and of the New Kingdom of Mexico or whatever other region suits her."[7]

Finally Spain realized she had to settle her difficulties with the United States alone. Since her colonies in the Western Hemisphere were still in revolt, she reconciled herself to losing Florida in exchange for a settlement of other disputes with the United States.

Americans knew that Spain would have to cede East Florida, for she could not control or adequately govern the colony. Escaped slaves found refuge there, and British agents operated there freely, selling arms and encouraging Indians to resist American encroachments. By not controlling the Indians, the United States said, Spain violated Pinckney's Treaty. Spain in turn complained that Americans were transgressing neutrality by aiding the rebelling Spanish colonies in the Americas.

The Adams–Onís Negotiations

These South American revolutions, signifying that Spain's empire was disintegrating, offered the United States the opportunity of realizing long-held expansionist desires without war. The Spanish minister in Washington, Don Luis de Onís, was supposed to help in keeping the empire intact by preventing the United States from recognizing the rebelling colonies. He had come to the United States in 1809, but because Napoleon had overthrown the Spanish monarchy, years passed before Madison's government received him. Madison finally accepted his credentials in December 1815 after the restoration of the monarchy. Then Onís began conversations with Secretary of State Monroe on the question of East Florida. Onís also had powers to discuss the undetermined boundaries of the Louisiana Purchase, particularly the western frontier and the ownership of Texas. He launched his talks with Monroe by stating that Spain would recognize American title to portions of West Florida already taken, if the United States would accept the Mississippi River as its western boundary and thus give up Louisiana.

By the time John Quincy Adams became secretary of state and took up negotiations in December 1817, however, Onís was prepared to modify his demands. He suggested a western boundary for the United States at about the middle of the Louisiana Territory. Adams countered with a proposal that placed that boundary in Texas, gave the United States both the Floridas, and relieved Spain from payment of damages claimed by Americans. Before Adams and Onís could reconcile their differences, two incidents in East Florida disrupted the negotiations.

In the summer of 1817 some military adventurers, who claimed authority from various revolutionary governments in Latin America, had captured Amelia Island. One of them, who said he represented the revolutionary regime in Mexico, claimed East Florida for that government in the fall of that year. This was all that President Monroe needed to move into East Florida himself, for the "no-transfer resolution" of January 1811, under which Mathews had acted, gave him authority to take Florida if a foreign power should try to seize it. Since Mexico was a foreign nation, Monroe sent troops to Amelia Island and took possession in December while Adams and Onís were negotiating.

The United States then followed that violation of Spanish sovereignty with another. Creek Indians and their Seminole cousins from Florida had frequently attacked Americans in American territory and then fled into Spanish Florida. After those Indians had massacred a party of Americans on the Apalachicola River late in 1817, Monroe ordered Andrew Jackson to punish them and if necessary to pursue them into Spanish Florida. If they took refuge behind Spanish forces, however, he was to withhold his attack and notify the War Department.

Pinckney's Treaty obligated Spain to restrain the Indians within the borders of her possessions. Since she was incapable of doing so, the United States was justified in allowing Jackson to pursue them into Florida, but Jackson hoped to do more. In January 1818 he told the president he wanted to seize all of Florida as the United States had taken Amelia Island. "This can be done," he wrote, "without implicating the Government; let it be signified to me . . . that the possession of the Floridas would be desirable to the United States, and in sixty days it will be accomplished."[8]

Jackson made good his boast. In March 1818 he invaded Florida with three thousand men, pushing the Indians before him. He seized the fort and town of St. Marks, captured and executed two British subjects on charges that they had aided enemies of the United States, and then captured Pensacola. Since he executed the two British subjects under ill-defined powers their deaths might have touched off a serious crisis with England if she had not then faced more pressing diplomatic problems in Europe.

England's foreign minister, Robert Castlereagh, told the American minister in London, that "such was the temper of Parliament, and such the feeling of the country, that he believed WAR MIGHT HAVE BEEN PRODUCED BY HOLDING UP A FINGER."[9] England, however, never held the finger up, and Spain realized again that England would not support her against the United States, either in boundary disputes or in keeping the United States from recognizing the independence of her rebelling colonies.

Jackson finished his Florida campaign in May 1818 and returned to Nashville. He had done more than win an Indian war. He had conquered a Spanish province that Monroe had coveted since he had helped acquire Louisiana in 1803, but Jackson's intemperate actions embarrassed the president. Monroe could not now grasp what he wanted to take because he feared the international repercussions.

Monroe then denied that he had given Jackson authority to take East Florida. Jackson believed that he had and insisted, years later, that a congressman from Tennessee, Mr. John Rhea, an old friend, had written him stating that the president approved his plan for conquest. Jackson said he had burned the letter according to Monroe's instructions. Most of the evidence, though controversial, supports Monroe in the argument, but there is little doubt that Jackson did what Monroe desired in conquering Florida.

The public applauded Jackson's invasion, but political enemies did not. Congress investigated his deeds, but ultimately four resolutions of condemnation failed by substantial majorities. All of the cabinet except

John Quincy Adams wanted to disavow Jackson, or to discipline him. Adams argued that the government must sustain him, and it did. For political reasons, Monroe went along with Adams and then attempted to mollify the furious Jackson.

Onís, too, was furious. He demanded an indemnity and said he would sign no treaty until the United States punished Jackson, disavowed his "outrage," and restored East Florida to Spain. Adams defended Jackson, justifying the invasion as self-defense. He insisted that Spain must either control Florida or cede it. Florida, he said, is "a derelict, open to the occupancy of every enemy, civilized or savage, of the United States, and serving no other earthly purpose than as a post of annoyance to them." [10]

Actually, Spain had already decided to concede more for an understanding with the United States, though Jackson's invasion forced her to do now what she knew she must do eventually. She could not keep Florida from a country as hostile as the United States. The alternative to cession appeared to be a war Spain did not want, for she had no allies to help her and her hands were already full with the revolutions in South America. In January 1818 Britain had offered to mediate, but the United States had refused. Now circumstances appeared to give Spain no choice but cession.

Therefore, when Monroe appeased Spanish honor by agreeing to restore the territory Jackson had overrun, Spain proceeded with the disrupted negotiations. Spain was ready as she had been earlier to cede the Floridas if the United States would agree to a satisfactory western boundary, but now in October 1818 Onís was willing to concede a boundary farther west than he had previously proposed. Adams then suggested that the boundary between American and Spanish territory in North America be drawn all the way to the Pacific Ocean. Onís agreed to accept Adams's proposal for the western boundary of the United States at the Sabine River, the eastern edge of Texas, but said he had no authority to extend the line to the Pacific.

In January, Onís received new instructions, sent in October and prompted by Jackson's invasion, to concede the United States a boundary to the Pacific. Then the negotiations went rapidly until February 22, 1819, when Adams and Onís signed the completed treaty.

The Florida or Transcontinental Treaty

By that agreement, sometimes called the Adams-Onís Treaty, sometimes the Florida Treaty, and sometimes the Transcontinental Treaty, Spain ceded East and West Florida without payment, though the United States agreed to assume the claims of its own citizens against Spain to the extent of $5 million. The treaty defined the western boundary of Louisiana, and by it Spain surrendered her claims to the Oregon country to the United States and agreed to a northern boundary at the forty-second parallel to the

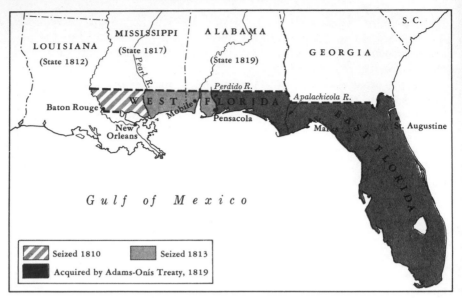

EXPANSION INTO THE FLORIDAS, 1810–1819

Pacific Ocean. The United States reluctantly gave up its shadowy claim to Texas. That was about all Spain got out of the treaty, except for peace and the settlement of claims.

The Senate approved the treaty unanimously two days after Adams signed it, and Monroe ratified it the next day. Americans liked the treaty. "The fact has long been evident," an influential journal commented, "that a sovereignty over these countries was needful to our peace and quietness, and that we would possess them by fair or foul means—by treaty or by force. We have preferred the former, and Spain has happily agreed to do that which her own interest prompted—for the Floridas, though so valuable to us, have always been a real incumbrance on her." [11]

Spain, however, did not seal the bargain immediately. Fearing that the United States would recognize the independence of her rebelling colonies, she delayed ratification for almost two years. Before ratifying, Spain demanded a pledge that the United States would not aid or recognize the independence of the colonies. The United States refused. "As a necessary consequence of the neutrality between Spain and the South American provinces," Adams told the new Spanish minister in Washington, "the United States can contract no engagement not to form any relations with those provinces."

Irked at the delay, Andrew Jackson wanted to enforce the treaty "at the mouth of the cannon." Adams thought the use of force would be justified. Wanting to avoid war, the Spanish king finally ratified the treaty in October 1820.

Since a limitation within the treaty said it had to be ratified within six months, Monroe sent it to the Senate for a second time. Before the Senate could act, opposition to the treaty arose in the West. With Henry Clay as their spokesman, Westerners demanded that the cession of Texas be included in its provisions. The government, however, refused to hold out for Texas, though not because it was unwilling to buck Spanish resistance. It feared that the issue of Texas would arouse an internal controversy over the territorial limits of slavery.

The opposition, though vocal, was not strong. The Senate gave the treaty its second approval by a big majority on February 19, 1821. Three days later, exactly two years from the date of signature, ratifications were exchanged. That completed the fourth step. All the Floridas, and more, now belonged to the United States.

John Quincy Adams was proud of the treaty he had negotiated. "It was, perhaps, the most important day of my life," he said when he signed it. His was in fact a transcontinental treaty, stretching American claims from the Atlantic to the Pacific Oceans. "The acknowledgment of a definite boundary to the South Sea," he wrote, "forms a great epoch in our history." [12]

THE TRANSCONTINENTAL LINE OF THE ADAMS-ONÍS TREATY

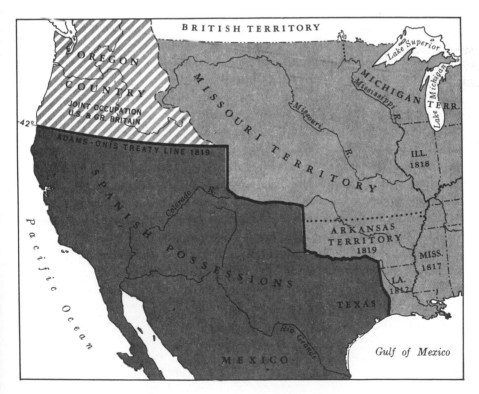

The Holy Alliance and Spain's Colonies

Adams also helped shape the diplomacy of the Monroe Doctrine, a development connected in principle with his transcontinental treaty. To understand how the United States formulated this most famous of its doctrines, it is necessary to follow a few developments in the international politics of Europe after the fall of Napoleon in 1815.

At the Congress of Vienna, the major powers tried to reconstruct Europe as it had been before Napoleon by restoring the old balance of power and maintaining it through the Quadruple or Grand Alliance. Great Britain, Russia, Prussia, and Austria had formed that alliance in March 1814 and renewed it in November of the following year to preserve the territorial arrangements made at Vienna and to prevent Napoleon from returning to France. Three years later, when a reconstructed France was admitted, the agreement also became known as the Quintuple Alliance.

Under that arrangement the five powers met at fixed intervals to discuss the peace and politics of Europe. Altogether they sponsored four congresses, the last of which met in Verona in 1822 and broke up with the Grand Alliance in virtual dissolution. Yet that alliance launched the stabilizing Concert of Europe, and its congresses began the modern system of conference diplomacy.

In addition to this broad arrangement, Alexander I of Russia induced the sovereigns of Austria and Prussia in September 1815 to join him in the Holy Alliance, a vague treaty designed apparently to buttress the political alliance and uphold autocracy. Those three sovereigns invited other rulers to come in, and most of them did. The prince regent of England would have done so, but as a constitutional ruler without independent power could not. The members of the Holy Alliance even invited the United States to join, but it politely refused.

Thus, both England and the United States were outside the Holy Alliance. Yet England belonged to the Grand Alliance and supported the balance of power it had created. Since Europe's statesmen at first did not take the Holy Alliance seriously, that coalition meant little to nonmembers such as England and the United States. Prince Clemens Metternich of Austria dismissed it as a "loud-sounding nothing," but later changed his mind, and Castlereagh considered it mystical nonsense. Nonetheless, the public confused the Holy Alliance with the Grand Alliance and acquired the habit of calling the combination of powers the Holy Allies. Regardless of precise title, the European Allies functioned as enemies of liberal government.

A New World problem that persistently concerned the allies was what should be done about Spain's rebelling colonies. The Grand Alliance in 1814 had restored Ferdinand VII to the Spanish throne, but he failed to regain the allegiance of his colonies which continued their fight for independence. Disturbed by this challenge to a legitimate monarchy, the European sovereigns wanted to see a strong effort made to re-establish Ferdinand's old authority in the Americas, but England did not.

England's motive was mainly economic. Before Napoleon's invasion Spain had monopolized the commerce of her colonies, but during the war those colonies had opened their ports to British and other foreign trade. England's trade with them, and to a lesser extent that of the United States, too, had prospered. Thus England, and the United States also, wished to continue that Latin-American trade and did not want Spain to re-establish her commercial monopoly. Both countries, therefore, had a stake, primarily commercial, in the independence of the Spanish-American colonies. The sympathy of the European monarchs for Ferdinand's plight appeared to endanger that stake.

At the first congress of the Concert of Europe, held at Aix-la-Chapelle in 1818, Britain said she would not assist, except through peaceful mediation, in restoring the Latin-American colonies to Ferdinand. At the second congress, held at Troppau in 1820, Prince Metternich suggested that the Allies had a sacred duty to crush revolution wherever it appeared. The British government would not accept Metternich's reactionary doctrine, but Russia, Prussia, and Austria did.

In that same year four liberal revolutions, in Naples, Piedmont, Spain, and Portugal, appeared to convert the Holy Alliance into a real compact. The tsar, with a million men under arms, was eager to send some of them to smother the uprisings in Italy. At this time the Grand Allies dissuaded him, but at their congress in Laibach in 1821 they sent an Austrian army to crush the revolutionaries in Piedmont and Naples. If the Allies, Holy or otherwise, could smash revolution in Europe, it seemed logical that they could do the same in the Americas.

Even before the meeting of the first European congress, President Monroe and Secretary of State Adams fearfully anticipated just such a development. They knew that the United States alone could do little to stop the Allies if they should try to defeat the revolutions in Spanish America. Monroe's government, moreover, was not even ready to offer the Spanish colonies the support of recognizing their independence, especially not before it had completed the Adams-Onís Treaty.

Yet from the beginning of the long struggle the United States had watched the Spanish-American movements for independence with growing compassion. The American people sympathized with the revolutionaries because they saw a resemblance between their own revolution against George III and the wars against Ferdinand VII. American publicists gave the struggles of the Spanish-American liberators, Simón Bolívar, José San Martín, and others, wide circulation. The drama and continental sweep of the Latin-American battles, swirling among snow-clad mountains and fought in steaming jungles, gripped the imagination.

Reflecting, in part at least, the sympathy of its people, the govern-

ment of the United States received agents from the revolutionary governments cordially, but always unofficially, and sent its own agents to care for
its interests in Spanish America. It did not, however, intervene in the revolutionary wars. Instead, it assumed a position of official neutrality in 1815
between Ferdinand and the rebels and in so doing recognized the belligerency of the Spanish-American states. Toward the more important question
of recognition of independence, it adopted a policy of watchful waiting.

At the same time, the United States permitted the revolutionaries to
buy supplies and war materials within its borders and allowed their ships to
use its ports. So widespread was public sympathy for the colonials and so
defective the neutrality laws, that violations of neutrality were common.
The Spanish Americans outfitted and equipped privateers in North American ports and then sailed them against Spain, a power friendly to the
United States. These infractions of neutrality were so embarrassing to the
government while Adams was negotiating with Onís that in March 1817
and April 1818 it passed new and stronger neutrality laws.

Many Americans, moved by the epic struggle to the south, demanded
that the government recognize the independence of the Latin states.
Speaker of the House Henry Clay, their foremost spokesman, urged such
recognition and attacked Monroe and Adams for hesitating. In a moving
speech on March 25, 1818, he pleaded with Congress for recognition of the
United Provinces of the Rio de la Plata (Argentina) and gave American
sympathies their fullest expression.

"We behold the most sublime and interesting objects of creation; the
loftiest mountains, the most majestic rivers in the world . . . and the
choicest productions of the earth," he said. "We behold there a spectacle
still more interesting and sublime—the glorious spectacle of eighteen millions of people, struggling to burst their chains and to be free." [13]

Despite Clay's thrilling speech, Congress would not act for practical
reasons. It was then interested mainly in Florida and other Spanish borderlands that Adams was trying to obtain peacefully.

Later, but before the Monroe administration was ready, Congress did
act. In May 1820 the House of Representatives, under Clay's leadership,
passed a resolution calling for the appropriation of funds for the expenses of
diplomatic agents in the Spanish-American states which had already declared independence, but the administration ignored the resolution.

Monroe and Adams had good reasons for hesitating. Premature recognition would offer Spain a cause for war they did not want, particularly
over the question of recognition. They had to decide on their own under
what conditions they could recognize the independence of the Latin-
American republics without grievously offending Spain and endangering
the acquisition of East Florida. International law offered no clear precedent.

Adams finally worked out a formula. The United States, he said,
should recognize the Spanish-American states "when independence is es-

tablished as a matter of fact so as to leave the chance of the opposite party to recover their dominion utterly desperate." While this formula made good sense, it did not relieve Monroe and Adams from speculating that Spain and the European Allies might so strongly resent recognition they would go to war against the United States.

In the following year, 1821, before Monroe and his advisers could make a decision, a Greek revolution against Turkey broke out and complicated the question of recognition. The statesmen of Europe thought that the tsar would use the Greek war of independence to gain a foothold in the Mediterranean. This problem, along with French intervention in Spain to crush the liberal revolution there, led to arrangements for another congress in the fall of 1822.

John Quincy Adams, meanwhile, had observed Britain's reluctant drift away from the Grand Alliance and her cautious resistance to the principles of the Holy Alliance. Adams believed that division of Europe into two camps, one constitutional and the other autocratic, enhanced the security of the United States. He realized that the British government would now do almost anything reasonable to avoid a break with the United States. With this understanding and with the European situation in mind, in January 1821 he bluntly explained his position to the British minister in Washington.

At that time the minister questioned Adams about American claims to the area of the Columbia River. Great Britain, he said, had a prior claim there. Adams insisted that she did not. "And how far would you consider," the minister said, "this exclusion of the right to extend?" "To all the shores of the South Sea," Adams replied. "And in this," the English diplomat asked, "you include our northern provinces on this continent?" "No," Adams, answered, "there the boundary is marked, and we have no disposition to encroach upon it. Keep what is yours, but leave the rest of this continent to us."[14]

Here Adams stated the noncolonization principle that he would place in the Monroe Doctrine. Six months later, in a violently anti-British July Fourth address, he restated the principle.

A few months later Russia gave Adams another opportunity to expound his noncolonization idea. Russia had long claimed a stretch of America's northwest coast, but did not try to enforce her claim until 1799 when she chartered the Russian-American Company and gave it exclusive trading rights and jurisdiction along the coast as far south as fifty-five degrees north latitude. The company planted settlements north of that line and in 1812 moved south into Spanish California. It set up a trading post, called Fort Ross, on Bodega Bay just north of San Francisco.

The American government, while apprehensive, never showed much concern about Fort Ross, but was alarmed by an imperial ukase the tsar issued on September 14, 1821. With that decree the Russian government, on behalf of the Russian-American Company, extended its exclusive claim to Russian America down the Pacific Coast to the fifty-first parallel and forbade all foreign ships, on penalty of confiscation, to come within one hundred Italian miles of the coast north of that parallel. Therefore Russia's claim extended into the Oregon country claimed by both the United States and Britain. Luckily, Russia never enforced the ukase, and when the United States and Britain protested, she invited them separately to negotiate a settlement in St. Petersburg.

Adams used his protest against Russia's new claim to reiterate the noncolonization principle. He told the Russian minister in Washington on July 17, 1823, that "we should contest the right of Russia to *any* territorial establishment on this continent, and that we should assume distinctly the principle that the American continents are no longer subjects for any new European colonial establishments."[15] A few days later he embodied the same idea in instructions to the American ministers in Russia and Britain.

Although the ukase gave Adams the opportunity of again stressing noncolonization, Russia apparently was not his primary target. He appeared to aim his announcement primarily at Britain, whom he considered a more menacing territorial rival than Russia.

Cautious Recognition

Meanwhile, with the Adams-Onís Treaty ratified, the time for watchful waiting toward the Latin-American wars had ended. Impressive military victories of the Spanish-American patriots had made it clear that according to the Adams formula Spain's plight in the colonies was "utterly desperate." Events in Europe, moreover, made war over recognition unlikely. News of Bolívar's victory at the Battle of Carabobo in June 1821, which destroyed Spanish power in Colombia and Venezuela, had prodded the United States government into bringing recognition to a decision.

Even though Monroe favored recognition he still hesitated. Congress had to prompt him before he wrote the special message recommending recognition of the independence of the United Provinces of the Rio de la Plata (Argentina), Colombia, Chile, Peru, and Mexico which he sent to Congress on March 8, 1822. Since Spaniards and patriots were still fighting in parts of South America, he said the United States should observe "the most perfect neutrality" between Spain and the patriot governments. Congress responded by appropriating $100,000 to maintain the expense of "such Missions to the independent nations on the American continent" as the president might deem proper.[16] The president signed an act establishing those missions on May 4.

Monroe was so cautious that he waited almost a year before appointing ministers to the United Provinces of the Rio de la Plata and to Colombia. He wished to measure Europe's reactions to recognition before taking the last step. United States policy toward the new governments, as given in the instructions to those two ministers, called for support of republicanism against monarchy, for their complete separation from Europe, for trade with the United States on the most-favored-nation terms, and for their acceptance of the doctrine of freedom of the seas.

Like many decisions in foreign policy, Monroe's actions mixed caution with boldness. They were bold because the United States became the first nation outside of Latin America to recognize the Spanish-American republics. They were cautious because the United States did not give the Spanish-American patriots tangible assistance such as arms, men, or money. "We do not see the probability of any particular benefit to the [patriots] or to the United States from the act," the *National Gazette* said on March 11. With recognition, the United States simply announced officially that it believed Spain had lost her colonies. That recognition did not deter Spain or the European Allies. Only force could do that. Those Allies still hoped, through peaceful accommodation, or perhaps through force, to save the colonies for Ferdinand.

Spain protested, but the Spanish Americans were pleased with the recognition. It marked a turning point in their long struggle. Even though not backed by tangible aid, it gave moral support and offered official evidence of the sympathy of American people.

In their recognition of Spanish-American independence, Monroe and Adams had also taken advantage of the division among Europe's leaders over policy toward the Greek war of independence. As the Grand Alliance prepared for the Congress of Verona in the fall of 1822, that division had a marked effect on both American and European diplomacy. Meanwhile, Castlereagh committed suicide and George Canning became Britain's foreign minister on September 9.

When the congress assembled in October at Verona, a French army stood on the Spanish border ready to rescue Ferdinand VII, whose reactionary rule had sparked a revolution, from the rebels who held him prisoner. Canning warned the Allies that England would not take part in any collective intervention in Spain. The Allies, despite England's objections, authorized France to intervene. On April 6, 1823, a French army plunged into Spain and in a few months occupied most of the country.

Americans were alarmed, fearing that the Holy Allies might next attempt to smother revolution in Spanish America. That fear haunted American statesmen in the summer and fall of 1823. It also bothered Canning. He had hoped that England's prestige would keep the French out of Spain and that his warning would stop the Allies from meddling in Spanish America. Like his predecessor, he followed a policy of neutrality between Spain and her colonies to preserve the Spanish-American market for English traders. In the summer of 1823 that policy appeared to have failed.

John Quincy Adams, like Canning himself, did not believe that the

Allies would in fact invade the Spanish-American republics. He was more concerned about Cuba, fearing that as the Spanish crisis mounted England might rush to the defense of Spain's revolutionary regime and then demand Cuba as a reward. Adams had ideas of his own about the future of that island. He told the American minister to Spain that if Cuba separated itself from the mother country it "can gravitate only towards the North American Union." Then he wrote, "you will not conceal from the Spanish government the repugnance of the United States to the transfer of the island of Cuba by Spain to any other power." This time Adams had applied the no-transfer principle directly to a Spanish possession.

Canning's Overtures

The United States had several times suggested a joint Anglo-American policy on the Spanish colonies. The British had never responded favorably, but in the fall of 1823 Canning himself took the lead. On August 16, he began conversations with Richard Rush, the American minister in London. These conversations furnished the impulse for the Monroe Doctrine.

First, Rush raised the question of possible French intervention in Spanish America. He was pleased, he said, that England would not allow France to snuff out the freedom of the Spanish republics. Then Canning asked if the United States would cooperate with England in upholding that anti-intervention policy. Cooperative *"action,"* he said, would not be necessary. If France knew that England and the United States supported the same policy, that knowledge would be enough to check her designs on Spanish America.

Several days later, on August 20, Canning explained in "unofficial and confidential" terms what he considered the basis for an understanding. He said that Britain believed "the recovery of the Colonies by Spain to be hopeless," but recognition was a matter of "time and circumstances." England, however, was "by no means disposed to throw any impediment in the way of an arrangement between them and the mother country by amicable negotiations." England did not desire to acquire any part of them, but "could not see any portion of them transferred to any other Power with indifference."

"If these opinions and feelings are," Canning added, "as I firmly believe them to be, common to your government with ours, why should we hesitate mutually to confide them with each other, and to declare them in the face of the world?" Then he asked, are you "authorised to enter into negotiation and to sign any convention upon this subject?"

Rush replied three days later that the American government agreed with Canning's sentiments, but that his instructions did not permit him to commit his government without advance approval. If Canning would promise immediate instead of future recognition, however, Rush was will-ing "to make a declaration, in the name of my Government, that it will not remain inactive under an attack upon the independence of those States by the Holy Alliance."[17] He knew such a commitment would exceed his instructions and that his own government might disavow him, but he was prepared to take full responsibility. Canning answered that his government was not yet ready for recognition. Rush, therefore, forwarded Canning's proposal to Washington without further action.

Meanwhile, Canning received word that as soon as the French com-pleted their campaign in Spain the European Allies planned to call a new congress to deal with the problem of Spanish America. He then renewed his overtures. The United States, he said, was the leading power on the American continent. "Were the great political and commercial interests which hung upon the destinies of the new continent," he asked, "to be can-vassed and adjusted in this hemisphere, without the co-operation or even knowledge of the United States?" Rush stubbornly insisted that he would sign a joint declaration only if Canning would pledge England to an imme-diate recognition of the South American states. Since the British govern-ment was not yet willing to break openly with the powers of Europe and time was running out, the discussion ended.

The Polignac Memorandum

France took Cádiz, the last liberal stronghold in Spain, on September 30, 1823, and thus completed the destruction of the constitutional revolu-tion. That alarming news did not reach London until October 10, but Canning, unwilling to wait for the uncertain official American response to his overtures, had already acted alone to soften its impact. Although he believed that the French could not intervene successfully in Spanish America against the opposition of British sea power, he now thought they planned to try. Early in October, therefore, he had begun talks with Prince Jules de Polignac, the French ambassador in London, warning him against any French interference in Spanish America.

The prince explained that France disclaimed any intention of appro-priating any part of the Spanish possessions in America. She asked for nothing more than the right to trade there on the same terms as Britain. "She abjured, in any case," he said, "any design of acting against the Colo-nies by force of arms."[18] Polignac's assurances, embodied in a memorandum concluded on October 12, removed the threat of European interference in Spanish America.

While Canning and Polignac were talking, Rush's first dispatches car-rying Canning's overtures arrived in the United States. Monroe and Adams looked them over, and then Monroe turned to his Virginia friends, former presidents Jefferson and Madison, for advice. He disliked the idea of deserting the principle of nonentanglement, yet he asked Jefferson, "If a case can exist in which a sound maxim may, and ought to be departed from, is not the present instance precisely that case?" Then he added, "My own impression is that we ought to meet the proposal of the British government."[19]

Jefferson agreed with the president. "Great Britain," he said, "is the nation which can do us the most harm of any one, or all on earth; and with her on our side we need not fear the whole world." He, as did Madison, urged Monroe to "join in the declaration proposed."[20] With that advice, Monroe was prepared to link American policy with that of Britain.

Meanwhile, on October 16, Russia's minister in Washington told Adams that Russia would not recognize the rebel governments and that she was pleased with America's neutral policy toward the Spanish-American wars. To the secretary of state that note seemed to imply that if the United States championed Spanish-American freedom, the tsar would support Spain and France in South America.

The cabinet met on November 7 to discuss Canning's overtures and the Russian "crisis." Secretary of War John C. Calhoun suggested giving Rush discretionary authority to make a joint declaration with Canning, even if it pledged the United States never to acquire Cuba or Texas. Even though the suggestion agreed with Monroe's own ideas, Adams disagreed. Although the United States had no designs on Cuba or Texas, he said, one day those provinces might want to join the Union. The government, he thought, should not therefore tie itself with a joint declaration. Deeply impressed, Monroe said he did not wish to take an action which might subordinate the United States to Britain.

Adams still believed, and rightly so, that the European Allies would not invade South America, but he wanted the United States to take the lead from Britain as the protector of Spanish-American independence. Thus, as a presidential candidate, he would not appear to have truckled to Britain and would seem to have gained access to commercial advantages in South America. He thought Monroe should, therefore, take a stand against Russia, France, and the Holy Alliance, and at the same time refuse Britain's overtures. "It would be more candid," he said, "as well as more dignified, to avow our principles explicitly to Russia and France, than to come in as a cock-boat in the wake of the British man-of-war."[21] After some debate, the cabinet agreed with him, and his ideas governed the writing of a reply to Canning and to the Russian minister.

Adams then instructed Rush to decline Canning's proposal for a joint declaration, but assured the British minister that the United States accepted his stated principles except the one concerning recognition. He insisted that the Spanish colonies "were of *right* independent of all other nations, and that it was our duty so to acknowledge them." Then he added that the United States "could not see with indifference, any attempt by one or more powers of Europe to restore those new states to the crown of Spain, or to deprive them, in any manner whatever of the freedom and independence which they have acquired." He did not, however, rule out the idea of a joint declaration. Emergency conditions, he said, might make such an announcement necessary.

Monroe and his advisers did not know of the Polignac Memorandum. When the news reached the United States in mid-November that France had crushed the constitutional revolution in Spain, Monroe himself feared that the Allies would next attack Spanish America. Therefore, he again talked of a joint declaration with Britain.

In a cabinet meeting a few days later, Calhoun shared the president's alarm. The Holy Allies with ten thousand men, he said, could restore Mexico and all South America to Spain. Adams, however, was still not alarmed and still opposed linking American action with Britain. "I no more believe that the Holy Allies will restore the Spanish dominion upon the American continent," he declared, "than that the Chimborazo will sink beneath the ocean." [22]

Two days later, on November 17, the Russian minister gave Adams another note. The tsar's policy, the note said, was "to guarantee the tranquillity of all the states of which the civilized world is composed." That policy, he indicated, included support of Spain's supremacy in Latin America.

Adams now connected the Russian problem with Canning's overtures, and wished to answer both Russia and Britain in notes that clearly asserted his country's policy in the Western Hemisphere. Later, he felt, the notes could be published. The president had different ideas. He wanted to announce that policy in his annual message to Congress on the State of the Union. His word was final. On November 21, therefore, Monroe read a draft of his message to the cabinet.

That draft outlined foreign affairs as Adams had sketched them for the president the week before, but went beyond the secretary's draft. The message, Adams said, now "alluded to the recent events in Spain and Portugal, speaking in terms of the most pointed reprobation of the late invasion of Spain by France, and of the principles upon which it was undertaken by the open avowal of the King of France. It also contained a broad acknowledgment of the Greeks as an independent nation, and a recommendation to Congress to make an appropriation for sending a Minister to them."

Adams urged the president not to take so strong a stand. It would, he explained, be a grave departure from the principles of George Washington. It would be "a summons to arms—to arms against all Europe, and for objects of policy exclusively European—Greece and Spain."

On the next day, when alone with the president, the secretary pressed his case with greater urgency. "The ground that I wish to take," he advised, "is that of earnest remonstrance against the interference of the European powers by force with South America, but to disclaim all interference on our part in Europe; to make an American cause, and adhere inflexibly to that."[23] Monroe then changed his message to meet Adams's suggestions.

The Monroe Doctrine

The president delivered his views to the world on December 2, 1823, in two widely separated passages in his message to Congress. He announced as a principle "that the American Continents, by the free and independent condition which they have assumed and maintain, are henceforth not to be considered as subjects for future colonization by a European power." This, the noncolonization principle, was the work of Adams.

Then in his own words Monroe referred to the Holy Allies and declared "that we should consider any attempt on their part to extend their system to any portions of this Hemisphere, as dangerous to our peace and safety. With the existing Colonies or dependencies of any European power, we have not interfered, and shall not interfere. But with the Governments who have declared their Independence, and maintained it, and whose Independence we have, on great consideration, and on just principles, acknowledged, we could not view any interposition for the purpose of oppressing them, or controlling in any other manner, their destiny, by any European power, in any other light than as the manifestation of an unfriendly disposition towards the United States."

The Monroe Doctrine stated nothing new. It summed up old principles and applied them to immediate circumstances. It was a theoretical justification of a policy of self-interest and was concerned basically with three principles: noncolonization, meaning that no European power could in the future form colonies in either North or South America; nonintervention, which warned Europe against meddling in American affairs and said "hands off"; and noninterference in European affairs, which implied that Europe's political system was distinct from that of the Western Hemisphere.

The Monroe Doctrine also had a fourth principle not stated in the message but expressed in supporting documents. It was the no-transfer principle that had been American policy since 1811.

Monroe's words had no real threat of force behind them, but the president and Secretary Adams both knew that British policy opposed European intervention in Spanish America. They could, therefore, make their bold pronouncement without fear and without force of their own. To be effective, the Monroe Doctrine needed the support of the British fleet, which indirectly it had. Yet Monroe, not knowing of the Polignac Memorandum, believed he was addressing himself to an immediate crisis. It was the French memorandum, agreed upon two months before the president's message, and not the Monroe Doctrine, that had removed the danger of intervention by the Holy Allies, a danger that probably never truly existed.

Unaware that the Allies had decided against intervention and that hence the Monroe warning was directed against a nonexistent danger, most Americans accepted it at face value and greeted it warmly. They did not, however, refer to the principles of 1823 as the Monroe Doctrine until more than a quarter of a century later. Congress, furthermore, despite administration efforts to gain its endorsement, refused to make the doctrine anything more than a presidential statement of policy. As such, through the years, it grew into one of the nation's enduring foreign policies.

European statesmen, however, did not take Monroe's message seriously. They considered it an empty threat meant to influence domestic politics. The Russian government said the doctrine "merits only the most profound contempt." Metternich condemned Monroe's words as mere "indecent declarations" which cast blame and scorn on the institutions of Europe most worthy of respect. Although the message made most of them angry, none of the European powers protested. Their statesmen, who were aware of the substance of the Polignac Memorandum before learning of Monroe's message, rightly regarded that memorandum as the decisive document in Spanish-American affairs.

Britain's reaction to the American doctrine differed from that of the European statesmen. Since his overtures to Rush had been largely responsible for its announcement, Canning at first considered it a reflection of his own diplomacy. As he examined it closely, however, the noncolonization clause came to irk him. In March 1824, therefore, he published the Polignac Memorandum, giving it wide circulation in Latin America, to show that Britain and not the United States was the first and real protector of Spanish-American freedom.

Even in Latin America, as a result, the reaction to Monroe's doctrine was not generally enthusiastic. The liberal thinkers there received it cordially, and the governments of Colombia and Brazil endorsed it, but conservative leaders, and even some of the liberals, on second thought were cool to it. They knew that if any outside force had saved their independence, it was the British fleet, not Monroe's blast on the republican trumpet. When several of the new states, among them Colombia, Brazil, and Mexico, approached the United States for an alliance or assistance based on Monroe's ideas, the immediate practical emptiness of the doctrine became clear. The United States turned them down.

The Panama Congress of 1826

Within a few years of Monroe's message, the United States again showed its reluctance to carry out the doctrine's broad principles and even admitted its inability to do so. In December 1824 Simón Bolívar, hoping to form an inter-American organization to protect the newly independent states of Latin America against possible attack from Europe, called those states to a congress to be held in Panama in October of the following year. Although Bolívar himself, who considered Britain a better source of protection, had not included the United States, several of the Latin governments invited it to participate. They wished to draw the United States into an agreement supporting the principles of the Monroe Doctrine.

John Quincy Adams had now become president, in part as a result of accomplishments in foreign policy, and Henry Clay, a former champion of Latin-American independence, his secretary of state. They accepted the invitations, and Adams nominated two delegates to attend the conference. The nominations immediately ran into trouble. For domestic reasons stemming from the bitterness engendered by the presidential election of 1824, Adams's enemies were willing to do almost anything to oppose and injure him. In Congress they tried to block participation in the Panama Conference but cloaked their opposition with a mantle of principle, saying that participation would violate Washington's and Jefferson's advice against foreign entanglements. Southerners, for instance, were hostile to participation because they feared that the conference would call for the establishment of relations with the Negro republic in Haiti and the abolition of the slave trade by the nations of the Americas.

Finally, the opposition was overcome. The Senate confirmed the delegates in March 1826, and the House then appropriated funds for the mission, but Congress had debated so long on the issue of participation that the delegates never reached Panama. One of them died on the way, and the other, upon learning that the meeting had adjourned, never went to Panama.

Even if the commissioners had been able to participate in the Panama Congress, it is clear that they could have done nothing to uphold the principles of the Monroe Doctrine. In nominating them, for instance, Adams had assured the Senate that the mission was "neither to contract alliances, nor to engage in any undertaking or project importing hostility to any other nation." It would only be permitted to accept an agreement reaffirming the noncolonization principle, but without any commitment from the United States. Even that limited gesture was too much for the Senate, which tacked an amendment to its approval expressing opposition to any commitment. There must be, the Senate said, no "departure from the settled policy of this government, that, in extending our commercial relations with foreign nations, we should have with them as little political connexion as possible."

The Panama Conference itself accomplished little. All that can be said for it is that it was a forerunner of the Pan-American movement and hence had launched an idea that did not die.

British statesmen, meanwhile, had concluded that the Monroe Doctrine had been designed in a spirit unfriendly to their country, but approved of the nonintervention principle because it fitted their own objectives. Despite the weakness of the American claim, Canning felt, moreover, that he could not allow the United States to pose as the protector of Spanish-American freedom without further action by his government on behalf of the Latin Americans. He persuaded his government to recognize the independence of the Spanish-American republics, which it did in December 1824. More than a year and a half later, Canning claimed credit for preserving the freedom of those republics. "I called the New World into existence," he boastfully told Parliament, "to redress the balance of the Old."[24]

The Monroe Doctrine had also stimulated another reaction in Canning. He and other British statesmen had been so upset by the noncolonization principle, that he abandoned a plan for joint negotiations with the United States at St. Petersburg concerning Russia's claims on the northwest coast of North America. Therefore, the United States engaged itself in separate negotiations with the Russians and concluded a convention with them in April 1824, that resolved the conflicting claims. Britain signed a similar treaty to February 1825.

In these treaties Russia agreed to make no settlements south of the line fifty-four degrees forty minutes north latitude on the west coast of North America, and the United States and Britain promised to establish none north of that line. Those treaties thus left the United States and Britain as the only claimants to the Oregon country. Although the Monroe Doctrine was in part, at least, directed against Russia, she did not limit her claims in North America or make a treaty with the United States because of it. Other reasons, mainly more important stakes in the Balkans, motivated her statesmen.

VII

Spur of Destiny

For about twenty years, from the middle of the 1820s to the early 1840s, the United States was not entangled in any major diplomatic crisis. Europe's rivalries did not threaten it and its people were not themselves looking for foreign adventures. Instead, Americans devoted themselves mainly to populating a continent and to domestic politics. Nonetheless, a number of frustrating foreign problems demanded the attention of their government. One of them concerned trade with Britain's colonies in the West Indies. Although minor in itself, that problem became important because John Quincy Adams and Andrew Jackson made an issue of it in domestic politics.

The West Indian Trade

Since independence, the United States had tried to break into Britain's mercantilist system so as to secure freedom of trade, and by 1815 had largely succeeded. The commercial convention of that year with Britain and Jay's Treaty had placed commerce between the United States and the British Isles on a reciprocal most-favored-nation basis and had admitted American ships to the ports of the British East Indies, but had not allowed Americans to trade with Britain's West Indies.

Resenting the exclusion, the United States enacted retaliatory trade legislation against the British in 1817, 1818, and 1820. By 1820, in fact, it had ended direct trade with the British West Indies and had blocked the importation of West Indian products through Canada, New Brunswick, Nova Scotia, and even England.

At first the legislation had no effect. The actions of the American Congress, a London newspaper explained, "affect, in truth, so small and so inconsiderable a portion of our general trade, as to be worthy of no other notice than as indicating the spirit in which they originate." True enough, the West Indian trade with the United States was small but the planters of those islands, who suffered from its loss, considered it important.

With the support of those who advocated a broad program of free trade, the planters petitioned Parliament to resume direct commerce with the United States. Yielding finally to the pressure, Parliament in July 1822 opened certain ports in the West Indies to American merchants. The terms, however, were restrictive and contingent on the American government granting similar treatment to British ships in its ports.

Delighted with these concessions, Secretary of State John Quincy Adams wanted more. Congress, therefore, enacted legislation on March 1, 1823, that opened American ports to British ships carrying goods directly from the West Indies and from other recently unlocked ports and gave the president authority to meet British restrictions on that trade with a discriminatory tariff of his own on certain of the colonial products imported in British ships. Accordingly, President Monroe imposed a tariff that would remain in effect until Britain should give up her intercolonial preferences. The United States, in other words, wanted its ships admitted into the West Indies on the same terms as British ships and cargoes.

Since legislation offered no solution to the West Indian problem, the two governments tried unsuccessfully to reach a settlement in 1824 through negotiation. Believing that colonial preference within the empire was a domestic matter, the British still would not allow Americans unrestricted trade in the Indies, though they were willing to make other concessions. Colonial preference, the British held, was essential in maintaining their sea power.

Despite the failure of the negotiations, Parliament made certain limited concessions in the West Indian trade in 1825 after Adams became president. They would apply, however, only if the United States removed its discriminations against British shipping.

Assuming wrongly that the pressure in Parliament from the West Indian planters would force the British government to make further concessions, Adams refused to compromise. As a result, Britain in July 1826 excluded all American ships from the West Indies until the United States should repeal its discriminatory duties.

Adams, meanwhile, had decided to soften his demands. Early in July he sent Albert Gallatin to London to negotiate an agreement on the West Indian question and other problems. Although Gallatin had conciliatory instructions which gave him the power to agree to a reciprocal suspension of discriminatory legislation, he arrived too late. The British had again closed the West Indies to American shipping. When Gallatin tried to reopen the question he got nowhere. George Canning, the foreign minister, would not even discuss it.

Although Adams himself now felt that "there should be an act of

Congress totally interdicting the trade with all the colonies, both in the West Indies and North America," he decided that if Congress would accept trade in the West Indies without complete reciprocity, he would also. Congress offered no support. Instead, political enemies attacked Adams's West Indian diplomacy. He was, one of them pointed out, "very unfortunate in this affair & [he] will find it difficult to resist the imputation of having trifled with a very valuable portion of commerce." And, the critic added, *"You may rest assured that the re-election of Mr. Adams is out of the question."*

Nonetheless, as required by law, Adams issued a proclamation on March 17, 1827, closing the nation's ports to ships coming from any of Britain's colonies in the Americas. A month later he tried once more to negotiate, this time on the basis of accepting the West Indian trade virtually on Britain's terms, but the British were still unwilling to reopen their ports in the West Indies. One critic pointed out that Adams and his advisers, "after huckstering for an unattainable shadow till they lost the substance," then became "willing and anxious to do what they grossly neglected to do when they had the power."

Finally, the West Indian controversy helped ruin Adams politically. His loss of that trade in 1826 and his failure to regain it in 1827 became an important issue in the election of 1828 that swept Andrew Jackson into power.

When Jackson took over the government in March 1829, the British West Indies were still closed to American ships, but political conditions in both England and the United States had changed enough to make a settlement of that question appear possible. Early in 1827, Canning, whom Adams considered "an implacable, rancorous enemy of the United States," had died. Canning's successor, Lord Aberdeen, held a friendlier view of the United States and wanted to settle the controversy.

Although in the past Jackson had often expressed hatred of the British, his attitude toward the old enemy had softened. He, too, wanted a settlement. His secretary of state, Martin Van Buren, went so far as to inform the British that the American people had repudiated the views of the Adams administration.

After some delay in preliminary negotiations, Jackson, with the support of Congress, gave up the demand that Britain abandon her policy of colonial preference before the United States would remove its discriminatory duties. Through a proclamation of October 5, 1830, he declared the retaliatory duties repealed and opened American ports to British ships on the same terms as American ships. Two days after receiving Jackson's proclamation, the British government issued an order in council opening its West Indies to direct trade with the United States, but subject to duties it might choose to impose. This was called the "reciprocity of 1830." Although a compromise settlement that allowed only a limited trade, it resolved another Anglo-American controversy without serious loss to the United States.

Claims Against France

Another problem that had defied Adams and that Jackson also finally settled was that of the claims of American citizens against France for destruction of their property between 1803 and 1815 in the Napoleonic wars. Americans had tried unsuccessfully to settle their claims since 1815, although Europeans had similar claims, and France had paid them. Understandably, Americans felt the sting of discrimination.

Soon after becoming president, Jackson took up the cause of the American claimants and after involved negotiations arrived at a settlement. In a treaty of July 4, 1831, France agreed to pay twenty-five million francs in six annual installments, but her government could make no payments until the legislative chambers approved the treaty and voted the money. Since many Frenchmen considered the amount to be paid as unnecessarily high, the chambers would not execute the treaty.

Therefore, when Jackson's secretary of the treasury drew a draft on the French government for the first installment in February 1833, France's minister of finance refused payment because the legislature had neither approved the treaty nor appropriated money for it. When Jackson pressed the French to execute the treaty, the king explained to the American minister in Paris that "unavoidable circumstances" alone had prevented it, but added that "it will be faithfully performed."

Despite those assurances, in April 1834 the French chamber of deputies defeated a bill appropriating the money. Jackson bristled, ordered the navy ready for sea duty, and in his annual message of December asked Congress to support strong measures against France. The United States, he said, would not permit solemn treaties "to be abrogated or set aside." He recommended "that a law be passed authorizing reprisals upon French property in case provisions shall not be made for the payment of the debt at the approaching session of the French Chambers."[1]

Even though the Senate, under Whig leadership, refused to back the president in a policy of reprisals, his words angered and hurt the French. They recalled their minister in Washington and suggested that the American minister leave Paris. He sailed shortly after for the United States, leaving the Paris legation to a *chargé d'affaires*.

The French chambers finally voted the money but said it could not be paid until the American government satisfactorily explained the harsh language in the president's annual message. Jackson refused. "We would not permit any foreign nation to discuss such a subject," he said. "Nor would we permit any or all foreign nations to interfere with our domestic concerns, or to arrogate to themselves the right to take offense at the mode, or manner, or phraseology of the President's message or any official communication between the different co-ordinate or other branches of our government."[2]

Since neither France nor the United States would now retreat, they broke off diplomatic relations. Jackson was convinced that he had a popular issue and that the people stood behind him. They shouted as one, from Maine to Florida, he said, "No apology, no explanation—my heart cordially responds to that voice." His advisers finally overcame his stubborn pride and persuaded him to soften his attitude.

In his annual message of December 1835, therefore, Jackson denied he had intended "to menace or insult the Government of France." Yet he also said that "the honor of my country shall never be stained by an apology from me for the statement of truth and the performance of duty." Since neither country wanted to prolong this minor tempest and neither wanted to back down first publicly, in January 1836 they both accepted a British offer to mediate. Then the British mediator announced that France accepted the explanation in Jackson's recent message as satisfactory. That settled the matter. France paid her installments, Jackson sent France a gracious message, and the two countries resumed cordial relations.

Although both Frenchmen and Americans had talked of war and made warlike preparations, the claims dispute never reached the stage of a real war crisis. This episode illustrated the tremendous influence that the personality of a strong president, such as Jackson, had on foreign policy. His attitude could magnify an unimportant issue into a minor crisis and even arouse the American people into thinking about war with a friendly nation.

The Caroline *Incident*

About a year and a half after Jackson's blunt diplomacy had disposed of the claims question, his successor, Martin Van Buren, had to deal with a crisis in relations with Great Britain that the United States did not settle until the signing of the Webster-Ashburton Treaty in 1842. The immediate difficulties began with two rebellions in Canada in 1837.

Even though the British authorities quickly suppressed the rebellions, the rebel cause aroused widespread sympathy among Americans who mistakenly identified the uprisings with their own revolution against England. One New York newspaper reflected American sentiment when it reported that "99 out of 100 people here wished success to the Canadians."[3] Many Americans hoped that Canada would declare herself independent and were willing to help in driving the British from North America.

Concerned over the violent feelings on both sides of the border, President Van Buren issued a proclamation on November 21, 1837, calling on

Americans to remain neutral. Since the proclamation had no force behind it, Van Buren sent no troops to the frontier to guard American neutrality. Less than a month later, William Lyon Mackenzie, a defeated leader of the rebellion in Upper Canada, fled across the border and established head-quarters in Buffalo. He rapidly raised funds and recruited volunteers for a "patriot" army to fight the British in Canada.

With a small band of his "patriots" Mackenzie then moved to Navy Island on the Canadian side of the Niagara River. There he ran up the rebel flag, set up a provisional government, and attracted other recruits, many of them Americans. Soon his "army" numbered almost a thousand. To carry supplies from the New York shore, the "patriots" engaged an American-owned steamboat of forty-six tons, the *Caroline.* The Canadian authorities decided to prevent its use as a supply ship and on the night of December 29 sent a force of fifty men under the command of a naval officer to destroy the *Caroline.*

Since the *Caroline* was not at Navy Island, the raiders continued across the river to the New York side where they found the ship was tied to a dock. While overcoming the crew and some passengers, they killed one American and wounded several others. Then they set fire to the ship and towed it out into the river where it sank.

On the American side of the frontier the attack aroused more anti-British feeling. Extremists demanded retaliation. Some, like those in Rich-ford, Vermont, resolved it was the right of every American *"who can,* to cross the line into Canada, and volunteer to help the *patriots* to obtain their liberties, and execute justice on their oppressors, and those who have shed innocent blood in the United States."[4] Fearing that the flaming sentiment along the border might lead to war, moderate Americans urged mutual forbearance.

As soon as Van Buren himself learned of the *Caroline* attack, he sum-moned Major General Winfield Scott to take command of the border area. "Blood has been shed," he told Scott; "you must go with all speed to the Niagara frontier."[5] On the following day, January 5, 1838, the president issued another proclamation, this time warning that all those "who shall compromit the neutrality of this Goverment by interfering in an unlawful manner with the affairs of the neighboring British provinces will render themselves liable to arrest and punishment under the laws of the United States, which will be rigidly enforced."

At the same time, Secretary of State John Forsyth protested "the de-struction of the property and assassination of citizens of the United States on the soil of New York" to the British minister in Washington. The United States, Forsyth said, would demand redress. The Englishman did not argue the matter, but referred it to his superiors with his own point of view. "If the Americans either cannot or will not guard the integrity of their own soil or prevent it from becoming an arsenal of outlaws and assassins," he wrote, "they have no right to expect that the soil of the United States will be respected by the victims of such unheard of violence."

Taking the position that the *Caroline* raiders had acted in self-defense and legally under the rules of international law, the British government would not accept responsibility for the act or meet the American demands for redress. It took the whole affair coolly and did as little about it as had the United States about Jackson's execution of two British subjects in his Florida raid twenty years earlier. The diplomatic problem raised by the *Caroline* incident, therefore, remained unsettled.

Border Strife and Secret Societies

Strife and tension along the frontier did not end either. Extremists and Canadian refugees in the United States kept alive the threat of armed invasion into Canada. After the failure of the "patriots" to foment revolution in Canada they resorted to secret societies, organizing five of them in 1838 and 1839. The first of these, the Canadian Refugee Relief Association formed in New York in March 1838 sought to embroil the United States in a war with Britain. Since the United States was suffering from the effects of the Panic of 1837, recruits for the societies were not difficult to find among the unemployed who sympathized with the rebel cause, particularly when the organizations offered a cash bounty and free land.

The Refugee Association's first act sought to avenge the *Caroline*. Shouting "Remember the *Caroline*," some twenty-two of its followers, disguised as Indians, in the early morning hours of May 29, 1838, captured the British steamboat *Sir Robert Peel* in American waters of the St. Lawrence, routed the passengers and burned the ship. The association followed this with two blundering attacks on Canada along the Niagara frontier. Then its activities ended. Most of the secret societies, in fact, were short-lived. They died after the fiascoes of their first attacks.

The largest and most feared of those societies, the Hunters and Chasers of the Eastern Frontier, however, lasted longer than most, and at its height had about fifty thousand members. Originating in Vermont, it spread its "Hunters Lodges" across the northern part of the United States, into Canada, and even into some of the southern states. Its avowed purpose was to eliminate British monarchial rule from North America and each member had to take an elaborate secret oath pledging him "never to rest till all tyrants of Britain cease to have any dominion or footing whatever in North America."[6]

Like those of the other secret societies, the raids of the "Hunters," organized by Americans and launched from American soil, ended ingloriously. Understandably, the attacks enraged Canadians, invited reprisals, and kept alive the threat of war. Moderate elements in the United States were disgusted and alarmed. "The game of pirating upon our neighbors has been carried far enough," one American newspaper said early in 1839. "Neither Canada nor Great Britain can stand it much longer. The United States would not."

Although Van Buren, anxious to avoid war, tried to prevent Americans from attacking Canada, his actions were inadequate. Congress, moreover, offered little assistance. In March 1838 it amended the Neutrality Act of 1818 in order to provide punishment for those engaging in the illegal raids, but the amendments added little to the president's existing powers. Even Winfield Scott, though successful in curbing certain minor activities, proved unable to check the more dangerous sorties, such as those of the "Hunters."

Finally, by the end of 1839, the activities of the secret societies died down and the frontier tension eased, but Van Buren's efforts, which included a visit to the border in June, were not the only reason the attacks stopped. The raiders in time grew disgusted with their leaders, realized the futility of the invasions, and took fright at the severe treatment Canadian authorities meted out to prisoners.

Controversy over Alexander McLeod

The relative calm on the frontier did not last long. In the following year, the case of Alexander McLeod revived the tension. New York authorities arrested McLeod, a deputy sheriff from Niagara, Upper Canada, on November 12, 1840, charging him with arson and the "murder" of Amos Durfee, the American killed during the *Caroline* raid. The authorities might have freed McLeod on the bail offered by the Canadian government, but a mob prevented the release by training a cannon on his cell.

Brushing aside the question of guilt or innocence, the British government made it a matter of national honor to secure McLeod's release without trial. The attack on the *Caroline,* the British minister in Washington insisted, was "the publick act of persons obeying the constituted authorities of Her Majesty's Province." Even if McLeod had participated in the raid, the British government argued, he himself could not be held responsible for what had occurred since he had acted under the official orders of his superiors. In taking this position, the British government did what it previously had refused to do. It now assumed responsibility for the *Caroline* attack.

Secretary of State John Forsyth would not accept the British argument. Neither he nor the president, he said, was "aware of any principle of international law, or indeed of reason or justice" giving legal immunity to offenders even though they "acted in obedience to their superior authorities."

The dispute dragged on, but when Daniel Webster became secretary of state in March 1841 under the Whig president William Henry Harrison, and a month later under John Tyler, he reversed the position Forsyth had taken. He agreed with the British that international law did not justify punishing as criminals those who acted under military orders, but pointed out that the federal government had no power to interfere with the jurisdiction of the New York courts.

Supported by a ruling of the Supreme Court of New York, the state authorities said the trial must go on. Justice must take its course regardless of the international repercussions. Even though he insisted on upholding the rights of his state, New York's governor, William H. Seward, assured Webster confidentially that he would pardon McLeod if found guilty.

Webster needed that support because McLeod's case had aroused angry nationalistic outbursts on both sides of the Atlantic. Earlier the American minister in London, at the urging of Lord Palmerston, Britain's foreign secretary, had written to the president that "the excitement is indeed violent among all Parties & the case is treated as one of the most monstrous character. Some . . . talk of seizing and retaliating upon Americans here. One thing is certain, if McLeod is executed, there will be *immediate war*! Of this you may rest assured." This threat of war was probably an exaggeration, but feelings were violent.

In the United States, members of Congress debated angrily and the opposition attacked Webster for his subservience toward Britain. Americans demanded redress for the *Caroline*. That, from their point of view, was the essence of the McLeod case. "Sir—the waves of Niagara have extinguished the fires of that vessel," one congressman from Tennessee said— "they have silenced forever the agonizing shrieks of her remaining crew— but the cry for vengeance still comes up from her deep and agitated bosom, in tones louder than the thunder of her own mighty cataract." [7]

A change of ministry in England in September 1841 then helped to ease the crisis. Lord Aberdeen, as conciliatory as Webster toward the case, replaced the truculent Palmerston as foreign secretary. Finally, on October 12, a New York court in Utica acquitted McLeod. After his release, the troubles arising from the Canadian rebellions died down.

Since the British had admitted responsibility for the *Caroline* attack, the questions of its legality, or reparation, and of apology, remained. Webster and a special emissary from Britain, Lord Ashburton, took them up in their negotiations in 1842. Although Ashburton insisted that the *Caroline* raiders had invaded American territory in self-defense, he admitted that "what is perhaps most to be regretted is that some explanation and apology for this occurrence was not immediately made." Webster took this as a satisfactory apology. Since the United States accepted the destruction of the *Caroline* as an act of self-defense and admitted that the ship had engaged in illegal activity, it demanded no indemnity.

To prevent similar conflicts between federal and state jurisdiction in the future, Webster, with President Tyler's support, drafted a bill to cover such cases. Congress passed it on August 29. That act gave the Federal courts jurisdiction in all cases where aliens were charged with crimes committed under the authority of a foreign government.

Again, aroused passions and questions of prestige and national honor had magnified minor issues into a prolonged crisis between two friendly peoples. Fortunately, sane statesmanship and goodwill on both sides finally kept the crisis within the bounds of a peaceful settlement.

The Maine Boundary Dispute

Before the McLeod controversy had waned, difficulties over the northeastern boundary led to another minor Anglo-American crisis. The United States and Britain both claimed some twelve thousand square miles of land between Maine and New Brunswick. No one had run the boundary in that area because for nearly sixty years the United States and Britain had been unable to agree on the location of the line, described vaguely in the treaty

THE SETTLEMENT OF
THE MAINE BOUNDARY
CONTROVERSY, 1842

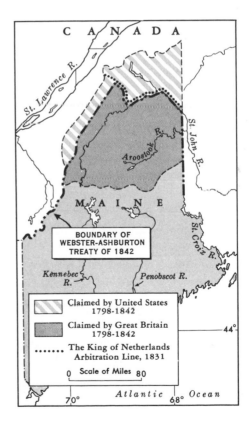

of peace at the end of the American Revolution. After trying a number of times to agree on a boundary through direct diplomacy, the two countries submitted the dispute in 1827 to the arbitration of the king of the Netherlands, who could not reach a judicial decision on the evidence available to him and hence decided on a compromise line in January 1831.

Technically, as arbitrator, the king should have decided between the opposing claims on the basis of the evidence. Since he had not and had essentially split the difference, Britain and the United States agreed that he had exceeded his authority, but Britain was willing to accept the compromise if the United States would. Maine, however, protested against what it considered a loss of territory rightfully its own, and thus when President Jackson asked the Senate's advice, it voted in June 1832 not to accept the king's recommendations.

In the next decade population in Maine and New Brunswick increased, and railroads became an important means of travel. Rail traffic between Canada proper and the maritime provinces would be most direct if it passed through the border area. The rebellions of 1837, moreover, had shown the need for an all-weather route, for military purposes, from Halifax on the Atlantic shore to Quebec, located inland. The best route ran from St. John, on the mainland, through the disputed territory.

Toward the end of the decade a new crisis flared up in that very area, now considered strategically important. Late in 1838 lumberjacks from New Brunswick began cutting timber there, in the fertile valley of the Aroostook River. In February 1839 a land agent from Maine with a party of two hundred men attempted to expel the lumberjacks. In a night clash the New Brunswick men captured fifty of the Americans and threw them into jail. Both Maine and New Brunswick mustered their militia, and Congress appropriated $10 million for the protection of Maine and authorized the president to call for fifty thousand volunteers.

For a while it looked as if the trivial and bloodless "Aroostook War" of 1838–1839 might erupt into a real conflict, but neither side wanted that. President Van Buren, therefore, again called on Winfield Scott who went to the Aroostook country and in March 1839 arranged a truce. Since the truce gave each side possession of the territory it actually occupied without endangering its claim to the disputed land, Maine remained in nominal control of the Aroostook Valley.

Since Britain and the United States now recognized that the unsettled boundary might at any time produce another crisis, the time appeared ripe for a negotiated settlement. Before they could begin negotiations, however, another controversy, this time primarily involving the South, created new tensions stemming from the old problems of the slave trade and freedom of the seas in time of peace.

The Creole *Incident*

Early in November 1841 a cargo of 135 slaves aboard the *Creole,* an American ship sailing from Virginia for slave markets in New Orleans revolted, killed one of the white men, overpowered the ship's officers and crew, and forced the mate to put into Nassau in the Bahamas, a British port. Authorities there hanged the murderers but allowed the other Negroes to retain the freedom they had won when they reached free British soil. When the United States demanded surrender of the Negroes, the British authorities refused to give them up. That refusal, coupled with Britain's efforts to stop the African slave trade, infuriated Southerners.

The United States had outlawed that trade in 1808 but had not enforced its own laws. Britain had abolished the slave trade a year earlier, freed all slaves under her flag in 1833, and thereafter carried on a vigorous international crusade against slavery. Through treaties with other nations, her cruisers stopped suspected slave ships on the seas, but the United States would not allow those cruisers to stop and search ships flying the American flag. John Quincy Adams when he was secretary of state clearly expressed the American view. The British minister in Washington once asked him if he could conceive of a more atrocious evil than the slave trade. "Yes," Adams uaid, "admitting the right of search by foreign officers of our vessels upon the seas in time of peace; for that would be making slaves of ourselves." [8] To Americans the right of visit and search brought back bitter memories of impressment during the Napoleonic wars.

After 1839 the United States became the only major maritime power not obligated by treaty to allow the British to crush the slave trade wherever they found it, even if carried on by foreigners using the American flag. After that date, in fact, more and more of the slave ships used the American flag to protect their trade. "The chief obstacle to the success of the very active measures pursued by the British government for the suppression of the slave trade on the [African] coast," a governor of Liberia wrote in 1839, "is the *American flag.* Never was the proud banner of freedom so extensively used by those pirates upon liberty and humanity as at this season." [9]

As the British increased their activities, the guns of their cruisers stopped many slave ships flying the American flag that were not American. They also mistakenly detained legitimate American ships, thus creating exacerbating incidents. Americans, particularly Southerners, became more determined than ever to resist any interference with legitimate commerce and with freedom of the seas.

Then the British framed a doctrine allowing them to stop ships in time of peace. They called it the "right of visit." Under this principle, while disclaiming the right of search in time of peace, the British said they would board only ships "strongly suspected of being those of other nations unwarrantably assuming the American flag." The United States argued that the new doctrine was the old "right of search" in disguise and that it violated the freedom of the seas. That doctrine, in effect, merely increased American determination to prevent the British from stopping any American ships. In 1841 along with the *Creole* case and the border tension, it added to the martial fever in the United States.

Lord Ashburton's Mission

War sentiment and hatred of Britain in the winter of 1841–42, therefore, were strongest on the frontier, in the South, and among Democrats. Whigs and businessmen in the seaport cities were neither martial nor anti-British. They profited from their trade with England, and most of them believed that their prosperity depended on continued peace with her.

Secretary of State Daniel Webster was himself a Whig who shared the sentiments of his party's primary supporters. In his policies he catered to American business and worked to uphold his announced principle that "no difference shall be permitted seriously to endanger the maintenance of peace with England." Not long after he took office, therefore, he let the British know that his government was willing to settle the most serious controversy, that of the Maine boundary, through negotiation and a treaty.

England's foreign secretary, Lord Aberdeen, also wanted peace and realized that something had to be done to clear away the difficulties. He took advantage of Webster's offer and, as we have seen, sent a friend as a special envoy to the United States, "one who would be peculiarly acceptable to the United States as well as eminently qualified for the trust," and empowered him to make a treaty on the boundary question and to settle the other problems.

Lord Ashburton, Alexander Baring, was well suited for his mission. His wife was an American, he had many social and business connections in the United States, and earlier in his life had even lived there. Also, Webster knew him. The secretary had met Ashburton and many of Britain's leading statesmen and businessmen when he visited England in 1839 for some American concerns. Therefore, when Ashburton arrived in Washington in the spring of 1842, he could meet informally and cordially with Webster to settle Anglo-American problems. In the words of a contemporary observer, they dispensed with the "mere etiquette, the unnecessary mystery and mummeries of negotiations." [10]

At the outset, on the question of the Maine boundary, the two men decided to put aside the documentary evidence and the arguments of almost sixty years and to work out an agreement on a new line. To reach a compromise they had to overcome two main obstacles. On the British side, the snag was the proposed military road from Halifax and St. John to Quebec. Ashburton's instructions insisted that any settlement must assure it to Britain.

On the American side, the impediment was the claim of Maine and Massachusetts to the whole of the disputed land. Before 1820 Maine had been a part of Massachusetts, and after the separation Massachusetts had retained ownership of half of the public lands in the disputed area. Both states were politically important, both insisted that the federal government could make no settlement without their consent, and both opposed a compromise boundary. Before Webster could make a settlement, therefore, Maine and Massachusetts had to agree to accept a surrender of lands they considered rightfully theirs. Webster won them over in a carefully worked out campaign of propaganda, persuasion, and coercion.

First, the secretary of state launched a newspaper campaign in Maine designed to win the people's consent to a compromise boundary. To finance Webster's propaganda, President Tyler placed $17,000 in State Department "secret service" funds at his disposal. Next, the secretary persuaded Maine and Massachusetts to send commissioners to Washington to participate in working out a settlement.

Then, as Webster said later, he delivered his "grand stroke." [11] He knew that at the peace negotiations in Paris in 1785 Benjamin Franklin had marked a map "with a strong red line" to indicate the boundary, but neither he nor anyone else had been able to find a copy of the marked map in the American archives. An authentic copy of that map would have proved which side had the stronger claim.

Webster did not really care who had the better legal title. What he wanted was a successful negotiation. From a secondhand dealer he picked up an old map with markings on it that supported Britain's claims and then backed it with evidence supplied by his friend Jared Sparks, a professor at Harvard College. Sparks had seen a map in the French archives he thought was Franklin's red-line map. From memory and his notes he marked a map of Maine and sent it to Webster. It, too, conceded almost half of the disputed land to Britain. Those maps fitted the objectives of the secretary's diplomacy.

Webster showed the old map, marked according to Sparks's memory, to the Maine and Massachusetts commissioners and forced them to agree to the compromise he wanted. They realized that the map, if authentic, destroyed their case. Then the federal treasury paid Maine and Massachusetts $150,000 each and expense money to compensate them for the lands they surrendered. Having overcome the "states' rights" opposition, Webster then concluded a treaty with Ashburton. In addition, they exhanged notes covering the various other questions in dispute.

The Webster-Ashburton Treaty

The treaty, signed on August 9, 1842, divided the disputed territory, giving Britain some five thousand square miles including the site of the proposed military route. The United States received some seven thousand square miles, including the Aroostook Valley and the right to navigate the St. John River through New Brunswick. Since he obtained the coveted military and railroad route, Ashburton was willing to make concessions elsewhere.

Ashburton conceded most of the American claim to some 150 square miles of disputed territory at the head of the Connecticut River in New Hampshire. He also surrendered a narrow strip of land on the forty-fifth parallel along the northern borders of New York and Vermont that rightfully belonged to Britain. This land was important because the original surveyors of the line had made a mistake. At the northern end of Lake Champlain, at Rouse's Point, New York, the United States had built a fort that cost about $1 million. That structure, named Fort Montgomery but commonly called "Fort Blunder," was, as a new survey showed, in Canadian territory, about a half mile north of the true line. Ashburton agreed to keep the boundary at the old line and the United States retained its costly fort.

Ashburton's most important boundary concession lay in the West, in a disputed area between Lake Superior and the Lake of the Woods. There, he gave up some sixty-five hundred square miles of "wild country" that he considered of "little importance to either party." The important thing, he believed, was "that some line should be fixed and determined." That region contained the iron ore fields of Minnesota, including the eastern part of the rich Mesabi Range.

A second treaty, signed on the same day but later consolidated with the other to form one agreement, provided for the extradition, or mutual surrender, of fugitive criminals between the United States and Canada and for the cooperation of the British and American navies in suppressing the slave trade. The Canadians and the British hoped the extradition agreement would help to end border troubles. "If you can succeed," the governor general of Canada wrote Ashburton in July, "in making some arrangements by which we may be able reciprocally to give up our own respective delinquents you will have done more for the peace and quiet of These Provinces than I perhaps shall ever be able to do."

As to the slave trade, Britain suggested that each nation allow the naval vessels of the other a limited "right of visit" on suspected slave ships flying their flags. So strong was American sentiment against the right of search in any form that Webster would not even discuss it, but he did agree to commit the United States to take stronger measures against its own nationals engaged in the slave trade. The treaty also obligated the United States to keep a naval force of eighty guns in African waters under an independent command that would cooperate with the British in suppressing the slave traffic. Until the Civil War the United States never kept its part of the bargain and the slave trade continued to flourish under the illegal protection of the American flag.

The treaty did not mention the *Caroline* and *Creole* cases. Webster and Ashburton included them in the notes they exchanged, which did not have the binding qualities of the treaty itself.

Since the compromises did not give Americans all that they wanted, Webster expected strong opposition to the treaty in the Senate. With the Senate, and with the country as a whole, he employed the same tactics he had used with Maine and Massachusetts. Even before he signed the treaty, he had enlarged his propaganda campaign on its behalf. By the time the treaty reached the Senate, therefore, he had built up considerable public support for it.

Webster's propaganda stressed two main themes, one positive and one negative. He pointed out that the treaty would end all difficulties with Britain to the advantage of the United States and warned that even if the terms were not fully satisfactory, the United States had no choice but to accept them as the alternative was war. His propaganda was successful. Most newspapers, Whig and Democratic, accepted the treaty as an instrument of peace.

Still, some senators, particularly Democrats, were not satisfied. In a secret session of the Senate Thomas Hart Benton, a Democrat from Missouri, denounced the treaty as sacrificing the interests of the West and South to those of the Northeast. Some other Democrats supported his views, but Webster and President Tyler had sent the red-line map to the Senate along with the treaty, and it overcame most of that body's resistance. The Senate approved the treaty on August 20, 1842, by a vote of thirty-nine to nine, the largest majority it had ever given a treaty. All but one of the opposing votes were Democratic.

While astute propaganda made the Webster-Ashburton Treaty popular in the United States, Canadians, and some Englishmen, attacked it. In Parliament, Lord Palmerston denounced it as the "Ashburton Capitulation" and said later that it was "one of the worst and most disgraceful treaties that England ever concluded." [12] When Englishmen learned of Webster's red-line map, they assumed that Ashburton could have forced better terms from the Americans, so they condemned him in even harsher terms than before for allegedly selling out his country.

Later, after both the United States and England had ratified the Webster-Ashburton Treaty, debates in Parliament revealed that England all along had possessed a copy of the original map authentically marked. Since that map confirmed the American claim, as did two other copies that turned up in later years, it silenced the treaty's opponents. Although the United States had in fact surrendered land it rightfully owned, the sacrifice had not been entirely one-sided. England and the United States had both adjusted to political and economic realities. Britain had made important concessions elsewhere, and to the United States the minerals of Minnesota were more important in the long run than the timber of New Brunswick.

Since both countries had strong economic and business ties with the other, war probably would not have occurred even if the agreement had not been concluded. Nonetheless, the Webster-Ashburton Treaty cleared up festering difficulties and closed incidents that had led men on both sides of the Atlantic to talk of war.

The Oregon Question

One important problem that Webster and Ashburton had discussed but failed to settle was that of dividing the Oregon country, a wilderness on the Pacific Coast north of California and forty times the size of the disputed land between Maine and New Brunswick. Agreement on that division proved difficult because, in part, Ashburton's instructions were uncompromising. Since insistence on an agreement over Oregon appeared likely to endanger the Maine settlement, the Webster-Ashburton Treaty contained nothing on the West Coast problem. "It must," Ashburton wrote to his superior, "therefore, I fear, sleep for the present."

At that time, neither Ashburton nor Webster considered the Oregon question urgent or a threat to peace. "I much doubt," Ashburton said, "whether the Americans will for many years to come make any considerable lodgment on the Pacific." [13] He believed, as did Webster, that an independent republic would rise on the Pacific and would remove the Oregon question as a source of Anglo-American friction.

Webster considered the whole Northwest as poor country and virtually valueless to the United States, and certainly not worth serious trouble with Britain. Like most Whigs, moreover, he feared the results of national expansion. He accepted the doctrine that antedated the Republic, namely, that a democracy in annexing distant territories did so at its own peril. "In seeking acquisitions, to be governed as Territories, & lying at a great distance from the United States," he wrote to an expansionist, "we ought to be governed by our prudence & caution; & a still higher degree of these qualities should be exercised when large Territorial acquisitions are looked for, with a view to annexation." [14] With these ideas running through their heads Webster and Ashburton found it relatively easy to let the Oregon problem sleep for a while.

A few years later, however, political developments in the United States and a great migration to Oregon created such tension with England that again war appeared probable if the problem were not settled by negotiation. The basic source of difficulty was that neither the United States nor Britain had clear title to the whole Oregon country.

The conflicting claims of both countries went back many years. Americans held that Captain Robert Gray's discovery of the Columbia River in 1792, the official expedition of Lewis and Clark that descended the

Columbia in 1805, and John Jacob Astor's Pacific Fur Company post (the first American settlement in Oregon, planted in Astoria near the mouth of the Columbia in 1811) gave them possession of the river's entire valley to the fifty-first parallel. The British had seized Astor's post in 1813 but had restored it to the United States in 1818. By the Adams-Onís Treaty, the United States had also succeeded to all of Spain's claims, based on early voyages and explorations, north of the forty-second parallel. Up to the time of the Webster-Ashburton negotiations, however, the United States had been willing to compromise by limiting its claim to the forty-ninth parallel.

The Louisiana Purchase had given the United States still another, though not legal, claim stating that the Oregon country was a natural extension of Louisiana. In the words of Albert Gallatin, "the United States claimed a natural extension of their territory to the Pacific Ocean, on the grounds of contiguity and population, which gave them a better right to the adjacent unoccupied land than could be set up by any other nation."

With sound reasoning the British dismissed all the American claims, except those based on Gray's and Lewis and Clark's explorations, as inconsequential. They acknowledged American rights of first discovery of the Columbia but said that the discoveries of their own explorers in the region, going back to Sir Francis Drake's voyage in 1579, Captain James Cook's in 1778, and Captain George Vancouver's in 1792, gave them a stronger claim since they had followed exploration with occupation. As for the Spanish claims in the Oregon country, Britain said that Spain had surrendered them in the Nootka Sound Convention of 1790. The American claims based on Spain's rights, therefore, had no standing.

Since the claims stemming from discovery and exploration were confused, the British suggested that the Oregon country be divided on the basis of possession. Britain offered this solution for many years, but the United States would never accept it.

When the United States had negotiated the Convention of 1818 with Britain, it had refused to divide Oregon, as Britain had suggested, on a boundary that followed the Columbia River to the sea. Nor had Britain been willing to extend the boundary of forty-nine degrees from the Rocky Mountains to the Pacific Coast. Therefore, in that treaty, as we have seen, the two countries had compromised their rival claims by agreeing to leave the region open to both Americans and Englishmen for ten years without prejudicing the claims of either country.

In the following year the Adams-Onís Treaty had established the southern boundary of the Oregon country at the forty-second parallel. Then the American and British treaties with Russia in 1824 and 1825 had set the northern boundary at fifty-four degrees forty minutes. By 1827 the United States and Britain were the only rivals for that land, and its boundaries were clear. They ran westward from the Rocky Mountains to the sea and north from the forty-second parallel to the parallel of fifty-four degrees forty minutes.

In that year, on August 6, since Britain and America could not decide on a division of the country and since open or "joint" occupation had produced no serious friction, they agreed by treaty to extend the open occupation indefinitely. Each country could end the arrangement by giving a one-year notice of intention to do so.

To obtain a settlement on the line of the Columbia River, the British were willing, however, as they had been in 1818, to make a concession on the Pacific Coast north of the Columbia. George Canning, the British foreign minister, offered Albert Gallatin, the American negotiator, the Olympic Peninsula adjoining the Strait of Juan de Fuca. He made the offer to meet the American demand for harbors inside the strait, particularly for a harbor that could be used as a naval base. Since the area offered was an enclave with no overland connection with the United States and surrounded on every side by British territory or by waters the British navy could dominate, Gallatin rejected the offer. With shrewd foresight he favored postponing a settlement "until the citizens of the United States shall have acquired a respectable footing in the country."

Hudson's Bay Company and the Columbia River

Americans were slow in settling in the Oregon country. Until 1842 Britain had profited more from open occupation than had the United States. Since 1807 British trading companies had continuously controlled the whole region north of the Columbia. After 1821, except for a few American trappers, the Hudson's Bay Company, exercising exclusive trading and administrative privileges granted it by the British government, alone occupied most of the disputed land. It controlled a series of posts located on the banks of rivers that cut through the region.

Its main post in Oregon was Fort Vancouver, located on the north bank of the Columbia River opposite the Willamette River. The Columbia, Hudson's Bay contended, was the central transportation system of the Oregon country. The company insisted that Britain's continued possession of that river was essential for preserving its fur trade in Oregon. That trade, until the mid-1840s, shaped the objectives of British diplomacy in Oregon.

Even though the Hudson's Bay Company held scattered posts south of the Columbia, the fur trade there was less important than in the north, and the British government had long given up its claims there. The United States held unchallenged claims to the land between the forty-second parallel and the Columbia River. Yet Americans would not, as the British had long insisted they should, accept a division of the Oregon country at the Columbia, partly because they sought a good harbor on the Pacific Coast.

From the Columbia south, the Oregon coast, rugged, rocky, and wild, contained no port accessible even to the smallest seagoing ships.

The American desire for a harbor, despite the personal indifference of Webster and Ashburton to the fate of Oregon, had proved to be one of the main obstacles to a compromise boundary. "What they are principally looking to is to have a harbour of their own on the Pacific," Ashburton wrote. "The mouth of the Columbia is a barred and indifferent harbour, but they say that the estuary to the North of it, entered, I believe, by the Strait of Juan de Fuca is the only good harbour on this part of the coast, and hence the obstinacy with which they have hitherto persisted in carrying the boundary line further north."[15]

Since Ashburton's instructions had insisted on the Columbia River as a boundary, and the United States had demanded a harbor on the Pacific Coast, Webster had concluded that the best way to settle the Oregon question would be to take a new approach. With President Tyler's support, Webster told Ashburton that the United States might make a settlement if Britain would persuade Mexico to cede to the United States part of her province of California, including the magnificent harbor of San Francisco. Then the American need for a port on the Pacific Coast would be met; the United States would no longer have to insist on a harbor in the Strait of Juan de Fuca; and they themselves could make a treaty dividing the Oregon country at the Columbia River. All this could be done without loss to either Britain or the United States. Only Mexico would lose.

This tripartite plan had fascinated Ashburton, who reported it to his government. The British government, however, would not act on it, and nothing came of it.

Although some Americans wanted a harbor on the Pacific primarily for strategic reasons (in particular, for a naval base), Webster's plan also reflected the determination of some Americans who desired such a port for commercial reasons—to build a trade with Asia. The mouth of the Columbia did not offer such a harbor.

In June 1842, a few weeks after Ashburton had forwarded the tripartite plan to London, Lieutenant Charles Wilkes, U.S. Navy, who had been away from the United States for four years exploring the Pacific area, returned and reported on his explorations of the Oregon coast. He aroused a new public interest in Oregon and shattered any possibility that the United States might surrender its claims north of the Columbia as proposed in the tripartite plan. Wilkes told of the perilous bar at the mouth of the Columbia. "Mere description," he reported, "can give little idea of the terrors of the bar of the Columbia; all who have seen it have spoken of the wildness of the scene, and the incessant roar of the waters, representing it as one of the most fearful sights that can possibly meet the eye of the sailor."

Of the Strait of Juan de Fuca and its sea arms to the east, Wilkes told a different story. "Nothing can exceed the beauty of these waters, and their safety: not a shoal exists within the Strait of Juan de Fuca, Admiralty Inlet, Puget Sound, or Hood's Canal, that can in any way interrupt their navigation by a seventy-four gun ship," he wrote. "I venture nothing in saying, there is no country in the world that possesses waters equal to these."[16] Since those were the only harbors in the Oregon country that ships could enter or leave in any season of the year, he suggested that the United States demand a boundary north of forty-nine degrees so as to include Vancouver Island and the harbors of the strait. Such a boundary became a primary objective in America's Oregon diplomacy.

The Great Migrations of 1843 and 1844

Until the Webster-Ashburton Treaty and Wilkes's return, most Americans, except in the West, had shown little concern over the Oregon question or over the region itself. American settlers had not challenged the Hudson's Bay Company for possession, but some Americans, particularly in the Old Northwest, had always been interested in Oregon. In the 1830s a few bold men had pioneered the way to Oregon overland via the Oregon Trail and laid the basis for later great migrations. Still, the efforts of early Oregon promoters such as those of the Boston school teacher Hall J. Kelley and the Cambridge businessman Nathaniel J. Wyeth, and of missionaries such as the Protestant Marcus Whitman and the Catholic Father Pierre de Smet, brought only a few American pioneers to Oregon. In 1840 there were only sixty families, consisting of missionaries, trappers, and Canadians who had been employed by the Hudson's Bay Company, settled in the Willamette Valley that ran south from Fort Vancouver on the Columbia.

Although the earlier promoters, even with enthusiastic letters, speeches, and pamphlets on Oregon, had brought few settlers, they had publicized the region widely. After 1835 government writers and travelers who had visited Oregon had advertised the rich agricultural possibilities of the land, particularly of the Willamette Valley. That valley, the writers said, was the most desirable part of Oregon, and it lay outside territory claimed by the Hudson's Bay Company. Americans could settle there under their own flag.

The publicity of a decade lured the first large party of pioneers, more than a hundred, over the Oregon Trail in 1842. In the next two years almost two thousand people fleeing years of depression following the Panic of 1837 and seeking virgin land, took to the Oregon Trail. These settlers demanded that the United States annex Oregon.

In the United States, meanwhile, Westerners and other Oregon enthusiasts expressed disappointment over Webster's failure to settle the Oregon question in his negotiations with Ashburton. When Westerners heard rumors of the tripartite plan, moreover, they voiced angry disapproval. "Oregon Conventions" then sprang up throughout the West demanding immediate occupation of all of Oregon. One such convention meeting in Cincinnati in April 1843 concluded that "the rumored negotiation for a surrender of any part of Oregon for an equivalent in California was dangerous to peace and a repudiation of Monroe's doctrine." Western expansionists wanted all of Oregon and California. Those expansionists met in a national convention in Cincinnati in July and "resolved that the right of the United States to the Oregon territory, from 42° to 54° 40' north latitude, is unquestionable, and that it is the imperative duty of the General Government forthwith to extend the laws of the United States over said territory."

The Oregon question had now captured the minds of Democratic expansionists. The migrations of 1843 and 1844 and the rapidly increasing strength of the American position in Oregon led them to challenge Britain's claim to any of that country. Members of Congress took up the cry for the whole of Oregon. They proposed various warlike measures, such as fortifying the Oregon Trail, immediately abrogating the joint occupation treaty of 1827, and setting up a territorial government in Oregon.

Even President John Tyler, a Southern expansionist, responded to the fresh demand for all of Oregon. "After the most rigid and, as far as practicable, unbiased examination of the subject," he said in his annual message of December 1843, "the United States have always contended that their rights appertain to the entire region of country lying on the Pacific and embraced within 42° and 54° 40' of north latitude." In July 1844, as the "Oregon fever" in the United States mounted, the British suggested another attempt to settle the Oregon question. Finally, Tyler's last secretary of state, John C. Calhoun, turned down a British offer to arbitrate. He preferred a policy of "masterly inactivity" whereby American pioneers would clinch the claim to Oregon. Yet, as late as 1845 the Hudson's Bay Company still exercised almost unchallenged dominion north of the Columbia. American settlements were still concentrated in the Willamette Valley.

Polk's Oregon Policy

The popular cry for the "whole of Oregon," in the presidential campaign of 1844, made the diplomacy of the Oregon question a domestic issue. Western Democrats and other expansionists exploited it and the nationalist sentiment it aroused to nominate their candidate, James K. Polk of Tennessee. At its convention in Baltimore, the Democratic party accepted the demands of its expansionists by resolving in its platform "that our title to the whole of the territory of Oregon is clear and unquestionable; that no portion of the same ought to be ceded to England or any other power; and that the re-occupation of Oregon and the re-annexation of Texas at the earliest practicable period are great American measures." [17] That resolution implied what was not so—that all of Oregon rightfully belonged to the United States.

Since that resolution linked the Oregon question with that of Texas and hence balanced the objectives of southern and western expansionists, it has been referred to as the "Bargain of 1844." While it may not have resulted from a formal bargain, it expressed the sentiments of expansionists from those regions. Texas and Oregon became foremost issues in the campaign, but Texas more than Oregon helped bring Polk into office.

Although Polk had won only a narrow victory, he took it as a mandate to press for as much of Oregon beyond the Columbia River as he could get. He had identified himself fully with the platform demanding the whole of Oregon and was prepared to carry out his party's expansionist demands. In his inaugural address, he delivered a bellicose warning to Britain. "Our title to the country of the Oregon is 'clear and unquestionable,' " he said, "and already are our people preparing to perfect that title by occupying it with their wives and children." [18]

More than the words, the tone and official character of Polk's inaugural speech aroused talk of war in England. He had now spoken not as a politician seeking election, but as president. As an answer to Polk the London *Times* declared that Englishmen were "prepared to defend the claims of this country to the utmost, wherever they are seriously challenged." Yet Lord Aberdeen, Britain's foreign secretary, as in the Maine crisis, sought a means to preserve peace through compromise.

While committed politically to demanding all of Oregon, Polk privately preferred compromise to war. Even in his belligerent speech he had not insisted on the "whole" of Oregon. All of Oregon, he told Richard Pakenham, the British minister in Washington, on July 12, 1845, really belonged to the United States, but since preceding administrations had several times offered to settle on the forty-ninth parallel he was willing to concede the same boundary. Influenced, no doubt, by nationalistic outbursts in England calling for the defense of British claims, Pakenham made the mistake of rejecting the offer without referring it to his government. Secretary of State James Buchanan, according to Polk's instructions, then withdrew the offer and the administration again took up the claim to all of Oregon.

Britain's rejection of his offer, Polk asserted in his first annual message to Congress in December, "afforded satisfactory evidence that no compromise which the United States ought to accept, can be effected." The American title "to the whole Oregon territory," he maintained, was supported by the "irrefragable facts and arguments"; hence he asked for authority to give the one year's notice abrogating the treaty of joint occupation and for power to extend the protection of American laws over settlers in Oregon. Apparently with California as well as Oregon in mind, he restated the noncolonization principle of the Monroe Doctrine. Polk's stand now appeared uncompromising, but he had not said he *must* have all of Oregon and that he would settle for nothing less.

Aberdeen, who was himself willing to negotiate a settlement on a boundary at the forty-ninth parallel, meanwhile reproved Pakenham for rejecting Polk's offer on his own responsibility and directed the minister to offer arbitration. Pakenham did so twice, but the president turned him down. Polk now held that Britain had to make concessions and that the people were behind a bold policy toward Oregon. When a South Carolina congressman expressed fear that the bold policy might lead to war, Polk told him "that the only way to treat John Bull was to look him straight in the eye; that I considered a bold and firm course on our part the pacific one." [19] In fact, he wanted the power to end the treaty of joint occupation as a means of putting pressure on Britain, not as a preliminary to war.

Manifest Destiny

While Congress debated Polk's proposals, the "Oregon fever" reached its peak. The "true title" to Oregon, wrote John L. O'Sullivan, editor of the New York *Morning News,* lay in "our manifest destiny to overspread and to possess the whole of the continent which Providence has given us. . . ." A week later a member of Congress picked up O'Sullivan's newly coined phrase of manifest destiny. Our title to Oregon, he told the House of Representatives, now appeared founded on *"the right of manifest destiny to spread over the whole continent."* [20]

A congressman from Illinois said he had little regard for "musty records and the voyages of old sea captains, or the Spanish treaties," since the United States had a better title to Oregon "under the law of nature and of nations." God, Americans said, preferred to be on the side of morality than law.

Others advanced the right of "geographical predestination" in claiming all of Oregon. Vast distances separated it from England; it was contiguous to the United States. Obviously, they pointed out, nature meant that land for Americans. The *Democratic Review* summed up that theory in two lines of verse:

> The right depends on the propinquity,
> The absolute sympathy of soil and place. [21]

Agrarian nationalists of the Midwest now talked more and more of fighting for "the whole of Oregon."

Many Americans, particularly Whigs, did not want to fight for Oregon to the line of fifty-four degrees forty minutes. They ridiculed those who did by calling them "fifty-four forties." In derision they coined the phrase "fifty-four forty or fight," though it probably started as the pun referring to "Political Principles of President Polk," "P.P.P.P. Phifty-Phour Phorty or Phight." This, for example, appeared in an opposition paper in Cleveland:

> Don't you phurious phifty phour phorties pheel phleasantly phlat and phool-ish at the phunny phizzle out of your phearless phile leader, who phortiphied his claim to the whole of Oregon by repeated official declarations that 'our title is clear and unquestionable?' Phoor phellows![22]

Expansionist Democrats of the Old Northwest then adopted the slogan of "fifty-four forty or fight" as their own.

Even though Polk appeared the spokesman of the northwestern agrarian nationalists, their demands alone did not finally shape American policy toward Oregon. Men of commerce, many of them Whigs with their eyes on the trade of Asia, still wanted Oregon but were willing to compromise for a line below fifty-four forty. "It is the key to the Pacific," a New York congressman said of Oregon. "It will command the trade of the isles of the Pacific, of the East, and of China." In the same month a New Englander told Congress what merchants wanted. "We need ports on the Pacific," he asserted. "As to land, we have millions of acres of better land still unoccupied on this side of the mountains." Business groups and merchants still wanted the Strait of Juan de Fuca and its harbors but did not want to fight for more.

Spokesmen for the merchants and Whigs, who viewed with alarm the possibility of war with England, pointed out that the United States could get the harbors and still compromise. A boundary at the forty-ninth parallel would give the United States access to the strait. With Texas safely in the Union as of December 1845, Southerners now joined the merchants of the Northeast in favoring a compromise. They, too, were unwilling to risk war with England by demanding more than forty-nine degrees. "Possessed, as by this line we should be, of the agricultural portion of the country, of the Straits of Fuca, and Admiralty Inlet," Jefferson Davis of Mississippi said, "to American enterprise and American institutions we can, without a fear, intrust the future."[23] Democratic expansionists of the Northwest considered the willingness of southern Democrats to compromise a breach of faith and treachery to the party.

In 1845, especially following the annexation of Texas, concern for the future of California, held by a weak Mexico but being overrun by American pioneers, convinced many of the men of commerce who wanted a harbor that America's true manifest destiny lay in California. Many Americans who coveted San Francisco Bay now urged a compromise on Oregon. Fearing incorrectly that England had designs on California, they believed that a compromise on Oregon would ease alleged English pressure on Mexico to obtain California. "We must surrender a slice of Oregon," the New York *Herald* maintained, "if we would secure a slice of California."

By early 1846 those who desired a compromise settlement had blunted demands for all of Oregon. They stressed the maritime and agricultural advantages of California as compared to those of Oregon. "Oregon is but a bleak, barren waste," the Nashville *Union* explained, "compared with California." Many disciples of manifest destiny who preferred California now denounced those in Congress who still insisted on all of Oregon, even at the cost of war with England. The California expansionists, too, were willing to settle for a boundary at forty-nine degrees.

Congress reflected the growing sentiment for peace and compromise on Oregon. After debating more than four months, it finally passed a joint resolution in April, authorizing the president to terminate the agreement of joint occupation, but with a preamble stressing it was a resolution intended to bring peace, not war. Referring to opinion in Congress, the New York *Herald* captured what was probably the prevailing sentiment of most Americans in these words:

> This is the line that we define,
>   The line for Oregon;
> And if this basis you decline,
>   We go the "whole or none,"
> We go the "whole or none," Lord John,
>   Up to the Russian line;
> Then, if you're wise, you'll "compromise"
>   On number forty nine.[24]

Aberdeen's Domestic Problems

Within a week, in accord with the congressional resolution, Polk gave England the required year's notice abrogating the joint occupation treaty of 1827, but with it expressed hope that a friendly settlement would be promoted. Realizing that the Senate would now probably back a compromise settlement, Polk also hoped that his action would induce England to renew negotiations on Oregon on the basis of a compromise. The notice had the desired effect.

Lord Aberdeen welcomed Polk's friendly suggestion and immediately prepared an offer acceptable to most Americans. Since he held a low estimate of Oregon's worth—a "pine swamp," he called it—and had long favored a settlement at forty-nine degrees, the foreign secretary did not want to fight for that wilderness. Yet Britain's claims to the region between the Columbia River and forty-nine degrees were superior to those of the United States. To give the region to the Americans meant, to most Englishmen, an unwarranted surrender. Aberdeen's problem, therefore, was a domestic one of persuading the British people, his own government, and the opposition party, to accept a retreat to the forty-ninth parallel.

Aberdeen finally won support for his Oregon policy through convincing argument, a careful propaganda campaign, and unexpected developments in Oregon and England. Throughout 1845 American pioneers had continued flocking to Oregon. By the end of that year about five thousand had settled there. Yet all but a handful lived in the Willamette Valley. The Hudson's Bay Company, which still exercised almost unchallenged dominion north of the Columbia, nonetheless viewed their presence with alarm. Some of the settlers were frontiersmen who made their own law with pistol and rifle, hating the company for standing in the way of American control of the region. More than once they had threatened to storm Fort Vancouver and put its well-dried pine timbers to the torch. In defense, the company posted guards and mounted cannon, for inside the fort in that year were goods valued at £100,000.

Earlier, because of the decline of the fur trade in the Columbia area, the company had decided to shift its center of operations in Oregon north to Vancouver Island. It began moving in 1845, and fear of an American attack probably hastened the move. It was obvious now that the Columbia River was no longer vital to the company's fur trade. That move destroyed one of the main arguments for retaining the region between the Columbia and the forty-ninth parallel. Investigators from the Royal Engineers and the Royal Navy who had surveyed the Oregon situation agreed, moreover, in their reports submitted at this time, that England could not hold the region against attack and that inevitably Americans would overrun it.

All this strengthened Aberdeen's view that Britain would lose nothing vital in settling at forty-nine degrees. After those developments, Sir Robert Peel, the prime minister, and the cabinet were willing to support Aberdeen's policy.

At the same time, in England the movement for free trade and repeal of the corn laws, special tariffs on grain, helped overcome the resistance of the opposition party. Lord John Russell, the Whig opposition leader, supported Peel's Tory government in its efforts to repeal the corn laws and wanted no war that would interfere with that trade reform. Lord Palmerston, the former Whig foreign secretary and a belligerent nationalist, however, had often denounced Aberdeen's foreign policies as cowardly and as "truckling" to American pressure. He would allow no retreat in Oregon.

In 1845, Palmerston's warlike utterances did not fit the times. Most Englishmen wanted peace. In December, when Peel's Tory government fell from power, a war scare followed the news that Palmerston would again become foreign secretary. Lord John Russell could not form a government to take over, as other Whig leaders refused to serve in the cabinet with Palmerston. Peel, therefore, headed the government again. Russell then spoke boldly in favor of a compromise on Oregon and in February 1846 secretly told Aberdeen and the Tories that he would, in effect, accept any Oregon treaty they drafted.

Aberdeen and Peel had also launched a propaganda campaign to win public opinion to their Oregon policy. The Tory press, and even some Whig journals, took up Aberdeen's arguments that England could get all that was worth fighting for by retreating to Vancouver Island and forty-nine degrees. With that boundary and with the island she could still have fine ports, access to the Strait of Juan de Fuca, and keep the peace.

Through press propaganda, Aberdeen apparently convinced his countrymen that Britain's claims to Oregon had flaws, that Oregon was not worth a war, that the fur trade there was dying, that the Columbia River was not necessary for commerce, and that American claims to good harbors on the Pacific Coast were reasonable. The London *Examiner,* a leading Whig newspaper, published an article in April 1845 describing the valley of the Columbia as barren wasteland and urging a settlement at forty-nine degrees. "The value of the whole territory in fee simple would not be worth the expense of one year's war," another London journal announced later that year. Then in January when the ostensibly independent London *Times* took up Aberdeen's arguments, most of the press did also, and the Tory government won its propaganda campaign. When Polk's notice terminating joint occupation reached him, therefore, Aberdeen could respond with the knowledge that he had the people's support for a compromise settlement.

The Oregon Treaty

Aberdeen then sent Polk a draft treaty offering a boundary at forty-nine degrees to the middle of the channel between the mainland and Vancouver Island and thence south through the Strait of Juan de Fuca to the Pacific Ocean. This left all of Vancouver Island to the British. The treaty also provided for free navigation of the Columbia for the Hudson's Bay Company and for protection of certain of its property rights in the disputed area.

That draft treaty reached Polk on June 6, a few weeks after Congress had declared war on Mexico. Even so, the president objected to it at first, but his cabinet persuaded him to follow the unusual procedure of submitting it to the Senate for its advice before deciding either to accept or reject it. There, some of the "fifty-four forty" Westerners shouted their dismay at the "surrender" of American land, but they were now an impotent minority. By a vote of thirty-eight to twelve the Senate on June 10, 1846, advised the president to accept the proposed treaty. Five days later Secretary of State Buchanan and the British minister in Washington signed it. Then, on June 18, the Senate by a vote of forty-one to fourteen gave its formal consent to the treaty without adding a single change. The president ratified it on the next day.

Polk had retreated from the line of fifty-four forty and accepted a compromise on forty-nine degrees for several reasons. He was convinced, apparently, that the British would not give up more than forty-nine de-

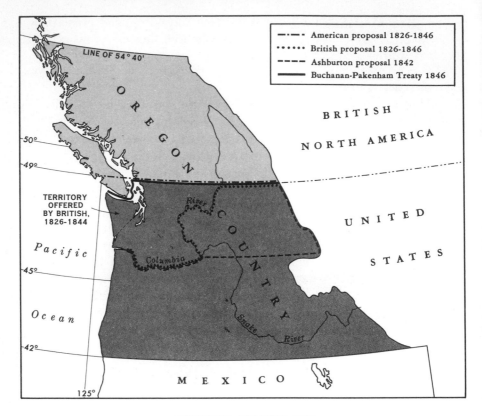

DISPUTED OREGON, 1846

grees without war, and neither he nor the people as a whole wanted a war with England. In fact, he had hoped to clear up the Oregon question before going to war with Mexico. Since taking office, Polk had been willing to settle on the forty-ninth parallel, including ports in the Strait of Juan de Fuca, and had several times said so. But he had not dared admit that openly as he feared public opinion, aroused by the expansionist cries for all of Oregon, would not support him. He could not publicly abandon the Democratic platform of 1844, yet he could not risk breaking up his party over the issue of 54° 40'. When popular opinion appeared to shift in favor of peace, he safely retreated to forty-nine degrees.

To the "fifty-four forties" the Oregon treaty appeared a surrender. To nationalistic Englishmen, who had long expected more, it smacked of capitulation. On the basis of claims and possession, the English made the real sacrifice. Yet both countries obtained what they really wanted—good ports and land for future populations. Most important, the English-speaking peoples had again settled a bitter quarrel peacefully.

Tallyrand—engraving from a painting by F. Gérard (Librairie Hachette)

The Transfer of Louisiana to the United States, December 20, 1803
(Samuel H. Kress Collection)

Napoleon in His Study, by Jacques-Louis David

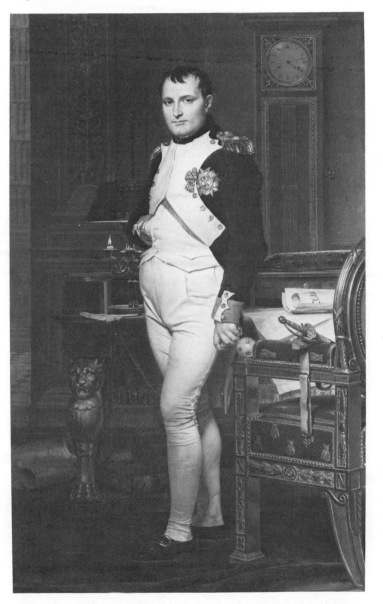

The Battle of New Orleans

The signature of the Treaty of Ghent Between the United States and Great Britain in the Old Carthusian Monastery at Ghent, Christmas Eve, 1814, by Sir Amèdée Forestier (Smithsonian Institution)

John Quincy Adams (Harvard University)

The Oregon Trail (Public Roads Administration)

Scott at Vera Cruz, 1847 (New York Historical Society)

William H. Seward
(Library of Congress)

U.S. Army Landing
at Baguiri, Cuba

863,956
WORLDS CIRCULATED YESTERDAY
The
"Circulation Books Open to All."
World.
"Circulation Books Open to All."
863,956
WORLDS CIRCULATED YESTERDAY

VOL. XXXVIII. NO. 13,331.
NEW YORK, THURSDAY, FEBRUARY 17, 1898.
PRICE

MAINE EXPLOSION CAUSED BY BOMB OR TORPEDO?

Capt. Sigsbee and Consul-General Lee Are in Doubt---The World Has Sent a Special Tug, With Submarine Divers, to Havana to Find Out---Lee Asks for an Immediate Court of Inquiry---Capt. Sigsbee's Suspicions.

CAPT. SIGSBEE, IN A SUPPRESSED DESPATCH TO THE STATE DEPARTMENT, SAYS THE ACCIDENT WAS MADE POSSIBLE BY AN ENEMY.

Dr. E. C. Pendleton, Just Arrived from Havana, Says He Overheard Talk There of a Plot to Blow Up the Ship---Capt. Zalinski, the Dynamite Expert, and Other Experts Report to The World that the Wreck Was Not Accidental---Washington Officials Ready for Vigorous Action if Spanish Responsibility Can Be Shown---Divers to Be Sent Down to Make Careful Examinations.

The New York World *a day after*

New York World Records the Explosion of the *Maine* (Department of State)

Theodore Roosevelt During the Spanish-American War

The Signing of the Peace Protocol with Spain at the White House, Painting by
Theobald Cliartrau, 1899 (White House)

HARPER'S WEEKLY
JOURNAL OF CIVILIZATION

VOL. L.   New York, Saturday, February 3, 1906   No. 2563

THE BUSY SHOWMAN.—III.

Ladies and Gentlemen: I have the great pleasure this week of submitting to your favorable consideration my latest Foreign Exhibit. Certain envious side-show men at the other end of Pennsylvania Avenue criticise this Exhibit on the ground that it is without precedent. But precedents don't concern me. Besides, my predecessors, although worthy enough in a sense, were not enterprising. You need anticipate no so-called "entanglements" as the result of this Exhibit. It is my business to give a good and varied show, and I know my business. Otherwise I should not enjoy your distinguished patronage and universal approval. I warn you against all side shows. This is the only Original Grand Exhibition. Trusting to see you promptly in your seats next week, and thanking you for your kind attention, I am Very Truly Yours

Teddy's Big Stick (*Harper's Weekly*, February 3, 1906)

VIII

Texas and California

That same expansionist fervor, expressed in the phrase manifest destiny, that had sent Americans swarming over the Oregon Trail, had driven others into Texas. Between 1800 and 1820, while Texas still belonged to Spain, the first frontiersmen had drifted across the Sabine River. Some were armed invaders intent on destroying Spanish control, others were settlers who squatted on the land illegally, appropriating farms near Nacogdoches in east Texas or to the north on the south bank of the Red River. Whether filibusters or settlers, most of them were tough and unruly, and all paid little attention to international boundaries.

Spain did not want those or any other Americans in Texas. She had expected Texas to serve as a buffer against such intruders, a barrier protecting her other lands to the west and south. Yet she did not force those squatters from Texas, for in those years that province was virtually unguarded and lightly populated. In 1820 only three small Spanish outposts guarded the entire province, and cattle far outnumbered its several thousand people. If it were to prosper and form a screen against Americans, Texas needed people.

As early as 1801 Spanish authorities had talked of attracting immigrants to Texas, but fearing that most of them would come from the United States, they did nothing. Inaction prevailed until December 1820 when Moses Austin, a Connecticut-born Yankee who had settled in the West, asked permission to bring three hundred settlers into Texas. The authorities there, now serving a liberal Spanish government, in January 1821 reversed previous policy and approved.

Later that year Mexico won independence from Spain, and Texas became a Mexican province. Mexico's relations with the United States in that year of independence were unusually cordial. Mexicans were grateful for aid Americans had given them in their revolution and believed that friendship with the United States was firmly rooted. Their statesmen realized, moreover, that the growing strength of the United States stemmed, in part at least, from a steady flow of immigrants. Since few would leave Mexico's settled regions, Mexico's authorities decided to follow the American pattern in populating Texas. They inaugurated a policy of encouraging foreigners to settle the province.

Mexican Policies in Texas

Meanwhile, on his way to Missouri to recruit colonists, Moses Austin died. His twenty-seven-year-old son Stephen then took over the task of building a colony, and since many Americans wanted Texas land, he had no difficulty. After settling his colonists in Texas, however, he encountered difficulty over his land grant which he finally overcame after making a special trip to Mexico City. There, the new Mexican government in April 1823 confirmed his grant under terms which set a pattern for future grants. Those terms allowed young Austin to bring into Texas three hundred families who would agree to become Mexican subjects and accept the Catholic religion. Each family, without cost, could have one square league, or 4,428 acres, of land. In addition to receiving a bonus in land proportionate to the number of settlers he brought, Austin, for his services, could collect 12½ cents an acre from the settlers.

Under those terms Austin's colony grew and prospered, and others tried to imitate his success. They were encouraged, furthermore, by the Mexican government which enacted a liberal national colonization law in August 1824 that in effect gave the states of the Mexican nation the unoccupied land within their borders to dispose of as they wished. The law's main restrictions were minor. It said foreigners, without official permission, could not settle within twenty leagues of an international boundary or ten leagues from the coast, and that no one could obtain more than eleven square leagues of land.

Under that law the state of Coahuila-Texas, of which Texas was a district, adopted its own land law in the following March. It opened Texas to those of "Christian and good moral character" who would swear allegiance to Mexico, offered them special tax exemptions, and gave responsibility for handling immigration to land agents, or *empresarios*. The law promised handsome rewards in land to the successful *empresario*, and in general followed the pattern of Austin's grant.

News of that law sent American speculators flocking into Coahuila-Texas for land grants. Most of them wanted only a quick profit by selling their rights to others. Only a few lived up to the contracts they received. The sincere *empresario* found colonists easily, for the Mississippi Valley teemed with prospective settlers who wished to escape the still deadening effect of the depression following the Panic of 1819. Since most pioneers did not have cash in a lump sum, land prices in the United States for them were high. The Land Act of 1820, for instance, required a cash payment of $1.25 an acre. Across the United States border, an easy journey by land or sea, Mexico now offered rich land for a few cents an acre.

Even the speculators and those responsible *empresarios* who failed as colonizers lured hundreds of pioneers into Texas through their newspaper advertisements and personal recruiting. By 1830 American settlers numbered about eight thousand. Mexico's policy of populating Texas through the bait of cheap land was succeeding, but that very success now caused alarm. The "Texas fever" that swept the lower Mississippi Valley would not stop. Yet Mexico, already experiencing difficulty with some Americans in Texas, now wanted to halt the immigration.

Although most of the settlers were loyal to the Mexican government, some conflict between them and the Mexican authorities was bound to arise. All but a few of the Americans in Texas were Southerners who either had brought Negro slaves with them or who expected to acquire some later to work their lands. The Americans, therefore, were shocked when the state of Coahuila-Texas in 1827 obtained a constitution calling for the gradual freeing of all bond servants; two years later Mexico's president decreed slavery abolished everywhere. They were able, however, to exert enough pressure to force the Mexican authorities to exempt Texas from the anti-slavery laws. Although the Americans had won a concession, the slavery question created a lasting ill will.

Religious differences, in time, also brought on difficulties. To own land, Protestant Americans had to become Catholics. Since their desire for land was stronger than religious scruples, the early settlers outwardly at least accepted Mexico's official religion. Since Mexican authorities did not force them to attend Catholic churches, they did not have to become practicing Catholics, and few did. Later settlers, particularly illegal squatters who had taken no oath of allegiance to Mexico, ignored the law allowing none but Catholics to worship publicly. They wanted their own Protestant churches, which they went ahead and built in defiance of law. The authorities did nothing to prevent them from worshipping as they pleased and even conceded limited religious toleration. Yet most Americans resented the religious restrictions, and Mexican officials were angered by resistance to their laws.

Armed clashes between American settlers and Mexican authorities added to the mutual distrust. One of the most serious of those early conflicts broke out in the autumn of 1826 when Haden Edwards, an *empresario,* tried to remove American and Mexican squatters from his land grant in east Texas. Taking the side of the squatters, the Mexican authorities annulled Edwards's contract and ordered him from the country. His brother, Benjamin W. Edwards, then gathered a handful of men, rode into Nacogdoches, and under a red and white flag inscribed "Independence, Liberty, and Justice" on December 16 proclaimed the Republic of Fredonia, stretching "from the Sabine to the Rio Grande." The Edwards brothers had counted, mistakenly, on outside help. "Our friends in the United States," Benjamin said, "are already in arms, and only waiting for the word." Stephen F. Austin, at the head of a small army acting for the Mexican authorities, quickly snuffed out the Fredonian rebellion.

That revolt did irreparable harm to relations between Americans and the Mexicans. To some Americans in Texas, Haden Edwards, a speculator contemptuous of Mexicans and Mexican law, in time appeared a martyr who suffered at the hands of a tyrannical government. Mexicans probably remembered the shape of conquest in Florida and saw in the Fredonian rebellion evidence that aggressive Americans intended to take Texas by force, even though Austin and other Americans loyal to Mexico had helped to suppress it. Fear and distrust, nevertheless, continued to cloud relations between Americans and Mexicans.

American Immigration

The diplomacy of the American government, at the time, added to Mexican distrust and led Mexican officials to suspect the United States of encouraging Americans to colonize Texas as part of a plot to annex the province. Ever since John Quincy Adams in his treaty with Luis de Onís in 1819 had given up the vague American claims to Texas, Americans, mostly Westerners, had demanded that the government recover that province. When Adams became president in 1825, he tried unsuccessfully to obtain as much of Texas as he could by instructing his minister to Mexico, Joel R. Poinsett, to negotiate a new boundary. Then in 1827 Poinsett offered $1 million for all of Texas, but Mexico would not sell.

Adams's successor, Andrew Jackson, also tried to acquire Texas through diplomacy and purchase. He instructed Poinsett to try again for Texas and increased the offer to $5 million, but still Mexico refused to sell. Jackson replaced Poinsett with Anthony Butler, an unprincipled minister who for six years resorted to various shady devices to get Texas. He attempted to bribe Mexican officials into selling, tried to force an unpayable loan on them with Texas as security, and urged the president to seize eastern Texas by force. Mexico's rulers did not know the details of Butler's unsavory schemes, but were aware that he had orders to secure Texas at any cost.

Butler's mission, moreover, began right after the pro-Jackson press had launched a campaign urging and predicting the acquisition of Texas. A Mexican officer at Nacogdoches reported in December 1829 that Americans were recruiting "colonists" to revolutionize Texas. There is, he said, "no other subject of conversation on the frontier but the views of President Jackson to take possession of Texas."

Since the blundering Jacksonian diplomacy, the ominous press campaign, and the threatening frontier rumors followed on the heels of the alarming Edwards revolt, the Mexican government reviewed its immigration policy in Texas. A Mexican official who had investigated the situation made a report in January 1830 and sounded the alarm against losing Texas to the United States. "Either the government occupies Texas *now,*" he warned, "or it is lost forever." [1] He suggested that the government encourage Mexican and European immigrants to come to Texas, that it create an economic bond between Texas and the rest of Mexico by stimulating trade, and that it strengthen old garrisons and establish new ones in the province.

In April the Mexican congress incorporated those suggestions into a law. Although never fully enforced, that law, in addition, prohibited further American immigration into Texas. Nonetheless, Americans kept coming, most of them illegally. The Texas border was too long for Mexico to police adequately. The new law thus had the effect of barring serious immigrants selected by responsible *empresarios* and of encouraging lawless adventurers who respected no authority, Mexican or American, to take their chances in Texas.

Serious trouble began in 1831 when the Mexican government planted garrisons at strategic points among the Texans to prevent the spread of American colonies. The settlers hated them, particularly some of the renegade American commanders who showed less regard for them than did the Mexicans. In 1832 Mexican soldiers clashed several times with settlers and blood flowed. In that year Texans demanded that Mexico repeal its anti-immigration law and grant them privileges of self-government, especially that it give Texas the status of a state separate from Coahuila. Then they organized "committees of safety" to build up public support for their program.

Late in 1833 the Mexican congress offered substantial concessions and repealed the anti-immigration law, but it would not grant separate statehood. The state of Coahuila-Texas also granted some concessions. In 1834, as a result, peace reigned in Texas. With the borders open once more, a new "Texas fever" swept the Mississippi Valley and land-hungry Americans again rushed into Texas. By the end of 1835, Americans in Texas numbered about thirty thousand and Mexicans about three thousand. Culturally and ethnically, Texas was becoming an American province. In some of the prosperous American settlements one listened in vain for the soft sounds of the Spanish tongue. In others, it seemed an alien and strange sound. The political allegiance to Mexico City of the Americanized province was tenuous.

The Texas Revolution

Mexico's weak control over its province became clearly evident after April 1834 when Antonio López de Santa Anna, an unprincipled adventurer, made himself dictator of Mexico. He repudiated existing reforms and attempted to establish a centralized government. In Texas he tried to enforce measures that appeared repressive. So some forty Texans, members of a minority war faction, on June 30, 1835, captured a Mexican fort and garrison at Anahuac on Galveston Bay. When Santa Anna moved to punish the attackers, "committees of safety and correspondence" sprang up in the American communities and armed resistance became a revolution.

On November 3, while still professing loyalty to Mexico, the Texans met at San Felipe de Austin, drafted a "Declaration of Causes" that compelled them to take up arms, set up a provisional government, and appointed Andrew Jackson's friend, the frontier fighter Sam Houston, commander of their army. A few months later, on March 2, 1836, the government adopted a declaration of independence and the Republic of Texas was born.

Santa Anna, meanwhile, marched into Texas. At San Antonio his army of some four thousand besieged fewer than two hundred Americans who stood off his forces for thirteen days behind the adobe walls of an abandoned mission, the Alamo. Finally, with the dawn of March 6, the Mexicans swarmed over the walls. The Americans inflicted a heavy toll, but by noon the last man was dead. From that day "Remember the Alamo" became a cry of revenge for Americans in Texas.

A few weeks later the Texans suffered another loss. A force of three hundred and fifty men under the command of James W. Fannin, Jr., surrendered to a superior Mexican army near Goliad. In violation of the surrender terms, the Mexicans on March 27 shot the prisoners. Like the slaughter at the Alamo, the massacre at Goliad sent volunteers flocking to join Houston's army.

At first Houston retreated eastward before Santa Anna's forces. Then suddenly, on April 21, just west of the San Jacinto River near Galveston Bay, Houston, with his army swollen to almost eight hundred men, turned. The Texans charged the unprepared Mexicans during the siesta hour and within thirty minutes slaughtered more than six hundred and captured over seven hundred, including Santa Anna. The Texan losses were negligible, nine killed, thirty-four wounded.

Houston later set Santa Anna free, but before he did, the Mexican leader signed two treaties. One declared hostilities ended and called for Mexican forces to evacuate Texas. The other, a secret treaty, pledged his support for an independent Texas with a boundary at the Rio Grande River. Those agreements meant nothing, for the Mexican congress repudiated them as soon as it learned of Santa Anna's capture. Nonetheless, since the Mexican forces remaining in Texas after the Battle of San Jacinto had already retreated into Mexico, that battle had won Texas a *de facto* independence.

American Aid and Neutrality

The Texans had not won their independence unaided. When they started the revolution, they had sought and expected help from the American people, and Americans as individuals or in groups, wholly sympathetic to them, had responded liberally. As early as October 1835 the people of New Orleans, for instance, had organized a Texas committee to recruit volunteers and raise money. It helped raise three "volunteer" companies which within two months were fighting in Texas. Before the end of November, cities in most western and southern states, and even in northern states such as New York and Pennsylvania, were holding mass meetings in support of the Texans. Those cities organized "Texas committees" that solicited money and brought together bands of "emigrants" to fight in Texas. "Emigrate to Texas!" urged a speaker at a Philadelphia meeting. "It abounds in game of all kinds. You will find plenty of employment for as many rifles and muskets as you can get there."

The revolutionary authorities in Texas had sent special commissioners into the United States to take advantage of popular enthusiasm and to lure emigrants to Texas with promises of handsome land grants. Those commissioners obtained money through donations and loans. Some capitalists, eager to speculate in Texas lands, even made contracts with the Texans under the guise of "loans" whereby they would take bargain-price land in repayment. The loans tied powerful American financiers to the Texan cause, for repayment would come only with victory. With the money they raised, the commissioners bought arms, medicines, and other supplies and shipped them to Texas. Without such support the Texans probably could not have defeated Mexico.

Mexico realized the importance of the American aid and protested. The American government answered that it tried to enforce its neutrality laws prohibiting the raising of hostile forces against a friendly state. When the Texas revolution began, in fact, President Jackson ordered the district attorneys, "when indications warranted," to prosecute violators of neutrality, but they and other government officials generally disregarded their instructions. Some of them so openly sympathized with the Texans that they connived at violations of the laws. Public opinion favoring the Texans, particularly in the South and West, was so strong that even if the government had made strenuous efforts to stop the Texas volunteers, which it did not, it would have had difficulty doing so. In contrast to Jackson, during the Canadian rebellion of 1837, Martin Van Buren made strong efforts to enforce American neutrality, but Britain was powerful and could retaliate. Mexico was weak.

An Independent Texas

In addition to expecting American aid, Texans had hoped to join the United States. As soon as they began fighting, in fact, they appealed to Jackson to recognize their independence or to annex them. Although he personally wanted Texas, the president reacted cautiously and did nothing immediately. If the United States annexed Texas, war with Mexico would follow. Equally ominous was the question of slavery. It made immediate annexation impossible. After the Battle of San Jacinto, Texas asked to be annexed on terms calling for recognition of property in slaves. Abolitionists feared that Texas might add four or five slave states to the Union and argued that the Texas revolution was part of a conspiracy by slave owners and those in power in the United States to gain more slave territory.

"People of the North!" the foremost anti-Texas abolitionist declared, *"Will you permit it?* Will you sanction the abominable outrage; involve yourselves in the deep criminality, and perhaps the horrors of war, *for the establishment of slavery in a land of freedom;* and thus put your necks and the necks of your posterity under the feet of the domineering tyrants of the South, for centuries to come?"[2] Despite such charges, only circumstantial evidence, not hard proof, supports the conspiracy theory.

Northern Whigs opposed the annexation, charging that Jackson and Houston had plotted the Texas revolution to add one or more Democratic states to the Union. The president feared, with reason, that annexation would create so great a political upheaval that it might destroy the Union. The same fears did not, however, apply to recognition of independence. Yet Jackson hesitated in this, too, for in the approaching election of 1836 he did not want to weaken the chances of his handpicked candidate, Martin Van Buren. To recognize Texas would appear to align the administration with slavery, might split the Democrats, and would imperil Van Buren's chances for the presidency. Jackson also delayed recognition for another reason. He hoped, apparently, to acquire Texas through direct negotiations with Mexico as represented by Santa Anna, but that plan failed.

Meanwhile, petitions calling for immediate recognition of an independent Texas poured into Congress from all over the Union, north and south. In response, both houses of Congress in July 1836 passed resolutions favoring recognition. In a special plebiscite a few months later, Texans overwhelmingly favored annexation to the United States as soon as possible. Finally, on March 3, 1837, the day before he left office and after Van Buren had been elected, Jackson recognized the independence of Texas.

Many in Texas and in the United States regarded that recognition as merely a preliminary to annexation. The Texan minister in Washington, Memucan Hunt, therefore, formally offered Texas for annexation on August 4. Van Buren rejected the offer. "If the overture of General Hunt were even to be reserved for future consideration," Secretary of State John Forsyth explained, "it would imply a disposition to espouse the quarrel of Texas with Mexico, something wholly at variance with the spirit of the treaty of amity with Mexico and contrary to the uniform policy and obvious welfare of the United States."[3]

Van Buren feared the political opposition of the Whigs and abolitionists. Already the American Antislavery Society had circulated anti-Texas petitions, securing thousands of signatures, and the legislatures of northern states were passing anti-Texas resolutions. Then, while occupied with the trials of the Panic of 1837 and the difficulties on the Canadian border, he made it clear that he wanted no additional troubles from Texas. In October 1838, therefore, Texas formally withdrew her offer of annexation and followed a course of independence.

Mexico refused to recognize Texan independence and continually threatened invasion. The government of Texas, therefore, sent agents to Europe to gain recognition from the major powers. With their support it hoped to force Mexico to recognize its independence, a plan only partially successful. France granted official recognition in October 1839; Britain in November 1840; and lesser European countries did the same later, but repeated efforts to gain Mexican recognition failed. Mirabeau B. Lamar, an expansionist and the second president of Texas, therefore, tried unsuccessfully to extend the borders of Texas to the Pacific Ocean and thereby create a republic that could stand on its own among the powers of the world.

When Sam Houston became president of Texas for the second time late in 1841, he found an empty treasury, a heavy debt, and war with Mexico. In 1842, as a consequence, he approached the American government with two offers on the possibility of annexation. President John Tyler, a pro-slavery Virginian, favored annexation as did a majority of his cabinet. He might have accepted one of the offers if he had been certain of getting a treaty of annexation through the Senate. He had even told his secretary of State, Daniel Webster, that "could the North be reconciled to it, could anything throw so bright a lustre around us?" Webster, a Northern Whig, however, was opposed to annexation. He would do nothing that would add more slave territory to the Union.

After Webster resigned, in the spring of 1842, Tyler went ahead with plans for annexation, motivated in part by the standard southern argument that the United States must acquire Texas before Britain succeeded in winning a dominant influence over the Texan government and in abolishing slavery there. This argument carried weight because the British desired an independent Texas that would act as a barrier to the expansion of the United States and that would balance its power in North America. They also wished to relieve their mills from an uncomfortable dependence on southern cotton grown by slaves.

English abolitionists believed, furthermore, that Britain, through financial and other assistance could persuade Texas to free her slaves and to remain independent. Texas could then sell her cotton grown by free men to England, and the English manufactured goods could go to Texas without climbing a tariff wall. To keep Texas from rushing into the arms of the United States, Britain tried unsuccessfully, therefore, to persuade Mexico to recognize Texas as independent.

Houston's actions also gave the impression that the United States might lose Texas. When Mexico in February 1843 offered political autonomy and separate statehood if Texas would return to Mexican rule, Houston hinted that a return might be possible if Mexico granted a temporary armistice. Santa Anna, again president of Mexico, granted the armistice and late that year began negotiations with the Texans. Those negotiations, as Houston hoped they would, aroused stronger annexationist sentiment in the United States and alarmed Tyler. He now wanted annexation for two main reasons: as an extension of the area of slavery and as a popular issue to help elect him president in 1844.

The Upshur-Calhoun Treaty

In June 1843, Tyler had appointed Abel P. Upshur, a pro-slavery fellow Virginian, secretary of state. According to Tyler, there was no man "whose energies of body and mind were more unremittingly devoted to" annexing Texas than Upshur. To counter British policies, the new secretary offered Texas a treaty of annexation in October. "Texas must not be permitted to throw herself into the arms of England under any impression that this government or this people is either hostile, or even cold, toward her," he had said.[4]

At first Houston refused the offer but later consented to negotiations. He imposed two conditions: protection from the United States in case Mexico attacked, and assurances that the treaty would gain approval from the Whig Senate. Upshur offered military and naval protection from the moment the treaty was signed and said a poll of the Senate assured a two-thirds approval. Since Tyler had hoped to prevent the annexation plan from stirring up the antislavery forces, Upshur negotiated secretly.

Before completing the negotiations, Upshur went on a presidential cruise aboard the warship U.S.S. *Princeton* on January 28, 1844. During the firing exercises, a twelve-inch cannon called the "Peacemaker" exploded while the secretary was watching it, killing him and leaving the Texas treaty unfinished. Tyler then appointed the South's foremost defender of slavery, John C. Calhoun, secretary of state. Now sixty-two years old and approaching the twilight of a long and active career, Calhoun did not want the position but accepted because his southern friends told him they needed his influence to secure Texas and thereby advance the cause of slavery. Thus, with the idea of winning a victory for slavery, Calhoun on April 12 signed the treaty of annexation that Upshur had negotiated.

Then, a few days later, Calhoun took a step that linked the treaty publicly with the expansion of slavery. He had long resented the efforts of British abolitionists to end slavery in Texas. In answering a note from Lord Aberdeen explaining British policy on Texas and slavery, therefore, he defended the annexation treaty, but did not limit himself to an ordinary defense. He went out of his way to praise slavery as a positive good. The United States, he said, must annex Texas to prevent it from falling under the influence of the British who would wipe out slavery there and threaten the "peculiar institution" in the neighboring southern states of the Union.

Calhoun's note, addressed to the British minister in Washington, Richard Pakenham, when published with the treaty of annexation aroused immediate opposition in the North. There, people urged their senators to vote against the Upshur-Calhoun Treaty and defeat the planned expansion of slavedom. Calhoun had aroused the very controversy that Tyler and Upshur had tried to avoid in their secret negotiations.

President Tyler submitted the agreement to the Senate on April 22, on the eve of the presidential campaign and before the parties held their conventions. The rising public opposition to the treaty fused itself with the politics of the campaign. Whigs and Democrats both passed over Tyler as a candidate. The leading Whig candidate was Henry Clay, and for the Democrats, Van Buren. Both men, while the Texas treaty was before the Senate, publicly opposed immediate annexation. The Whigs, as expected, nominated Clay and thus committed the party against immediate annexation. Unwilling to accept Van Buren's stand against annexation, the Democrats nominated the avowed expansionist James K. Polk. In their platform they demanded "the reannexation of Texas." With their candidate and platform, therefore, the Democrats became the party of expansion.

When the Senate on June 8 voted on the treaty, the influence of the campaign and of Calhoun's note seemed clear. Whig Senators, since their standard-bearer was against it, as were their constituents, could not support the treaty. Offended by the defeat of their candidate, the Van Buren Democrats would not vote at this time for a treaty he had opposed. Therefore, with only southern support, the treaty failed by a vote of thirty-five to sixteen. Although Texans had expected the defeat, they resented it. The negotiations had cost them their temporary armistice, for Mexico resumed hostilities.

Two developments helped reverse the defeat. First, annexationists perhaps mistakenly, viewed Polk's election as a mandate for expansion. "It is the will of both the people and the States," Tyler told Congress in his annual message in December, "that Texas shall be annexed to the Union promptly and immediately."[5]

Secondly, Lord Aberdeen contrived, as soon as he had heard of the Upshur-Calhoun Treaty in May, to block American annexation. He approached the French government, proposing that Britain, France, Mexico,

Texas, and perhaps the United States, join in a "diplomatick Act," or treaty, guaranteeing the boundaries of Texas and hence preventing her from joining the Union. If the United States persisted in trying to acquire Texas, Aberdeen told the Texans, England "would go to the last extremity . . . in support of her opposition to the annexation," if France were "perfectly agreed." [6]

Even though France agreed to join England in this bold proposal, in effect pledging both countries to guard Texan independence by war if necessary, they never adopted it. The British and French ministers in the United States warned against the plan. European intervention, particularly before the presidential election, they said, would strengthen the expansionist forces in the United States. Polk's election then showed the depth of expansionist fervor, and Aberdeen lost interest in the plan. That expansionist sentiment so alarmed the French that they told the British the annexation of Texas hardly seemed "of sufficient importance to us to justify our having recourse to arms in order to prevent it."

The Anglo-French designs, particularly Lord Aberdeen's scheme, aided rather than hindered annexation, for when Americans heard of these plans, they took them as proof that England was willing to go to war to keep the United States from having Texas. Many Americans, apparently, then decided that Texas must be theirs, with or without slaves.

Annexation by Resolution

Although sensitive to the shift of opinion in favor of annexation, Tyler knew that he could not obtain a two-thirds majority in the Senate to approve a treaty. When Congress assembled in December, therefore, he suggested annexation by joint resolution, which required only a simple majority in both houses. A resolution calling for annexation passed in the House of Representatives on January 25, 1845, by a vote of 120 to 98, and in the Senate on February 27, by 27 to 25.

In both houses the vote followed party, rather than sectional, lines. All the Democrats voted in favor of the resolution, and all but two Whigs opposed it. Tyler signed it on March 1, three days before leaving office. Two days later he sent word to his diplomatic agent for Texas, Andrew J. Donelson, to invite Texas to join the Union under the terms of the resolution.

Since the Constitution said "new states may be admitted by the Congress into this Union," the resolution invited Texas to come into the Union as a state, and not as a territory. Other terms allowed Texas, when she had enough population, to make as many as four states out of her territory. She could retain her own public lands, but had to pay her own public debt and would come into the Union as a slave state.

The Mexican minister in Washington protested the resolution, calling it an act of aggression that deprived his country of an integral part of her territory, demanded his passports, and quit his post. The British and French, meanwhile, made another effort to prevent annexation. In May they finally persuaded Mexico to agree to recognize the independence of Texas, if that province would agree "not to annex herself or become subject to any country whatever."

Texas now had to make her decision. Some Texans, particularly Sam Houston, did not like the American terms, but public opinion overwhelmingly favored annexation. President Anson Jones, who had assumed office in December, submitted the American offer to his congress, along with the Mexican treaty, sponsored by the British and French, offering peace and recognition. That congress, on June 16, chose unanimously to join the United States. Three weeks later, on July 4, a popularly elected convention ratified that decision and accepted a constitution for a new state of Texas. On December 29 President Polk signed the final resolution that brought Texas, after waiting nine years, formally into the Union. "The final act in this great drama is now performed," Anson Jones said. "The Republic of Texas is no more." [7]

The Opening of California

Another Mexican province that lay in the path of manifest destiny was California, a land of majestic mountains, barren deserts, and rich valleys, stretching along the Pacific shore south of Oregon. Spain had used California as she had Texas, as a buffer protecting her provinces in Mexico from foreign encroachments, particularly from southward-moving Russians. Spain's control over California had never been firm. Fifteen hundred miles of desert, made doubly formidable by bands of Apaches, Yumas, and other fierce desert Indians, separated California from the seat of Spanish authority in Mexico City. Spain's officials had maintained infrequent communication with California only by sea.

The first Americans to reach California had also come by sea. A few of them arrived before 1800, mostly New England merchant adventurers seeking sea otter skins to use in their trade with China, but the sea otter trade did not become important until after the turn of the century. Since they were engaged in a clandestine commerce forbidden by Spanish authorities, those Yankee traders, as well as the men of the New England whaling ships who visited the province, built no lasting ties with California. Nevertheless, those men publicized it when they returned to New England.

After California became a Mexican province in 1821, it retained its semiautonomous status. In the 1820s and 1830s, the Californians, mainly men of Spanish blood who had settled the province, rebelled about ten times against incompetent governors Mexico sent north to rule them. Turmoil and revolution in Mexico added to their spirit of independence. Isolated and virtually autonomous, California had developed its own way of life. Few Californians had any strong sense of loyalty to their Mexican rulers.

In these decades of political ferment Americans gained a firm foothold in California. Some of the first Americans to reach that province in the Mexican period sought furs, particularly beaver pelts. They broke California's isolation by piercing the mountain and desert barrier protecting its eastern side. The first of these path-finding "mountain men," Jedediah S. Smith, reached California late in 1826. Others followed. Then for about a decade the fur traders pushed into the rich valleys and coastal lands, blazing the major transcontinental trails into the territory. They opened California by land and advertised what they saw.

While certain fur traders were coming by land, other Americans, New Englanders, came by sea for the "hide and tallow trade." The Mexican government opened California's ports to foreign traders in hides and tallow, but until 1827 the British, through an agreement with the Mexican government, monopolized that trade. Then, after the agreement expired, American traders swarmed into the ports. The crews of the Boston hide ships, since they sometimes spent two or three years in acquiring a cargo, obtained an intimate knowledge of the California coast. In the early 1830s, American shippers planted agents in the ports to buy hides and to store them in warehouses until a company ship called for them.

Except for a few sailors who had remained from earlier visits, those agents became the first permanent American residents in California. They bought ranches, became Catholics, married Mexican wives, and adopted Mexican ways. They liked California. In letters they sent home they told of the good life they lived and praised the virtues of their adopted land. Others who visited California or who settled there, British and American, wrote books and articles and also publicized the province, praising the climate, fertile soil, and the magnificent bay of San Francisco. Richard Henry Dana, Jr., for example, made the hide and tallow trade famous in his classic, *Two Years Before the Mast*. Appearing in 1840, this book, along with other accounts, aroused an intense American interest in California, a land now reputed to be a "pioneer's paradise."

To restless Americans harried by depression, those accounts had magnetic appeal. Equally attractive were the political reports which pointed out that most of the land was thinly populated, the government inadequate, and Mexico's hold on the province "miserably weak and ineffective." In addition, military defenses were virtually nonexistent. Only a handful of pioneers, the accounts implied, could drive out the backward Mexicans and make the lush valleys American. In the wake of the "Oregon fever," as a result, a lesser fever for California began to rise in the Middle West in the 1840s.

The first landseekers from the Midwest arrived in 1841. Then, after the mass western migrations of 1843, trains of covered wagons rolled into California in increasing numbers. Those people did not settle among the Californians along the coast but squatted illegally in the Sacramento Valley and established their own way of life.

Although the Californians had been friendly to the small number of Americans who had earlier settled among them, they now became alarmed by the large-scale invasion, particularly since the Protestant newcomers, unlike the Americans already in the province, brought with them an unconcealed contempt for Mexicans, a hatred of Catholics, and a disregard for Mexican law. Friction between the alien American invaders and the Mexican authorities, therefore, developed almost immediately.

Efforts to Purchase California

Before the covered wagons had started moving into California, American diplomacy had tried to acquire that province from Mexico and in effect contributed to the bitter state of Mexican-American relations. That "incompetent rascal" Anthony Butler suggested buying the province in 1835. Through him Andrew Jackson tried to purchase San Francisco Bay and northern California for $500,000, but Butler's negotiations failed. Mexico would no more part with California than she would with Texas.

After Mexico got rid of Butler, Jackson nonetheless persisted in trying to obtain San Francisco Bay, the portion of California he considered most desirable. In 1836 he sent William A. Slacum, a naval officer, to investigate the Pacific Coast. Slacum too insisted that the United States must have the bay of San Francisco.

Early in the following year, while discussing a possible mediation between Mexico and Texas with Santa Anna, Jackson said he was willing to offer $3,500,000 for California lying north of thirty-eight degrees of latitude, assuming mistakenly that such a boundary included all of San Francisco Bay. At the same time, he urged Texas to extend her boundaries to include California. If Texas acquired control of San Francisco Bay, the main harbor on the Pacific Coast, he thought, New England and other commercial sections of the North would accept Texas. "He is very earnest and anxious on this point of claiming the Californias," the Texan minister in Washington wrote, "and says we must not consent to less." [8]

After Jackson left the White House in 1837, direct efforts to acquire California ceased. Van Buren did nothing diplomatically, but he did send Lieutenant Charles Wilkes of the navy to the Pacific. In the fall of 1841 Wilkes visited San Francisco Bay, traveled through the surrounding country, and gathered detailed information on the life of the province. Most of all he was impressed by San Francisco Bay, "one of the finest, if not the very best harbor in the world." Wilkes's activities aroused the suspicions of Californians, who believed his expedition was part of an American program of annexation.

John Tyler revived the question of acquiring California. His minister to Mexico, Waddy Thompson, urged annexation. "I would like to be instrumental in securing California," he explained. His dispatches described it as "the richest, the most beautiful, the healthiest country in the world." The harbor of San Francisco, he said, was "capacious enough to receive the navies of all the world" and was destined to control the trade of the entire Pacific. "I am profoundly satisfied," he wrote in one letter, "that in its bearing upon all the interests of our country, agricultural, political, manufacturing, commercial, and fishing, the importance of the acquisition of California cannot be overestimated." [9]

Tyler and Secretary of State Webster supported Thompson's plans and authorized him to negotiate a treaty for the acquisition of the province. Webster considered San Francisco Bay more valuable than all of Texas. In his "tripartite plan," as we have seen, he was even willing to sacrifice Oregon north of the Columbia River for that bay and northern California.

Thompson's ideas for acquiring California probably would not have succeeded anyway, but the rash act of Commodore Thomas Ap Catesby Jones, the commander of an American naval force in the Pacific, gave Mexico new cause to fear the United States and hence removed any chance of success for Thompson's plans. While in Peru, Jones received news that led him to believe that the United States was at war with Mexico, and that Mexico intended to cede California to Britain. He quickly sailed for Monterey, California's provincial capital, reaching it on October 18, 1842. Although he found no sign of war, everything was "normally dilapidated," he said; he captured the town and raised the American flag. Two days later, finding that he had been mistaken, he restored Monterey to the Mexican authorities and apologized.

Although Jones's behavior created little ill will in California, it aroused a violent reaction in Mexico City. It forced Thompson to admit that it was now "wholly out of the question to do anything as to California." Still, American desire for California persisted and, after Calhoun became secretary of state, that desire grew more intense for the following reasons: the accelerating rate of American immigration, fear of English designs on the province stemming from the activities of British agents there, and reports that California would separate from Mexico to become an independent republic.

The mounting interest in California led President Tyler to appoint Thomas O. Larkin, a New Englander who had become Monterey's wealthiest merchant, American consul in California. Larkin formally opened his consulate in April 1844 and reported on all that happened there, particularly on political developments. He urged Calhoun to acquire California, and the secretary tried to buy it, but his efforts, like the earlier ones, failed.

President Polk, like Calhoun and Tyler, wanted California and at practically any cost. Soon after his inauguration in 1845 he apparently told his secretary of the navy that he placed the acquisition of California on the same plane as the "Oregon question." It would be, he said, one of the "four great measures" of his administration. As in the acquisition of the Oregon Territory, Polk's desire to obtain California reflected the gospel of manifest destiny. Scarcely two weeks after his inaugural, newspapers were saying the Rio Grande would not stop the westward march of the Anglo-Saxons. "The process by which Texas was acquired," a Baltimore paper said, "may be repeated over and over again."

Mexico's reaction to the annexation of Texas, however, complicated Polk's efforts to acquire California peacefully. In taking over Texas, the United States inherited her smoldering state of war with Mexico, for ever since Tyler had made it clear that his plans to annex were serious, Mexico had said annexation would be cause for war. After Tyler signed the resolution of annexation, therefore, Mexico had broken off diplomatic relations. The Mexican press warned that American greed had marked all of Mexico for its prey. "Union and war" should be our answer, one paper declared. Although the Mexican government made some preparations for war, it was so rocked by revolutions that it could not at that time launch hostilities against the United States, nor even defend itself.

Grievances against Mexico

Mexico's periodic revolutions, on the other hand, had given the United States cause for grievance. Those disturbances had destroyed American lives and property in Mexico. In one uprising alone, in 1835, Mexican forces had executed twenty-two Americans without trial. In addition, Mexico owed Americans money for munitions and supplies they had sold to her during her revolt against Spain from 1810 to 1821. Beginning in the days of Andrew Jackson, the American government had taken up the claims of its citizens and had demanded payment.

A claims commission of Americans and Mexicans, established by treaty in 1839, had finally worked out a partial settlement whereby Mexico agreed to pay slightly over $2 million in twenty installments over five years. She made only three payments before defaulting at the end of April 1843. Mexico was not unwilling to pay the debts but with an empty treasury was unable to do so. When Polk became president, expansionists had taken up the claims question, denouncing Mexico for alleged perfidy. In pressing the claims Polk did not, however, demand cash. If Mexico would recognize the annexation of Texas with a boundary at the Rio Grande, he would accept that recognition in place of cash payment for the claims.

Polk was willing to make that offer because the Texan, and hence the American, claim to the Rio Grande boundary was dubious. Texas had claimed the Rio Grande as her western and southern boundary when she gained independence and had forced Santa Anna to recognize that frontier boundary by treaty, but the Mexican government had repudiated that treaty and refused to recognize any boundary with Texas. Since Texas's southern boundary, under both Spanish and Mexican rule, had never extended beyond the Nueces River, her claim to the Rio Grande was weak. Yet when Texas voted to join the Union, Polk accepted her claim to the line of the Rio Grande as legitimate and was determined to uphold it.

Before annexation, neither Mexico nor Texas had occupied the area between the Nueces and the Rio Grande, an almost unsettled no man's land between two states technically at war. As far as Mexico was concerned, there was no dispute over that land between the rivers. All of Texas was Mexican. She denied the existence of Texas as an independent state and claimed that Texas did not have the power to annex herself to the United States.

In July 1845, immediately after Texas voted to join the Union, Polk ordered Brigadier General Zachary Taylor to take several thousand troops from the Louisiana border into Texas to occupy the debatable region south of the Nueces. Taylor was instructed not to disturb Mexican settlements or attack Mexican troops "unless an actual state of war should exist." By the end of the month, Taylor had camped his army near the town of Corpus Christi at the mouth of the Nueces River. By October that force had increased to four thousand men, half of the entire American army and the largest concentration of troops since the end of the War of 1812, thirty years earlier. Taylor's troops remained in the heat of Corpus Christi for eight months.

Polk, meanwhile, sought ways to acquire California and at the same time settle the claims and boundary questions. This required bargaining with Mexico, which he could not do without reopening diplomatic relations. In April, therefore, he had sent William S. Parrott, a confidential agent, to Mexico to see if the government there would agree to resume those relations and reopen negotiations for settling the difficulties between the two countries.

In August, Parrott wrote several times that the Mexican government would accept an American minister. Polk decided, as a result, to send John Slidell of New Orleans on a secret mission to Mexico with full diplomatic powers. Before sending him, the president wanted official assurance from the Mexican government that it would resume diplomatic relations. The Mexicans obliged on October 15, saying they would receive any "commis-

Line according to act of Texas Congress, Dec. 19, 1836, and claimed by U.S. as part of Texas, 1845-1848

Texas Annexation, 1845

THE BOUNDARIES OF TEXAS,
1836–1848

sioner" sent to Mexico City "with full powers to settle the present dispute in a peaceable, reasonable, and honorable manner." Polk received the assurance on November 9 and immediately dispatched Slidell on his mission.

Slidell's instructions allowed him to offer a choice of four settlements. The United States would assume the claims if Mexico would accept the Rio Grande boundary. If the boundary included New Mexico, the United States would pay $5 million in addition. If Mexico would also sell California, the United States would pay $25 million, or if she would sell only part of California north of Monterey, the United States would give $5 million more. Slidell could conclude a treaty if Mexico accepted any one of the proposals, but he could make no settlement that excluded the Rio Grande boundary.

When Slidell arrived in Mexico City on December 6, the government of President José Joaquín Herrera was in danger of collapse. Since news of Slidell's mission had leaked and had aroused a violent opposition to the negotiation, the Herrera government did not dare recognize him, let alone negotiate. "You know," the Mexican foreign minister told Slidell, "the opposition are calling us traitors for entering into this arrangement with you." [10]

The Herrera government had to reject Slidell or fall. It announced, therefore, that it could not accept a minister with full powers, but only a special "commissioner" empowered to settle the Texas question alone. Slidell's rejection did not save the Herrera regime. It fell on the last day of December. Although Polk would not change Slidell's commission, he instructed him to approach the new Mexican government, which Slidell did and was again rejected. In March 1846, therefore, he left Mexico, convinced that only force would win American objectives.

Many Americans shared Slidell's feelings. All during the summer and autumn months of 1845, tension with Mexico had mounted. Some impetuous Americans had demanded war. In August one politician reported from Philadelphia that he had heard "nothing else talked of but war with Mexico." [11] News of Slidell's rejection stimulated an even more violent reaction. The United States, a New Orleans paper said, "are now left no alternative but to extort by arms the respect and justice which Mexico refuses to any treatment less harsh." [12]

Behind Mexican stubbornness, many Americans believed, stood the power of Britain and France, but particularly of Britain. Polk, too, found this possibility easy to believe. During the summer and fall of 1845, he had heard disturbing reports from American officials in Britain, Mexico, and California of British designs on California. "England must never have California," the consul at Liverpool said. [13] Parrott reported from Mexico City that British intrigue had blocked him. The British, he warned, wanted California. Thomas O. Larkin wrote from Monterey that the British and French had designs on California.

Even though the British government itself had no such designs, rumors had reached Polk that England and France would recognize the Californians as independent if they would agree never to annex themselves to the United States. Since the Californians in February 1845 had defeated the forces of a Mexican governor, demonstrating the ineffectiveness of Mexican rule, such tales appeared to have substance. Regardless of the rumors, it seemed California was becoming an international derelict.

As in the case of Texas, fear of English intervention aroused a wide enthusiasm for expansion into California. Newspaper editors, Democratic and Whig, warned against British designs, saying that the province must become American, if only to limit Britain's power.

To counter alleged British influence, Polk appointed Larkin his secret agent in California. "The future destiny of that country," Secretary of State James Buchanan wrote to Larkin, "is a subject of anxious solicitude for the Government and people of the United States." The president, therefore, "could not view with indifference the transfer of California to Great Britain or any other European Power." If, on the other hand, he added, the Californians "should desire to unite their destiny with ours," we would receive them as "brethren." [14]

Larkin's instructions told him, in effect, to persuade native Californians to part voluntarily from Mexico and place themselves under American protection. Polk had also sent additional warships to join the Pacific squadron with orders to take San Francisco if war broke out with Mexico.

Then, in his first annual message to Congress in December, Polk revived the Monroe Doctrine, directing it against Britain and France. With California in mind, he said "that the people of this continent alone have the right to decide their own destiny. Should any portion of them, constituting an independent state, propose to unite themselves with our Confederacy, this will be a question for them and us to determine without any foreign interposition."[15] In warning against European diplomatic interference in North America, Polk thus expanded the Monroe Doctrine.

A month later, on January 12, 1846, Polk learned that Herrera's government had refused to receive Slidell and hence realized that his plans for purchasing California and the Southwest were failing. The president now became convinced that only a policy of force would impress Mexico. On that same day he ordered General Taylor to march his forces across the no man's land to the north bank of the Rio Grande.

The War with Mexico

On February 13 Polk received dubious assurance that a show of force would bring Mexico to terms. A friend of Santa Anna, who had just returned from a visit to the former dictator, then in exile in Havana, told him that Santa Anna intended to return to Mexico soon to resume power. If Polk aided Santa Anna financially, the friend said, the exiled general, once he assumed power, would be willing to sell part of the Southwest and part of California. "The U.S. would never be able to treat with Mexico," however, he added, "without the presence of an imposing force by land and sea."[16]

Impressed by the suggestions of Santa Anna's agent, Polk wanted to send Mexico an ultimatum. If it were rejected, then he would be ready for "aggressive measures." Since the Oregon crisis was smoldering, Secretary of State Buchanan persuaded him not to start a war with Mexico until he was sure there would be none with England. General Taylor's forces, meanwhile, had brought the nation to the verge of war.

Taylor's army began the move to the Rio Grande on March 8, 1846, and twenty days later four thousand American soldiers stood on the banks of the river. In April, Mexican troops began arriving in large numbers across the river and gathering in the town of Matamoros until they numbered well over five thousand. Tension built up. On April 23 Mexico's president proclaimed a "defensive war" against the United States. Two mornings later, American dragoons clashed with Mexican cavalry on the north side of the Rio Grande. The Americans counted sixteen killed or wounded.

Before that blood had been shed, Polk had decided on war. He had received word of Mexico's final refusal to accept Slidell on April 7, but had waited until Slidell could report to him in person before asking for a declaration of war. Slidell arrived in Washington on May 8, still convinced that only force would bring Mexico to terms. On the next day, a Saturday, Polk told his cabinet that on Tuesday he wanted to send a message to Congress recommending a declaration of war because Mexico had rejected Slidell and had not paid the claims. All of the president's advisers agreed except George Bancroft, the secretary of the navy, who said if Mexican forces committed an "act of hostility" then he would favor immediate war. That night news arrived telling of the clash on the Rio Grande. Polk now had an "act of hostility."

The president immediately called another meeting of his cabinet and that Sunday prepared the war message he sent to Congress on Monday, May 11. That message recited accumulated grievances of twenty years against Mexico and stressed her "breach of faith" in refusing to receive Slidell. Those offenses, he said, had already exhausted the "cup of forbearance." "But now," he added, "after reiterated menaces, Mexico has passed the boundary of the United States, has invaded our territory, and shed American blood upon American soil." Despite "all our efforts to avoid it," he insisted, war now "exists by the act of Mexico herself." [17]

Polk's policy toward Mexico had been a combination of sabre rattling, intrigue, and unpalatable peace offers. If he had not been an expansionist, determined to have California and the Southwest, he might have worked harder to keep peace, but peace would not have given him California and the other western lands. To obtain them he did not flinch at the prospect of war, even on the flimsy pretext of unpaid claims and a rebuffed diplomat.

On the day after Polk's message, a resolution authorizing the president to declare war against Mexico passed the House of Representatives by a vote of 174 to 14 and the Senate by 40 to 2. All the Democrats voted for war, joined by 47 Whigs in the House and 16 in the Senate.

"Mr. Polk's War," as critics called it, soon became unpopular. Whigs and some Democrats opposed it. Northern Whigs and abolitionists viewed the war as a conspiracy hatched by slaveholders and Southerners in the Polk administration. A Whig convention in New Hampshire declared that it was being waged "for the dismemberment of a sister republic upon pretexts that are false, and for a purpose that is abhorrent to all feelings of humanity and justice." Abraham Lincoln, then a young Whig congressman from Illinois, asked repeatedly in his "spot resolutions" that the president name the "spot" on American soil where American blood had been spilled. The New England poet, James Russell Lowell, even recommended northern secession:

> Ef I'd *my* way I hed ruther
> We should go to work an' part,—
> They take one way, we take t'other,—
> Guess it wouldn't break my heart. [18]

Opposition to the war upset Polk. He had expected a short easy conflict that, as Santa Anna's friend had said, would quickly force Mexico to sell him the territory he wanted. In his memoirs Thomas Hart Benton, the Democratic senator from Missouri, wrote that the administration "wanted a small war, just large enough to require a treaty of peace, and not large enough to make military reputations, dangerous for the presidency."[19] The two leading generals were Whigs.

On May 13 the secretary of the navy told the commander of the American naval squadron off Vera Cruz, "If Santa Anna endeavors to enter the Mexican ports, you will allow him to pass freely." Polk hoped to make an immediate peace with Santa Anna on the terms Santa Anna's agent had proposed in February. Santa Anna returned to Mexico, but did not keep his bargain with Polk. Instead, he took command of the Mexican army and directed the war against the United States. Polk then decided "to prosecute the war with vigor," and it became long, costly, and bloody.

A few of Mexico's leaders counted on opposition to war within the United States to help them, had an exaggerated estimate of their military prowess, or had nurtured unfounded expectations of European aid, primarily from England and France. They had desired war and expected victory. But most knowledgeable Mexicans were aware of their country's military impotence and were reluctant to fight. As they expected, Mexico found herself on the defensive from the beginning and met nothing but defeat. Polk launched a triple thrust against her. General Taylor's army struck across the Rio Grande into northern Mexico. Another smaller force under General Stephen W. Kearny moved west to conquer New Mexico and to occupy California. The third army, under General Winfield Scott, in March 1847 went by sea to Vera Cruz and then fought inland to Mexico City to dictate terms of peace.

Developments in California, meanwhile, looked as if they might make that province a second Texas. The activities of settlers, who continued to arrive in large numbers, and of a young American army officer, John Charles Frémont, upset Larkin's plans to win California through peaceful persuasion. In the summer of 1845, the War Department had sent Frémont deep into Mexican territory with a well-armed party of sixty-two men. Ostensibly his task was to find a shorter land route to California, and "in arranging this expedition," Frémont wrote later, "the eventualities of war were taken into consideration."

Frémont's "exploring" expedition reached California in December 1845 and after spending two months there retreated into Oregon when the California authorities threatened to fight. In May 1846 a special messenger from Polk overtook Frémont. What secret or verbal orders that messenger brought are unknown, but Frémont marched his men back into California and made camp "to await positive orders in regard to the war" with Mexico.[20]

Then, within a few weeks, some of the newer American emigrants in the Sacramento Valley revolted against the Mexican rulers and in June set up the California Republic with a flag depicting a bear as their emblem. Frémont supported this bear flag revolt, and took over its leadership. Thus, when he learned that war had broken out, northern California, partly through his efforts, was already in American hands. In July, when Commodore Robert F. Stockton took command of American naval and military forces in California, he and Frémont conquered the rest of the province. General Kearny arrived in December in time to help crush a revolt against American authority in southern California. By January 13, 1847, all resistance had ceased, and California was an American province.

With the conquest of California, Polk placed the American flag over all the territory he had included in his war objectives. He wrote in his diary repeatedly after the war started that Mexico must cede New Mexico and California. Despite her defeats Mexico would make no peace treaty on Polk's terms.

The Mission of Nicholas P. Trist

Polk needed an early treaty because tensions over slavery and expansion threatened to disrupt the Union. Whig opposition to the war had become so fierce early in 1847 that the president did not dare declare his aim of annexing New Mexico and California. In mid-April he decided to send an inconspicuous executive agent, Nicholas P. Trist, to join Winfield Scott's army in Mexico. Moving toward Mexico City with the army, Trist could take advantage of Scott's victories and of any sudden opportunity Mexico offered to make a treaty that would cede California and the Southwest.

The president used Trist, chief clerk in the department of state, and not a more prominent person because Trist was a loyal Democrat who held a position of no political importance and therefore could begin negotiating with the Mexicans without arousing factional resentment in Polk's own party. Through use of an executive agent, moreover, Polk kept all power in his own hands and could take full credit for any successful negotiation. Yet Trist had ability, intelligence, and previous diplomatic experience with Latin Americans, and spoke Spanish fluently.

Trist's instructions, dated April 15, were like Slidell's and told him to secure the Rio Grande boundary, California, and New Mexico. In addition, he was to acquire what the Mexicans called Baja, or Lower, California and the right of transit across the Isthmus of Tehuantepec. The territorial acquisitions were to serve as the war indemnity in place of cash, but Trist could offer Mexico as much as $30 million beyond assumption of claims for all that he demanded. Since Polk had not yet disclosed his territorial aims publicly, the instructions demanded absolute secrecy.

Trist reached Vera Cruz early in May and immediately quarrelled with General Scott, a Whig who distrusted Polk. Scott believed that the administration was trying to degrade him by placing a mere clerk over him. At first Scott and Trist argued so bitterly that they gave up speaking to each other. For days, thereafter, they bombarded each other and Washington with angry letters.

In his early efforts to negotiate, Trist came to realize that he needed Scott's cooperation to succeed and hence made overtures to him. The general responded cordially so that overnight the two men cast aside their enmity and became friends. Scott now called Trist "able, discreet, courteous, and amiable," and said, "I am perfectly willing that all I have heretofore written to the Department [of War] about Mr. Trist, should be suppressed." Scott, Trist told his wife, was "the soul of honour and probity, and full of the most sterling qualities of heart and head."[21]

As the American army paused before the gates of Mexico City in August, Santa Anna, through the British legation, asked for an armistice. Believing the chance of concluding a peace treaty justified an armistice, Scott and Trist granted one. Before Trist could forward to Polk the results of his preliminary negotiations in which he appeared willing to accept something less than the Rio Grande boundary, the armistice broke down. Therefore, Scott advanced, and on September 15 his marines patrolled the streets of the capital.

Before the end of September, Polk heard of the August armistice. Trist, it appeared, was ignoring his instructions. "Mr. Trist is recalled," Polk explained in his diary, "because his remaining longer with the army could not, probably, accomplish the objects of his mission, and because his remaining longer might, & probably would, impress the Mexican Government with the belief that the U.S. were so anxious for peace that they would ultimate[ly] conclude one upon the Mexican terms. Mexico must now first sue for peace, & when she does we will hear her propositions."[22] The president was now convinced that Mexico would make peace only if the United States increased the tempo of the war, and he urged Congress to do that.

For the first time since the beginning of the war, moreover, Polk announced his aim of territorial gain, stressing the need to acquire New Mexico and California. He told Congress on December 7, 1847, that "the doctrine of no territory is the doctrine of no indemnity; and, if sanctioned, would be a public acknowledgment that our country was wrong, and that the war declared by Congress with extraordinary unanimity was unjust, and should be abandoned." The Whigs did not agree, and on January 3, 1848, the House of Representatives declared, by a vote of eighty-five to eighty-one, that the war had been "unnecessarily and unconstitutionally begun by the President of the United States."

At the same time, the long war and the refusal of Mexico to make a peace treaty aroused some Democratic expansionists to demand all of Mexico. "Schemes of ambition, vast enough to have tasked even a Roman imagination to conceive," a Virginia senator told Congress on January 3, "present themselves suddenly as practical suggestions." The "all-Mexico movement" did not sway Polk from his own more limited, but still vast, objectives. He had never wanted, he had said in his December message, "to make a permanent conquest of the Republic of Mexico, or to annihilate her separate existence as an independent nation." [23] Polk, in effect, desired a peace treaty before the election of 1848 because he wanted to take the war out of politics.

Trist, meanwhile, on November 16, 1847, had received Polk's letters ordering him home. He was ready to obey even though Santa Anna had fled and a new Mexican government that appeared ready to negotiate a satisfactory peace had assumed power. Mexican officials, the British legation, and General Scott, however, all asked him to negotiate a treaty before leaving. Trist, therefore, disregarded the president's instructions and remained.

Trist wrote to Polk and Secretary of State Buchanan explaining his decision. It still left the administration, he said, at "perfect liberty to dis-

ACQUISITIONS FROM MEXICO, 1848

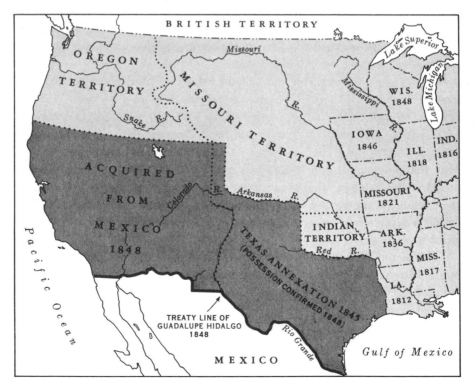

avow his proceeding, should it be deemed disadvantageous to our country."
Then, after some delay, he sat down with the Mexican commissioners.

The Treaty of Guadalupe Hidalgo

Night and day, all through January 1848 Trist negotiated. Finally,
on February 2, in the little town of Guadalupe Hidalgo near Mexico City,
he signed a treaty in which Mexico recognized the American conquests.
The United States paid $15,000,000 and assumed the claims of its own
citizens up to $3,250,000. The Treaty of Guadalupe Hidalgo gave the
United States the Rio Grande boundary, California, and an area comprising
Nevada, Utah, New Mexico, Arizona, and parts of Wyoming and Colorado. This was the minimum Polk had authorized Trist to accept in April.
Yet, including Texas, Mexico had lost half of her national territory.

When Polk first heard of his clerk's insubordination, he concluded
that Trist and Scott had conspired to embarrass him. "Mr. Trist has acted
very badly," the president said when he received the treaty. Then as he
went through it, he recorded in his diary "if on further examination the
Treaty is one that can be accepted, it should not be rejected on account of
his bad conduct."[24] Polk did not reject it. He accepted his repudiated emissary's treaty because the state of politics made peace necessary and because
it gave him his territorial objectives.

In the Senate, Democrats who clamored for the whole of Mexico and
Whigs who wanted none of Mexico's territory opposed the treaty. Ex-
tremes, as Polk remarked, "sometimes meet and act effectively for negative
purposes." They could not, nevertheless, block the treaty. The Senate on
March 10 gave its consent by a vote of thirty-eight to fourteen. A few days
later, a disgruntled Whig wrote that the peace treaty "negotiated by an
unauthorized agent, with an unacknowledged government, submitted by
an accidental President to a dissatisfied Senate, has, notwithstanding these
objections in form, been confirmed."[25]

After Mexico ratified the treaty, Polk told Congress that "the results
of the war with Mexico have given the United States a national character
which our country never before enjoyed." New Mexico and California, he
said, "constitute of themselves a country large enough for a great empire,
and their acquisition is second only in importance to that of Louisiana in
1803."[26] An intangible result, as the future would show, was an intensified spirit of "militarism and racism that coarsened democratic sensibilities" in American society.[27]

I X

Young America

In the decade following peace with Mexico, internal affairs, primarily the sectional conflict over slavery, dominated politics. Yet American diplomacy had to deal with a number of scattered problems, a few of which might have burst into serious crises. One of them concerned the control of transit routes across Central America for a possible interoceanic canal.

The new empire in the West had made the United States a major power in the Pacific and pointed to the need for a canal linking California and Oregon with the Atlantic coast. The discovery of gold on California's American River in January 1848 and the ensuing rush that quickly expanded the population in the state dramatized this need.

Bidlack's Treaty

As if by coincidence, during the Mexican War the United States had acquired transit rights across the Isthmus of Panama. New Granada, which became the state of Colombia, had been nervously watching Britain expand her control over the Mosquito Coast of nearby Nicaragua and then move threateningly toward the isthmus, at that time a province of New Granada. To forestall any lunge toward Panama, Granadan officials turned to the United States for help, offering it transit rights on the same terms enjoyed by their own people if the United States would guarantee the "perfect neutrality" of the isthmus in time of war, guarantee Granadan sovereignty over it, and maintain a free transit. On December 12, 1846, Benjamin A. Bidlack, the American *chargé d'affaires* in Bogotá, on his own initiative signed a treaty with New Granada that included those terms. President Polk accepted it and the Senate, which feared the entangling commitment but desired the transit more, finally approved in June 1848.

In urging ratification, the Granadans had called attention to the nonintervention principle of the Monroe Doctrine. In that case, Polk did not act in the name of that doctrine; but in regard to the Yucatán peninsula (presently a part of Mexico), he expanded the doctrine with what has been called the "Polk Corollary." In March 1848 local authorities in Yucatán had offered their land to the United States, to Britain, and to Spain. Fearing that one of the other powers might accept the offer, Polk sent a special message to Congress on April 19 that cited the Monroe Doctrine, indirectly suggested American occupation of the peninsula, and in effect expressed opposition to the transfer of territory in the New World to a foreign power even with the consent of the inhabitants. Nothing came of the Yucatán proposal as the new government there withdrew the March offer.

Nonetheless, Polk's concern over Central America reflected a growing rivalry with Britain, at that time the dominant power in the Caribbean. The British, in fact, noted this new extension of American power with increasing uneasiness. Since Bidlack's Treaty gave the United States special rights over one of the two best routes for a possible interoceanic canal, they sought control over the other. That second route, long considered the better of the two, went through Nicaragua, beginning on the east coast at San Juan, at the mouth of the San Juan River. In January 1848 the British, who controlled the east coast of Nicaragua through a protectorate over the Mosquito Indians, a tribe that lived there, had seized San Juan from the Nicaraguans and had renamed it Greytown.

When Nicaragua appealed to the United States for help, Polk sent a diplomatic agent, Elijah Hise, to Central America. He vied with Britain for control of the Nicaraguan route. On June 21, 1849, Hise made an unauthorized treaty with Nicaragua, giving the United States exclusive rights over the Nicaraguan route and committing it to a guarantee of Nicaragua's sovereignty.

On the west coast of Central America the Gulf of Fonseca dominated one of the possible Pacific Ocean approaches to the Nicaraguan route. In the gulf lay Tigre Island, belonging to Honduras. Hise's successor, Ephraim G. Squier, signed a treaty with Honduras on September 28, 1849, temporarily giving the United States that island for a naval base. Squier also negotiated another treaty with Nicaragua, modifying the Hise treaty.

To block American control over the Nicaraguan route, the British agent in Central America signed a treaty with Costa Rica, protecting that country's claim to the northern bank of the San Juan River. Then in October a British naval officer seized Tigre Island. Although this act aroused resentment in the United States, the Whig president, Zachary Taylor, did not retaliate and did not ratify the Hise and Squier treaties. The British government, too, was more peacefully inclined than its agents. It disavowed the seizure of Tigre Island and did not accept the treaty with Costa Rica.

Neither Britain nor the United States wanted the other to have exclusive control over canal routes in Central America; yet, if they persisted in their rivalry, it seemed as if one of the minor crises might lead to a larger conflict. "We are deeply anxious to avoid any collision with the British Government in relation to this matter," Taylor's secretary of state, John M. Clayton, wrote, "but that collision will become inevitable if great prudence be not exercised on both sides." Both countries, therefore, agreed to try to settle their differences in Central America through diplomacy.

The Clayton-Bulwer Treaty

In December 1849 the British government sent a new minister to the United States, Sir Henry Lytton Bulwer, who promptly began negotiations with Clayton to adjust the Central-American difficulties. Finally, on April 19, 1850, they signed a treaty that denied either country exclusive control over the canal routes. Both parties also agreed not to build fortifications along a canal route, not to exercise dominion over any part of Central America, and to guarantee the neutrality of any canal when built.

Since the treaty was a compromise with purposely ambiguous wording, both countries could accept it without appearing to surrender to the other. After the Senate had approved the treaty on May 22, Clayton and Bulwer tried to clarify some of the ambiguities through an exchange of notes interpreting the commitments of their respective countries. Bulwer said Britain did not regard the treaty as applying "to Her Majesty's Settlement at Honduras or to its dependencies."[1] Clayton accepted that interpretation with qualifications and went ahead with the exchange of ratifications. Nonetheless, disputes arose.

Americans believed that under terms of the treaty the British had agreed to give up their protectorate over the Mosquito Indians. Claiming that the treaty's provisions applied only to any extension of dominion in Central America, Britain rejected the American view and retained her protectorate. Then in March 1852 she converted some islands in the Bay of Honduras into the "Colony of the Bay Islands." That act again aroused American indignation. Americans claimed that it violated both the Clayton-Bulwer Treaty and the Monroe Doctrine, and Democrats in Congress attacked the treaty itself as ineffectual.

Thus, like many compromises, the Clayton-Bulwer Treaty was unpopular, but it was not, as many Americans believed, a surrender to British imperialism. In the 1850s the United States was not strong enough to defy Britain's naval power in upholding its claim to an exclusive control over a canal route through Central America. Yet with the Clayton-Bulwer Treaty the United States attained a legal equality with Britain in an area vital to its security, and in that sense, therefore, the treaty was a gain for American diplomacy.

Despite the treaty, Anglo-American rivalry continued all through the 1850s. In 1854 it sparked a minor crisis when, during disorders in Greytown, the American minister there suffered insult and a small injury. In July, an American naval officer demanded reparation and an apology. When they did not come, he bombarded the town and destroyed it. The British government considered the bombardment an outrage, one "without parallel in the annals of modern times," it said, and sought a disavowal. The United States not only refused to disclaim it, but President Franklin Pierce went so far as to defend the deed in his annual message to Congress in December.

Britain meanwhile became so deeply involved in the Crimean War, that she did not press the issue. Sharp division in American opinion also helped to ease the crisis. In particular, the British found some consolation in the denunciations of the brutal bombardment printed in the American press. Then the activities of American filibusters and capitalists in Central America led the British to believe that the United States intended to flout the Clayton-Bulwer Treaty.

As the California goldfields attracted travelers over the Central-American transit routes, American capitalists tried to profit from the heavy traffic. A group of them hauled passengers across Panama and financed a railroad there that began construction in 1850 and finished in 1855. To the north, the capitalist Cornelius Vanderbilt and some associates developed a rival route through Nicaragua. With a monopoly over the Nicaraguan route, the Vanderbilt company became a formidable competitor to the Panama line.

Violence and disorder in both Nicaragua and Panama, meanwhile, had threatened to interrupt and at times did disrupt traffic, leading to demands that the United States police the routes. Nothing came of that idea, but in 1854 William Walker, a Southern filibuster, or adventurer, often called the "grey-eyed man of destiny," added to the turmoil. He landed in Nicaragua with fifty-eight followers called "the American Phalanx" and in time, with the aid of officials of the Vanderbilt company, made himself dictator of Nicaragua.

England feared that Walker was playing the "Texas game" in Central America in violation of the Clayton-Bulwer Treaty. President Pierce recognized Walker's government in May 1856, saying he did so to make satisfactory arrangements for keeping the Nicaraguan transit route open. In June, however, Secretary of State William L. Marcy explained that Pierce had recognized Walker's government because Britain had aided that adventurer's enemies. The United States, Marcy asserted, "could not remain entirely inactive and see Great Britain obtain complete ascendancy in all the states of Central America." Yet Walker denied that he intended to annex Nicaragua to the United States. He dreamed, instead, of a federal government with himself at its head, embracing all of Central America and Cuba, but his followers thought they were fighting to bring Nicaragua into the Union. At a celebration in August 1856, for instance, they drank to such toasts, as "The American Eagle. May she drop her feathers in Nicaragua." [2]

Antislavery Northerners believed, as did the British, that Walker was trying to add more slave territory to the Union, an assumption based on impressive evidence. In September 1856 Walker decreed the reestablishment of slavery in Nicaragua and planned to revive the slave trade. The object of the decree, he said, was "to bind the Southern States to Nicaragua as if she were one of themselves." Southern expansionists were pleased and expressed approval of Walker's exploits. They had even written into the Democratic platform of June of that year that "the people of the United States cannot but sympathize with the efforts which are being made by the people of Central America to regenerate that portion of the continent which covers the passage across the interoceanic isthmus."

Walker's artificial government could not, however, last without outside support. He had made enemies of the neighboring Central-American states, which had joined in an alliance against him, and had antagonized Vanderbilt by siding with that entrepreneur's enemies in his own transit company. A vengeful Vanderbilt switched his ships to the Panama crossing and cut off Walker's supplies and the flow of recruits from the United States. In addition, he threw his support to the Central-American alliance which drove the filibuster from Nicaragua in May 1857.

Walker contributed nothing but more disorder to the jungle of Central-American diplomacy in the 1850s. The expansionist Democrat, James Buchanan, several times wanted to take advantage of that chaos by sending American troops into Central America to keep the transit routes open, but Congress would not support him. Walker tried again to take over Central America but finally died before a Honduran firing squad in September 1860 after a British officer had surrendered him to his enemies.

After Walker's downfall, Britain and the United States adjusted most of their differences in Latin America. By means of treaties with Honduras and Nicaragua in 1859 and 1860, Britain gave up her Mosquito protectorate and returned the Bay Islands to Honduras. "Our relations with Great Britain are of the most friendly character," Buchanan could therefore say in his annual message of December 1860. "The discordant constructions of the Clayton and Bulwer treaty between the two Governments," he pointed out, have been settled "entirely satisfactory to this government." [3]

The Tehuantepec Question

The transit routes across Central America were not the only ones that interested the United States in the 1850s. At the beginning of that decade many Americans considered the route across the Isthmus of Tehuantepec in Mexico the most practicable for a railroad connection between the East coast and California. Interest in that route grew out of the Mexican War. Polk had authorized Trist to pay as much as $15 million for transit rights across that isthmus, but Mexico would not include those rights in the Treaty of Guadalupe Hidalgo.

After the war, the same reasons that impelled Americans to acquire transit concessions in Central America led them to seek similar rights across Tehuantepec. In January and in June 1850 the United States signed two transit treaties with Mexico. The opposition of Mexican public opinion to any transit treaty with the United States destroyed the first agreement, and the American Senate's insistence on amendments that were unacceptable to Mexico killed the second. When the American minister in Mexico threatened to use force if a treaty were not agreed to, the Mexican minister of foreign relations said, "Your government is strong; ours is weak. You have the power to take the whole or any portion of our territory. . . . We have not the *faculty* to resist. We have done all we could to satisfy your country. . . . We can do no more."[4] If the Mexican government had surrendered to the American demands, it would have fallen immediately, so strong were anti-American passions in Mexico.

When the United States slightly modified some of its demands, the Mexican government finally signed a new treaty on January 25, 1851, and the American Senate approved it, but no Mexican congress dared accept it. Then in December Millard Fillmore's secretary of state, Daniel Webster, heard that the Mexican senate planned to give Britain the concession across Tehuantepec. He warned against it, saying that the United States "could not see with indifference that isthmus . . . under the sway of any European state."[5]

The situation in Mexico changed when Santa Anna again became president in April 1853. By that time the Tehuantepec project had become enmeshed in other Mexican-American problems. Franklin Pierce, an expansionist who had become president a month before Santa Anna had returned to power, wanted to settle all outstanding issues with Mexico. Those problems included a dispute over New Mexico's southern boundary, destructive Indian raids into Mexico from the United States—raids the United States was obligated to prevent under the terms of the Treaty of Guadalupe Hidalgo—and the Tehuantepec question. Pierce also wanted more Mexican land. He planned, therefore, to merge all those issues into a negotiation for Mexican territory. Since Santa Anna needed money to finance his despotic regime, Pierce thought that he would be willing to sell his country's land and settle the other problems for money.

The Gadsden Purchase

To handle the negotiations, Pierce appointed James Gadsden, a South Carolina politician and railroad promoter, minister to Mexico in May 1853.

Along with Jefferson Davis, the secretary of war and perhaps the most powerful man in the Pierce administration, Gadsden wanted some of the Mexican land for a proposed southern railroad to the Pacific Ocean. He arrived in Mexico City in August and immediately began negotiations with Santa Anna.

Using threats of force, Gadsden urged the Mexicans to cede a large part of northern Mexico and Baja California. American absorption of that territory, he said, was inevitable; Mexico had better sell to avoid future troubles. The Mexicans, however, would part with no more than the minimum necessary for the proposed railroad. On December 30, Gadsden signed a treaty whereby Mexico sold the southern parts of Arizona and New Mexico, including a disputed region near El Paso called Mesilla Valley, for $20 million, $15 million to be paid to Mexico and $5 million to American citizens to satisfy claims against Mexico.

The Senate added amendments that reduced the money to ten million, all to go to Mexico, annulled the provision of the Treaty of Guadalupe Hidalgo that made the United States responsible for Indian depredations, and settled the Tehuantepec question. The amended treaty gave Americans the right to use any means of transit across the Isthmus of Tehuantepec, and the American government the right to protect the transit by force. Santa Anna accepted the amended treaty and exchanged ratifications on June 30, 1854. Even he, however, could not get away with such a treaty. That sale forced his removal in August of the following year.

The Gadsden Purchase was the last acquisition from powerless Mexico, but Mexicans never forgot the land hunger of their northern neighbor. A later dictator of Mexico coined an aphorism covering his country's plight. "Poor Mexico," he said, "so far from God and so near the United States."

Annexationist Sentiment in Canada

Mexico was not the only neighbor who seemed destined for annexation during the 1850s. Canada appeared willing to join the United States of her own will. Annexationist sentiment in Canada had its roots in two related problems, one political and the other economic.

Political unrest, stemming from the two rebellions of 1837 against Canada's government, had combined with an economic depression in 1846–1847 to give strength to the movement for annexation. After the rebellions, Britain through various political reforms had given Canada a limited measure of responsible government. In Canada's general election of 1848 those reforms led to the overwhelming defeat of the Tory Loyalists, the party of merchants and professional men who had long controlled government affairs. These men took their defeat with a bitterness that expressed itself in a special hatred for the French-Canadians who had in effect voted them out.

The economic problem was related to the political one. Under Britain's mercantilist laws, Canada's products, mainly raw materials such as wheat, timber, and fish, had had a favored market in England protected from foreign competition. In 1846, England had repealed her corn laws and had opened her markets to the world without favored treatment for Canadians or anyone else. Loss of that protected market had caused serious economic distress in Canada. "Three-fourths of the commercial men are bankrupt, owing to Free-trade," Lord Elgin, who became Canada's governor general in 1847, wrote; "a large proportion of the exportable produce of Canada is obliged to seek a market in the States. It pays a duty of twenty per cent on the frontier. How long can such a state of things be expected to endure?" [6]

Some conservative Tory Loyalists, with their center of activity in Montreal, believed that annexation to the United States would solve their problem. It would, they thought, open the vast American market to their produce and bring a "new day" in their political life by making the French-Canadians an impotent minority in the population of a greater United States. The annexationists, however, were themselves a minority among Canadians. Nonetheless, they expressed their views in a manifesto "to the people of Canada" issued from Montreal early in October 1849. It called for a "friendly and peaceful separation from British connexion, and a union upon equitable terms with the great North American confederacy of sovereign states." Within a few days it gained more than a thousand signatures from Montreal's financial and political leaders.

Americans, mainly those in the North and East, followed Canada's annexation movement with approval. In 1849, for example, the Vermont legislature passed a resolution saying that the annexation of Canada "is an object in the highest degree desirable to the people of the United States." Yet these apostles of manifest destiny did not stir up a widespread annexationist sentiment in the United States, and the Whig administration of Zachary Taylor did nothing to encourage the Canadian annexationists. Taylor followed a cautious policy because the South did not want Canada. If Canada entered the Union she would add more free-soil states, making the slaveholding South a smaller sectional minority than it was. The administration, therefore, wished to avoid any action that might have caused the South to secede and split the Union.

Even Northerners who wanted Canada did not attempt to arouse popular emotions, for they saw no need to rush. They believed annexation was inevitable. The Toledo *Blade* expressed their attitude when it said that "when the fruit is fully ripe it will fall into our lap without any exertion on our part." [7]

The British government, however, opposed the annexation movement and instructed its administrators in Canada to discourage it. Those officials, such as Lord Elgin, saw in reciprocal free trade with the United States the best means of allaying the annexationist sentiment. To obtain that reciprocity they had to persuade the United States to lower its tariffs against Canadian products, but Americans would not consider doing so without gaining something in return. Specifically, Americans desired increased fishing privileges off the coast of Britain's maritime provinces and free navigation of the St. Lawrence River and Canada's canals.

Canada tried to work out some kind of legislative agreement that would meet the American terms and permit free trade, but her efforts failed because the American Congress would not reciprocate. At this time the United States was more concerned with other problems, particularly with slavery. Finally, the British decided to exert pressure to bring about a trade agreement, mainly by enforcing restrictions on American fishermen imposed by the Convention of 1818. Before 1852 British authorities in the maritime provinces had been lenient in interpreting that convention, but in that year several provinces demanded equivalent privileges from the United States in reciprocal free trade. They would not open their fisheries to Americans, beyond narrow treaty requirements, without those concessions.

In June the British ordered naval protection for their fisheries in North America to force observance of the convention and to prevent encroachments by Americans. That order, as well as the seizure of fishing vessels that violated treaty restrictions, angered Americans, particularly New Englanders. Secretary of State Daniel Webster said the British action would disrupt the "extensive fishing business of New England" and warned that it would be "attended by constant collisions of the most unpleasant and exciting character, which may end in the destruction of human life, in the involvement of the Government in questions of a very serious nature, threatening the peace of the two countries."[8] President Millard Fillmore then announced that he was willing to settle the questions of reciprocal trade, the fisheries, and navigation of the St. Lawrence River and the canals.

That suited the British, who had been willing to exchange navigation of the St. Lawrence and the fisheries for the privilege of bringing the products of their North American colonies into the United States without paying duties, but Britain and the United States could reach no agreement in 1852 and 1853. As the fishing season of 1854 approached, therefore, conflict in the northern waters appeared likely, for the United States had also sent warships to those waters to protect American interests, but with orders to avoid trouble if possible.

The Marcy-Elgin Treaty

Finally, after Secretary of State Marcy made an overture, the British sent Lord Elgin, accompanied by a commission, to the United States in May 1854 to negotiate a treaty. Elgin and his staff approached their task as accomplished diplomats. His snobbish young secretary said that the treaty they negotiated "floated through on champagne," though "a lot of senators" preferred brandy-and-water and cigars.

"Lord Elgin pretends to drink immensely," his secretary disclosed, "but I watched him [at a party], and I don't believe he drank a glass between two and twelve. He is the most thorough *diplomat* possible,—never loses sight for a moment of his object, and while he is chaffing Yankees and slapping them on the back, he is systematically pursuing that object."[9]

In the Marcy-Elgin Treaty, signed on June 5, 1854, the United States obtained almost all that it had desired in the fisheries. That agreement allowed Americans to fish the inshore waters of all the maritime provinces except Newfoundland, and in return offered British subjects the privilege of fishing along the Atlantic shore as far south as Albemarle Sound, North Carolina, at the thirty-sixth parallel. Americans, the treaty said, could use the St. Lawrence and the Canadian canals between the Great Lakes and the sea on the same terms as British subjects, while those subjects obtained free navigation of Lake Michigan.

The reciprocity provisions, of most importance to the Canadians, admitted a larger number of agricultural products, seafoods, and raw materials into both the United States and the British North American provinces duty free. This reciprocity treaty, the first the United States ever negotiated, was to run for ten years. After that, either party could terminate it with a year's notice. The Senate, won over by Lord Elgin's diplomacy, approved the treaty on August 4.

Northerners still believed that Canada would someday join the United States and that the treaty would not injure annexation. They were wrong. Reciprocity brought increased trade between Canada and the United States, ended the waning talk of annexation, helped to relive Canada's economic distress, and immediately eased tension in the fishing grounds.

Neutrality and the Crimean War

The next minor quarrel with Britain involved a violation of American neutrality growing out of the Crimean War. Heavy losses in fighting the Russians led Parliament in December 1854 to authorize the enlisting of foreigners for the British army. The British minister in the United States, John F. Crampton, and consuls in various cities worked out a scheme for obtaining soldiers in the United States by paying their expenses to Halifax in Nova Scotia where the recruits enlisted. Acting cautiously, Crampton followed American legal advice and tried not to violate the neutrality laws that prohibited recruiting in the United States for, and by, foreign countries at war. Some of his agents were not as careful. They openly advertised for recruits and violated the laws.

At first American authorities were indulgent, but when segments of the public denounced the recruiting, Secretary of State Marcy protested to the British government, which then ordered the recruiting stopped. Meanwhile, in September 1855 the American government had arrested and convicted a British agent whose trial brought out evidence implicating Crampton and British consuls in New York, Philadelphia, and Cincinnati in violations of American neutrality.

The attorney general and the government took the position that violation of domestic laws was not the basic issue. "The main consideration," he said, "is the sovereign right of the United States to exercise complete and exclusive jurisdiction within their own territory; to remain strictly neutral, if they please."[10] President Pierce asked the British government to recall Crampton and the three consuls, but it refused. On May 28, 1856, therefore, the day before the opening of the Democratic presidential convention at which he sought the nomination, Pierce dramatically expelled Crampton and revoked the exequaturs, or written orders, of the consuls.

Pierce's action caused hard feelings in England, but the British did not retaliate by dismissing the American minister in London. They did, however, delay naming a new minister to the United States for ten months, until after Pierce went out of office. When Crampton went home, moreover, he was knighted.

Sympathy for Europe's Liberals

While Americans resented Britain's interference in their internal politics they did not hesitate to meddle, or consider meddling, in European affairs. In 1848 Germans, Italians, Frenchmen, and Hungarians, motivated by liberal and nationalistic sentiments, revolted against their monarchical rulers. Most of the revolutionaries tried, or hoped, to establish republican governments. In March the people of Venice, seeking to overthrow Austrian rule, proclaimed a republic. The American consul in Turin urged the sending of "an American ship of war" to break the Austrian blockade of the city. Nothing came of the proposal, and the Austrians crushed the Venetian Republic. Similarly French troops smashed the Roman Republic, proclaimed in February 1849. Many Americans urged recognition of the Roman Republic. Margaret Fuller, a brilliant and scholarly New England writer who was early devoted to the idea of women's freedom, who committed herself to Italy's liberation, and who tended the wounded in a hospital in Rome, tried to promote American aid, but stimulated mainly sympathy. Under the leadership of Lajos Kossuth, Hungarians set up a republic in April 1849. The Austrians destroyed it too. By the following year all the liberal revolutions had failed.

Americans sympathized with all the liberal revolutionary movements, but the Italian and Hungarian struggles particularly appealed to them because in these countries rebel leaders used the American Revolution as a kind of model. American intellectuals were profuse in their admiration of

Giuseppe Mazzini, an Italian patriot who organized a Young Italy movement that was esteemed and copied throughout Europe. With the movement Mazzini hoped to liberate Italy from foreign rule and make it a republic similar to the United States. Americans also greatly admired Kossuth, and the United States had even planned to recognize his government if it could survive.

When the Austrian government learned of the contemplated recognition it protested against American interference in its domestic affairs. Daniel Webster, again secretary of state, this time under Millard Fillmore, used the protest as an opportunity to win the plaudits of American nationalists and gain support for the compromise of 1850. "I wished to write a paper which should touch the national pride," he said, "and make a man feel *sheepish* and look *silly* who should speak of disunion." [11]

In his note to Johann Georg Hülsemann, the Austrian *chargé* in Washington, Webster defended the projected recognition, upheld republican principles, and bombastically exalted the status of the United States. "The power of this republic at the present moment," he boasted, "is spread over a region one of the richest and most fertile on the globe, and of an extent in comparison with which the possessions of the house of Hapsburg are but as a patch on the earth's surface." [12] Webster pleased Americans but infuriated the Austrians. Indeed, a New York newspaper announced, "if the Austrian minister does not like our interference in the affairs of Hungary, he may go home as soon as he pleases."

The American government next turned its attention to Kossuth himself. A number of the revolutionary leaders, such as Giuseppe Garibaldi, Italy's foremost rebel nationalist, and a defender of the Roman Republic, had made their way to the United States as refugees. Garibaldi had received an American passport and had had an American corvette, which he did not use, placed at his disposal. So it was not unprecedented when the American government helped secure Kossuth's release from two years of imprisonment in Turkey, where he had fled from Hungary, and sent a naval vessel to bring him to New York where in December 1851 he received a tumultuous welcome.

When Kossuth visited Washington, he dined with President Fillmore and received a banquet from Congress. There Webster said that Americans would rejoice in seeing a model of the United States on the lower Danube and that Hungary ought to be "independent of foreign powers."

Kossuth's welcome, as well as Webster's speech, offended the Austrian government, which demanded Webster's dismissal. Fillmore refused to remove his secretary of state. As a result, American relations with Austria remained strained until Webster died in October 1852.

The only other serious friction with Austria in the nineteenth century came the following year in the case of Martin Koszta, a Hungarian refugee who had taken first papers declaring his intention of becoming an American citizen. While on a visit to Turkey, Koszta was abducted by Austrian authorities and thrown into chains aboard an Austrian brig in the harbor at Smyrna. On July 2, 1853, the commander of an American sloop of war in the harbor delivered an ultimatum to the Austrians and forced Koszta's release, an act that led to a harsh diplomatic exchange between the Austrian and American governments. Secretary of State Marcy's nationalistic, if not legally correct, defense of Koszta pleased many Americans.

This cocky nationalism in the Koszta case grew out of the excitement over liberal and nationalistic movements in Europe, such as "Young Italy," "Young Germany," and "Young Ireland," which had stimulated a radical movement in 1852 within the Democratic party called "Young America." European immigrants, particularly from Germany and Ireland, imbued with republican ideals had flocked into the Democratic party, supported the movement, and urged cooperation with republican movements in Europe. John Crampton's description of the movement is as good as any. He said "the 'Young America' or 'Manifest Destiny' Party" was composed of "those who possess extreme democratic doctrines in the usual sense of the word . . . ; and also those who urge it to be a duty, as well as the true policy of the United States to intervene in the affairs of Foreign Nations in support of Democratic & Republican Principles."

The Young America group urged a vigorous foreign policy, and Franklin Pierce had stressed such a policy in his inaugural address in order to please that wing of his party. Marcy had reflected the bumptious nationalism of Young America when in a "Dress Circular" he had asked American diplomats not to wear uniforms, but to appear in the courts of Europe "in the simple dress of an American citizen." [13] He had also told them not to employ foreigners in their legations and to use only "the American language." The aggressive foreign policy urged by the "Young America" Democrats, however, can best be seen in the efforts to acquire Cuba.

Quest for Cuba

Long before the era of manifest destiny and of Young America, some American statesmen were convinced that Cuba, and Puerto Rico also, were destined to belong to the United States. Spain appeared unable to hold very long the meager remnants of her once magnificent empire in the New World. Henry Clay had explained in 1825 what became established policy. The United States, he said, "could not see with indifference" Cuba passing into the hands of any other European power, meaning England or France. In June 1837, when the government heard rumors that Britain was negotiating with Spain for Cuba in exchange for a loan, the American minister in London had protested and reiterated American policy. He told the British foreign secretary that *"it was impossible that the United States could acqui-*

esce in the transfer of Cuba from the dominion of Spain to any of the great maritime powers of Europe." [14]

During the war with Mexico some expansionists had included Cuba among their objectives. "Cuba must be ours!" a New York newspaper had said. "We want its harbors for our ships to touch at to and from Mexico—for the accommodations of American and English transatlantic steamers—for its products and trade, and as the Grand key to the Gulf of Mexico. Give us Cuba, and our possessions are complete." [15]

After the war, Cuba, lying athwart Central-American transit routes to newly acquired California, became more than ever an object of American concern. Responding to the demands of proslavery Democratic expansionists, Polk in June 1848 offered to buy Cuba for as much as $100 million dollars. News of the projected purchase leaked and Spanish newspapers protested. The Spanish minister of state then refused to negotiate. "Sooner than see the Island transferred to *any power,*" he had said, the people of Spain "would prefer seeing it sunk in the Ocean."

During the succeeding Whig administrations of Presidents Taylor and Fillmore, the proslavery expansionists could not obtain official support for annexing Cuba. Some of them, therefore, turned to filibustering expeditions against the island with the idea of detaching it from Spain and ultimately bringing it into the Union. The leading filibuster was a Cuban exile, General Narciso López. At one time he had held high office under Spain in Cuba, but in the summer of 1848, after Spanish authorities had found him involved in a plot to overthrow their rule on the island, he had fled to the United States.

López planned to invade Cuba with a force of Americans, Cuban exiles, and various adventurers, and to arouse the people there to revolution against Spain. Most of his support came from Southerners who wanted to bring Cuba into the Union as a slave state. López organized his first expedition in New York in 1849. It was composed of the "most desperate creatures as ever were seen," a government agent said, toughs who "would murder a man for ten dollars." [16] Federal authorities broke up the expedition in September before it left the city.

Undaunted, López shifted his headquarters to New Orleans where the climate was more congenial to his plotting. Since some of the lower South's most important political leaders supported him, he had little trouble in recruiting more than five hunded men. Slipping through a cordon of American and Spanish warships, López and his band landed in Cuba on May 18, 1850, and captured the Spanish garrison at Cárdenas, but the Cubans did not rally to his banner as he had expected. The expedition then retreated before Spanish lancers and fled to Key West, Florida. Although he had failed again, the South greeted López as a hero.

President Fillmore, however, was determined to stop the filibustering. "We instigate no revolutions," he announced, "nor suffer any hostile military expeditions to be fitted out in the United States to invade territory or provinces of a friendly nation."[17] Nevertheless, López organized a third expedition, again composed mostly of Southerners, and the federal authorities failed to stop him. He landed near Havana on August 11, 1851, with over four hundred men and fell into a trap. The Spaniards captured or killed all the invaders, including López whom they garroted publicly in Havana. Before dying he shouted defiantly: "My death will not change the destiny of Cuba!"

The Spaniards also executed some of the American prisoners, including the son of the attorney general of the United States, while ultimately letting others go. The executions infuriated Southerners. Mobs in New Orleans wrecked the Spanish consulate, and in Mobile they assaulted shipwrecked Spanish sailors. Already embittered by the filibustering expeditions, the Spanish government demanded redress for the attacks and for the destruction of Spanish property. Finally, in 1852, the Spanish and American governments worked out a settlement whereby the United States apologized and paid for some of the damage.

Meanwhile, Spain had sought European help in defending Cuba against the filibusters. After the first expeditions, she had asked Britain and France several times for support and to guarantee her possession of Cuba. Although concerned about the fate of Cuba, Britain and France would not intervene directly in Spain's quarrel. After López's death, however, Britain became interested in a plan whereby she, the United States, and France would join in making a treaty declaring that none of them would try to acquire Cuba. In April 1852 the British and French formally asked the United States to agree to such a three-power treaty.

Before preparing an answer, Secretary of State Webster told the British and French ministers in Washington of "his own entire concurrence in their views with regard to Cuba," but he died without delivering a formal reply. In November, the presidential elections brought victory to Franklin Pierce and the Young America expansionists. Fillmore and his new secretary of state, Edward Everett, agreed finally to reject the proposed treaty.

In his nationalistic reply to the British and French ministers, Everett stressed the strategic significance of Cuba to the United States and said that the president would not enter the treaty because "he considers the condition of Cuba as mainly an American question."[18] Everett's note ended the Whig effort to deal with the Cuban question. Pierce and his Young America and Southern supporters next took up the question.

Pierce frankly wanted Cuba. "The policy of my Administration," he said in his inaugural, "will not be controlled by any timid forebodings of evil from expansion." Referring to Cuba, though not by name, he explained that "the acquisition of certain possessions" was "eminently important for our protection." [19] In trying to carry out a vigorous foreign policy, Pierce appointed avowed expansionists to important cabinet and diplomatic posts. Secretary of State Marcy believed that an expansionist record would help him in obtaining the next Democratic presidential nomination. Pierre Soulé, Pierce's minister to Spain, was a French-born radical from Louisiana who aspired to the leadership of Young America and who was an outspoken advocate of taking Cuba for the expansion of slave territory. He had defended and supported López and his filibusters. Soulé believed that the main objective of his mission was to acquire Cuba.

In its very first year the Pierce administration appeared to expect a filibustering expedition to free Cuba from Spain. John A. Quitman, an extreme proslavery Southerner who had been governor of Mississippi, began organizing just such an expedition in 1853. He had grandiose plans and dreamed of a southern empire of slavery that would include Cuba and Mexico. He and other Southerners feared that Spain, encouraged by England, would free slaves in Cuba and "Africanize" the island in the manner of Haiti. His filibuster would prevent that.

According to a Whig newspaper, Quitman had gathered a war chest of one million dollars, an army of some fifty thousand men, and equipment that included twelve ships, eighty-five thousand arms, and ninety field pieces by the summer of 1854. At first the Pierce administration supported his undertaking. The plan was, apparently, to make Cuba independent and then to bring it into the Union as a slave state like Texas, but Quitman and his formidable force never sailed. The politics of the slavery controversy forced the administration to withdraw its support. Still, Quitman would not abandon his project.

The events that finally led to its abandonment began on February 28, 1854, when Spanish authorities in Cuba confiscated the cargo of the American steamship *Black Warrior* for a technical violation of port regulations she had ignored with impunity on at least seventeen previous voyages. This appeared to be the needed "incident" that could serve as an excuse for war and the taking of Cuba by direct force. American excitement ran high, and on March 15 Pierce asked Congress for authority "to obtain redress for injuries received, and to vindicate the honor of our flag." [20] The time appeared ripe for strong action against Spain, for Britain and France were preparing to go to war against Russia and did so on March 28. With their military forces committed to the Crimea, they probably would not interfere with any American effort to take Cuba.

Marcy instructed Soulé in Madrid to demand an apology and $300,000 as indemnity for injuries sustained by the *Black Warrior*. The impetuous Soulé then went beyond his instructions. On April 8 he delivered the demand for an indemnity as a forty-eight-hour ultimatum. Suspecting that he had exceeded his instructions, the Spanish foreign minister ignored the ultimatum and finally settled the *Black Warrior* affair directly with the ship's owners. The Pierce administration went along with the settlement because of domestic developments.

A month earlier, on March 3, the Senate had approved the Kansas-Nebraska bill and Pierce's party then tried to force it through the House of Representatives. Since that bill favored the South and aroused intense opposition in the North, Pierce did not now dare launch a war to grab Cuba as additional slave territory. Congress, moreover, would not support him. The Kansas-Nebraska bill passed the House late in May and Pierce signed it on May 30. On the following day he issued a proclamation warning that the government would prosecute those who violated the neutrality laws. It appeared to crush what remained of Quitman's filibustering plans.

Pierce next tried to acquire Cuba through purchase and intimidation. On April 3 Marcy authorized Soulé to offer as much as $130,000,000 for Cuba. If Spain refused to sell, he told Soulé, "you will then direct your efforts to the next most desirable object, which is to detach that island from the Spanish dominion and from all dependence on any European power."[21] The administration apparently desired a revolution in Spain that would make Cuba independent. Despite Soulé's tampering with rebellion, that plan also failed. The administration then tried other methods. In August Marcy instructed Soulé to confer with James Buchanan, the minister to Great Britain, and with John Y. Mason, the minister to France, to make plans that would advance the efforts to acquire Cuba.

The three ministers met supposedly in secrecy from October 9 to 18, first in Ostend, Belgium, and then in Aix-la-Chapelle, Rhenish Prussia. They signed their report, later known as the Ostend Manifesto, on the last day and sent it to Marcy by confidential messenger. That dispatch, drafted by Buchanan from Soulé's notes, restated old arguments as to why Spain should sell Cuba and why the United States should buy it. It compared the alleged "Africanization" of Cuba to a neighbor's burning house, a fire that justified tearing down the building if there were no other means of preventing the flames from destroying one's own house. Under the circumstances, "by every law, human and Divine," it said, "we shall be justified in wresting it [Cuba] from Spain, if we possess the power."

Since the report was not a public statement of policy but a secret dispatch to the secretary of state, it was not in any sense a "manifesto." News of the meeting and of the report leaked and stimulated unsavory publicity that shocked Europeans and Americans. The Ostend Manifesto proved to be the high point of American efforts to acquire Cuba in the 1850s. The dispatch reached Washington on November 4, 1854, just as the administration suffered defeats in the mid-term congressional elections. Since the blatant efforts of the Young America diplomats to acquire Cuba contributed to those defeats, the administration retreated from its aggressive Cuban policy.

On November 13 Marcy wrote to Soulé, that "damned little French-man," repudiating the Ostend Manifesto and told him to cease efforts to buy Cuba. Since this was a repudiation of Soulé himself, the minister resigned a month later. Then the administration finally convinced Quitman to give up the filibustering plan he had never fully abandoned. Hostile congressmen forced publication of a trimmed version of the Ostend Manifesto in the following March, a publication that aroused new criticism at home and in Europe of American efforts to "steal" Cuba.

"Cuba at any cost," one newspaper headline shouted in referring to the Ostend Manifesto. Horace Greeley's New York *Tribune* called it "The Manifesto of the Brigands." "What could have got into able and intelligent men," a Democratic senator asked, "to write such a letter?" Although the criticism, blundering diplomacy, and the obvious proslavery character of Pierce's Cuban policy killed any chance of obtaining Cuba, the Democrats did not stop trying.

Pierce's successor, James Buchanan, won election on a platform that called for annexation of Cuba. An expansionist, he tried several times to interest Congress in proposals to buy the island, but with no success. With aggressive foreign policy he hoped to divert the nation from its preoccupation with slavery. "The great desire to acquire Cuba and to throw before the country a new and exciting topic, one which will override all others, and cover up the errors of this administration," a Southern diplomat wrote, "is the policy of the Democratic Party." Buchanan, like Pierce, failed in his foreign policy, particularly toward Cuba, because his policy appeared to advance the interests of slavery.

China Trade

During the decades in which the diplomacy of manifest destiny and Young America was capturing public imagination, dramatic events unfolded in the Far East that were ultimately to have a profound influence on American foreign policy. American diplomacy, while not usually at the center of those events, had a part in them. Actually, American interest in the Far East did not erupt suddenly in those decades. It had begun quietly a half-century earlier.

After losing the markets in the British empire, the newly independent American traders sought new outlets, one of which appeared to be China. The *Empress of China,* a ship of 360 tons owned by a group of New York merchants, slipped out of New York's harbor on February 22, 1784, with a cargo of ginseng, raw cotton, and furs and sailed directly for China. She returned in May of the following year with a cargo of silk, tea, and porcelain. Since the voyage brought a profit of some 25 percent of the original investment, other ships, primarily from New England, entered the

China trade. By 1800, American merchants had built a modest but profitable commerce with China.

Since those who went to China bought more than they sold, the American trade with China, like that of other Western nations, was not a balanced one. A main reason for that was China's economic self-sufficiency. The Chinese considered their civilization superior to that of the West and had far less desire for Western products than the Westerners had for their goods. The Chinese would buy a few luxury items such as the ginseng root, clocks, watches, and furs, but little else. Westerners made up the balance in their purchase of Chinese goods, such as tea and silks, by bringing great quantities of silver.

American ships usually did not sail directly for China. They would leave New England with batches of the ginseng root and cargoes of rum, kettles, hatchets, and arms. Then they would sail around Cape Horn and up the Pacific Coast as far north as the Columbia River. There, and along the way, they would barter rum and hardware with the Indians for furs, usually the pelt of the sea otter or seal. With furs and ginseng, and also kegs of silver dollars obtained on Mexico's Pacific coast, Americans sailed for China.

The Chinese, who considered Westerners barbarian inferiors and were not anxious to trade with them, restricted Western traders to the port of Canton. Within the port the Chinese government regulated commerce through a monopoly it granted to a group of merchants called the Co-hong. Americans and other foreigners could trade only with the merchants of the Co-hong and only in factories, or trading posts, located outside the walls of Canton. They could not go into the interior or even spend the night in Canton.

Despite those restrictions, American trade with China increased rapidly during the first half of the nineteenth century and reached its peak during the era of the swift clipper ship between 1850 and 1855. America's trade with China was second only to that of Britain, but it was only a small fraction of the United States's total foreign commerce. For those who participated in it, however, the profits were good, particularly after British merchants found a market for opium in China. That narcotic reversed the balance of trade. The Chinese smoked so much opium that American ships and those of other Western nations soon sailed away from China with quantities of silver as well as with silks and porcelains.

Alarmed at the loss of silver and the evils of opium, which officials said "flows and poisons the land," the Chinese government tried to enforce regulations prohibiting traffic in the drug. But British merchants, interested in maintaining their established market, urged their government to force the Chinese to continue accepting the import of opium, whether or not their own government approved. Other British interests, representing a new manufacturing class seeking enlarged markets for its goods, especially textiles, demanded that their government force the Chinese government to accept the principle of free trade for all merchants dealing in any commodities. Since the British manufacturers framed their demands in terms of free trade, they won support from manufacturers and traders in other countries and spearheaded a new international development in China.

This drive of Western commercial interests, backed by the British government, came to a crisis in 1839 when a Chinese official seized and destroyed a large stock of British opium. The ensuing controversy developed into the Opium War of 1839–1842. Victory in this one-sided struggle enabled the British to force the Treaty of Nanking of August 29, 1842, on the Chinese. That treaty, and other agreements that immediately followed, changed the international status of China and of American trade and diplomacy there.

The British compelled the Chinese to recognize them as equals and to pay not only for the destroyed opium but also for Britain's costs in fighting the war. The indemnity for the Opium War, as well as others imposed later, burdened the Chinese government with an international debt it could not pay under its existing system of taxation. In order to raise money for payment, China, with the aid of Europeans, later created a special customs service. The customs officials collected dues at the flat rate of 5 percent of the value of all goods that penetrated the country. This rate, imposed by treaty, deprived China of control over her own trade.

Beginning with the Treaty of Nanking, the British, and then other foreigners, secured the right to trade freely in four ports in addition to Canton. Since China opened them under treaties forced upon her, these became known as the "treaty ports." In the ports foreigners usually lived in international settlements or national concessions under local self-government. Since Europeans considered Chinese law barbarous, they forced the Chinese to give Western consuls in the international settlements jurisdiction over their own people and even over Chinese who brought civil suits against Europeans. Since those legal rights, known as "extraterritoriality," impinged on China's sovereignty, the treaties upholding them came to be known as the "unequal treaties."

Under a separate treaty signed in October 1843, the British established the most-favored-nation principle in China's foreign relations. That principle, of particular value to Americans, said that any privilege any country won from the Chinese would accrue automatically to other countries having treaties with them.

Unable to withstand the military power of the Western nations, China by the 1860s became something of an international colony of those powers who had merchant ships trading on her coasts and naval power to support them. Britain's victory in 1842, therefore, inaugurated a new international system for the control of that country. That pattern of unequal treaties limited China's sovereignty and gave the treaty powers special rights there that laid the basis for American commercial and diplomatic policy in China. The United States, as one of the treaty powers, profited from the system.

Negotiations with China

Before the new developments had transformed China's international status, American interest in China had been almost wholly commercial. Major Samuel Shaw, the American government's first representative in China, appointed consul in Canton in 1786, had no diplomatic status. Like all consuls serving in China before 1854, he did so without salary and his interests were commercial. The Chinese government did not officially recognize the American consuls but considered them as head merchants. Those consuls had no authority over American traders in China. Unlike the British government, the American government in the first half of the nineteenth century did little to help its traders in China.

Since the American merchants at Canton did not expect support from the government and were satisfied with the status of their trade there, the first American diplomatic mission to Asia did not even attempt to open formal relations with China. In January 1832 Andrew Jackson commissioned Edmund Roberts, a merchant from New Hampshire who had traded in the area of the Indian Ocean and had served in the consular service, as a special agent to make commercial treaties with Cochin-China, Siam, Muscat, and Japan. When Roberts arrived in Canton, the Chinese refused to recognize his official status. They ordered the American warships accompanying him to "unfurl their sails and return home; they will not be permitted to delay and loiter about, and the day of their departure must be made known. Hasten, hasten!"[22]

Roberts failed in Cochin-China but succeeded in negotiating treaties with Siam and Muscat in 1833 that opened those countries to American trade on terms of the most-favored-nation principle and with fixed tariff charges. Believing himself and his mission inadequately prepared for negotiations with the Japanese, he did not go on to Japan as planned. Instead, he returned to the United States with his two treaties. In 1835, Jackson sent him back to Asia to exchange ratifications and to negotiate a treaty with Japan. At Macao, on his way to Japan, Roberts died of the plague in June 1836. Although results of his diplomacy were meager, he had for the first time placed American trade with an Asian nation on a treaty basis.

The first American treaty with China stemmed from the Opium War and the Treaty of Nanking. During hostilities, the United States had remained neutral and had watched developments with sympathy for the Chinese, and American merchants at Canton had carried on their trade with greater profit than usual. Yet they asked for protection and the American government sent a naval squadron, under the command of Commodore

Lawrence Kearny, to Chinese waters. Six weeks after the Treaty of Nanking, Kearny asked the Chinese authorities to place Americans "upon the same footing as the merchants of the nation most favored."[23] A Chinese official assured him that American interests would be safeguarded since foreign trade would "be regulated uniformly by one rule, without the least partiality to be manifested toward any one." Although the Chinese acted on their own initiative in insisting on the most-favored-nation clause in their later Treaty of the Bogue with Britain, some writers have believed that Kearny's suggestion may have had some influence on their action.[24]

Realizing that the Treaty of Nanking had changed China's international status and the conditions of trade, American merchants in China feared that they might not be able to enjoy fully the commercial privileges the British had extorted from the Chinese. Although Americans were building their own industrial system behind tariff walls, they embraced the principle of worldwide trade. They did not wish to be excluded from trading with China on the same basis as others. Therefore, they pressed their government to open diplomatic relations with China to protect their commercial interests there. "How much of our tobacco," one congressman said in hopes of gaining more trade in China, "might be there chewed, in place of opium!"

President Tyler responded favorably to the merchants and others, and in May 1843 he appointed Caleb Cushing, a Whig lawyer of Newbury, Massachusetts, and a member of the committee on foreign affairs of the House of Representatives, the first commissioner to the Chinese empire. Cushing, who arrived at Macao in February of the following year, had instructions to obtain the same commercial privileges by treaty, without using force, that Britain had obtained through war. He was to "signify, in decided terms and a positive manner, that the Government of the United States would find it impossible to remain on terms of friendship and regard with the emperor, if greater privileges or commercial facilities should be allowed to the subjects of any other Government than should be granted to the citizens of the United States."[25]

Even though the Chinese had already granted most-favored-nation privileges to foreigners, they did not wish to negotiate another treaty. Why make a treaty, they said, "when the Americans have already been given all the advantages in trade which have been conceded to the English?" Backed by four warships and using indirect threats, Cushing nonetheless persuaded the Chinese to sign an agreement on July 3, 1844, at Wanghia, a village near Macao.

The Treaty of Wanghia gave Americans the same privileges the British had forced from China, including fixed tariff duties and most-favored-nation guarantees. Cushing also gained some privileges that went further than those of the British, particularly in the matter of extraterritoriality. The British had won extraterritorial rights only in civil matters; the American treaty extended those rights to criminal cases as well. So superior was Cushing's treaty to that of the British that through the operation of the most-favored-nation principle, it became the basic treaty for Western nations in their relations with China for the next fourteen years.

The Treaty of Wanghia, approved unanimously by the Senate, placed policy toward China on a firm foundation. It marked the end of an era of economic relations without benefit of diplomatic protection for Americans in China and the beginning of American participation in the international politics of the Far East.

After the Treaty of Wanghia, American interest in China, stimulated by the new official relations, grew rapidly. Possibilities of increased trade helped draw the attention of merchants and others to the Pacific Coast. From the Pacific shores, they said, the United States would be able to tap the riches of Asia as would no other nation, and China would provide a vast market for American products.

Then, with the acquisition of the Oregon Territory and California, Americans turned even more intently toward the Pacific and Asia. Traders, and particularly missionaries, flocked to China. They found a land racked by turmoil and controlled by an officialdom that had nothing but contempt for foreigners such as themselves. In 1849, the smoldering discontent of the masses with the rule of the Manchu dynasty burst into a long and bloody civil war called the Taiping Rebellion. Although the Taiping rebels, under a visionary leader who gave his cause a pseudo-Christian character, failed to destroy the dynasty at Peking, they conquered large parts of China and in 1853 established themselves at Nanking where they ruled for a decade. Before the Taipings collapsed in 1864, the rebellion took a toll estimated at twenty million lives.

Many Americans, particularly missionaries, at first mistakenly considered the Taiping uprising a truly Christian movement that might strengthen China and give it a new regime that would break down hostility to the West. Secretary of State Marcy, for instance, spoke of "the wonderful events in China, events which threaten the overthrow of the Tartar rule, and the establishment in its stead of a government more in accordance with the tenets of Christianity."

In time, however, American officials concluded that overthrow of the Manchus would be inimical to American interests, meaning commerce, their main concern. It appeared logical, therefore, for the American government to abandon its initial sympathy for the Taipings and to support the authority of the imperial government that had offered most-favored-nation treatment in trade.

Yet, even while imperilled by the Taipings, the imperial government's contempt for foreigners led it to evade its treaty obligations. The Treaty of Wanghia, for example, had called for direct diplomatic relations between the signatories, but Chinese officials rebuffed all advances from the

United States. Although Americans lacked the military power in Asia necessary to force their diplomats upon the Chinese, the British and the French did not. In 1857, they went to war to compel the Manchu government to carry out its agreements and give them further privileges. In the conflict called the *Arrow* War they easily defeated China.

Britain had asked the United States to join the alliance against China, but the American government refused, preferring a policy of neutrality. It did, however, send a naval squadron to Chinese waters that on one occasion met Chinese belligerence with force. Some Americans felt that the United States, like Britain and France, should have resorted to a policy of military coercion. "Diplomatic intercourse can only be had with this government," the American diplomatic official in China said, "at the cannon's mouth."[26] He recommended cooperation with Britain and France.

Although the United States had remained neutral in the fighting, it, along with Russia, sent diplomatic representatives to cooperate with the British and French in negotiating new treaties with China. The Treaties of Tientsin, signed by the four powers with China in 1858, opened eleven more ports to foreign trade and residence, enlarged the principles of the treaty settlement of 1842–1844, and conceded foreigners the right of diplomatic representation at Peking, the capital. Later negotiations legalized the traffic in opium and established the 5 percent tariff limit on imports into China. Britain's Treaty of Tientsin now became the basic document in China's international relations.

Through the most-favored-nation principle, the United States in its Treaty of Tientsin, signed on June 18, 1858, gained the privileges Britain and France had had to fight to obtain. It thus followed a policy that has been called "hitch-hiking" imperialism, one that took the benefits of British and French imperialism while incurring none of the risks. When further friction led Britain and France to renew war with China in 1859 and their troops occupied Peking, the United States again profited from concessions they forced the Chinese to make. "The English barbarians," the Chinese imperial commissioner wrote to the emperor, "are . . . full of insidious schemes, uncontrollably fierce and imperious. The American nation does no more than follow in their direction."

Although Americans did not use force in China and did not stake out their own concessions in the treaty ports, they accepted the fruits of battle. American merchants lived in the concessions held by other countries and claimed the privileges of the unequal treaties.

Another group of Americans who claimed those privileges were missionaries. Those missionaries, mostly Protestant, began arriving in China in the 1830s. Since they could not go inland and seldom at first learned to speak Chinese, they worked primarily among the Co-hong merchants and Chinese servants of the Western traders. Later, some missionaries learned Chinese, acted as interpreters for diplomatic officials, and held minor diplomatic posts. Few at that time saw virtue in China's social system. To them the Chinese were "benighted heathen," whom they somehow had to save.

The missionaries converted few Chinese but did transmit Western culture to China in a limited way. Through treaty provisions forced on the Chinese, they won the right to build churches and hospitals in China, but the protection they demanded and their aggressive tactics antagonized the Chinese. Even if they had been more circumspect, they would probably have caused trouble since their Christian religion was in effect a revolutionary force that required converts to turn against the traditional Chinese way of living and thinking.

More important than the missionaries' influence on the Chinese was their role in interpreting China to America. Through their official reports, books, and magazines they gave Americans hungry for information a special view of China and helped to create a philanthropic concern in her that was perhaps as important as the economic interest. Despite their faultfinding, they aroused a sympathy for China that influenced foreign policy and long remained with Americans.

Anson Burlingame and the Cooperative Policy

After the Treaties of Tientsin, Abraham Lincoln's secretary of state, William H. Seward, followed a policy of cooperating with the other treaty powers in China. The main principles of that cooperative policy were that the United States would not seek Chinese territory, would not interfere in China's political struggles "further than to maintain our treaty rights," and would act diplomatically with the other powers in upholding those rights. The man who inaugurated and carried out that policy was Anson Burlingame, the first American minister to reside in Peking. Burlingame, a former congressman from Massachusetts who obtained his post as a political reward, arrived in China in October 1861.

Soon after his arrival, Burlingame realized that China's weakness would encourage other Western nations to partition her. He tried, therefore, to preserve China's territory, and hence equal commercial opportunity, by working closely with the British, French, and Russian ministers in Peking. That cooperative policy, designed to safeguard American commercial interests and hold China to a strict observance of the treaties, helped keep foreign powers from taking full advantage of her weakness. Since it was based on personalities and did not appeal equally to the self-interest of all the powers, it lasted only a few years.

Burlingame's charm and efforts to help China understand the ways of the West won the confidence of the Chinese, whom he had long urged to send diplomatic representatives abroad. When he retired in 1867, therefore, they asked him, in his private capacity, to serve as a special minister abroad "for the Management of China's Diplomatic Relations"[27] with the treaty powers. Associated with him and having equal status were a Chinese and a Manchu envoy. Burlingame's own objective in this mission was to revive the cooperative policy by securing direct support from the treaty powers. He also wanted to win sympathy in the West for China.

Acting for China, Burlingame signed a treaty with Secretary of State Seward on July 28, 1868, that added eight articles to the American Treaty of Tientsin. The Burlingame Treaty reaffirmed American privileges in China, disavowed any desire to intervene there, and gave the Chinese the most-favored-nation privileges of travel, visit, and residence in the United States. That was its most significant feature, the opening of the United States to unrestricted Chinese immigration. Burlingame continued his mission to the capitals of Europe but died of pneumonia in St. Petersburg in February 1870 before completing it.

The Burlingame mission and relations with China up to that point left Americans with the impression that China was particularly friendly to the United States. "Of all the great powers who have had treaties with them," the *Nation* wrote of the Chinese, "America stands alone as their constant friend and adviser, without territorial aspirations, without schemes of self-aggrandizement—the unpretending but firm advocate of peace and justice."[28] Burlingame's successor at Peking wisely pointed out that such was not the case. The dominant attitude of the Chinese, he said, was one of "antipathy and distrust" toward all foreigners. The Chinese considered Americans, who profited from the concessions gained by British and French arms, the "accomplices in the acts of hostility committed by those powers."

Early Trade with Japan

While developing policy in China in the wake of British policy there, the United States took the lead in opening relations with Japan. Until the California rush, American interest in Japan had been incidental to commercial concern in China. When Americans did turn their attention to Japan, they found a people who had insulated themselves from the outside world for two and a half centuries.

In the sixteenth century Japan had traded with merchants from Spain, Portugal, Holland, and England, and had allowed Christian missionaries, primarily Catholic, to work among her people. At the beginning of the seventeenth century, however, a warrior clan, the Tokugawa, seized power and clamped an ironfisted dictatorship on the country. The Tokugawa isolated Japan from outside influences that might have threatened their rule.

In particular the Japanese feared the military power of the Western nations. They considered Christianity a symbol of that power, a subversive force and a menace to their rule. The Tokugawa, therefore, expelled Westerners and persecuted Christians. By 1638 they had rooted out Western influence and with blood and fire had eliminated Christianity. They left one window open to the outside world, the port of Nagasaki. After 1790 they allowed the Dutch, on the tiny island of Deshima in Nagasaki's harbor, the privilege of bringing in one ship a year.

The first American ships entered Japanese waters in the 1790s. Between 1797 and 1809, during the Napoleonic wars, the Dutch were cut off from their Japanese trade and hired American ships to make their annual voyages to Nagasaki. Then, as the China trade increased, ships sailing the great circle route from San Francisco frequently passed Japan's shores, and in the 1820s American whalers began cruising in Japanese waters. The captains of those ships wanted to use Japanese ports to take on fresh water and supplies, but the Japanese would not allow them to enter. Storms frequently wrecked American ships on Japan's rocky coasts. Since Japanese law decreed death for foreigners entering the country, officials, while not always enforcing the death penalty, imprisoned shipwrecked sailors as criminals and treated them cruelly.

In the 1830s and 1840s American traders in China tried unsuccessfully a number of times to extend their commerce to Japan. During this period the United States made several official efforts, the first being that of Edmund Roberts, to open relations with Japan, but these failed. The American government wanted the right to use a Japanese port of call for supplies for the China ships and also desired humane treatment for shipwrecked sailors. It therefore instructed Commodore James Biddle, who exchanged ratifications of the Treaty of Wanghia, to proceed to Japan and open negotiations for a treaty of commerce. Biddle sailed for Japan and in July 1846 anchored his two ships at Edo Bay, later called Tokyo, and immediately found himself surrounded by hostile ships. The Japanese rudely rejected his overtures for a treaty and warned him "to depart immediately, and to consult your own safety by not appearing again upon our coast." Biddle withdrew, his mission a failure.

Within a few years, as Americans populated the Pacific Coast, their interest in Japan, as in China, increased rapidly. The steamships, then beginning to push the sleek clipper ships from the China trade, needed coaling stations in Japan, and the traders, more than ever, wanted a foothold in Japan.

The time was ripe for forcing Japan to end her isolation. Russian and British warships were appearing in Japanese harbors, and through the Dutch at Deshima the Japanese knew of what was happening in China and elsewhere in the world. They were aware that the United States had conquered Mexico and had become a Pacific Ocean power. As ships of the Western nations converged on Japan, she appeared ready for a decided change in her foreign relations and for a remarkable internal revolution. The action of the American government triggered the change.

A naval officer who returned to the United States in 1851 after visiting Nagasaki reported that Japan was ready for a commercial treaty. We should try to make one, he recommended, "if not peaceably, then by force."[29] In March 1852, therefore, Millard Fillmore placed Commodore Matthew C. Perry in command of a naval expedition to Japan and appointed him special envoy to that country. Perry spent almost a year studying Japan from books and navigation charts he purchased from the Dutch, and in acquiring sample goods from American merchants to show to the Japanese. Then, on July 8, 1853, he led his squadron of four "black ships," two of them steamers, to the entrance of Edo Bay, his gun decks cleared for action. Although Perry's visit was no surprise to the Japanese, his steamers, belching black smoke and sailing against the wind, caused an uproar in Edo.

Perry's instructions told him to obtain a treaty that would protect shipwrecked sailors and open ports to traders and to American ships needing coal and other supplies. He also had orders to survey Japanese coastal waters if possible, to be firm, and to display "some imposing manifestations of power," but not to use force except in self-defense. When he got in touch with Japanese officials at Uraga, only twenty-seven miles from Edo, they urged him to withdraw to Nagasaki. He refused, threatened to advance directly to Edo, gave them a letter from the president addressed to the emperor, which they accepted because of his threat, and said he would return in the spring with a "larger force" for an answer. He then spent a few days surveying the waters of the bay and sailed south to pass the winter in China.

On his way south Perry took possession of the Bonin Islands. At Okinawa, in the Ryukyus, he established a coaling station and a year later, on July 11, 1854, made a treaty with the ruler of those islands, giving the United States other privileges there. Perry was an overseas expansionist who wanted the United States to take and hold the Bonins, the Ryukyus, and the island of Formosa. "I assume," he said, "the responsibility of urging the expediency of establishing a foothold in this quarter of the globe, as a measure of positive necessity to the sustainment of our maritime rights in the east."[30] Pierce's expansionist administration, ironically, rejected his proposals.

First Treaties with Japan

While Perry was in China the Tokugawa shogun, the real ruler of Japan, died and power fell to a less able successor. Perry's demand that the shogunate open the country to foreign trade threw Japanese officials into consternation. The shogunate took the unprecedented step of submitting the American proposals to the emperor at Kyoto, a mere figurehead, and his anti-shogun lords. They insisted on continuing the policy of seclusion and rejecting the demands, but the new shogun's advisers, fearing the power of Perry's ships, decided to receive the Americans amicably.

Thus, when Perry sailed into Edo Bay on February 12, 1854, with seven warships, several months earlier than he had planned because he feared Russian maneuvers in Japanese waters, he met a cordial reception. At the town of Kanagawa on March 31, Perry signed a simple treaty of friendship, Japan's first with a Western nation. It fell far short of establishing full diplomatic and trade relations, allowing Americans only a restricted trade under the immediate control of Japanese officials at two isolated ports. Japan also agreed to treat shipwrecked sailors humanely and to allow an American consul to reside at Shimoda, one of the ports.

This Treaty of Kanagawa said nothing about extraterritorial rights or a coaling station, but it allowed the United States most-favored-nation treatment and hence laid the foundation for future demands. The most significant feature of that treaty was that it ended Japan's long policy of seclusion.

Perry had not really opened Japan's doors; he merely unlocked them. Yet he set in motion forces in and out of Japan that transformed that country. His Treaty of Kanagawa served as a signal for Britain, Russia, and Holland to make similar treaties with Japan within a few months. Through the working of the most-favored-nation principle, the United States automatically obtained all the additional concessions Japan gave them.

As the Treaty of Kanagawa allowed, President Pierce in August 1854 appointed Townsend Harris consul-general to reside at Shimoda. Harris was a New York merchant of ability who had had considerable experience in Asia, and was, moreover, "a sound, reliable and influential Democrat." He had authority to negotiate a commercial treaty and was aware of the historic importance of his mission. "I shall be the first recognized agent from a civilized power to reside in Japan," he said as he approached the Japanese shore. "This forms an epoch in my life, and may be the beginning of a new order of things in Japan. I hope I may so conduct myself that I may have honorable mention in the histories which will be written on Japan and its future destiny."[31] He arrived at Shimoda aboard a warship in August 1856.

From the outset Harris encountered hostility that would have discouraged a person with less fortitude. Fearing difficulties with the people if a foreigner were stationed among them, Japanese officials asked him to return to the United States. Harris refused. Then they tried to force him to leave through harassment. The stationed guards around the temple he used as his home and obstructed his servants when they shopped. Harris, however, stayed on and through patience and tact gradually won the confidence of the Japanese.

Harris's main objective was to open the doors Perry had unlocked. Ten months after his arrival, Harris finally took a first step by persuading the Japanese to sign a convention on June 17, 1857. Basically, it clarified disputed points in the Treaty of Kanagawa and reinforced and expanded privileges, as in matters of trade and extraterritoriality, that Americans were already enjoying through the most-favored-nation principle.

While an improvement on Perry's treaty, the Convention of Shimoda still did not give the United States the commercial treaty it desired. To obtain such an agreement, Harris played on Japanese fears of Britain, France, and Russia, warning that as soon as Britain and France ended the *Arrow* War with China, they would send fleets to Japan and demand concessions by force. The United States, he said, did not want possessions in Asia. "If you accept the treaty I now offer you, no other country will demand more," he told the shogun's prime minister in January 1858. "If I display the treaty to the Europeans, they will desire to conclude identical treaties, and the matter will be settled by the mere sending over of a minister."

Therefore, the Japanese signed a full commercial treaty with the United States on July 29, aboard an American warship in Edo Bay, the first such agreement they made with any Western nation. "The pleasure I feel in having made the treaty," Harris wrote, "is enhanced by the reflection that there has been no show of coercion, nor was menace in the least used by me to obtain it."[32] The agreement opened several more ports to American trade and residence, recognized extraterritoriality for Americans in civil as well as criminal matters, established a fixed tariff, and called for diplomatic representation at the capitals of both countries by each signatory. Other Western nations quickly signed similar treaties a few months later, but Harris's carefully drawn document became the basic one in Japan's foreign relations until 1894.

Since Harris's treaty called for the exchange of ratifications in Washington, in February 1860 Japan used an American warship to carry a mission of seventy-one and the ratified treaty to the United States. Following the exchange, Abraham Lincoln appointed Harris minister to Japan, a post he held until he resigned two years later.

Meanwhile, the shogunate's efforts to enforce the American treaty and those made by other foreign nations in 1858, brought to the surface long-smoldering resentment against the Tokugawa clan. Feudal lords hostile to the Tokugawa directed some of the discontent against the government for opening the country to foreign trade and residence and part of it against the foreigners. Resentment against the Tokugawa and against the foreigners now became synonymous. "Honor the emperor—expel the barbarians" became a popular slogan, taken up especially by the emperor's court at Kyoto and the feudal clans of the west. The antiforeignism was strongest after the signing of the treaties to about 1865.

During this period the shogunate appeared to act in good faith in attempting to comply with the treaties. Understanding the difficulties confronting the shogunate, which was losing its power to the lords from the feudal clans in western Japan, Harris himself did not hold it responsible for the acts of its opponents. While the Japanese considered all treaties as "necessary evils," Harris told Secretary of State Seward, "there is no doubt that the Japanese regard us in a more friendly light than any of the other powers with whom they have come in contact." Not sharing Harris's views of the Japanese, other foreign diplomats favored a tough policy.

Seward urged a similar policy, believing that the Japanese might otherwise expel foreigners from the treaty ports. He told Harris that "very large interests, not of our own country only, but of the civilized world, are involved in retaining the foothold of foreign nations already acquired in the Empire of Japan."[33] On his own responsibility, however, Harris softened the tough policy Seward wanted.

Meanwhile, the nobles at the emperor's court in Kyoto disregarded the treaties. They decided, with the shogun as a virtual prisoner, that on June 25, 1863, they would begin once again to close the country and expel foreigners. When the shogun attempted to carry out an imperial decree to that effect, foreign diplomats warned him that their governments would resist. Harris's able successor, Robert H. Pruyn, sided with those diplomats and told the shogunate that closing the ports would lead to war with the United States, as well as with the other powers.

"You will represent to the minister of foreign affairs," Seward told Pruyn, "that it is not at all to be expected that any of the maritime powers will consent to the suspension of their treaties, and that the United States will cooperate with them in all necessary means to maintain and secure the fulfillment of the treaties on the part of the Japanese government."

Serious attacks against foreigners took place in June and July when the lord of the Choshu clan, whose holdings overlooked the narrow Straits of Shimonoseki, took upon himself enforcement of the expulsion decree by firing on American, French, and Dutch ships in the strait. An American warship, the *Wyoming,* in Yokohama at the time, then sailed to Shimonoseki and sank an armed steamer and a brig belonging to the Choshu. Pruyn believed that the prompt retaliation strengthened the hand of the shogunate and discouraged other antiforeign lords from launching similar attacks.

Nevertheless, the haughty Choshu lord remained defiant until September when an allied fleet of warships, nine British, four Dutch, three French, and one American, bombarded Shimonoseki heavily. The American ship, a rented steamer with a few guns, merely went along in a gesture of cooperation. The Shimonoseki expedition broke the back of the antiforeign movement and gave fresh courage to the vacillating shogun, who told foreign diplomats that Japan would respect the treaties. The shogunate then accepted responsibility for the Choshu incident and in October 1864 concluded a convention with the injured nations, agreeing to pay an indemnity of $3 million, of which the American share was $750,000. Since its share was in excess of the loss sustained, the United States refunded the money in 1883 in a gesture of friendship.

In November 1865 the shogunate informed the foreign powers that the emperor had at last sanctioned the treaties of 1858 and would revise tariffs downward. That weakened the antiforeign elements. In 1868 the western clans overthrew the Tokugawa shogunate and restored the emperor to nominal power. The imperial government then switched from its support of antiforeignism to a policy of encouraging increased foreign intercourse.

Principles of American Policy

American policy in Asia as it developed in the first half of the nineteenth century was based on two related principles: equal commercial opportunity and most-favored-nation treatment. In Japan, those principles helped transform the country and in China they later developed into the open door policy. Since the United States did not have a powerful navy available for duty in Asia and no property or leased holdings there, it followed a policy of hitch-hiking imperialism in China. It favored peace, free trade, and a reliance on treaties, because such a policy benefited American commerce. Yet in Japan it had not hesitated to use threats of force.

The United States cooperated with European powers and accepted the results of their imperialism because such a policy brought profits to its commerce and aided American missionary enterprise. Although many Americans have believed that the peaceful policy of abstention won friends in both China and Japan, it seems doubtful.

The policies of free trade and cooperation with European powers in the Far East were the opposites of American policies in other parts of the world. At home Americans, behind a protective tariff wall, denied other countries the right of free trade. In Latin America they upheld the principles of hands off as embodied in the Monroe Doctrine, and toward Europe they followed the principles of isolation and nonentanglement. Yet they were consistent: everywhere they followed a policy of self-interest.

X

The Civil War

While diplomats were shaping Far Eastern policy, internal politics brought the United States to its greatest crisis. Abraham Lincoln's election in November 1860 led South Carolina to secede from the Union on December 20. By February 1, 1861, Mississippi, Florida, Alabama, and Louisiana had followed her. When Lincoln became president on March 4, therefore, his main problem was the secession crisis. He made his position clear in his inaugural address. "I have no purpose, directly, to interfere with the institution of slavery in the States where it exists," he said, but added that "no State, upon its own mere motion, can lawfully get out of the Union."[1]

Lincoln's secretary of state, William H. Seward of New York, had his own ideas on how to meet the crisis. He had been Lincoln's main rival for the Republican nomination and believed that he instead of Lincoln should rightfully have been president. Convinced that he had the most ability in the administration, he considered himself a prime minister who would make policy while the untried Lincoln accepted the role of figurehead. On April 1, therefore, a mere three weeks after inauguration, Seward sent Lincoln a memorandum headed "Some Thoughts for the President's Consideration."

"We are at the end of a month's administration," Seward said, "and yet without a policy either domestic or foreign."[2] He suggested filling the gap with a policy of hostility or war against Spain, France, Britain, and Russia—one that would win back the loyalty of the seceded states and avoid a civil war. Lincoln put aside his secretary's proposal and did nothing to create foreign enemies for his government. He told Seward that he himself would conduct the government with "the advice of all the Cabinet."

Less than two weeks later, with the dawn of April 12, Southern cannon opened fire on Fort Sumter in Charleston's harbor. Two days later the tired smoke-stained garrison surrendered. On the following day, Lincoln called for seventy-five thousand militia for three months' service and for a special session of Congress. Four years of civil war had begun.

Belligerent Status for the South

Other Southern states, eleven in all, joined the secession movement. On April 19 Jefferson Davis, president of the Confederacy, offered to commission privateers to prey on Union shipping. Two days later Lincoln proclaimed a blockade of Southern ports and announced that the Union would treat privateers as pirates. Lincoln wanted to regard the war as a mere domestic quarrel, one that would not involve foreign nations and would thus avoid questions of neutral rights. Lincoln's proclamation of blockade, however, violated his own theory. The Union, according to international law, could not impose a blockade without a state of war and without placing restrictions on neutral shipping that would give the Confederacy belligerent rights.

News of Lincoln's blockade proclamation reached London on May 4, and England immediately recognized the flaw in the Union's theory. "The Northern party in fact," an English writer said, "demanded that we should recognize a state of war by admitting their blockade, and at the same time deny a state of war by treating Southern vessels as pirates." The British cabinet decided quickly to treat the civil conflict as a full-fledged war. On May 13 Queen Victoria issued a proclamation of neutrality recognizing the belligerency of the Confederacy, meaning that England accepted the South as having a responsible government capable of conducting war.

Lincoln, Seward, and the people of the North objected to Britain's neutrality proclamation first as unfriendly and then as "premature." Charles Francis Adams, Lincoln's minister to Great Britain, arrived in London just as the queen issued the proclamation. He considered it the first step toward foreign recognition of the Confederacy as an independent nation, which it was not. It was merely a customary proclamation of impartial neutrality, similar in principle to the position the United States had taken during the Canadian rebellion of 1837. Other European governments considered Britain's action proper. They followed her example and also accorded the South belligerent rights. From the beginning, therefore, the Civil War raised the old questions of maritime rights between belligerents and neutrals.

Although the maritime questions were old ones, the Civil War reversed the traditional positions of the United States and Britain. For the first time, the United States held the position of big navy power and its opponent that of small navy belligerent. For the first time England was the major neutral, and for the first time also the United States insisted on the rights of the belligerent rather than on the privileges of the neutral.

Another unique feature of the diplomacy of the Civil War was that the European nations for the first time could apply a body of international law covering maritime rights that had been adopted at the end of the Crimean War. The principles adopted in the Declaration of Paris of April 1856 abolished privateering, stated that a neutral flag covered all enemy goods except contraband, that neutral goods, except contraband, were free from capture under an enemy flag, and that a blockade was binding only if strong enough to prevent ships from entering enemy ports.

The Declaration of Paris embodied most of the neutral principles the United States had upheld since achieving independence. Yet when the European powers had asked the United States to adhere to the declaration, it had refused because it would not give up the right of privateering. At the time the United States believed that in a war with a stronger naval power it would need privateers to supplement the striking power of its small navy.

In the Civil War, however, privateering gave an advantage to the South, which had no navy. A week after Jefferson Davis said he would commission privateers, therefore, Secretary Seward offered to adhere unconditionally to the Declaration of Paris which would now benefit the Union. Speaking for the other powers as well as for herself, Britain would accept only a conditional adherence, saying that the ban on privateering would not apply during the Civil War. One reason for this statement was that the South, when approached informally about accepting the declaration, had said it would adhere to the principles of Paris except for the article on privateering.

In practice privateering did not help the South. The European nations closed their ports to both Northern and Southern ships of war and their prizes. The Confederacy, with its own ports blockaded, as a result had no ports where it could send prizes. It tried privateering in 1861, but after that year it gave up the effort; blockade-running proved more lucrative.

Seward had refused the offer of the European powers for a conditional adherence to the principles of the Declaration of Paris, but he told the British that the United States would follow them in practice. After the South's unsuccessful efforts at privateering, it also followed those principles during the course of the war.

The Question of Recognition

Agreement on maritime principles did not, however, solve the major diplomatic problem of the Civil War: would Europe, primarily England and France, recognize the Confederacy as an independent nation? The North's primary objective was to prevent such recognition. The South's aim was to win it, mainly through European political intervention. Although recognition depended more on the success of Confederate arms than on diplomacy, the material advantages to be derived from it were considered important enough to help bring victory to the South. Northern diplomacy and intelligence activities, as well as victories in battle, helped prevent such recognition.

Europe's recognition of the South's belligerency had given the Confederacy the status of a nation for purposes of fighting the war. Southern statesmen hoped from the beginning that England and France would take the next step and aid them in the same way France had helped the fighting colonies in the American Revolution. "England will recognize us," Jefferson Davis had said on the way to his inaugural, "and a glorious future is before us." With hopes high the South tried immediately to aid its armies through diplomacy. It sent agents, without official status, to Europe to work for recognition, to float loans, to spread propaganda, and to buy ships and supplies. European statesmen would not receive the Confederates officially. "I shall see the Southerners when they come," the British foreign secretary, Lord John Russell, wrote to his minister in Washington, "but not officially, and keep them at a proper distance." [3]

To add new strength to the South's diplomatic offensive, Jefferson Davis in August 1861 appointed James M. Mason of Virginia a special commissioner to England and John Slidell of Louisiana a commissioner to France to replace Confederate agents already there. Those veteran diplomats ran the blockade from Charleston to Havana, where they took passage on the British mail steamer *Trent* for the neutral port of St. Thomas in the Danish West Indies. From St. Thomas they expected to sail for England.

Capture of the Trent

Meanwhile, in the West Indies Captain Charles Wilkes, commanding the Union sloop of war *San Jacinto* recently returned from an African cruise, heard that the Confederate commissioners were on the *Trent*. On his own responsibility, as the *Trent* steamed through the Bahama channel on November 8, he overhauled her, fired two shots across her bow, and over the protests of the British captain plucked Mason and Slidell from her decks. Wilkes then took the two agents to Boston where they were imprisoned.

Wilkes's bold deed created great excitement in both England and the United States. Northerners, hungrily seeking some kind of a victory, rejoiced over the capture of two important Confederates and the insult Wilkes had given England. Cheering crowds in Washington serenaded Wilkes at his home as "the hero of the *Trent*"; the House of Representatives voted him a gold medal; and the secretary of the navy commended him for his "brave, adroit and patriotic conduct." The Northern press almost unanimously praised him. "As for Commodore Wilkes and his command," *The New York Times* said, "let the handsome thing be done. Consecrate another *Fourth* of July to him." [4]

Resenting the insult to their flag, Englishmen shook with anger. They suspected Seward, whom they distrusted, of wanting to provoke an international war and believed that Wilkes had acted under orders. Ships of the Royal Navy cleared their decks for action and eight thousand troops boarded transports for Canada. Henry Adams, a son of the American minister to Britain, wrote to his brother from London: "This nation means to make war. Do not doubt it." [5]

A Northern politician working in England to counter Southern propaganda was alarmed by London's grim excitement. "If it be not too late," he wrote to Lincoln, "let me beseech you to forbear—to turn if need be the other cheek, rather than smite back at present."

European statesmen—French, Italian, Prussian, Danish, and Russian—all agreed that the United States had done the wrong thing. Wilkes, according to international law, could stop and search the *Trent,* and if he discovered contraband, he could take the ship into port for judgment by a prize court. He compounded his blunder by taking only Mason and Slidell while allowing the *Trent,* which carried Southern diplomatic dispatches that might be considered contraband, to proceed. His act, moreover, smacked of impressment, a practice the United States had always denounced.

Although knowing little of the fine points of international law, President Lincoln grasped the difficulties of the case. At first he had been pleased by the capture, but he soon realized that his country held a weak position. He did nothing to encourage public rejoicing. "One war at a time," he told Seward. Yet the president did not like to retreat before British threats and hence sought a solution that would not appear a surrender. That was difficult. The British cabinet insisted that a "gross outrage and violation of international law has been committed." "The danger of a collision," Lord Russell told an American politician, "might be averted by the surrender of the rebel commissioners."

Prime Minister Palmerston and Russell drew up an ultimatum threatening war. When Prince Albert, Queen Victoria's dying consort, read the dispatch, he cautioned restraint and toned it down. The revised instructions sent to the British minister in Washington, dated November 30, 1861, and approved by Victoria, demanded release of the two prisoners and a suitable apology. If the United States did not indicate compliance within seven days, the minister had orders to break off diplomatic relations and return to London, but he also had private instructions not to threaten war.

Lincoln's cabinet met on Christmas Day to consider the British demands. Finally, after long discussion, all eight members agreed that the government must release Mason and Slidell. It was a wise decision. Failure to meet English demands probably would have meant war, and victory for the South. Although Lincoln feared political consequences arising from public anger over the surrender, public reaction, except for the anti-British press, was less violent than he and his advisers had expected.

One reason for the relatively calm reaction was the tone of Secretary

Seward's reply of December 26 to Lord Russell, which he immediately released to the newspapers. Seward admitted that Wilkes had made a mistake and promised to release Mason and Slidell. But, the secretary said, Wilkes had been correct in seizing the Confederates since "persons, as well as property, may become contraband."[6] This was a novel and untenable interpretation of contraband. Wilkes erred, Seward himself wrongly pointed out, in not sending the ship to an American port as a prize. In forcibly removing men from the decks of a neutral ship, Seward added, Wilkes had been guilty of doing what Britain had long practiced despite American protests.

"We are asked to do to the British nation," Seward said, "just what we have always insisted all nations ought to do to us."[7] Great Britain, according to his note, at last appeared to accept the principles of neutrality concerning impressment that the United States had defended in 1812.

Lord Russell accepted Seward's note as satisfactory, despite its masterly confusion of legal concepts, though he said he did not assent to all of the secretary's reasoning. Despite the furor the *Trent* affair had created, neither the British government nor the people really wanted a war with the United States. Such a war would have opened Canada to invasion, would have placed the British merchant marine at the mercy of American privateers, and would have aligned Britain, the leader of the world crusade to stamp out slavery, on the side of the slaveholding South. To the satisfaction of both England and the United States, Lincoln's government thus peacefully overcame its first major diplomatic crisis of the war.

That crisis brought no benefit to the South. When the Confederate commissioners arrived in England at the end of January 1862, public interest in them had almost disappeared. In referring to them the London *Times* had said, "We should have done just as much to rescue two of their own Negroes."[8]

King Cotton

The South's main diplomatic weapon, other than the power of its armies, was the coercive economic power of cotton, on which English and French textile industries were dependent. In England alone some five million people, about a fifth of the population, in one way or another relied on the textile industries for a living. The South supplied about 80 percent of England's raw cotton. The *Times* of London said that "so nearly are our interests intertwined with America that civil war in the States means destitution in Lancashire."[9] Southerners believed that England and France's dependence on their cotton would force those countries to recognize the Confederacy as independent and to end any long war by intervening on their side.

Without the South's cotton, a South Carolina senator had claimed, "England would topple headlong and carry the whole civilized world with her, save the South. No, you dare not make war on cotton. No power on earth dares to make war upon it. Cotton is king!"[10] These were the principles of the king cotton theory, a Southern article of faith comparable to the states' rights doctrine.

So much an article of faith was the theory that the South could not wait for the North's blockade to take effect. It tried to produce an immediate cotton famine with an embargo. "Let the blockade be effectual," a Southern spokesman said in the summer of 1861; "the stricter the better; the sooner will it be over; the sooner will rescue from Europe reach us; the sooner will the strong hand of the 'old country' remove our difficulties."[11] So the South at first actually welcomed the Union blockade.

In the first year of the war state and local officials in the South, and the people themselves, prevented the export of cotton. Southerners refused to plant a new crop and before the end of the war as a matter of patriotic duty had burned some two and a half million bales of cotton. Later, as its forces blockaded and occupied Southern ports, the North helped to strangle the export of cotton. During the entire war only a trickle of Southern cotton reached Europe. Yet neither England nor France, nor any other European nation, recognized the Confederacy. They did not for many reasons, but one reason stemmed from a fatal flaw in the king cotton theory.

In normal times English and French brokers stored a one-year supply of cotton, but when the Civil War began their warehouses bulged with bales good for two and a half years. Bumper crops in the years immediately preceding the war and the fact that the South had already shipped its 1860 crop had built up the surplus. Thus the war itself, the South's self-blockade, and the North's blockade came as a boon to British and French cotton brokers. They profited from the high wartime prices cotton brought. The war, in fact, saved England's cotton industry from a severe panic and in some instances turned impending ruin into glowing prosperity. A long war, therefore, worked to the advantage of cotton industrialists.

As the British and French textile manufacturers exhausted their stored cotton supplies, Europeans had found, by late 1862, substitutes in cotton from India and Egypt and in linen and woolen goods. Moreover, as its armies captured cotton, the Union made strenuous efforts to ship it to England to help alleviate the shortage.

Nevertheless, the working class suffered as thousands of English and French cotton spindles stopped. Tens of thousands of British textile operators had no work because of the "paralysis of the cotton trade." In Lancashire the mills ran half-time for a while, then two days a week, and finally they stopped. At times hundreds of hungry unemployed cotton operatives stood around the newspaper offices staring at bulletin boards, searching for news of the end of the war. In France the textile industry in fifteen departments was prostrate; 300,000 people were destitute. In Rouen alone, some 30,000 operatives out of 50,000 were unemployed.

Starving British workers, however, did not agitate for intervention in the war, mainly because they were divided in their sympathies, and because poor relief, public and private, and some supplied by Northern philanthropists, helped ease their suffering. Some favored the Union cause, viewing it as the champion of free against slave labor. But many millhands, motivated by economic self-interest, and some by conviction, sided with the Confederacy. As for France, her economic ties to the North were generally stronger than those to the South. By 1863, moreover, the war began definitely to favor the North, and other pressures for English and French intervention eased.

Some students of Civil War diplomacy have maintained that Britain did not intervene to break the cotton shortage because she considered wheat or cereals from the North more important than cotton. If Britain had intervened, that would have meant war with the United States and the consequent cessation of the flow of wheat during bad harvests. Since the British needed Northern wheat more than Southern cotton, this theory holds, they did not dare intervene. Critics of the theory have pointed out that England was able to obtain wheat from the interior of Russia and elsewhere without real difficulty. She bought it from the United States in large quantities because it was cheaper and because she could use wheat as a medium of international exchange when she sold war supplies to the Union.

Another theory, also based on economic motivation, has held that England's swollen war profits weakened the coercive power of king cotton. Both North and South bought most of their supplies from England, giving handsome rewards to her munitions makers. Soaring textile prices also offered huge gains to cotton brokers and industrialists, and to linen and woolen manufacturers. Britain's shipowners profited from the South's destruction of the Union's merchant marine, their main prewar rival. Some English shipowners even rejoiced over the war. According to the war profiteer theory, therefore, England profited from the Civil War to such an extent that she did not want to intervene and thereby kill prosperity.

Still another reason why Britain and France did not intervene was that of divided opinion among their people. Their upper classes had long believed that the American democratic experiment would collapse. "Democratic institutions," the *Times* of London said after Lincoln's election, "are now on their trial in America." The impending collapse of American democracy did not displease Europe's aristocracy. England's governing elite, for instance, had much in common with the South's planter class and little sympathy for the more democratic society of the North. "You know," an upper-class character in Disraeli's novel *Lothair* said, this Southern colonel "is a gentleman; he is not a Yankee. People make the greatest mistakes about these things." Most of Britain's leaders, men like Prime Minister Palmerston and Foreign Secretary Russell, favored the South. They were convinced at first that the South's independence was inevitable.

Britain's liberal humanitarians favored the Union. Yet even some of them wavered when Lincoln explained that he did not intend to declare war on slavery. British liberals, men like John Bright and Richard Cobden, saw the Civil War as the test of democracy and shared the desire of sections of the working classes for a Northern victory. Even though without the right to vote, pro-Union working people influenced the government through mass meetings and other demonstrations. "It is the duty of the working-men," one mass meeting resolved in January 1862, "to express their sympathy with the United States in their gigantic struggle for the preservation of the Union."

One old rhyme even had the workingmen sing:

Our mules and looms have now ceased work, the Yankees are the cause.
But we will let them fight it out and stand by English laws;
No recognizing shall take place, until the war is o'er;
Our wants are now attended to, we cannot ask for more.[12]

Mediation Offers

The attitude of Britain's upper classes toward the Civil War contributed to another crisis for the North in the fall of 1862. Secretary Seward had insisted from the beginning that foreign intervention would mean enlarging the war and that the Union would reject all offers of mediation. If Europe intervenes, he said in July 1862, "this civil war will, without our fault, become a war of continents—a war of the world." Yet after the crushing Northern defeat in the Second Battle of Bull Run, August 29–30, England's rulers were more convinced than ever that the Union cause was hopeless. On September 14, therefore, Palmerston suggested to Russell that the time had come for Britain and France to propose a joint mediation to the Union government "on the basis of a separation."

Three days later, Lord Russell replied that he agreed and suggested that "in the case of failure, we ought ourselves to recognize the Southern States as an independent State."[13] Meanwhile, General Robert E. Lee followed the Confederate victory at Bull Run with an invasion of Maryland. Union forces under General George B. McClellan stopped the Confederates on September 17 in the Battle of Antietam.

Palmerston learned of the results at Antietam at the end of September and on October 22 told Russell "that we must continue merely to be lookers-on till the war shall have taken a more decided turn." The British cabinet, therefore, voted against Russell's mediation scheme, which, if carried out, would probably have meant war with the Union.

A Southern victory at Antietam might have changed the course of the war. Instead, that battle delivered a mortal wound to Confederates chances for diplomatic recognition. Possible English intervention depended fundamentally on the success of Southern arms. Antietam, because of its diplomatic significance, was thus one of the decisive battles of the war.

Lord Russell's scheme was not the only effort at mediation. Emperor Napoleon III of France and the French upper classes also favored the Confederacy and believed that the North could not defeat the South. Napoleon had talked of mediation soon after the Civil War began. In October 1861 he had approached the British with a proposal for joint intervention to break the Northern blockade. Lord Russell would not consider it. "But we must wait," he told Palmerston on October 17. "I am persuaded that, if we do anything, it must be on a grand scale. It will not do for England and France to break a blockade for the sake of getting cotton." [14]

Napoleon was always ready to recognize the Confederacy and intervene if England would support him. He dared not risk a lone intervention because of divided opinion at home. Basically, then, the South's hopes for direct foreign intervention rested with England.

Shortly after collapse of the British mediation scheme, Napoleon made his most determined bid to intervene. Would Britain and Russia act jointly with France, he asked, in proposing a six-month armistice and a suspension of the blockade? The plan would have assured independence for the South. The North was certain to reject it. Britain and Russia would have nothing to do with it.

Later, in February 1863, Napoleon offered a friendly mediation, suggesting that Northern and Southern representatives meet on neutral ground to discuss peace terms. Seward promptly rejected the offer and both houses of Congress supported him with a joint resolution of March 3, denouncing mediation as "foreign interference." The emperor, deeply involved in Mexico, then gave up the idea of interfering directly in the Civil War.

One of the reasons Lord Russell had given for not joining Napoleon's armistice proposal, as advanced formally in November 1862 was Russia's refusal to join. Whether or not Russia participated would probably have made little difference, yet all during the war Northerners had gratefully received expressions of Russian goodwill. Russia would do nothing that would weaken the United States as a counterweight to Britain. She wanted to remain on good terms with the Union so she could use its ice-free ports as bases for cruisers in case of war with England.

This was Russia's motive when she sent her Baltic fleet to New York in September 1863 and her Pacific squadron to San Francisco in the following month. The threat of a European war over troubles in Poland, which would pit Russian ships against the British fleet, prompted the visits which ended in April 1864. Northerners viewed the naval visits as a demonstration of Russian support for the Union cause and greeted the Russians enthusiastically as friends who had come to help in time of need. The fleet visits did boost Northern morale, and even Union prestige abroad. They also contributed to the legend of long-standing Russian friendship for the United States. "God bless the Russians," the secretary of the navy had written.[15]

The Slavery Question

The issue of slavery profoundly affected diplomatic moves during the Civil War. Lincoln knew that Europe's liberals and humanitarians were disappointed because he had not converted the war into a crusade to end slavery. Southern statesmen, too, realized that a main obstacle to obtaining foreign support was slavery. As early as May 1861 the first Southern commissioners in England had reported that "the public mind here is entirely opposed to the Government of the Confederate States of America on the question of slavery, and that the sincerity and universality of this feeling embarrass the Government in dealing with the question of our recognition." Antislavery sentiment in France, a Confederate agent disclosed, was a "deep-rooted antipathy, rather than active hostility, against us."[16]

Lincoln's stand on slavery was directed toward winning the support of Republicans, War Democrats, and loyal border slave states. The effect on foreign policy was at first of secondary concern. Finally, however, he had to take European opinion into account. Since his armies had failed to conquer and the fear of foreign intervention haunted him, the president believed in the summer of 1862 that he had to take some drastic action to save the Union. Charles Francis Adams reported from London in July that a definite stand against slavery would greatly strengthen the Union position in Europe.

On July 22 Lincoln assembled his cabinet. "I have got you together to hear what I have written down," he said. Then he read a proclamation he had prepared as a war measure freeing slaves in the rebelling states. Seward suggested that the time was not right for the proclamation because of military reverses. It should, he said, be "borne on the bayonets of an advancing army, not dragged in the dust behind a retreating one."[17] Recognizing the logic of the argument, the president put the paper in his pocket and waited for the right time.

All through the summer Lincoln waited anxiously for a victory so that he could issue his preliminary Emancipation Proclamation. Although the Battle of Antietam was more a draw than a victory, he used it to herald emancipation. On September 23 newspapers carried Lincoln's announcement that on January 1, 1863, all slaves in any state in rebellion would be free. The proclamation did not apply to slaves in the border and loyal slave states.

The immediate reactions at home and abroad to the emancipation policy disappointed the Union government. Northern critics and British liberals said the proclamation did not go far enough; Southerners and their sympathizers denounced it as a desperate effort to achieve victory through the incitement of slaves to rebellion; and European skeptics pointed out that it was not a broad humanitarian gesture, but a limited war measure. A few of Britain's liberals, however, were pleased. "I wish the 1st of January to be here, and the freedom of the Slaves declared from Washington," John Bright told an audience at Rochdale. "This will make it impossible for England to interfere for the South, for we are not, I hope, degraded enough to undertake to restore three and one half millions of Negroes to slavery."

Although disappointed in the criticism of his new slavery policy, Lincoln remained firm and on January 1, 1863, issued the final proclamation. Immediate public reaction to it was mixed, but ultimately its effect abroad, particularly in England, proved decisive in winning public opinion to the North. In France liberals hailed it, and in England Charles Francis Adams reported it had created a wide sympathetic influence. "It has rallied all the sympathies of the working classes," he said, "and has produced meetings the like of which I am told, have not been seen since the days of the corn laws." Another American in London reported that "the President's Emancipation policy is working here" and more than anything else has helped prevent war with England.[18]

From many of those meetings came resolutions commending Lincoln's action. Reports from Spain, Switzerland, and elsewhere told of popular approval of his policy. Yet the Emancipation Proclamation had little immediate effect on the slaves themselves. It applied only to areas the Union government did not control and left slavery undisturbed where the government could control it.

Finally, with defeat appearing certain, the South itself offered to abolish slavery if England and France would offer recognition. In December 1864, at the suggestion of Judah P. Benjamin, the Confederate secretary of state, Jefferson Davis sent Duncan F. Kenner, a Louisiana planter, to Europe with the offer of abolition. Napoleon was willing to accept it, but not alone. "He is willing and anxious to act with England," Slidell wrote, "but will not move without her."[19] For England the offer came too late, even in the opinion of pro-Confederate Englishmen.

All during the war Southerners had been aware of Europe's hostility to slavery. This last futile diplomatic effort was an official recognition that slavery had been a serious handicap in their quest for foreign support.

The Union Blockade

Another vital factor that contributed to the South's ultimate defeat was the Union blockade. Lincoln tried to strangle the South with the greatest commercial blockade yet undertaken, stretching the Union navy over thirty-five hundred miles of coast from Alexandria on the Potomac River to the Mexican border at the mouth of the Rio Grande River. In past maritime wars, the United States had complained of Britain's wide-ranging blockades as being ineffective, as being mere "paper blockades," for under international law a blockade, to be binding on third parties, had to be effective. In other words, the blockading nation had to station enough ships outside blockaded ports to make their use clearly dangerous. The South argued, as had the United States against England, that the Union blockade was never effective enough to be binding under international law.

When the Civil War started, the blockade was in fact a blockade in name only. The Union navy had only about ninety ships on its register. Some were not seaworthy and others were old wooden sailing ships. Only twenty-four of its steamers were fit for service. Almost all the seaworthy ships were widely dispersed, but the South began the war without a navy. Thus, the North could, and did, use anything that would float and could mount a few guns as blockade ships. Later, the Union government bought and built ships for purposes of blockade and used them to cover the entire Confederate coast, with its many rivers, bays, and inlets.

Since Napoleon would not act without British support, the main problem in maintaining the blockade was whether or not Britain would respect it. "You will not insist that our blockade is to be respected, if it be not maintained by a competent force," Secretary Seward told Charles Francis Adams. But, he added, "the blockade is now, and it will continue to be, so maintained, and therefore we expect it to be respected by Great Britain."[20] Despite Southern protests and the fact that at first the blockade was ineffective, Britain accepted it as binding because her statesmen realized it was to her long-term interest to encourage the United States in upholding the principle of a loose, but legal, blockade.

As early as November 1861, the British minister in Washington said the blockade was "very far from being a mere Paper Blockade. A great many vessels are captured; it is a most serious interruption to Trade."[21] The *Times* of London pointed out that "England is too great to be often neutral, and should not forget that the arguments she might now employ against her neighbour might, we know not how soon, be retorted against herself with all the force of admissions." England, therefore, accepted Seward's reasoning that "the true test of the efficiency of the blockade will be found in its results."

Since the North could not legally blockade the ports of a neutral country, it resorted to another practice acceptable to the British, one designed to stop blockade leaks through neutral ports. It restricted neutral rights through the doctrine of "continuous voyage" first used by the British in 1805. As in the blockade itself, the United States went beyond the British practice in applying that doctrine.

Taking advantage of its immense coastline with its many shallows and indentations, the South pierced the blockade with specially constructed blockade-runners that ran all during the war and supplied Southerners with at least minimum necessities. British ships from London and Liverpool, for example, sailed for Havana, Nassau, or other neutral ports in the West Indies with blankets, arms, and ammunition. From the West Indies the small, swift blockade-runners would carry the goods to Confederate ports.

The Union navy tried to stop that trade by seizing neutral ships for breach of blockade before they reached the West Indies on the ground that the "ultimate destination" of their cargoes was a blockaded port. The United States Supreme Court in two notable opinions at the end of the war, that of the *Bermuda* in December 1865 and the *Springbok* in December 1866—both British ships—upheld the doctrine that goods sent from one neutral port to another but destined ultimately for a blockaded port, were in fact making a "continuous voyage" to the belligerent port and hence were legally subject to seizure.

In a third opinion in December 1866, that of the British merchant ship the *Peterhoff,* the Supreme Court sanctioned an enlarged interpretation of the doctrine of continuous voyage. When captured, the *Peterhoff* was on her way to Matamoros, Mexico, across the Rio Grande from Brownsville, Texas, with a cargo destined for the Confederacy. Since the goods would not go through a blockaded port and would complete the last lap of their journey overland, no breach of blockade was involved. Nevertheless, as the cargo was destined for the Confederacy, the Court said the voyage was continuous and ruled that the contraband goods in the cargo were liable to seizure.

European jurists attacked the American practice of expanding the doctrine of continuous voyage, but the British, even though they suffered most of the property losses through Union captures, did not protest. They were pleased with the American reversal on neutral rights, being again concerned with their own long-term interests.

The Confederate Navy

Although British maritime policy generally favored the Union, Northerners believed that in one important area Britain failed to fulfill the obligations of a neutral: the building of warships, and of their equipment, for the Confederacy in her shipyards and factories. One reason for the diplomatic difficulties that arose over this serious problem was that international law had not yet clearly defined a belligerent's right to build or buy warships in a neutral nation. Another reason was that Northerners resented Britain's loose interpretation of her own neutrality laws.

When the Civil War began, the South, without a navy and without its own means of building one, had planned to build one in neutral ports, primarily British. The United States had at the time one of the world's largest merchant fleets and wanted to prevent the South from creating a navy that might destroy its merchant fleet and break the blockade. Britain's neutrality law, the Foreign Enlistment Act of 1819, modeled after the American neutrality law of 1818, forbade the equipping and arming of ships in British ports for a belligerent's use. Britain's interpretation of her own law, however, allowed her shipbuilders to construct ships for belligerents if the builders did not themselves arm and equip them.

Taking advantage of England's loose neutrality laws, Captain James D. Bulloch, a Confederate agent with naval experience and a knowledge of maritime and international law, made arrangements with English firms for the building of unarmed warships for his government. During his first month in England, he made a contract for the steamer *Oreto,* supposedly a merchant ship destined for a firm in Palermo. That ship left Liverpool in March 1862 and at Nassau several months later took on British armament and equipment to become the Confederate cruiser *Florida.* On July 29, another of Bulloch's powerful ships, the *Enrica* or "No. 290," steamed out of Liverpool. Off the Azores she took on English guns and supplies, and even an English crew, and became the Confederate commerce destroyer *Alabama.*

The *Florida,* the *Alabama,* and other Confederate raiders, such as the *Shenandoah,* burned and sank over 250 Union merchant ships. By forcing shipowners to sell their ships or transfer them to foreign registry, the Confederates practically drove the Northern merchant fleet from the seas. The career of the *Alabama,* the most successful raider, in particular angered Northerners. It was, they said, a British ship, built in Britain, armed with British guns, manned by a British crew, and allowed purposely to escape from Liverpool by an unfriendly British government. Could anyone call this neutral conduct?

Charles Francis Adams had tried to prevent the *Florida* and *Alabama* from leaving England. He and the American consul at Liverpool had given evidence to British officials that the *Florida* was intended for Confederate service, but the crown's law officers said that the American minister had not presented "sufficient proof," so the ship sailed unmolested.

The case of the *Alabama,* however, was different. Adams had gathered a mass of affidavits as the ship neared completion, exposing her true character, and had given them to the proper British officials. The evidence convinced the queen's counsel, who advised "detaining the vessel." "It appears difficult," he said, "to make out a stronger case of infringement of the Foreign Enlistment Act." Then, on July 31, 1862, after a critical delay caused by the derangement of the queen's advocate, Lord Russell sent telegrams to Liverpool and nearby ports to stop the *Alabama.* He had, however, acted too late. The ship was gone.

Although Northerners believed that British officials had connived at the *Alabama's* escape and hence had violated neutrality, there was no convincing evidence to support that view. Later, Charles Francis Adams himself said that he believed Lord Russell had sincerely tried to prevent the ship's escape.

Before the *Alabama*'s escape, Captain Bulloch had contracted with her builders, Laird Brothers of Birkenhead, for two armored steamers, each to mount four nine-inch rifled guns in turrets and an iron ram, or "piercer," at the bow. Those armored ships, known as the Laird rams, would have been a greater menace to the Union than the *Alabama*.

The raiders destroyed commerce but in themselves could not determine the course of the war. Potentially more powerful than any ship in the Union navy, the Laird rams could, when completed, crush the wooden blockade ships, breach the blockade, and prolong the war.[22] The secretary of the navy said the departure of the rams must be stopped at all hazards. "We have no defense against them," he warned. "It is a matter of life and death." As the rams became ready for delivery to the Confederates in 1863 they touched off the last major diplomatic crisis of the Civil War.

The watchful Charles Francis Adams presented Lord Russell with persuasive evidence of the true character of the Laird rams and urged him to seize them immediately. Finally, on September 5, he warned that if the rams escaped, he would regard it "as practically opening to the insurgents full liberty in this kingdom" to build a navy. "It would be superfluous in me," he said, "to point out to your Lordship that this is war."[23]

The threat was unnecessary. Russell had already ordered the rams held. He told Adams on September 8 that "instructions have been issued which will prevent the departure of the two ironclad vessels from Liverpool." Later, the British government bought the rams for the Royal Navy. It had never intended allowing the rams to depart. Lord Russell had merely waited for decisive evidence before seizing them.

One reason why the British on their own initiative seized the rams was the fear of retaliation. In July 1862, at the time of the *Alabama*'s escape, Congress considered a bill empowering the president to commission privateers. The administration revived the privateering bill in January 1863 as the Laird rams crisis became serious. The bill became law on March 3. Since the South had no merchant marine that privateers could attack, it appeared that the Union intended to use a "flood of privateers" against neutral shipping, primarily British, if the blockade were broken. Lord Russell saw in this the danger of clashes with the Union that would lead ultimately to war. Then, if war came, the entire British merchant fleet would be prey to the privateers. This, in essence, was the threat used to offset that of the Laird rams.

The British government, therefore, tried a new and tighter neutrality policy. On April 5, 1863, it seized the *Alexandra,* another commerce raider intended for the Confederacy, on the ground she was about to violate the neutrality law. "The orders given to watch, and stop when evidence can be procured, vessels apparently intended for the Confederate service will, it is hoped," Russell wrote on April 7, "allay the strong feelings which have been raised in Northern America by the escape from justice of the *Oreto* and *Alabama*."[24]

By June, moreover, alarm over what future *Alabamas* might do to British commerce in a war replaced Britain's earlier satisfaction over the destruction of the rival Northern merchant fleet. In September the *Times* of London demanded that the government make the sale of warships to belligerents clearly illegal. If England were at war, it said, then "any power with a little money or credit, however otherwise insignificant, might purchase in the ports of any maritime State a squadron sufficient to occupy a large portion of our navy." For these and other reasons, including the victories of Union armies, the British enforced a more rigid neutrality policy, seized the Laird rams, and ended their last diplomatic crisis with the North.

The Laird rams crisis, however, did not end Confederate efforts to build a navy. When Britain began tightening her neutrality policy, Confederate agents, with the approval of Napoleon III, tried to build ships in France. In April 1863 Captain Bulloch and John Slidell drew up contracts for four cruisers to be built at Nantes and Bordeaux. In June, Bulloch signed a contract with a French firm for two formidable double-screw ironclad rams. If the rams had gone to sea under the Confederate flag, the American consul-general in Paris said later, "they would not only have opened every Confederate port to the commerce of the world, but they might have laid every important city on our seaboard under contribution."

Those ships never sailed for the Confederate navy. Through the activities of secret agents who bribed French clerks in the employ of business firms with whom the Confederates dealt, Union diplomats in France gathered documents showing that the ironclads were being built for the South. The Northern minister in Paris then protested and showed the emperor the indisputable evidence. Since the emperor would not now allow the ironclads to be delivered, the shipbuilders sold them to Denmark and Prussia who were at war with each other. When Denmark refused one of the rams, it finally reached the Confederates, who named it *Stonewall,* but the war ended before they could make use of it. Thus, although the French government itself had encouraged the South more than had the British government, France contributed far less to the Confederate navy.

When General Robert E. Lee met General Ulysses S. Grant in the village of Appomattox Courthouse on April 9, 1865, to discuss terms of surrender, the Union had already won the diplomatic war. The United States was fortunate in its foreign relations. The Union lost only its large merchant fleet that had already begun a decline as ships of steam and iron were replacing those of wood and sail. Union diplomacy, moreover, had proved itself competent and effective.

X I

Expansion and Arbitration

During the Civil War Spain and France attempted to regain lost influence in North America. Spain temporarily reannexed the Dominican Republic, which had won a precarious independence in 1844 after revolting against Haiti's control. Fearing that without help from a strong power independence from Haiti's Negro rulers could not last, the republic's whites had sought protection, and even annexation, at different times from Britain, France, the United States, and Spain.

Although the Spanish government did not at first seek to regain the island republic's territory, in 1860 some Spanish officials acting on their own made arrangements to take it over. Deeply involved in the slavery crisis, James Buchanan did nothing to stop the Spaniards. On March 18, 1861, therefore, the Dominican Republic's president proclaimed his country annexed to Spain. On April 2, Secretary of State William H. Seward sent a note to Spain invoking the principles of the Monroe Doctrine, threatening reprisals, and asking her to get out of the Dominican Republic.

Seward's words had no effect. Spain's queen, supported by a revived nationalism at home, on May 19 proclaimed the Dominican Republic once again Spanish territory. Spain said she would defend her hold on the island republic with all means at her disposal. Occupied with the problems of the Civil War, Seward, therefore, could do nothing more than he did on June 19; he protested the annexation as violating the Monroe Doctrine, Spain replied that she had occupied the country at the request of the Dominicans and refused to recognize the validity of the doctrine.

Within two years, when Spain's rule proved disappointing, the Dominicans revolted and asked the United States to assist them and to recognize their independence from Spain. Seward, who would not heed the insurgent pleas, followed a policy of strict neutrality toward the revolution.

Since the Union was trying to prevent European nations from recognizing and helping the Confederacy, he could not afford to recognize Dominican independence or aid the insurgents there. In reprisal, Spain might recognize the Confederacy.

Finally, guerrilla resistance, heavy costs, and yellow fever among her troops caused Spain to reverse her Dominican policy. Her last troops left Dominican soil in July 1865. Neither American threats nor fear of the Monroe Doctrine had forced Spain to end her rule; the resistance of the Dominican people was the critical factor.

In another intervention, however, Spain voluntarily accepted the Monroe Doctrine. In a quarrel with Peru, a Spanish naval squadron seized the Chincha Islands off Peru's coast in April 1864. Seward protested the seizure in May and spoke of the danger to "the general peace of nations." Spain had no designs on those islands. As soon as she heard of the seizure she disavowed it. In August her minister of state said Spain would not question the Monroe Doctrine "in or against Peru." "If President Monroe were alive and on the spot," he added, "he should see nothing running counter to his famous declaration." [1]

Triple Intervention in Mexico

While Spain intervened in the Dominican Republic, France attempted to create a puppet empire in Mexico. That effort was a far more menacing challenge to the Monroe Doctrine than anything Spain could do. The French intervention had its roots in the civil strife that had disrupted Mexico since she had achieved independence from Spain.

From 1858 to 1861, in what is known as the War of the Reform, two factions struggled for control of Mexico. One side, headed by the Zapotec Indian, Benito Juárez, was liberal, republican, anticlerical, and friendly to the United States. This faction had agreed, in the McLane-Ocampo Treaty of December 14, 1859, to make Mexico a virtual protectorate of the United States by giving it the right to intervene and exercise a police power in Mexico. The United States Senate, divided by the slavery issue, had, however, rejected the treaty in May 1860. The other Mexican faction, supported by the landed aristocracy and the church hierarchy, was conservative, fearful of the United States, and friendly to Europe. It wanted a monarchy, with some European prince on the throne.

During the Mexican civil war, guerrilla bands destroyed property owned by Englishmen, Spaniards, Frenchmen, and Americans, and killed some foreigners. Foreign governments expected Mexico to pay for those losses and also debts various Mexican governments had owed them, threatening to force payment.

Finally, the liberals emerged victorious. Juárez, in a black coach and simple black clothes, entered Mexico City as constitutional president on

January 11, 1861. For the first time, a civilian ruled Mexico. Since his administration was without money, on July 17 it declared a suspension of two years on payments to foreign creditors, though Juárez was willing to compensate for damages that could be proved genuine. Therefore, on October 31, Britain, France, and Spain signed a convention in London calling for a joint expedition against Mexico to force her to pay her debts. They said they would not take Mexican territory, tamper with her independence, or interfere with the right of Mexicans to choose their own government.

The European nations asked the United States, also one of Mexico's creditors, to join them. Secretary Seward tactfully refused. The United States, he said, preferred to avoid foreign alliances and wished to retain the goodwill of its Mexican neighbor, but, he added, the president did not question their right to use force to redress their grievances.

Spanish troops landed in Mexico in December, and in January 1862 English and French detachments joined them. After some disagreements, the three powers dissolved their alliance, and England and Spain withdrew from Mexico in May. Napoleon III, however, had plans of his own. Conservative Mexican exiles in France had convinced him that the Mexican people would welcome French troops, a monarchy, and the stability they would bring. He therefore kept his soldiers in Mexico and made impossible demands on Juárez's government. He demanded an indemnity, payment of debts to France, and redemption at face value of certain bonds a Swiss banker and owner of Mexican mines had obtained from the conservative government at about one-twentieth of their worth. Napoleon then sent to Mexico some thirty thousand fresh troops who drove Juárez's guerrilla forces before them and in June 1863 occupied Mexico City.

Maximilian in Mexico

Napoleon planned to create a Catholic monarchy in Mexico, linked to France. It would, he thought, counterbalance the United States in North America and be "an insuperable barrier" to further American expansion southward at Mexico's expense. France would benefit, he believed, through special financial privileges. He himself might at the same time win back some of the Catholic goodwill in France that he had lost in supporting Italian unification against the Pope.

As Napoleon desired, an assembly of notables, composed of Mexican conservatives, invited Archduke Maximilian, thirty-one-year-old brother of Austria's Hapsburg emperor, to become emperor of Mexico. Maximilian had insisted as a condition of acceptance that the people should vote their approval of the offer. The French occupation forces, terrorizing the liberal opposition, organized favorable plebiscites. On April 10, 1864, therefore, Maximilian, gentle-hearted but naïve, signed an agreement known as the Convention of Miramar. Napoleon had made the terms. He promised to support Maximilian with French troops until 1867. In return, Maximilian pledged himself to pay for the intervention and debts Mexico owed France.

With his beautiful young wife, Carlota, a Belgian princess, Maximilian arrived in Mexico City in June. Maximilian had grand ideas. He wanted to be a benevolent ruler who would regenerate strife-torn Mexico, but from the beginning his empire was a disappointment. Only French bayonets kept it from falling apart. Juárez's guerrilla forces still fought and controlled large areas of the countryside.

Americans, North and South, had been watching developments in Mexico with special concern. Lincoln's government disliked the French intervention but at first did nothing. It did not even register a formal protest, not daring to alienate France and thereby drive her to recognize the Confederacy. Seward himself moved cautiously. He told the American consul in Paris that "we are too intent on putting down our own insurrection, and avoiding complications which might embarrass us, to seek for occasion of dispute with any foreign power."[2]

Yet when the French asked Seward at the end of 1863 to recognize the monarchical regime that had been proclaimed in July, he refused to do so, saying that the United States would maintain strict neutrality in the war between France and Mexico. The Union continued to recognize Juárez as the head of Mexico's legitimate government, whereas most European governments recognized the empire. In his correspondence with the French, Seward did not mention the Monroe Doctrine, but its principles were implicit in many of the statements he made expressing opposition to foreign intervention.

Confederate statesmen offered to jettison the doctrine and support Maximilian in exchange for French recognition of the Confederacy's independence. Maximilian himself sympathized with the South. In January 1864 Jefferson Davis even appointed a minister to "His Imperial Majesty, Maximilian," but hoping to avoid difficulties with the Union, would not receive the Confederate agent when he arrived in Mexico. Then the Confederates threatened an "offensive and defensive alliance" with the North after the war to force Maximilian from Mexico if he and France did not recognize the Confederacy. Still, the French and Maximilian would not deal officially with the South.

In the North, meanwhile, as Union armies smashed their way to decisive victories, the government became bolder in denouncing French intervention. "Only the influence of executive moderation holds the popular action under restraint now," Seward told the American minister in France on February 8. Reflecting popular sentiment, the House of Representatives resolved unanimously on April 6 that the United States considered the French action in Mexico as "deplorable" and would not "acknowledge any monarchical Government erected on the ruins of any republican Government in America under the auspices of any European Power."[3]

"I think," the American minister in Paris told Seward two weeks later, that "the European press generally looks upon those resolutions as implying that the United States Government will not rest satisfied with the condition of things established by the French in Mexico." The French minister of foreign affairs, aware of the resolution, greeted the American minister at their next meeting with this question. "Do you bring us peace, or bring us war?" Seward assured the French that the congressional opinions were "not in harmony with the policy of neutrality, forbearance, and consideration which the President has so faithfully pursued."[4]

Maximilian and Napoleon both realized that the fate of their Mexican empire probably hinged on the outcome of the Civil War. Maximilian tried on his own, therefore, to win Union recognition through diplomacy and propaganda, hoping that Lincoln would appreciate his efforts to bring stability to Mexico. With the end of the Civil War and Lincoln's death, Maximilian's hope for accommodation died. He could expect no consideration, though he tried to obtain it, from Lincoln's successor, Andrew Johnson. On accepting the nomination for vice president, Johnson had threatened to "attend to this Mexican affair" after the war by using Union soldiers to wipe out the French. Other Americans shared his views. The Chicago *Tribune* even boasted that "California alone would drive Maximilian from Mexico if our government would give her permission."

The United States could now afford to state its policy in stronger terms. United and powerful, it had a formidable navy and a battle-hardened army. Generals Ulysses S. Grant, William T. Sherman, and others wanted to lead their veterans against the French in Mexico. American troops massed on the Mexican border, and veterans enlisted as volunteers in Juárez's forces. Seward believed, however, that he could get the French out of Mexico peacefully, through diplomacy. His tone toward France became increasingly firm.

When the French suggested recognition of Maximilian in exchange for withdrawal, Seward refused. French authority in Mexico, he said on November 6, is in direct antagonism to the policy and basic principles of the American government. That language upset the French minister of foreign affairs. "If you mean war," he asked, "why not say so frankly?"

Seward persisted. In polite terms, a month later, he asked the French to withdraw from Mexico, and on February 12, 1866, requested "definitive information of the time when French military operations may be expected to cease in Mexico." He still did not mention the Monroe Doctrine.

Napoleon, who had grown tired of the Mexican venture, announced on February 22 that he would withdraw his troops. "What I really want," he told the American minister in France, "is to get out of Mexico altogether." The intervention there was a costly failure, but he wanted to retreat as gracefully as possible and not appear openly to violate the terms of the Convention of Miramar. He had written Maximilian a month earlier that "though the departure of our troops may prove a momentary cause of weakness, it will have the advantage of removing all pretext for intervention on the part of the United States."[5] On April 5, therefore, Napoleon announced that he would pull out his troops in three detachments, one in November, another in March 1867, and the last in the following November. He withdrew, in fact, sooner than he had promised. The last French soldiers left Mexico on March 12.

Maximilian, the victim of bad advice, would not leave. Despite the entreaties of Napoleon and of friends to flee to the safety of Europe, he chose to fight to the end. Finally, Juárez captured him at Queretaro. Seward and the kings of Europe begged Juárez to spare the fallen Hapsburg, but the Indian leader insisted that Maximilian must die and serve as a warning to other would-be conquerors of Mexico. As decreed by a court-martial, Maximilian fell before a Mexican firing squad on June 19, 1867.

There are many puzzling questions in this tragedy, but one is of particular concern to American diplomacy. Did fear of the United States force Napoleon to give up the Mexican adventure? A number of circumstances apparently contributed to his decision. Since the expedition was costly and had never been popular in France, Napoleon probably tried to appease domestic critics by withdrawing his troops, which were needed in France anyhow since war with Prussia threatened. Finally, and probably most important, he could not ignore the increasing hostility of the United States and its formidable military position in North America. Whatever the precise reason for French withdrawal, it marked an impressive victory for the Monroe Doctrine.

Even though the American government had not invoked the doctrine by name, that victory won respect for the Monroe Doctrine in Europe. What had done so was not the doctrine's principles but America's increased power and knowledge that the United States could, and probably would, prevent European nations from intervening in the affairs of its neighbors. The French withdrawal also elevated the status of the Monroe Doctrine at home. From that time on the American people regarded it as a fundamental principle of national policy.

Seward in the Caribbean

While Seward had striven to ease France out of Mexico, he had also tried to carry out a program of expansion. The Civil War had, for some, buried the expansionist fervor of manifest destiny and Young America of the 1850s, but it had not destroyed the visions of empire held by Seward and others. Seward was a prewar expansionist who had written in 1846 that "our population is destined to roll its resistless waves to the icy barriers of the north, and to encounter oriental civilization on the shores of the Pacific."[6] He held similar and larger views in the 1860s, after the war. As secretary of state under Andrew Johnson he made a number of attempts to annex new territory.

Since the Union navy had encountered difficulties in controlling Confederate blockade-runners and cruisers in the Caribbean during the Civil War, Seward and American naval officers believed that the United States should acquire a naval base on one of the Caribbean islands. In January 1866 Seward took a month's cruise to the West Indies, ostensibly for his own health and for that of his son. While there, he visited islands suitable for naval bases. One that impressed him was St. Thomas in the Danish West Indies, or Virgin Islands. The fine harbor there was, in fact, his first stop.

Seward had first expressed interest in buying the three islands of that group to the Danish minister in Washington, General Waldemar R. Raasloff, about a year before the cruise. Having just lost two provinces in a war with Prussia, the Danes did not want to sell at that time. Before Seward's cruise, however, a new Danish ministry had come to power and had authorized Raasloff to negotiate a sale. The secretary returned from his cruise on January 28, and the next day began discussions with Raasloff, who suggested $20 million "as the abolute minimum price" for the islands. The negotiations dragged on and then shifted to Copenhagen. By July 1867 the United States and Denmark agreed on $7.5 million as the price for two of the islands.

Before signing a treaty ceding them, Denmark insisted on allowing the people there to vote on annexation. Seward at first objected, saying the vote would cause unnecessary delay, but finally yielded and a treaty of transfer was signed at Copenhagen on October 24.

The treaty was unpopular in the United States. Congress considered the purchase extravagant and unnecessary. On November 25 a congressman from Wisconsin offered a resolution denouncing "any further purchases of territory." The House of Representatives immediately passed it. "I intend to serve notice upon the kingdom of Denmark" the congressman said, "that this House will not pay for that purchase."[7] In the same month an earthquake and a hurricane devastated the Danish islands, leading many Americans to question more than before the alleged advantages of acquiring them.

Despite popular opposition, President Johnson and Seward went ahead with the treaty. In two plebiscites in January 1868 the people of both islands voted overwhelming approval of the annexation. At the end of that month the Danish government ratified the treaty, but in the United States the treaty could not get by the Senate, where Johnson had sent it in December.

General Raasloff, who had become Denmark's minister of war, returned to the United States in December 1868 to use his "personal influence" with the Senate. He appeared before the Senate Committee on

Foreign Relations, gave dinners for its members, and hired American propagandists to explain the alleged advantages of the treaty to the people. He wasted his efforts. The Senate committee opposed the treaty unanimously, but out of consideration for Raasloff, tabled it instead of recommending rejection.

Raasloff even sought the help of Ulysses S. Grant when Grant became president, but failed to get it. "That is entirely Seward's plan," Grant said, "with which I desire absolutely nothing to do." Later, in March 1870, the Senate Committee on Foreign Relations gave the Danish treaty an adverse report and that ended the matter.

While trying to buy the Danish islands, Seward also attempted to acquire a naval base in the Dominican Republic, on spacious Samaná Bay on the east coast of the island. Since it could command the Mona Passage into the Caribbean, American expansionists called it the "Key of the West Indies."

Expansionists, in fact, had long desired that bay. President Pierce had sent a special agent, William L. Cazneau, to the Dominican Republic in July 1854 to negotiate a commercial treaty and to buy or lease the bay. "Such a place in the occupancy of the United States, constantly resorted to by our steamers and other vessels," his instructions said, "could not fail to give stability to the Dominican Republic."[8] Cazneau obtained the treaty on October 5, but Britain and France persuaded the Dominican government to omit the cession of Samaná Bay and to make other changes. The United States would not accept the mutilated treaty and recalled Cazneau in December.

After the Spanish intervention, the republic's rulers, chronically in need of money, offered to sell the bay and then the entire country to the United States. Seward, with Johnson's support, was eager to buy. He visited the island, stopping at Haiti as well as at the Dominican Republic, on his health cruise and induced the president to say in his annual message of December 1868 that the people "of the two Republics of the island of St. Domingo" wanted to annex themselves to the United States. Haiti had not offered itself, but its ruler was willing to cede the harbor of Môle St. Nicholas and adjacent land if the United States would assume that country's debt to France.

As in the case of the Danish islands, Congress opposed the annexations. "We cannot have colonies, dependencies, subjects," the New York *Tribune* had declared in denouncing Seward's projects, "without renouncing the essential conception of democratic institutions."[9] Supporting those sentiments, the House of Representatives defeated a resolution authorizing a protectorate over Haiti and the Dominican Republic on January 13, and on February 1 voted decisively against another calling for annexation of the Dominican Republic.

Seward's plans to obtain naval bases in the Caribbean failed because legislators, absorbed in recovery from the Civil War and in industrial growth at home, would not support his expansionist program. "The true interests of the American people," the Philadelphia *Press* had said appropriately, "will be better served at this important period of our national history by a thorough and complete development of the immense resources of our existing territory than by any rash attempts to increase it."

Despite lack of popular support, not all of Seward's schemes failed. He also wanted to expand into the Pacific and tried unsuccessfully to buy the Hawaiian Islands. In 1867 he did succeed in annexing the atoll-enclosed Midway Islands, located about a thousand miles northwest of Hawaii. Seward's other annexation, Alaska, far more impressive than the tiny Midways, also took the American flag to the Pacific.

Annexation of Alaska

When Russia offered to sell Alaska, or Russian America, antiexpansionist sentiment in the United States appeared strong enough to prevent a purchase. The tsarist government wished to sell because it considered Alaska an economic liability and indefensible against a strong naval power such as Britain.

During the Crimean War, Britain and Russia had agreed to neutralize Alaska, but that conflict had convinced Russian statesmen they could not hold it in a future war. The Russian minister to the United States, Baron Edouard de Stoeckl, had recommended selling Alaska to the United States in December 1856. Other Russian statesmen did the same. The government, therefore, had instructed Stoeckl to forward any offer the United States might make for the province. He reported in January 1860 that the assistant secretary of state and a senator from California had asked him if Russia would sell Alaska. They said President Buchanan favored purchasing the province and was willing to pay as much as $5 million. Since the Russian government was not yet prepared to make a final commitment, and the Civil War intervened, nothing came of informal negotitions.

In December 1866 a council of ministers in St. Petersburg discussed the future of Alaska. Russia had administered Alaska through the Russian-American Company, a trading company whose charter had expired in 1862 and which now faced bankruptcy. If Russia wanted to retain Alaska, she either had to subsidize the company or take over direct administration of the unprofitable territory. The government decided to sell.

Since Russia wanted to strengthen American friendship and counterbalance Britain, the United States was the logical customer. The Russian government, therefore, commissioned Stoeckl, who was in Russia at the time, to return to Washington to sell Alaska for no less than $5 million, a moderate price when one considers that the Russians knew of the existence of gold there. Stoeckl was convinced that Americans would some day take over Alaska as they had Oregon and California. When they learned of the gold, he thought, they would probably swarm into the province in great numbers, and Russia would not be able to stop them. Fortunately for Russian policy, Stoeckl returned to the United States at a time when Seward eagerly sought new territories.

Seward's expansionist views did not have widespread support; except for some on the Pacific Coast, few Americans even knew of Alaska's existence. Yet in January 1866 the legislature of the Washington Territory (which had been carved out of the Oregon Territory thirteen years before) sent President Johnson a statement urging an agreement with Russia that would give American fishing vessels, whose crews wanted to buy fuel, water, and provisions, visiting privileges in Alaskan ports. Not knowing of Russia's decision to sell, Seward tried to use the petition as the means of persuading her to give up Alaska. Stoeckl arrived in New York in February 1867 and soon after dropped a hint through a friend of Seward's that Russia, if persuaded, might sell Alaska. That was all that Seward needed to move quickly.

On his arrival in Washington, about March 8, Stoeckl went immediately to the State Department. Seward brought up the fishing petition and Stoeckl assured him that Russia would not grant the desired privileges. Seward then asked if Russia would sell Alaska and Stoeckl said yes. After Seward obtained the president's approval, the two men began swift negotiations.

Seward offered $5 million; Stoeckl asked for $7 million. Realizing that the secretary had set his heart on the purchase, Stoeckl refused to lower the price. Seward finally agreed to $7 million and later offered an additional $200,000 to obtain Alaska free of all claims by the Russian-American Company. The two men then sealed the bargain, and Stoeckl used the new transatlantic cable to obtain the tsar's approval.

On Friday night, March 29, Stoeckl called the secretary of state at his home. "I have a dispatch, Mr. Seward, from my Government by cable," he said. "The Emperor gives his consent to the cession. Tomorrow, if you like, I will come to the department, and we can enter upon the treaty."

Seward, with a satisfied smile, said, "Why wait till to-morrow, Mr. Stoeckl? Let us make the treaty to-night." [10]

Then, in the middle of the night after they had aroused startled secretaries, Seward and Stoeckl went to the State Department. Lights burned steadily until four o'clock in the morning of March 30, when they signed the treaty. Later that day the president sent a special message to a surprised Senate asking approval for "a treaty for the cession of Russian America."

Seward and Stoeckl had kept their negotiations so secret that no one, except a handful of people in Washington, had suspected that the United States was seriously considering the purchase. News of Seward's treaty, therefore, surprised the American people. Newspaper editors tried hastily to uncover available information on Alaska and to comment on the treaty.

Anti-administration papers explained to an ignorant public that Alaska's only products were icebergs and polar bears. They called it "Seward's Folly," "Frigidia," "Walrussia," and "Johnson's Polar Bear Garden." "Will the newly acquired coast be erected into a territory?" the New York *Evening Post* asked. "Or are we to invent and add to our present system a colonial policy . . . ?" The New York *Tribune* said disparagingly, "We have more territory than we want." Yet most newspapers lauded the purchase and urged Senate approval of the treaty.

The Senate was hostile. Charles Sumner, chairman of its Committee on Foreign Relations, even advised Stoeckl to withdraw the treaty rather than risk rejection. Stoeckl refused. Despite antagonism, Seward believed that he could win enough popular support to force the treaty through the Senate. He launched a nationwide campaign to convince the people that Alaska was worth its price. It had, his propaganda said, known resources in fish, furs, and lumber, and its commercial and strategic importance in the Pacific Ocean area justified the purchase. Seward used another effective argument, that of Russian friendship. Since Russia wanted to sell and the administration had already agreed to buy, the argument went, America's debt of gratitude to her for support during the Civil War called for completion of the treaty.

Sumner, an expansionist who desired Canada and wished to "squeeze England out of the continent," now became the secretary's most powerful ally in obtaining Senate support for the Alaska treaty. Sumner also wished to retain Russia's friendship. "It is difficult to see," he said in a memorable three-hour speech in defense of the treaty, "how we can refuse to complete the purchase without putting to hazard the friendly relations which happily subsist between the United States and Russia." He explained too that Alaska "extends the base of commerce with China and Japan" and serves as a stepping stone to Asia.[11]

Seward also advanced four other main reasons for approving the treaty: special commercial advantages that possession of Alaska would bring to the Pacific Coast, extension of American dominion, spread of republican institutions, and Britain's exclusion from this part of the American continent. The Senate approved the treaty on the same day, April 9, 1867, by a majority of twenty-seven to twelve. So far, Seward's policy of secret diplomacy, swift action, and propaganda, had worked admirably.

One hurdle still remained. The House of Representatives had to appropriate the money. Impeachment proceedings against Johnson so delayed consideration of the appropriation that it appeared the House would not take favorable action. One reason for opposition to the appropriation arose from an alleged contract an American had made with a Russian agent to provide military supplies during the Crimean War. Since conditions of the contract were not clear, the Russian government would not pay the American. Therefore, he had advanced his claim for payment through the state department. Certain congressmen took up the inflated claim and insisted on holding up the Alaska appropriation until the Russian government agreed to pay it.

Some anti-Johnson congressmen opposed the treaty for other reasons. "Alaska, with the Aleutian Islands," a representative from New York said, "is an inhospitable, wretched, and God-forsaken region, worth nothing, but a positive injury and incumbrance as a colony of the United States." There was, however, considerable open support for it from the West Coast where men appreciated the value of the Alaskan fisheries with their abundant codfish, halibut, and salmon. A number of West Coast representatives also stressed that possession of Alaska would aid trade in the Pacific.

While trying to win support for the treaty, Stoeckl spent large sums on publicists, lobbyists, and on propaganda, and even bribed congressmen. He reported to his own government that he had spent most of the $200,000 that had been added to the purchase price for "secret expenses."

The American government, meanwhile, had already taken formal possession of Alaska and raised the flag over Sitka on October 18, 1867. When the House of Representatives was ready to take final action in the summer of 1868, it was thus confronted with an accomplished fact. "Shall the flag which waves so proudly there now be taken down?" a congressman asked. "Palsied be the hand that should dare to remove it! Our flag is there, and there it will remain." This proved a decisive argument. On July 23 the House approved the appropriation.

Unlike other continental annexations, there was never any popular demand for Alaska, yet Seward's "educational campaign" had undoubtedly convinced a number of Americans that Alaska would be an economic asset and had created some public support for the purchase, particularly among those who believed it was a bargain the government should not pass up. In a few decades the returns to the American people from gold production, from the fisheries, and from furs alone far surpassed the purchase price. Later, Alaska and its adjacent islands, stretching far into the Pacific, were recognized as being invaluable strategic assets. "Seward's Folly," a majestic domain of nearly 600,000 square miles, more than twice the size of Texas and almost equal to one-fifth of the rest of the United States, has proved a bargain second only to the purchase of Louisiana.

Agitation for Canada

In urging the acquisition of Alaska, Seward and other Republican expansionists had argued that it would bring the annexation of Canada one step closer. This argument was nothing more than the renewal of an old but apparently still popular demand. On July 2, 1866, for instance, an expansionist had gone so far as to introduce a bill in the House of Representatives making provision for Britain's North American provinces to come into the Union. "I know that Nature designs that this whole continent, not merely these thirty-six states," Seward himself claimed in a speech in Boston in June 1867, "shall be, sooner or later, within the magic circle of the American Union."

Although related to the annexationist agitation of the 1840s and 1850s, this renewed demand for Canada stemmed in part at least from Union resentment against Britain during the Civil War. "Let them [the British] remember, however, that when the termination of our civil conflicts shall have arrived," the New York *Herald* had warned six years earlier, ". . . Four hundred thousand thoroughly disciplined troops will ask no better occupation than to destroy the last vestiges of British rule on the American continent, and annex Canada to the United States." [12]

Northerners channeled some of the hostility they felt for Britain against Canada, even though Canada and Britain's other North American provinces at first sympathized with the Union. One reason for this ill feeling was that the Civil War had created some special problems in relations with Canada and had even reopened some old grievances. Canadians resented the fact that Northerners openly recruited or forced their young men into the Union army. When Union military police invaded Canada to take back deserters, Canadian authorities protested and resisted, but those resentments appeared minor in comparison with Northern anger against Canada.

Most Northerners believed that Canada, like England, had sympathized with the Confederacy. They resented this, but what angered them more was the use Confederate agents had made of Canadian soil. Early in the Civil War Canada became a refuge for Confederate soldiers who escaped from Northern military prisons. Later in the war Confederate agents raided Union border towns, using the British provinces as their bases. They made their biggest raid near the end of the war. Under orders of the Confederate War Department, some twenty Confederates fell upon the tiny village of St. Albans, Vermont, on October 19, 1864. They set fires, robbed banks, wounded two people, killed one, and fled back across the border.

This raid inflamed Northern public opinion as nothing had since the *Trent* affair. Lincoln's government had talked earlier of giving Britain the required six-month notice terminating the Rush-Bagot Agreement. Now the government decided to act. Confederate activities on the Great Lakes and the "insufficiency of the British Neutrality Act," Seward said, compelled the United States to take that step, which, however, was never completed, since the Civil War was drawing to a close and the Union had not placed any armaments on the lakes. In March 1865, therefore, Seward told the British that his government was willing to allow the Rush-Bagot Agreement to remain in effect, and the British agreed.

The Marcy-Elgin Treaty of 1854 did not survive the accumulated grievances of the war. Reflecting public sentiment, the New York *Herald* had said, "it becomes one of the first duties of the new Congress to manifest its resentment at the unfriendly and dishonest treatment by doing away with the treaty under which Canada derives such advantage from us."[13] Congress passed a joint resolution in January 1865 calling for repeal of the reciprocity treaty, and the president then gave Britain the necessary six-month notice of termination.

With this notice, expansionist newspapers, such as the Philadelphia *Press* and Philadelphia *Inquirer,* reported "a growing feeling in Canada in favor of annexation to the United States." The Toronto *Globe,* two years later, charged Seward with abrogating the treaty to facilitate the annexation of Canada.

Even though many Americans believed that the inevitable destiny of the British in provinces of North America was union with the United States, most Canadians did not want to become Americans. True, some Canadians still saw in annexation a solution to their economic and social problems, but theirs was a minority view. Sentiment for annexation was generally localized and sporadic. Annexationist agitation in the United States, in fact, strengthened Canadian nationalism and the movement toward confederation in Britain's North American provinces.

Some Canadians believed that American expansionists were so intent on annexation that they encouraged a society of Irish-Americans, called the Fenian Brotherhood, to invade Canada. Although the organization began in 1858 in New York, with the aim of forcing Ireland's independence from Britain, its activities did not reach threatening proportions until 1866. In that year the Fenians launched a series of raids into Canada with the idea of annoying England and involving the United States in a war with her that might lead to Irish independence. Some Fenians even talked of conquering Canada.

The Fenians held conventions in the United States, organized a government for their future republic, raised uniformed "armies," and even had an anthem, the "Fenian Marseillaise." It went:

> Away with speech, and brother, reach me down that rifle gun
> By her sweet voice, and hers alone, the rights of man are won
> Fling down the pen; when heroic men, pine sad in dungeons lone,
> 'Tis bayonets bright, with good red blood, should plead before the throne.[14]

Radical Republicans encouraged the Fenians in order to embarrass Andrew Johnson; Democrats courted the Irish vote, and some Americans considered the Fenian assaults just reprisal for the Confederate raids of the Civil War. The American government allowed the Fenians to demonstrate and did not prevent their raids. "In fact this Fenian demonstration is probably winked at by the U.S. Government," the Montreal *Gazette* remarked, "in the hope that it may produce terrorism in these colonies, which may favour their annexation projects; but in this they again commit an error, which will put further off the desired object." [15]

The Fenians made their first large incursion in May 1866 when eight hundred of them, mostly Civil War veterans, crossed the Niagara River from Buffalo and occupied the Canadian village of Fort Erie. They defeated a force of inexperienced Canadian volunteers but then retreated before organized military forces. The Canadians suffered twelve dead and the Fenians eight, plus other casualties. President Johnson did not issue a proclamation forbidding violations of the neutrality act until five days after the raid.

Four years later the Fenians staged their last raid from St. Albans. "Fenians," their leader said, "the eyes of Ireland are upon you." Seventy-five Canadians drove back two hundred of them at the border with one volley of rifle fire. Before the smoke had cleared, the United States marshal from Vermont dashed among the Fenians and arrested their "general" for violating the neutrality law.

Since the United States had tolerated the Fenians for years, Canadians believed there would have been no raids if the government had tried seriously to prevent them instead of acting after the invasions began. In comparison to the vigilant action of their own government against Confederate raiders, the American enforcement of neutrality laws seemed amazingly lax. The Canadian government had paid promptly for the damage of the St. Albans raid, but the United States had ignored Canada's bills for the damages inflicted by the Fenians. Some Americans, like Charles Sumner, took the view that the British flag in Canada had caused the Fenian troubles. If England would withdraw and allow the United States to annex Canada, they said, the threat of Fenian incursions would end.

Fenian activity and annexationist agitation in the United States in 1866 had been sufficiently menacing to solidify the movement for confederation in the British provinces, a movement expansionists did not like. The House of Representatives objected in a resolution in May 1867, but the Canadians went right ahead. Under the British North American Act of 1867, which went into effect on July 1, they formed a nation, the Dominion of Canada. Ironically, fear of the United States, of expansionism, and support of Fenian threats, had given Canadians the final impulse to form the national union.

Johnson-Clarendon Convention

While Canada was demanding payment for Fenian damages, the United States insisted on compensation for losses it had suffered in the Civil War because Britain had been lax in enforcing her neutral obligations. As early as October 1863 Charles Francis Adams had asked Lord Russell to arbitrate claims arising from the depredations of the *Alabama* and other Confederate cruisers. Russell refused. In 1865, when the United States wanted to discuss the *Alabama* claims, covering losses from all Confederate raiders, Russell, who was then prime minister, again refused. "England," he said, "would be disgraced forever if a foreign government were left to arbitrate whether an English secretary of state had been diligent or negligent in his duties."

Russell resigned in June 1866 and a more conciliatory government came to power. It reflected the view of many Englishmen who felt that previous governments had been shortsighted in ignoring the American claims. They realized the danger when the House of Representatives voted unanimously in July to modify the neutrality laws so as to permit Americans to sell ships to belligerents. If the Americans changed their neutrality laws and if Britain went to war, say with Russia, cruisers built in America flying the flag of the tsars might destroy the British merchant fleet.

Aware of those ominous possibilities, the new British foreign secretary offered to arbitrate the *Alabama* claims. Since Seward insisted on including Britain's alleged "premature" recognition of the Confederacy as a grievance and the British would not consider debating whether or not that recognition was justifiable, negotiations collapsed.

In 1868 a new British ministry under William E. Gladstone came to power, and Reverdy Johnson, a former senator from Maryland, succeeded Adams as minister to Britain. Johnson arrived in London in August and immediately tried to conciliate the British, but his impolitic speeches infuriated radical Republicans in the Senate.

"I like some things that Mr. Reverdy Johnson says," a friend wrote to Senator Sumner, "but he made a terrible mistake in calling Mr. Roebuck his friend, and shaking hands with him and Mr. Laird—Roebuck had done everything in his power to break up the American Union." Roebuck had been Parliament's chief advocate for recognition of the Confederacy, and Laird was the unrepentant builder of the *Alabama*.

Under precise instructions from Seward, Johnson worked out an agreement with the British known as the Johnson–Clarendon Convention. Signed on January 14, 1869, it covered all claims held by both sides since 1853 but offered settlement for individual claims only, without recognizing the indirect losses Americans had suffered from the Confederate raiders. It contained no apology for the *Alabama*'s escape. For those reasons and others essentially political, the Senate rejected it on April 13 by a vote of fifty-four to one.

On that same day, before the Senate had voted, Charles Sumner denounced the agreement and attacked England in a long speech. The convention, he said, included only a small part of England's wartime debt to the United States. He presented three bills. The first, for direct damage wrought by Confederate sea raiders, he estimated at $15 million. The second, for indirect damage to the merchant fleet from increased insurance rates and loss of revenue from commerce driven from American ships, amounted to $110 million. And the third, for England's "premature" recognition of belligerency and aid to the South which allegedly had doubled the duration of the war, he estimated at half the cost of the Civil War, or $2 billion. His total bill amounted to a staggering $2.125 billion. Although Sumner did not say it, what he sought in payment was Canada.

Sumner's speech, published in newspapers and in pamphlet form, received wide circulation and stimulated excitement on both sides of the Atlantic. Rather than cede Canada to pay for the bloated claims, the British were willing to fight. Sumner's swaggering speech and the rejection of the Johnson–Clarendon Convention aroused widespread resentment in Britain, blocking further negotiation over American claims. The most serious obstacle was British conviction that Sumner's ideas represented the policy of Ulysses S. Grant's new administration.

Even though President Grant in May 1869 appointed a close friend of Sumner, the historian John Lothrop Motley, minister to Britain, Sumner's ideas did not, as he himself thought they would, dominate the administration's foreign policy. Grant's capable secretary of state, Hamilton Fish of New York, like Sumner desired Canada, but he took firm control of foreign policy and followed a discreet course.

When Motley, contrary to Fish's instructions, presented the views of Sumner's speech to the British as the basis of administration policy, Grant decided quickly that "Motley must be dismissed at once." Fish agreed that Motley deserved dismissal but persuaded the president to retain him. By keeping Motley, the secretary tried to avoid further discredit to the Grant administration in England and an immediate rupture with Sumner. Therefore, Fish merely reprimanded Motley and told him to inform the British that whenever they wished to renew discussion of the *Alabama* claims, they should take the negotiations to Washington. In this way Fish bypassed Motley.

Hamilton Fish obtained his opportunity to renew negotiations on July 8, 1869, when Sir John Rose, a distinguished Scotsman and Canada's minister of finance, visited him. Rose had come to Washington to discuss a number of Canada's problems, particularly trade reciprocity. "At dinner," Fish told his diary next day, "Mr. Rose and I conversed on the subject of the *Alabama* Claims, etc."[16] Rose wanted to settle those claims as well and suggested that Britain might send a special mission to Washington to negotiate an agreement.

Upon his return to England, Rose discussed the *Alabama* claims and other American questions with leading statesmen there who were now prepared to adopt a more conciliatory policy. In July 1870 the Franco-Prussian War erupted, and in October Russia took advantage of it by repudiating provisions of the Treaty of Paris of 1856 that limited her fleet on the Black Sea. War between Russia and Britain appeared probable. In such a conflict, British statesmen feared, *Alabamas* built in America might swarm over the seas against their shipping. For those and other reasons the British were now willing to negotiate.

As Fish suggested, Grant's annual message announced that when Britain wanted a settlement of the claims controversy, the United States would consider it "with an earnest desire for a conclusion consistent with the honor and dignity of both nations."[17] Grant also referred to disputes with Canada. When the British decided to negotiate, therefore, they agreed beforehand to lay the basis for a general arbitration covering Canadian-American differences as well as the *Alabama* claims. The *Times* of London expressed widespread sentiment, saying that "this constant speculation, this supposition that war may come is half as bad as war itself. What we want is settled peace and the conviction that peace will remain until there is just and sensible cause for war."

In rejecting the Johnson–Clarendon Convention, the United States had injured British pride, and Britain could not with dignity reopen negotiations directly. She first sent Rose to Washington unofficially on a confidential mission. He arrived in January 1871. The British government, he told Fish, was willing to place all matters in dispute before a joint commission empowered to make a settlement by treaty. The United States agreed.

A month later, on February 27, a joint high commission held its first meeting in Washington. On the commission were five Americans headed by Secretary Fish, four British, and one Canadian statesmen. After meeting formally thirty-seven times, the commissioners signed a treaty on May 8.

Treaty of Washington

The Treaty of Washington contained four main problems to be settled by arbitration. Its foremost agreement covered the *Alabama* claims. In it the British expressed regret "for the escape, under whatever circumstances, of the *Alabama* and other vessels from British ports, and for the depredations committed by those vessels."[18] The treaty called for an international tribunal of arbitration consisting of five men that would meet in Geneva to settle the *Alabama* claims.

To facilitate the settlement, the British agreed to three rules defining neutral obligations that were to guide the arbitrators. The first said that a neutral government had to use "due diligence" to prevent ships, which it believed intended to make war on another nation, from arming and leaving its ports. Secondly, it had to prevent any belligerent from using its ports as bases for naval operations or sources of supplies, arms, or recruits. Thirdly, it had to exercise "due diligence" over all persons in its jurisdiction to prevent violation of those obligations.

Those rules were not part of international law at the time of the Civil

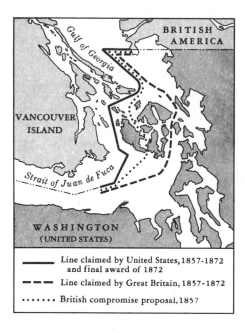

THE SAN JUAN ISLANDS
CONTROVERSY, 1872

War. Since they were retroactive, Britain in effect made an advance surrender of her case. She did that to establish precedent for the future. The
treaty said nothing about indirect claims, but the British commissioners
were convinced the United States had abandoned them.

The second major provision, which the Canadians considered the most
important of all, covered American fishing rights in Canadian waters. The
fisheries dispute stemmed from American abrogation of the Marcy-Elgin
Treaty in 1866. Canada had wanted to renew the treaty, but the United
States, committed to a policy of high protective tariffs, had rebuffed overtures for any kind of trade reciprocity. Canadians, therefore, retaliated with
tariffs of their own on American coal, lumber, bread, and other items.
Their most serious reprisal excluded Americans from the rich inshore
fisheries and denied them the right to buy bait and provisions in Canadian
ports. In January 1870 Canada's government had abolished previously generous privileges for American fishermen and had returned to the restricted
privileges of the Convention of 1818, enforcing them to the letter.

Under the Treaty of Washington Americans secured the right to use
the Canadian fisheries for at least ten years, and Canadian fishermen obtained similar rights along the American coast to the thirty-ninth degree of
north latitude. Since the United States obtained the larger advantages, the
treaty provided for an international arbitration commission to decide on
how much it should give Canada in additional compensation.

The third main question embraced by the treaty was a controversy in the Northwest over a group of islands, the largest of which was San Juan, in the channel separating Vancouver Island from the mainland. Since terms of the Oregon treaty defining the boundary were vague, the United States and Britain had long argued over who rightfully owned the islands. The Washington Treaty turned the San Juan controversy over to the German emperor for arbitration.

Less significant than the other three, the fourth agreement called for a mixed commission to settle other British and American claims distinct from the *Alabama* claims, particularly those arising from American seizure of British property during the Civil War. Since the British agreed to compensate Canada separately for damages arising from the Fenian raids, the Canadians did not press those claims during negotiations, and the treaty said nothing about them.

Americans were pleased with the treaty. The New York *Tribune* called it a "triumph of American principles and American diplomacy." It received Senate approval without much trouble in May 1871 by a vote of fifty to twelve. Canadians called it a "betrayal" of their interests, and one of their newspapers said it was a "wanton sacrifice of honour" and a "disgraceful capitulation." [19] Yet, after long debate, their parliament approved it.

As the Treaty of Washington provided, the five men comprising the international tribunal of arbitration selected to settle the *Alabama* claims met in Geneva on December 15 to hear the arguments. Boldly and unexpectedly the American case revived the claim for indirect damages, demanding payment of the full cost of the Civil War after the Battle of Gettysburg with 7 percent interest.

The British reacted angrily to the "enormous and intolerable" demands. Since they had assumed that claims for indirect damages were dead by mutual agreement, they accused the United States of trickery and refused to allow the arbitrators to consider them. Prime Minister Gladstone told Queen Victoria on January 30 that the American case presented claims and pretensions "such as it is wholly incompatible with national honour to admit or to plead to before a Tribunal of Arbitration." If the United States did not give up its swollen claims, the British press urged, the government must abandon the arbitration.

Secretary Fish had included indirect claims because he feared the Senate and public opinion, which, he thought, would cry out in protest against any case that did not include them. Merely by presenting the inflated demands he could satisfy them, forestall criticism, and allow the tribunal to reject them once and for all.

Despite British protests, therefore, Fish would not withdraw the exaggerated claims. "We are content to let the Tribunal pass upon the indirect claims," he told the British minister in Washington, "and if it rejects them we shall make no complaint; but we will never allow Great Britain or any other Power to dictate what form our Case shall take or what claims we shall advance."[20] Since Fish insisted on the indirect claims as a matter of political necessity and the British government, as a matter of national honor and political necessity, refused to consider them, the arbitration appeared doomed.

"It is all over. This is the end of the Treaty," the American minister in London said after a sleepless night. "Very well, sir," his ardent young secretary answered. "We shall fight Great Britain: and, thank God, we are ready for it!"[21]

Finally, five months later, as panic hit the stock markets and Americans and Englishmen again muttered words of war, statesmen groping for peace found a solution. Charles Francis Adams, the American member of the tribunal of arbitration, persuaded the other arbitrators to consider the indirect demands, even though those claims were not within their jurisdiction. In an extrajudicial or "advisory" opinion in June 1872, the tribunal declared the indirect claims invalid under recognized rules of international law and thus ended the controversy. Fish accepted the declaration, the British agreed to present their case, and the arbitration continued.

The tribunal held its final session on the afternoon of September 14 and announced its decision. Britain, it said, according to the rules of "due diligence" was responsible for the damage the *Alabama,* the *Florida,* and the *Shenandoah* had wrought and awarded the United States an indemnity of $15.5 million. Sir Alexander Cockburn, the British arbitrator scowled, refused to sign the award, and filed a dissent. After the tribunal finished its work, applause filled the crowded hall, but Cockburn did not listen. He snatched his hat and rushed to the door. The British government itself did not protest the award. A year later it gave the United States a check for the full amount.

None of the other arbitrations under the Treaty of Washington created a major diplomatic crisis. In the case of the San Juan Islands, the German emperor in October 1872 decided on a boundary that gave the disputed islands to the United States.

After meeting in Washington and Newport, Rhode Island, over a period of two years, the general claims commission in September 1873 dismissed all American claims and awarded the British $1,929,819, primarily for illegal seizures of British property, imprisonment, and other losses during the Civil War.

After long delay, the fisheries commission, composed of three arbitrators, met in Halifax in June 1877 to hear American and Canadian arguments. In November it awarded Canada $5.5 million to compensate for fishing privileges conceded to the United States. Americans considered the sum excessive, and their commissioner, like Cockburn, refused to sign the award and filed a dissent, but the United States paid.

"While nearly every other nation of the world settles its difficulties with other powers by the dreadful arbitrament of the sword," the Halifax commissioners said in final judgment of the Treaty of Washington, "England and America, two of the most powerful nations upon the earth, referred their differences to peaceful negotiation and made an epoch in the history of civilization." The commissioners exaggerated somewhat. Yet the Treaty of Washington, with its arbitrations, was a noteworthy victory for diplomatic negotiation. Although it did not dispel all frictions, it ended an era of ill will in relations with Britain and Canada and ushered in a decade of peace undisturbed by claims, recurring border clashes, and boundary disputes.

Grant and the Dominican Republic

The Treaty of Washington, the outstanding accomplishment in the Grant administrations, was not typical of Grant's own approach to foreign affairs. Usually he left matters of foreign policy to Secretary of State Fish, but in the case of the Dominican Republic he himself took an active interest. Soon after assuming office, Grant fell under the influence of speculators who wanted to annex the Dominican Republic for their own gain. The president also set his heart on the annexation, he explained later in memoirs, because he wished to send blacks where they could be "governed by their own race."

To take up where Seward had left off and to lay the basis for another annexation agreement, Grant sent his military secretary, General Orville E. Babcock, to the island in July 1869 as a special executive agent. Even though Babcock possessed no diplomatic powers, he signed an informal agreement on September 4 committing the United States to annex the Dominican Republic and to pay $1.5 million to cover its public debt, or to buy Samaná Bay for $2 million. He also pledged the president "privately to use all his influence" with Congress in winning acceptance for the idea of annexation. The agreement, made according to Fish's instructions, was little more than a memorandum embodying the terms of annexation, but Grant and the Dominican president considered it virtually a treaty.

Although not as enthusiastic about Babcock's agreement as Grant was, Fish sent Babcock back to the Dominican Republic with two draft treaties. The first provided for annexation of the republic as a territory with promise of ultimate statehood. The Dominicans had to agree to annexation by plebiscite, which they did. As an alternative, the second treaty gave the United States a ninety-nine-year lease of Samaná Bay with an annual rental fee and with the right of purchase at any time for $2 million. Since Babcock still had no diplomatic powers, a consular agent signed the two treaties for the United States on November 29.

Grant was so anxious to gain Senate approval of the treaty that on Sunday evening, January 2, 1870, he called on Sumner at his home.

"Now, I am told that you are chairman of the Judiciary Committee, before whom such matters come," Grant said, "and that if you will aid it the thing can be accomplished." Sumner corrected the president several times, informing him that he was chairman of the Foreign Relations Committee. Before Grant left, he erroneously thought he had won Sumner's support for the acquisition. On January 10, therefore, the president sent the two Dominican treaties to the Senate.

Using whatever influence he could exert, Grant lobbied in person for the annexation treaty. He would summon senators and ask their support. "I hear you are a member of the Senate Committee that has the San Domingo treaty under consideration," he told one, "and I wish you would support that treaty. Won't you do that?"[22] Despite the president's pressure, most senators disliked the treaty. After long debate, the Senate killed it on June 30. The Senate did not vote on the second treaty.

Sumner's opposition infuriated Grant. Since he regarded Sumner as chiefly and treacherously responsible for the treaty's defeat, he retaliated by immediately removing Sumner's friend Motley from his post in London. Later, in March 1871, Grant used his influence to depose Sumner as chairman of the Foreign Relations Committee.

Grant did not give up easily. He tried in several ways to revive the annexation scheme but could not or would not bypass Congress. In October 1871 the Dominican minister of foreign relations suggested a lease of Samaná Bay through an executive agreement that would not require Senate approval. "I will not be a party," Grant said, "to any such arrangement." He was now resigned to the fact that the Dominican question was unpopular. "We will drop the matter," he added, "and leave the whole question for Congress and the people." "Thus," a pleased Hamilton Fish told his diary, "a troublesome, vexatious, and unnecessary question is, as I trust, finally got rid of."

Forestalling Intervention in Cuba

Even more vexing than the Dominican question were problems raised by a rebellion in Cuba, called the Ten Years' War, that began in the fall of 1868. The rebels declared their independence from Spain in October and formed a shadowy provisional government for a republic. When Grant took office, no one knew how well organized the rebel government was or how effective its fighting forces. Soon, however, it became clear that the rebels had no organized army but fought the Spaniards in savage hit-and-run guerrilla warfare.

Cuban exiles and refugees in the United States stimulated sympathy for the rebel cause. Those Cubans, their American friends, and many newspapers urged intervention to aid the rebels. Since the Cuban government was little more than a shadow, Secretary of State Fish opposed intervention. He could not, under international law, justify recognizing it as a belligerent and much less as the government of an independent nation. He had, moreover, criticized England's "premature" recognition of Confederate belligerency and could hardly, with far less justification, recognize Cuban belligerency.

To forestall the interventionists, Fish offered to mediate the "civil war" in July 1869. He urged Spain to give Cuba independence for payment by the Cubans of an indemnity of about $150 million guaranteed by the United States. Spain delayed acceptance and finally the mediation plan died. Grant, anxious to recognize Cuban belligerency partly because he considered it proper revenge for Spanish recognition of Confederate belligerency during the Civil War, decided to take matters into his own hands.

One of the staunchest advocates of intervention was General John H. Rawlins, secretary of war and a close friend of Grant. He apparently persuaded the president to recognize Cuban belligerency, for on August 14, 1869, Grant asked Fish to proclaim neutrality and hence recognition, but the secretary put aside Grant's signed proclamation. Rawlins died on September 6, thus easing the pressure on Grant and Fish for recognition. Occupied with the problem of the Dominican Republic and other matters, the president forgot about his proclamation. Fish even persuaded him, in his annual message in December, to say that the rebellion in Cuba "has at no time assumed the conditions which amounted to a war in the sense of international law, or which would show the existence of a *de facto* political organization of the insurgents sufficient to justify a recognition of belligerency."

Most Republicans in Congress did not like the president's words; they preferred intervention. In February 1870 they began massing support for a joint resolution calling for recognition of Cuban belligerency. Public reaction, particularly as reflected by the New York press, appeared to favor the congressional interventionists.

Fish was alarmed. Recognition probably would mean war with Spain. He asked the unpredictable president, therefore, to fight the interventionist offensive by sending a special message, which Fish wrote, to Congress denouncing the folly of recognition. If Grant would not go ahead with the declaration, he said, he would resign. Grant yielded and on June 13 sent the message, one of his ablest, to Congress. "The question of belligerency," he said, "is one of fact, not to be decided by sympathies for or prejudices against either party. The relations between the parent state and the insurgents must amount in fact to war in the sense of international law."

When a resolution calling for recognition came to a vote in the House of Representatives three days later, it failed. Fish's policy had won a victory, and for three years the intervenionist tide receded.

The Virginius *Affair*

From the beginning of the war in Cuba the United States had been embarassed by filibustering expeditions that rebels and their American sympathizers had launched from American soil. More than once those expeditions had touched off nasty incidents. The most serious occurred in October 1873 when a Spanish gunboat captured the *Virginius,* a rebel steamer flying the American flag, on the open sea between Cuba and Jamaica. The Spanish captain brought the ship into Santiago and there, after hasty court-martial trials, the authorities shot as pirates fifty-three of the passengers and crew, some of them Americans and Englishmen. More executions would probably have followed if the commander of a British warship, the *Niobe,* had not hurried to Santiago from Jamaica and threatened to bombard the city if the killings did not stop.

Some Americans clamored for war. Even those who had cared nothing for the Cuban rebels now resented the insult to their flag. The government strengthened coastal fortifications and prepared the navy for hostilities. Yet most Americans appeared to demand redress, not war. On November 14, Fish telegraphed a virtual ultimatum to the Spanish government, demanding a salute to the American flag, release of the *Virginius* and her survivors, payment for the killings, and punishment of guilty officials. If Spain did not meet those demands, he said, the United States would sever diplomatic relations. The next step would be war. "If Spain cannot redress the outrages perpetrated in her name in Cuba," Fish said later, "the United States will." [23]

Fish soon learned that the *Virginius* belonged to Cubans, was fraudulently flying the American flag, and was carrying arms and filibusters contrary to American law. Therefore, he dropped the demand for a salute to the flag. Nonetheless, since no recognized state of war existed and the Cuban rebels did not have belligerent rights, Spain had no authority under international law to seize the ship on the seas.

Spain released the *Virginius* and the surviving prisoners, admitted that the seizure had been illegal, and in May 1875 paid an indemnity of $80,000 to go to the relatives of the executed Americans. The American people apparently accepted the *Virginius* settlement as fair.

The continuing butchery in Cuba led the United States to make one more effort to intervene. In November Fish asked the Spanish government to end the war by giving Cuba self-government. If Spain did not, he said, "the time is at hand when it may be the duty of other governments to intervene." [24] He sent copies of his proposal to England and the other principal nations in Europe asking that they too exert pressure on Spain to make peace.

Spain then made necessary concessions and promised specific reforms, but not self-government. The European governments, meanwhile, would not support Fish's proposal. At home, critics said Fish's approaches to the European nations violated the spirit of the Monroe Doctrine. Thus, the plan for cooperative intervention failed.

In 1878, Spain forced peace in Cuba and promised further reforms, such as colonial autonomy. Yet there was no true peace, merely a long truce. The reforms proved inadequate, and the Cubans were still determined ultimately to win their independence.

XII

Pugnacious Diplomacy

During the 1880s and 1890s the Department of State dealt with a number of problems that in themselves may be considered minor but when lumped together reveal a new pattern of behavior in international affairs. This pattern shows that foreign affairs were assuming an increasingly complicated role in the conduct of national policy. It suggests that despite the varied nature of most of those problems, they *either* stemmed from or were involved in issues of domestic politics, *or* the policymakers, and even the people, exhibited a fresh brashness, a pugnacious and at times a scarcely restrained nationalism, a kind of chip-on-the-shoulder attitude toward even minor issues of foreign policy. In some instances, both characteristics, prominent in the diplomacy of the eighties and nineties, can be seen in the American approach to a single problem.

Toward an Interoceanic Canal

This sharpened sense of national concern for status in the world, while evident in Seward's and Grant's expansionist projects, can also be discerned in the government's changed attitude toward building a canal across Central America. In the decades following the Civil War the government had shown a quickening interest in such a canal. In June 1867 Seward had concluded a treaty with Nicaragua that gave the United States transit rights across that country, but rights that were not exclusive. Two years later, in January 1869, he negotiated the first canal treaty with Colombia. Since Columbia's concessions were restricted, the Senate refused consent to ratification.

With the opening of the Suez Canal in the following November, and the subsequent transformation of communications and trade between Europe and Asia, public interest in a Central-American waterway mushroomed.

Grant himself took an interest in the project. "The subject of an interoceanic canal to connect the Atlantic and Pacific oceans through the Isthmus of Darien," he announced in his first annual message, "is one in which commerce is greatly interested." [1] Other presidents had favored a canal under international control, but he was the first to declare his support for a waterway owned and controlled exclusively by the United States.

Hamilton Fish now took up where Seward had left off and in January 1870 made another treaty with Colombia, one that gave the United States sole right to construct a canal across Panama. Since the Colombian senate added unacceptable amendments, that treaty, too, collapsed.

After United States naval survey expeditions had explored possible canal routes, as called for by a Senate resolution of March 1872, Grant appointed an interoceanic canal commission to evaluate the work of individual survey parties and recommend the best route for a waterway. Four years later it reported a unanimous decision in favor of a route through Nicaragua.

American interest in a canal now lagged for a few years. In 1879 when Ferdinand de Lesseps, the enterprising French builder of the Suez Canal, organized a private stock company with a concession from the Colombian government to build a sea-level canal across the Isthmus of Panama, interest suddenly picked up. Americans now became alarmed. They did not like the idea of a canal owned and operated by Europeans in their own backyard. In Congress, and in the press too, angry citizens denounced the project as a violation of the Monroe Doctrine.

Aware of public hostility and shocked by the extent of official disapproval of his enterprise, de Lesseps visited the United States in February 1880 to promote support for his canal and to allay government fears. He talked with President Rutherford B. Hayes and Secretary of State William M. Evarts, hoping to gain consent for his undertaking, but they did nothing to encourage him.

On March 8, three days after his conversation with de Lesseps, who was still in the United States, Hayes delivered a special message to Congress, written by Evarts, in which he announced that "the policy of this country is a canal under American control. The United States cannot consent to the surrender of this control to any European power or to any combination of European powers." A canal across the isthmus, he added, "would be the great ocean thoroughfare between our Atlantic and our Pacific shores, and virtually a part of the coast line of the United States." [2]

That attitude, reflecting Grant's views, now became national policy. A month later, the House of Representatives asked the president to take steps to abrogate the Clayton-Bulwer Treaty, the main obstacle to carrying out that policy.

Concerned over American hostility, the French government meanwhile had assured the United States that the de Lesseps project was a private one and that it did not intend to support the undertaking in any way. De Lesseps's engineers began work on the canal in February 1881, and the United States did nothing to interfere. Two years earlier, however, a group of American promoters had organized a company to build a competitive canal through Nicaragua. This company tried to gain government support but failed.

Since the Clayton-Bulwer Treaty stood in the way of a canal controlled exclusively by the United States, Secretaries of State Evarts, James G. Blaine, and Frederick J. Frelinghuysen, all tried to amend or abrogate it. Blaine's arguments were particularly vigorous. That treaty, he said, injures the spirit of the Monroe Doctrine and "impeaches our rightful and long established claims to priority on the American continent."[3] Since Britain would not surrender any of her rights under the treaty, Frelinghuysen disregarded it and on December 1, 1884, signed a treaty with General Joaquín Zavala of Nicaragua to supersede Seward's treaty of 1867.

That new treaty gave the United States exclusive right to build a canal across Nicaragua, to be owned jointly. In return, the United States guaranteed Nicaragua's territorial integrity and agreed to a permanent alliance. For the first time the United States included in a treaty the principle of a canal constructed and owned by the government, and for the first time it deliberately took a step that violated the Clayton-Bulwer Treaty.

The Senate rejected the Frelinghuysen-Zavala Treaty by a close vote in January 1885 and then proceeded to reconsider it. Two months later Grover Cleveland became president. On March 13, following the advice of his secretary of state, Thomas F. Bayard, he withdrew the treaty from the Senate. If the Senate had approved it, a quarrel with England would probably have followed.

Cleveland did not adopt the policy of his immediate predecessors for a waterway controlled exclusively by the United States. The canal, he said in his first annual message, "must be for the world's benefit—a trust for mankind, to be removed from the chance of domination by any single power, nor become a point of invitation for hostilities or a prize for warlike ambition."[4]

Despite failure of the Frelinghuysen-Zavala Treaty and the lack of government assistance, the American promoters went ahead in 1887 with their own plans for a Nicaraguan canal. With a concession from Nicaragua's government and under an act of Congress, they incorporated the Maritime Canal Company of Nicaragua. They no longer feared the rival French canal at Panama, for de Lesseps's company went bankrupt in February 1889 and in May, with about two-fifths of the digging completed, stopped construction.

The Maritime Canal Company began work in October 1889 using some of the equipment from Panama. That company soon ran out of money and asked the American government to finance its project. Since such aid would make the canal almost a government project and would violate the Clayton-Bulwer Treaty, Congress again refused to offer support. Work stopped and in August 1893 the subsidiary construction company went bankrupt. The Maritime Canal Company, though it tried, never resumed work.

Failure of the private companies in Panama and Nicaragua convinced many Americans that only the government had the resources necessary to build a canal. The main obstacle to such a canal, built and owned by the American government, was still the Clayton-Bulwer Treaty.

Blaine's Latin-American Policy

United States concern over a canal in the 1880s reflected a new governmental interest in all of Latin America. By that time the larger countries of South America, although plagued by wars, had achieved a higher level of political stability than in the past and had become more important commercially. In the United States stepped-up industrialism had reached the point where manufacturers sought new markets and new sources of raw materials for their factories. One of the Americans who keenly desired to promote trade with Latin America was James G. Blaine, James A. Garfield's secretary of state.

Since Blaine had been the outstanding Republican leader and Garfield merely a fortunate dark-horse candidate, Blaine believed that he, not Garfield, deserved to be president. Blaine had spent a quarter of a century in public life, but in that time had had no experience in foreign affairs. Yet he became secretary of state in March 1881 with the intention of functioning as the administration's prime minister. Since Garfield gave him a free hand in foreign affairs, Blaine was able, during that short tenure, to put his own "spirited foreign policy" into practice.

Blaine's policy toward Latin America had two main objectives: promotion of peace and increased trade. Both were in a sense anti-European. Peace, he believed, could be maintained by eliminating opportunities for European intervention in the Americas, an objective that called for effort on his part to try to end turbulence and wars then sweeping over parts of Latin America. As for trade, even though Latin-American states sold raw materials to the United States, they bought most of their manufactured goods from Europe. Blaine wanted to redress that unfavorable balance.

Blaine made his first effort to advance both trade and peace in his relations with Mexico. He assumed that the government there had now acquired a stability hitherto unknown. He wanted Mexico's prosperity to grow, he said, aided by Americans who wish to "take an active share in the prosecution of those industrial enterprises for which the magnificent resources of Mexico offer so broad and promising a field."[5] Later in that same month, however, an old boundary quarrel between Mexico and Guatemala blocked the launching of his Mexican policy.

On June 15 Guatemala appealed to the United States for aid. Blaine then offered his country's good offices for an arbitration. Believing rightly that he sided with Guatemala, Mexico flatly refused his offer. Blaine's attempted peacemaking not only failed but also angered Mexico and contributed nothing to closer trade relations.

Another territorial quarrel, this one in South America, seemingly presented the secretary with another opportunity to advance his peace policy. In 1879 Chile had gone to war against Bolivia and Peru over rival claims to a desert region rich in guano, a valuable fertilizer, and nitrates. In this conflict, called the War of the Pacific, Chile was overwhelmingly victorious by January 1881. She took over the nitrate territories and refused to give them up, but despite the defeat no Peruvian government would make a peace treaty.

When Blaine took office he immediately tried to work out a treaty between the belligerents. As in the Mexican dispute, he hoped to prevent or restrict any large cession of territory. Since Chile was determined to keep Peru's nitrate beds as an indemnity for her victory, he found himself in the position of partisan peacemaker. The American ministers in Chile and Peru, moreover, complicated Blaine's diplomacy; each became a partisan of his host country. Blaine tried, therefore, to arrange a settlement by sending a special envoy to the belligerent countries. Since Chile would agree to no settlement unless the nitrate lands were ceded to her, and Blaine opposed such terms, his peacemaking again failed. All that he accomplished was to earn Chile's ill will.

In the peace treaties of 1883 and 1884 with Peru and Bolivia that finally ended the War of the Pacific, Chile obtained, with some minor restrictions, the territories she demanded. Although many Americans regretted the fate of Peru and Bolivia, apparently the only way that Blaine or anyone else could have saved them from Chile was with force, which the United States had never intended to use.

The Pan-American Idea

Ironically, Blaine's outstanding accomplishment in Latin-American relations, the launching of the Pan-American movement, grew out of his effort to exert moral pressure on Chile in favor of Peru through cooperation with other Latin-American nations. Before an assassin's bullet had struck down Garfield in July 1881, Blaine had persuaded him to call a meeting of those states in Washington, ostensibly to discuss the general problem of preventing war in the Americas. The basic idea of a conference, however, did not originate with Blaine. In the United States it went back to Henry

Clay who had suggested a league of American states in 1820. In Latin America, Simón Bolívar had made the first effort to bring those states together in his futile Panama Congress of 1826.

Blaine's Pan-Americanism contained two basic ideas: that the American states, mainly because they vaguely supported principles of republican government, should discuss common problems, and that they should seek cooperation in matters of peace and trade. It also included hope that the conference, as a dramatic stroke of statesmanship, would save his Latin-American policy and enhance his stature as a candidate for the presidency.

Garfield's successor, Chester A. Arthur, reluctantly consented to go ahead with the gathering, and on November 28 Blaine sent invitations to all the independent Latin-American countries except Haiti. He announced the conference for November of the following year. Three weeks later Arthur replaced him with Frederick J. Frelinghuysen, a man whose politics were more congenial to Arthur's.

Secretary Frelinghuysen said the conference would "create jealousy and ill will" among those nations not invited, and "peace, the object sought by such consultation, would not be promoted." He was in fact more disturbed by Blaine's bungling intervention, touched by rumors of scandal, in the hostilities between Chile and Peru. Therefore, he abruptly withdrew the invitations.

The Pan-American idea did not die. Seven years later, in May 1888, Congress asked President Cleveland to call a conference of American states to promote trade and preserve peace. Its scope was wider than that of Blaine's original conference. Congress's resolution called for an American customs union and uniform trade regulations to promote free trade in the Western Hemisphere. Cleveland's secretary of state, Thomas F. Bayard, sent out the invitations in July.

Several months later Benjamin Harrison defeated Cleveland for the presidency and appointed Blaine his secretary of state. Thus Blaine, who eight years earlier had revived the Pan-American idea, welcomed the delegates from seventeen Latin-American states to the first inter-American conference that opened in Washington on October 2, 1889. He was chosen president of the conference.

With the idea of showing off the size and immense resources of the United States and hence promoting trade, the government sponsored a railroad tour of some five thousand four hundred miles for the Latins. At the end of forty-two days the exhausted delegates returned to Washington, duly impressed with the nation's wealth.

The work of the conference itself was disappointing. It rejected the proposal for a customs union and instead recommended that the countries desiring to do so negotiate separate reciprocal trade treaties. It adopted a plan for arbitration of all disputes and various resolutions. Few of the Latin-American countries had enough interest in the agreements to ratify them.

Before the conference closed on April 19, 1890, it became entangled in domestic politics, and Blaine's critics had attacked it. Calling it "Mr. Blaine's Congress," one paper for instance had said it would "accomplish nothing as long as the Republican party remains in power and continues to be the champion of high protection."

Realizing that Blaine wanted to take their Latin-American trade from them, Europeans also viewed the conference skeptically. A French paper pointed out that it had accomplished nothing practical. "Wholly platonic recommendations, which even so encountered a good deal of dissent, all the main proposals aborted—there is the balance sheet of the Pan-American Congress," it concluded.[6]

The critics were too harsh. The conference had not failed in everything. In establishing the International Bureau of the American Republics, later called the Pan-American Union, for the exchange of economic, scientific, and cultural information, it made a lasting contribution to the Pan-American movement. Even more important was the precedent of the gathering itself. It was the first of many conferences wherein matters of common interest to the American republics were discussed. Blaine left his own imprint on these early conferences. They avoided political matters and devoted themselves to the promotion of trade.

Blaine himself tried immediately to advance the trade objective. He opposed the protective McKinley tariff bill of 1890, calling certain of its provisions a "slap in the face to South Americans with whom we are trying to enlarge our trade." When the tariff became law on October 1, it contained a limited reciprocity clause his efforts had helped secure. Under it, Blaine negotiated a number of reciprocity agreements with Latin-American governments, but before the limited reciprocity had a fair trial a hostile Congress repealed it in 1894.

The Itata Incident

Within a year of the conference Blaine encountered new difficulties in his Latin-American policy, again in relations with Chile. Since his failure to mediate the War of the Pacific to the benefit of Peru, Blaine and the United States had been unpopular in Chile. In January 1891 a civil war broke out in Chile between her president on one side and the supporters of her congress on the other, who revolted against the president's efforts to increase executive power at the expense of the legislature.

The rebels, who controlled the Chilean navy, sent a steamer to San Diego, California, to obtain arms. Charging that the ship, the *Itata*, had violated neutrality laws, Federal authorities detained it on May 5. The next day the crew overpowered the American deputy marshal on board and sailed for Chile. Aware of the precedent of the *Alabama*'s escape and indignant over this affront to American authority, President Harrison sent a cruiser after the *Itata* to bring it back by force if necessary. Even though the cruiser failed to overtake the *Itata,* there was some danger it might clash with a Chilean cruiser designated to convoy the transport.

When the *Itata* reached Chile, rebel authorities surrendered her to the United States. American courts later released the ship, saying it had not violated the neutrality laws, but the damage to relations with Chile had already been done. The revolutionists won the war with arms from Germany, despite the fact that the United States had denied them guns when desperately needed. "Since the unfortunate incident of the *Itata,*" the American minister in Chile wrote, "the young and unthinking element of those who were in opposition to the Government have a bitter feeling against the United States."[7] The former rebels resented the hostility the United States government had shown to their cause and in particular the threat of force it had used in recovering the *Itata*.

The Baltimore *Affair*

While this anti-United States feeling was still running high, the captain of the U.S.S. *Baltimore,* one of three warships sent to Chile to protect American interests there during the civil war, gave shore leave in Valparaiso to 117 of his crew. That evening, October 16, 1891, Chilean hostility against the United States exploded in a street fight in the "Maintop," the city's tenderloin district, where a mob beat, stoned, and knifed American sailors, killing two and wounding others. The skipper of the *Baltimore* placed full blame on the Chileans. The Chilean authorities argued that neither country was responsible since the affair was a drunken brawl between American and Chilean sailors.

When news of the fight reached the United States, it aroused demands for retaliation. Accepting the interpretation of his naval officer, President Harrison took the view that it was not a mere sailors' brawl but a premeditated assault sparked by hatred of Americans that demanded "prompt and full reparation."

Concerned lest his Pan-American and reciprocity programs be damaged, Blaine wanted to play down the incident. He wished to "make a friend of Chile—if that is possible," but Harrison, a former soldier intensely proud of the flag and the uniform, regarded the attack as so serious that it required vigorous action. When Blaine offered his views in a cabinet meeting, the president, gesturing emphatically, said, "Mr. Secretary, that insult was to the uniform of the United States sailors."[8]

Chile was slow in making amends. In his annual message of December 9, therefore, Harrison threatened strong action. That threat angered Chile's foreign minister who publicly insulted Harrison and his government. Both countries now prepared for war and the *Baltimore* affair spawned the most serious crisis in Latin-American affairs since the French invasion of Mexico.

Since Blaine and the United States had proposed arbitration of disputes at the inter-American conference, Chile suggested that kind of settlement for the *Baltimore* crisis, but Americans would not think of it. "When the United States is willing to submit the question of the murder of her sailors in uniform to arbitration," an American naval officer in Valparaiso wrote in his journal, "I must look for other employment—the navy won't any longer suit me." [9] Harrison's private secretary recorded in his diary that "the President stated that all members of the Cabinet are for war."

In trying to find a diplomatic solution for the crisis, Blaine had to overcome the opposition of a Navy Department anxious for war. At its head stood Benjamin F. Tracy, one of the ablest secretaries of the navy and one of Harrison's most trusted advisers. An expansionist who viewed the navy as an instrument for imperialism, Tracy was carrying out a "big navy" program and replacing old wooden ships with fast modern ones, armored with steel.

The president backed Tracy against Blaine, often substituting his own notes to Chile, which were stronger in tone and fitted navy policy, for those of Blaine and the State Department. During this crisis the navy practically made foreign policy. An English diplomat in Washington wrote, for instance, that the United States was on the verge of war and that Blaine "has prevented war with Chile so far, and may do so still; but the President and the Navy are bent on it." [10]

Ignoring the views of his secretary of state, Harrison sent Chile an ultimatum on January 21, 1892, demanding suitable apologies or he would terminate diplomatic relations. He waited four days and no reply came. On Sunday, January 24, he worked all day on a "war" message, which he sent to Congress the next day.

Without allies and fearing destruction by the more powerful United States, Chile had already wisely decided to give in to the American demands. Her note of surrender and apology arrived in the United States on Tuesday, January 26. That ended the crisis. Later, Chile paid $75,000 to the injured men and to relatives of the dead sailors.

Although satisfactory to the United States, the settlement humiliated Chileans who resented the threat of naked force used against them. The *Baltimore* affair long embittered relations with Chile and throughout Latin America reawakened suspicions of United States imperialism. It wiped out whatever friendly feeling for the United States Blaine's inter-American conference may have stimulated. Latin Americans believed that the United States had interfered in Chile's domestic politics and had hectored her into paying an unjust indemnity.

Other nations, too, had observed the new bellicose tone of American foreign policy. A British student of American affairs wrote that "the moral for us is: what will the U.S. be like when their fleet is more powerful, if the administration acts in a similar manner?"[11] The British had reason to be concerned, for the next important problem in the Latin-American policy of the United States, over a disputed boundary between Venezuela and British Guiana, directly involved them, and the United States again displayed a jingoistic vigor.

Chinese Immigration

Meanwhile another problem, that of restricting Chinese immigration, had become of national concern. Before 1848 there were probably no more than fifty Chinese in the entire United States. After the discovery of gold in California thousands of laborers from densely populated southern China flocked to California to escape poverty at home and perhaps acquire wealth in a strange land. At first Californians welcomed the Chinese, who worked long hours in the mines or as cooks and launderers in the miners' camps. Yet from the beginning Chinese suffered discrimination from racial prejudice written into local laws.

After employment in the mining areas slackened, Chinese filled demands for cheap labor in the building of the Central Pacific Railroad, the western link of the transcontinental line. From 1860 to 1870 that railroad's construction company employed over ten thousand men, nine-tenths of them Chinese. When railroad construction ended, the Chinese laborers sought work wherever they could in a flooded labor market, becoming competitors for jobs with native-born Americans and with the increasing number of European workers who were coming to the United States. Californians, and others on the Pacific Coast, now added an economic argument to that of prejudice, saying that the Chinese were depriving whites of their livelihood and were lowering the white standard of living.

After 1870 Caucasian hostility led to demands for exclusion of Chinese laborers from the United States, and a social and economic problem became a political and diplomatic one. Since the Chinese were concentrated in the Pacific Coast states, mostly in California, historians have usually viewed the problem as sectional. The panic of 1873 caused increasing unemployment on the Pacific Coast and intensified hostility against the Chinese, leading to mob violence. Striking out blindly against economic forces they did not understand and seeing in the Chinese helpless scapegoats, working men attacked them.

Since the slogan "The Chinese Must Go" had become popular on the Pacific Coast, reflected a national racism, and would bring votes, both Republicans and Democrats included demands for action against Chinese immigration in their national platforms of 1876. In that year, aware of the political possibilities of the issue, Congress appointed a special committee to investigate Chinese immigration.

At the same time California's laborers sought economic relief through politics. In 1877 they organized their own party, the Workingmen's Party of California. That summer, leaders of the new party held mass meetings in San Francisco's sandlots and denounced the allegedly twin evils of capitalism and Chinese laborers. The most colorful of those sandlot orators, an Irish-born agitator named Denis Kearney, preached an anti-Chinese doctrine of violence. After one meeting of some six thousand workingmen, hoodlums among them invaded San Francisco's Chinatown, burned buildings, sacked fifteen laundries, and broke windows in the Methodist mission there. Usually, however, the Chinese suffered more from economic boycotts and job discrimination than from mob violence.

Californians were more interested in trade with China than were the people of any other section of the country; yet they were willing to sacrifice benefits that trade would bring rather than continue to accept the Chinese. They were in the forefront of those who demanded that Congress ban Chinese immigration.

The main obstacle to exclusion was the Burlingame Treaty that allowed the Chinese to migrate freely to the United States. That obligation did not appear to bother Congress. In February 1879 it passed the fifteen passenger bill, which said no ship could bring more than fifteen Chinese to an American port at any one time.

People of the Pacific Coast deluged President Rutherford B. Hayes with petitions urging him to sign the bill. Others, particularly in the East, wanted him to veto it. The New York Chamber of Commerce, for example, denounced the bill as "establishing a bad precedent; as an unworthy political concession to the lawless spirit of a single State; as tending to degrade the national character in the sight of all other nations." [12]

"Our treaty with China forbids me to give it my approval," Hayes, who favored "suitable" Chinese restriction, wrote in his diary. "The treaty was of our asking." [13] On March 1, therefore, he vetoed the bill. Even so, the fifteen passenger bill was a turning point in immigration policy. It was only a matter of time before Chinese restriction would become national law. Hayes and Secretary of State Evarts realized that. Therefore, they sent a special mission to China to revise the Burlingame Treaty and obtain the legal right to restrict Chinese immigration.

Chinese Exclusion

James B. Angell, president of the University of Michigan, who headed the commission, had discussed Chinese immigration with Secretary Evarts. Restriction, he had told Evarts, would probably win popular support. Any absolute prohibition, he warned however, would be "diametrically opposed to all our national traditions and would call down the censure of a very large portion if not a majority of our most intelligent and high-minded citizens."[14]

Angry over the mistreatment of their people in California, officials of the Chinese Foreign Office would not consider prohibition, but finally agreed to some limitations on the immigration of laborers. On November 17, 1880, the commission signed two treaties with China. The first, a commercial agreement, contained a noteworthy clause prohibiting Americans from trading in opium in China.

The other, the immigration treaty which modified the Burlingame Treaty, was itself China's major concession. It gave the American government the right to "regulate, limit, or suspend," but not to prohibit, entry of Chinese laborers into the United States. The "limitation or suspension," the treaty said, should be "reasonable" and should apply only to Chinese who "may go to the United States as laborers, other classes not being included in the limitation." Congress approved both treaties. Then it passed an act suspending Chinese immigration for twenty years.[15] President Chester A. Arthur believed that under terms of the Angell Treaty twenty years was not "reasonable" and vetoed the bill in April 1882.

Since Congress did not succeed in overriding the veto, it hurriedly passed another bill suspending the flow of Chinese laborers for ten years and declaring that "hereafter no state court or court of the United States shall admit Chinese to citizenship." The president signed the legislation on May 6. Two years later Congress amended and strengthened the law. The act of 1882, usually called the Chinese exclusion law, marked a radical departure on ethnocultural grounds from the nation's policy of offering a haven to the peoples of all nations. It also violated the spirit of treaties with China and created ill will in China, which grew as anti-Chinese violence spread throughout the American West. One of the most serious outbreaks was a massacre in Rock Springs, Wyoming, in September 1885. A white mob attacked the Chinese quarter there, burning and destroying property, murdering twenty-eight Chinese, and seriously wounding fifteen others. The Chinese minister in Washington complained. Secretary Bayard expressed regret and promised an investigation.

While the government investigated the Rock Springs massacre, the people of Seattle, Washington Territory, took the law into their own hands and expelled the Chinese from their homes, chanting "The Chinese Must Go." "The Civilization of the Pacific Coast," one newspaper declared, "cannot be half-Caucasian and half-Mongolian." Even soldiers sent to protect the Chinese beat them up and cut off their queues. "The chances are," another paper remarked, "that the people will be called on to protect the Chinese."[16]

After almost six weeks of continuous anti-Chinese agitation, mass meetings, and newspaper propaganda, the people of Tacoma, Washington Territory, also resorted to mob violence against the Chinese. Abetted by local authorities, they expelled two hundred Chinese on November 3 and burned their property. President Cleveland warned the people of the Washington Territory by proclamation against mob violence and ordered federal troops there to "preserve order."

The Chinese government demanded redress for the injuries its people had suffered. When Secretary of State Bayard explained that the federal government could not interfere with the administration of local and state laws unless allowed by the Constitution, the Chinese could not understand. Why, they asked, should dual government protect wrongdoing in the United States and not offer the same immunities to Chinese authorities when Chinese mobs injured Americans and other foreigners? Chinese provincial and local authorities had several times indemnified Americans for losses incurred through riots.

Bayard answered some of the complaints in February, saying that he was himself outraged by attacks on Chinese. Since private individuals, not federal officials, had made them, the government denied responsibility or obligation for redress. Out of "generosity and pity," however, the president might ask Congress to offer assistance to those Chinese who had suffered losses from mob violence.

Those Chinese who returned home reported the humiliations they had suffered in the United States, and their stories contributed to the stirring up of anti-American mobs in China. So worried did the American minister in Peking become over possible retaliatory attacks against Americans that he asked the government to send warships to Canton and other ports "to give what protection and asylum they can to American citizens who may become the objects of mob-assault in that region."[17]

China was then weak. She had no warships to send to San Francisco and Seattle to protect her citizens there. She therefore expressed willingness to make a treaty prohibiting Chinese laborers from emigrating to the United States if the government would guarantee the safety of Chinese already there and would pay for past injuries and losses. In February 1887 Congress offered payment for the losses at Rock Springs but said nothing about responsibility.

Finally, on March 12, 1888, Bayard and the Chinese minister in Washington signed a treaty excluding Chinese laborers from the United States for twenty years. The United States agreed, as a gesture of friendship, to pay the Chinese government an indemnity of $276,619 for losses through mob violence, but without admitting the federal government's responsibility. In essence, with the treaty China agreed to recognize the principle of exclusion that Americans had enacted into law six years earlier. The Senate amended the treaty, approved it, and enacted legislation to carry it into effect, but China did not ratify it. For the first time in the history of a treaty, the Chinese Foreign Office said, the people protested. A mob in Canton demonstrated against the treaty.

Without waiting for China to indicate her reaction to the treaty, but assuming rejection, William L. Scott, Cleveland's friend and campaign manager, introduced a bill into the House of Representatives excluding Chinese laborers. It passed quickly, and Cleveland, anxious to win votes in the presidential campaign of that year, signed it on October 1.

The Scott Act prohibited Chinese who had gone home for a visit from returning and abrogated the Angell Treaty without the courtesy of notifying the Chinese government beforehand. In the past China's own foreign relations had been motivated by prejudice and antiforeignism. Now, ironically, the United States had permitted racial prejudice and political opportunism to take the place of statesmanship in policy toward the Chinese.

China protested but that made little difference. Since President Harrison, who succeeded Cleveland, and Secretary of State Blaine favored exclusion, they ignored protests and virtually broke off diplomatic relations with China. In the spring of 1889, the Supreme Court declared the Scott Act constitutional but said it violated the Angell Treaty. In July the Chinese minister in the United States said he was shocked by the fact that American law allowed the government to "release itself from treaty obligations without consultation with, or the consent of, the other party to what we had been accustomed to regard as a sacred instrument."

With the Geary Act of May 5, 1892, Congress extended the provisions of the Scott Act for another ten years and strengthened Chinese exclusion. The Supreme Court a year later declared that law, the most stringent of the anti-Chinese legislation, constitutional. The Chinese government protested against the injustice of the law, but the American government ignored the protests. It continued, however, to demand special rights through unequal treaties for American merchants and missionaries in China.

Finally, on March 17, 1894, in exchange for more lenient enforcement of the exclusion laws, China signed a treaty that "absolutely prohibited" Chinese laborers from emigrating to the United States for ten years. It was almost identical to the unratified treaty of 1888, and either country could renew it for another ten years unless either gave formal notice of termination.

Since Congress again renewed the exclusion laws in April 1902 without consulting China, this time indefinitely, the Chinese government gave formal notice in January 1904 of intention to terminate the treaty of 1894 the following December. On April 27, therefore, Congress amended the act of 1902 by omitting previous reference to treaty obligations. Chinese exclusion, based on an unfounded theory of Chinese inferiority, remained national policy. "Congress had done its work so well," Secretary of State John

Hay wrote, "that even Confucius could not become an American—though he should seek it with prayers and tears."[18]

In parts of China, hatred of Americans, sparked by rising nationalism, burned deeply. In 1904 and 1905 people boycotted American goods, and anti-American feeling swept through treaty ports and several provinces. Even though the United States was the only great power that had not used force against China, it was, because of its exclusion policy and mistreatment of Chinese, the first country whose goods and people were boycotted.

"The Chinese people are in earnest," the Chinese ambassador said. "Your exclusion act is humiliating. They would prefer to pay a huge indemnity or surrender a slice of territory rather than be insulted and menaced as they are by the attitude of the United States."[19] Racial and cultural prejudices, shared and catered to by politicians, had sown ill will among the Chinese. Although no one knew how much, it seems clear that those domestic actions had also injured American foreign policy in China.

The Northeast Fisheries

While people of the West Coast were fighting for Chinese exclusion, those of New England found the old problem of the Canadian fisheries as irritating as ever. They had always resented the large award Canada had received under the Treaty of Washington and had disliked some of its other fisheries provisions. On March 3, 1883, by joint resolution, therefore, Congress abolished the special privileges of that treaty as of July 1, 1885. American fishing rights in Canadian waters would then rest on the obsolete Convention of 1818. Since July fell in the middle of the fishing season, and sudden termination might create friction and misunderstandings between Canadians and American fishermen, Secretary of State Bayard worked out a "temporary diplomatic agreement" in June 1885 that allowed Americans to continue fishing in Canadian waters under terms of the Treaty of Washington.

The agreement obligated President Cleveland to ask Congress for authority to appoint Americans to a joint commission with the British to settle the whole question. Cleveland requested the authority in December. Since he was a Democrat, and Republicans controlled Congress, he was refused. During the next fishing season Canadian and Newfoundland officials strictly enforced and even went beyond rules of the Convention of 1818, seizing American fishing craft and arresting their crews for true and alleged violation of regulations.

At the end of that season, therefore, Bayard offered to negotiate permanent understanding on the issue through a joint commission that would study the problem. Congress, meanwhile, had passed a bill, which the president approved in March 1887, authorizing him at his discretion to retaliate against Canadians by suspending their trading privileges in the United States. Even though Cleveland signed the bill, he had no intention of using it as anything but a lever to force concessions from Britain and Canada.

Perhaps Cleveland's lever worked, because the British immediately agreed to negotiation in Washington by a joint commission. Bayard headed the American commissioners, and Joseph Chamberlain led the British representatives who met in November. After long negotiation, they signed a compromise treaty in February 1888. Although this agreement promised the end of this old problem, it encountered strong opposition in the Senate.

Cleveland signed the treaty on February 20 and transmitted it to the Senate the same day, urging approval, but 1888 was an election year and New Englanders and other Republicans, who narrowly controlled the Senate, would not allow a Democratic president to win credit for settling the long-festering dispute. "The better the treaty," one of the commissioners wrote, "the worse it is likely to fare at the hands of the extreme men who do not mean that the Administration shall get any help from it."[20] In criticizing the agreement, opponents tried to make it appear a surrender to the British and thus place the president in a weak position with Irish-American voters and other anglophobes. In a strictly party vote on August 21 Republican senators killed the treaty.

In a political countermove two days later, Cleveland sent a strong message to Congress, ostensibly aimed at Canada but designed to embarrass the Senate, urging Congress to grant him power to strike against Canadian trade. "And above all things," he said, "the plan of retaliation, if entered upon, should be thorough and vigorous."[21] Fearing business losses and injury in the presidential election, the Republicans would not grant him the retaliatory power he requested.

Even though the death of the Bayard-Chamberlain Treaty embittered Canadians, it did not lead to conflict over the fisheries because the commissioners had also agreed to a two-year working arrangement, or *modus vivendi*. Although never fully satisfactory, the arrangement continued, with renewals, for several years. Yet partisan politics and sectional interests had destroyed the opportunity for permanent settlement of a long smoldering dispute.

Sackville-West

In Pomona, California, a Republican fruit grower named George Osgoodby read Cleveland's retaliatory message on the fisheries question and suspected it of being an electioneering device designed to catch votes among Irish-Americans and New Englanders. He therefore sent the British minister in Washington, Sir Lionel Sackville-West, a letter saying he was a naturalized American who had been born an Englishman and signed it

Charles F. Murchison. He asked "privately and confidentially" if Cleveland's foreign policy would in the long run "favor England's interests" and if he should vote for Cleveland.

Lord Sackville blundered into Osgoodby's trap. He replied in September 1888 that he favored Cleveland. Republican campaign managers obtained Sackville's letter and shortly before the election published it. In the furor that followed, Democrats and Republicans both denounced the diplomat for interfering in America's domestic politics. Republicans said his letter proved that Cleveland was a tool of Britain. Democrats demanded that Cleveland dismiss Sackville. "Now kick out Lord Sackville with your biggest boot of best leather, and you've got 'em," a Democratic editor advised Cleveland. *"Hesitation is death."* [22]

The president in effect followed that advice. First he demanded Sackville's recall. "The President feels deeply this conduct of the British Minister," Bayard told the British foreign secretary, "and the sentiment of both political parties is in concurrence that his usefulness in this country has ended." [23]

The foreign secretary refused to recall Sackville without having the opportunity to examine the complaint against him. Cleveland then dismissed the unfortunate diplomat to show that he and the Democratic party were in no way subservient to Britain. Nonetheless, Republican campaign orators insisted that the administration had always been pro-English. "They have given Sir Sackville the shake, and now all that remains for you to do," a prominent Republican told campaign audiences, "is to give Mr. Cleveland the sack." [24]

The British were angry because they believed that the president had sacrificed Sackville-West for political reasons and not for any wrongdoing. They refused to send another minister to the United States until after Cleveland left the White House.

The German Pork Dispute

Another question stemming from domestic developments, but more economic than political, was that of pork exports to Europe. By 1881 Britain, France, Austria, Italy, Turkey, Greece, and Germany restricted, or prohibited, imports of American pork and pork products such as ham, bacon, and lard, alleging that those meats were infected with trichinosis, a parasitic disease harmful to man and hence dangerous to the health of their people. The German ban was the one most offensive to the United States and touched off a dispute that spread over a decade.

One reason for bitterness between Germany and the United States over the pork products was that both countries had adopted a protective tariff as national policy at about the same time, the United States after the Civil War and Germany in 1879 in the decade after her unification. Germany's protective policy was essentially agrarian, while that of the United States was industrial. Both Germany and the United States in this period became industrial nations, but Germany also changed from a food exporting to a food importing nation. The United States soon became the world's greatest exporter of pork products.

The restrictions on pork struck hard at American farmers and the great meat packing industry of the Midwest. The hog raisers and meat packers exerted considerable pressure on the Department of State and Congress to persuade Europeans to lift their restrictions. Some believed that the Germans used "dreadful parasites" as an excuse to enable their hog raisers to maintain high prices for native pork. When the German government planned total exclusion of American pork products, the American minister in Berlin advised in January 1883 that "the only argument that would be effective against the measure would be fear of reprisals." In March, Germany went beyond restriction and excluded all American pork products.

Hog raisers, among them German-Americans who had settled in the pork centers of the Midwest, cried for relief and denounced the German government. What particularly irked Americans was that Germany banned only American pork—"and that," one paper said, "on a pretext which, being officially set up by a responsible government, tends to injure the reputation of American hog products in all other countries."[25]

Since Chancellor Otto von Bismarck considered the large landowners, who produced pork and resented low-priced American competition, pillars of the German monarchy, he wanted to protect them. "It is absolutely necesssary for us people of Europe," he told an American journalist in July 1884, "to protect ourselves in time against your competition, for whenever the point arrives that the United States is not checked in its inroads on our agriculture, complete ruin will overtake our landholding classes."

Americans demanded retaliation against Bismarck's policy, but that did not prove necessary. Beginning in 1886, Congress met most of the German complaints by passing laws subjecting meats to rigid inspection before export. Those laws gave Germany the excuse to remove the ban on American pork without appearing to surrender to threats of retaliation. Yet such a threat, particularly as embodied in a new tariff, was more effective than the inspection laws.

In this period, Germany profited from the export of beet sugar to the United States. Republican protectionists came to power when Benjamin Harrison became president in 1889. On October 1, 1890, Congress passed the McKinley tariff empowering the president to impose a duty on German sugar. Germany suggested that it would accept the meat inspection laws as satisfactory and remove the ban on pork if the United States would not impose a duty on German sugar under the new tariff. The United States accepted this compromise in an exchange of declarations with a German diplomat at Saratoga, New York, on August 22, 1891. The "Saratoga Agreement" ended the pork dispute.

The New Orleans Affair

Shortly before the settlement of the pork controversy, the United States ran into a quarrel with Italy, another newly unified European power. A large number of Italians had settled in New Orleans where in October 1890 unknown assassins killed a popular police chief. Most people believed that the murderers had come from the local Sicilian population. The authorities rounded up suspects, all of them Italians or of Italian origin, and brought them to trial. The jury failed to convict anyone. To onlookers aroused by the crime and influenced by antiforeign prejudice, the verdict appeared unjust. A mob of six to eight thousand, led by prominent citizens, rushed to the jail. Within twenty minutes, without restraint from state or local law officers, who stood by, the mob systematically lynched eleven of the suspects. Three were Italian subjects, and the others were naturalized Americans or had declared their intentions of becoming citizens.

Baron Francesco Saverio Fava, the Italian minister in Washington, immediately protested to Secretary of State Blaine, denouncing the inaction of New Orleans authorities and asking him to take "precautions" against further violence to the Italian colony there. Blaine expressed regret and sent a telegram to the governor of Louisiana asking him to protect Italian subjects from further mob violence and to investigate the lynchings.

That action did not satisfy the Italian government. It wanted official assurance that the guilty parties would be brought to trial and that an indemnity for the families of the mob victims would be paid. The Italian demands placed the federal government in a dilemma similar to those in the cases of mob violence against the Chinese. "The recent outbreak in New Orleans against the Italians," William Howard Taft, then solicitor general, wrote, "has raised some rather embarrassing international questions, and emphasizes the somewhat anomalous character of our Government, which makes the National Government responsible for the action of the State authorities without giving it any power to control that action."[26]

After a few weeks of fruitless negotiation, the Italian government recalled Baron Fava and the United States called home its minister from Rome. The Italian press attacked the United States, and mass meetings in Italy demanded satisfaction for the New Orleans violence. In the United States, Baron Fava's recall turned the affair into a front-page sensation. While most newspapers advised moderation, some spoke of war, reflecting the rising militancy and pugnacious nationalism in this period

Although serious, the situation did not create any real danger of war. Italy's premier, Marquis Antonio Starabba di Rudini, had to deal with aroused public emotions. Since his coalition government was unstable, he had recalled Fava to impress his own people with a show of energy and not particularly with the intention of exerting unreasonable pressure on the United States. The fact that a grand jury sat for two months in New Orleans and failed to indict any of the leaders of the lynch mob made his domestic position even more difficult.

After public tempers had cooled, both governments attempted to find a peaceful settlement. President Harrison and Secretary Blaine sought a constitutional means of enabling the federal government to prosecute leaders of the mob, but they uncovered no law giving the federal courts jurisdiction. They did, however, find an indirect way of meeting Italian demands for an indemnity.

In his annual message in December, Harrison in effect offered an apology, and in April 1892, after extended negotiations, Blaine said the "lamentable massacre at New Orleans" obligated the United States to pay a satisfactory indemnity. The president, he added, had instructed him to offer $25,000 to the families of the victims and hoped that the indemnity would compensate for the tragedy and that Italy and the United States might resume friendly relations. The Italian government accepted the indemnity and immediately restored full diplomatic relations.

In paying the indemnity Harrison circumvented the usual procedure of asking Congress for an appropriation. He took the money from the contingent fund of the Department of State for "expenses." Since Congress on previous occasions had been reluctant to pay indemnities, the St. Paul *Pioneer-Press* said the action was "proper and wise." If the question of an appropriation had gone to Congress, it pointed out, it "would have been fought and delayed and haggled over until all the graciousness was taken out of the act."[27] Some members of Congress were dissatisfied. They believed that Harrison had usurped their prerogatives and had violated precedent.

Despite the passions it aroused, the brief New Orleans affair was a minor diplomatic incident, but it exposed the struggle between Congress and the president for control of foreign policy and emphasized the constitutional gap in cases of mob violence against aliens. According to international law, the federal government is obligated to protect aliens, but under the Constitution states have the main responsibility for maintaining public order, including the protection of aliens and their property from mob violence.

Bering Sea Controversy

In contrast to its inadequate powers to protect aliens from mob violence, the federal government in the 1880s tried to stretch its domestic laws beyond the traditional three-mile limit of national jurisdiction in order to protect fur seals in the North Pacific. One of three surviving seal

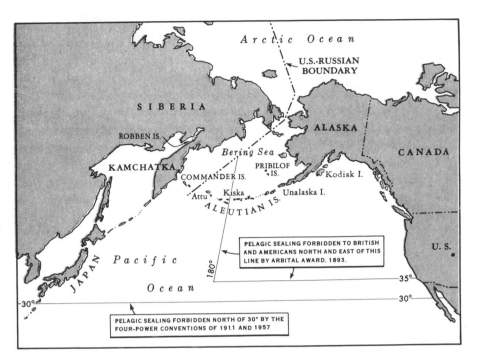

THE BERING SEA SEAL CONTROVERSY

herds would spend each summer on two of the Pribilof Islands in the Bering Sea that the United States had acquired from Russia with the purchase of Alaska. Almost from the beginning the United States took the position that since the seals had their breeding grounds on American territory, they were American property wherever they went, even beyond the three-mile limit. In 1870 it gave the Alaska Commercial Company, a private concern, the sole right to hunt male seals on the Pribilof Islands for twenty years.

In 1881 and 1882 American and Canadian hunters, attracted by the high prices seal skins were bringing, defied the monopoly and began hunting seals as they swam or floated beyond the three-mile limit, a practice called pelagic sealing. That practice, on a commercial scale, threatened to exterminate the herd. Since seals are polygamous, and only about one male for each hundred females is necessary to propagate the herd, hunters could slaughter the males with profit and without endangering the species. While the seals swam, however, hunters could not easily distinguish male from female. Since the cow-mother roamed the sea searching for food while the bull remained on the beach, over 80 percent of the seals the pelagic hunters killed were females. The hunters did not always recover mortally wounded animals and all the others they killed. Each female they killed, moreover, usually had an unborn pup within her and a nursing pup on land that would die if she did not return. For every seal the pelagic hunters killed and recovered, therefore, about four others died.

To stop the indiscriminate slaughter, American officials in August 1886 began seizing ships engaged in pelagic sealing. They arrested Canadians on the theory that the Bering Sea was a closed sea, a *mare clausum,* covered by American laws that Canadians had violated. Britain immediately protested, and a long diplomatic dispute ensued. The British insisted that the Bering Sea was not a closed area and that American revenue cutters had no right to take their vessels on the high seas.

Americans became angry because the pelagic sealing did not stop, and Canadians fumed over the seizure of their ships. Newspapers in both countries demanded drastic action. In 1887 Secretary of State Bayard tried unsuccessfully to settle the controversy through international agreement.

When Blaine became secretary of state for the second time in 1889, he took up the dispute. Instead of claiming that the Bering Sea was a closed sea, he maintained that pelagic sealing threatened to destroy the Pribilof herd and hence violated good morals and involved permanent injury to the United States. He then argued that through long-continued acquiescence of all nations, Russia had acquired a preeminent right over the seals in that sea beyond the three-mile limit, and that the United States had succeeded to that prescriptive right.

Britain rejected Blaine's arguments of prescriptive right. She insisted, as before, that pelagic sealing did not justify taking foreign vessels on the high seas. International law allowed such seizures in time of peace only by mutual agreement, or if the ships were pirate craft. The British said that if the United States continued to interfere with their flag on the seas they would take strong action, but they also offered to submit the whole sealing question to an impartial arbitration.

After arguing for over a year, the United States and Britain signed a treaty on February 29, 1892, which submitted the dispute to seven arbitrators. The Senate approved the treaty in March, and a year later the arbitral tribunal met in Paris.

In August 1893 it announced that every one of the major points was decided against the United States. It denied any right of American jurisdiction over the Bering Sea, upheld freedom of the seas in time of peace, and destroyed the theory that the United States had a "property right" in the seals of the Bering Sea. Later, in June 1898, the United States paid $473,151 to Britain for claims concerning her ships that had been seized by American revenue cutters.

Pelagic sealing continued, and after 1900 the Japanese took an even greater toll of the herd than did the Canadians. Some of the Japanese sealers even poached within the three-mile limit. In July 1906, for instance, Japanese hunters landed on one of the Pribilofs and began slaughtering seals.

American authorities fired on the poachers, killing five and wounding two, and took five prisoners.

To avoid more dangerous international incidents and to save the seals, the United States offered important concessions to Japan and Canada if they would agree to stop their nationals from pelagic sealing. Since Russia was losing seals from a herd she controlled, she was ready to join any international agreement to save the seals. The four Pacific powers, Russia, Japan, Britain, and the United States, signed the North Pacific Sealing Convention on July 7, 1911. Each of them promised to prohibit their own nationals from pelagic sealing, and the United States agreed to give Japan 15 percent of the seal skins it took each year from the Pribilof herd and a similar amount to Canada.

In the years following the convention, the herd increased rapidly and Japan, Canada, and the United States profited from the regulated killing of the males. Japan, however, was not satisfied. She claimed that the seals were injuring important fisheries and in October 1940 denounced the convention by giving the one-year notice. Canada and the United States continued to forbid pelagic sealing to their own citizens. On February 9, 1957, after negotiating for two years, Russia, Japan, Canada, and the United States signed another North Pacific Sealing Convention. This one prohibited pelagic sealing, allowed visit and search, gave Japan and Canada 15 percent of the Russian and American annual kill, and provided for a cooperative research program under a four-power fur seal commission.

XIII

Dawn of a New Destiny

The last two decades of the nineteenth century also witnessed an intensification of the spirit of expansion. It is often called the new manifest destiny. Like earlier expansionism it was based on a belligerent nationalism, but also on recently acquired industrial wealth and notions of racial superiority. Although distinctive, this imperialism was not truly new or unique. Some of its ideas were implicit in the manifest destiny preceding the Civil War, and others were similar to those of contemporary European imperialisms.

This new manifest destiny differed from previous expansionism in its concern for its unvarnished racism, overseas markets, its claim to scientific foundations, and its popularity. Its scientific credentials rested on the work of the English naturalist, Charles R. Darwin, mainly on two of his books published twelve years apart, *On the Origin of Species* (1859) and *Descent of Man* (1871). The central idea in his theory of evolution was "natural selection," or that the struggle for life favored those who possessed characteristics enabling them to survive at the expense of their fellows.

Other men, particularly the self-made English philosopher and sociologist Herbert Spencer and his American disciple, sociologist William Graham Sumner, took Darwin's ideas and applied them to people in social, economic, and political situations. This became Social Darwinism, which popularized such terms as the "survival of the fittest" in the "struggle for existence." If the "fittest" survived among humans and animals, the same might hold true for nations. This was an attractive doctrine for a vigorous and expansive people such as Americans of the late nineteenth century.

American writers and thinkers quickly took up the gospel of Social Darwinism and made it a part of their expansionist philosophy. The bumptious nationalism of the new manifest destiny, with or without the racism of Social Darwinism, was evident, for instance, in the *Baltimore* affair with

Chile and in the reaction to Italian protests over the New Orleans lynchings. Among Americans prominent in preaching expansionism, Anglo-Saxon supremacy, or in working nationalist ideas into thinking on foreign policy were historian John Fiske, Congregational clergyman Josiah Strong, political scientist John W. Burgess, and naval officer Alfred Thayer Mahan.

Basic to the new manifest destiny was the dogma of Anglo-Saxon superiority. Since Anglo-Saxons were preeminent, the racial theory went, they must expand to show their fitness. John Fiske advanced that idea and made it popular, particularly in his essay "Manifest Destiny," published in *Harper's Magazine* of March 1885. He presented the same idea in a book that year, and he repeated it in lectures in cities throughout the nation.

In that same year Josiah Strong published *Our Country: Its Possible Future and Its Present Crisis,* a book that sold over 175,000 copies. With missionary zeal Strong emphasized social reform wrapped in civilizing nationalism. America's progress and greatness, he wrote, "are the results of natural selection," and he went on, "this powerful race will move down upon Mexico, down upon Central and South America, out upon the islands of the sea, over upon Africa and beyond. And can anyone doubt that the result of this competition of races will be the 'survival of the fittest'?" In his *Descent of Man,* Darwin himself had written that probably the backward races would disappear before the advance of higher civilizations. "We must not forget," a prominent journalist wrote, "that the Anglo-Saxon race is expansive."

Members of the Anglo-Saxon cult recognized a powerful bond of race and culture with England and preached a *rapprochement* that became an unwritten alliance in the beginning of the twentieth century. "There is," a former secretary of state wrote in 1898, "a patriotism of race as well as of country." [1] The unwritten alliance with England was perhaps the most important and enduring feature of the new manifest destiny.

Mahan also desired close ties with England. After he published his book *The Influence of Sea Power upon History, 1660–1783* in 1890, he became the nation's foremost exponent of expansion and naval power. Since America's industrial growth demanded new markets and sources of raw materials, he announced in books and articles, the United States needed a large merchant marine protected by a great navy to compete in the worldwide struggle for commerce. To support that expanded sea power, he said, the United States also required overseas bases and colonies. Other nations, mainly the great powers of Europe, were scrambling for colonies in Asia, Africa, and among the islands of the Pacific Ocean. The United States must not be left behind in the march toward greatness.

Some were not impressed by the ideas of the new imperialists and the arguments of the Social Darwinists. Critics exposed the flaws in their theories. Social Darwinism, critics said, was like a circle. It led nowhere. It defined power in terms of survival and explained survival in terms of power and strength. "You might infer, to hear them buzz," a critical historian wrote a few years later, "that only the fittest survive, or, to put it conversely, the fact that you survive is proof that you are the 'fittest.' "[2]

The critics were right in arguing that the Social Darwinists were mistaken in ignoring the struggle of people with their environment and in emphasizing the battle of people with people. They and the apostles of the new manifest destiny were also mistaken in interpreting "fittest" in terms of force, implying that the strongest and most brutal survive. Darwin himself defined the fittest as those who adapted themselves best to existing conditions. Natural selection seldom operates among people. Since there is nothing "natural" about nations, and nations are made of people, the theory cannot logically apply to international relations.

Yet, as Mahan said, "whether they will or not Americans must now begin to look outward." He and others foresaw the possibilities of naval and commercial greatness in the Pacific Ocean. Beginning in 1883 Congress made successive appropriations for a modern battle fleet, but the United States had already started its overseas expansion in the Pacific. There, among the islands of Samoa and Hawaii, Americans saw the first bloom of the new manifest destiny.

Early Interest in Samoa and Africa

American interest in Samoa, an archipelago of fourteen islands located south of the equator in the central Pacific, about halfway between Honolulu and Sydney, Australia, went back beyond the era of the new expansionism. Yankee traders, American whalers, and even warships stopped there.

The United States, however, did not investigate the islands until Lieutenant Charles Wilkes of the navy led an official exploring expedition there in October 1839. Wilkes was especially impressed by the harbor of Pago Pago on Tutuila, one of the larger islands. Before leaving, he appointed an Englishman as American consul in Samoa and made an agreement with native chiefs covering trade and the protection of foreigners on the islands.

During the next thirty years English missionaries and traders and German merchants established themselves on the islands, mainly on Upolu, the second largest island. By 1870 the Germans owned most of the land and controlled most of the commerce, principally in copra.

Although the American government did nothing to establish a foothold in Samoa, a group of land speculators from Honolulu and San Francisco had moved in and in 1868 organized the Polynesian Land Company. Through dubious methods, they acquired large tracts of land from natives on Upolu and Tutuila. Those speculators tried unsuccessfully to persuade the United States to take over the islands so they could strengthen their claims to the land.

In 1870 a New York shipbuilder, who had organized a steamship line to run from San Francisco to Australia, tried unsuccessfully to obtain a subsidy from the government. Nonetheless, in the following year he sent an agent to Samoa to see if Pago Pago could be used as a coaling station for his ships. That agent called Upolu the "garden spot of the Pacific" and reported Pago Pago to be "the most perfectly landlocked harbor that exists in the Pacific Ocean."

The agent's report, stating that New Zealand and Germany were scheming to annex the islands, aroused the Navy Department. The rear admiral in command of the Pacific fleet, therefore, sent Commander Richard W. Meade to survey the harbor of Pago Pago. "I think some kind of treaty with the native chiefs will be necessary to frustrate foreign influence," Meade wrote, "which is at present very active in this matter, seeking to secure the harbor."[3]

On his own authority on February 17, 1872, Meade made a treaty with the chief of Pago Pago which gave the United States exclusive control of the harbor for a naval station. Three months later President Grant submitted the unauthorized agreement to the Senate. The Senate would not approve. Yet Meade's unratified treaty marked the beginning of closer relations between Samoa and the United States, and aroused German and British suspicions.

A group of Samoan chiefs, probably guided by American expansionists, next petitioned the United States to annex their islands or establish a protectorate over them. Now curious about Samoa, Grant in June 1873 sent a friend, Colonel Albert B. Steinberger, as a confidential agent to investigate.

Steinberger returned to the United States in December with letters from native chiefs that again asked the president to extend a protectorate over Samoa. Steinberger then went back to the islands as Grant's special agent but soon gave up that post to make himself premier of the kingdom of Samoa, an office he held until deposed in 1876.

Following Steinberger's departure, native warfare and international rivalry rocked the islands, and rumors circulated that either Germany or England would annex them. Preferring American control and encouraged in this sentiment by the American consul in the islands, the Samoan chiefs sent an envoy, M. K. Le Mamea, to the United States to offer their country for annexation. The Senate, Le Mamea was told, would not approve a treaty of annexation, so he and Secretary of State Evarts signed a treaty of peace and friendship on January 17, 1878, the first such agreement Samoa made with any major power. It gave the United States the right to establish a naval station at Pago Pago in return for a promise that the American government would use its good offices in disputes between Samoa and third powers. Since the treaty committed the government to little, the Senate gave its consent.

Not to be outdone, Germany in January and Britain in August 1879 signed treaties with Samoa giving them naval stations. The native chiefs then asked the three treaty powers to exercise a joint protectorate over the islands, which the powers did informally as the result of a convention their consuls signed at Apia on Upolu on September 2. Although the convention never went to the Senate for approval, the American government accepted it as an executive agreement and abided by its terms.

At this time Germany's chancellor, Otto von Bismarck, had a distaste for colonies. In December 1879, for example, he warned the British not to seize the islands, saying "we are not seeking anything *exclusively,* but wish to protect our interests there."[4] Four years later, Bismarck changed his mind about colonies. Beginning in April 1884 with a protectorate over part of Southwest Africa that caused friction with Britain, Germany grabbed colonies wherever she could. The imperial rivalry over African territory, especially the Congo basin, was more important to Germany and England than the fate of Samoa. This imperialism in Africa, part of the pattern that included contemporaneous expansion in the Pacific, also attracted the United States.

In 1876 King Leopold II of Belgium created the International Association for the Exploration and Civilization of Central Africa and two years later the International Association of the Congo to control and exploit the Congo River basin. Leopold feared, with good reason, that Britain and Portugal would act to shut him out of Central Africa by closing the mouth of the Congo. Aware that American leaders desired to share in the trade of the Congo, he sought to use them to enhance his position in the Congo. He asked the American government to grant the international association, which was in effect a private corporation, formal recognition. President Chester A. Arthur, with Senate concurrence, did so in April 1884, calling Leopold's association "a friendly Government." American recognition, quickly followed by recognition from other powers, gave the association a status it had previously lacked and drew the United States into the international politics of African colonialism.

In September when Bismarck, along with the French, decided to call a conference in Berlin on the political and commercial problems of the Congo, he therefore logically invited the United States, the first nation to recognize Leopold's possession. With the ostensible purpose of promoting equal trading privileges for Americans in the Congo, Arthur's administration accepted the invitation. Many in the United States, even within Arthur's party, opposed this dabbling in the "internal affairs of other continents." Why, one critic asked, should the United States help convert the Congo into "a monarchy for some impecunious European princes?"[5]

The Berlin Conference on African Affairs convened in November 1884 and completed its work the following February. It considered three main topics: free trade in the Congo area, free navigation of the Congo and

Niger rivers, and rules for establishing future European colonies in Africa. It also formally recognized the international association as the Congo Free State with Leopold as sovereign. The American delegates, who were active and influential throughout the proceedings, signed the general act, or convention, that embodied these results. But American adherence was never ratified. President Grover Cleveland refused to support what he considered an unwarranted entanglement. A special agent who had been sent to the Congo to investigate the situation apparently summed up the conventional wisdom of the time. "I do not believe," he wrote, "that Americans want or should want anything to do with Central Africa."[6] Nonetheless, for the first time American diplomats had participated in an international conference concerned with issues and territorial rivalries outside the Western Hemisphere.

Opposition to entanglement in European rivalries did not apply to Samoa. There tripartite control of the government brought no peace. The islands seethed with the intrigues of the three rival consuls and the turmoil of native wars. In keeping with Bismarck's new colonialism, in November 1884, while the more important fate of the Congo was being decided in Berlin, the German consul forced a treaty on Samoa's king that made his land a German protectorate. Disregarding the treaty, the king appealed to England and the United States for protection. Since Germany now appeared determined to seize the archipelago, Cleveland's secretary of state, Thomas F. Bayard, announced American opposition to German or any other foreign control of the islands.

Samoa's Fate

By the summer of 1886, Germany and the United States both recognized that their rivalry in Samoa threatened their peaceful relations. When Bayard suggested a three-power conference to deal with the Samoan problem, Britain and Germany accepted. At the conference, which met in Washington in June and July 1887, the United States suggested equal control by the three powers under a plan that would assure Samoa's independence. Since her commercial interests in the islands outweighed those of the other powers, Germany demanded preponderant political influence, and Britain supported her position in exchange for concessions elsewhere in the South Pacific. Since the United States opposed the German demand and insisted on Samoan autonomy, the conference adjourned without accomplishing a thing.

In Apia, meanwhile, international rivalry intensified. The Germans had sent four warships, declared war on the Samoan king, deported him, and entrenched their own puppet king. A native chief, encouraged by British and Americans, revolted against the puppet government. In December 1888 the rebels ambushed a detachment of German sailors, killing twenty and wounding thirty. Swearing vengeance, the Germans shelled and burned rebel areas, including American property.

Americans who had never before heard of Samoa now became aroused by reports of German violence there. A wave of anti-German feeling swept over the United States, and leading newspapers demanded a vigorous defense of American interests in Samoa. Some spoke of war. One of them was convinced that "Germany in this affair has simply played the highwayman."[7] In the midst of this excitement President Cleveland placed the Samoan situation in the hands of Congress. "I have insisted," he said in expressing his suspicions of Germany, "that the autonomy and independence of Samoa should be scrupulously preserved. . . ."[8] Congress then voted $500,000 for the protection of American life and property and $100,000 for developing the harbor at Pago Pago.

Debates on the appropriations brought up the whole question of policy in Samoa. Expansionist senators made it clear that they would not abandon the foothold there. The United States, they insisted, needed naval bases and overseas possessions to strengthen and maintain its position in the Pacific. The "sound and fury" over distant islands alarmed some liberals who opposed deep involvement.

The Nation suggested abandoning Samoa to Germany. "The more the matter is looked into," it said, "the more plainly does it seem, on our part, an outbreak of sheer Jingoism and meddlesomeness in other people's affairs." True enough, the United States had no vital interest in the islands, but the new manifest destiny, espoused by expansionist Republican senators, demanded a more aggressive policy.

Believing that existing tension was dangerous and Samoa not worth a possible clash with the United States, Chancellor Bismarck of Germany suggested that the United States, Britain, and Germany resume the disrupted negotiations of 1887 in Berlin. Cleveland and Bayard agreed but left the conference details to Benjamin Harrison's incoming administration.

In Apia, meanwhile, one British, three German, and three American warships crowded the harbor, and their sailors glowered at each other over ready guns. Then, on March 16, 1889, before any ship could get out to sea, a hurricane struck the harbor, sinking or beaching the six German and American warships with a tragic loss of life. Only the British *Calliope*, by forcing steam on her boilers, battled her way through mountainous waves to open sea and safety. The hurricane blew away the immediate crisis between Germany and the United States. "Both paused aghast," Robert Louis Stevenson wrote in his classic account of Samoan affairs; "both had time to recognise that not the whole Samoan Archipelago was worth the loss in men and costly ships already suffered."[9]

When delegates of the three powers met in Berlin in April, they were apparently sobered by the effects of the hurricane. After negotiating for six weeks, they signed a treaty on June 14 that established condominium, or three-power control of Samoa, though the fiction of Samoan independence was still maintained. "We see but one serious fault in the treaty," the New York *Herald* said. "It is that it involves us in agreements with European Governments which are contrary to the fixed policy of this country."

That was true enough, but the United States accepted this departure from its traditional policy of nonentanglement because the apparent alternative—German control of Samoa—was unacceptable to expansionists and others. Despite opposition of a strong minority, therefore, the Senate approved the treaty.

Since the rivalry and intrigue of the three powers continued and the natives resented their rule, the protectorate never worked well. "Who asked the Great Powers to make laws for us," a native orator asked; "to bring strangers here to rule us? We want no white officials to bind us in the bondage of taxation."

Cleveland, who had returned to power in 1893, deplored the entangling condominium. "Our participation in its establishment against the wishes of the natives," he said in his annual message of the following year, "was in plain defiance of the conservative teachings and warnings of the wise and patriotic men who laid the foundations of our free institutions."[10] He suggested withdrawal, but Congress would not follow his recommendations.

Early in 1899 civil war broke out in Samoa. The Germans supported one side, and the British and Americans the other. This time British and American warships fired on rebel villages, destroyed German property, and suffered the loss of sailors in a Samoan ambush.

Anti-German feeling had now become so strong that many Americans blamed only Germany for the difficulty in Samoa. "Does she want to fight?" a senator from Nevada asked. "If so, she may be accommodated." Anti-imperialists, however, denounced American policy and demanded withdrawal. "The Americans have one more evidence of what empire-building means," an editor explained. "It means shelling defenseless native villages, making our flag the symbol of high-handed interference."[11] Since British and American sailors stood shoulder to shoulder in the Samoan conflict, some Americans and Englishmen saw in this more evidence of a growing intimacy between their two countries.

With Republican expansionists now in power under William McKinley, the United States abandoned the theory it once held that Samoan independence was the object of its policy. When Germany suggested partition of the islands, therefore, McKinley and Secretary of State John Hay agreed. "Our interests in the Archipelago were very meagre," Hay wrote to a friend, "always excepting our interest in Pago Pago, which was of the most vital importance. It is the finest harbor in the Pacific and absolutely indispensable to us."[12]

Germany, Britain, and the United States settled the Samoan question in a convention they signed on December 2 in Washington. The United States acquired Tutuila and some lesser islands. Germany obtained the other islands. To compensate the British for surrender of their claims, Germany gave them the Tonga Islands, also islands in the Solomon chain, and concessions in West Africa.

The Senate approved the treaty. The Navy Department was pleased with Pago Pago, and some newspaper editors rejoiced "that the United States is now finally divorced from all political entanglements with either Germany or England." Anti-imperialists protested. "We blot out, then," a Democratic senator said, "a sovereign nation, a people with whom we have treaty relations, and divide the spoils." [13]

In February 1900 President McKinley placed the islands under the Navy Department, and in April the chiefs of Tutuila ceded their island to the United States. Other chiefs did the same in 1904. During the First World War, New Zealand seized the German islands and retained them. The United States did not formally accept its islands as full-fledged possessions until February 1929, when Congress confirmed the Samoan cessions by joint resolution.

Hawaii's Special Status

American policy in Hawaii, much more than that in Samoa, focused public attention on expansion in the Pacific. An archipelago of seven major islands in the eastern half of the North Pacific, about two thousand nautical miles from San Francisco, Hawaii was closer to the United States than to any other major power.

American interest in Hawaii, or the Sandwich Islands, also grew out of the early days of the China trade. Those islands offered a delightful halfway resting place for sailors weary of the sea, a source of fresh supplies, and a trade in sandalwood, a product that brought large profits in China.

Even before Americans had started visiting the islands, English, French, Spanish, and Russian ships stopped there. Some of the sailors from those and from American ships liked the islands so well that they stayed permanently, forming the nucleus of a foreign colony. Early in the nineteenth century, Honolulu, on the island of Oahu, became an important trading center, often called the "Crossroads of the Pacific."

In 1819 American whalers came to the islands and soon gave Hawaii a commercial importance that aroused the interest of the American government. At about the same time, in April 1820, the first band of New England missionaries landed in the islands. Those "Pilgrims of Hawaii" soon converted the natives to Protestant Christianity, and even more than traders, whalers, and planters, they and their children made Hawaii, in effect, a Pacific frontier of the United States. Those missionaries also came to dominate political life of the islands, becoming self-appointed advisers to the native government.

Americans, however, did not threaten Hawaii's independence, as did agents of other countries. Under the influence of American missionaries, the Hawaiian government passed a law in April 1831 banning Catholic priests from the islands and also persecuted native Catholics. Considering herself the protector of Catholic missions in the Pacific, France took the anti-Catholic laws in Hawaii as serious affronts and sent a frigate to Honolulu in 1839. The captain forced two treaties on the Hawaiian government, allowing Catholics freedom of worship and giving special trade concessions to France.

This successful use of force impressed the Hawaiian government with the need of gaining guarantees of its independence, especially from Britain, France, and the United States. American policy became clear when Hawaiian commissioners presented their plea to Secretary of State Daniel Webster in December 1842.

Although Webster would make no treaty guaranteeing independence, he stated that "the United States . . . are more interested in the fate of the islands, and of their Government, than any other nation can be." American policy, he added, opposed any kind of foreign control over the Hawaiian Islands.[14]

In the following year an unofficial and unsuccessful attempt of a British naval officer to take over Hawaii as a protectorate led the acting secretary of state to protest and to declare that the United States might be justified in using force to keep the islands out of European hands. Six years later in August 1849, another French intervention led the United States to sign a commercial treaty with the Hawaiian kingdom that formally recognized its independence. After that, some Americans, particularly on the newly acquired Pacific Coast, clamored for annexation.

Franklin Pierce was willing to oblige, and in 1854 his agent in Hawaii negotiated a treaty of annexation that Secretary of State Marcy never completed because it called for large annual annuities to the king and royal family and for Hawaii's entrance into the Union as a state. Many native Hawaiians, moreover, also opposed annexation because of American racial attitudes, citing the position of blacks in the United States as representative of the contempt for colored peoples.

Marcy next tried to draw Hawaii closer to the United States with a trade reciprocity treaty negotiated in July 1855. Fearing competition from Hawaiian sugar, Louisiana cane planters opposed it. The Senate, therefore, killed it.

After the Civil War high tariffs threatened to deprive Hawaiian sugar of its main market in California. The Hawaiian government therefore sought another reciprocity treaty. Although Secretary of State Seward preferred annexation, he welcomed the overtures as a step toward annexation and negotiated such a treaty in May 1867. It, too, failed in the Senate. Ironically, some senators voted against it because they feared that reciprocity might make the islands prosperous and thus prove a barrier to annexation.

In 1872 depression struck Hawaii's sugar industry. So desperate were the planters that they were willing to offer Pearl Harbor to the United States in exchange for a reciprocity treaty. That proved unnecessary. In January 1875 the United States signed a reciprocity treaty that ran for seven years and allowed Hawaiian sugar to enter the country free of duty. The Senate, this time fearing that another refusal might drive Hawaii into the arms of Britain, approved, adding an article that pledged the kingdom not to lease or dispose of any of its territory to any other power. That treaty, by making the islands economically dependent on the United States, marked a turning point in relations with Hawaii.

Reciprocity triggered a vast expansion in sugar, creating a boom that brought far-reaching changes to the Hawaiian kingdom. To meet the ensuing labor shortage, planters imported cheap contract labor, mostly Chinese and Japanese. The Asian influx alarmed Americans who disliked the change in the racial composition of the islands. Native Hawaiians, on the other hand, resented the Americanization of the islands, a process strengthened by reciprocity. Hence they attacked reciprocity. In the United States powerful sugar refiners in the East and cane planters in Louisiana also opposed it.

Even though the American government was sensitive to that opposition and realized that reciprocity brought its people no genuine economic benefits, it was friendly to the idea because through reciprocity Hawaii had in effect become its strategic outpost in the Pacific. In December 1884, therefore, the United States signed a convention extending reciprocity for another seven years. After considerable delay, the Senate finally approved the new treaty in January 1887, but added an amendment giving the United States the exclusive right to use Pearl Harbor as a naval station. Despite its dislike of the amendment, Hawaii accepted the treaty. Hawaiian independence, it now appeared, could not last.

Although white Hawaiians, many of them sons of American missionaries, in effect controlled the islands, native Hawaiians resented their rule and were more alarmed than ever by the virtual protectorate the United States had come to exercise over them. Determined to retain independence, some of them started a movement calling for "Hawaii for the Hawaiians." When Secretary of State Blaine offered Hawaii a new treaty in 1889 which in fact would have converted it into an American protectorate, native leaders protested so loudly that their government dropped the project.

In the following year an economic crisis added to the political unrest. The McKinley tariff that became law in October removed the duty on raw sugar imported into the United States and gave American producers a bounty of two cents a pound, thus wiping out the advantage the Hawaiian product had enjoyed over other foreign sugar. The effect in Hawaii was disastrous. Sugar production dropped precipitously, property values fell, and workers lost their jobs or took wage cuts.

During this period of tension, actually in January 1891, a politically experienced and strong-willed princess, Liliuokalani, became queen. She disliked the dominant influence of whites in the government and the constitutional safeguards they had imposed. In particular, she sympathized with the native movement of "Hawaii for the Hawaiians." By royal decree on January 14, 1893, she unsuccessfully attempted to replace the existing constitution with a new one that would return greater political power to the natives.

Previously sugar planters and industrialists, most of them Americans, had opposed annexation because they feared that American laws would cut off their supply of Asian labor and hence bite into their profits. The McKinley tariff and "Queen Lil" changed their views. Annexation now seemed the only safeguard for their property and profits. A small group of American Hawaiians in Honolulu, therefore, had organized an annexation club. News of the queen's arbitrary decree drove the annexationists to action. They decided to overthrow the monarchy, establish a provisional government, and ask for American annexation. The American minister in Honolulu, John L. Stevens, a close friend of Secretary Blaine and an ardent annexationist himself, agreed to support the revolutionists.

Revolution, Independence, and Annexation

On January 16 the revolutionists asked Stevens to land troops when necessary. "We are unable," they said, "to protect ourselves without aid, and therefore pray for the protection of the United States forces."[15] The queen and her advisers became alarmed and on that same day declared they would make no changes in the constitution, except through legal means, but the queen's retreat came too late. That afternoon Stevens ordered over 150 armed men from the cruiser *Boston,* then in Honolulu's harbor, to land and protect American lives and property. Instead, they took up positions that intimidated the queen's forces.

On the next day, the revolutionary committee of safety proclaimed the monarchy abolished and established a provisional government "to exist until terms of union with the United States of America have been negotiated and agreed upon." Stevens immediately recognized this regime, which thirty hours before had considered itself so weak that it needed American protection. Under protest, the queen then surrendered her authority, saying she yielded "to the superior force of the United States" which Stevens had used against her.[16] Within three days the bloodless revolution was over.

Five white commissioners from the new government immediately left for Washington to negotiate a treaty of annexation. As soon as they arrived in San Francisco the American press spread the story of the Hawaiian revolution over the nation. Expansionists welcomed it. "The popular verdict is clear, unequivocal, and practically unanimous," the New York *Tribune* announced. "Hawaii is welcome."

Less than two weeks after the revolution, Stevens himself wrote that "the Hawaiian pear is now fully ripe, and this is the golden hour for the United States to pluck it."[17] On that same day he hoisted the American flag and proclaimed Hawaii a protectorate. Secretary of State John W. Foster later disavowed that act, but the American flag continued to fly over government buildings in Honolulu.

Himself an imperialist, Foster quickly signed a treaty with the commissioners on February 14 that would incorporate Hawaii into the Union as a territory. The next day President Harrison submitted it to the Senate, saying that the United States had no hand in the revolution, that the Hawaiian government offered annexation voluntarily, and that, therefore, his government had no alternative but to accept the treaty. Aware of Democratic opposition, the Senate would not act in the two weeks remaining in Harrison's administration.

Five days after he became president for the second time, Grover Cleveland, on the advice of Secretary of State Walter Q. Gresham, withdrew the treaty from the Senate. Two days later he appointed a special commissioner, James H. Blount, a retired congressman from Georgia, to investigate the overthrow of the monarchy and to seek a guide for administration policy. Immediately after arriving in Hawaii, Blount repudiated the protectorate Stevens had proclaimed, hauled down the flag, and launched a thorough investigation.

In his report, Blount condemned Stevens's role in the revolution, saying that "the undoubted sentiment of the people is for the Queen against the Provisional Government, and against annexation." Gresham now wanted to reverse Stevens's policy. "Should not the great wrong done to a feeble but independent State by an abuse of the authority of the United States," he asked the president, "be undone by restoring the legitimate government? Anything short of that will not, I respectfully submit, satisfy the demands of justice."[18]

Accepting Blount's findings and Gresham's advice, Cleveland condemned the American role in the revolution as morally wrong. He replaced Stevens with a new minister who had secret instructions to restore Liliuokalani to her throne if she would grant amnesty to the revolutionists. Although the former queen at first was unwilling, saying angrily that "my decision would be, as the law directs, that such persons should be beheaded and their property confiscated," she ultimately agreed to Cleveland's terms.[19]

Sanford B. Dole, the son of a missionary and president of the provisional republic, refused to restore the monarchy. The president of the

United States, he said ironically, had no right to interfere in the domestic affairs of Hawaii. Many Americans, even Democrats, sided with Dole. "The Democratic party," the Atlanta *Constitution* announced, "has not been in the habit of restoring monarchies anywhere."[20]

The question of annexing Hawaii, meanwhile, had set off a strident debate on imperialism in Congress and in the press. Expansionists lauded imperialism and urged annexation for strategic reasons, but anti-imperialists, including Cleveland himself, attacked the wisdom of acquiring alien peoples and territory outside the continent.

Since Cleveland could restore Liliuokalani only through force, and Congress would not support him in a policy of bloodshed, he did nothing more after Dole's rebuff and allowed the provisional government to continue without American interference. That government established the Republic of Hawaii on July 4, 1894, under a constitution authorizing its president, whenever possible, to make a treaty of union with the United States. Cleveland promptly recognized the new republic.

The Republic of Hawaii never intended independence to be permanent, nor did expansionists in the United States. In 1896, for instance, the Republican campaign platform announced that "the Hawaiian Islands should be controlled by the United States."[21] When Republicans returned to power in March 1897, even though William McKinley himself was not at first an expansionist, they were prepared to carry out their commitment on Hawaii.

Those imperialists, moreover, were alarmed by possible Japanese control of the islands through immigration. Between 1883 and 1896 so many Japanese had crowded themselves into Hawaii that by 1897 they comprised about one-fourth of the population and were steadily increasing. The Japanese government disliked the discriminatory laws directed against its people in Hawaii, and as early as March 1893 had asked the government there to give them voting rights along with whites and native Hawaiians.

Hawaii's relations with Japan blossomed into a crisis in March 1897 when Hawaiian authorities arbitrarily refused to admit about twelve hundred Japanese immigrants who had already reached the islands. Japan protested and in May sent a warship to Honolulu. Rumors of war in Honolulu, an observer said, were as "thick as creditors around the Government building on pay day." Many in Hawaii now looked upon annexation as a necessary shield against Japan. The government, therefore, appealed to the United States for protection and urged annexation. Then, on June 16, a little over three months after taking office, McKinley sent another treaty of annexation to the Senate.

While the Senate had the treaty under consideration, Japan protested, saying annexation would upset the *status quo* in the Pacific and endanger Japanese rights in Hawaii. That protest played into the hands of the administration which used fear of Japanese action to gain Senate approval.

"We cannot let those Islands go to Japan," the president told a senator. "Japan has her eye on them."[22] If something were not done, he added, there would soon be another revolution, and Japan would gain control. Secretary of State John Sherman went so far as to instruct the American minister in Honolulu to announce a provisional protectorate pending annexation if Japan used force.

"The annexation of Hawaii is for the benefit of the Hawaiian, the Latin, and the Anglo-Saxon races of these Islands," the *Hawaiian Star* announced. "It is not and does not pretend to be for the benefit of the Asiatics. It is meant as a bar to the Asiatics."[23] Japan ultimately withdrew her protest and accepted an indemnity of $75,000 as a settlement of claims against the Hawaiian government.

Opposition from anti-imperialist Democrats and producers of beet sugar, meanwhile, had blocked the treaty in the Senate. Champ Clark, a Democratic congressman from Missouri, said "manifest destiny" was "the specious plea of every robber and freebooter since the world began, and will continue to be until the elements shall melt with fervent heat." Nonetheless, the expansionist fervor that marked the Spanish-American War drew Hawaii into the Union.

In this war the Hawaiian government made no pretense of being neutral. It did all it could to aid the United States. Despite this, Republican expansionists argued that they needed Hawaii as a base under American control for ships and troops going to the Philippines. At one time McKinley appeared ready to annex Hawaii by executive decree as a war measure. "We need Hawaii just as much and a good deal more than we did California," he told his secretary. "It is manifest destiny."[24]

Spurred on by manifest destiny and war fever, Congress hastily drew up a joint resolution of annexation. It passed both houses by July 6, 1898, and the president signed it the next day. A month later, on August 12, the Hawaiian Islands became American territory.

In acquiring Hawaii, the United States completed a process it had started many years before. Yet it also broke the pattern of past foreign policy since Hawaii, later the fiftieth state, was the first important overseas acquisition.

The Venezuelan Boundary Dispute

While dealing with the results of the Hawaiian revolution, Cleveland had become embroiled in a dispute over a boundary in South America that at first had nothing to do with the United States. The quarrel involved ownership of fifty thousand square miles of sparsely settled jungle, an area slightly larger than the state of New York, claimed by both Venezuela and the British in Guiana. That land had been in dispute long before Venezuela had become an independent nation. No one had ever drawn a satisfactory boundary. In 1841 Sir Robert Schomburgk, a British geographer, surveyed the territory for the British government and drew a boundary favorable to his employer. Venezuela protested and refused to make a settlement along the Schomburgk line. Both countries then agreed not to encroach on the disputed territory.

After 1875 a few settlers, gold miners and others, filtered into the area and friction between Venezuelan authorities and those of British Guiana developed. Both countries advanced inflated claims to the land. Since Venezuela was the weaker party, she repeatedly asked the British to arbitrate the whole area in dispute, but they were willing to do so only for the territory west of, or beyond, the Schomburgk line. The Venezuelans, therefore, appealed to the United States for help and attempted to invoke the principles of the Monroe Doctrine.

Beginning in 1887, after a rupture in relations between Venezuela and Britain, the United States more than once offered to assist in arbitrating the boundary. The British refused the American good offices, persisting in their stand that the territory inside the Schomburgk line was not open to arbitration. This was the situation when Cleveland became president for the second time in March 1893.

The change in administrations left Harrison's minister to Venezuela, William L. Scruggs, without a diplomatic job. In August 1894 the Venezuelan government hired him as legal adviser and propagandist to work in Washington. He immediately wrote a pamphlet entitled *British Aggressions in Venezuela, or the Monroe Doctrine on Trial*. It presented only the Venezuelan side of the dispute and linked it with the Monroe Doctrine, now a revered American policy. He published the booklet in October, selling it on newsstands and distributing it free to newspaper editors, members of Congress, governors, and other leaders of opinion. Before December it ran through four editions.

Scruggs did not rely solely on his pamphlet to arouse American opinion in support of Venezuela and the Monroe Doctrine. In January 1895 he persuaded his congressman to introduce a resolution urging Britain and Venezuela to arbitrate. It passed both houses unanimously, and Cleveland signed it on February 20. Then the press took up the cause of the Monroe Doctrine. To the New York *Tribune* the problem was "perfectly simple." Venezuela owned the land and Britain was trying to take it.[25]

At this time a seemingly unrelated episode, the Corinto affair, intruded on relations with Britain. In April about four hundred British marines occupied the port of Corinto in Nicaragua in an effort to collect compensation for harsh action Nicaragua had taken in 1894 against several British subjects and a vice consul. Nicaragua appealed to Cleveland, asking him to intervene against an alleged violation of the Monroe Doctrine. Secretary of State Gresham replied that since Britain did not intend to occupy Corinto permanently, the Monroe Doctrine was not in danger.

Newspapers kept the Corinto affair in the headlines by denouncing England's strong-arm tactics in dealing with Nicaragua and criticizing the Cleveland administration for permitting the British to act as they pleased. "What is the most amazing and embittering," one complained, "is that this act of British aggression is consummated with the assent and sanction of the American Administration."[26]

Nicaragua finally made arrangements for payment of the indemnity, and so the British left Corinto on May 2. That did not end the matter for Cleveland. Political opponents, and even some Democrats, attacked his foreign policy for being weak and pro-British. The Corinto affair and political criticism, as well as fear of foreign political and economic encroachments in Latin America, now influenced Cleveland's policy toward Venezuela. To aid the Democratic party and enhance his own political stature, friends urged him to meet the attacks of his critics by taking a strong stand in support of Venezuela.

Olney's "Twenty-Inch Gun"

Shortly before the British left Nicaragua, therefore, Cleveland asked Gresham to prepare a note on the Venezuelan question, but the secretary died before completing it. Richard Olney, a strong-willed, brusque, and vigorous lawyer from Boston, who had been attorney general, took over as secretary of state on June 10 and in a few weeks finished the Venezuelan document. While Olney prepared his note, an article by Henry Cabot Lodge, a young Republican senator from his own state, appeared in a national magazine. Lodge declared that "the supremacy of the Monroe Doctrine should be established and at once—peaceably if we can, forcibly if we must."[27] He wanted the United States to halt British imperialism in Venezuela.

Olney's note, his first important state paper, was similar in spirit to Lodge's article. Cleveland, who later dubbed it a "twenty-inch gun," liked the note and said it was "the best thing of the kind" he had ever read. He "softened" it a bit, but still it remained forceful and essentially as Olney had written it. The secretary sent it to the American ambassador in London on July 20.

Olney asked Britain to submit the disputed territory to arbitration and to accept his own extreme interpretation of the Monroe Doctrine which he called a "doctrine of American public law." By holding territory claimed by Venezuela, he said, Britain violated that doctrine and justified American intervention in the dispute. "Today the United States is practically sovereign on this continent, and its fiat is law upon the subjects to which it confines its interposition," he emphasized. That is so, he went on, because "in addition to all other grounds, its infinite resources combined with its isolated position render it master of the situation and practically invulnerable as against all other powers." He asked the British to reply before the president addressed Congress in the session that would open in December.[28]

With its time limit and belligerent tone the note had the characteristics of an ultimatum. In referring to rumors of a ninety-day ultimatum, one English journal said mockingly. "Isn't it awful? But it might be still more awful if we only knew what the blessed Monroe Doctrine was, or what on earth the United States government has got to do with a quarrel between Great Britain and another independent state."[29]

The impatient Olney received no reply for four months. On December 2, Congress convened without an answer to Olney's note. For various reasons, the British had delayed their response but had intended to send it before Congress met. Because they miscalculated the date set for Congress to convene, the reply, dated November 26, did not reach Olney until December 7.

Lord Salisbury, Britain's foreign secretary, was an experienced diplomat and a blunt aristocrat as self-righteous about British honor as Olney was about American policy. Salisbury said the Monroe Doctrine had no validity under international law, could not bind Britain, and did not apply to the Venezuelan boundary dispute. Britain, he added, was willing to arbitrate only the land beyond the Schomburgk line. He made not a single concession.

Salisbury's reasoning was clear and logical, more so than Olney's. The imperious tone of his two notes, with their cutting sentences, however, infuriated Cleveland and Olney. After Olney drafted a special message, Cleveland sat up all night rewriting it and sent it to Congress on December 17. He said that Britain had refused to arbitrate, and in truculent passages written by Olney he recommended strong action. He requested authority to appoint an independent commission to investigate and decide where the boundary should be and for power to enforce its decision. "In making these recommendations," the president declared, "I am fully alive to the responsibility incurred, and keenly realize all the consequences that may follow."[30]

That was the language of war, which neither Cleveland nor Olney truly wanted. Cleveland's menacing use of the investigating commission was, in fact, probably less a threat of war than a means of forcing the British to arbitrate the entire disputed region.

Congress instantly applauded the message and gave Cleveland the authority he requested. The House of Representatives voted unanimously for the boundary commission and appropriated $100,000 for its expenses. A wave of warlike enthusiasm swept over the country. "It is the call to arms," the Washington *Post* cried out; "the jingoes were right after all, and it is not to be the fashion henceforth to sneer at patriots and soldiers." The Springfield *Union* joined in with, "Good for Mr. Cleveland!"

Yet some Americans and a few of their newspapers denounced the message. Moderates, fearful of war, urged peace. The governor of Massachusetts wrote the president, for instance, that "public opinion here is extremely strong and earnest in favor of a peaceful and honorable solution of the difficulty." [31]

English politicians, moreover, did not respond to Cleveland's message with nationalistic explosions of their own. Nor did the British people. Few of them knew or cared anything about Venezuela. Lord Salisbury and his supporters did not want war. He realized that he had underestimated Cleveland's determination to force a solution. Backed by a favorable public opinion and anxious to allay the unexpectedly violent American sentiment, the British government reopened the subject of arbitration.

Britain's reasons for backing down are complex, but two stand out: she wanted to retain American friendship and feared the power of a united Germany who was challenging her industrially and on the seas. In Europe Britain had no friends, so she did not want to make another enemy in the American people. Her own people considered war with the United States virtually unthinkable.

At this time, furthermore, Britain's troubles with the Boers, or Dutch settlers in South Africa, came to a head. An Englishman, Dr. Leander Starr Jameson, led an armed raiding party into the Boer republic of the Transvaal. The Boers repulsed the raiders on January 3, 1896, and Germany's kaiser sent an open telegram to Paul Kruger, president of the Transvaal, congratulating him on thwarting the "Jameson raid." The kaiser implied ominously that Germany supported the Boers in their quarrel with England.

That telegram aroused British anger. Englishmen shouted defiance of Germany and prepared for war. The German war scare, although it followed Britain's decision to back down on the Venezuelan matter, diverted attention from that crisis and made easier a retreat on Venezuela and hence reconciliation with the United States. "War between the two nations, England and the United States," the British colonial secretary announced "would be an absurdity as well as a crime."

After long negotiation with the United States, Britain agreed to submit the entire disputed territory to an arbitration tribunal of five men under a formula excluding areas that settlers had held for fifty years. Britain and Venezuela signed a treaty of arbitration in February 1897 that embodied the fifty-year formula. The American boundary commission then disbanded and turned its work over to the new tribunal.

In October 1899 the arbitration tribunal handed down a unanimous award that gave Britain about 90 percent of the territory in dispute. The settlement followed the Schomburgk line, but with two important exceptions. Venezuela received some five thousand square miles in the interior on the headwaters of the Orinoco River, but more important strategically, she gained the mouth of the Orinoco and hence control of that great river. The award, nonetheless, was a diplomatic compromise that favored Britain and embittered Venezuela.

Even though the award failed to recognize the wide claims of Venezuela that American editors and jingoes had championed, American opinion seemed generally satisfied with it. Cleveland and Olney had successfully challenged England and had persuaded her to recognize the predominant position of the United States in the Western Hemisphere. Americans were more interested in this diplomatic victory over Britain than in the merits of the boundary settlement itself.

Britain's satisfaction is also understandable. Even though the British had retreated on the principle of arbitration, they had won most of what they desired in the settlement. They had, after all, wanted to fix the boundary at the Schomburgk line for many years. They had at the same time retained American friendship without great sacrifice. Even though the United States and Britain had appeared close to war, the Venezuelan crisis marked the beginning of a new Anglo-American *rapprochement* that heralded the birth of a strong but unofficial alliance.

For the United States alone, the Venezuelan crisis marked the hardening of a militant and belligerent nationalism. Americans accelerated their efforts to build a large and powerful navy. They took a new interest in foreign policy and in affairs abroad. They were ready to back their now expanded view of the Monroe Doctrine with force. Although the United States had long had the potential for being a world power, the Venezuelan crisis showed that it was willing and capable of acting as one. The powers of Europe would now have to take the possible reaction of the United States into consideration when they planned major moves in foreign policy.

The Olney-Pauncefote Convention

During the Venezuelan crisis some Americans and some Englishmen believed that their countries might not have come so close to war if they had been committed to a general arbitration treaty. They were shocked by the irresponsible talk of war that had spread over the United States. American and British efforts to negotiate an arbitration treaty were not new. They had begun in 1873 and Cleveland himself had a great interest in arbitration. Nothing definite happened, however, until after the Venezuelan crisis.

Secretary Olney and Sir Julian Pauncefote, British ambassador in Washington, signed a general arbitration convention on January 11, 1897. It committed their countries for five years to submit to arbitration, within certain limitations, all disputes they failed to settle through diplomacy. Much public sentiment appeared to support the treaty, and Cleveland and Olney tried to mobilize that opinion to impress the Senate, but opposition was strong. Referring to Canada and the West Indies, the Chicago *Tribune* claimed that Americans wanted "to get rid of foreign influence on the North and South American continents. . . . We don't want to be tied up with any general arbitration treaty." Disturbed by Senate opposition to the treaty, the English *Saturday Review,* on the other hand, lamented that America was "misrepresented by its stupid and mischievous Congress."[32]

William McKinley, Cleveland's Republican successor, supported the treaty and in his inaugural address said he hoped the Senate would approve it. The Senate, reflecting popular distrust of Britain and unwilling to surrender any of its control over foreign policy through an advance commitment to arbitration, defeated the treaty in May. Despite disappointment in the ruling elites of both England and the United States, defeat of the convention did not impair the newly strengthened friendship with Britain.

XIV

That Splendid Little War

Another crisis in nearby Cuba brought the new manifest destiny more dramatically to the attention of the American people than had Samoa or. Hawaii. The crisis began with a worldwide depression in 1893, followed by an American tariff law of 1894 that raised duties on raw sugar, the backbone of Cuba's already depressed economy, to a level 40 percent higher than under the previous tariff. The new tariff wrecked Cuba's sugar market and brought crushing poverty and more misery to the island. Economic exhaustion, added to smoldering discontent with Spain's misrule since the end of the Ten Years' War—a discontent fanned by Cuban exiles in the United States—led the Cubans in February 1895 to revolt against their Spanish rulers.

Since the United States had long been interested in Cuba, the insurrectionists found it relatively easy to arouse American feelings against Spain. Americans showed their temper a few weeks after the revolt began when they learned that on March 8 a Spanish gunboat had fired on an American steamer, the *Alliança,* about six miles off Cuba's coast. That attack made the Cuban revolution headline news in practically every newspaper in the country and set off a wave of jingoism. A senator from Alabama wanted to "despatch a fleet of warships to Havana" to avenge insult to the flag.[1] Other Americans clamored for similar action. After that, incident after incident embittered relations with Spain and built up sympathy for the Cuban rebels.

Capitalizing on American sympathy, Cubans established revolutionary committees, or *juntas,* in the United States, with general headquarters in New York, in order to spread propaganda, raise funds, and to recruit and outfit filibustering expeditions. Joseph Pulitzer's New York *World* and William Randolph Hearst's New York *Journal,* which were locked in a circulation war that fed on sensationalism, dramatized the rebellion as a struggle between good and evil. Seldom, if ever, reporting Spanish actions in a favorable light, Hearst and Pulitzer's "yellow" journals used stories of Spanish atrocities to increase circulation. When there were no suitable incidents, their reporters sometimes dressed up the latest rumors as dispatches. At the same time, both journals preached intervention and urged a foreign policy of imperialism. Throughout the country other newspapers, though their influence was not exercised through sensational journalism, demanded the same policy, calling on Americans to accept their destiny by assuming obvious responsibilities in Cuba.

The religious press, mostly Protestant, joined the crusade against alleged Spanish barbarism, as did some of the business press, but many financial and trade journals opposed the clamor for war. Whether the yellow press created a mood of imperialism or merely expressed the existing sentiment of the people, it preached what many Americans wanted to hear. For some Americans the revolution in Cuba offered an excuse for an imperialism ostensibly based on humanitarian principles.

Precarious Neutrality

Given the attitude of the American people and the nature of the struggle in Cuba, the United States found it difficult to hold to a policy of neutrality. The government patrolled its own coasts at considerable expense to prevent smugglers, filibusters, and gunrunners from reaching Cuba's shores, but some always got through.

Ignoring the usual rules of warfare, the revolutionists in Cuba inaugurated a scorched earth policy, plundering and destroying loyalist property and burning sugar plantations, many of them owned by Americans. Cubans aimed to drive their masters from the island by exhausting Spain's resources. At the same time Cubans charged Spaniards with following a policy of calculated brutality, and Americans, seeing only one side of the conflict, believed the revolutionaries.

Some recently naturalized Americans, formerly Cubans, fought the Spaniards. When captured, they demanded protection of the American flag. In almost every case when the American government intervened officially in their behalf, the Spanish government cooperated. But Spain, understandably bitter, accused the American government of failing to uphold its neutrality since most of the money and munitions that kept the rebellion aflame came from the United States. Without American assistance, she said, the rebellion would die.

In the first year of the rebellion Spain made little headway against Cuban forces. In February 1896, therefore, she sent an energetic and ruthless general, Valeriano Weyler, to Cuba with orders to crush the rebels. To fight fire with fire he instituted a harsh concentration camp policy designed to control rebels who appeared peaceful farmers in the day and fought as guerrillas at night. Although no more drastic than similar measures used by other commanders at other times in fighting guerrilla armies and no more brutal than the tactics of the rebels themselves, Weyler's policy outraged Americans. Since sanitation was primitive and Spanish administration bad, many of the men, women, and children herded into concentration camps died from malnutrition and disease.

The yellow press played up the misery of Cubans in the camps, denounced Weyler's methods, and labelled him "Butcher." Most Americans knew him by no other name; even statesmen referred to him as "Butcher" Weyler.

Grover Cleveland opposed demands for intervention. In June 1895 he had issued a proclamation of neutrality recognizing the existence of insurrection in Cuba, but not the belligerency of the rebels. That policy, he believed, was the best way of enforcing neutrality laws and protecting American interests, but it did not satisfy Congress. In the following April both houses, motivated by partisan political considerations, overwhelmingly passed a concurrent resolution favoring recognition of Cuban belligerency and calling on the president to offer the nation's friendly offices "to the Spanish Government for the recognition of the independence of Cuba."[2] Since such action was an executive function, Cleveland ignored the resolution. He was more concerned, however, over talk that Congress might try to force him to recognize Cuba, which might have brought on war with Spain.

Two days before final passage of the resolution, Secretary of State Olney offered to mediate the quarrel between Spain and her rebelling colony. Fearing that the United States wanted Cuba for itself, Spain refused the offer, and that summer her statesmen drew up a plan for joint action by Europe's major powers to prevent the United States from intervening. "The question is a Spanish one," the Spaniards pointed out, "but the interests it touches are not Spain's alone, but all Europe's." The plan fell through, and American demands for intervention increased.

There were jingoes and imperialists in both political camps, but in the Republican party the jingoes shaped the platform of 1896. "We believe," that platform stated, "that the government of the United States should actively use its influence and good offices to restore peace and give independence to the Island," meaning Cuba.[3] Foreign policy was by no means the main issue of the campaign, but imperialists believed that the Cuban revolution offered a rare opportunity to drive Spain from the Western Hemisphere. An articulate coterie of publicists, naval strategists, and nationalist politicians, mostly in the Republican party, did not want to lose that opportunity and urged intervention.

The Republican who won the presidency, William McKinley, was no imperialist. He was a small town Ohio politician who had advanced far in politics under the wing of the Cleveland capitalist Marcus A. Hanna. An affable, handsome man who made friends easily and won the affection of those close to him, McKinley paid little attention to foreign affairs. He wanted peace. There will be "no jingo nonsense under my administration," he said. In his inaugural address he virtually ignored foreign policy. "We want no wars of conquest," he announced; "we must avoid the temptation of territorial aggression." McKinley was not one to inspire men, yet, as someone remarked, if men would not die for him they were happy to vote for him. He usually accommodated himself to pressures of public opinion and politics.

In September 1897, through the American minister in Madrid, Mc-Kinley offered his good offices to Spain to restore peace in Cuba. The United States, the minister said, "had no intention of annexing the Island of Cuba, nor did it aspire to the responsibilities of a protectorate." [4] Yet the offer carried the threat of intervention if Spain did not reverse her policy in Cuba.

Even though a new and liberal Spanish government had come to power in October, it turned down the president's offer. It did, however, inaugurate reforms in Cuba: it recalled Weyler, granted Cubans political rights similar to those held by Spaniards, and promised eventual home rule.

The rebels spurned Spain's concessions. Home rule no longer satisfied them; they wanted complete independence. Yet Spain's conciliatory attitude softened the sentiment of the American government, if not of the yellow press and the people. "No War with Spain—All Indications Point to Peace," the Washington *Post* announced in its headline of November 6. In his first annual message in December, McKinley recognized Spain's new efforts and urged his people to give her a "reasonable chance" to effect satisfactory changes. He seemingly repudiated intervention. "I speak not of forcible annexation," he said, "for that cannot be thought of. That, by our code of morality, would be criminal aggression." [5]

The Maine Goes Down

Spanish loyalists, who ran the Cuban economy and government and who opposed even the thought of being ruled by native Cubans, also attacked the new liberal policy. On January 12, 1898, some of them rioted in Havana's streets shouting, "Viva Weyler." Fearing attacks on Americans, Fitzhugh Lee, the interventionist American consul-general in Havana, suggested sending several warships to Key West, Florida. From there they could easily sail to Havana if needed. Even though tension in Havana eased and Lee advised against sending warships to the city, the second-class battleship *Maine,* which was in fact a sleek armored cruiser, entered Havana's harbor on the morning of January 25. The president, American officials insisted, had sent the *Maine* not as a threat but as "an act of friendly courtesy." The visit, nonetheless, displeased the Spaniards in Havana and added new tensions to an already taut situation there.

Then, as the *Maine* lay at anchor, what might have been a trifling incident became an outrage. On February 9 Hearst's *Journal* published a private letter written by Enrique Dupuy de Lôme, the Spanish minister in the United States, to a friend in Cuba. That document, filched by an insurgent spy and placed into the hands of a Hearst reporter, proved a sensation. President McKinley, Dupuy de Lôme wrote, is weak, "a would-be politician who tries to leave a door open behind himself while keeping on good terms with the jingoes of his party." [6]

The fact that a Spaniard dared criticize an American president, particularly in contemptuous terms, whipped the jingoes and the yellow press to fury. Within twelve hours, before the United States demanded Dupuy de Lôme's recall, he resigned. The Spanish government accepted the resignation, but his unwittingly indiscreet comments had already irreparably harmed Spanish-American relations.

Less than a week later, news from Havana gave the nation another shock. On the night of February 15, something or somebody blew up the *Maine,* killing 260 men. The interventionist journals flooded the country with "war extras," even though the captain of the *Maine* himself had suggested that "public opinion should be suspended until further report." "THE MAINE WAS DESTROYED BY TREACHERY," the New York *Journal* announced in a massive headline, and offered diagrams to prove its conclusion. [7] "The slightest spark," the secretary of the navy noted in his diary, "is liable to result in war." On March 9 Congress rushed through a unanimous vote for an appropriation of $50 million for war preparations.

On March 17, in the midst of the *Maine* hysteria, a conservative and respected Republican senator from Vermont and a former secretary of war, Redfield Proctor, made a speech reporting on the death and misery he had seen in concentration camps in Cuba. Weyler's cruelties and loss of the *Maine,* he said, did not move him as did "the spectacle of a million and a half people, the entire native population of Cuba, struggling for freedom and deliverance from the worst misgovernment of which I ever had knowledge." [8]

Those who were not impressed by the exaggerations of the yellow sheets believed Proctor and concluded that something had to be done about Cuba. "Senator Proctor's speech," the *Wall Street Journal* observed two days later, "converted a great many people in Wall Street, who have heretofore taken the ground that the United States had no business to interfere in a revolution on Spanish soil." There was no question, it said, about the accuracy of Proctor's statements: "they made the blood boil."

Eleven days after Proctor's speech a naval court of inquiry published its findings that a submarine mine had blown up the *Maine.* The people, already believing Spain guilty, were now convinced. War fever spread from coast to coast. The yellow journals called for war and even the religious press joined the chorus. "And if it be the will of Almighty God, that by war the last trace of this inhumanity of man to man shall be swept away from this Western Hemisphere," the *Evangelist,* a Presbyterian journal, announced, "let it come!" [9]

On March 28, the same day on which the president announced the court's findings, the American minister in Madrid presented the Spanish government with a virtual ultimatum. It suggested an immediate armistice until October 1, with an end to the concentration camp policy and American mediation of the revolution. The minister asked for a reply in a few days. What the United States wanted, Assistant Secretary of State William R. Day made clear in a subsequent telegram, was an independent Cuba.

Spain Attempts Negotiation

Anxious to avoid war, the Spanish government in its reply three days later met most of the American demands. It ordered the end of the concentration camp policy and said it would grant an armistice if the rebels asked for one. Rejection of American mediation and the issue of the armistice, which the rebels, confident of ultimate American intervention, would not ask for, made the reply unsatisfactory. The United States wanted an unconditional armistice, that is, actual independence. If the Spanish government did not accept McKinley's demands in full, a disastrous war appeared certain; if it conceded all, an angry public would probably overthrow it and perhaps the monarchy also.

In her dilemma Spain appealed to the major European powers for help, but none offered direct assistance. Although anxious to prevent war between Spain and the United States, the German foreign minister was blunt. "You are isolated," he told the Spanish ambassador, "because everybody wants to be pleasant to the United States, or, at any rate, nobody wants to arouse America's anger; the United States is a rich country, against which you simply cannot sustain a war." [10] The pope, however, offered to mediate the Cuban conflict and Spain, desperately looking for a way out, was willing to grant an armistice if he asked for it. An armistice sponsored by the Vatican would not appear to the Spanish people an ignominious surrender to an American ultimatum.

The American minister in Madrid cabled the president on April 5 that Spain had agreed to stop hostilities under the pope's terms. "I believe this means peace"; and he added, "I believe that you will approve this last conscientious offer for peace." For a moment the people of Europe seemed convinced that the threat of war between Spain and the United States had subsided, and all breathed more easily. McKinley, however, sent a noncommittal reply, indicating that all now depended on Congress.

Despite their previous reluctance to interfere, the great powers of

Europe—Britain, Germany, France, Austria-Hungary, Russia, and Italy—
at the urging of Austria backed by Germany, tried to avert war through an
amicable intervention. The ambassadors of the European powers in Washington, acting in a body, presented McKinley with a joint note on April 7
appealing "to the feelings of humanity and moderation of the President and
of the American people" to preserve peace with Spain. The American government knew beforehand that the collective act of the European powers
was not a serious one. It knew definitely that England would not interfere
with American plans. In his reply McKinley spoke of fulfilling "a duty to
humanity" and would concede nothing.

Two days later the European powers exerted greater pressure on Spain
than they had on the United States. On the same day Spain, on her own
initiative, ordered an end to hostilities in Cuba, thus meeting virtually all
of McKinley's demands except American mediation. "I hope that nothing
will now be done to humiliate Spain," the American minister in Madrid
wired the next day, "as I am satisfied that the present government is going,
and is loyally ready to go, as fast and as far as it can. With your power of
action sufficiently free you will win the fight on your own lines." [11]

McKinley, despite his personal desire to avert war, did not feel he had
freedom of action. He would not buck the popular outcry for war and the
jingoes of his own party. War, the Richmond *Times* said, "would undoubtedly have a wholesome effect in knitting the bonds of the Union closer
together, and in allaying sectional and class strife." Consciously, or uncon-
sciously, many Americans agreed with that idea, and they swelled sentiment for intervention in Cuba. If they did not give the people the war
they wanted, Republican politicians believed, then the people in the approaching fall elections would turn them out of office. The president himself feared that if he did not act, Congress would pass a war resolution over
his head and humiliate him and his party. Thus McKinley, even though
most of his cabinet and certain leading Republican senators favored peace,
yielded to the war hawks.

The Onset of War

On April 11, two days after Spain's final capitulation, McKinley sent
Congress his message recommending forcible intervention. He had prepared this six days earlier but had delayed delivering it until Americans in
Cuba were evacuated. He spoke "in the name of humanity, in the name of
civilization"; said he had exhausted every effort to relieve intolerable conditions in Cuba; and asked Congress for authority to use the army and navy
to end hostilities there, in effect, a request for war. In two brief para-
graphs, added to the end of a speech covering nine printed pages, he mentioned Spain's surrender on the points that ostensibly were the causes for
war. [12]

On that same day Spain made one more desperate try for European assistance. Her plea brought forth another effort from the Austrian government which urged the powers to take diplomatic action on behalf of Spain. Three days later the ambassadors of the great powers met in the British embassy in Washington where they prepared a joint note with the idea of pressuring the United States. Spain's concessions, they held, made armed intervention unjustifiable.

This was as close as Spain could come to achieving the European intervention on her behalf that she desired. The powers never delivered the note, mainly because Britain, who sought American friendship, and the German kaiser, who considered the move pointless, opposed this last-minute diplomatic intervention. "It seems very doubtful whether we ought to commit ourselves to a judgment adverse to the United States," the British Foreign Office said, "and whether in the interests of peace such a step would be desirable." [13]

That episode reflected the attitude of the foreign powers. None of the countries of continental Europe were friendly to the United States. Most of them disliked America's badgering of impotent Spain. England, the American ambassador in London wrote, "is the only European country whose sympathies are not openly against us." [14] There is, however, no basis to the story that the powers had created a new concert of Europe to intervene in the New World and that only British friendship thwarted it.

Although there were many reasons for Britain's friendliness, one was especially significant as it also formed the basis for an Anglo-American *rapprochement* at the turn of the century. Since Britain's delicate international position left her without friends, she could not afford to alienate the United States. So conspicuously friendly were the British, that many Americans suspected a secret Anglo-American alliance. Irishmen in New York were so concerned that they organized an Anti-British Alliance Association of the United States.

In Congress, meanwhile, the fate of Spain's empire was being debated and the president's influence over his party being shattered. McKinley's reasons for leading the country to war had a hollow ring, but a Congress eager for a fight not only gave them its full support but wished to go beyond them. On April 19, after a long harsh wrangle over a Senate amendment recognizing the insurgent republic, one that would have infringed the president's constitutional prerogatives of recognizing a foreign state, Congress passed a joint resolution without that recognition. It declared Cuba independent and authorized intervention. An amendment proposed by Senator Henry M. Teller of Colorado pledging the United States not to annex Cuba passed without dissent. The Teller amendment, more than McKinley's high-sounding phrases, reflected some of the humanitarian impulse behind the drive to war. The president signed the resolution of intervention on the following day. Spain, in desperation after receiving a three-day ultimatum, declared war on April 24, and Congress, the next day, declared war to have existed since April 21, when McKinley had established a blockade.

Why did this war come when leading statesmen on both sides did not want it? Some historians, particularly economic determinists, blame vested and expansionist business interests, but many American investors in Cuba desired peace. They wanted to save their property from the destruction of war, and business interests in the United States were divided; many opposed war until it came. Even the *Maine*'s destruction did not change their desire for peace.

"We here in Washington," war-bent Theodore Roosevelt had written to a friend in disgust, "have grown to feel that almost every man connected with the big business interests of the country is anxious to court any infamy if only peace can be obtained and the business situation be not disturbed."[15] American businessmen were far more concerned with recovery from an industrial depression that had gripped the country from 1893 to early 1897 and with opportunities of economic expansion at home than they were with expansion abroad.

In accord with their own sentiments and with what they considered to be public opinion, American political leaders, as much as any other force, brought McKinley to a decision for war, particularly after destruction of the *Maine*. Newspapers, the people, and the politicians demanded it. McKinley headed a businessmen's administration that did not want war. "I did all that in honor could be done to avert the war," he said three years later, "but without avail." He probably sincerely believed that, but he cannot be absolved from blame. He chose war rather than risk the breakup of his party. No president, regardless of political and popular pressures, can evade responsibilities that are his in leading his people into war. If McKinley, who had shown courage in bucking political pressure up to a point, had had the sterner qualities of leadership in time of crisis, he could have tried, at least, to hold Congress in check and to overcome the popular hysteria.

Ten Weeks of Warfare

As to the war capabilities of Spain and the United States, they were unequal. Spain's main asset was a misguided concept of national honor. On paper her military power appeared formidable. She had almost 200,000 troops in Cuba and a navy that contained more armored cruisers and torpedo boats than did the American navy, but the United States had more battleships and its navy was newer and better disciplined. Spain's ships were hardly seaworthy, were based thousands of miles from the scene of fighting, and her leaders were haunted by anticipation of defeat.

Even before the war started, Admiral Pascual Cervera, commander of

Spain's main naval squadron, recorded privately: "We may and must expect a disaster. But . . . I hold my tongue and go forth resignedly to face the trials which God may be pleased to send me."[16]

With most Americans, apparently the war was popular. They entered it lightheartedly, their young men marching off to the strains of "The Stars and Stripes Forever." Despite this gay martial spirit of its people, the United States was militarily unprepared. The army totalled only 28,183 officers and men, scattered in small detachments from coast to coast. It had enough rifles of a new type for the regulars, but the 200,000 volunteers the president had called into service received outmoded rifles that fired a black-powder cartridge. The army lacked necessary equipment for a field campaign—shoes, blankets, tents—and could get no light khaki cloth. So the soldiers fought a hot summer campaign in Cuba in heavy blue winter uniforms.

The casualty lists softened the war spirit, but Spain proved a feeble opponent and the fighting was mercifully short. She appeared to have placed her trust almost wholly on outside help, on European intervention that never came.

The first blows of the war, which proved to be the most important ones, did not fall on Cuba but in Asia, on Spain's Philippine Islands. One day, two months before the outbreak of war, Theodore Roosevelt, then assistant secretary of the navy, became acting secretary for three or four hours while the secretary was away. At this time, the traditional story goes, he took a grave responsibility upon himself and may have influenced the course of history. He cabled Commodore George Dewey, in command of the Asiatic Squadron, orders to prepare for "offensive operations in the Philippine Islands."

Since Roosevelt's deed reflected standard naval policy, it did not, in fact, shape events. Dewey would have prepared his ships with or without Roosevelt's orders. Nonetheless, those instructions stood. After war began and a British proclamation of neutrality forced him to leave Hong Kong, the White House ordered Dewey to proceed to the Philippines to destroy or capture the Spanish fleet there. "While we remained at war with Spain," Dewey explained later, "our purposes [was] to strike at the power of Spain wherever possible."[17] And strike he did. As soon as he received the president's orders, he set out full steam for the Philippines. On the night of April 30 his ships entered Manila Bay and at dawn destroyed the Spanish fleet there; but the Spanish garrison in Manila remained intact. "The guns of Dewey at Manila have changed the destiny of the United States," the Washington *Post* announced prophetically. "We are face to face with a strange destiny and must accept its responsibilities. An imperial policy!"[18]

Two days before Dewey's victory, Admiral Cervera, in a state of despair, had steamed out of the Cape Verde Islands with four armored cruisers and three destroyers for Cuban waters. His officers sensed impending doom. "I think it undoubted," one of them wrote to the prime minister, "that the sacrifice of these naval forces will be as certain as it will be fruitless and useless for the termination of the war."[19] Since no one knew the destination of Cervera's ships, panic gripped cities along the Atlantic coast. Fear followed the joy of Dewey's victory. "Telegrams, letters, and statesmen representing the imperilled localities poured into the War Department," the harassed secretary of war wrote. "They wanted guns everywhere; mines in all the rivers and harbors on the map."

The brooding Cervera had not planned offensive operations. On May 19 he led his ships into narrow landlocked Santiago Bay, and an American fleet promptly bottled him up. After two hard-fought engagements, an American army began closing in on the city of Santiago on July 1. Cervera was now caught between American land and sea forces. Two days later, on orders from his superiors, he led his ships from the harbor to meet senseless death and destruction to preserve Spanish "honor." The American naval forces suffered only two casualties, one man killed and another wounded. News of the Santiago victory reached the United States on July 4. Independence Day commemorations expanded into victory celebrations throughout the nation. Santiago surrendered on July 16, and later American troops took over Puerto Rico. After ten weeks of fighting, the war was over.

In the Philippines, meanwhile, Dewey waited for reinforcements. He did not have the troops to take Manila. After stopping to take Guam in the Spanish Marianas, an American expeditionary force on June 30 reached the Philippines. While Dewey had been waiting, several countries, including Germany and Britain, had sent warships to the Philippines. Germany had sent a squadron more powerful than Dewey's. Friction over blockade measures and other issues broke out between Dewey and the German commander. Since Dewey's relations with the British were unusually friendly, a legend emerged from Manila that the British had saved Dewey from attack by the German forces by threatening to support him in any battle. Although the Germans were anxious to take the Philippines for themselves, they had not intended to provoke war or to threaten Dewey. He did not, therefore, have to be saved by the British.

Peace Terms

With her fleets destroyed and her forces stranded in Cuba and the Philippines, Spain finally conceded that further resistance was useless and sued for peace. McKinley dictated terms on July 30, 1898, demanding complete surrender of Cuba, cession of Puerto Rico, one island in the Marianas (Guam), and occupation of the city and harbor of Manila pending final disposition of the Philippines.

Even though the terms seemed severe, Spain accepted them and signed the preliminary peace protocol on August 12, protesting sadly that "this demand strips us of the very last memory of a glorious past and expels us . . . from the Western Hemisphere, which became peopled and civilized through the proud deeds of our ancestors." John Hay, soon to become secretary of state, commented in a far different mood. "It has been a splendid little war," he wrote; "begun with the highest motives, carried on with magnificent intelligence and spirit, favored by that Fortune which loves the brave."[20]

Formal peace negotiations began in Paris on October 1. Secretary of State William R. Day headed the American commission of five. Two facts stand out in the composition of that commission. Four of the five commissioners were expansionists committed to a "large policy" of imperialism, and the fifth eventually came around to the view of the others. Three were ranking members of the Senate Foreign Relations Committee. Realizing that he might run into difficulty obtaining Senate approval for the treaty, McKinley set something of a precedent by including senators in the peace commission.

The Spanish commissioners accepted demands for Cuban independence, cession of Puerto Rico, and after strong protests even agreed to assume the Cuban debt of some $400 million, but they balked at demands for the Philippines. Since the United States had not conquered them, Spain said, it could not rightfully claim them in the peace settlement. Manila did not surrender to American and Filipino forces until August 13, the day after signing of the peace protocol.

Internal problems also complicated the status of the Philippines. Before the war Spain had crushed a revolt of Filipino patriots. After the battle of Manila Bay, an American warship brought General Emilio Aguinaldo, exiled leader of the Filipino insurgents, to Manila where Dewey had encouraged him to lead a new revolt against the Spaniards. Aguinaldo had organized rebel forces under the impression that the United States would liberate the Philippines from Spanish rule, as it had pledged itself to a free Cuba. On August 6 he had announced the independence of the Philippine Republic and sought foreign recognition.

Dewey, however, had cabled that the "republic" represented only a faction and could not keep order in the area it allegedly controlled. Expansionists, moreover, had already mounted a campaign demanding that the United States keep the Philippines. They were unwilling to surrender them to allegedly uncivilized natives when those islands could serve as a portal to the rich trade of the Orient. Naval interests, too, emphasized the commercial and strategic importance of the Philippines, suggesting that Germany or Japan would take them if the United States did not.

Industrial and commercial interests important within the Republican party now swung behind an expansionist policy that many businessmen had formerly opposed. The religious press also threw its support behind an "imperialism of righteousness." Commercial expansion, a prominent Presbyterian leader explained, was "a necessary part of the great outward impulse of civilization, the missionary movement welcomes it as an ally." The Chicago *Times-Herald*, a paper close to the administration, said, "We find that we want the Philippines" and added that "the people now believe that the United States owes it to civilization to accept the responsibilities imposed upon it by the fortunes of war." [21]

McKinley once again went along with what he considered representative public opinion. After returning from a speechmaking trip to Chicago, Omaha, and other points in the Middle West during the congressional campaigns, when he carefully measured the response to his remarks on assuming colonial burdens, he concluded that the American people wanted to annex the Philippines. He told the peace commissioners, therefore, that the Philippines stood on a "different basis than did Cuba." The war, he explained, "has brought us new duties and responsibilities which we must meet and discharge as becomes a great nation," and incidental to tenure in the Philippines is "the commercial opportunity to which American statesmanship cannot be indifferent." [22]

McKinley decided to surrender to manifest destiny by taking all of the Philippines, but only after praying for divine guidance. "And one night late it came to me this way . . . ," he told a visiting group of Methodist clergymen, "(1) That we could not give them back to Spain—that would be cowardly and dishonorable; (2) that we could not turn them over to France or Germany—our commercial rivals in the Orient—that would be bad business and discreditable; (3) that we could not leave them to themselves—they were unfit for self-government—and they would soon have anarchy and misrule over there worse than Spain's was; and (4) that there was nothing left for us to do but take them all, and to educate the Filipinos, and uplift and Christianize them." And then, he added, "I went to bed . . . and slept soundly." The Irish satirist, Finley Peter Dunne, or "Mr. Dooley," commented, "An' yet, tis not more thin two months since ye learned whether they were islands or canned goods." [23]

Not strong enough to resist, but protesting American demands as violations of the protocol, Spain, therefore, reluctantly parted with the Philippines for $20 million. Technically she gave up the islands as a war indemnity. With the signing of the Treaty of Paris on December 19, the United States took in the fruits of its "splendid little war." For the first time it brought under its flag a distant land and alien masses without offering the hope of future statehood. Not all Americans, not all senators, and certainly not all Filipinos, were pleased.

Many Americans considered annexation of the Filipinos without their consent unconstitutional and a perversion of the idealistic crusade to free Cuba. Even before McKinley had submitted the Treaty of Paris to the Senate, the foes of expansion opened a great debate on the future of American foreign policy. A group of them in Boston had grasped the initiative by launching an Anti-Imperialist League. Other cities formed similar leagues. The leaders of the anti-imperialist cause were distinguished, including industrialist Andrew Carnegie, labor leader Samuel Gompers, university presidents Charles W. Eliot of Harvard and David Starr Jordan of Stanford, numerous other intellectuals, and writers such as Hamlin Garland and Mark Twain.

The Republican president of one of the anti-imperialist leagues argued that territorial expansion into the Pacific would lead ultimately to war. "For us, independence in policy, peace, and self-assertion will be impossible," he said, "if we enter into the islands of the east." Whether or not such views were sound, the movement had a fatal weakness. It failed to attract a large popular following.

There could be no stopping the march of the flag, a Republican imperialist had argued in a campaign speech. "It is God's great purpose made manifest in the instincts of our race, whose present phase is our personal profit, but whose far-off end is the redemption of the world and the Christianization of mankind."[24]

Expansionist Americans were supported by the British prophet of the new imperialism, Rudyard Kipling, who in February 1899 urged acceptance of the task of civilizing lesser colored peoples, especially the Filipinos:

> Take up the White Man's burden—
> Send forth the best ye breed—
> Go bind your sons to exile
> To serve your captives' need;
> To wait in heavy harness,
> On fluttered folk and wild—
> Your new-caught, sullen peoples,
> Half-devil and half-child.[25]

"Rather poor poetry, but good sense from the expansionist standpoint," Theodore Roosevelt wrote to his friend Henry Cabot Lodge.[26]

Lodge, the junior senator from Massachusetts, led the Senate fight for the Treaty of Paris. "I confess," he wrote, "I cannot think calmly of the rejection of that Treaty by a little more than one-third of the Senate. It would be a repudiation of the President and humiliation of the whole country in the eyes of the world, and would show we are unfit as a nation to enter into great questions of foreign policy."[27]

Faced with determined opposition in the Senate, the administration made support of the treaty a party issue and used its patronage power freely. That was not enough, for the senior senator from Massachusetts, George F. Hoar, a Republican and an anti-imperialist, led the fight against the treaty. To annex the Philippines, he insisted, would be a dangerous break with the past, a violation of American ideals, and a departure from the principles of the Declaration of Independence. The country's greatest asset, he and other anti-imperialists pointed out, was its heritage of freedom. To take the Philippines would deny that heritage. They agreed with William Jennings Bryan that no nation could endure half-republic and half-colony. They reminded the people that the United States had gone to war as a liberator, not as a conqueror.

Ironically, at a critical moment the treaty received unexpected aid from Bryan, then leader of the Democratic party. Although opposed to imperialism and acquisition of the Philippines, he wanted the Senate to accept the treaty so as to make the peace official. Later, if the Democrats won the election of 1900, the United States could give the Philippines their freedom. He urged Democratic senators, therefore, to vote for the treaty. Whether or not Bryan's aid was decisive is questionable, but by the narrow margin of 57 to 27, one more vote than the necessary two-thirds, the Senate approved the treaty on February 6, 1899. Lodge called it the closest, "hardest fight I have ever known."

Carnegie was among those who overstressed Bryan's influence. "One word from Mr. Bryan," he wrote later with lasting bitterness, "would have saved the country from disaster. I could not be cordial to him for years afterwards. He had seemed to me a man who was willing to sacrifice his country and his personal convictions for party advantage."[28]

Filipinos and Destiny

Two days before the Senate had approved the treaty, Aguinaldo's forces revolted against American rule. The Filipinos, the most Christian people in Asia, did not want to be "uplifted and Christianized" by Americans. The army, therefore, began civilizing them with rifle and bayonet. "These Filipinos must be taught obedience," the Washington *Star* said, "and must be forced to observe, even if they cannot comprehend, the practice of civilization."[29] Before the United States succeeded in stamping out the revolt, which lasted four years, it used more troops than in the Spanish war, expended $600 million dollars, and sacrificed over four thousand lives. Americans found their soldiers resorting to brutal repressive measures, just as the Spaniards had done in Cuba. They too used forms of torture and concentration camps to break the fighting spirit of the insurrectionists.

Already skeptical of the Philippine venture, many Americans showed their anger in a renewed outburst of anti-imperialism. From the beginning, in fact, opinion on the Philippines was so divided that a week after approving the peace treaty the Senate defeated a resolution calling for independence only by the casting vote of the vice-president. Mark Twain, seared by the Philippine conquest, suggested changing the flag with "the white stripes painted black and the stars replaced by the skull and cross bones." A more powerful denunciation of imperialism came from the pen of the young poet William Vaughn Moody:

> Lies! Lies! It cannot be! The wars we wage
> Are noble, and our battles still are won
> By justice for us, ere we lift the gage.
> We have not sold our loftiest heritage.
> The proud republic hath not stopped to cheat
> And scramble in the market-place of war. . . .
> Ah no!
> We have not fallen so.[30]

Bryan, the Democratic candidate, tried to make imperialism the paramount issue in the presidential campaign of 1900. His party's platform announced "that any government not based upon the consent of the governed is a tyranny; and that to impose upon any people a government of force is to substitute the methods of imperialism for those of a republic."[31] McKinley had an answer. "Do we need their consent," he asked, "to perform a great act for humanity?"

With McKinley again their standard-bearer, Republicans went to the people with the slogan, "Don't haul down the flag." "Who," Senator Hoar asked, "shall haul down the President?"[32] Nonetheless, imperialism made no headway as a primary issue, for Republicans insisted that free silver, or currency, was the main issue. The country was prosperous and apparently did not want to repudiate the results of war. McKinley won the presidency with a more impressive vote than in 1896.

"The war with Spain makes the United States a World Power," more than one observer remarked. "She is no longer a self-centered provincial country, but an imperial nation."[33] Actually, the Spanish-American War did not itself make the United States a world power; the nation already had potential for such status. War and the treaty offered foreigners, and more important, Americans themselves, the occasion to recognize that status. "We are face to face with a strange destiny," the Washington *Post* had remarked in a perceptive editorial. "The taste of empire is in the mouth of the people even as the taste of blood in the jungle. It means an imperial policy, the Republic renascent, taking her place with the armed nations."[34]

The war marked one of the important turning points in foreign policy. From that time on Americans could no longer look merely inward. The United States had established its dominance of the Caribbean and had extended its influence to the shores of Asia. It had become a recognized world power through its own inherent strength; that strength affected the international politics of all great powers of the world. Even if it wanted to, the United States in the new century could not remain aloof from the politics of the rest of the world.

XV

Open Door and Big Stick

During the years of the new manifest destiny, events in Asia transformed the context of American policy in that part of the world. In 1894–95 Japan fought China for control of Korea. Since the Sino-Japanese War was remote, the fighting did not at first alarm Americans. "The deplorable war between China and Japan," Secretary of State Walter Q. Gresham told the Japanese, "endangers no policy of the United States in Asia."[1] Nonetheless, the United States did not ignore the conflict. China tried to draw the United States into it by requesting American mediation, but Japan protested. So Grover Cleveland's government remained neutral. It did, however, land troops in Korea to protect missionaries, sent warships to Chinese waters, and after China's defeat became involved in peace negotiations.

Japan's victory brought her status as a great power and appeared to confirm the Western view of China as a giant unable to defend himself. That victory also prompted Russia, Germany, and France to intervene. In April 1895 they forced Japan to relinquish territory on the mainland that she had taken from China. This triple intervention opened a fresh chapter in China's relations with Japan and the West.

In the next three years the great powers scrambled for economic concessions and spheres of political interest. China became a market for Western investment, principally railroad and mining capital, as well as for trade. "The various powers," China's dowager empress said, "cast upon us looks of tigerlike voracity, hustling each other in their endeavors to be the first to seize upon our innermost territories." Hungrier than ever, imperialists appeared ready to make good their threats to dismember China. By 1899, with the Manchu government helpless to resist, the West had reduced parts of the country to semicolonial status. By this time the threatened partitioning of China alarmed the American government and especially some American business interests.

Trade with China had not amounted to much, never more than 3 percent of the United States's total foreign commerce. Yet businessmen and others believed that the Chinese market offered opportunity for a vast future trade. That was one reason why American commercial interests had approved of keeping the Philippines. In China there were 400 million people, more than five times as many as in the United States, a Massachusetts business journal explained. Their wants were increasing every year. "What a market!"

Future trade in that market would depend on equal commercial opportunity for all nations, including such things as equal customs duties and harbor dues, or what was commonly called the open door, a privilege Americans had enjoyed since the Treaty of Wanghia. Partitioning China into spheres of influence, and eventually colonies with their exclusive privileges, would mean the end of the open door and of American hopes for a growing portion of China's trade.

Great Britain's Position

Russian, German, and French expansion in China alarmed the British more than it did the Americans. Britain had controlled most of China's foreign trade, some 80 percent of it, and had always supported the open door. As European powers began to stake out their spheres of influence, however, British opinion divided. Some British officials feared that European rivals would close the door in their own spheres and that British trade would suffer. Others believed that European imperialists would bring order to the interior, and that British trade might even thereby prosper within foreign spheres. For strategic and political reasons, still other Englishmen did not like any spheres and naval leaseholds controlled by others.

In spring 1898 the British reacted to the new international situation in China with a threefold strategy. They stressed the importance of retaining the open door, secretly sought an agreement with some other power to block Russia's penetration, and worked out plans for their own sphere of influence in the Yangtze Valley, or as one of their statesmen said, they prepared themselves "to pounce the moment anyone else pounces." They realized that the old doctrine of the open door was not really appropriate to the new situation in China where the powers sought mining and railway concessions and other opportunities for capital investment, and not merely trade. Yet the British continued to support the open door because they still profited from trade more than any other nation and did not want their traders excluded anywhere.

On March 8, therefore, about a month before the beginning of the Spanish-American War, the British government confidentially invited the United States to cooperate in maintaining the open door, asking in effect:

"Will you stand with us in our China policy?" It said nothing about spheres of influence and special investment privileges within them.

McKinley rejected the British overture. He was at the time concerned primarily with the Cuban crisis, did not wish to espouse for political reasons what appeared to be a British policy, did not think new developments in China seriously threatened American interests there, and did not wish to depart from the "traditional policy" of avoiding foreign entanglements.

John Hay, American ambassador to England and an anglophile, did not like the administration's rebuff. He was not at the time concerned with China or American policy there, but with relations in England. He wanted to cooperate closely with England whenever an opportunity arose. Late in September Hay became secretary of state.

That summer, though still professing to support the principle of the open door, the British went into the concession business in a big way by carving out the largest sphere of influence yet in the Yangtze Valley and by obtaining several strategic leaseholds. During that winter, especially after the Treaty of Paris had confirmed the United States as an imperialist power in Asia, American opinion on the open door changed. Lord Charles Beresford, a member of Parliament and a representative of the Associated Chambers of Commerce of Great Britain, visited the United States after a tour of China and Japan and urged American and British cooperation in preserving the open door. He desired "free and equal commercial relations for all time in the Orient" and to save China from partition. His speeches and a book he wrote at the time, *The Break-Up of China,* popularized the idea of the open door among Americans.

The American Position

Although already well-established in America's Asian policy, the open door now became especially attractive to businessmen with their expanded visions of trade in China. That trade through the recently acquired Philippines, they argued, depended on preserving China as a free market. American missionaries, rejoicing over annexation of the Philippines and fearing antiforeignism stirred up by the concession hunters, also urged a stronger policy in China. The McKinley administration, sensitive to business views, began reacting to the new pressures. Secretary of State Hay, for instance, told Congress that the sale of American products in China should not be endangered by exclusive privileges for other powers, meaning that the door should remain open to Americans.

As his adviser on Far Eastern affairs Hay had chosen a friend, William W. Rockhill, who had served in China and Korea. Rockhill took up his new duties in the spring of 1899. That June an old friend from Peking, an

Englishman named Alfred E. Hippisley, who worked for the Chinese government in the Imperial Maritime Customs Service, visited the United States and discussed China's situation with him.

Hippisley urged that the American government "do what it can to maintain the Open Door for ordinary commerce in China."[2] He accepted the spheres of influence as positive facts but wanted the United States to approach the powers and obtain assurances that they would adhere to the principle of the open door within their own spheres. Since England was no longer greatly disturbed about the open door, Hippisley did not speak for the British government. He was concerned over probable breakup of the customs service, the financial ruin, and threatened partitioning of China.

Rockhill listened to Hippisley's ideas with sympathy. He preferred, in fact, to go further than Hippisley proposed. "You know what my views are about the position the United States should take in China," he said; "I would like to see it make a declaration in some form or other, which would be understood by China as a pledge on our part to assist in maintaining the integrity of the Empire."[3] Both men realized that such a broad policy was unrealistic. The American government, for political and traditional reasons, could not support it. Therefore, they restricted their plan to maintaining the open door for trade within the spheres.

Hippisley shrewdly suggested that the McKinley administration could deliver a diplomatic stroke that would win popular support and bring it political advantage. "The public need know nothing of the steps taken by the Sec. of State," he wrote, "till the negotiations have been consummated, and the announcement then that the U.S. had secured China's independence and so served the cause of peace & civilization would be a trump card for the Admin. and crush all the life out of the anti-imperialism agitation. . . ."[4]

The Open Door Notes

Hay, probably remembering Britain's earlier overture and himself already favorable to the open door idea, liked the Hippisley-Rockhill plan. In August, therefore, he authorized Rockhill to go ahead with Hippisley's suggestion and to draft notes for the great powers in Asia. Rockhill drew up instructions for the American ambassadors to the powers based on a memorandum drafted by Hippisley a week before. Hay and McKinley approved the Rockhill notes virtually without change. Hay sent them, the first open door notes, to Britain, Germany, and Russia on September 6 and in November to Japan, France, and Italy.

Hay said nothing about preference and monopoly in mining, railroad, and other capital investments in the spheres of influence. He asked the powers merely to allow equal commercial opportunity within the spheres, not to interfere with the treaty ports in them, not to impede collection of

Chinese customs duties, not to charge discriminatory railroad rates or harbor dues, and to cooperate with the United States in securing support of the other powers for the principle of the open door. Even though the notes were moderate and limited in scope, merely by sending them the United States breached its theoretical policy of noninterference in the affairs of major powers.

Only Italy, who did not have a sphere, fully accepted Hay's suggestions. The other countries answered evasively with faint gestures of approval. Yet six months later, in May 1900, Hay announced that the powers had given him satisfactory assurances and that he regarded them as "final and definitive." He thus placed the powers publicly on record as supporting the open door and left the American people with the impression that he had achieved a diplomatic triumph, one that had prevented the breakup of China by predatory powers. The press supported his policy and praised him warmly. Some newspapers called it a "diplomatic victory" and others a "victory for civilization."

Hay had not won a victory. He had merely announced his country's support of the open door, a principle other powers had refused to accept without qualification. Even if they had supported it on Hay's terms, there could have been no real equality of commercial opportunity in China so long as the spheres of influence, meaning special financial and investment privileges, continued to exist. Only force could destroy the spheres, and Americans, or their leaders, were unwilling to use arms and become more directly entangled in the international politics of Asia. Hay's policy thus represented a pious expression of American economic and political self-interest. Ironically, it suited the Chinese attitude of treating all barbarians alike and setting them against each other. Moreover, the open door and the still-potent policy of isolation were incompatible.

Just as Hay announced his satisfaction with replies to the open door notes, an antiforeign, anti-imperialist uprising, fomented by a secret society that Westerners called Boxers and encouraged by the imperial government, broke out in China. The Boxer Rebellion offered an opportunity for the first real test of Hay's open door policy.

In June 1900, powerful bands of Boxers, armed with swords and spears, overran Peking, rioting and pillaging throughout the city. Joined by imperial troops, they laid siege to foreign legations in the city. The siege lasted until August 14, when an international rescue expedition of some twenty thousand soldiers lifted it. The United States contributed some twenty-five hundred men to the rescue force. The need "to secure for our merchants, farmers, and wage-workers the benefits of the open market," Theodore Roosevelt argued, made sending troops into China legitimate.

While concerned over the fate of Americans in Peking, Hay did not overlook the broader implications of the Boxer uprising. He realized that some of the powers, Russia and Germany in particular, would use the troubles as an excuse to expand their spheres of influence. When the Boxers attacked Russians in Manchuria, for example, the Russian minister of war was pleased. "This will give us an excuse for seizing Manchuria," he said. Hay decided, therefore, on another announcement.

Hay's Circular of 1900

In his earlier notes Hay had merely implied the desirability of maintaining China's integrity. In the middle of the Boxer crisis he sent a circular note to the powers informing them that the United States wanted to "bring about permanent safety and peace to China, preserve Chinese territorial and administrative entity, protect all rights guaranteed to friendly powers by treaty and international law, and safeguard for the world the principle of equal and impartial trade with all parts of the Chinese Empire." [5]

Unlike the earlier notes, this July circular did not ask for replies. Hay thereby enlarged his earlier position and announced it as American policy to the other powers without asking them formally to join in upholding it. The complete open door policy thus comprised the notes of 1899 and circular of 1900. It included the two principles of equal commercial opportunity for foreigners and their respect for China's independence.

The circular, announced one day before the meeting of the Democratic national convention, won public approval. In the election year of 1900 it struck an idealistic note in foreign policy that contrasted sharply with the harsh campaign in the Philippines and the shrill charges of anti-imperialists. "Nothing so meteoric," according to Henry Adams, "had ever been done in American diplomacy." [6]

Hay's notes had practically no effect on the great powers, however. Those powers used the Boxer troubles to increase their influence in China. By the end of October, Russia, for instance, had won military control over Manchuria and appeared ready to convert her sphere there into a protectorate. That posture threatened both principles of the open door. Nonetheless the general threat to China's independence seemed less formidable than before.

Although given lip service by most of the powers the open door policy did not prevent partition. At first, as William Vaughn Moody described the situation in his poem "The Quarry,"

> Came many brutes of prey, their several hates
> Laid by until the sharing of the spoil. [7]

Finally, however, jealousies and rivalries among the powers became so strong that they could not agree on how to dismember the quarry. Each potential partitioner feared a first move that might set off a chain reaction and then a world war. So each hesitated to strike.

Hay himself realized that he had made no true converts to China's territorial integrity. "There is . . . not a single power we can rely upon," he complained later, "for our policy of abstention from plunder and the Open Door." There was something sanctimonious and even false in that lament. The United States in its own Asian possession, the Philippines, did not allow the open door it asked others to permit in their spheres. Furthermore, in December 1900 only five months after announcing his concern for China's territorial entity, Hay too joined the concession hunters. He secretly instructed the American minister in Peking to try to obtain a naval coaling station at Samsah Bay on China's coast opposite the northern tip of Formosa. Since Japan regarded Fukien, facing Formosa, as her own sphere of influence, she blocked the move, reminding Hay of his concern for China's territorial integrity.

Meanwhile, Rockhill had gone to China as a special commissioner and then became minister in Peking. He too became disillusioned with the open door policy. "England has her agreement with Germany," he wrote, "Russia has her alliance with France, the Triple Alliance comes in here, and every other combination you know of is working here just as it is in Europe. I trust it may be a long time before the United States gets into another muddle of this description."[8]

Hay and Rockhill had begun to realize that the United States, with the acquisition of the Philippines and its expanded open door policy, had entered the entanglements of world politics through the back door of Asia. This was a logical outcome of the new manifest destiny and overseas expansion. The irony of it all was that Americans believed that the open door policy was a triumph of idealism over power politics, a policy that saved China.

While the powers negotiated settlement of the Boxer Rebellion, Russia pressed China secretly for separate agreement on Manchuria that would increase her control over that province. The Russian moves alarmed Britain and the United States, but especially Japan, who asked the American government what steps it would take to uphold the open door in Manchuria. Hay replied that the United States was "not prepared to attempt singly, or in concert with other Powers, to enforce these views in the east by any demonstration which could present a character of hostility to any other Power."[9] That showed Japan, who considered Manchuria worth fighting for, that the United States would not go beyond words.

Hay continued to use words. In April he asked Russia for assurances that she would not discriminate against American enterprise in Manchuria. For a while diplomatic pressure appeared to work. Russia eased her own pressure on Manchuria, but renewed it in November. So Britain and Japan signed their first alliance in January 1902, a five-year treaty aimed at Russia. That alliance readjusted power relationships in the Far East and also caused a shift within the European political system.

Meanwhile, after McKinley's death, Theodore Roosevelt retained Hay as secretary of state and accepted the open door as the basis of American policy in Asia. Not adequately informed by the diplomatic service, Hay received news of the Anglo-Japanese alliance as a surprise. When Russia, under pressure from the alliance, agreed in April to evacuate her troops from Manchuria, he seemed satisfied. He had not, apparently, grasped the warlike significance of that alliance.

Russia did not keep her word. Instead of removing troops, she pressed new demands on China. If China had met them, they would have ended all pretense of an open door in Manchuria. Russia's actions also threatened negotiations Hay had begun with China for a commercial treaty. After Russia vaguely assured Hay that she "had never opposed the development of foreign commerce in Manchuria," he went ahead with the Chinese treaty embodying the open door principles, concluding it on October 8, 1903. Yet, when China appealed for America's good offices in her difficulties with Russia, he refused to be drawn directly into the complicated international politics of Manchuria. He had already told President Roosevelt that he believed American "public opinion" would not support cooperative action "which would seem openly hostile to Russia."

Japan as a World Power

At this point, Japan sought an understanding with Russia that would give her a free hand in Korea where she feared Russian encroachments even more than in Manchuria. Russia would not agree. Japan broke off negotiations and on February 8, 1904, launched a surprise attack on the Russian fleet at Port Arthur, declaring war two days later. All the fighting in the Russo-Japanese War took place on Chinese soil, thereby endangering what remained of the open door policy.

As soon as hostilities began, Roosevelt reaffirmed that policy. He asked Japan and Russia to respect "the neutrality of China and in all practical ways her administrative entity," but said nothing about Korea. The Russian ambassador in Washington asked later why the United States should wish to deprive Russia of Manchuria and not Japan of Korea. Since neither the Russian nor the Japanese reply was satisfactory, Roosevelt's request accomplished nothing. But Hay, again bluffing, announced that the belligerents had given proper assurances. A year later Roosevelt, through Hay, circularized the neutral powers asking them to respect "the integrity of China and the 'Open Door' in the Orient." All responded favorably, but the most dangerous threats to the open door would come from Russia and Japan.

In the war Roosevelt and the American people favored the Japanese. "Public opinion in this country," a contemporary survey announced, ". . . supports the position assumed by Japan—that Russia shall give her a free hand in Korea and guarantee Chinese sovereignty in Manchuria." [10] Roosevelt said later, in an assertion historians have considered dubious, that on the outbreak of hostilities he had notified Germany and France that he would "promptly side with Japan and proceed to whatever length was necessary on her behalf" if the European powers intervened against her. [11] "I like the Japanese," he explained more than once. [12] They had, he maintained, the kind of fighting stock he admired.

Yet as the war went on, with one Japanese victory following another, Roosevelt changed his views. He decided that the best situation for the open door and America's interest in the Far East would be a balance of power between Russia and Japan, not a triumph that would make Japan supreme in eastern Asia. He tried, therefore, to mediate a peace that would not drive Russia completely out of eastern Asia.

Roosevelt's opportunity came through the Japanese. Despite their victories, they desperately needed peace. They had failed to break the Russian armies, and their government was on the verge of bankruptcy. Even though Roosevelt had been trying for several months to bring the war to an end, he imposed one condition when the Japanese indicated they wanted him to arbitrate—that they support the open door. In April 1905 the Japanese government assured him "that Japan adheres to the position of maintaining Open Door in Manchuria and of restoring that province to China." [13] That statement was the closest to what might be called a pledge that he received on the open door.

A month later the Japanese asked Roosevelt on his own "initiative to invite the two belligerents to come together for the purpose of direct negotiation." [14] He then approached the tsar who also needed peace. The tsar's funds were exhausted, he could obtain no more credit from French bankers, and revolutionary movements at home, where the war was never popular, threatened the entire war effort and his regime as well. He therefore accepted the peace proposal.

Roosevelt then immediately offered his good offices to both countries. In August the belligerents met at Portsmouth, New Hampshire. As a basis for peace, Russia withdrew from Korea and surrendered her special interests in southern Manchuria. The most serious obstacles to a treaty were Japan's demands for all of the island of Sakhalin and a large monetary indemnity. Russia refused to consent to either and threatened to break up the conference and renew hostilities. Roosevelt, even though he remained pro-Japanese, then persuaded Japan to give up her demand for an indemnity and arranged a compromise that gave half of Sakhalin to Japan.

"Peace Arranged; Japan Gives In," the *New York Times* headline announced the next day. Russia and Japan signed the Treaty of Portsmouth on September 5. Almost everybody praised Roosevelt's diplomacy. "The President's prestige throughout the world is beyond anything that he can imagine," a friend wrote. "Without regard to party or section," *Public Opinion* said, "the papers praise him for his skill and tact in holding the conference together till an agreement could be reached." He had become, it added, "the most popular man in the world."[15] In the following year Roosevelt received the Nobel Peace Prize for his role at the Portsmouth conference.

Ominously, the Japanese people did not join the popular acclaim for Roosevelt's peacemaking. They had counted on an indemnity and believed that he had robbed them of their compensation for victory. Since the Japanese government knew that it had made an unpopular peace, it used Roosevelt as the scapegoat. It did not dare tell the people it could not continue the war. The people, therefore, turned against the United States. Anti-American riots swept over Japan.

Shortly after, Americans began to lose sympathy for Japan. Her demands at the peace conference, the stiffness of her diplomats, and the limited success of Russian statesmen in trying to win American public opinion through careful handling of public relations, helped make the Portsmouth conference, in the long run, a turning point in Japanese-American relations. Thus, for the second time in Asia, the United States had played an important role in the international politics of the great powers, and for the second time results were unsatisfactory.

It was fitting, nonetheless, that the increasingly powerful United States should have had a hand in the Treaty of Portsmouth, one of the more important treaties of the modern world. It recognized that for the first time an Asian nation had defeated a major European power. That victory aroused, in time, a latent nationalism in many parts of Asia and in a sense marked the beginning of the end of European predominance there. It confirmed Japan's status as a world power. It also assured Japan's dominance in southern Manchuria and Korea, a fact of considerable significance for the United States.

The Taft-Katsura Agreed Memorandum

In Korea, Japan made no pretense of upholding the open door. Her influence in this country had been gradually increasing since 1895, despite Russia's opposition. With the Treaty of Portsmouth it became an exclusive control. When the Russo-Japanese War began, Korea had proclaimed independence but took no measures to defend it. She believed apparently that the United States and the other great powers of the West would guarantee her independence. When Japan went ahead and converted Korea into a protectorate, Britain and the United States, however, acquiesced and hence abandoned the idea of the open door for Korea. "We can not possibly interfere for the Koreans against Japan," Roosevelt told Hay. "They couldn't strike one blow in their own defence." [16] Since Roosevelt knew that he could not prevent Japan's action, he realistically accepted the inevitable.

Japan's victories over Russia had caused some uneasiness in the United States over the safety of the Philippines. While on a trip to the Philippines, Secretary of War William Howard Taft, under Roosevelt's instructions, stopped off at Tokyo. In conversations there with Count Taro Katsura, Japan's prime minister, he brought up concern over the Philippines and also said that he believed Japanese suzerainty over Korea would contribute to lasting peace in the Far East. Katsura, in turn, disavowed any aggressive Japanese designs against the Philippines. Following this exchange of views on July 27, 1905, an "agreed memorandum" of the discussion was drawn up, which some have called the "Taft-Katsura Agreement." Although the memorandum was not a formal agreement, it did embody the president's ideas. He cabled Taft that the conversation was absolutely correct and that "I confirm every word you have said." [17]

When England renewed her alliance with Japan in August, she too recognized Japan's "paramount political, military, and economic" interests in Korea. A few months later, actually on November 24, the United States instructed its minister in Seoul to close the legation there, thus becoming the first nation to recognize Japan's complete control. Japan had now sealed the door in Korea with the approval of the United States. Actually, since Hay had first announced the open door policy, Korea's door had never been opened very much.

Anti-Japanese Prejudice

Despite the Taft-Katsura memorandum, developments within the United States added to Japanese-American antagonisms engendered by the Portsmouth treaty. In October 1906 San Francisco's school board segregated some ninety-three Japanese children in a special school. That move climaxed a series of discriminations against the Japanese in California where the white citizenry wanted to exclude them as it had the Chinese. The Japanese already there suffered from racial prejudice, restrictive legislation, boycotts, and riots. Their mistreatment fed a bitter anti-Americanism in Japan just as the Chinese discrimination a year earlier had sparked an anti-American boycott in China.

Japan protested "the condition of the affairs in San Francisco," saying that the segregation of Japanese children because of race was "an act of discrimination carrying with it a stigma and odium which it is impossible to overlook." Roosevelt realized that relations with the proud and sensitive Japanese had now become the major problem in American foreign relations. He saw the contradiction in America's position. On the one hand the United States sought equal commercial treatment in Asia, and on the other it closed its door to Asian immigrants and discriminated against them. At the same time, even though Japan had assured him she would uphold the open door in Manchuria, her statesmen saw American support of the open door there as an obstacle to their own plans for exploiting Manchuria and actually closing the door there.

War between Japan and the United States, it seemed to foreign observers, was not improbable. Roosevelt recognized the danger. "The infernal fools in California, and especially in San Francisco," he told his son, "insult the Japanese recklessly, and in the event of war it will be the Nation as a whole which will pay the consequences."[18] So he pursued a firm but conciliatory policy toward the Japanese, working to adjust differences peacefully. His policy can be summed up in the words of the old West African proverb he was fond of quoting, "Speak softly and carry a big stick." For a while he negotiated patiently with the Japanese but always held in reserve the power of the navy, his big stick.

First, Roosevelt told the Japanese that he opposed the discriminatory action of the San Franciscans and assured them he would deal with the matter. He investigated the segregation and in his annual message in December told Congress that the school board's action was a "wicked absurdity," and suggested legislation conferring the right of naturalization on the Japanese. Roosevelt's attitude pleased the Japanese but enraged West Coast Japanophobes.

Since the action of the school board was local and beyond the jurisdiction of the federal government, unless the courts held that it violated a commercial treaty of 1894 with Japan, Roosevelt could not use his office to effect an immediate easing of the crisis. He therefore exerted his personal influence with the Californians and at the same time tried to reach a diplomatic settlement with the Japanese. He invited San Francisco's mayor and the entire school board to Washington where he persuaded them to rescind the segregation order in exchange for a promise to stop the immigration of Japanese laborers.

With the Japanese, the president tried more than once to obtain a treaty whereby they and the United States would exclude each other's laborers, but Japan would not agree. Finally, in return for an understanding that the United States would not stigmatize the Japanese as inferiors by barring them by law, Japan agreed voluntarily to withhold passports from her laborers seeking to enter the American mainland. This executive arrangement, worked out with Japan's ambassador in Washington through an exchange of notes in 1907 and 1908, became known as the Gentlemen's Agreement. Through it Roosevelt recognized the justice of Japan's case and at the same time upheld the right of the United States to determine its own immigration policy.

Yet anti-Japanese agitation on the Pacific Coast did not end. Rumors of war circulated in foreign capitals. The best information in France, England, and Germany, Roosevelt wrote, "is that we shall have war with Japan and we shall be beaten." [19] He went so far as to send orders to General Leonard Wood, commanding American troops in the Philippines, to prepare to meet a Japanese attack. In October he again sent Taft to Tokyo. The secretary of war reported on the eighteenth that "the Japanese Government is most anxious to avoid war."

Then, to overcome the continuing crisis, Roosevelt prepared a demonstration of naval power and made concessions to Japan, seemingly at China's expense, in Manchuria. He decided to send the battleship fleet, the second largest in the world, on a world cruise to impress Japan with the futility of war with the United States. Many Americans, particularly those on the East Coast, protested. They considered the cruise dangerous. It might, instead of easing the crisis, actually provoke war. The fleet, they said, should remain in home waters, to protect the country. Roosevelt persisted, personally reviewing the fleet on the eve of its departure in December 1907 and handing the commanding officer sealed orders.

After the fleet had arrived in the Pacific, the emperor invited it to visit Japan. When the ships dropped anchors in Tokyo's waters, the people gave them a tumultuous welcome, the high point of the entire cruise. "The fleet made a vivid and far-reaching impression," a correspondent of the Chicago *Tribune* reported. "It caused the Japanese to realize the formidable power of the United States, as nothing else could possibly have done." Roosevelt himself believed the same thing. "Every particle of trouble with the Japanese Government and the Japanese press," he wrote later, "stopped like magic as soon as they found that our fleet had actually sailed, and was obviously in good trim."

The Root-Takahira Agreement

While the fleet was on its cruise Roosevelt took other steps to dispel the crisis. On May 5, 1908, he concluded a five-year treaty of arbitration with Japan. Although a limited agreement, excluding all questions of "vital interest," it was a peaceful gesture. More important were the notes Secretary of State Elihu Root exchanged with the Japanese ambassador in Washington, Baron Kogoro Takahira, after the fleet left Yokohama.

In the Root-Takahira Agreement, signed November 30, the United States and Japan promised to respect each other's possessions in the Pacific area, to support the "existing *status quo*," and to uphold "by all pacific means at their disposal the independence and integrity of China and the principle of equal commercial opportunity for commerce and industry of all nations in that Empire."[20] In case of a threat to those principles the two countries agreed to communicate with each other in search of an understanding on action they would take.

On the surface, the ambiguous executive agreement appeared to be a victory for the open door. Actually, it was a self-contradictory declaration designed to ease mutual antagonisms. The existing *status quo,* in effect, recognized Japan's special position in south Manchuria. No evidence supports the thesis that the agreement was a bargain in which the United States surrendered the open door in Manchuria in exchange for Japanese support of its principles in China proper, and another renunciation of aggressive tendencies toward the Philippines. Some Americans, however, recognized it as essentially a concession to the realities of Japan's position in Asia.

Roosevelt's policy closed another chapter in the history of the open door with a realistic appraisal of America's position. Manchuria and Korea were of secondary concern to American foreign policy. Trade there was negligible, and Americans would not support an Asian war at this time merely for idealistic reasons. To Japan, on the other hand, the closed door in Korea and southern Manchuria was vital. She had gone to war twice to advance and hold her interests in those areas and presumably would do so a third time if necessary.

Roosevelt felt that a limited retreat on the open door was a small price to pay for a general agreement with Japan and for peace in an area where the United States had no essential interests. He made this clear in a long letter to his successor explaining his view on Far Eastern policy.

"The Open Door policy in China was an excellent thing," Roosevelt said, "and I hope it will be a good thing in the future, so far as it can be maintained by general diplomatic agreement; but, as has been proved by the whole history of Manchuria, alike under Russia and under Japan, the 'Open Door' policy, as a matter of fact, completely disappears as soon as a powerful nation determines to disregard it, and is willing to run the risk of war rather than forego its intention."[21] That was the heart of the matter. It was not in the interest of the United States to risk war over principles not vital to its foreign policy.

Cuba's Status

In addition to thrusting the United States into the morass of Far Eastern politics, the Spanish-American War left it in control of Cuba and dominant in the Caribbean. Expansionists wanted to insure that dominance by annexing Cuba and thereby brush aside the embarrassing Teller amendment. "I cannot believe it an evil for any people," the assistant secretary of state announced, "that the Stars and Stripes, the symbol of liberty and law, should float over them." Europeans believed the United States would take Cuba as it had the Philippines.

The occupation of Cuba and the behavior of the McKinley administration appeared to give substance to European fears. The United States never recognized the government of the Cuban rebels and ignored the claims of rebel leaders that Cuba was an independent nation. The Philippine insurrection, however, weakened imperialist demands for Cuba, and hence McKinley went ahead with plans for an independent Cuba, but one tied firmly to United States Caribbean policy. Cuba, he told Congress, "must needs be bound to us by ties of singular intimacy and strength."

General Leonard Wood, an expansionist who wanted to annex Cuba, took over as American military governor in December 1899. With an iron hand he introduced needed reforms in education, sanitation, public works, and government, hoping to bind the island to the United States. "Clean government, quick, decisive action and absolute control in the hands of trustworthy men, establishment of needed legal and educational reforms," he told his friend Theodore Roosevelt, "and I do not believe you could shake Cuba loose if you wanted to."[22]

Despite the benefits that Wood's rule conferred, most Cubans resented it, preferring the freedom they thought should be theirs. Weary Cubans expressed their feeling in doggerel:

> Don't eat, don't spit;
> Don't scratch, don't smoke;
> Arrive very early;
> Depart almost by night.
> There is no time for lunch
> Nor anything other than writing;
> He who wishes to work here
> Is he who wishes to die.[23]

Cuban demands for freedom and the pressure of anti-imperialists at home led Wood to call Cuban leaders together in Havana in November 1900 to adopt a constitution. They drew up a constitution based in part on that of the United States but did not, as Wood had asked them to do, provide for special future relations with the United States. Jealous of the independence that appeared within their grasp, Cubans feared that the United States desired a protectorate over their country.

Since the McKinley administration was unwilling to accept a truly independent Cuba, Secretary of War Elihu Root brought together administration ideas on what Cuba's connection to the United States should be, and Orville H. Platt of Connecticut, chairman of the Senate Committee on Foreign Relations, attached them as a "rider" to the army appropriation bill of March 2, 1901. They became law as the Platt Amendment.

That amendment authorized the president to end military occupation as soon as a Cuban government established itself under a constitution that defined future relations with the United States. Its main provisions prevented Cuba from making financial or diplomatic agreements with foreign powers that would impair independence, gave the United States legal right to intervene in Cuban affairs, forced Cuba to ratify all acts of the American military government, allowed the United States to buy or lease coaling or naval stations in Cuba, and required Cuba to embody those terms into a permanent treaty with the United States.

At first the Cuban constitution makers rejected the Platt Amendment, but the United States made it clear that its troops would continue to occupy the island until the Cubans accepted the Platt terms. Root tried to mollify the Cubans. "The Platt Amendment," he maintained, "is not synonymous with intermeddling or interference with the affairs of the Cuban Government."[24] The United States would intervene only to maintain proper government and to preserve Cuba's independence. Under pressure, the Cubans reconsidered, and then reluctantly accepted the Platt Amendment, making it an appendix to their constitution. Later, on May 22, 1903, they also accepted it as part of a treaty they signed with the United States.

Since that agreement was one-sided, forcing obligations only on Cuba and giving rights only to the United States, it impaired Cuba's sovereignty and made the island a virtual protectorate of the United States. Europeans, as did Latin Americans, considered the Platt Amendment a step toward annexation. "Of the independence of Cuba nothing remains," a Paris newspaper said; "of the promises of the United States equally little." A Berlin paper said the amendment was "the beginning of absolute control by the Americans," a view shared by General Wood and other expansionists. To the surprise of the world, however, Roosevelt withdrew American troops in May 1902 and ended the first Cuban intervention.

That withdrawal did not dispel sentiment for annexation. Several senators, for instance, introduced legislation calling for direct admission of Cuba into the Union as a state. In Cuba itself, the next few years saw bitter strife leading to open rebellion. In September 1906 at the request of Cuba's president, Roosevelt reluctantly exercised the right of intervention under the Platt Amendment, and American troops again patrolled Havana's streets.

The United States sent another governor to the island, one the Cubans grew to hate, comparing his extensive powers to those of "the Czar of Russia added to the Shah of Persia and the Grand Turk."[25] In April

1909, after bringing forced peace and stability, the United States, again to the surprise of foreigners, withdrew its troops and ostensibly left Cuba to the Cubans. In its second intervention the United States had shown that it intended to maintain its strategic security in the Caribbean and would not hesitate to use force in doing so.

The Interoceanic Canal

More important than control of Cuba was command of possible canal routes across Central America. Protection of the approaches to a future canal, the heart of United States Caribbean policy, had in fact prompted insistence on the Platt Amendment.

During the Spanish-American War, the voyage of the battleship *Oregon* from Puget Sound around Cape Horn to Cuban waters had captured public imagination and dramatized need for a canal that would cut sailing time from one coast to another by at least a third. The new island possessions in the Pacific and the Caribbean, moreover, made construction of such a waterway appear more important than ever to national security. McKinley had pointed out that need for a canal in his annual message of December 1898 and had added that "our national policy now more imperatively than ever calls for its control by this Government."[26]

Failure of the French and American companies to build waterways at Panama and Nicaragua had convinced the United States that construction of an interoceanic canal was beyond the resources of private capital. If one were to be built, the government would have to do it. As McKinley had pointed out, however, the government wanted to control any canal it would build. The main obstacle to such control was still the Clayton-Bulwer Treaty of 1850.

Congress appeared ready to disregard the Clayton-Bulwer commitment and to authorize the building of an exclusively American canal through Nicaragua. Such action would have damaged increasingly friendly relations with Britain, a possibility that alarmed Secretary of State John Hay. He urged the British government, therefore, to negotiate a revision of the treaty. Since Britain's Caribbean interests no longer appeared as vital as they once were, it was willing, but for a price.

In return for a more liberal treaty, the British wished the United States to make concessions in a controversy over the boundary between the Alaskan panhandle and British Columbia. Finally, after holding up canal negotiations for a year and after a temporary settlement of the boundary controversy in the fall of 1899, the British foreign secretary suggested taking up the canal treaty on America's terms. He yielded because he knew the United States was so determined to have its canal that it would go ahead in defiance of the Clayton-Bulwer Treaty and because the Boer War had exposed the weakness of Britain's international position. "America seems to be our only friend just now," the British ambassador in Washington reported, "& it would be unfortunate to quarrel with her."[27]

As a result, Hay and Sir Julian Pauncefote, the British ambassador, signed a treaty on February 5, 1900, amending the Clayton-Bulwer agreement by permitting the American government to construct and control an interoceanic canal. The treaty also called for a neutralized waterway and barred the United States from fortifying it.

When the text of the Hay-Pauncefote Treaty became public, influential newspapers and politicians attacked it. Theodore Roosevelt, at the time governor of New York, expressed a major objection. "I do not see why," he wrote, "we should dig the canal if we are not to fortify it so as to insure its being used for ourselves and against our foes in time of war."[28] The Detroit News commented that "another of the administration's 'great diplomatic victories' has been won—by the British government."[29]

In approving the treaty, almost a year later, the Senate wrote the major objections into three amendments which the British refused to accept. Still anxious to strengthen American friendship and not truly caring if the United States fortified its canal, the British finally negotiated another treaty, which Hay and Pauncefote signed on November 18, 1901. This second Hay-Pauncefote Treaty gave the United States what it desired by expressly superseding the Clayton-Bulwer Treaty and by saying nothing about fortifications. By tacit agreement the British expected the United States to fortify any canal it built. Since the second treaty cleared the way for an exclusively American canal, the Senate on December 16 overwhelmingly approved it.

Britain surrendered to American demands without exacting equivalent concessions because she could no longer maintain supremacy in the Caribbean in the face of American naval construction and because she sought to retain American friendship. In the next few years, in fact, Britain reduced her garrisons in the West Indies and withdrew her naval squadron from the Caribbean, leaving the United States supreme in that strategic sea.

The United States now had to decide where it would build the canal. That proved a thorny problem. A French corporation, the New Panama Canal Company, had taken over rights and assets of the bankrupt de Lesseps organization. The canal company hoped to sell its rights and costly equipment, rotting and rusting in the jungle, to the United States if Colombia would give her consent.

The Nicaraguan government had canceled the concession of the Maritime Canal Company and was eager to negotiate with the American government for canal rights through its land. Thus, the United States had a choice of two routes, each of which ultimately gained powerful supporters in Congress.

Most congressmen had long preferred the Nicaraguan route. Two official commissions, one in 1895 and another in 1899, had investigated that route and reported in its favor. Even before the second commission had made its report, the Senate had passed a bill calling for a canal through Nicaragua. If that bill passed in the House of Representatives, a Panama canal appeared doomed, and the stockholders of the New Panama Canal Company would get nothing.

To advance its interests, the canal company employed a prominent New York lawyer and lobbyist, William Nelson Cromwell, as general counsel. Wise in the ways of politics, Cromwell made friends with important politicians, particularly with powerful Mark Hanna who had become a senator from Ohio. Cromwell even contributed $60,000 to the Republican campaign fund of 1900. As a result, the Republican platform called for an isthmian canal, but the Democratic platform favored one through Nicaragua.

In part through Cromwell's influence, it appears, the House defeated the Nicaraguan canal bill. In its stead, the House called for a new investigation of both routes, giving Panama equal status with Nicaragua. President McKinley then appointed a new commission to determine the best route for a canal.

That commission found many advantages in the Panama route. It was shorter than the Nicaraguan route, ships would be able to travel over it in slightly more than one-third the time it would take to go through a Nicaraguan canal, and construction and maintenance costs would be less. But the New Panama Canal Company wanted $109 million for its assets, whereas the commission said $40 million would be a fair price. In November 1901, therefore, the commission recommended the Nicaraguan route.

The Hepburn Bill and Spooner Amendment

Acting on the commission's report, on the following January 9 the House passed the Hepburn bill authorizing the president to secure necessary rights for a Nicaraguan canal and appropriating funds for construction. Fearing complete loss, the New Panama Canal Company quickly lowered the price for its assets to $40 million. President Roosevelt, who at first had favored the Nicaraguan route, now preferred Panama. He reconvened the canal commission and ordered it to reconsider its recommendation. It submitted a supplementary report on January 18 favoring the Panama route if Colombia would agree to suitable arrangements.

Ten days later Senator John C. Spooner of Wisconsin, acting for the administration, offered an amendment to the Hepburn bill. The Spooner amendment authorized the president to pay not more than $40 million for the holdings of the New Panama Canal Company and to begin construction of a canal through Panama. If he could not arrive at satisfactory terms with either the French company or Colombia within a "reasonable time," he was to proceed with the Nicaraguan canal.

Supporters of the Panama route had also launched a careful propaganda campaign. Philippe Bunau-Varilla, formerly chief engineer of the de Lesseps company and at the time a speculator and large stockholder in the New Panama Canal Company, had come to the United States a year earlier to work for the Panama route. A dynamic man, skillful in public relations, he was fired with the idea that the canal had to go through Panama to vindicate the judgment of his countryman, de Lesseps. Through lectures, pamphlet writing, and newspaper publicity he advanced his idea. Even though he and Cromwell disliked each other, they managed between them to persuade important politicians to support the Panama route.

Still, advocates of the Panama route might have lost out if they had not been able to take advantage of an act of nature. On May 2, 1902, while Congress was considering the rival routes, volcanic Mont Pelée on the Caribbean island of Martinique erupted, spewing tons of lava and ash, destroying a city, and killing some 30,000 of its people. Twelve days later a report reached the United States that Mt. Momotombo, an old volcano in Nicaragua about one hundred miles from the proposed canal line, had become active and that an accompanying earthquake had wrought destruction in a nearby town.

When Nicaragua's president denied that the old volcano was active, Bunau-Varilla obtained Nicaraguan postage stamps showing Momotombo "belching forth in magnificent eruption," and presented each senator with a stamp and this comment: "An official witness of the volcanic activity on the Isthmus of Nicaragua."[30] The Senate then adopted the Spooner amendment, the House concurred, and the amended Isthmian Canal Act became law on June 28.

The Hay-Herrán Treaty

In attempting to obtain other rights it considered essential for control of a Panama canal, the United States ran into difficulties. The president of Colombia, José Manuel Marroquín, an eighty-year-old intellectual of limited political experience, had a weak grip on his office. Colombian political conditions were such that if he granted the United States the privileges it sought, some of his enemies would accuse him of surrendering his country's sovereignty to imperialists. If he did not meet American demands, he might lose the canal to Nicaragua, and some of his enemies would damn him for not bringing it and expected economic benefits to Colombia. Even worse, if he did not yield, it appeared that the United States might take Panama by force.

Finally, Marroquín instructed Dr. Tomás Herrán, his *chargé* in Washington, to make a treaty on the best terms he could get. After Secretary of State Hay delivered an ultimatum threatening to deal with Nicaragua unless Colombia accepted American terms, Herrán signed a treaty on January 22, 1903. It gave the United States a lease of one hundred years on a strip six miles wide across the isthmus for $10 million gold and an annual rent of $250,000 beginning in nine years. The Senate approved the treaty on March 17, but Colombians in Bogotá objected to the terms. Marroquín, nevertheless, submitted the treaty to the Colombian senate which had the right to accept or reject it. Despite a threat of retaliation by Secretary Hay if Colombia did not ratify, that senate unanimously rejected the Hay-Herrán Treaty on August 12.

Colombians maintained rightly that the treaty infringed on their country's sovereignty, but the real obstacle to ratification was money. Colombians wanted to modify the treaty so that the New Panama Canal Company would pay them $10 million and the United States would increase its payment to $15 million. The American government refused to consider any amendments. The Colombian senate, moreover, argued that the New Panama Canal Company's franchise, which ran to 1910, was illegal and would by law expire the following year. After it expired, Colombia could take over the company's assets and herself sell them to the United States for $40 million. Since Panama was part of the national domain, Colombia had acted within her rights.

Yet Colombia's tactics infuriated Roosevelt, who had decided that he must have the Panama route. "I do not think that the Bogotá lot of jack rabbits," he told Hay, "should be allowed permanently to bar one of the future highways of civilization." [31] He was prepared to recommend to Congress that the United States buy the French rights, occupy the isthmus in defiance of Colombia, and "proceed to dig the canal," but such extreme action proved unnecessary.

Before Colombia had rejected the Hay-Herrán Treaty, her maneuvering had alarmed Cromwell, Bunau-Varilla, and officials of the New Panama Canal Company. Moreover, the people of Panama, who had expected great benefits from the canal, feared that if it should go to Nicaragua, the isthmus would sink into insignificance. Since they had long been discontented with rule from isolated Bogotá and had often revolted against it, they were prepared to take drastic action to insure the canal for their area. A small group of them, linked closely with officials of the New Panama Canal Company, had even made plans for seceding from Colombia if she rejected the Hay-Herrán Treaty. The conspirators had approached Cromwell in New York, and he had assured them of support.

The plans did not go well until Bunau-Varilla returned to New York from Paris in September 1903. He met with some of the conspirators in the Waldorf-Astoria Hotel and promised $100,000 to support a revolution. In October he talked with Secretary Hay and President Roosevelt. Even though they made no promises, he assured himself from Roosevelt's sentiments that "as certain as if a solemn contract had been signed between us" the president would take advantage of a revolution to win his canal rights.[32] Bunau-Varilla, therefore, sent word to the schemers in Panama that the United States would not allow their revolution to fail.

Hay had told the president that if a revolt broke out in Panama the United States must act "to keep the transit clear." "Our intervention," he added, "should not be at haphazard, nor, this time, should it be to the profit, as heretofore, of Bogotá."[33] He had in mind a twisted interpretation of Bidlack's Treaty of 1846.

The original purpose of that treaty had been to block some outside power, primarily Britain, from seizing Panama, and not to protect a secessionist movement. During numerous uprisings in Panama prior to 1903, the United States had landed troops there at least six different times to protect the free transit, but only with the consent of Colombian authorities. Hay now intended to use the treaty against Colombia herself.

The Panama Revolution and Canal Settlement

Late in October 1903, the United States ordered several warships to Central-American waters, and on November 2 orders went to their commanders to seize the Panama railroad, keep the free transit, and prevent Colombia from landing troops within fifty miles of the isthmus if a revolution broke out. On the following day, according to plan, the revolution began. It was sparked by a motley army of less than a thousand composed of section hands from the Panama Railroad, a subsidiary of the French canal company, the fire brigade of the city of Panama, and bribed deserters from Colombia's garrison in Panama. The governor of Panama submitted to arrest, a key Colombian naval commander accepted a bribe to sail away, and troops from the U.S.S. *Nashville* prevented loyal Colombian forces from suppressing the uprising. In thus maintaining the free transit, Americans insured the success of the virtually bloodless revolution.

The next day, November 4, Panama declared herself independent. The government at Bogotá then asked the United States to help it recover its estranged province, promising to ratify the Hay-Herrán Treaty as signed. The American government rejected the offer, and on the same day, November 6, Hay instructed the consul-general in Panama to extend *de facto* recognition to the new Republic of Panama. *De jure* recognition followed a week later when Roosevelt officially received Bunau-Varilla as Panama's first minister to the United States, a post the Frenchman had forced from Panama as part of the bargain he had made in financing the revolution. On November 18, only fifteen days after the revolution, Hay signed a treaty with Bunau-Varilla on terms similar to those of the Hay-Herrán Treaty, only more favorable to the United States.

Under the Hay-Bunau-Varilla Treaty the United States guaranteed Panama's independence and obtained a grant in perpetuity of a canal zone ten miles wide instead of six. That treaty made Panama the second United States protectorate in the Caribbean. Panama accepted the treaty and the Senate, even though the president had acted contrary to the Spooner amendment in dealing with Panama instead of Colombia, approved it on February 23, 1904.

Roosevelt's big stick diplomacy had gained him the right to build the vital canal on bargain terms, but it also incurred the hatred of Colombians, ultimately increased resentment throughout Latin America against Yankee imperialism, and caused a split in opinion at home. Liberals reacted with shame and shock to Roosevelt's action, calling it "disgraceful" and "pi-

PANAMA AND THE CANAL ZONE, 1903

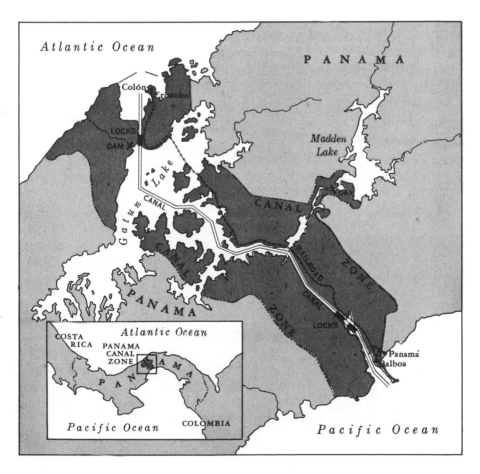

racy," but expansionists, particularly Republicans, were pleased and praised his policy. The Detroit *News* spoke candidly. "Let us not be mealy-mouthed about this," it said. "We want Panama." [34]

Sensitive to criticism, the president was quick to defend his policy, saying that "the recognition of the Republic of Panama was an act justified by the interests of collective civilization" and that he had received a mandate from civilization to take Panama. There is a story that in a cabinet meeting, while justifying his policy, he turned to Secretary Elihu Root. "Well," he demanded, "have I answered the charges? Have I defended myself?" "You certainly have, Mr. President," Root replied. "You have shown that you were accused of seduction and you have conclusively proved that you were guilty of rape." [35]

Later Roosevelt boasted, "I took the Isthmus, started the canal and then left Congress not to debate the canal, but to debate me." [36] The most logical explanations for his ruthless policy appear to be his impatient desire to "make the dirt fly" before the election of 1904, his contempt for Latin Americans, and his view that the end justified the means. If he had been more considerate of the political dilemma of a weak neighbor and less impatient, he probably could have obtained the necessary treaty rights from Colombia without compounding ill will in Latin America.

The United States began construction on the canal in May 1904 and ten years later opened it to the ships of the world. Roosevelt's Republican successor, William H. Taft, tried to placate Colombia and to obtain her recognition of Panama's independence, but she refused. She asked repeatedly for arbitration of the legality, according to treaty and international law, of American action in the Panama revolution. The American government persistently refused, saying it would not arbitrate a matter of national honor.

Woodrow Wilson's administration tried more effectively to mollify Colombia and hence improve Latin-American relations. In April 1914 it negotiated a treaty with Colombia expressing regret for the American role in the Panama revolution and offering $25 million in compensation. Roosevelt denounced the treaty as blackmail, and his friends in the Senate, notably Henry Cabot Lodge, blocked it. In 1921, two years after Roosevelt's death, the Senate revived that treaty but without the expression of regret. Lodge now insisted that compensating Colombia would improve commercial relations. The real reason for the Republican change appeared to be the extensive oil fields discovered in Colombia. Payment of the indemnity, it seemed, would ease the way to oil concessions that resentful Colombians had denied American companies while granting them to foreign rivals.

The Senate approved the treaty on April 21, and the United States paid Colombia $25 million, the same amount she had appeared willing to accept in 1903 in exchange for canal concessions. The belated payment at least showed that the United States, despite the materialistic concern in the

Senate, was willing to admit doing Colombia an injustice and willing to compensate her for it.

The Virgin Islands

In its Caribbean policy the United States would not allow any political disturbance to threaten control of the approaches to its planned canal, and it was especially sensitive to possible European encroachments. Control of the Caribbean required suitable naval bases that it did not have at the end of the Spanish-American War. The base acquired in Puerto Rico appeared inadequate for large naval forces, and the government had not yet made arrangements with Cuba for one at Guantanamo. The United States, therefore, desired additional bases, particularly in the port of St. Thomas in the Danish West Indies.

Prompted by rumors that Germany sought bases in the Caribbean and that she might acquire the Virgin Islands, the United States signed a treaty with Denmark in 1902 for the sale of those islands for $5 million. The Senate approved the treaty, but the upper house of Denmark's parliament rejected it by one vote. Some Americans believed that German influence had spoiled the sale.

European Intervention in Venezuela

At the same time, while Congress was considering the rival canal routes, a dispute in Venezuela created new tension between Germany and the United States. Venezuela's unscrupulous dictator, Cipriano Castro, had defaulted on some foreign debts. After futile negotiations, Germany and Britain, whose nationals appear to have suffered most abuse, completed plans by November 1902 to use force to bring Castro to terms.

Both countries were careful not to offend the United States. Germany had first informed the American government of her decision to punish Castro, giving assurances she did not intend to seize Venezuelan territory. Britain advised the United States of her plans in November, and the American government raised no objections.

At first Roosevelt himself saw nothing wrong in the Europeans using force. "If any South American State misbehaves towards any European country," he had written while still vice president, "let the European country spank it."[37] The Monroe Doctrine, he said later, did not protect rulers like Castro from deserved punishment. "We do not guarantee any state against punishment if it misconducts itself," he announced in his first annual message to Congress, "provided that punishment does not take the form of the acquisition of territory by any non-American power."[38]

On December 7 Britain and Germany served ultimatums on Venezuela. Within the next few days their naval forces captured four Venezuelan gunboats; the Germans destroyed two because they were unseaworthy. The British landed troops at La Guayra, both countries blockaded Venezuela's main ports, and the British bombarded forts at Puerto Cabello. Italy joined the blockade on December 16.

Since Castro knew he could expect no sympathy from Secretary Hay, he immediately appealed to the American people for help and tried to associate American interests, especially the Monroe Doctrine, with those of Venezuela. Then he appealed for arbitration through the American government. Hay merely forwarded the appeal to Britain and Germany "without comment."

American public opinion, meanwhile, began to turn against Germany. It grated sensibilities, the New York *American* said, "to see an American republic kicked and cuffed by a brace of European monarchies." Hay, therefore, abandoned his passive attitude and urged the European powers to arbitrate. Desiring to remain on good terms with the United States, both Germany and Britain had already decided to arbitrate, but with reservations as to certain of the claims against Castro.

Roosevelt asserted later that he had compelled a reluctant Germany to arbitrate by delivering an informal ultimatum to her ambassador in Washington threatening to send Admiral Dewey and the fleet to Venezuela. There is doubt as to whether or not he did. In any case, it is clear that Americans suspected German motives. Roosevelt may well have exerted pressure, for Dewey, in command of fleet maneuvers in the Caribbean in December 1902, did prepare to defend American interests there. A few months later Dewey himself told newspaper reporters that he saw in the maneuvers "an object lesson to the Kaiser, more than to any other person." [39]

Once the European powers had agreed to the principle of arbitration, a peaceful solution to the intervention appeared certain. Hay, to the president's delight, persuaded the powers to submit their grievances to the International Court of Arbitration at The Hague. "It seems to me," Roosevelt wrote to former President Cleveland, "that you have special cause for satisfaction in what we have succeeded in accomplishing this time in connection with getting England and Germany explicitly to recognize the Monroe Doctrine in reference to their controversy with Venezuela and in getting all of the parties in interest to accept arbitration by the Hague Court." [40]

Nonetheless, the principle behind the intervention alarmed some of the Latin-American countries, who considered it a dangerous precedent. Argentina's minister for foreign affairs, Luis M. Drago, sent a note to the United States suggesting as something of a corollary to the Monroe Doctrine that the use of armed forces by a European nation to collect public debts from an American nation was wrong. Although the American government did not at the time accept the Drago Doctrine, later when the Sec-

ond Hague Conference in 1907 embodied it in modified form in a convention, the United States supported it.

Meanwhile in January 1903, before the Venezuela arbitration began,
the guns of Fort San Carlos at Maracaibo fired on one of the blockading
German ships. A few days later several German ships bombarded and destroyed the fort. "Are people in Berlin crazy?" an angry Roosevelt asked.
"Don't they know that they are inflaming public opinion more and more
here?"[41] He was right. Anti-German sentiment swept the country.

Reluctant to arouse more American resentment, the Germans reduced
their cash demands and hastened the arbitration negotiations. The powers
lifted their blockade on February 14.

Several features stood out in the Venezuela intervention. Most Americans, showing a widespread distrust of Germany, apparently considered
that country the villain of the entire affair. Secondly, the episode gave the
Monroe Doctrine new dignity at home and in Europe.

England's prime minister, in an effort to dispel American resentment
created by the intervention, paid public homage to the Monroe Doctrine.
"We welcome any increase of the great influence of the United States of
America upon the great Western Hemisphere," he said. Then he added, "I
believe it would be a great gain to civilization if the United States of
America were more actively to interest themselves in making arrangements
by which these constantly recurring difficulties between European Powers
and certain States in South America could be avoided."[42] This advice was
not lost on Roosevelt, for out of the Venezuela experience grew his determination to formulate a corollary to the Monroe Doctrine that he sub-
sequently applied to the Dominican Republic.

The Roosevelt Corollary

The Dominican Republic, like Venezuela, had borrowed heavily from
foreigners. Torn by frequent civil strife, it was unable to pay its public
debt of some $32 million. Europeans claimed about $22 million. The
Dominican government recognized the claims of foreigners in agreements
that pledged the income from some of its customshouses to the payment of
those debts, but civil wars continued. Late in 1903 American, French, and
Italian forces stepped in briefly to protect the interests of their nationals. A
few months later it was clear that the Dominican Republic was bankrupt
and that European powers might intervene as they had in Venezuela to
force some kind of debt settlement.

Roosevelt no longer held to the view that Latin-American misbe-
havior justified European intervention. The award of the tribunal in the
Venezuela debt case had shown that those who used force could expect
preferred payment of their claims, for, as one State Department official

said, it "put a premium on violence."[43] The United States, therefore, sought an alternative to European naval demonstrations in the Caribbean.

The president then decided to intervene himself to prevent European use of force and possible control of territory in the Caribbean, an idea implicit in the Platt Amendment and various British suggestions. He expressed his idea publicly in May 1904. Any nation that paid its debts and kept itself in order, he wrote, need not fear interference from the United States, but brutal wrongdoing would require intervention "by some civilized nation, and in the Western Hemisphere the United States cannot ignore this duty."

Republicans and nationalists approved Roosevelt's theory as a necessary extension of the Monroe Doctrine, but Democrats and anti-imperialists denounced it as "a flagrant exhibition of jingoism" and as a policy of trying to boss the world. Roosevelt insisted that he spoke only the simplest common sense. "If we are willing to let Germany or England act as the policemen of the Caribbean, then we can afford not to interfere when gross wrongdoing occurs," he told Root. "But if we intend to say 'Hands off' to the powers of Europe, sooner or later we must keep order ourselves."[44] That was the essence of what came to be known as the Roosevelt Corollary to the Monroe Doctrine.

Under pressure from the United States, meanwhile, the Dominican government had made arrangements to pay its debt to an American concern, the Santo Domingo Improvement Company, in monthly installments guaranteed by customs collected at certain ports. When the Dominicans failed to meet the first payment, one of the Improvement Company's agents took over collection of customs at Puerto Plata in October. European nations protested and appeared ready to use force to collect the debts of their own nationals. In his annual message in December Roosevelt then reaffirmed his corollary, adding that "in the Western Hemisphere the adherence of the United States to the Monroe Doctrine may force the United States, however reluctantly, in flagrant cases of such wrongdoing or impotence, to the exercise of an international police power."[45]

A few weeks later Hay pointed out the danger of European intervention to the Dominican government and asked if it wished the United States to take charge of the collection of duties. The Dominicans agreed, and in January 1905 the two countries signed an agreement giving the United States control of the customs. The United States said it would give 45 percent of the revenues to the Dominican government and allot the balance to foreign creditors. It also guaranteed that republic's territorial integrity. Fearing that the executive agreement would invade the Senate's treaty prerogative, Congress protested. Roosevelt's minister in the republic, therefore, embodied most of the terms of the arrangement in a protocol, but omitted the territorial guarantee.

The president submitted the protocol, with a special message urging approval, to the Senate in February, pointing out that "those who profit by the Monroe Doctrine must accept certain responsibilities along with the rights which it confers; and that the same statement applies to those who uphold the doctrine." Democrats objected to the protocol and blocked consideration, so the Senate closed its session in March without approving it. Roosevelt was furious. The Senate's power over treaties should be like the president's veto, he said, "it should be rarely used."[46]

Undaunted, Roosevelt reverted to his original plan of an executive agreement, and in April completed a *modus vivendi* with the Dominicans placing their country in American hands. For more than two years Americans collected Dominican customs, made payments on the republic's debts, and gave it an unaccustomed financial stability. The protecting guns of American warships discouraged revolutions, so that the Dominicans also enjoyed an unusual political stability.

Democrats and others opposed making the Dominican Republic another Caribbean protectorate and denounced Roosevelt's arrangement as unconstitutional. Republicans, and apparently most Americans who thought about it, approved the Roosevelt Corollary. The Senate, therefore, after bitter debate, finally consented to the essential terms of the executive agreement in another treaty of February 1907, and the Dominican receivership continued. Most foreign creditors were willing to see it continue since it paid them a reasonable return on their debts.

Elihu Root and Latin America

Even though Latin Americans showed no widespread opposition to the Roosevelt Corollary, they resented Roosevelt's highhanded actions, his contemptuous statements about them, and his assumption of superiority. Elihu Root, who had succeeded Hay as secretary of state in July 1905, wanted to counteract the adverse effect of Roosevelt's policies upon Latin America. He suggested a goodwill trip, and the president, who had become concerned about the resentment because it appeared to affect the expansion of investment and trade in Latin America, endorsed the idea. Root, therefore, attended the Third Inter-American Conference which opened at Rio de Janeiro late in July 1906 and on the way visited seven Latin-American countries.

In his address to the conference, Root assured Latin Americans that the United States had no aggressive designs against them and sought only their cooperation. "We wish for no victories but those of peace," he said; "for no territory except our own; for no sovereignty except over ourselves."[47] Even though the secretary's words in Rio de Janeiro and elsewhere in Latin America were reassuring, neither he, nor any other American statesman, could soften the distrust of the United States. The crowds that cheered him and the champagne toasts in his honor were demonstrations of hospitality and esteem for him, not signs of goodwill toward the United States.

Latin Americans could not forget Panama, the Platt Amendment, and the Roosevelt Corollary. Many of them were economically and otherwise dependent on the United States, and they lived under the shadow of the big stick. What universal power, some asked themselves, gave the United States "the mission to put in order those who live in disorder?" A few expressed a view that "lesser" peoples of later years were to voice again and again. "If we live in disorder," they said, "we live in our own house, and nobody has the right to meddle in it."

United States policy in the Caribbean clearly worked for the advancement of its own interests there, and in the long run for the protection of the Latin Americans. Few could deny, however, that it was an arrogant policy, insensitive to the rights of the Latin Americans. The United States in the beginning of the twentieth century was young as a great power and overused its strength.

XVI

Britain's Rapprochement and Dollar Diplomacy

With the Open Door policy the United States had become involved in the international rivalries of Europe in Asia. Acting in support of similar principles—the Open Door, the balance of power, and peace—Theodore Roosevelt also intervened in imperial politics in North Africa.

Rivalries in Morocco

The United States had no direct interest in North Africa, particularly in Morocco, a center of European rivalry. American trade there was small and strategic interest negligible. Yet in 1880 the United States had participated in a conference in Madrid dealing with the abuse of extraterritoriality that threatened to extinguish Morocco's independence. At that time Britain and Spain wished to uphold Morocco's integrity whereas France did not. Since Germany was not yet interested in colonies and anxious to divert French attention from Alsace and Lorraine, provinces lost in the Franco-Prussian War, she supported France at the conference. The resulting treaty, therefore, merely defined extraterritorial protection without providing means to correct abuses, and thus allowed France to tighten her grip on Morocco. The United States signed the Madrid treaty precisely because it required no binding commitment.

In the quarter of a century that followed, France and Britain dissolved their colonial rivalry. By agreements reached in 1904 Britain accepted French plans to take over Morocco, and France acquiesced in British control of Egypt. This marked the beginning of an *entente cordiale* designed to withstand the rising might of Germany. In the years after 1880, German foreign policy changed. Germany, too, competed for African colonies and built up a considerable trade in Morocco.

Concerned over Morocco's fate and over the *entente,* Germany decided early in 1905 to oppose the extension of France's power. She insisted on an international conference to decide the future of Morocco. Since the United States had treaty rights there, the German chancellor, Bernhard von Bülow, sought Roosevelt's support for an Open Door in Morocco and a conference. Roosevelt gave a noncommital answer, but von Bülow interpreted it as meaning that the president had "drawn a parallel between maintaining the Open Door in China and in Morocco." [1]

Taking advantage of Russia's absorption in war with Japan and her inability to aid her French ally, von Bülow decided to test the *entente.* He persuaded a reluctant kaiser, William II, to visit the sultan at Tangier. The kaiser arrived in March and delivered a belligerent speech which in effect told France that Germany intended to take part in any Moroccan settlement. This speech infuriated the French foreign minister, Théophile Delcassé, who was willing to risk war by taking over Morocco anyway. England supported him, but Delcassé's policy created apprehension in Paris. Since France was poorly prepared, the premier, Pierre-Maurice Rouvier, was unwilling to gamble on war without Russian support. The cabinet, therefore, voted unanimously against Delcassé, forcing him to resign in June. To avert war, Rouvier conciliated Germany, but still hoped to avoid a conference. Germany's show of strength, however, humiliated France.

In an effort to seal her triumph, Germany urged Roosevelt to intervene by persuading France and England to agree to a conference. Roosevelt promised his help and asked the Germans to moderate their demands. He asked the French to accept a conference and convinced them that he wanted to prevent war and not to serve the interests of Germany.

The kaiser, meanwhile, promised Roosevelt that in any differences of opinion at the conference between Germany and France, he would support any decision the president considered fair. When Roosevelt told the French of the kaiser's promise they agreed to the conference which met in January 1906 in Algeciras, a small seaport in southern Spain.

At home, critics attacked the president for joining the Moroccan negotiations. Even Secretary of State Elihu Root believed that American interests in Morocco were insufficient to warrant participation. Nevertheless, Roosevelt went ahead.

At the conference France insisted on making Morocco a protectorate. Germany wanted several powers, including herself, placed in control and ultimately a partition with a share for herself. Although officially neutral, Roosevelt sympathized with the French and told them so. Germany therefore found herself practically alone in her demands. Only Austria-Hungary supported her. Germany had blundered in insisting upon a conference. Instead of driving a wedge between France and England, she had strengthened the *entente*. Even the United States seemed to believe that Germany was trying to drive France to war.

When Germany refused to come to terms, Roosevelt offered a compromise that preserved the principle of international control but gave the substance of power in Morocco to France. He persuaded Germany to accept the compromise by recalling the kaiser's promise to him. Although on the surface both countries seemed satisfied with the General Act of Algeciras, signed in April 1906, it proved ultimately to be a diplomatic defeat for Germany.

Pleased with his role in the negotiations, Roosevelt was convinced that the conference had prevented a war that had seemed imminent.

In adhering to the Act of Algeciras, Secretary of State Root insisted that the United States had no political interest in Morocco and assumed no obligation to enforce the settlement. Yet when the treaty reached the Senate later in the year, critics again attacked Roosevelt and demanded more reservations. When the Senate finally consented to the treaty in December, it reiterated in a formal reservation that adherence did not mean a departure from traditional nonentanglement policy.

How significant Roosevelt's role was in keeping the peace is not clear. One point, however, is evident: on the theory that a threat to world peace justified American intervention, he had openly broken the tradition of avoiding problems of European politics. He realized, as did some of his contemporaries, that the United States, now a recognized great power, could not entirely avoid the tensions of Europe. His intervention in Morocco foreshadowed a significant shift in American foreign policy toward closer ties with the Anglo-French *entente*.

Yet, Roosevelt's venture into Europe's diplomacy for a while seemed nothing more than a temporary aberration. When Germany and France again appeared on the verge of war in another Moroccan crisis in 1911, President William H. Taft remained aloof.

The Hague Peace Conferences

In the first decade of the twentieth century many Americans believed that the United States had an obligation to help maintain world peace. The government, therefore, evinced an interest in peace projects, disarmament, international organization, and arbitration. Yet, when the tsar of Russia, Nicholas II, called an international conference of twenty-six nations to meet at The Hague in 1899 to discuss disarmament and the prevention of war, the American government did not at first show much interest. It finally yielded to the pressures of a peace movement, emphasizing disarmament and arbitration, that had already gathered considerable strength among the reformers of the period, and sent a delegation to The Hague peace conference.

The conference failed to achieve its major objective of disarmament, but did adopt conventions and declarations designed to humanize war. Its most noteworthy achievement was a permanent court of arbitration, a panel of slightly over a hundred individuals upon whom nations could call to act as arbitrators. The countries which signed the convention did not pledge themselves to use the court, and none were willing to accept arbitration as a means of settling those disputes that usually led to war. Another point worthy of note was the support American delegates consistently gave to Great Britain.

The United States was particularly reluctant to surrender any control over vital national issues to the court. When the Senate approved various agreements signed at the conference, such as those dealing with the outlawing of inhumane weapons, it insisted again that those commitments could not require the United States to depart from its nonentanglement policy. The Senate attempted to do what was virtually impossible—to draw a line between political and nonpolitical international obligations.

After the First Hague Conference a widespread discussion of international organization gave new hope to the leaders of the peace movement. Some talked of holding periodic peace conferences and others suggested improvements in the permanent court of arbitration. In September 1904, President Roosevelt promised members of a private peace society that he would ask the nations of the world to participate in a second conference at The Hague. The United States appeared ready to take the lead in the movement for world peace, but the Russians wanted to sponsor the conference, so Roosevelt stepped aside. The tsar called the Second Hague Conference which met in 1907. This time, at the insistence of the United States, the conference included representatives from the Latin American nations, making a total of forty-four participating states.

The second conference, too, failed to achieve either a reduction or limitation of armaments. Secretary of State Root wanted to replace the old ineffective permanent court with a true court that would sit in regular session with a small staff of genuine jurists, but the conference would not accept the American proposal. The conference did adopt a number of minor conventions dealing with such matters as restrictions on the right of capture in naval war, which the United States ratified.

Arbitration Treaties

In setting up the permanent court of arbitration the First Hague Conference had reflected a broad international interest in the settlement of disputes through arbitration. A few years after the conference, in 1904, Secretary of State John Hay negotiated ten bilateral arbitration treaties that obligated the United States in advance to arbitrate through the Hague court certain kinds of disputes not settled by diplomacy. Even though the treaties were broad and would not deal with disputes that actually brought on wars, the Senate would not approve them without drastic change.

Jealously guarding its prerogative in foreign relations, the Senate insisted that it had to approve every special agreement defining the questions at issue in each arbitration. In other words, it regarded each arbitration agreement as a treaty and would not surrender the power of defining the arbitration to the president, as called for in the original Hay treaties. Since Hay believed that the Senate amendments made the treaties meaningless and the president agreed with him, Roosevelt withdrew the treaties from the Senate. Since we already have the power to make special arbitration treaties, Roosevelt said, to pass "these amended treaties does not in the smallest degree facilitate settlements by arbitration, to make them would in no way further the cause of international peace."[2]

Hay's successor, Elihu Root, took a different view of the Senate's position. He believed that weak arbitration treaties were better than none and converted Roosevelt to his thinking. In the year following the Second Hague Conference Root negotiated twenty-four bilateral treaties with the leading nations of the world except Germany. All treaties were similar to Hay's except that the special agreement defining the scope of each arbitration needed the approval by the usual two-thirds vote of the Senate. Most of the pacts had a limit of five years, and most were renewed at the end of the five years.

Critics pointed out that the Root treaties were so narrow in scope they could contribute little to settling significant international disputes. Yet, the Senate would not go beyond the Root formula.

William H. Taft believed in the peace movement. In the interests of peace he wanted to go beyond the Root treaties. "I do not see," he said, "why questions of honor may not be submitted to a tribunal supposed to be composed of men of honor who understand questions of national honor."[3] He instructed Secretary of State Philander C. Knox, therefore, to negotiate general arbitration treaties with Britain and France that included even questions of "national honor" as subjects for arbitration. Those two treaties, signed in August 1911, and designed to serve as models, said all "justiciable" questions—meaning in Taft's view infringements of legal rights under the principles of international law—not settled by diplomacy should go to the Hague court or some other suitable tribunal. In any dispute a joint high commission would decide whether or not a question at issue was "justiciable" and whether it could be submitted for arbitration.

The advocates of peace organized a nation-wide campaign to win the Senate's approval, and Taft himself appealed directly to the people. As jealous as ever of any infringement of its treaty power, the Senate amended the treaties, reserving to itself the right to determine whether or not an issue was "justiciable." Since Taft would not ask Britain and France to accept the crippling amendments that excluded virtually every issue of importance from arbitration, he did not ratify the treaties. He recalled a few years later that the Senate "had truncated them and amended them in such a way that their own father could not recognize them."[4]

"Cooling Off" Treaties

Despite defeat of the Taft treaties, friends of peace gained renewed hope when Woodrow Wilson became president—hope that international disputes might be settled without resort to war. Both Wilson, and his secretary of state, William Jennings Bryan, approached the problem with evangelical zeal. Although the idea was not original with him, Bryan had long advocated the use of joint commissions to determine disputed facts in international controversies. When he accepted the secretaryship one of his conditions was that the president must give him a free hand to negotiate treaties for the maintenance of peace.

Soon after taking office, Bryan began negotiating a series of conciliation pacts entitled "Treaties for the Advancement of Peace," but popularly called "cooling off" treaties. They supplemented the Root treaties by committing signatory nations to submit all disputes not capable of settlement through diplomacy, even those touching questions of "national honor," to permanent international commissions for investigation. During the period of investigation, usually one year, neither party would begin hostilities. The disputants could either accept or reject the commission's recommendation. The basic idea behind the pacts was that of delay in time of acute tension.

Bryan's first "cooling off" treaty, with El Salvador, was signed in August 1913. By October of the following year he had concluded twenty-nine others, among them treaties with Britain, France, and Italy. Germany refused to negotiate a treaty. Since the recommendations of the investigating commissions were not binding and the pacts committed the United States to little more than a period of delay, the Senate approved most of them. Cynics condemned the treaties as unrealistic, but Bryan considered them the outstanding achievement of his long career.

Anglo-American Rapprochement

During the era of this peace movement the new Anglo-American *rapprochement* grew stronger. There were, nonetheless, a number of lesser conflicts that Britain and the United States had to resolve before they could cement their new friendship. One of these arose out of the Boer War.

When war broke out in October 1899 between Britain and the Boer republics of South Africa, the British found themselves widely disliked. The peoples and governments of Europe appeared solidly pro-Boer. The attitude of the United States, therefore, was especially important to Britain.

Most Americans, but particularly those of Dutch, German, and Irish blood, in contrast to government policy, sympathized with the Boers. Since Britain was the dominant sea power and the United States a leading neutral, incidents over British seizures of American ships aroused strong feelings. So strong was sentiment against Britain that in the election of 1900 the Democrats tried to make an issue of government sympathy for Britain. Their platform condemned "the ill-concealed Republican alliance with England" and extended "sympathy to the heroic burghers in their unequal struggle to maintain their liberty and independence." [5]

When Roosevelt became president the Boers hoped that this young man with a Dutch name might show more understanding of their cause than had McKinley and Hay, but they were disappointed. "The downfall of the British Empire," he had written before becoming president when the English were faring badly in the war, "I should regard as a calamity to the race, and especially to this country." [6] Roosevelt, too, turned his back on the Boers and favored a British victory.

One reason for America's friendly policy toward Britain, despite the sentiment of the people, was Britain's own friendliness during the Spanish-American War. At the time, moreover, imperialism was fashionable, and the American government could not justifiably condemn the British when it had rebels of its own to crush in the Philippines. The firmness of official American friendship for Britain strengthened the Anglo-American *rapprochement*.

Some Englishmen had feared that the United States might take advantage of their trouble in Africa by forcing a settlement of disputes over the Clayton-Bulwer Treaty and the Alaskan boundary, and were gratified when no such move was made. Yet, even though Britain defeated the Boers, her distresses ultimately forced her to resume the stalemated negotiations over the Clayton-Bulwer Treaty and to express a willingness to compromise on the issue of the Alaskan boundary. Thus in the American disputes with Canada she was more willing to make concessions than was Canada.

Alaska's Frontier

The most serious controversy with Canada, and hence with Britain, since the London government was responsible for the dominion's external affairs, grew out of differing interpretations of the vague boundary between Alaska's panhandle and Canada. According to the Anglo-Russian Treaty of 1825, part of which was incorporated into the Russo-American Treaty of 1867 giving Alaska to the United States, the boundary ran inland thirty miles from the Pacific Ocean. For over seventy years the United States, Russia, and Britain had assumed that the boundary followed the irregularities of the coastline.

After the discovery of gold in the region of Canada's Klondike River, near Alaska, Canada challenged the old interpretation. She insisted that the boundary did not follow the windings of the coast but instead ran in a relatively straight line from the outer limits of the coast cutting across the tips of land projections and the mouths of inlets. What made Canada's interpretation significant was that the best route to her interior region and to the gold fields lay through the Alaskan panhandle, mainly through the Lynn Canal which controlled the trade of the interior into the gold fields and also gave Canada access to the sea.

Under the Canadian interpretation ports at the head of the canal would have fallen on the Canadian side of a boundary cutting across the canal. This would have broken American control of the trade of the interior. Americans considered the Canadian claim preposterous, believing it had been trumped up because of the gold discoveries. Canadians denied the charge, saying they had long neglected their claim because it was in a remote region that was virtually inaccessible prior to the gold discoveries. Still, it seemed that Canada and Britain sought a generous settlement over the boundary in exchange for concessions elsewhere.

Since thousands of rough goldseekers from all over the world, but mainly from the United States, had stampeded to the Klondike, a settlement of the boundary dispute appeared urgent. Those men might get out of hand and touch off a conflict between American and Canadian authorities. The United States and Britain agreed to submit the dispute, along with other Canadian problems, to a joint high commission which met in Quebec in August 1898. For political reasons the Canadian commissioners demanded an American retreat at the Lynn Canal. Also for political reasons, primarily pressures from the Pacific Coast, the Americans could not retreat, and the commission failed to settle the boundary problem.

The British offered to arbitrate but the United States refused. In October 1899, therefore, Secretary Hay negotiated a temporary agreement, or *modus vivendi*, with Britain that pleased no one but brought stability to the Alaskan frontier. Later when Britain tried to obtain concessions on the Alaskan boundary in return for canal concessions in Central America, the United States refused. And, in March 1902 Roosevelt ordered troops to southern Alaska to prevent disturbances among the miners.

Since the Canadians, too, dreaded outbreaks and the British feared that the dispute might endanger the new *rapprochement*, they desired a settlement. John Hay negotiated and on January 23, 1903, signed a treaty with Sir Michael Herbert, the British ambassador in Washington, calling for a panel of six "impartial jurists of repute," three to be chosen by the president and three by Britain's king, to define the boundary by majority vote.

The shipping and trading interests of the state of Washington denounced the Hay-Herbert Treaty as endangering American control of the

Lynn Canal, and opposition in the Senate appeared so strong that for a while it looked as if the agreement would die there. Senator Lodge, who supported the treaty, overcame opposition by obtaining the names of the commissioners the president intended to appoint and confidentially revealing them to his colleague: Secretary of War Elihu Root; a former senator from the state of Washington, George Turner; and Lodge. Since all three were known to be firmly committed to the American case, the partisan selections infuriated the Canadians. Sir Michael was "disgusted and disheartened." "Everything in this country," he said, "is subservient to politics, and really an ambassador in Washington needs more than an ordinary stock of patience."[7]

Roosevelt had not desired unbiased jurists, though he had asked two justices of the Supreme Court to serve who had refused. He said he had consented to the commission only out of friendship to England, wishing her to be able to retreat gracefully from the untenable position "in which she has been placed by Canada." Perhaps the Louisville *Courier-Journal* summarized the American view: "It is not likely that England will get anything she is not entitled to from that trio," it predicted.[8]

England appointed Lord Chief Justice Richard E. W. Alverstone, and two prominent Canadian jurists. After some preliminary haggling, the Alaska Boundary Tribunal convened in London in September. Since the American commissioners adamantly upheld the claim of their government and the Canadians adhered as strongly to their position, the decision rested with Alverstone who in effect assumed the role of an arbitrator rather than that of a jurist.

Even before the tribunal met, Roosevelt let the British know that if the commissioners did not decide in favor of the United States he would run the boundary by force. "The plain fact is that the British have no case whatever," he told Lodge, "and when this is so Alverstone ought to be satisfied, and indeed must be satisfied with the very minimum—simply enough to save his face and bring an adjustment."[9] British officials passed on Roosevelt's threats to use the "big stick" to Alverstone.

Instructed to avoid a deadlock, Alverstone voted with the Americans. Although the United States gained a narrower coastal area than its commissioners demanded, the award, announced on October 2, favored its claims. Canada received only two of four disputed islands. The United States retained an unbroken coastal strip and control of the strategic Lynn Canal. The decision was diplomatic rather than judicial. The Canadians were so bitter they refused to sign the award, while Americans were delighted with the decision. The British were sick of the whole dispute and pleased to have it out of the way. Seven years later Roosevelt maintained that "the settlement of the Alaskan boundary settled the last serious trouble between the British Empire and ourselves, as everything else could be arbitrated."[10]

Fisheries Settlement

What Roosevelt said was essentially true. Yet the oldest dispute with Britain, over the fishing grounds of the North Atlantic, remained unsettled while he was in the White House and jeopardized the stability of the new *rapprochement*.

Since Britain had several times renewed the *modus vivendi* of 1888, allowing American fishing vessels to buy bait and other supplies in the harbors of Canada and Newfoundland under a licensing system, the dispute lay quiet for ten years. Canada and Newfoundland resented the *modus vivendi* because it offered privileges to the United States without giving them equivalent concessions. In 1898, they suggested a permanent settlement of the old controversy. If the United States would repeal its tariff on their fish, the British dominions said, they would agree to remove the restrictions on American fishermen imposed by the Anglo-American Convention of 1818.

Finally, on November 8, 1902, John Hay and the prime minister of Newfoundland signed a treaty giving Americans free fishing privileges in the waters of Newfoundland and allowing fish and some other products of that province free access to the American market. The New England fishing interests opposed the treaty. Influenced by that opposition, led by Henry Cabot Lodge, the Senate killed the treaty in 1905. In June of that year, Newfoundland's parliament retaliated with a law terminating the *modus vivendi* and placing punitive restrictions on American fishing vessels in its waters. In May of the following year Newfoundland enacted additional discriminatory legislation against American fishing ships.

Anxious to keep the fisheries controversy from becoming more serious, Secretary of State Elihu Root visited Newfoundland and Canada. In September 1907, he arranged another temporary agreement with Britain that allowed Americans to continue fishing in the waters of Newfoundland but under restricted conditions. Then, in the following April, he signed a general arbitration treaty with Britain under whose terms both countries formally agreed in January 1909, to submit the fisheries problem to a panel of five judges from the permanent court of arbitration at The Hague, including one American and one Canadian judge. The tribunal delivered its award in September 1910. Although Root regarded the decision as a "great and substantial victory" for the American case, it was a compromise that gave something to both sides.

The most important feature of the award sustained Britain's right to make and enforce local fishing regulations, but the regulations had to be reasonable. If the United States contested their reasonableness, then the objections would go to a permanent mixed fishery commission that would determine who was right. The British had long claimed the right, challenged by Americans, to exclude American fishermen from all bays regardless of size. The tribunal ruled that bays less than ten miles wide at the mouth were inshore waters and hence closed to American fishermen. When the mouth exceeded ten miles, the area of local jurisdiction was three miles along the shore of the bay and Americans could fish in the bay beyond the three-mile limit.

An Anglo-American commission signed a convention in July 1912, modifying the Hague award, but confirming its essential points. This resolved the most vexatious problems of the longest dispute in the history of American foreign policy. Later in the twentieth century other controversies over fisheries caused friction, but they never truly endangered American friendship with Canada.

Reciprocity of 1911

Another problem, related to that of the fisheries, that had long troubled relations with Canada was that of trade reciprocity. Since the abrogation of the Marcy-Elgin Treaty in 1866, Canada had sought some kind of reciprocal trade agreement, but the United States had refused all proposals. Republicans, who had controlled the government most of the time in the years since the Civil War, upheld the principle of a protective tariff almost as a matter of party faith. In 1909 they passed the Payne-Aldrich Tariff, a protectionist measure that struck at Canada with special severity. Canadians threatened retaliation.

To avoid a tariff war if nothing more were done, President Taft and Prime Minister Sir Wilfrid Laurier, the head of Canada's Liberal government, signed an agreement on January 26, 1911, for commercial reciprocity. It allowed most of Canada's main products, primarily agricultural, to enter the United States subject to no duties or to low ones, and American manufactures could go into Canada on the same terms. Since the agreement was not a treaty, it was to go into effect by concurrent legislation, meaning that a simple majority in both houses of Congress could make it law.

The reciprocity bill won approval in the House of Representatives without delay, but the Senate, sensitive to the opposition of lumber, fish, and agriculture interests, adjourned in March without acting on it. Regarding the bill as one of the most important measures of his administration, Taft called Congress into special session in April. Despite continued opposition by protectionists and by many in his own Republican party, he got the bill through the Senate in July with the aid of Democratic votes.

In urging passage, Taft and other supporters of the bill gave the impression that free trade would lead to the annexation of Canada. "The amount of Canadian products we take," the president said privately, "would make Canada only an adjunct of the United States."[11] He repeated similar ideas publicly, and a number of congressional and newspaper supporters used the same argument.

In Canada public sentiment had changed and reciprocity became a party issue. Liberals supported it and Conservatives, backed by manufacturers, railroads, and other financial interests, opposed it. This forced the prime minister to dissolve parliament and to call a general election. The main issue was reciprocity, but propaganda, feeding on a latent distrust of the United States and on an aroused nationalism, reduced it to the issue of choosing between the United States or the empire.

The inept statements of Taft and American congressmen proved to be valuable campaign material for the Conservatives. One editor said that "the answer from the Canadian people is that Canada is, and intends to remain, British."[12] So it was. The Canadians rallied round the flag and in September gave the Conservatives a decisive victory. Later, the Conservative party defeated the reciprocity bill in parliament.

The defeat of reciprocity did not precipitate a tariff war with Canada or harm the Anglo-American *rapprochement,* but it embarrassed the Taft administration and smothered trade reciprocity for a quarter of a century. After the election of 1911 American relations with Canada became distinct from those with England.

Panama Tolls Controversy

Another controversy with England arose from differing interpretations of the Hay-Pauncefote Treaty over toll payments for the use of the Panama Canal as it approached completion. The canal should be open to the ships of all nations "on terms of entire equality," the treaty read, so that there would be no discriminatory charges against any nation. In August 1912, Congress exempted American ships engaged only in the coastwise trade, as from California to New York, from payment of tolls. Viewing the exemption as a violation of the Hay-Pauncefote Treaty and breach of faith that would lead to higher tolls for foreign ships, the British protested. They asked for adjudication of the dispute under the arbitration treaty of 1908.

President Taft refused, saying that "when the treaties are properly construed, owning the canal and paying for it as we do, we have the right and power, if we choose, to discriminate in favor of our own ships."[13] Other Americans believed the United States was bound by honor not to discriminate.

In the presidential campaign of 1912 the platforms of both the Democratic and Progressive parties supported the exemption. Yet even though President Wilson had approved the exemption during the campaign, he soon became convinced that the British had a good case and that the nation's honor was at stake. He also realized that arbitration would require a treaty and that the mood of the Senate was such that it probably would not give the necessary two-thirds approval. Fortunately, he obtained the support of Henry Cabot Lodge, who suggested repeal of the clause which made the trouble.

Wilson followed that procedure. He met with the Senate Foreign Relations Committee in January 1914 and pointed out that he needed British support for the tolls controversy. When he went before a joint session of Congress in March to ask for repeal of the exemption, he referred to the difficulties in Mexico, but not specifically. "I ask this of you in support of the foreign policy of the administration," he said. "I shall not know how to deal with other matters of even greater delicacy and nearer consequence if you do not grant it to me in ungrudging measure."[14]

The House of Representatives repealed the exemption a few weeks later, but the Senate debated two months and did not do so until June 11. That repeal was more than just a victory for Wilson's foreign policy. It settled the last important controversy with Britain before the *rapprochement* met the test of the First World War.

Dollar Diplomacy in Asia

These years preceding the First World War also saw a change in the concept of the Open Door. Priding itself on close relations with business, the Taft administration wanted American capital to expand into foreign fields. The president and his secretary of state, Philander C. Knox, were particularly eager to have dollars penetrate China for profitable investment, an area where dollars had refused to go of their own accord.

This policy of seeking to open China for investment became known as Dollar Diplomacy. It was, Taft claimed, a policy of substituting dollars for bullets, "an effort frankly directed to the increase of American trade upon the axiomatic principle that the Government of the United States shall extend all proper support to every legitimate and beneficial American enterprise abroad."[15] Others defined Dollar Diplomacy in expansionist terms as a financial aspect of the Open Door doctrine.

Dollar Diplomacy had its roots in the Roosevelt period. In the summer of 1905 Edward H. Harriman, a railroad financier, who controlled a large part of American shipping in the Pacific, visited Japan. There he made arrangements to purchase a controlling interest in the South Manchuria Railway, which Japan hoped to acquire at the end of the Russo-Japanese War.

Harriman explained his plan to the American minister in Tokyo. "There's no doubt about it," he said. "If I can secure control of the South Manchuria Railroad from Japan, I'll buy the Chinese Eastern from Russia, acquire trackage over the Trans-Siberian to the Baltic, and establish a line of steamers to the United States. Then I can connect with the American transcontinental lines, and join up with the Pacific Mail and the Japanese transpacific steamers. It'll be the most marvelous transportation system in the world. We'll girdle the earth." [16]

After the peace with Russia, Japan backed out of her arrangement with Harriman, which she had never signed. She decided to exploit her railroad properties in Manchuria herself, basically with Japanese and Chinese capital. Harriman did not abandon his idea, but it might have died if Willard Straight, then consul-general at Mukden, Manchuria, had not kept it alive.

Harriman had met Straight, a restless young diplomat, while in Asia and was impressed by his "character and force." Straight distrusted the Japanese and believed that their control of southern Manchuria threatened potential American interests there. He was convinced that meager investments accounted for lack of United States power in that part of the world. Believing that investments would lead to American political influence in Manchuria, he wrote to Harriman in 1906, stressing profitable opportunities there. Straight even devised a plan for a railroad to compete with Japan's South Manchuria Railway. He told Harriman of his plan, but the financial panic of 1907 in the United States made investment capital scarce, so Harriman rejected Straight's idea.

Meanwhile, in July 1907 Japan and Russia signed two conventions, one of them secret, that recognized northern Manchuria and Outer Mongolia as Russian spheres of influence and southern Manchuria and Inner Mongolia as Japanese spheres. These agreements, though not clear at the time, threatened the Open Door and opportunities for foreign investment in Manchuria. Realizing he could do nothing to stop the Russians and the Japanese without using force he did not have, President Roosevelt did not challenge their predominance in Manchuria.

Straight, however, wanted to block the Japanese. He kept in touch with Harriman, urging him to invest in China. Nothing happened until the end of the panic when Harriman asked Secretary of State Root to recall Straight for consultation on opportunities for investment in Manchuria. " 'Wall Street' is feeling confident again and is looking for the investment of capital in foreign lands," the chief of the State Department's Far Eastern Division said. "It has turned to Manchuria and wants the latest advice on the situation up there. . . ." [17]

Straight returned to the United States in September 1908 with ideas that fitted the objectives of Dollar Diplomacy. In November he became acting chief of the Division of Far Eastern Affairs. While in Washington, he worked to maintain Harriman's interest in Manchuria's railroads and tried to gain (for his own schemes) the support of New York bankers, who sought investment abroad.

Serving as a link between the Department of State and Harriman, Straight aided in arrangements for a loan to China, through Harriman's banking associates, Kuhn, Loeb and Company, to finance a program of eco-

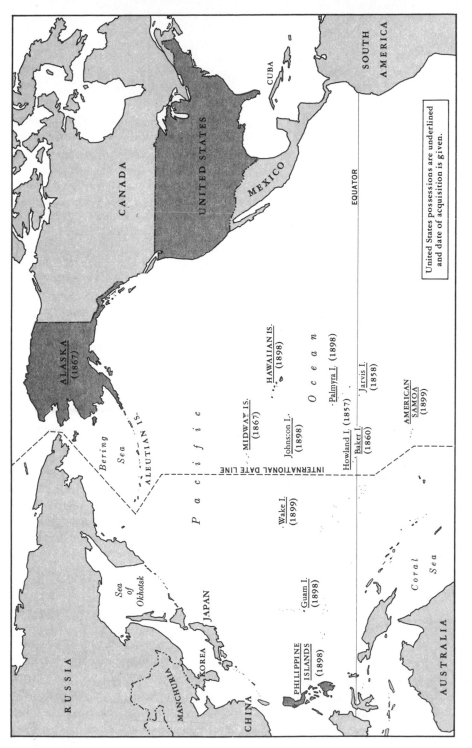

THE AMERICAN EMPIRE IN THE PACIFIC, 1910

United States possessions are underlined and date of acquisition is given.

nomic reform. He also tried to pave the way for Harriman and the bankers to buy the South Manchuria Railway and Russia's Chinese Eastern Railway in northern Manchuria. As long as Roosevelt was in the White House, however, Straight's ideas received scant attention from the government.

When Taft became president, the ideas of Straight and Harriman gained official support. Taft and Knox believed that the government should aid private enterprise in seeking markets and investment opportunities abroad. They also felt that in pumping capital into China they would block Japan's policy there, help preserve China's administrative integrity, and extend the principles of the Open Door.

When China signed an agreement with English, French, and German bankers in June 1909, known as the Hukuang Railway loan, to finance the construction of railroads in southern and central China, the Taft administration sought a share of the loan for American bankers. Straight, who resigned from the Department of State that same month, immediately went to work for the banking group that became "the official agent of American railway financing in China."

Since the Taft policy threatened a potentially lucrative financial monopoly, the Europeans resisted the American attempt to intervene. Therefore, Taft himself sent a telegram to the Chinese prince regent demanding a share of the railroad loan for the American bankers. China and the powers finally admitted the American bankers in May 1910, and what had been a three-power consortium became the first four-power consortium.

Willard Straight, meantime, while working to obtain the Chinese loan, also kept alive his earlier plan for the purchase of the railroads in Manchuria. He and Harriman tried to buy the Chinese Eastern Railway from Russia so they could expand the line southward, threaten Japan with competition, and force her to sell the South Manchuria Railway that Harriman really wanted. But Harriman, the one American financier intensely interested in Manchuria, died in September 1909.

Without Harriman the American bankers hesitated to support the financing of railroads in Manchuria. So Straight attempted to lure capital and the government into activity in Manchuria. He managed to transfer the interest of the bankers to Manchuria, and since the Taft administration feared that Japan's control of trade, railroads, and mineral deposits in southern Manchuria would freeze out American economic rights, he also succeeded in involving the government in Manchurian affairs.

Knox's Neutralization Scheme

Late in October 1909 Secretary of State Knox, aware of Harriman's and Straight's activities, told the American banking group of a plan to "neutralize" Manchuria's railroads. He wanted an international syndicate to lend money to China to purchase all the Manchurian railroads, with the syndicate supervising them during the term of the loan. If Britain found the plan impracticable, then he would ask her to support an alternative idea of building a line to compete with Japan's South Manchuria Railway. This neutralization scheme, Knox thought, would preserve the Open Door in Manchuria and help China gain control there. It would, he said privately, "smoke Japan out" of her dominant position in southern Manchuria. Knox's plan and Straight's ideas fitted together so well that they appeared to be part of a grand design.

In November Knox approached England first with the idea of having her present his plan to her Japanese ally. If Japan refused to cooperate, she would then find herself stigmatized as an enemy of the Open Door in Manchuria. Since Britain's main concern was the rising power of Germany in Europe, she relied on her alliance with Japan for support in Asia and, since concluding an *entente* with Russia in 1907, looked to Russia and France for aid in Europe. She would do nothing to alienate either Japan or Russia, for those two countries resented Knox's transparent scheme to deprive them of their spheres of influence in Manchuria. When he asked Japan and Russia to join his plan, they rejected it in January 1910, with notes so similar as to indicate collaboration. Since France supported the British position, all the powers but Germany opposed the neutralization scheme.

Knox's blundering scheme drove Russia and Japan together to tighten their grip on Manchuria. In July, they announced, as they had three years earlier, that they had signed a treaty promising mutual consultation to preserve the *status quo* in Manchuria and cooperation in developing its railroads. They had also concluded a secret convention reaffirming their spheres of influence and promising "common action" to defend them. Their announcement just about crushed China's hopes in Manchuria.

Thus, American policy antagonized Japan and Russia and lost the confidence of China. Moreover, since Roosevelt had, in effect, acquiesced in a closed door there, Taft and Knox had reversed his Far Eastern policy. Their failure also aroused the ire of the American banking group. Since the opposition of the other powers precluded financial success, the bankers threatened to withdraw from the whole of China. Instead of opening the door to American investment in Manchuria and China, Dollar Diplomacy virtually closed it.

Still, the Taft administration did not abandon its policy. China had, meanwhile, revived an old scheme for currency reform as part of a larger program of general reform. Since American bankers were at the time still interested in making loans, the State Department decided to use the currency reform as a means of restoring shattered prestige in China. Taft invited England, France, and Germany to participate, and a second four-power consortium drew up a Chinese Currency Reform and Industrial Development Loan in April 1911. That loan was never floated.

A month later the first four-power consortium finally reached an agreement on the Hukuang Railway loan. Although accepted by the Chinese government, the Hukuang loan, for thirty million dollars, was unpopular with the people who resented foreign economic exploitation of their country. Instead of being used immediately to build railroads, it helped touch off a revolution that overthrew the Manchu dynasty.

Six-Power Consortium

After their revolution of 1911, the Chinese set up a republic in February 1912. Desperately in need of money, the new government turned to the members of the four-power consortium for aid. The bankers were willing to make a loan for the reorganization of China's government, but Britain and France wanted their Japanese and Russian allies to share in it. Japan and Russia, therefore, became members of a six-power consortium in June. In enlarging the consortium the powers recognized the Japanese and Russian spheres in Manchuria and Mongolia. The Taft administration, as a result, accepted Japan's dominant position in southern Manchuria and abandoned the Open Door in that region.

Before the six-power consortium could complete its agreement with China, the American banking group lost its desire to participate. Agents of the bankers reported that the international market could not handle a large amount of Chinese bonds. That news, coupled with Chinese opposition to several features of the proposed loan and fear of the incoming Wilson administration, finally led the banking group to decide that it must have full government support or it would give up its share of the loan.

Five days after Wilson took office, representatives of the American bankers, Straight among them, interviewed Secretary of State Bryan. They said their group would not go through with its share of the reorganization loan unless the administration asked it to do so and indicated it would use force, if necessary, to make China live up to the contract.

Wilson and Bryan discussed the loan problem in two cabinet meetings. Then the president issued a statement directly to the press. His administration, he said, would not ask the bankers to participate "because it did not approve the conditions of the loan or the implications of responsibility on its own part," and he added, "the conditions of the loan seem to us to touch very nearly the administrative independence of China itself." [18]

Wilson thus repudiated Dollar Diplomacy, and the bankers withdrew from the first four-power consortium and from the six-power consortium. The other members of the six-power consortium went ahead without the American bankers and concluded a loan for the reorganization of the Chinese government in April 1913.

Wilson's decision on the loan led foreign statesmen to wonder if he would adopt a similarly independent policy in recognizing the new Chinese republic. Secretary Knox had followed a policy of cooperating with the other powers who desired concessions from the Chinese government as the price of recognition. American public sentiment, sympathetic to China's republican form of government, favored recognition. So in February and April of 1912 Congress passed resolutions adopting a republican form of government and urging Taft to extend early recognition. Knox resisted those pressures, believing that his cooperative policy served the national interest better than would individual action. Taft's government, therefore, retired with the United States maintaining only *de facto* relations with the Chinese republic.

When Wilson took office, he was anxious to extend *de jure* recognition independently of other powers. Before doing so, however, he offered the powers a chance to join him. Since only four Latin American states accepted Wilson's offer, the United States on May 2, 1913, became the first of the great powers to recognize the Chinese republic. In acting alone, Wilson repudiated another of the Taft-Knox policies.

California Land Laws

When a new crisis arose over the status of Japanese aliens in California, Wilson did not show the same benevolent attitude toward Japan as he had toward China. Prejudice in California was an old problem. Every California legislature from 1907 to 1913 had considered discriminatory measures against Japanese. In March 1913 anti-Japanese agitation erupted with particular force when both Democrats and Republicans catered to the racial feeling of voters by introducing legislation designed to bar Japanese from owning land.

Many governments prohibited foreigners from acquiring property. The Japanese government objected not to the legislation itself, but to the injustice of its discriminatory features. Japan demanded treatment for her nationals equal to that accorded other aliens in the United States and resented the laws that stigmatized Asians as inferiors.

Since Wilson himself favored exclusion of foreigners, he did not attempt to stop the Californians from enacting their discriminatory laws. He merely asked them to act so "as to offend the susceptibilities of a friendly nation as little as possible."[19] He even suggested a means of keeping Japanese from possessing real estate in California without violating a Japanese-American commercial treaty of 1911.

At first the California legislators followed Wilson's suggestion by drawing up an alien land bill indirectly prohibiting Japanese from owning land in the state. Later, they substituted another bill directed specifically against Japanese. Japan protested the proposed law and newspapers carried reports of a mass meeting in Tokyo demanding war rather than have the nation submit to humiliation by California.

Alarmed by the developments in the West and by the war agitation in Japan, Wilson appealed publicly to the California legislators in April not to embarrass the federal government with a law that openly discriminated against Japanese. He also sent Bryan to California to plead for moderation with lawmakers and the governor. Since Wilson took a narrow view of the federal government's authority over the police powers of a state, he would go no further. He would not use federal power to coerce a state. Therefore, even though Bryan begged the Californians to modify their proposed legislation, they would not.

As the tension with Japan increased, the California legislature on May 3, 1913, passed an Alien Land Bill depriving aliens "ineligible to citizenship" of the right to own land except as guaranteed by treaty. Other aliens, however, were still allowed to own land.

Considering the law an affront to national honor, the Japanese government on May 9 lodged a strong protest with the Department of State. So violent was the reaction in Japan, that the Joint Board of the Army and Navy, the highest defense agency in the United States, began preparations for war and wanted to order several warships to the Philippines to protect them against any surprise attack from Japan. Bryan and Wilson wished to avoid any move that might arouse more excitement in Japan; hence the president refused to send the warships.

Bryan tried to persuade California's governor to veto the Alien Land Bill, but the governor signed it and it became law on May 19. The president, at the same time, assured newspaper reporters that talk of war was foolish and that the crisis would be overcome amicably. He and Bryan tried to conciliate the angry Japanese as best they could. The secretary told them that what California had done did not represent national policy.

Since Wilson and Bryan did not deny the justice of the Japanese complaints against the discriminatory features of the land law, they helped to ease the wound in Japan's pride. Bryan told the Japanese "that nothing is final between friends" and that "a satisfactory solution can be found for all questions if the parties approach the subject with patience and in the right spirit."[20] Gradually the tension in both Japan and the United States eased.

Twenty-One Demands

When the First World War spread to Asia, it endangered the Open Door in China and intensified tensions between Japan and the United States. Japan entered the war on the Allied side in August 1914. Her navy seized German islands in the Pacific north of the equator, the Marianas (except Guam), the Carolines, and the Marshalls. Her army invaded the Shantung Peninsula and expelled the Germans from their leasehold there.

In the fighting on Shantung the two main belligerents, Japan and

Germany, violated China's neutrality, but Japanese violations were more flagrant. Helpless to protect herself, China appealed to the United States, as a champion of the Open Door, to intervene on her behalf. While expressing friendship for China, Acting Secretary of State Robert Lansing replied that the United States could not become entangled in international difficulties. Yet some Americans shared Chinese fears that Japan intended not only to remain in the Shantung province but also to use it as a base for taking over other portions of China.

In January 1915, within a month after completing her conquests, Japan showed that the Chinese and American fears were sound. Taking advantage of the involvement of the other great powers except the United States in the European war, she presented the Chinese government with the Twenty-One Demands, a document that would have transformed China into a vassal state. Although the Japanese had warned China to keep the demands secret, Chinese authorities let their substance leak to the United States.

In March Bryan sent a note to Japan that reflected both Wilson's concern that the Japanese were going too far and his own effort to be conciliatory. Bryan objected to several of the demands, but added, in Shantung, southern Manchuria, and eastern Inner Mongolia, "the United States frankly recognizes that territorial contiguity creates special relations between Japan and these districts."[21] At this time the president neither approved nor disapproved of the demands. To the Chinese and Japanese it appeared that the United States, the only great power in a position to block the Japanese if it so desired, no longer championed the Open Door policy. As Japan's pressure on China increased, however, Wilson changed his position. "I feel," he explained, "that we should be as active as the circumstances permit in showing ourselves to be champions of the sovereign rights of China. . . ."[22]

Japan gave in to American protests by abandoning or modifying her more obnoxious demands. The Chinese, nevertheless, still balked at accepting all of the remaining terms, so on May 7 the Japanese resorted to an ultimatum. Concerned over American rights in China, Bryan, two days after China had accepted the ultimatum, sent identical notes to Japan and China. He said the United States could not recognize any agreement between them "impairing the treaty rights of the United States and its citizens in China, the political or territorial integrity of the Republic of China, or the international policy relative to China commonly known as the Open Door policy."[23] Although the note had little effect on the Japanese, other than to increase anti-American sentiment among them, it announced a nonrecognition principle the United States would use again. Meanwhile, in two treaties signed on May 25, China formally agreed to most of the Twenty-One Demands.

Significantly, although American protests had helped in preventing Japan from reducing China to a protectorate, Japan had won a commanding position in China. Wilson, like Roosevelt before him, realized he could not lead the American people into a war to defend distant China and the principle of the Open Door.

The Lansing-Ishii Agreement

While the war in Europe continued to sap the energies of the Allied powers, Japan exploited her victory with a program of loans designed to insure economic dominance over China. Since the nations fighting in Europe had no surplus capital to invest, they were forced to abandon their active interest in China's finances and hence could not prevent Japan's economic penetration. As early as December 1916, therefore, the Europeans turned to the United States, urging it to return to the consortium Wilson had abandoned. The United States, the British and French pointed out, was the only country with available investment capital that could stop the Japanese.

Since American bankers did not consider China a good place for investment, Wilson found that he could not counter Japan's financial expansion in China through private investment. In the fall of 1917, after the United States and China had both entered the war, Wilson yielded to the urgings of the British and French, and decided to use a new consortium to offset Japan's gains in China. Once more a president had to convert American bankers into agents of diplomacy.

Noting this change in policy, the Japanese decided to ask for a statement on the American attitude toward their expansion in China. In September they sent one of their ablest diplomats, Viscount Kikujiro Ishii, to the United States as the head of a special mission, ostensibly to discuss cooperation in the war against Germany. Actually, Secretary of State Robert Lansing and Viscount Ishii debated conflicting Japanese and American objectives in China.

Ishii wanted Lansing's public recognition of Japan's "special interests" in China as "paramount interests." Lansing would not agree. He defined "special interests" as growing out of geographical propinquity but not as giving Japan title to rights beyond those belonging to any other nation. Lansing and Ishii finally compromised by putting the secretary's restrictive interpretation of "special interests" into a secret protocol of October 31, 1917. "The Governments of Japan and the United States," that protocol said, "will not take advantage of the present conditions to seek special rights or privileges in China which would abridge the rights of the subjects or citizens of other friendly states." [24] That protocol was kept secret for eighteen years.

On November 2, Lansing and Ishii signed the protocol and in an exchange of notes publicly reaffirmed that their countries respected the Open Door and the territorial integrity of China. The heart of their agreement, however, was the statement recognizing that "territorial propinquity creates special relations between countries, and consequently the Government of the United States recognizes that Japan has special interests in China, particularly in the part to which her possessions are contiguous." [25]

The ambiguity of the Lansing-Ishii Agreement allowed each signatory to construe it to suit its own purposes. Acting as though the secret protocol did not exist, Japan interpreted the agreement as a recognition of her "paramount" position in China and hailed Viscount Ishii for winning a "great diplomatic victory." The United States interpreted the agreement as Japan's pledge to respect the Open Door and China's independence. Since the agreement without the protocol appeared to nullify the Open Door and to surrender more to Japan than she really got, Americans who considered their country a friend of China viewed it as a diplomatic blunder. Believing the United States had betrayed them, the Chinese protested the agreement. What the agreement actually did was to make a temporary public concession to Japan that helped alleviate Japanese-American tension during the war.

Wilson's Four-Power Consortium

Wilson had not, as some assumed, given up the principle of the Open Door or diplomatic defense of China's sovereignty. He still hoped to restrict Japan's capital investment in China through international means. A week after exchanging notes with Ishii, Secretary Lansing cabled the American minister in China that the government was considering a new consortium to aid China in a program of economic reconstruction. On July 8, 1918, the American bankers he had invited to join the consortium agreed to consider loans to China on two conditions. The aid, they said, must be broadly international, including British, French, and Japanese bankers, and the American government must announce that the loans were being made at its suggestion.

Wilson's government immediately accepted the banker's conditions and two days later sent the plan to Britain, France, and Japan with an invitation to join the new consortium. All ultimately agreed to participate, but Japan, resenting the American challenge to her program of gaining a financial monopoly in China, did so only after obtaining recognition of her "special position" in southern Manchuria and Mongolia. Discussions between the powers on the consortium plan went on during the peace conference in Paris at the end of the First World War and continued until October 1920, when the final compromise agreement was signed.

Wilson had viewed the new four-power consortium as a means of weakening Japan's planned hegemony over China by strengthening the principle of the Open Door. Ironically, China refused salvation through the new consortium, preferring to seek loans in the world market where she could borrow on the best terms available. Nonetheless, the new four-power consortium was significant in marking a reversal of Wilson's stand of 1913 on Dollar Diplomacy.

XVII

Missionary Diplomacy

As they had done in China, President Taft and Secretary of State Knox encouraged American bankers to invest in Latin America, particularly in the republics of the Caribbean area. The objectives of their Dollar Diplomacy in the Caribbean differed from those in China, but had similar characteristics. In addition to advancing their own foreign policy, they wanted to bring the peoples of the Caribbean economic and political stability.

The republics of Central America and the Caribbean had always been turbulent, but their unrest had not threatened any strategic United States interest. As the Panama Canal neared completion, however, the United States became increasingly sensitive to any disturbances that might invite European nations to intervene to protect their investments in the area. So Taft and Knox, like Theodore Roosevelt, refused to tolerate disorders in the Caribbean.

Actually, the Taft administration went futher in its interventions than had Roosevelt under his corollary to the Monroe Doctrine. Taft tried to preserve order and prevent European intervention by pressuring governments of Caribbean countries to keep new European capital out and to force capital already there to leave. American dollars, with assurances of protection from the government, could then go into the republics. In theory, those countries would gain peace and stability, the United States government would forestall outside intervention in the sensitive canal area, and American investors would earn profits.

Intervention in Nicaragua

Taft's intervention in Nicaragua offered the clearest example of dollar diplomacy in action. American investment in Nicaragua was small in comparison to that in some other Caribbean republics, but because of Nicaragua's proximity to the canal, the United States was particularly sensitive to any disturbance there. Yet, Nicaragua's dictator, José Santos Zelaya, who had ruled since 1893, turned his country into the most turbulent of Central America. His ambition had been to dominate the five republics of Central America. From 1894 to 1908 he had led his country into a number of petty wars with its neighbors. In 1907 he invaded Honduras and removed her president; later, he endangered El Salvador and Guatemala. He also threatened American business investments in his country.

In May 1909, Zelaya financed Nicaragua's entire debt through an international syndicate of European investors formed in London, and pledged the nation's customs income and other properties to payment of the loan. This loan and Zelaya's general anti-Americanism suggested a willingness to turn Nicaragua's economy over to Europeans. If he failed to pay the debt, the Europeans had the right to take over the country's major source of revenue.

Several months later a revolution, apparently partly stimulated and financed by American firms, broke out against Zelaya. During the battles of the following month, Zelaya's forces captured and executed two Americans fighting with the insurgents. On December 1 Knox sent the Nicaraguan *chargé* in Washington a scorching note condemning Zelaya as a tyrant. Knox then dismissed the *chargé* and broke off relations with Zelaya's government. Since Zelaya realized he could not withstand the hostility of the United States, he resigned a few weeks later and fled to Mexico.

Fighting continued, but by August 1910 the insurgents had the country under control. The new president, Adolfo Díaz (a former bookkeeper of an American mining company in his country), who had the support of Americans in Nicaragua and of the Taft administration, turned to the United States for aid in stabilizing the republic's precarious finances. His minister in Washington, Salvador Castrillo, signed a convention in June 1911 with Knox that would have turned Nicaragua into a protectorate if the agreement had been accepted by the United States Senate.

The Knox-Castrillo Convention sought to create a stable currency by refunding the Nicaraguan debt with American loans and by pledging Nicaragua's customs revenues to the payment of the debt. Nicaragua agreed to place the administration of her customs houses during the life of the loan in the hands of an official approved by the president of the United States. This plan, it was hoped, would remove an incentive to revolution since the customs houses would no longer be one of the prizes of victory. Since American bankers would float the loan, it would also eliminate a main cause for European intervention in behalf of creditors.

So desperate was Nicaragua's plight that in less than a month after the signing of the convention, she defaulted her foreign debt contracted in 1909. American bankers encouraged by the Department of State "unofficially" took over control of Nicaragua's finances. In September the bankers made a short-term loan to the Nicaraguan government, promised to negotiate a settlement with the European creditors, and set up a receivership for the customs. In December an American army officer, approved by President Taft, took over as Nicaragua's collector of customs.

Since the Senate, in May 1912, refused to approve the Knox-Castrillo Convention, the bankers continued their private customs receivership. In June they made an agreement with Nicaragua's European creditors, mostly British, whereby they would pay off the debt with part of the customs revenues. Taft and Knox thus maintained a protectorate through private agencies.

When a revolt against Díaz broke out in July, imperilling American investments, he asked for armed assistance. Maintaining that intervention was necessary to protect the lives and property of foreigners, the Taft administration landed over twenty-five hundred marines and bluejackets from eight warships in Nicaragua, crushed the revolt, and saved Díaz. The United States then stationed a warship and a legation guard of a hundred marines in Nicaragua to discourage future revolutions.

Realizing that Dollar Diplomacy was unpopular in Latin America, Knox in March had made a good will tour through most of the Caribbean republics. But, in view of his interventionist policy, Knox's tour did little to win the trust of Latin Americans.

By the beginning of 1913 American control over Nicaragua was firm, but the republic's treasury remained shaky. Nicaragua, therefore, sought an alternative to the Knox-Castrillo Convention that might bolster her finances. In February she signed a treaty with the United States ceding potential naval bases and the exclusive right to build, control, and operate a canal through her territory in exchange for the small sum of three million dollars to pay her debts, but the United States Senate refused to approve the agreement.

Honduras

Meanwhile, similar motives had led Taft to intervene in the affairs of other Central American countries, which with the exception of El Salvador, had defaulted on their foreign debts. Since Knox feared that the European creditors might seize customs houses, he wanted to establish control over the revenues of the Central American republics.

While drawing up his unsuccessful convention with Nicaragua, Knox also tried to promote a reorganization of Honduras' finances. By 1909 Honduras' defaulted foreign debt, with accumulated interest, had become so large that it probably could never be repaid. After long negotiations the foreign creditors, mostly British, agreed to accept a few cents on the dollar from money Honduras would obtain from an American loan guaranteed by a customs collectorship. In January 1911 Knox signed a treaty with Honduras establishing the collectorship, but both the Honduran congress and the American Senate rejected it. In Honduras, therefore, Knox's Dollar Diplomacy failed.

At that time Knox also expressed willingness to aid in financial reforms in all the Central American countries, but the republics did not welcome his offer. In 1911, Costa Rica forestalled possible American intervention by making a new loan agreement with her European creditors. Guatemala's dictator, who had been particularly notorious in his treatment of foreign creditors, negotiated with a group of American bankers for a loan to refund his foreign debt. Despite the efforts of the Department of State in support of the agreement, it was never completed.

Lodge Corollary

Another problem grew out of a commercial development in Mexico's isolated Baja California. On that province's west coast lay the large natural harbor of Magdalena Bay in which the United States had long been interested as a potential naval base, but had not exploited because the area around the bay lacked adequate water. Nonetheless, a strong foreign naval power in possession of the bay would pose a threat to the security of California and to the Panama Canal.

In 1911 a group of Japanese in San Francisco offered to buy a large tract of land on the shores of Magdalena Bay, and a fishing concession, from an American company that owned them. Since American policymakers assumed that a Japanese colony at the bay would endanger national security, particularly the canal, the Department of State ordered the American company to stop the negotiations because they violated the Monroe Doctrine.

In February 1912 Henry Cabot Lodge, chairman of the Senate Committee on Foreign Relations, revived the issue of Magdalena Bay. In a speech against Taft's arbitration treaties, he warned of "some great Eastern power" taking possession of a harbor on Mexico's west coast for naval or military purposes. The Los Angeles *Examiner,* a Hearst newspaper, took up the theme of a Japanese threat by printing a "Tokio dispatch" revealing "practical completion of plans for establishment of a big Japanese colony at Magdalena Bay."[1] The Mexican government, on the following day, denied all rumors of Japan gaining a foothold in Baja California, and the Japanese government on April 6 denied interest in a settlement at the bay.

William Randolph Hearst, nonetheless, would not give up his concern over the "yellow peril." His Los Angeles newspaper chartered a steamer and sent three reporters and a photographer to Magdalena Bay to get "facts, and nothing but the facts." The reporters found two Japanese living near a fish cannery on an island off the bay.

Secretary Knox told Lodge that the charges in the press concerning

Japanese intrigue were groundless and would likely injure relations with Japan. Yet Lodge insisted upon clarifying American policy toward colonization by foreign states. Though convinced that the Japanese government was not involved in negotiations over Magdalena Bay, he and his committee decided that the Senate should declare its attitude.

On August 2, 1912, by a vote of fifty-one to four, the Senate adopted a resolution submitted by Lodge disapproving the transfer of harbors or other strategic sites in the Americas to any private company connected with a government outside the American continents. That resolution, though it mentioned neither Japan nor the Monroe Doctrine, was significant because it extended the principles of the doctrine to an Asian power, specifically Japan, and to private companies having connections outside the Western Hemisphere.

Missionary Zeal

Since Woodrow Wilson and William Jennings Bryan had been critical of intervention in the Caribbean, Latin Americans expected them to reverse Republican policy. Only a week after taking office Wilson denounced Dollar Diplomacy in the Caribbean. He went further in the promise of a new Latin American policy in a speech at Mobile, Alabama, in October 1913. Speaking of a "spiritual union" between the American continents, he foresaw the day when foreign creditors would lose their grip on the Latin republics, and announced that "the United States will never again seek one additional foot of territory by conquest."[2]

The record of the Wilson administration in Latin American affairs did not fit the pattern of the president's words. In the Caribbean and Mexico the commitments of the past and the inconsistencies of its own policies so entangled the administration's program that it carried out a series of interventions more extensive than any under Theodore Roosevelt and Taft. Those interventions also grew out of an attitude of moral superiority and a missionary zeal to do good. Eager to help the peoples of the Caribbean republics and Mexico improve their lot, Wilson and Bryan thought of their interventions as actions in behalf of helpless friends they were trying to save from internal anarchy and foreign dangers.

If any country needed salvation according to the Wilson formula, it was Nicaragua. As soon as Wilson had taken office, the government of Adolfo Díaz tried to renegotiate the unsuccessful canal treaty it had made with Knox. The treaty that emerged from the new negotiations contained provisions similar to those of the Knox convention, but went further, giving the United States the right to intervene in Nicaragua in the same manner that the Platt Amendment had in Cuba.

Since the Platt Amendment clause had aroused opposition in the Senate, the treaty that Bryan finally signed in August 1914 with Emiliano

Chamorro, Nicaragua's minister in Washington, and that the Senate approved two years later, omitted the provision allowing American intervention. The removal did not in fact change American policy; the United States intervened virtually at will in Nicaragua's affairs.

When Costa Rica, El Salvador, and Honduras protested the Bryan-Chamorro Treaty as infringing on their rights, the United States ignored their objections. Under Wilson, as under Taft, therefore, the United States continued to control Nicaragua's finances, a control supported by a small occupation force of marines.

The Dominican Republic

Conditions in the Dominican Republic, where for a number of years there had been relative stability under the United States customs receivership established in 1907, also offered the Wilson administration an opportunity to advance its Latin American policy. In September 1913 another revolution broke out. Even though the United States supported the government in power, the rebels triumphed almost everywhere.

By the summer of 1914 conditions became so bad that Wilson intervened. He arranged an armistice and sent a commission to the republic to investigate. The commission suggested reforms, and Secretary Bryan urged the Dominicans to grant the United States control over finances and the armed forces, a greater power over their country than the treaty of 1907 allowed.

Meanwhile, the commission worked out a plan whereby elections under American supervision were held in November. One of the revolutionary leaders was elected president, but his rule proved unsatisfactory, and revolution erupted again in May 1916. After repeated warnings that the United States would not stand for continued armed anarchy, American marines landed and occupied the capital city.

The United States then insisted on a treaty giving it control of the republic's finances and armed forces, but the Dominicans refused. Marines, therefore, took over the entire country by November and established a military government.

In authorizing military rule, Wilson said he did it "with the deepest reluctance," but had to do it because he was "convinced that it is the least of the evils in sight in this very perplexing situation."[3] The customs receivership remained in effect, but it now turned over its revenues to the American military governor who exercised all the functions of government, as though he were president. At one time he even exchanged diplomatic correspondence with the United States.

Although there was some armed resistance to the occupation, on the whole it brought stability to the country. Yet, it was a peace based on naked force that fostered among Dominicans a deep-seated distrust of the United States.

Haitian Protectorate

Violence, revolution, and Wilson's missionary zeal also brought American bayonets to Haiti. Various foreign governments had several times landed troops there to protect their nationals during disturbances. Hoping to stabilize finances and forestall further European intervention, the Department of State asked the Haitians to sign a treaty in July 1914 giving the United States control of the customs. In December continued disturbances led marines to take a half million dollars from a Haitian bank controlled by Americans to a United States warship to keep it from falling into the hands of Haiti's latest dictator.

In January 1915 another revolution brought more chaos. Agreeing that they could not long postpone intervention, Wilson and Bryan sent a commission to negotiate a treaty giving them a naval base and control of the customs. Before the commission arrived in Haiti, a new government under General Vilbrun Guillaume Sam came to power. Sam refused to negotiate. In fact, it soon became clear that no Haitian government would willingly agree to the extensive control of the republic the United States desired. Force appeared the only way to gain such control, a policy Bryan was reluctant to follow.

After Bryan had resigned, a new revolution presented the United States with an excuse for intervention. President Sam executed some 167 political prisoners. In retaliation, the people of Port-au-Prince dragged him from the French legation, where he had fled for sanctuary, and tore his body to pieces in the streets.

That bloody violence temporarily ended Haiti's independence. That afternoon, July 28, 1915, marines and bluejackets swarmed ashore and occupied Port-au-Prince. More troops came later and occupied the entire country. Since the *cacos,* professional fighters, retreated to the mountains and fought the occupation, the pacification became a war of extermination. Before the war ended, American troops had slaughtered over two thousand of the resisting Haitians.

Meanwhile, an American admiral took over control of Haiti's government, and the State Department forced a treaty on the Haitians that established a tighter control over them than the United States had imposed on any other Caribbean country, including Cuba. That treaty, signed on September 16, was to run for twenty years, and gave the United States command of Haiti's finances, armed forces, public works, foreign affairs, and the right to intervene in other ways to preserve Haiti's independence. The Senate approved it in February 1916 without a dissenting vote.

Two years later, through a controversial new constitution, the United

States tried to perpetuate the reforms it had introduced. The Haitians approved the constitution in a plebiscite conducted by American marines, but it failed to bring true stability and democratic government to Haiti.

Wilson's Pan-American League

The Wilson administration's missionary diplomacy differed from the Dollar Diplomacy of Taft and Knox primarily in its motivation. Bryan was even willing to offer federal money to unstable governments to advance foreign policy, but mainly as a substitute for his predecessor's guarantee of private investment. In August 1913 he had suggested lending money from the federal treasury to Nicaragua and to other Latin American countries at a low rate of interest to help in freeing them from the control of European creditors. Bryan's plan seemed too bold to the president, so he turned it down. Even though the United States may have feared it, there was no danger of serious European intervention in the Caribbean during the Wilson years.

Despite their reliance on force, Wilson and Bryan hoped that their policies would lead to peace and unity in the Americas. Wilson himself took the lead in trying to bind the countries of the Western Hemisphere together in a pan-American league in which they would agree to settle all their disputes by peaceful means and would guarantee each other's territorial integrity and political independence "under republican forms of government."

A leader in the peace movement had proposed such a treaty in 1910, as had the Colombian government in 1912, but the Taft administration had paid no attention to the proposal. Wilson, however, liked the idea. In December 1914, therefore, the Department of State drafted a treaty and circulated it among Latin American governments. Colonel Edward M. House, Wilson's personal adviser, saw the treaty as a model for the warring nations of Europe to copy when peace came. Brazil, Argentina, and at least six of the smaller Latin republics supported the pact, but Chile, fearing that under it she might lose lands she had conquered from Peru, opposed it, and the treaty failed.

Some students of Latin American relations have seen Wilson's Latin American policy, particularly his proposed pan-American pact, as marking a new day in relations with the southern republics. There is, however, little evidence to support the view that Wilson was willing to change national policy in the Caribbean or to renounce the so-called right of intervention, despite his support of the idealistic pan-American treaty.

Danish West Indies

Although it did not directly involve the Latin republics, Wilson's purchase of the Danish West Indies, now called the Virgin Islands, was

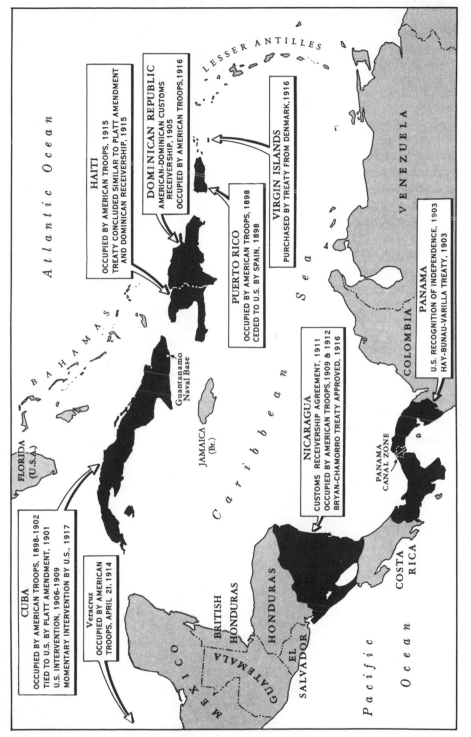

THE AMERICAN EMPIRE IN THE CARIBBEAN, 1898–1917

CUBA
OCCUPIED BY AMERICAN TROOPS, 1898–1902
TIED TO U.S. BY PLATT AMENDMENT, 1901
U.S. INTERVENTION, 1906–1909
MOMENTARY INTERVENTION BY U.S., 1917

Veracruz
OCCUPIED BY AMERICAN
TROOPS, APRIL 21, 1914

NICARAGUA
CUSTOMS RECEIVERSHIP AGREEMENT, 1911
OCCUPIED BY AMERICAN TROOPS, 1909 & 1912
BRYAN-CHAMORRO TREATY APPROVED, 1916

PANAMA
U.S. RECOGNITION OF INDEPENDENCE, 1903
HAY-BUNAU-VARILLA TREATY, 1903

HAITI
OCCUPIED BY AMERICAN TROOPS, 1915
TREATY CONCLUDED SIMILAR TO PLATT AMENDMENT
AND DOMINICAN RECEIVERSHIP, 1915

DOMINICAN REPUBLIC
AMERICAN-DOMINICAN CUSTOMS
RECEIVERSHIP, 1905
OCCUPIED BY AMERICAN TROOPS,1916

PUERTO RICO
OCCUPIED BY AMERICAN TROOPS, 1898
CEDED TO U.S. BY SPAIN, 1898

VIRGIN ISLANDS
PURCHASED BY TREATY FROM DENMARK,1916

Atlantic Ocean

LESSER ANTILLES

VENEZUELA

COLOMBIA

Caribbean Sea

JAMAICA (Br.)

Guantanamo Naval Base

BAHAMAS

FLORIDA (U.S.A.)

MEXICO

BRITISH HONDURAS

GUATEMALA

HONDURAS

EL SALVADOR

NICARAGUA

COSTA RICA

PANAMA CANAL ZONE

Pacific Ocean

another facet of his Caribbean policy. Some Americans had long feared that Denmark would sell her Caribbean islands to some other more powerful European power, particularly Germany, and that fear increased after the outbreak of the First World War. Secretary of State Robert Lansing told Denmark in the summer of 1916 that the United States would seize the islands if German control appeared imminent. Therefore in a treaty signed on August 4, Denmark agreed to sell her possessions for twenty-five million dollars.

The United States willingly paid five times more than it had offered for the three small impoverished islands in 1902 to keep them from falling into German hands, even though, because of other American holdings in the Caribbean, they were now of no real value as a naval base. As Lansing pointed out, their purchase was a kind of strategic insurance for security of the Panama Canal.

Mexican Revolution

More perplexing than the problems of the Caribbean, were developments in Mexico. In fact, they constituted Wilson's main concern in foreign affairs until the summer of 1915 when the war in Europe came to absorb most of his attention. Missionary diplomacy launched its most drastic intervention against Mexico, again with the idea of establishing a democratic government that would help an oppressed people meet pressing economic and social needs.

The Mexican problem began in 1911 when a revolution led by Francisco I. Madero, a young reformer educated in France and briefly at the University of California, overthrew the dictatorship of Porfirio Díaz. Madero planned to destroy the old order of privileges for the few, including foreign investors, and to reconstitute Mexican society on a new democratic base. Madero's leading general, Victoriano Huerta, betrayed him and led a successful counterrevolution against him. Although he denied it, Huerta apparently ordered Madero murdered in February 1913, an act that shocked Americans.

Henry Lane Wilson, the United States ambassador in Mexico City, urged President Taft to recognize Huerta's government, but Taft would not until Huerta promised concessions in other disputes. Other countries, among them Britain, France, and Germany, recognized Huerta's government.

As soon as Woodrow Wilson became president, Ambassador Wilson and others within the Department of State advised him to recognize Huerta's regime, pointing out correctly that the United States had usually extended *de facto* recognition to revolutionary governments. Believing that if he recognized Huerta he would be encouraging assassination throughout Latin America, the president departed from the traditional recognition policy. He advanced the doctrine that the United States would not recognize governments that came to power by force against the peoples' will and in violation of their country's constitution.

Huerta, moreover, did not control all of Mexico. On the day after he proclaimed himself provisional president, General Venustiano Carranza, a follower of Madero, began a new revolt in northern Mexico. Carranza and his followers, calling themselves Constitutionalists, swore to depose Huerta and to re-establish constitutional government.

President Wilson decided that Huerta must go, and offered to "mediate" the war in such a way as to eliminate Huerta. In August 1913, Wilson sent John Lind, a former Democratic governor of Minnesota acting as his personal agent, to Huerta to ask him to hold a fair election in which he would not be a candidate so that a constitutional government the United States could recognize would come to power. Wilson also sent a circular note to the powers asking them to urge Huerta to accept American mediation of the civil war. Huerta refused Wilson's demands.

Although not a serious threat, Huerta's outburst did represent the views of many Mexicans. Their country was not Nicaragua or the Dominican Republic; Wilson could not rule it through a puppet government supported by a few hundred marines. Yet Huerta gave Lind the impression that he would before long give up the presidency of Mexico, which was essentially what Wilson desired.

On August 27 Wilson went before a joint session of Congress and explained his policy toward Mexico. It was up to Huerta, he pointed out, to accept American mediation, and hence to resign. He would, Wilson said, pursue a patient policy of nonintervention and watchful waiting while "forbidding the exportation of arms or munitions of war of any kind" to either side in the Mexican civil war.[4]

Huerta soon showed he had no intention of abdicating. In October his troops dispersed congress and clamped a dictatorship on Mexico. That new act of violence shocked Wilson. He sent a circular note to governments with representatives in Mexico asking them to wihhold recognition from Huerta. Two weeks later he warned those governments that he would use whatever means were necessary to force Huerta from office. For six months Wilson now did all he could, short of war, to depose Huerta. His plan was simple and direct. He tried to isolate the dictator diplomatically and encouraged the Constitutionalists in their war against him.

Wilson exerted most pressure against the British, forcing them, in effect, to choose between American friendship and the Mexican oil they needed for their fleet. Since war in Europe seemed imminent and Wilson's good will would be worth more than Mexico's oil, the British government withdrew its support from Huerta.

Since Wilson found that he had either to allow the Constitutionalists to obtain arms or carry out his threats to depose Huerta with American troops, he recognized the belligerency of the Constitutionalists and in February 1914 revoked the arms embargo against them. His action strengthened Huerta. Many Mexicans who were formerly apathetic now rallied behind the dictator as the symbol of resistance to American domination. Force, which Wilson had been reluctant to use, now seemed to offer the only way of toppling Huerta.

Bloodshed at Veracruz

An incident at Tampico on April 9 gave Wilson the excuse. A whaleboat with seven sailors and one officer from the U.S.S. *Dolphin,* a warship, went ashore without Huerta's permission behind his Federalist lines to buy gasoline. A Federalist colonel arrested the Americans. When the Federalist commander in the area learned of the arrest, he immediately released the Americans and sent an apology to Admiral Henry T. Mayo, commander of the American squadron off Tampico, explaining that his subordinate had made a mistake.

The apology might have ended any further difficulty if Wilson had not decided to use it as a means of overthrowing Huerta. Admiral Mayo, on his own initiative, immediately demanded a twenty-one gun salute to the American flag, and the president supported the ultimatum. They thus converted a petty incident to an affront against national honor. Ironically, Wilson demanded the discharge of an international obligation from a government he would not recognize. Huerta resisted, saying he would salute only if the United States returned volley for volley.

Meanwhile, Wilson had ordered the North Atlantic battleship fleet to Tampico and on the afternoon of April 20 asked Congress for authority to use the armed forces. If war should come, he said, it would be only against "General Huerta and those who adhere to him and give him their support," not against the Mexican people.[5]

While Congress debated the president's request, news reached Washington that the German steamer *Ypiranga* was headed for Veracruz with a cargo of guns and ammunition for Huerta. Wilson decided to substitute the seizure of Veracruz for naval action at Tampico and immediately ordered the navy to seize the customs house at Veracruz to prevent the entry of the munitions. Mexican naval cadets and soldiers offered a determined resistance. The dead and wounded, mostly Mexican, totaled over four hundred. Americans took control of the city on April 22, and on the next day Congress authorized the use of armed forces.

Since Wilson insisted that he had invaded Veracruz to avenge a personal insult, but really had done it to hasten Huerta's downfall, few people understood why he had acted as he did. On the surface he appeared willing to start a war over a dubious point of honor. A London journal expressed the point well. "If war is to be made on points of punctilio raised by admirals and generals," it said, "and if the Government of the United States is to set the example for this return to mediaeval conditions it will be a bad day for civilization." [6]

Throughout Latin America, newspapers condemned the occupation of Veracruz as more evidence of imperialism, and mobs demonstrated against it. Even Carranza, a proud nationalist who hated Huerta, denounced it as foreign aggression. Most North Americans, apparently, did not approve the seizure and deplored the possibility of war. The thought of war also appalled Wilson, so he halted further offensive operations.

Argentina, Brazil, and Chile then stepped in with a timely offer to mediate the conflict. When Wilson and Huerta accepted their offer, most Americans were relieved. In agreeing to negotiate with a government he would not recognize, however, Wilson again acted inconsistently. That made little difference to the delegates of the A B C powers and of the United States who met with representatives from Huerta's government at Niagara Falls, Canada, from May 18 to July 2. Since Carranza refused to send a delegation, to permit Wilson to mediate the civil war, or to allow the Niagara delegates to determine the fate of Mexico's revolution, the conference accomplished nothing except to extricate Wilson from a difficult position.

Two weeks later, with his regime crumbling under pressure from Wilson and blows from internal foes, Huerta resigned. A month later Carranza's forces entered Mexico City, but the Constitutionalist coalition quickly fell apart and Mexico plunged into three more years of civil war. One of the leading Constitutionalist generals, an illiterate former bandit named Francisco Villa, drove Carranza from Mexico City and took over the government. In August the Wilson administration shifted its support to Villa, but Carranza fought back and in February 1915 returned to Mexico City. Meanwhile, Wilson switched to a policy of neutrality, insisting that the Mexicans should settle their own problems in their own way.

Yet within the United States, pressure for intervention mounted rapidly. The Hearst papers, the hierarchy of the Catholic Church, Theodore Roosevelt, and others, all clamored for action to stop loss of American life and property and attacks against the church. In June, therefore, Wilson again interfered by asking the Mexican leaders to compose their differences and stop their fighting. Carranza denied his right to meddle.

At the same time growing friction with Germany over the use of the submarine led administration leaders to try to avoid any overt action that would lead to war with Mexico. Secretary of State Robert Lansing turned to several Latin American states for help in settling the Mexican civil war. In August, he began a series of conferences with the six ranking Latin American envoys in Washington, representing Argentina, Brazil, Chile, Bolivia, Guatemala, and Uruguay, who appealed to rival Mexican leaders to compose their differences, but Carranza refused. Since he controlled most of Mexico and was growing stronger, Wilson and Lansing decided to recognize him. The United States and the six states of the pan-American conference formally recognized Carranza's regime as the *de facto* government of Mexico in October.

Relations with Carranza's government went relatively smoothly for several months, but Villa, who resented the recognition of Carranza, soon turned on his former friends and tried to embroil the United States in a war with Mexico. He hoped to return to power as a national hero fighting to prevent American conquest. On January 10, 1916, he stopped a train at Santa Ysabel in northern Mexico, removed seventeen young American engineers, and shot sixteen of them on the spot. Two months later he sent some four hundred raiders into Columbus, New Mexico. They shot everybody in sight, killing nineteen Americans, and burned the town.

The Pershing Expedition

The demand for military intervention then became so strong that Wilson could not resist it. Since Carranza's government was incapable of preventing Villa's outrages, orders went out to military commanders in Texas to prepare an expedition to pursue Villa into Mexico. Lansing negotiated a protocol with Mexico's representative in Washington on March 13 allowing the United States and Mexico in the future to pursue bandits across the international boundary. Two days later a punitive expedition, under the command of Brigadier General John J. Pershing, crossed the border, but with explicit orders not to attack Carranza's forces.

Pershing's force grew to more than six thousand men and penetrated more than three hundred miles into Mexico in pursuit of the elusive Villa. Since Carranza had thought only in terms of small forces with limited striking power, he expressed alarm at the size of Pershing's expedition and immediately took diplomatic action to force Pershing to withdraw.

In April an incident almost touched off war and prevented Pershing from retreating quietly. At the town of Parral, some 180 miles inside Mexico, American and Mexican soldiers exchanged fire, leaving forty Mexicans and two Americans dead. Mexican opinion now became so hostile to the American expedition that Carranza could not remain in power without taking steps to compel its withdrawal. Wilson would not retreat, but fortunately the generals in the field worked out a temporary compromise that prevented war.

In May, Villistas raided the little town of Glen Springs, Texas, killing three soldiers and a boy. When Wilson sent a new detachment into Mexico in pursuit of the raiders, Carranza concluded that a showdown must come and demanded the withdrawal of Pershing's forces under the threat of war. He then instructed his generals to prevent any new expeditions from entering Mexico and to resist Pershing's force if it moved in any direction but north toward the border. On June 18 Wilson called out the entire national guard and incorporated it into the army, and made other preparations for war. Two days later Secretary Lansing told the Mexican government that the United States would not recall its troops and warned that any attack on them would "lead to the gravest consequences." [7]

The next day, only a few hours after Lansing's message reached Mexico City, Mexican and American troops clashed again, at a place called Carrizal. Both sides suffered casualties. This appeared to be the final incident that would precipitate war. Wilson accused the Mexicans of deliberately attacking the Americans, which was not so, and even prepared a war message, but never delivered it. Neither he nor Carranza wanted war. The Mexican leader released the twenty-three American prisoners his troops had captured at Carrizal.

Realizing that a growing crisis with Germany was more serious, Wilson pleaded for peace. "Do you think the glory of America would be enhanced by a war of conquest in Mexico?" he asked on July 1. Three days later Carranza asked either for direct negotiations or Latin American mediation to end the tension. Since Lansing and Wilson preferred the direct negotiations, a joint high commission met in New London, Connecticut, in September and broke up in acrimony in January 1917. Although it failed to settle the controversy, it helped preserve the peace.

Since no issue vital to the security of the United States was at stake in Mexico, and since involvement in the European war seemed probable in the near future, Wilson decided to withdraw Pershing's troops to Texas. By the first week of February the last of the punitive expedition had left Mexico and the danger of war was over.

Mexico, meantime, had drawn up a new constitution and in March had elected Carranza president. The United States extended immediate *de jure* recognition by sending an ambassador. Mexico's revolution finally established a broad new social order and in time firm constitutional government. Historians still debate whether Wilson's meddling helped or hindered that revolution in achieving its objectives.

NOTES

CHAPTER ONE

1. Alexis de Tocqueville, *Democracy in America,* trans. by George Lawrence; J. P. Mayer and Max Lerner, eds. (New York, 1966), p. 114.
2. Arthur M. Schlesinger, Jr., *The Imperial Presidency* (Boston, 1973), pp. viii-ix.
3. New York, Oct. 13, 1789, in John C. Fitzpatrick, ed., *The Writings of George Washington* (39 vols., Washington, 1931–44), XXX, 446.
4. Quoted in Alexander DeConde, *The American Secretary of State: An Interpretation* (New York, 1962), p. 90.
5. *Ibid.,* p. 74.
6. Farewell Radio and Television Address to the American People, Jan. 17, 1961, *Public Papers of the Presidents of the United States, Dwight D. Eisenhower, 1960–61* (Washington, 1961), p. 1038.
7. Leo Bogart, *Silent Politics: Polls and the Awareness of Public Opinion* (New York, 1972), pp. 99–100.

CHAPTER TWO

1. Quoted in Charles de La Roncière, *Histoire de la marine française* (5 vols., Paris, 1899–1920), III, 300.
2. For analyses of mercantilism, see Jacob Viner, "Power versus Plenty as Objectives of Foreign Policy in the Seventeenth and Eighteenth Centuries," *World Politics,* I (Oct. 1948), 1–29 and Charles Wilson, " 'Mercantilism:' Some Vicissitudes of an Idea," *Economic History Review,* 2nd ser., X (Dec. 1957), 181–188.
3. Albert B. Hart and Edward Channing, eds., "The Articles of the Confederation of the United Colonies of New England, 1643–1684," *American History Leaflets,* No.7 (New York, Jan. 1893), p. 4.
4. The quotation is from Alison G. Olson, "The British Government and Colonial Union, 1754," *William and Mary Quarterly,* 3rd ser., XVIII (Jan. 1960), 26.
5. Max Savelle, "The Appearance of An American Attitude toward External Affairs, 1750–1755," *The American Historical Review,* LII (July 1947), 662.
6. Quoted in Gerald Stourzh, *Benjamin Franklin and American Foreign Policy* (Chicago, 1954), p. 120.
7. Moncure D. Conway, ed., *The Writings of Thomas Paine* (4 vols., New York, 1906), I, 88–89.
8. Quoted in Curtis P. Nettels, *The Roots of American Civilization: A History of American Colonial Life* (New York, 1938), p. 704.
9. Memorial of Feb. 29, 1776, in Louis L. Loménie, *Beaumarchais and His Times,* trans. by Henry S. Edwards (New York, 1857), p. 270.
10. Julian P. Boyd, "Silas Deane: Death by a Kindly Teacher of Treason?" *William and Mary Quarterly,* 3rd ser., XVI (April, July, and Oct. 1959), 185–187, 319–322, 324.

11. To Arthur Lee, March 21, 1777, in Francis Wharton, ed., *The Revolutionary Diplomatic Correspondence of the United States* (6 vols., Washington, 1889), II, 298.

12. Jan. 5, 1777, *ibid.*, p. 246.

13. Quoted in Helen Augur, *The Secret War of Independence* (New York, 1956), p. 259.

14. To Gouverneur Morris, Oct. 4, 1778, in John C. Fitzpatrick, ed., *The Writings of George Washington* (39 vols., Washington, 1931–44), XIII, 22.

15. Nov. 6, 1780, in Wharton, *Revolutionary Diplomatic Correspondence,* IV, 131.

16. Quoted in Frank Monaghan, *John Jay* (New York, 1935), p. 196.

17. Dec. 17, 1782, in Wharton, *Revolutionary Diplomatic Correspondence,* VI, 144.

CHAPTER THREE

1. Quoted in Harry R. Warfel, *Noah Webster: Schoolmaster to America* (New York, 1936), p. 60.

2. Quoted in John Fiske, *The Critical Period of American History, 1783–1789* (Boston, 1893), pp. 57–58.

3. Quoted in Frank Monaghan, *John Jay* (New York, 1935), p. 229.

4. John B. Sheffield, *Observations on the Commerce of the American States,* 6th ed. (London, 1784), p. 2.

5. "A Friend to Commerce" in the *Connecticut Gazette and the Universal Intelligencer* (New London, Conn.), Aug. 13, 1794.

6. Sheffield, *Observations on American Commerce,* p. 245.

7. Quoted in Gilbert Chinard, *Honest John Adams* (Boston, 1933), p. 199.

8. *Ibid.*, p. 217.

9. Quoted in George M. Wrong, *Canada and the American Revolution* (New York, 1935), p. 390.

10. Jan. 19, 1785, in Henry P. Johnston, ed., *The Correspondence and Public Papers of John Jay* (4 vols., New York, 1890–93), III, 138.

11. To Dr. Ramsay, Oct. 27, 1786, in Henry A. Washington, ed., *The Writings of Thomas Jefferson* (9 vols., Washington, 1853–54), II, 49.

12. Quoted in George H. Guttridge, *David Hartley, M.P.: An Advocate of Conciliation, 1774–1783* (Berkeley, Calif., 1926), p. 319.

13. To the Comte de Moustier, March 26, 1788, in John C. Fitzpatrick, ed., *The Writings of George Washington* (39 vols., Washington, 1931–44), XXIX, 447–448.

14. Quoted in Monaghan, *John Jay,* p. 257.

15. For the Monroe and Jay quotations, see *ibid.*, pp. 258–259.

16. To Thomas Jefferson, July 14, 1786, in Johnston, *Correspondence of John Jay,* III, 206.

17. To James Monroe, May 5, 1793, in Paul L. Ford, ed., *The Writings of Thomas Jefferson* (10 vols., New York, 1892–99), VI, 238.

18. The quotation on Jay and the poem are printed in the *Virginia Herald and Fredericksburg Advertiser,* July 3 and Aug. 11, 1795.

19. Quoted in Dice R. Anderson, "Edmund Randolph" in Samuel F. Bemis, ed., *The American Secretaries of State and Their Diplomacy* (10 vols., New York, 1927–29), II, 124.

20. For the quotation, see James Iredell to Mrs. Iredell, March 3, 1796, in J. Griffith McRee, *Life and Correspondence of James Iredell* (2 vols., New York, 1858), II, 462–463. Historians disagree as to the influence of Jay's Treaty on Pinckney's negotiations. For details, see Samuel F. Bemis, *Pinckney's Treaty: A*

Study of America's Advantage from Europe's Distress, 1783–1800 (Baltimore, 1926), pp. 249–331; Arthur P. Whitaker, *The Spanish-American Frontier, 1783–1795* (Boston, 1927), pp. 201–222; also, Whitaker's, "New Light on the Treaty of San Lorenzo," *Mississippi Valley Historical Review,* XV (March 1929), 435–454 and his "Godoy's Knowledge of the Terms of Jay's Treaty," *The American Historical Review,* XXXV (July 1930), 804–810.

21. To James Madison, July 7, 1793, in Ford, *Writings of Jefferson,* VI, 338–339.
22. "The Anas," March 12, 1792, *ibid.*, I, 188.
23. To the Committee of Public Safety, Dec. 27, 1794, in Stanislaus M. Hamilton, ed., *The Writings of James Monroe* (7 vols., New York, 1898–1903), II, 162–163.
24. Sept. 12, 1795, in *American State Papers, Foreign Relations* (6 vols., Washington, 1832), I, 596–598.
25. Dec. 11, 1796, *ibid.*, I, 746–747.
26. Printed in *The Herald: A Gazette for the Country* (New York), Dec. 3, 1796.
27. Quoted in Albert J. Beveridge, *The Life of John Marshall* (4 vols., Boston, 1916–19), II, 273.
28. James D. Richardson, ed., *A Compilation of the Messages and Papers of the Presidents, 1789–1897* (10 vols., Washington, 1896–99), I, 266.
29. Quoted in Alexander DeConde, "William Vans Murray and the Diplomacy of Peace: 1797–1800," *The Maryland Historical Magazine,* XLVIII (March 1953), 14.
30. To James Lloyd, Jan. 1815, in Charles F. Adams, ed., *The Works of John Adams* (10 vols., Boston, 1850–56), X, 113.

CHAPTER FOUR

1. To Rufus King, Feb. 15, 1797, Timothy Pickering Papers, Massachusetts Historical Society, Boston (Microfilm copy).
2. Quoted in E. Wilson Lyon, *Louisiana in French Diplomacy 1759–1804* (Norman, Okla., 1934), p. 104.
3. Henry Adams, *History of the United States of America during the Administrations of Jefferson and Madison* (9 vols., New York, 1889–1909), I, 400.
4. To James Monroe, May 26, 1801, in Paul L. Ford, ed., *The Writings of Thomas Jefferson* (10 vols., New York, 1892–99), VIII, 58.
5. Louis A. Pichon, to Talleyrand, Georgetown, Oct. 25, 1801, quoted in Alexander DeConde, *This Affair of Louisiana* (New York, 1976), p. 110.
6. April 18, 1802, in Ford, *Writings of Jefferson,* VIII, 144–145. This was the same policy Federalists had suggested five years earlier. If France should regain Louisiana, Timothy Pickering had said, "the United States could not fail to associate themselves with Great Britain, and make common cause against France." To C. C. Pinckney, Feb. 25, 1797, National Archives, Dept. of State, Diplomatic and Consular Instructions.
7. Gilbert Chinard, ed., *The Correspondence of Jefferson and Du Pont de Nemours* (Baltimore, 1931), pp. xxxiv–xxxvi.
8. Quoted in Bradford Perkins, *The First Rapprochement: England and the United States, 1795–1805* (Philadelphia, 1955), p. 163.
9. Jan. 13, 1803, Ford, *Writings of Jefferson,* VIII, 190.
10. Quoted in Lyon, *Louisiana in French Diplomacy,* p. 135.
11. Quoted in François Barbe-Marbois, *The History of Louisiana* (Philadelphia, 1830), p. 310.
12. Quoted in *ibid.*, p. 286.

13. Quoted in Charles E. Hill, "James Madison," *The American Secretaries of State and Their Diplomacy,* Samuel F. Bemis, ed., (10 vols., New York, 1927–29), III, 42–43.
14. To R. R. Livingston, Oct. 10, 1802, Ford, *Writings of Jefferson,* VIII, 173.
15. To Elbridge Gerry, Jan. 26, 1799, *ibid.,* VIII, 328.
16. Extract from a poem by David Humphreys, quoted in Ray W. Irwin, *The Diplomatic Relations of the United States with the Barbary Powers, 1776–1816* (Chapel Hill, N.C., 1931), p. 15.
17. To George Logan, March 21, 1801, Ford, *Writings of Jefferson,* IX, 220.
18. Quoted in Louis M. Sears, *Jefferson and the Embargo* (Durham, N.C., 1927), p. 178.
19. Jefferson to Lafayette, Feb. 24, 1809, *ibid.,* p. 137. There is, however, reason to believe that the embargo restrained rather than encouraged industrial growth. See Bradford Perkins, *Prologue to War: England and the United States, 1805–1812* (Berkeley, Calif.: 1961), p. 172.

CHAPTER FIVE

1. To William Pinkney, Jan. 3, 1809, quoted in Abbot Smith, "Mr. Madison's War: An Unsuccessful Experiment in the Conduct of National Policy," *Political Science Quarterly,* XVII (June 1942), 229–246.
2. *American State Papers, Foreign Relations* (6 vols., Washington, 1832), III, 386–387.
3. Quoted in Charles C. Tansill, "Robert Smith," in Samuel F. Bemis, ed., *The American Secretaries of State and Their Diplomacy* (10 vols., New York, 1927–29), III, 179.
4. The quotation is from the *Courier,* July 17, 1811, in Reginald Horsman, *The Causes of the War of 1812* (Philadelphia, 1962), p. 220.
5. Quoted in Julius W. Pratt, "James Monroe," in Bemis, *Secretaries of State,* III, 223.
6. John Quincy Adams to Thomas Boylston Adams, Sept. 29, 1812, in Charles Francis Adams, ed., "Correspondence of John Quincy Adams, 1811–1814," *Proceedings of the American Antiquarian Society,* New Series, XXXIII (April 1913), 120.
7. "A Fourth of July Ode" in Parke Godwin, *A Biography of William Cullen Bryant* (2 vols., New York, 1883), I, 106.
8. *American State Papers, Foreign Relations,* III, 590.
9. Quoted in Pratt, "Monroe," in Bemis, *Secretaries of State,* III, 270.
10. June 23 and 24, 1814, in James Madison, *Letters and Other Writings of James Madison,* published by order of Congress (4 vols., New York, 1884), III, 408.
11. Bayard to Robert G. Harper, Aug. 19, 1814, in Elizabeth Donnan, ed., "Papers of James A. Bayard, 1796–1815," *Annual Report of the American Historical Association, 1913* (2 vols., Washington), II, 318. *The Times* quotation is in Fred L. Engleman, *The Peace of Christmas Eve* (New York, 1962), p. 123.
12. Quoted in Samuel F. Bemis, *John Quincy Adams and the Foundations of American Foreign Policy* (New York, 1949), p. 205.
13. The quotations are from Dudley Mills, "The Duke of Wellington and the Peace Negotiations at Ghent in 1814," *The Canadian Historical Review,* II (March 1921), 25, 27–28.
14. Entry of Dec. 24, 1814, in Charles F. Adams, ed., *Memoirs of John Quincy Adams, Comprising Portions of His Diary from 1795 to 1848* (12 vols., Philadelphia, 1874–77), III, 126.

15. Quoted in Irving Brant, *James Madison: Commander-in-Chief, 1812–1936* (Indianapolis, 1961), p. 369.
16. Quoted in Alfred L. Burt, *The United States, Great Britain, and British North America* (New Haven, 1940), p. 389.
17. The building of land fortifications on the border by both sides did not end until 1872. See C. P. Stacey, "The Myth of the Unguarded Frontier, 1815–1871," *The American Historical Review,* LVI (October 1950), 2.
18. Quoted in John H. Powell, *Richard Rush: Republican Diplomat, 1780–1859* (Philadelphia, 1942), p. 119.

CHAPTER SIX

1. Quoted in Henry Adams, *History of the United States of America during the Administrations of Jefferson and Madison* (9 vols., New York, 1889–1909), III, 134.
2. Entry of May 6, 1811, in Charles Francis Adams, ed., *Memoirs of John Quincy Adams* (12 vols., Philadelphia, 1874–77), II, 261.
3. Quoted in Adams, *History of the United States,* V, 315.
4. See Rufus Kay Wyllys, "The East Florida Revolution of 1812–1814," *Hispanic American Historical Review,* IX (Nov. 1929), 420, and John A. Logan, Jr., *No Transfer: An American Security Principle* (New Haven, 1961), pp. 119–120, where the resolution and act are quoted.
5. The quotations are in Rembert W. Patrick, *Florida Fiasco: Rampant Rebels on the Georgia-Florida Border, 1812–1815* (Athens, Ga., 1954), pp. 13–14, 121, 130.
6. For Monroe's comments, see *ibid.,* pp. 121, 130.
7. Notes of June 18, 1818, to the Spanish ambassadors in London and Paris, quoted in Philip C. Brooks, *Diplomacy and the Borderlands: The Adams-Onís Treaty of 1819* (Berkeley, Calif., 1939), p. 105.
8. Jan. 6, 1818, in John S. Bassett, ed., *Correspondence of Andrew Jackson* (7 vols., Washington, 1926–35), II, 345.
9. Quoted in John H. Powell, *Richard Rush: Republican Diplomat, 1780–1859* (Philadelphia, 1942), p. 129.
10. The note of Nov. 28, 1818, is in the *American State Papers, Foreign Relations* (6 vols., Washington, 1832), IV, 539–543.
11. *Niles' Weekly Register,* XVI (Baltimore, Feb. 27, 1819), 3.
12. Entry of Feb. 22, 1819, Adams, *Memoirs,* IV, 274—275.
13. *Annals of Congress,* 15th Congress, 1st sess., II, 1476.
14. Entry of Jan. 27, 1821, Adams, *Memoirs,* V, 252–253.
15. *Ibid.,* VI, 163.
16. William S. Robertson, "Recognition of the Hispanic American Nations by the United States," *Hispanic American Historical Review,* I (Aug. 1918), 257.
17. The Canning and Rush quotations are in Powell, *Richard Rush,* pp. 158–160.
18. Quoted in Dexter Perkins, *The Monroe Doctrine, 1823–1826* (Cambridge, Mass., 1927), p. 118.
19. Oct. 17, 1823, in Stanislaus M. Hamilton, ed., *The Writings of James Monroe* (7 vols., New York, 1898–1903), VI, 324.
20. Oct. 24, 1823, in Paul L. Ford, ed., *The Writings of Thomas Jefferson* (12 vols., New York, 1904–05), XII, 319–320.
21. Entry of Nov. 7, 1823, Adams, *Memoirs,* VI, 179.
22. Entry of Nov. 15, 1823, Adams, *Memoirs,* VI, 185–186.
23. For the quotations, see *ibid.,* entries of Nov. 21 and 22, 1823, VI, 194–198.

24. Quoted in Harold W. V. Temperley, *The Foreign Policy of Canning, 1822–1827* (London, 1925), p. 154.

CHAPTER SEVEN

1. Message of Dec. 1, 1834, James D. Richardson, ed., *A Compilation of the Messages and Papers of the Presidents, 1789–1897* (10 vols., Washington, 1896–97), III, 106.
2. Quoted in John S. Bassett, *The Life of Andrew Jackson* (2 vols. in one, New York, 1928), p. 669.
3. Quoted in Albert B. Corey, *This Crisis of 1830–1842 in Canadian-American Relations* (New Haven, 1941), p. 28.
4. *Ibid.*, p. 38.
5. Quoted in Winfield Scott, *Memoirs of Lieut.-General Scott, LL.D.* (2 vols., New York, 1864), I, 307.
6. The full text of the oath is in Corey, *The Crisis of 1830–1842*, p. 76.
7. The two quotations are from Corey, *ibid.*, pp. 135, 137.
8. Entry of June 29, 1822, in Charles Francis Adams, ed., *Memoirs of John Quincy Adams* (12 vols., Philadelphia, 1874–77), VI, 37.
9. Quoted in Hugh G. Soulsby, *The Right of Search and the Slave Trade in Anglo-American Relations, 1814–1862* (Baltimore, 1933), p. 46.
10. Quoted in Oliver P. Chitwood, *John Tyler: Champion of the Old South* (New York, 1939), p. 310.
11. To Jared Sparks, March 11, 1843, in Claude H. Van Tyne, ed., *The Letters of Daniel Webster* (New York, 1902), p. 286.
12. Quoted in Frederick Merk, "British Politics and the Oregon Treaty," *The American Historical Review*, XXXVII (July 1932), 665.
13. Ashburton's quotations, dated June 29 and April 25, 1842, are from dispatches to Aberdeen and are in Frederick Merk, "The Oregon Question in the Webster-Ashburton Negotiations," *Mississippi Valley Historical Review*, XLIII (Dec. 1956), 395, 401.
14. To Waddy Thompson, June 27, 1742, in Van Tyne, *Letters of Webster*, p. 269.
15. To Aberdeen, April 25, 1842, quoted in Merk, "The Oregon Question in the Webster-Ashburton Negotiations," *Mississippi Valley Historical Review*, XLIII (Dec. 1956), 395.
16. Wilkes is quoted in Norman A. Graebner, "Maritime Factors in the Oregon Compromise," *Pacific Historical Review*, XX (Nov. 1951), 333.
17. *Niles' National Register*, LXVI (Baltimore, June 8, 1844), 227.
18. March 4, 1845, in Richardson, *Messages of the Presidents*, IV, 381.
19. Entry of Jan. 4, 1846, Milo M. Quaife, ed., *The Diary of James K. Polk: During His Presidency, 1845–1849* (4 vols., Chicago, 1910), I, 155.
20. Sullivan, Dec. 27, 1845, and Robert C. Winthrop, Jan. 3, 1846, are quoted in Julius W. Pratt, "The Origin of 'Manifest Destiny,' " *The American Historical Review*, XXXII (July 1927), 795, 796.
21. Quoted in Albert K. Weinberg, *Manifest Destiny: A Study of Nationalist Expansionism in American History* (Baltimore, 1935), p. 148.
22. July, 1846, quoted in Hans Sperber, " 'Fifty-four Forty or Fight': Facts and Fictions," *American Speech*, XXXII (Feb. 1957), 9.
23. Quoted in Norman A. Graebner, *Empire on the Pacific: A Study of American Continental Expansion* (New York, 1955), pp. 130–131.
24. New York *Herald*, April 6, 1846, quoted in Norman A. Graebner, "Polk,

Politics, and Oregon," East Tennessee Historical Society's *Publications,* No. 24 (1952), p. 17.

CHAPTER EIGHT

1. Quoted in Ray A. Billington, *The Far Western Frontier, 1830–1860* (New York, 1956), p. 118.
2. Benjamin Lundy quoted in Samuel F. Bemis, *John Quincy Adams and the Union* (New York, 1956), p. 356.
3. *Ibid.,* p. 359.
4. Quoted in Randolph G. Adams, "Abel Parker Upshur," in Samuel F. Bemis, ed., *The American Secretaries of State and Their Diplomacy* (10 vols., New York, 1927–29), V, 96.
5. James D. Richardson, ed., *A Compilation of the Messages and Papers of the Presidents, 1789–1897* (10 vols., Washington, 1896–99), IV, 344.
6. Quoted in Ephraim D. Adams, *British Interests and Activities in Texas, 1838–1846* (Baltimore, 1910), pp. 168–169.
7. Quoted in Herbert P. Gambrell, *Anson Jones: The Last President of Texas* (Garden City, N.Y., 1948), p. 419.
8. Quoted in Robert G. Cleland, *Early Sentiment for the Annexation of California, 1835–1846* (Austin, Tex., 1915), p. 17.
9. *Ibid.,* pp. 27–28.
10. Quoted in Norman A. Graebner, *Empire on the Pacific* (New York, 1955), p. 120.
11. *Ibid.,* p. 151.
12. New Orleans *Commercial Bulletin,* March 16, 1846, quoted in Justin H. Smith, *The War with Mexico* (2 vols., New York, 1919), I, 121.
13. Quoted in Graebner, *Empire on the Pacific,* p. 108.
14. Oct. 17, 1845, John Bassett Moore, ed., *The Works of James Buchanan* (12 vols., Philadelphia, 1908–11), VI, 275–277.
15. Dec. 2, 1845, in Richardson, *Messages of the Presidents,* IV, 398.
16. Milo M. Quaife, ed., *The Diary of James K. Polk: During His Presidency, 1845–1849* (4 vols., Chicago, 1910), I, 224–225.
17. The text is in Richardson, *Messages of the Presidents,* IV, 437–443.
18. Homer Wilbur, ed., *The Biglow Papers,* ser. 1, 4th ed. (Boston, 1889), p. 59.
19. Thomas H. Benton, *Thirty Years' View* (2 vols., New York, 1854–56), II, 680.
20. For details, see Richard R. Stenberg, "Polk and Frémont, 1845–1846," *Pacific Historical Review,* VII (Sept. 1938), 211–227; George Tays, "Frémont Had No Secret Instructions," *ibid.,* IX (June 1940), 157–171; and Werner H. Marti, *Messenger of Destiny: The California Adventures, 1846–1847, of Archibald H. Gillespie, U.S. Marine Corps* (San Francisco, 1960), pp. 37–42, which gives a full analysis of the Frémont-Gillespie episode.
21. Quoted in Graebner, *Empire on the Pacific,* pp. 198–199.
22. Entry of Oct. 5, 1847, Quaife, *Polk Diary,* III, 186.
23. Polk is quoted in Norman A. Graebner, "James K. Polk's Wartime Expansionist Policy," East Tennessee Historical Society's *Publications,* No. 23 (1951), pp. 43–44.
24. Entry of Feb. 19, 1848, Quaife, *Polk Diary,* III, 345.
25. Bayard Tuckerman, ed., *The Diary of Philip Hone, 1828–1851* (2 vols., New York, 1889), II, 347.
26. Message of July 6, 1848, Richardson, *Messages of the Presidents,* IV, 587–588.

27. See David M. Pletcher, *The Diplomacy of Annexation: Texas, Oregon, and the Mexican War* (Columbia, Mo., 1973), p. 579.

CHAPTER NINE

1. Mary W. Williams, "John Middleton Clayton," in Samuel F. Bemis, ed., *The American Secretaries of State and Their Diplomacy* (10 vols., New York, 1927–29), VI, 66.
2. Quoted in William O. Scroggs, *Filibusters and Financiers: The Story of William Walker and His Associates* (New York, 1916), p. 226.
3. James D. Richardson, ed., *A Compilation of the Messages and Papers of the Presidents, 1789–1899* (10 vols., Washington, 1896–99), V, 639.
4. Quoted in J. Fred Rippy, *The United States and Mexico* (New York, 1926), p. 55.
5. Quoted in James M. Callahan, *American Foreign Policy in Mexican Relations* (New York, 1932),p. 200.
6. Quoted in Lester B. Shippee, *Canadian-American Relations, 1849–1874* (New Haven, 1939), p. 6.
7. Quoted in Cephas D. Allin and George M. Jones, *Annexation, Preferential Trade, and Reciprocity: An Outline of the Canadian Annexation Movement of 1849–50* (Toronto, 1911), p. 384.
8. Quoted in Shippee, *Canadian-American Relations,* p. 44.
9. Quoted in Margaret O. W. Oliphant, *Memoir of the Life of Lawrence Oliphant and of Alice Oliphant, His Wife,* 2nd ed. (2 vols., Edinburgh, 1891), I, 120.
10. Quoted in Claude M. Fuess, *The Life of Caleb Cushing* (2 vols., New York, 1923), II, 167–168.
11. Kenneth E. Shewmaker, "Daniel Webster and the Politics of Foreign Policy, 1850–1852," *Journal of American History,* LXIII (Sept. 1976), 310.
12. For the text of the note, dated Dec. 21, 1850, see Daniel Webster, *The Writings and Speeches of Daniel Webster* (18 vols., Boston, 1903), XII, 165–178.
13. The circular was dated June 1, 1853; see Merle E. Curti, "Young America," *The American Historical Review,* XXXII (Oct. 1926), 54.
14. Quoted in Basil Rauch, *American Interest in Cuba, 1848–1855* (New York, 1948), p. 33.
15. New York *Sun,* July 23, 1847, quoted in *ibid.,* p. 59.
16. *Ibid.,* p. 114.
17. First annual message of Dec. 2, 1850, Richardson, *Messages of the Presidents,* V, 78.
18. Note of Dec. 1, 1852, quoted in Foster Stearns, "Edward Everett," in Bemis, *Secretaries of State,* VI, 130.
19. Richardson, *Messages of the Presidents,* V, 198.
20. Quoted in Roy F. Nichols, *Franklin Pierce: Young Hickory of the Granite Hills,* 2nd ed. (Philadelphia, 1958), p. 328.
21. Quoted in Ivor D. Spencer, *The Victor and the Spoils: A Life of William L. Marcy* (Providence, R.I., 1959), p. 321.
22. Quoted in Foster Rhea Dulles, *China and America: The Story of Their Relations since 1784* (Princeton, 1946), p. 17.
23. Quoted in Tyler Dennett, *Americans in Eastern Asia* (New York, 1922), p. 108.
24. John K. Fairbank, in *Trade and Diplomacy on the China Coast: The Opening of the Treaty Ports, 1842–1854* (Cambridge, Mass., 1953), pp. 195–196, points out

that the idea of equal treatment of barbarians is an old one in Chinese history and that Kearny's claim that he inaugurated the policy of equal treatment for the United States is weak.

25. Quoted in Dennett, *Americans in Eastern Asia,* p. 141.
26. Quoted in Dulles, *China and America,* p. 48.
27. Knight Biggerstaff, "The Official Chinese Attitude toward the Burlingame Mission," *The American Historical Review,* XLI (July 1936), 684.
28. Quoted in Dulles, *China and America,* p. 68.
29. Commander James Glynn quoted in Dennett, *Americans in Eastern Asia,* p. 257.
30. Quoted in *ibid.,* p. 272.
31. Quoted in Carl Crow, *He Opened the Door of Japan* (New York, 1939), p. 90.
32. Payson J. Treat, *Diplomatic Relations between the United States and Japan, 1853–1895* (2 vols., Stanford, Calif., 1932), I, 58.
33. Dec. 19, 1861, quoted in Dennett, *Americans in Eastern Asia,* p. 412.

CHAPTER TEN

1. Roy P. Basler, ed., *The Collected Works of Abraham Lincoln* (9 vols., New Brunswick, N.J., 1935–55), IV, 263, 265.
2. *Ibid.,* IV, 317.
3. Quoted in Ephraim D. Adams, *Great Britain and the American Civil War* (2 vols., London, 1925), I, 67.
4. *Ibid.,* I, 220n.
5. The secretary of the American legation in London felt the same way. "The excitement among the English people," he said on Dec. 6, 1861, "is strengthened daily and unless checked will drive the nation to war." Sarah A. Wallace and Frances B. Gillespie, eds., *The Journal of Benjamin Moran, 1857–1865* (2 vols., Chicago, 1949), II, 918.
6. Quoted in Frederic Bancroft, *The Life of William H. Seward* (2 vols., New York, 1900), II, 238.
7. *Ibid.,* II, 241.
8. Jan. 11, 1862, quoted in Adams, *Britain and the Civil War,* I, 238.
9. April 13, 1861, quoted in Frank L. Owsley, *King Cotton Diplomacy: Foreign Relations of the Confederate States of America,* 2nd ed., rev. by Harriet C. Owsley (Chicago, 1959), p. 11.
10. M. B. Hammond, March 4, 1858, *ibid.,* p. 16.
11. Quoted in *ibid.,* p. 24.
12. Quoted in Joseph H. Park, "The English Workingmen and the American Civil War," *Political Science Quarterly,* XXXIX (Sept. 1924), 452.
13. Quoted in Henry Adams, *The Education of Henry Adams* (Boston, 1918), p. 153.
14. Quoted in Spencer Walpole, *The Life of Lord John Russell* (2 vols., London, 1889), II, 344.
15. Entry of Sept. 25, 1863, Howard K. Beale, ed., *Diary of Gideon Welles* (3 vols., New York, 1960), I, 443. On Dec. 12 Welles wrote that "Our Russian friends are rendering us a great service," p. 484.
16. The quotations are in Owsley, *King Cotton Diplomacy,* pp. 530, 531.
17. Quoted in Henry W. Temple, "William H. Seward," in Samuel F. Bemis, ed., *The American Secretaries of State and Their Diplomacy* (10 vols., New York, 1927–29), VII, 76.

18. John M. Forbes, April 29, 1863, quoted in Douglas H. Maynard, "The Forbes-Aspinwall Mission," *Mississippi Valley Historical Review*, XLV (June 1958), 80.
19. March 6, 1865, quoted in Owsley, *King Cotton Diplomacy*, p. 538.
20. May 21, 1861, quoted in Bancroft, *Seward*, II, 170.
21. Nov. 29, 1861, quoted in Adams, *Britain and the Civil War*, I, 255.
22. Frank J. Merli, *Great Britain and the Confederate Navy, 1861–1865* (Bloomington, Ind., 1970), p. 252, points out that the blockade-breaking potential of the rams has been exaggerated.
23. Quoted in Brooks Adams, "The Seizure of the Laird Rams," *Massachusetts Historical Society Proceedings*, XLV (Dec. 1911), 297.
24. Quoted in Adams, *Britain and the Civil War*, II, 136.

CHAPTER ELEVEN

1. Quoted in Dexter Perkins, *A History of the Monroe Doctrine*, rev. ed. (Boston, 1955), p. 146.
2. To John Bigelow, Sept. 9, 1863, in Frederic Bancroft, *The Life of William H. Seward* (2 vols., New York, 1900), II, 426.
3. *Congressional Globe*, 38th Congress, 1st sess., p. 1408.
4. The quotations are in Bancroft, *Seward*, II, 429.
5. Quoted in Egon C. Corti, *Maximilian and Charlotte of Mexico*, trans. from the German (2 vols., New York, 1928), II, 580.
6. March 31, 1846, George E. Baker, ed., *The Works of William H. Seward* (5 vols., New York, 1853–84), III, 409.
7. Quoted in Theodore C. Smith, "Expansion after the Civil War, 1865–1871," *Political Science Quarterly*, XVI (Sept. 1901), 412–436.
8. Quoted in Charles C. Tansill, *The United States and Santo Domingo, 1798–1873: A Chapter in Caribbean History* (Baltimore, 1938), p. 178.
9. Quoted in Smith, "Expansion after the Civil War," *Political Science Quarterly*, XVI (Sept. 1901), 434.
10. The conversation is recorded in Frederick W. Seward, comp., *William Henry Seward: An Autobiography and Memoir of His Life, with Selections from His Letters* (3 vols., New York, 1891), III, 348.
11. The text of the speech is in Charles Sumner, *The Works of Charles Sumner* (15 vols., Boston, 1875–83), XI, 186–349.
12. Sept. 12, 1861, quoted in Lester B. Shippee, *Canadian-American Relations, 1849–1874* (New Haven, 1939), p. 158.
13. Nov. 9, 1864, quoted in *ibid.*, p. 178.
14. Quoted in William D'Arcy, *The Fenian Movement in the United States: 1858–1886* (Washington, 1947), p. 99.
15. Feb. 12, 1866, in Shippee, *Canadian-American Relations*, p. 220.
16. Quoted in Allan Nevins, *Hamilton Fish: The Inner History of the Grant Administration*, rev. ed. (2 vols., New York, 1957), I, 213.
17. Dec. 5, 1870, in James D. Richardson, ed., *A Compilation of the Messages and Papers of the Presidents, 1789–1899* (10 vols., Washington, 1896–99), VII, 102.
18. The expression of regret had the advantage of satisfying the United States without committing Britain to payment for damages. See Maureen M. Robson, "The *Alabama* Claims and the Anglo-American Reconciliation, 1865–1871," *Canadian Historical Review*, XLIII (March 1961), 11.
19. The Canadian reaction is summarized in Goldwin Smith, *The Treaty of Wash-*

ington, 1871: A Study in Imperial History (Ithaca, N.Y., 1941), pp. 91–113.

20. The Gladstone and Fish quotations are in Nevins, *Hamilton Fish,* II, 524–526.

21. Quoted in Frank W. Hackett, *Reminiscences of the Geneva Tribunal of Arbitration, 1872: The Alabama Claims* (Boston, 1911), p. 202n.

22. Carl Schurz, *The Reminiscences of Carl Schurz* (3 vols., New York, 1908), III, 307.

23. Quoted in Joseph V. Fuller, "Hamilton Fish," in Samuel F. Bemis, ed., *The American Secretaries of State and Their Diplomacy* (10 vols., New York, 1927–29), VII, 183.

24. Nov. 5, 1875, *ibid.,* p. 194. This instruction to the American minister in Madrid is usually known as "No. 266."

CHAPTER TWELVE

1. Dec. 6, 1869, in James D. Richardson, ed., *A Compilation of the Messages and Papers of the Presidents, 1789–1899* (10 vols., Washington, 1896–99), VII, 33.

2. *Ibid.,* VII, 585–586.

3. Quoted in Philip M. Brown, "Frederick Theodore Frelinghuysen," in Samuel F. Bemis, ed., *The American Secretaries of State and Their Diplomacy* (10 vols., New York, 1927–29), VIII, 28.

4. Dec. 8, 1885, in Richardson, *Messages of the Presidents,* VIII, 327–328.

5. To P. H. Morgan, June 1, 1881, *Foreign Relations of the United States, 1881,* p. 761.

6. The quoted newspapers are the New York *Herald,* April 16, 1890, and the *Revue Sud Américaine,* May 18, 1890, in A. Curtis Wilgus, "James G. Blaine and the Pan-American Movement," *Hispanic American Historical Review,* V (Nov. 1922), 702, 705.

7. Quoted in Osgood Hardy, "The *Itata* Incident," *Hispanic American Historical Review,* V (May 1922), 198.

8. Quoted in Albert T. Volwiler, "Harrison, Blaine, and American Foreign Policy, 1889–1893," *Proceedings of the American Philosophical Society,* LXXIX (Nov. 15, 1938), 640.

9. Dec. 31, 1891, in Robley D. Evans, *A Sailor's Log: Recollections of Forty Years of Naval Life* (London, 1901), p. 279.

10. Cecil Spring-Rice, Jan. 19, 1892, quoted in Volwiler, "Harrison, Blaine, and American Foreign Policy," *Proceedings of the American Philosophical Society,* LXXIX (Nov. 15, 1938), 645.

11. Spring-Rice, *ibid.,* p. 647.

12. Feb. 27, 1879, quoted in Charles C. Tansill, *The Foreign Policy of Thomas F. Bayard, 1885–1897* (New York, 1940), p. 129.

13. Quoted in Claude G. Bowers and Helen D. Reid, "William M. Evarts," in Bemis, *Secretaries of State,* VII, 253.

14. March 11, 1880, quoted in Tansill, *Bayard,* p. 132.

15. The text of the treaties is in Shirley W. Smith, *James Burrill Angell: An American Influence* (Ann Arbor, Mich., 1954), pp. 136–139.

16. The Seattle *Post-Intelligencer* of Sept. 11, 1885, and the Seattle *Call* of Nov. 9 quoted in Jules A. Karlin, "Anti-Chinese Outbreaks in Seattle, 1885–1886," *Pacific Northwest Quarterly,* XXXIX (April 1948), 114.

17. Charles Denby to Bayard, Feb. 27, 1886, quoted in Tansill, *Bayard,* p. 143n.

18. To Theodore Roosevelt, March 2, 1904, quoted in Howard K. Beale, *Theodore Roosevelt and the Rise of America to World Power* (Baltimore, 1956), p. 214.

19. May 21, 1905, quoted in Beale, *Theodore Roosevelt,* p. 218.
20. James B. Angell to Bayard, Feb. 24, 1888, quoted in Tansill, *Bayard,* p. 301.
21. Richardson, *Messages of the President,* VIII, 621.
22. Quoted in Allan Nevins, *Grover Cleveland: A Study in Courage* (New York, 1932), p. 430.
23. To Edward J. Phelps, Oct. 26, 1888, in Tansill, *Bayard,* p. 334.
24. John Sherman quoted in Nevins, *Cleveland,* p. 431.
25. New York *Herald,* March 17, 1883, quoted in Louis L. Snyder, "The American-German Pork Dispute, 1879–1891," *Journal of Modern History,* XVII (March 1945), 24.
26. March 18, 1891, quoted in Jules A. Karlin, "The Indemnification of Aliens Injured by Mob Violence," *Southwestern Social Science Quarterly,* XXV (March 1945), 35.
27. April 16, 1892, quoted in Karlin, *ibid.,* 242.

CHAPTER THIRTEEN

1. Richard Olney, "International Isolation of the United States," *Atlantic Monthly,* LXXXI (May 1898), 588. The journalist is A. Lawrence Lowell and is quoted in Richard Hofstadter, *Social Darwinism in American Thought,* rev. ed. (Philadelphia, 1955), p. 81.
2. William R. Thayer, quoted in Hofstadter, *Social Darwinism,* p. 198.
3. To the secretary of the navy, Jan. 21, 1872, quoted in George H. Ryden, *The Foreign Policy of the United States in Relation to Samoa* (New Haven, 1933), p. 57.
4. Quoted in Paul Kennedy, *The Samoan Tangle: A Study in Anglo-German-American Relations, 1878–1900* (New York, 1974), p. 23.
5. Quoted in David M. Pletcher, *The Awkward Years: American Foreign Relations under Garfield and Arthur* (Columbia, Mo., 1962), p. 322.
6. Quoted in *ibid.,* p. 345.
7. San Francisco *Examiner,* Nov. 27, 1888, quoted in Charles C. Tansill, *The Foreign Policy of Thomas F. Bayard, 1885–1897* (New York, 1940), pp. 99–100.
8. Message of Jan. 15, 1889, in James D. Richardson, ed., *A Compilation of the Messages and Papers of the Presidents, 1789–1899* (10 vols., Washington, 1896–99), VIII, 805.
9. *A Footnote to History: Eight Years of Trouble in Samoa* (London, 1892), p. 276.
10. Dec. 3, 1894, in Richardson, *Messages of the Presidents,* IX, 532.
11. New York *Evening Post,* April 6, 1899, quoted in Joseph W. Ellison, "The Partition of Samoa: A Study in Imperialism and Diplomacy," *Pacific Historical Review,* VIII (Sept. 1939), 268.
12. To Joseph H. Choate, Nov. 13, 1899, in William R. Thayer, *The Life and Letters of John Hay* (2 vols., Boston, 1915), II, 282.
13. Quoted in Foster Rhea Dulles, *The Imperial Years* (New York, 1956), p. 196.
14. Quoted in Sylvester K. Stevens, *American Expansion in Hawaii, 1842–1898* (Harrisburg, Pa., 1945), p. 3.
15. *Foreign Relations, 1894,* App. II, 1056.
16. The capitulation is printed in William A. Russ, Jr., *The Hawaiian Revolution (1893–94),* (Selinsgrove, Pa., 1959), pp. 95–96. Russ stresses that the queen surrendered to the U.S., not to the insurgents, pp. 349–350.
17. Feb. 1, 1893, quoted in Montgomery Schuyler, "Walter Gresham," in Sam-

uel F. Bemis, ed., *The American Secretaries of State and Their Diplomacy* (10 vols., New York, 1927–29), VIII, 244.

18. The report, dated July 17, 1893, is in *Foreign Relations, 1894,* App. II, 567–605. Gresham's plan, Oct. 18, 1893, is on p. 463.
19. Nov. 13, 1893, quoted in Schuyler, "Walter Gresham," in Bemis, *Secretaries of State,* VIII, p. 248.
20. Quoted in Allan Nevins, *Grover Cleveland* (New York, 1932), p. 558.
21. Kirk H. Porter, *National Party Platforms* (New York, 1924), p. 204.
22. Quoted in William A. Russ, Jr., *The Hawaiian Republic (1894–98): And Its Struggle to Win Annexation* (Selinsgrove, Pa., 1961), p. 320.
23. Sept. 9, 1897, in Stevens, *American Expansion in Hawaii,* p. 288.
24. Quoted in Margaret Leech, *In the Days of McKinley* (New York, 1959), p. 213.
25. Nelson M. Blake, "Background of Cleveland's Venezuelan Policy," *The American Historical Review,* XLVII (Jan. 1942), 263.
26. Philadelphia *Press,* April 30, 1895, *ibid.,* p. 264.
27. *American Review,* CLX (June 1895), 658.
28. Olney to Bayard, June 20, 1895, *Foreign Relations, 1895,* I, 545–562.
29. *St. James Gazette,* quoted in Blake, "Background of Cleveland's Venezuelan Policy," *The American Historical Review,* XLVII (Jan. 1942), 270.
30. Quoted in Nevins, *Cleveland,* p. 640.
31. For the quotations, see *ibid.,* pp. 641–642.
32. The papers, dated Jan. 12 and Feb. 15, 1897, are quoted in Nelson M. Blake, "The Olney-Pauncefote Treaty of 1897," *The American Historical Review,* L (Jan. 1945), 234–236.

CHAPTER FOURTEEN

1. John T. Morgan, quoted in Walter Millis, *The Martial Spirit* (Boston, 1931), p. 29.
2. Quoted in French E. Chadwick, *The Relations of the United States with Spain: Diplomacy* (New York, 1909), p. 438.
3. Kirk H. Porter, *National Party Platforms* (New York, 1924), p. 205.
4. The text of the note, dated Sept. 23, 1897, is in *Foreign Relations, 1898,* pp. 568–573.
5. James D. Richardson, ed., *A Compilation of the Messages and Papers of the Presidents, 1789–1899* (10 vols., Washington, 1896–99), X, 131.
6. *Foreign Relations, 1898,* p. 1007.
7. The captain and the *Journal* are quoted in Jacob E. Wisan, *The Cuban Crisis as Reflected in the New York Press, 1895–1898* (New York, 1934), pp. 389, 392.
8. The secretary of the navy and Proctor are quoted in Millis, *Martial Spirit,* pp. 111, 124.
9. The *Wall Street Journal* and the *Evangelist,* March 31, 1898, are quoted in Julius W. Pratt, *Expansionists of 1898* (Baltimore, 1936), pp. 246, 285.
10. April 5, 1898, von Bülow quoted in Orestes Ferrara, *The Last Spanish War: Revelations in "Diplomacy"* (New York, 1937), p. 127.
11. The quotations are from Chadwick, *Relations with Spain: Diplomacy,* pp. 571, 573, 575.
12. The text is in Richardson, *Messages of the Presidents,* X, 139–150.
13. Arthur Balfour to Julian Pauncefote, April 15, 1898, quoted in Charles S. Campbell, Jr., *Anglo-American Understanding, 1898–1903* (Baltimore, 1957), p. 35.

14. John Hay to Henry Cabot Lodge, April 5, 1898, in William R. Thayer, *The Life and Letters of John Hay* (2 vols., Boston, 1915), II, 165.
15. To Robert Bacon, April 5, 1898, quoted in Howard K. Beale, *Theodore Roosevelt and the Rise of America to World Power* (Baltimore, 1956), p. 60.
16. Quoted in Millis, *Martial Spirit,* p. 119.
17. Quoted in Louis Halle, *Dream and Reality: Aspects of American Foreign Policy* (New York, 1958), p. 184.
18. June 3, 1898, quoted in Foster Rhea Dulles, *America's Rise to World Power, 1898–1954* (New York, 1954), p. 43.
19. Quoted in Millis, *Martial Spirit,* p. 170.
20. To Theodore Roosevelt, July 27, 1898, in Thayer, *Hay,* II, 337.
21. Quoted in Millis, *Martial Spirit,* p. 317.
22. Quoted in Pratt, *Expansionists of 1898,* pp. 335–336.
23. Charles S. Olcott, *The Life of William McKinley* (2 vols., Boston, 1916), II, 110–111, and Finley Peter Dunne, *Mr. Dooley in Peace and in War* (Boston, 1899), p. 43.
24. Albert Beveridge quoted in Claude G. Bowers, *Beveridge and the Progressive Era* (Boston, 1932), p. 76.
25. *Collected Verse of Rudyard Kipling* (London, 1912), p. 321.
26. Jan. 12, 1899, in Henry Cabot Lodge, ed., *Selections from the Correspondence of Theodore Roosevelt and Henry Cabot Lodge, 1884–1918* (2 vols., New York, 1925), I, 384.
27. Quoted in John A. Garraty, *Henry Cabot Lodge: A Biography* (New York, 1953), p. 200.
28. *Autobiography of Andrew Carnegie* (Boston, 1920), p. 364.
29. Quoted in Foster Rhea Dulles, *The Imperial Years* (New York, 1956), p. 177.
30. "An Ode in Time of Hesitation," in Robert Morss Lovett, ed., *Selected Poems of William Vaughn Moody* (Boston, 1931), pp. 18, 24.
31. Porter, *National Party Platforms,* pp. 210–211.
32. Hoar is quoted in Robert L. Beisner, *Twelve Against Empire: The Anti-Imperialists, 1898–1900* (New York, 1968), p. 155.
33. Alva Adams, governor of Colorado, July 21, 1898, quoted in Marilyn B. Young, *The Rhetoric of Empire: American-China Policy, 1895–1901* (Cambridge, Mass., 1968), p. 97.
34. Quoted in Robert E. Osgood, *Ideals and Self-Interest in America's Foreign Relations: The Great Transformation of the Twentieth Century* (Chicago, 1953), p. 48.

CHAPTER FIFTEEN

1. Nov. 6, 1894, quoted in Alfred L. P. Dennis, *Adventures in American Diplomacy, 1896–1906* (New York, 1928), p. 175.
2. To Rockhill, July 25, 1899, quoted in Alfred Whitney Griswold, *The Far Eastern Policy of the United States* (New York, 1938), p. 65.
3. To Hippisley, Aug. 3, 1899, *ibid.,* p. 67.
4. To Rockhill, Aug. 21, 1899, *ibid.,* p. 71.
5. July 3, 1900, *Foreign Relations, 1900,* p. 299.
6. Henry Adams, *The Education of Henry Adams* (Boston, 1918), p. 392.
7. Robert Morss Lovett, ed., *Selected Poems of William Vaughn Moody* (Boston, 1931), p. 28.
8. To Hippisley, July 6, 1901, quoted in Griswold, *Far Eastern Policy,* p. 83.
9. Feb. 1, 1901, quoted in Dennis, *Adventures in American Diplomacy,* p. 242.

10. Quoted in Foster Rhea Dulles, *The Imperial Years* (New York, 1956), pp. 270–271.

11. To Cecil Spring-Rice, July 24, 1905, quoted in Tyler Dennett, *Roosevelt and the Russo-Japanese War* (Garden City, N.Y., 1925), p. 2.

12. See, for instance, letters to Meyer, Feb. 6, and Kennan, May 6, 1905, in Elting E. Morison, *The Letters of Theodore Roosevelt* (8 vols., Cambridge, Mass., 1951–54), IV, 1115, 1169.

13. Quoted in Dennett, *Roosevelt and the Russo-Japanese War,* p. 180.

14. Komura to Roosevelt, March 31, 1905, quoted in Howard K. Beale, *Theodore Roosevelt and the Rise of America to World Power* (Baltimore, 1956), p. 285.

15. Quoted in Dulles, *Imperial Years,* p. 276.

16. Jan. 28, 1903, in Morison, *Roosevelt Letters,* IV, 1112.

17. July 31, 1905, in *ibid.,* IV, 1293.

18. To Kermit Roosevelt, Oct. 27, 1906, in *ibid.,* V, 475.

19. To Elihu Root, July 23, 1907, in *ibid.,* V, 725.

20. *Foreign Relations, 1908,* p. 511.

21. To William H. Taft, Dec. 22, 1910, quoted in Griswold, *Far Eastern Policy,* p. 132.

22. Quoted in Carleton Beals, *The Crime of Cuba* (Philadelphia, 1933), p. 173.

23. Quoted in Russell H. Fitzgibbon, *Cuba and the United States, 1900–1935* (Menasha, Wis., 1935), p. 31n.

24. To Leonard Wood, April 3, 1901, quoted in Dennis, *Adventures in American Diplomacy,* p. 265.

25. The governor was Charles E. Magoon. The quotation is from Fitzgibbon, *Cuba and the United States,* p. 142n.

26. *Foreign Relations, 1898,* p. lxxii.

27. Pauncefote to Salisbury, Jan. 19, 1900, quoted in Charles S. Campbell, Jr., *Anglo-American Understanding, 1898–1903* (Baltimore, 1957), p. 190.

28. To Alfred T. Mahan, Feb. 4, 1900, in Morison, *Roosevelt Letters,* II, 1185.

29. Quoted in Dwight C. Miner, *The Fight for the Panama Route: The Story of the Spooner Act and the Hay-Herrán Treaty* (New York, 1940), p. 97.

30. Quoted in Miles P. Du Val, Jr., *Cadiz to Cathay: The Story of the Long Diplomatic Struggle for the Panama Canal,* 2nd ed. (Stanford, Calif., 1947), p. 165.

31. Aug. 19, 1903, quoted in Miner, *Panama Route,* p. 345.

32. Philippe Bunau-Varilla, *Panama: The Creation, Destruction, and Resurrection* (London, 1913), p. 312.

33. Sept. 13, 1903, quoted in Miner, *Panama Route,* p. 351.

34. Quoted in Dulles, *Imperial Years,* p. 251.

35. Quoted in Philip C. Jessup, *Elihu Root* (2 vols., New York, 1938), I, 404–405.

36. Speech of March 24, 1911, quoted in Du Val, *Cadiz to Cathay,* p. 438.

37. To Speck von Sternberg, July 12, 1901, in Morison, *Roosevelt Letters,* III, 116.

38. Dec. 3, 1901, in *Foreign Relations, 1901,* pp. xxxvi–xxxvii.

39. Dewey is quoted in Beale, *Roosevelt and the Rise to World Power,* p. 418.

40. Dec. 26, 1902, in Morison, *Roosevelt Letters,* III, 398.

41. Quoted by Albert W. von Quadt, Jan. 25, 1903, in Alfred Vagts, *Deutschland und die Vereinigten Staaten in der Weltpolitik* (2 vols., New York, 1935), II, 1595.

42. Lord Balfour, Feb. 14, 1903, quoted in Campbell, *Anglo-American Understanding,* p. 299.

43. Quoted in Dexter Perkins, *A History of the Monroe Doctrine,* 2nd ed. (Boston, 1955), p. 238.

44. The quotations are from letters to Elihu Root, May 20 and June 7, 1904, in Henry F. Pringle, *Theodore Roosevelt: A Biography* (New York, 1931), pp. 294–295.

45. Dec. 6, 1904, *Foreign Relations, 1904*, p. xli.

46. For the message, Feb. 15, 1905, see *ibid., 1905*, p. 334; Roosevelt's comment is in Pringle, *Roosevelt*, p. 296.

47. Quoted in James B. Scott, "Elihu Root," in Samuel F. Bemis, ed., *The American Secretaries of State and Their Diplomacy* (10 vols., New York, 1927–29), V, 217.

CHAPTER SIXTEEN

1. Quoted in Howard K. Beale, *Theodore Roosevelt and the Rise of America to World Power* (Baltimore, 1956), p. 359. In the preceding year the United States had shown some interest in Morocco by intervening in the case of Jon Perdicaris, allegedly an American citizen who had been kidnapped and held for ransom by a native chieftain. For details, see Alfred L. P. Dennis, *Adventures in American Diplomacy, 1896–1906* (New York, 1928), pp. 443–445 and Harold E. Davis, "The Citizenship of Jon Perdicaris," *Journal of Modern History*, XIII (Dec. 1941), 517–526.

2. To Shelby M. Cullom, Feb. 10, 1905, in Elting E. Morison, ed., *The Letters of Theodore Roosevelt* (8 vols., Cambridge, Mass., 1951–1954), IV, 1119.

3. Quoted in Henry F. Pringle, *The Life and Times of William Howard Taft* (2 vols., New York, 1939), II, 739.

4. Quoted in William Stull Holt, *Treaties Defeated by the Senate* (Baltimore, 1933), p. 235.

5. Kirk H. Porter, *National Party Platforms* (New York, 1924), p. 216.

6. To A. C. Cowles, Dec. 17, 1899, quoted in Beale, *Theodore Roosevelt*, p. 95.

7. Quoted in Henry F. Pringle, *Theodore Roosevelt: A Biography* (New York, 1931), p. 291.

8. Quoted in Charles S. Campbell, Jr., *Anglo-American Understanding, 1898–1903* (Baltimore, 1957), p. 313.

9. Oct. 5, 1903, in Morison, *Roosevelt Letters*, III, 616.

10. To A. T. Mahan, June 8, 1911, in Morison, *Roosevelt Letters*, VII, 280.

11. Quoted in Hugh L. Keenleyside and Gerald S. Brown, *Canada and the United States*, rev. ed. (New York, 1952), p. 267.

12. Quoted in Keenleyside and Brown, *Canada and the U.S.*, p. 271.

13. To H. S. Drinker, July 27, 1911, quoted in Pringle, *Taft*, II, 649.

14. Ray S. Baker and William E. Dodd, eds., *The Public Papers of Woodrow Wilson* (6 vols., New York, 1925–27), *The New Democracy*, I, 93.

15. Annual message of Dec. 3, 1912, quoted in Alfred W. Griswold, *The Far Eastern Policy of the United States* (New York, 1938), p. 134.

16. Lloyd C. Griscom, *Diplomatically Speaking* (Boston, 1940), p. 263.

17. Phillips to Rockhill, July 16, 1908, in Charles Vevier, *The United States and China, 1906–1913: A Study of Finances and Diplomacy* (New Brunswick, N.J., 1955), p. 72.

18. March 18, 1913, *Foreign Relations, 1913*, p. 170.

19. To James D. Phelan, April 9, 1913, quoted in Arthur S. Link, *Woodrow Wilson and the Progressive Era, 1910–1917* (New York, 1954), p. 85.

20. May 18, 1913, quoted in Arthur S. Link, *Wilson: The New Freedom* (Princeton, 1956), pp. 299–300.

21. March 13, 1915, *Foreign Relations, 1915*, p. 108.

22. To Bryan, April 14, 1915, quoted in Tien-yi Li, *Woodrow Wilson's China Policy, 1913–1917* (New York, 1952), p. 122.
23. May 11, 1915, in *Foreign Relations, 1915,* p. 146.
24. *Foreign Relations, The Lansing Papers, 1914–1920,* II, 450.
25. *Ibid.,* II, 446.

CHAPTER SEVENTEEN

1. April 1, 1912, quoted in Eugene K. Chamberlin, "The Japanese Scare at Magdalena Bay," *Pacific Historical Review,* XXIV (November 1955), 354.
2. The text, dated Oct. 27, 1913, is in Ray S. Baker and William E. Dodd, eds., *The Public Papers of Woodrow Wilson* (6 vols., New York, 1925–27), *The New Democracy,* I, 64–69.
3. To Secretary of State, Nov. 26, 1916, in *Foreign Relations, 1916,* p. 242.
4. The message is in Baker and Dodd, *Wilson Papers, New Democracy,* I, 45–51.
5. *Ibid.,* I, 101.
6. *Economist,* April 18, 1914, quoted in Arthur S. Link, *Woodrow Wilson and the Progressive Era, 1910–1917* (New York, 1954), p. 124.
7. To Secretary of Foreign Relations, June 20, 1916, in *Foreign Relations, 1916,* p. 591.

SUPPLEMENTARY READINGS

The following are suggestions for those who may wish to investigate the history of foreign relations in greater depth than is possible in a textbook. Although in need of updating, a still useful basic bibliography is Samuel F. Bemis and Grace G. Griffin, eds., *Guide to the Diplomatic History of the United States, 1775–1921* (Washington, 1935). Frank Freidel, ed., *Harvard Guide to American History* (rev. ed., 2 vols., Cambridge, Mass., 1974) contains numerous references to major diplomatic studies. *Foreign Affairs: An American Quarterly Review* publishes annotated bibliographies in each issue. It also publishes, under the title *Foreign Affairs Bibliography,* larger compilations. The first volume covered 1919–1932; subsequent volumes include writings for ten-year periods. Specialized guides are David F. Trask, Michael C. Meyer, and Roger R. Trask, comps., *A Bibliography of United States-Latin American Relations Since 1810: A Selected List of Eleven Thousand Published References* (Lincoln, Nebr., 1968); and Wilton B. Fowler, comp., *American Diplomatic History Since 1890* (Northbrook, Ill., 1974). U.S. Department of State, Office of External Research, *Foreign Affairs Research: A Directory of Governmental Resources* (Washington, 1969), lists what can be found in government agencies; and Laurence F. Schmeckebier and Roy B. Eastin, eds., *Government Publications and Their Use* (2nd. ed., Washington, 1969), explains usage. For selected periodical literature since 1955, see *Historical Abstracts* and *America: History and Life* published by the American Bibliographical Center, Santa Barbara, Calif. About a fifth of the annotated entries deal with foreign relations. See also Eric H. Boehm, ed., *Bibliographies on International Relations and World Affairs: An Annotated Directory* (Santa Barbara, 1965).

Most valuable among documentary collections is Department of State, *Papers Relating to the Foreign Relations of the United States,* volumes published regularly since 1861 under slightly varying titles. They contain selections from dispatches and instructions deposited in official archives. For earlier diplomatic documents see Francis Wharton, ed., *The Revolutionary Diplomatic Correspondence of the United States* (6 vols., Washington, 1889); *The Diplomatic Correspondence of the United States* (7 vols., Washington, 1833–34), which cover 1783–89; and Walter Lowrie and Matthew St. Clair, eds., *American State Papers, Class I: Foreign Relations* (6 vols., 1832–59), which cover 1789–1828. David Hunter Miller, ed., *Treaties and Other International Acts of the United States of America* (8 vols., Washington, 1931–48), contains notes on the negotiations as well as documents and is the best compilation for the years 1778–1863. Useful supplements are: William M. Malloy, ed., *Treaties, Conventions, International Acts, Protocols and Agreements between the United States and Other Powers, 1776–1937* (4 vols., Washington, 1910–38); Charles I. Bevans, comp., *Treaties and Other International Agreements of the United States of America, 1776–1949* (Washington, 1968); and the series entitled *United States Treaties and Other International Agreements* which began publication in 1950 on an annual basis and which contains arguments of various kinds with other countries; and U.S. Dept. of State, Historical Office, *American Foreign Policy: Current Documents* (Washington, 1956–), selection of principal speeches, diplomatic notes, etc. Also useful is *Documents on American Foreign Relations* published annually since 1938, first by the World Peace Foundation and since 1951 by the Council on Foreign Relations. Outstanding analyses of international law as it pertains to United States diplomacy are: John Bassett Moore, *A Digest of International Law* (8 vols., Washington, 1906);

and Green H. Hackworth, *Digest of International Law* (8 vols., Washington, 1940–44).

The basic work on concepts and themes traced historically is Alexander DeConde, ed., *Encyclopedia of American Foreign Policy: Studies of the Principal Movements and Ideas* (3 vols., New York, 1978). For a multivolume history of American diplomacy that focuses on secretaries of state, see Samuel F. Bemis, ed., *The American Secretaries of State and Their Diplomacy* (10 vols., New York, 1927–29). In 1963 Robert H. Ferrell took over as editor and by 1972 added eight new volumes to the series. Brief accounts of secretaries of state are in Norman A. Graebner, ed., *An Uncertain Tradition: American Secretaries of State in the Twentieth Century* (New York, 1961); and Frank J. Merli and Theodore A. Wilson, eds., *Makers of American Diplomacy* (2 vols., New York, 1974), which includes other policymakers too. Important other series are: *The American Foreign Policy Library* published by Harvard University Press under various editors and which more often stresses the politics of the country surveyed than it does American policy; *The American Diplomatic History Series,* edited by Armin Rappaport; *America in Crises* and *America and the World,* edited by Robert A. Divine. Since 1931 the Council on Foreign Relations has put out, usually a volume for each year, a survey on *The United States in World Affairs.* Alexander DeConde, *American Diplomatic History in Transformation* (Washington, 1976) is a pamphlet that analyzes themes and interpretations in the historical literature.

CHAPTER ONE

On the theory and conduct of diplomacy, see François de Callières, *On the Manner of Negotiating with Princes,* trans. from the French by A. F. Whyte (Boston, 1919); Harold Nicolson, *Diplomacy* (3rd ed., London, 1966); Nicolson, *The Evolution of Diplomatic Method* (New York, 1955); Ernest Satow, *A Guide to Diplomatic Practice,* 4th ed., Nevile Bland, ed. (New York, 1957); John E. Harr, *The Professional Diplomat* (Princeton, 1969); and John R. Wood and Jean Serres, *Diplomatic Ceremonial and Protocol: Principles, Procedures, and Practices* (New York, 1970). On international law and power in a context of diplomacy and diverse cultures, see Georg Schwarzenberger, *Power Politics: A Study of International Society* (rev. ed., New York, 1956); Charles de Visscher, *Theory and Reality in Public International Law,* trans. from the French by P. E. Corbett (Princeton, 1957); Percy E. Corbett, *Law in Diplomacy* (Princeton, 1959); Julius Stone, *Quest for Survival: The Role of Law and Foreign Policy* (Cambridge, Mass., 1961); Adda B. Bozeman, *Politics and Culture in International History* (Princeton, 1960); and Bozeman, *The Future of Law in a Multi-cultural World* (Princeton, 1971).

For American practice and procedures, see Thomas H. Etzold, *The Conduct of American Foreign Relations: The Other Side of Diplomacy* (New York, 1977); James L. McCamy, *The Administration of American Foreign Affairs* (New York, 1950); Graham H. Stuart, *American Diplomatic and Consular Practice* (2nd ed., New York, 1952); Arthur W. McMahon, *Administration in Foreign Affairs* (University, Ala., 1953); Thomas A. Bailey, *The Art of Diplomacy: The American Experience* (New York, 1968); Charles W. Thayer, *Diplomat* (New York, 1959); Warren F. Ilchman, *Professional Diplomacy in the United States, 1779–1939: A Study in Administrative History* (Chicago, 1961); H. Bradford Westerfield, *The Instruments of America's Foreign Policy* (New York, 1963); Joseph Frankel, *The Making of Foreign Policy: An Analysis of Decision Making* (London, 1963); Kurt London, *The Making of Foreign Policy: East and West* (Philadelphia, 1965); Burton M. Sapin, *The Making of United States Foreign Policy* (Washington, 1966); Thomas A. Bailey, *The Art of Diplomacy:*

The American Experience (New York, 1968); Ellis Briggs, *Anatomy of Diplomacy: The Origin and Execution of American Foreign Policy* (New York, 1968); and Richard A. Johnson, *The Administration of United States Foreign Policy* (Austin, Tex., 1971).

For self-interest, idealism, and realism, see George F. Kennan, *American Diplomacy, 1900–1950* (Chicago, 1951); Kennan, *Realities of American Foreign Policy* (New York, 1951); Hans J. Morgenthau, *In Defense of the National Interest: A Critical Examination of American Foreign Policy* (New York, 1951); Robert E. Osgood, *Ideals and Self-Interest in America's Foreign Relations: The Great Transformation of the Twentieth Century* (Chicago, 1953), all of which expound the realist position. Frank Tannenbaum, *The American Tradition in Foreign Policy* (Norman, Okla., 1955) and Dexter Perkins, *The American Approach to Foreign Policy* (rev. ed., Cambridge, Mass., 1962) defend idealism.

On the Constitution and the president, see Louis Henkin, *Foreign Affairs and the Constitution* (Mineola, N.Y., 1972); Edward S. Corwin, *The President's Control of Foreign Relations* (Princeton, 1917); Corwin, *The President: Office and Powers, 1787–1957: History and Analysis of Practice and Opinion* (4th ed., New York, 1957); Sidney Warren, *The President as World Leader* (Philadelphia, 1964); Edgar E. Robinson, *et al., Powers of the President in Foreign Affairs, 1945–1965* (San Francisco, 1966); Manfred Landecker, *The President and Public Opinion: Leadership in Foreign Affairs* (Washington, 1968); Thomas E. Cronin and Sanford D. Greenberg, *The Presidential Advisory System* (New York, 1969); James W. Davis, Jr., *The National Executive Branch: An Introduction* (New York, 1970); Raoul Berger, *Executive Privilege: Constitutional Myth* (Cambridge, Mass., 1974); Arthur M. Schlesinger, Jr., *The Imperial Presidency* (Boston, 1973); I. M. Destler, *Presidents, Bureaucrats, and Foreign Policy: The Politics of Organizational Reform* (Princeton, 1972); Rexford G. Tugwell and Thomas E. Cronin, eds., *The Presidency Reappraised* (New York, 1974); Louis W. Koenig, *The Chief Executive* (3rd ed., New York, 1975); and Richard E. Neustadt, *Presidential Power: The Politics of Leadership with Reflections on Johnson and Nixon* (New York, 1976). For the role of Congress, see Eleanor E. Dennison, *The Senate Foreign Relations Committee* (Stanford, Calif., 1942); Albert C. Westphal, *The House Committee on Foreign Affairs* (New York, 1942); Robert A. Dahl, *Congress and Foreign Policy* (New York, 1950); Daniel S. Cheever and H. Field Haviland, Jr., *American Foreign Policy and the Separation of Powers* (Cambridge, Mass., 1952); Holbert N. Carroll, *The House of Representatives and Foreign Affairs* (Pittsburgh, 1958); David N. Farnsworth, *The Senate Committee on Foreign Relations* (Urbana, Ill., 1961); Leroy N. Rieselbach, *The Roots of Isolationism: Congressional Voting and Presidential Leadership in Foreign Policy* (Indianapolis, 1966); Hugh G. Gallagher, *Advise and Obstruct: The Role of the United States Senate in Foreign Policy Decisions* (New York, 1969); and Francis O. Wilcox, *Congress, the Executive, and Foreign Policy* (New York, 1971).

On the secretary of state, Department of State, and Foreign Service, the following are helpful: Richard I. Werking, *The Master Architects: Building the United States Foreign Service, 1890–1913* (Lexington, Ky., 1977); William I. Bacchus, *Foreign Policy and the Bureaucratic Process: The State Department's Country Director System* (Princeton, 1974); Don K. Price, ed., *The Secretary of State* (Englewood Cliffs, N.J., 1960); Alexander DeConde, *The American Secretary of State: An Interpretation* (New York, 1962); Norman L. Hill, *Mr. Secretary of State* (New York, 1963); J. Rives Childs, *American Foreign Service* (New York, 1948); Graham H. Stuart, *The Department of State: A History of Its Organization, Procedure, and Personnel* (New York, 1949); Zara S. Steiner, *The State Department and Foreign Service: The Wriston Report—Four Years Later* (Princeton, 1958); Robert E. Elder, *The Policy Machine: The Department of State and American Foreign Policy* (Syracuse, N.Y., 1960); William Barnes and John H. Heath, *The Foreign Service of the United States: Origins, Develop-*

ment, and Functions (Washington, 1961); Smith Simpson, *Anatomy of the State Department* (Boston, 1967); W. Wendell Blancké, *The Foreign Service of the United States* (New York, 1969); John F. Campbell, *The Foreign Affairs Fudge Factory* (New York, 1971); and Robert D. Schulzinger, *The Making of the Diplomatic Mind: The Training, Outlook, and Style of United States Foreign Service Officers, 1908–1931* (Middletown, Conn., 1975).

For military, intelligence, and related topics, see Burton M. Sapin and Richard C. Snyder, *The Role of the Military in American Foreign Policy* (Garden City, N.Y., 1954); Roger Hilsman, *Strategic Intelligence and National Defense* (Glencoe, Ill., 1956); Walter Millis, *Arms and Men: A Study in American Military History* (New York, 1956); C. Wright Mills, *The Power Elite* (New York, 1956); William W. Kaufmann, ed., *Military Policy and National Security* (Princeton, 1956); Samuel P. Huntington, *The Soldier and the State: The Theory and Politics of Civil-Military Relations* (Cambridge, Mass., 1957); Walter Millis, *et al., Arms and the State: Civil Military Elements in National Policy* (New York, 1958); Paul Y. Hammond, *Organizing for Defense: The American Military Establishment in the Twentieth Century* (Princeton, 1961); Washington Platt, *National Character in Action: Intelligence Factors in Foreign Relations* (New Brunswick, N.J., 1961); David Wise and Thomas B. Ross, *The Invisible Government* (New York, 1964); Wise and Ross, *The Espionage Establishment* (New York, 1967); Thomas C. Schelling, *Arms and Influence* (New Haven, 1966); Donald A. Wells, *The War Myth* (New York, 1968); Merlo J. Pusey, *The Way We Go to War* (Boston, 1969); George Thayer, *The War Business: The International Trade in Armaments* (New York, 1969); Harry H. Ransom, *The Intelligence Establishment* (Cambridge, Mass., 1970); Bruce M. Russet, *What Price Vigilance: The Burdens of National Defense* (New Haven, 1970); Sidney Lens, *The Military-Industrial Complex* (Philadelphia, 1970); William Proxmire, *Report from Wasteland: America's Military Industrial Complex* (New York, 1970); David Wise, *The Politics of Lying: Government Deception, Secrecy, and Power* (New York, 1973); Victor Marchetti and John Marks, *The CIA and the Cult of Intelligence* (New York, 1974); Morton H. Halperin, *Bureaucratic Politics and Foreign Policy* (Washington, 1974); Halperin and Robert Borosage, *The Lawless State: The Crimes of the U.S. Intelligence Agencies* (New York, 1976); and Klaus E. Knorr, ed., *Historical Dimensions of National Security Problems* (Lawrence, Kans., 1976).

For public opinion, pressure groups, and the press, see Thomas A. Bailey, *The Man in the Street: The Impact of American Public Opinion on Foreign Policy* (New York, 1948), a stimulating pioneer study; Lindsay Rogers, *The Pollsters: Public Opinion, Politics and Democratic Leadership* (New York, 1949); Gabriel Almond, *The American People and Foreign Policy* (New York, 1950); V. O. Key, Jr., *Politics, Parties, and Pressure Groups* (4th ed., New York, 1958); Marquis Childs and James B. Reston, eds., *Walter Lippmann and His Times* (New York, 1959); Angus Campbell, *et al., The American Voter* (New York, 1960); James N. Rosenau, *Public Opinion and Foreign Policy* (New York, 1961); Bernard C. Cohen, *The Press and Foreign Policy* (Princeton, 1963); Louis L. Gersson, *The Hyphenate in Recent American Politics and Diplomacy* (Lawrence, Kans., 1964); Elmer E. Cornwell, Jr., *Presidential Leadership of Public Opinion* (Bloomington, Ind., 1965); Harwood L. Childs, *Public Opinion: Nature, Formation, and Role* (Princeton, 1965); Lloyd A. Free and Hadley Cantril, *The Political Beliefs of Americans: A Study of Public Opinion* (New Brunswick, N.J., 1967); John Hohenberg, *Between Two Worlds: Policy, Press, and Public Opinion in Asian-American Relations* (New York, 1967); James B. Reston, *The Artillery of the Press: Its Influence on American Foreign Policy* (New York, 1967); William O. Chittick, *State Department, Press, and Pressure Groups: A Role Analysis* (New York, 1970); Harold Mendelsohn and Irving Crespi, *The Polls, Television, and the New Politics* (Scranton, Pa., 1970); Leo Bogart, *Silent Politics: Polls and the Awareness of Public*

Opinion (New York, 1972); Bernard C. Cohen, *The Public's Impact on Foreign Policy* (Boston, 1973); Robert A. Divine, *Foreign Policy and U.S. Presidential Elections, 1940–1960,* (2 vols., New York, 1974); Michael Leigh, *Mobilizing Consent: Public Opinion and American Foreign Policy, 1937–1947* (Westport, Conn., 1976); and Russell W. Howe and Sarah H. Trott, *The Power Peddlers: How Lobbyists Mold America's Foreign Policy* (New York, 1977).

For aspects of the economic dimension, see Benjamin H. Williams, *Economic Foreign Policy of the United States* (New York, 1929); Raymond F. Micksell, *United States Economic Policy and International Relations* (New York, 1952); William A. Williams, *The Tragedy of American Diplomacy* (Cleveland, 1959); Herbert Feis, *Foreign Aid and Foreign Policy* (New York, 1964); Edward S. Mason, *Foreign Aid and Foreign Policy* (New York, 1964); Harry Magdoff, *The Age of Imperialism: The Economics of U.S. Foreign Policy* (New York, 1969); Ronald Radosh, *American Labor and United States Foreign Policy* (New York, 1969); John White, *The Politics of Foreign Aid* (New York, 1974).

Other books on topics pertinent to this chapter are: Cecil V. Crabb, *Bipartisan Foreign Policy: Myth or Reality?* (Evanston, Ill., 1957); Joseph C. McKenna, *Diplomatic Protest in Foreign Policy: Analysis and Case Studies* (Chicago, 1962); Robert Blum, ed., *Cultural Affairs and Foreign Relations* (Englewood Cliffs, N.J., 1963); Merle E. Curti, *American Philanthropy Abroad* (New Brunswick, N.J., 1963); Francis L. Loewenheim, ed., *The Historian and the Diplomat: The Role of History and Historians in American Foreign Policy* (New York, 1967); Peter Brock, *Pacifism in the United States: From the Colonial Era to the First World War* (Princeton, 1968); Brock, *Radical Pacifism in Antebellum America* (Princeton, 1968); Joseph H. de Rivera, *The Psychological Dimension of Foreign Policy* (Columbus, Ohio, 1968); Mira Wilkins, *The Emergence of Multinational Enterprise: American Business Abroad from the Colonial Era to 1914;* Wilkins, *The Maturing of National Enterprise: American Business Abroad from 1914 to 1920* (Cambridge, Mass., 1970, 1974); and Nathan Glazer and Daniel P. Moynihan, eds., *Ethnicity: Theory and Experience* (Cambridge, Mass., 1975).

CHAPTER TWO

For the diplomacy of the colonial era the basic monograph is Max Savelle, *The Origins of American Diplomacy: The International History of Angloamerica, 1492–1763* (New York, 1967). See also his *Empires to Nations: Expansion in America, 1713–1824* (Minneapolis, 1974); Fredi Chiappelli, ed., *First Images of America: The Impact of the New World on the Old* (2 vols., Berkeley, Calif., 1976); Felix Gilbert, *To the Farewell Address: Ideas of Early American Foreign Policy* (Princeton, 1961), valuable for analyses of the transference of ideas from Europe to America; Viola F. Barnes, *The Dominion of New England: A Study in British Colonial Policy* (New Haven, 1923); Harry M. Ward, *The United Colonies of New England, 1643–90* (New York, 1961); Ward, *"Unite or Die": Intercolony Relations, 1690–1763* (Port Washington, N.Y., 1971); Michael G. Kammen, *Empire and Interest: The American Colonies and the Politics of Mercantilism* (Philadelphia, 1970); William J. Eccles, *France in America* (New York, 1972); John H. Parry, *Trade and Dominion: The European Overseas Empires in the Eighteenth Century* (New York, 1971); Gustave Lanctot, *Canada and the American Revolution, 1774–1783,* trans. Margaret M. Cameron (Toronto, 1967); Zenab E. Rashed, *The Peace of Paris, 1763* (Liverpool, 1951); Robert L. Gold, *Borderland Empires in Transition: The Triple Nation Transfer of Florida* (Carbondale, Ill., 1969).

On revolutionary foreign relations the basic monograph is Samuel F. Bemis, *The Diplomacy of the American Revolution* (1935; 2nd ed., New York, 1957). For the diplomacy of peacemaking the basic study is Richard B. Morris, *The Peacemakers: The Great Powers and American Independence* (New York, 1965). Other important studies are Arthur B. Darling, *Our Rising Empire, 1763–1803* (New Haven, 1940); Helen Augur, *The Secret War of Independence* (New York, 1956); Richard W. Van Alstyne, *The Rising American Empire* (New York, 1960); Van Alstyne, *Empire and Independence: The International History of the American Revolution* (New York, 1965); Van Alstyne, *Genesis of American Nationalism* (Waltham, Mass., 1970); Lawrence S. Kaplan, *Colonies into Nation, 1763–1801* (New York, 1972); Elmer Bendiner, *The Virgin Diplomats* (New York, 1976); and Lawrence S. Kaplan, ed., *The American Revolution and "A Candid World"* (Kent, Ohio, 1977).

For aspects of British policy, see Vincent J. Harlow, *The Founding of the Second British Empire, 1763–1793* (London, 1952); Piers Mackesy, *The War for America, 1775–1783* (London, 1964); Paul C. Phillips, *The West in the Diplomacy of the American Revolution* (Urbana, Ill., 1913); Clarence W. Alvord, *The Mississippi Valley in British Politics* (2 vols., Cleveland, 1917); Alvord, *Lord Shelburne and the Founding of British American Goodwill* (London, 1926); Samuel F. Bemis, *The Hussey-Cumberland Mission and American Independence: An Essay in the Diplomacy of the American Revolution* (Princeton, 1931); Thomas P. Abernethy, *Western Lands and the American Revolution* (New York, 1937); Lawrence H. Gipson, *The Triumphant Empire: Thunder-Clouds Gather in the West, 1763–1766* (New York, 1961); Isabel de Madariaga, *Britain, Russia, and the Armed Neutrality of 1780: Sir James Harris's Mission to St. Petersburg During the American Revolution* (New Haven, 1962); and Jack M. Sosin, *Whitehall and the Wilderness: The Middle West in British Colonial Policy, 1760–1775* (Lincoln, Neb., 1969).

For French diplomacy, see Jonathan R. Dull, *The French Navy and American Independence: A Study of Arms and Diplomacy, 1774–1787* (Princeton, 1976); William C. Stinchcombe, *The American Revolution and the French Alliance* (Syracuse, N.Y., 1969); John J. Meng, *The Comte de Vergennes: European Phases of His American Diplomacy (1774–1780)* (Washington, 1932); and Edward S. Corwin, *French Policy and the American Alliance of 1778* (Princeton, 1916). For relations with Spain, Holland, Russia, and Germany, see Parker B. Thomson, *Spain: Forgotten Ally of the American Revolution* (North Quincy, Mass., 1976); Friedrich Edler, *The Dutch Republic and the American Revolution* (Baltimore, 1911); Nikolai N. Bolkhovitinov, *The Beginnings of Russian-American Relations, 1775–1815*, trans. Elena Levin (Cambridge, Mass., 1975); and Horst Dippel, *Germany and the American Revolution, 1770–1800: A Sociohistorical Investigation of Late Eighteenth Century Political Thinking*, trans. Bernard A. Uhlendorf. (Chapel Hill, N.C., 1977).

Useful biographical studies are Carl Van Doren, *Benjamin Franklin* (New York, 1938); Gerald Stourzh, *Benjamin Franklin and American Foreign Policy* (1954; 2nd ed., Chicago, 1969); Claude-Anne Lopez, *Mon Cher Papa: Franklin and the Ladies of Paris* (New Haven, 1966); Roger Burlingame, *Benjamin Franklin: Envoy Extraordinary* (New York, 1967); Cecil B. Currey, *Road to Revolution: Benjamin Franklin in England, 1765–1775* (Garden City, N.Y., 1968); Currey, *Code Number 72: Ben Franklin, Patriot or Spy?* (Englewood Cliffs, N.J. 1972), which is critical; David Schoenbrun, *Triumph in Paris: The Exploits of Benjamin Franklin* (New York, 1976); William E. O'Donnell, *The Chevalier de la Luzerne: French Minister to the United States, 1779–1784* (Bruges, 1938); Frank Monaghan, *John Jay* (New York, 1935); Page Smith, *John Adams* (2 vols., Garden City, N.Y., 1962); and Oliver P. Chitwood, *Richard Henry Lee: Statesman of the Revolution* (Morgantown, W. Virginia, 1967).

CHAPTER THREE

For analyses of the Confederation period, constitution making, and foreign relations, see Abraham D. Sofaer, *War, Foreign Affairs and Constitutional Power: The Origins* (Cambridge, Mass., 1976); Merrill Jensen, *The New Nation: A History of the United States during the Confederation 1781–1789* (New York, 1950); Gordon S. Wood, *The Creation of the American Republic, 1776–1787* (Williamsburg, Va., 1969); and Frederick W. Marks, *Independence on Trial: Foreign Affairs and the Making of the Constitution* (Baton Rouge, La., 1973).

Good accounts of politics and diplomacy in the Federalist years are in Arthur B. Darling, *Our Rising Empire;* Manning J. Dauer, *The Adams Federalists* (Baltimore, 1953); Nathan Schachner, *The Founding Fathers* (New York, 1954); Joseph Charles, *The Origins of the American Party System* (Williamsburg, Va., 1956); John C. Miller, *The Federalist Era, 1789–1801* (New York, 1960); Paul A. Varg, *Foreign Policies of the Founding Fathers* (East Lansing, Mich., 1963); and Lawrence S. Kaplan, *Colonies into Nation.*

On relations with Great Britain, see Samuel F. Bemis, *Jay's Treaty: A Study in Commerce and Diplomacy* (1923; 2nd ed., New York, 1962); Alfred L. Burt, *The United States, Great Britain and British North America from the Revolution to the Establishment of Peace after the War of 1812* (New Haven, 1940); Bradford Perkins, *The First Rapprochement: England and the United States, 1795–1805* (Philadelphia, 1955); Joanne L. Neel, *Phineas Bond: A Study in Anglo-American Relations, 1786–1812,* (Philadelphia, 1968); Jack L. Cross, *London Mission: The First Critical Years* (East Lansing, Mich., 1968); Helen Looze, *Alexander Hamilton and the British Orientation of American Foreign Policy, 1793–1803* (The Hague, 1969); Charles Ritcheson, *Aftermath of Revolution: British Policy Toward the United States, 1783–1795* (Dallas, 1969); Jerald A. Combs, *The Jay Treaty: Political Battleground of the Founding Fathers* (Berkeley, Calif., 1970); and J. Leitch Wright, Jr., *Britain and the American Frontier, 1783–1815* (Athens, Ga., 1975).

For relations with France, see Charles D. Hazen, *Contemporary American Opinion of the French Revolution* (Baltimore, 1897); Beverly W. Bond, *The Monroe Mission to France, 1794–1796* (Baltimore, 1907); Gardner W. Allen, *Our Naval War with France* (Boston, 1909); Durand Echeverria, *Mirage in the West: A History of the French Image of American Society to 1815* (Princeton, 1957); Alexander DeConde, *Entangling Alliance: Politics and Diplomacy under George Washington* (Durham, N.C., 1958); DeConde, *The Quasi-War: The Politics and Diplomacy of the Undeclared War with France, 1797–1801* (New York, 1966); Louis M. Sears, *George Washington and the French Revolution* (Detroit, 1960); Lawrence S. Kaplan, *Jefferson and France: An Essay on Politics and Political Ideas* (New Haven, 1967); Peter P. Hill, *William Vans Murray, Federalist Diplomat: The Shaping of Peace with France, 1797–1801* (Syracuse, N.Y. 1971); Harry Ammon, *The Genet Mission* (New York, 1973); and Albert H. Bowman, *The Struggle for Neutrality: Franco-American Diplomacy during the Federalist Era* (Knoxville, Tenn., 1974).

Important studies on relations with Spain are Samuel F. Bemis, *Pinckney's Treaty* (Baltimore, 1926); Arthur P. Whitaker, *The Spanish-American Frontier, 1783–1795: The Westward Movement and the Spanish Retreat in the Mississippi Valley* (Boston, 1927); Whitaker, *The Mississippi Question, 1795–1803: A Study in Trade, Politics and Diplomacy* (1934; reprinted, New York, 1962); Warren L. Cook, *Flood Tide of Empire: Spain and the Pacific Northwest, 1543–1819* (New Haven, 1973); and Lester D. Langley, *Struggle for the American Mediterranean: United States European Rivalry in the Gulf-Caribbean, 1776–1904* (Athens, Ga., 1975).

Noteworthy special and biographical studies are Charles M. Thomas, *American Neutrality in 1793: A Study in Cabinet Government* (New York, 1931); Charles S.

Hyneman, *The First American Neutrality: A Study of the American Understanding of Neutral Obligations during the Years 1792 to 1815* (Urbana, Ill., 1934); Vernon G. Setser, *The Commercial Reciprocity Policy of the United States, 1774–1829* (Philadelphia, 1937); Frederick B. Tolles, *George Logan of Philadelphia* (New York, 1953); Stephen F. Kurtz, *The Presidency of John Adams: The Collapse of Federalism, 1795–1800* (Philadelphia, 1957); Marshall Smelser, *The Congress Founds the Navy, 1787–1798* (Notre Dame, Ind., 1959); Henry M. Adams, *Prussian-American Relations, 1775–1871* (Cleveland, 1960); Felix Gilbert, *To the Farewell Address;* Julian P. Boyd, *Number 7: Alexander Hamilton's Secret Attempts to Control American Foreign Policy* (Princeton, 1964); Alfred W. Crosby, Jr., *America, Russia, Hemp, and Napoleon: American Trade with Russia and the Baltic, 1783–1812* (Columbus, Ohio, 1965); Marvin Zahniser, *Charles Cotesworth Pinckney: Founding Father* (Chapel Hill, N.C., 1967); Robert Ernst, *Rufus King: American Federalist* (Chapel Hill, N.C., 1968); Gerard H. Clarfield, *Timothy Pickering and American Diplomacy, 1795–1800* (Columbia, Mo., 1969); Gilbert L. Lycan, *Alexander Hamilton and American Foreign Policy: A Design for Greatness* (Norman, Okla., 1970); and Gerald Stourzh, *Alexander Hamilton and the Idea of Republican Government* (Stanford, Calif., 1970). See also pertinent works cited in the previous chapter.

CHAPTER FOUR

Although superseded in particulars, Henry Adams, *History of the United States of America during the Administrations of Jefferson and Madison* (9 vols., New York, 1889–1909) remains a basic work for this period. Its first four volumes deal with Jefferson's diplomacy. For fullest scholarly coverage of Jefferson and Madison in these years, see Dumas Malone, *Jefferson the President: First Term, 1801–1805* (Boston, 1970); Malone, *Jefferson the President: Second Term, 1805–1809* (Boston, 1974); and Irving Brant, *James Madison: Secretary of State, 1800–1809* (Indianapolis, 1953). See also Doris Graber, *Public Opinion, the President, and Foreign Policy: Four Case Studies from the Formative Years* (New York, 1968).

On the acquisition of Louisiana, see Alexander DeConde, *This Affair of Louisiana* (New York, 1976); Arthur P. Whitaker, *The Mississippi Question, 1795–1803* (New York, 1934); E. Wilson Lyon, *Louisiana in French Diplomacy, 1759–1804* (Norman, Okla., 1934, 1974), the most important studies dealing directly with the subject. Other pertinent books are: Charles C. Tansill, *The United States and Santo Domingo, 1798–1873* (Baltimore, 1938); Rayford W. Logan, *The Diplomatic Relations of the United States with Haiti, 1776–1891* (Chapel Hill, N.C., 1941); Ralph Korngold, *Citizen Toussaint* (New York, 1944, 1965); and George Dangerfield, *Chancellor Robert R. Livingston of New York, 1746–1813* (New York, 1960).

For Barbary warfare and diplomacy, see Ray W. Irwin, *The Diplomatic Relations of the United States with the Barbary Pirates, 1776–1816* (Chapel Hill, N.C., 1931); H. G. Barnby, *The Prisoners of Algiers: An Account of the Forgotten American-Algerian War, 1785–1797* (New York, 1966); Glenn Tucker, *Dawn Like Thunder: The Barbary Wars and the Birth of the U.S. Navy* (Indianapolis, 1963); Raymond W. Bixler, *The Open Door on the Old Barbary Coast* (New York, 1959); Louis B. Wright and Julia H. McLeod, *The First Americans in North Africa: William Eaton's Struggle for a Vigorous Policy against the Barbary Pirates, 1799–1805* (Princeton, 1945); and Gardner W. Allen, *Our Navy and the Barbary Corsairs* (Boston, 1905). Also important, but more for background and enrichment, are James Woodress, *A Yankee's Odyssey: The Life of Joel Barlow* (Philadelphia, 1958); David H. Finnie, *Pioneers East: The Early American Experience in the Middle East* (Cambridge, Mass.,

1967); and James A. Field, Jr., *America and the Mediterranean World, 1776–1886* (Princeton, 1969).

For maritime and other problems, see Bradford Perkins, *Prologue to War: England and the United States, 1805–1812* (Berkeley, Calif., 1961); Louis M. Sears, *Jefferson and the Embargo* (Durham, N.C., 1927); Walter W. Jennings, *The American Embargo, 1807–1809* (Iowa City, 1921); Robert G. Albion and Jennie B. Pope, *Sea Lanes in Wartime: The American Experience, 1775–1942* (New York, 1942); Eli F. Heckscher, *The Continental System: An Economic Interpretation* (Oxford, 1922); James F. Zimmerman, *Impressment of American Seamen* (New York, 1925); and I-Mien Tsiang, *The Question of Expatriation in America Prior to 1907* (Baltimore, 1942). See also pertinent studies by Burt, Darling, and Perkins cited for previous chapters.

CHAPTER FIVE

The second half of Henry Adams, *History of the United States,* offers a readable, detailed account of the politics and diplomacy of the war, but later studies have superseded important aspects of its scholarship. The most noteworthy of these are: Bradford Perkins, *Prologue to War: England and the United States, 1805–1812* (Berkeley, Calif., 1961) and *Castlereagh and Adams: England and the United States, 1812–1823* (Berkeley, Calif., 1964), now standard accounts; Reginald Horsman, *The Causes of the War of 1812* (Philadelphia, 1962); Roger H. Brown, *The Republic in Peril: 1812* (New York, 1964); Julius W. Pratt, *Expansionists of 1812* (New York, 1925), which advances the western war hawk theory; and Alfred L. Burt, *The United States, Great Britain, and British North America from the Revolution to the Establishment of Peace after the War of 1812* (New Haven, 1940). For the diplomacy of peacemaking, see Fred L. Engelman, *The Peace of Christmas Eve* (New York, 1962); Samuel F. Bemis, *John Quincy Adams and the Foundations of American Foreign Policy* (New York, 1949); and Frank A. Updyke, *The Diplomacy of the War of 1812* (Baltimore, 1915). Two scholarly military histories of note are: John K. Mahon, *The War of 1812* (Gainesville, Fla., 1972) and Reginald Horsman, *The War of 1812* (New York, 1969).

Other specialized studies or useful syntheses are: Victor A. Sapio, *Pennsylvania and the War of 1812* (Lexington, Ky., 1970); Samuel E. Morison, Frederick Merk, and Frank Freidel, *Dissent in Three American Wars* (Cambridge, Mass., 1970); Harry L. Coles, *The War of 1812* (Chicago, 1965); J. Mackay Hitsman, *The Incredible War of 1812* (Toronto, 1965); Patrick C. J. White, *A Nation on Trial: America and the War of 1812* (New York, 1965); Philip P. Mason, ed., *After Tippecanoe: Some Aspects of the War of 1812* (East Lansing, Mich., 1963); Alec R. Gilpin, *The War of 1812 in the Old Northwest* (East Lansing, Mich., 1958); and Alfred T. Mahan, *Sea Power in Its Relation to the War of 1812* (2 vols., Boston, 1905).

Noteworthy biographical studies are: Irving Brant, *James Madison: The President, 1809–1812* (Indianapolis, 1956); Brant, *James Madison: Commander-in-Chief, 1812–1836* (Indianapolis, 1961); Harry Ammon, *James Monroe: The Quest for National Identity* (New York, 1971); Raymond Walters, Jr., *Albert Gallatin: Jeffersonian Financier and Diplomat* (New York, 1957); Morton Borden, *The Federalism of James A. Bayard* (New York, 1955); and Bernard Mayo, *Henry Clay: Spokesman of the New West* (Boston, 1937).

CHAPTER SIX

Monographs and scholarly syntheses for the diplomacy and politics of the period are: Samuel F. Bemis, *John Quincy Adams and the Foundations of American*

Diplomacy (New York, 1949); Bradford Perkins, *Castlereagh and Adams: England and the United States, 1812–1823* (Berkeley, Calif., 1964); George Dangerfield, *The Era of Good Feelings* (New York, 1952); Dangerfield, *The Awakening of American Nationalism, 1815–1828* (New York, 1965); and William H. Goetzmann, *When the Eagle Screamed: The Romantic Horizon in American Diplomacy, 1800–1860* (New York, 1966).

For the Florida diplomacy see Robert W. Remini, *Andrew Jackson and the Course of American Empire, 1767–1821* (New York, 1977); Wanjohi Waciuma, *Intervention in Spanish Floridas 1801–1813; A Study in Jeffersonian Foreign Policy* (Boston, 1976); Rembert W. Patrick, *Florida Fiasco: Rampant Rebels on the Georgia-Florida Border, 1810–1815* (Athens, Ga., 1954); Philip C. Brooks, *Diplomacy and the Borderlands: The Adams-Onís Treaty of 1819* (Berkeley, Calif., 1936); Isaac J. Cox, *The West Florida Controversy, 1798–1813: A Study in American Diplomacy* (Baltimore, 1918); and Herbert B. Fuller, *The Purchase of Florida: Its History and Diplomacy* (Cleveland, 1906).

Noteworty studies dealing with recognition and other problems concerning the Latin American revolutions are: Edward B. Billingsley, *In Defense of Neutral Rights: The United States Navy and the Wars of Independence in Chile and Peru* (Chapel Hill, N.C., 1967); Harold F. Peterson, *Argentina and the United States, 1810–1960* (New York, 1964); Arthur P. Whitaker, *The United States and the Independence of Latin America, 1800–1830* (Baltimore, 1941); William S. Robertson, *France and Latin-American Independence* (Baltimore, 1939); Charles C. Griffin, *The United States and the Disruption of the Spanish Empire, 1810–1822* (New York, 1937); and J. Fred Rippy, *Rivalry of the United States and Great Britain over Latin America, 1808–1830* (Baltimore, 1929).

For the Monroe Doctrine the standard one-volume survey is Dexter Perkins, *A History of the Monroe Doctrine* (rev. ed., Boston, 1953), but more detailed and appropriate for this period is his *The Monroe Doctrine, 1823–1826* (Cambridge, Mass., 1927); and Ernest R. May, *The Making of the Monroe Doctrine* (Cambridge, Mass., 1975), which stresses the importance of domestic politics in shaping the doctrine. See also John A. Logan, *No Transfer: An American Security Principle* (New Haven, 1961) and Edward H. Tatum, *The United States and Europe, 1815–1823* (Berkeley, Calif., 1936); Walther Kirchner, *Studies in Russian-American Commerce, 1820–1860* (Leyden, 1975); Howard I. Kushner, *Conflict on the Northwest Coast: American-Russian Rivalry in the Pacific Northwest, 1790–1867* (Westport, Conn., 1975); Charles A. Manning, *Russian Influence on Early America* (New York, 1953); Semen B. Okun, *The Russian-American Company*, trans. from the Russian by Carl Ginsburg (Cambridge, Mass., 1951); and Benjamin P. Thomas, *Russo-American Relations, 1815–1867* (Baltimore, 1930). The influence of events in Greece is discussed in Joseph L. Grabill, *Protestant Diplomacy and the Near East: Missionary Influence on American Policy, 1810–1927* (Minneapolis, 1971); James A. Field, Jr., *America and the Mediterranean World 1776–1896* (Princeton, 1969); Stephen A. Larrabee, *Hellas Observed: The American Experience of Greece, 1775–1865* (New York, 1957); Harris J. Booras, *Hellenic Independence and America's Contribution to the Cause* (Rutland, Vt., 1936); and Myrtle A. Cline, *American Attitude toward the Greek War of Independence, 1821–1828* (Atlanta, Ga., 1930). Important biographical studies are: Harry Ammon, *James Monroe* and John H. Powell, *Richard Rush: Republican Diplomat, 1780–1859* (Philadelphia, 1942). See also pertinent titles cited for previous chapter.

CHAPTER SEVEN

Frank L. Benns, *The American Struggle for the British West India Carrying-Trade, 1815–1830* (Bloomington, Ind., 1923) gives the fullest coverage of the West Indies question. For the controversy with France, see Henry Blumenthal, *France and the United States: Their Diplomatic Relations, 1789–1914* (Chapel Hill, N.C., 1970); Blumenthal, *A Reappraisal of Franco-American Relations, 1830–1871* (Chapel Hill, N.C., 1959); and Richard A. McLemore, *Franco-American Diplomatic Relations, 1816–1836* (Baton Rouge, La., 1941). On relations with Africa, the slave trade and search at sea, see Alan R. Booth, *The United States Experience in South Africa, 1784–1870* (Capetown, 1976); Clarence C. Clendenen and Peter Duignan, *Americans in Black Africa up to 1865* (Stanford, Calif., 1964); Clendenen and Duignan, *The United States and the African Slave Trade, 1619–1862* (Stanford, Calif., 1963); Warren S. Howard, *American Slavers and the Federal Law, 1837–1862* (Berkeley, Calif., 1963); Hugh G. Soulsby, *The Right of Search and the Slave Trade in Anglo-American Relations, 1814–1862* (Baltimore, 1933); and William E. B. Dubois, *The Suppression of the African Slave Trade to the United States of America, 1638–1820* (New York, 1896).

For the issues of the Canadian frontier see Howard Jones, *To the Webster-Ashburton Treaty: A Study in Anglo-American Relations, 1783–1843* (Chapel Hill, N.C., 1977); Oscar A. Kinchen, *The Rise and Fall of the Patriot Hunters* (New York, 1956); Albert B. Corey, *The Crisis of 1830–1842 in Canadian-American Relations* (New Haven, 1941); and Samuel F. Bemis, *John Quincy Adams and the Foundations of American Foreign Policy* (New York, 1949). For the Oregon question, other aspects of Anglo-American relations, and manifest destiny, see David M. Pletcher, *The Diplomacy of Annexation: Texas, Oregon, and the Mexican War* (Columbia, Mo., 1973), the fullest scholarly study in a broad context; Frederick Merk, *Fruits of Propaganda in the Tyler Administration* (Cambridge, Mass., 1971); Merk, *The Oregon Question: Essays in Anglo-American Diplomacy and Politics* (Cambridge, Mass., 1967); Merk, *The Monroe Doctrine and American Expansionism, 1843–1849* (New York, 1966); Merk, *Manifest Destiny and Mission in American History: A Reinterpretation* (New York, 1963); Merk, *Albert Gallatin and the Oregon Problem* (Cambridge, Mass., 1950); Wilbur D. Jones, *The American Problem in British Diplomacy, 1841–1861* (Athens, Ga., 1974); Jones, *Lord Aberdeen and the Americas* (Athens, Ga., 1958); Edwin E. Rich, *Hudson's Bay Company, 1670–1870* (3 vols., New York, 1961) III, 657–734, dealing with the Oregon rivalry; John S. Galbraith, *The Hudson's Bay Company as an Imperial Factor, 1821–1869* (Berkeley, Calif., 1957); Norman A. Graebner, *Empire on the Pacific: A Study of American Continental Expansion* (New York, 1955); Melvin C. Jacobs, *Winning Oregon: A Study of an Expansionist Movement* (Caldwell, Idaho, 1938); Albert K. Weinberg, *Manifest Destiny: A Study of Nationalist Expansionism in American History* (Baltimore, 1935), a pioneer study in the influence of ideas on foreign policy; and Jesse S. Reeves, *American Diplomacy under Tyler and Polk* (Baltimore, 1907).

Two noteworthy general accounts are Charles S. Campbell, *From Revolution to Rapprochement: The United States and Great Britain, 1783–1900* (New York, 1974) and Kenneth Bourne, *Britain and the Balance of Power in North America, 1815–1908* (Berkeley, Calif., 1967). Useful biographical studies are: Charles Sellers, *James K. Polk: Continentalist, 1843–1846* (Princeton, 1966); Raymond Walters, Jr., *Albert Gallatin Jeffersonian Financier and Diplomat* (New York, 1957); Claude M. Fuess, *Daniel Webster and the Rise of National Conservatism* (New York, 1955); and Oliver P. Chitwood, *John Taylor: Champion of the Old South* (New York, 1939).

CHAPTER EIGHT

Many of the titles listed for the previous chapter are also pertinent to this one. For example, the best balanced scholarly study of the diplomacy of the Mexican War is David M. Pletcher's, *The Diplomacy of Annexation: Texas, Oregon and the Mexican War* (Columbia, Mo., 1973). Other important works are: Gene M. Brack, *Mexico Views Manifest Destiny, 1821–1846: An Essay on the Origins of the Mexican War* (Albuquerque, 1975); John H. Schroeder, *Mr. Polk's War: American Opposition and Dissent, 1846–1848* (Madison, Wis., 1973); Frederick Merk, *Slavery and the Annexation of Texas* (New York, 1972); Seymour V. Connor and Odie B. Faulk, *North America Divided: The Mexican War* (New York, 1971), which supports traditional American interpretations; Samuel E. Morison, Frederick Merk, and Frank Freidel, *Dissent in Three American Wars;* Glenn W. Price, *Origins of the War with Mexico: The Polk-Stockton Intrigue* (Austin, Tex., 1967), which stresses American intrigue; Otis A. Singletary, *The Mexican War* (Chicago, 1960), a brief synthesis; Thomas E. Cotner and Carlos E. Castañeda, eds., *Essays in Mexican History* (Austin, Tex., 1958); José Fernando Ramirez, *Mexico during the War with the United States,* Walter V. Scholes, ed., and Elliott B. Scherr, trans. (Columbia, Mo., 1950); Robert S. Henry, *The Story of the Mexican War* (Indianapolis, 1950) and Alfred H. Bill, *Rehearsal for Conflict* (New York, 1947), popular accounts; George L. Rives, *The United States and Mexico, 1821–1848* (2 vols., New York, 1913); Justin H. Smith, *The War with Mexico* (2 vols., New York, 1919), impressive in scholarship but marred by ethnocentric biases; and Ramón Alcaraz, *The Other Side: or Notes for the History of the War between Mexico and the United States,* Albert C. Ramsay, trans. and ed. (New York, 1850).

Important studies on more specialized topics are: George W. Smith and Charles Judah, eds., *Chronicles of the Gringos: The U.S. Army in the Mexican War, 1846–1848: Accounts of Eyewitnesses or Combatants* (Albuquerque, 1968); Joseph M. Nance, *Attack and Counterattack: The Texas-Mexican Frontier, 1842* (Austin, Tex., 1964) and *After San Jacinto: The Texas-Mexican Frontier, 1836–1841* (Austin, Tex., 1963); Stanley Siegel, *A Political History of the Texas Republic, 1836–1845* (Austin, Tex., 1956); William C. Binkley, *The Texas Revolution* (Baton Rouge, La., 1952); Joseph W. Schmitz, *Texan Statecraft, 1836–1845* (San Antonio, Tex., 1941); John D. P. Fuller, *The Movement for the Acquisition of All Mexico, 1846–1848* (Baltimore, 1936); Eugene C. Barker, *Mexico and Texas, 1821–1835* (Dallas, 1928); Robert G. Cleland, *Early Sentiment for the Annexation of California, 1835–1846* (Austin, Tex., 1915); Justin H. Smith, *The Annexation of Texas* (New York, 1911); and Ephraim D. Adams, *British Interests and Activities in Texas, 1838–1846* (Baltimore, 1910).

Biographical studies of consequence are: Charles G. Sellers, *James K. Polk: Continentalist, 1843–1846* (Princeton, 1966); Samuel F. Bemis, *John Quincy Adams and the Union* (New York, 1956); Ilerena Friend, *Sam Houston: The Great Designer* (Austin, Tex., 1954); Wilfrid H. Calcott, *Santa Anna* (Norman, Okla., 1936); Marquis James, *The Raven: A Biography of Sam Houston* (Indianapolis, 1937); Allan Nevins, *Frémont: The West's Greatest Adventurer* (2 vols., New York, 1928); Eugene C. Barker, *The Life of Stephen F. Austin* (Nashville, 1925); and Eugene I. McCormac, *James K. Polk: A Political Biography* (Berkeley, Calif., 1922).

CHAPTER NINE

For rivalry over Central America, see Robert E. May, *The Southern Dream of a Caribbean Empire, 1854–1861* (Baton Rouge, La., 1973); Mario Rodríguez, *A Palmerstonian Diplomat in Central America: Frederick Chatfield, Esq.* (Tucson, Ariz.,

1964); Albert H. Carr, *The World of William Walker* (New York, 1963); Thomas L. Karnes, *The Failure of Union: Central America, 1824–1860* (Chapel Hill, N.C., 1961); Lawrence Greene, *The Filibuster: The Career of William Walker* (Indianapolis, 1937); William O. Scroggs, *Filibusters and Financiers: The Story of William Walker and His Associates* (New York, 1916); Mary W. Williams, *Anglo-American Diplomacy, 1815–1915* (Washington, 1916); and Ira D. Travis, *The History of the Clayton-Bulwer Treaty* (Ann Arbor, Mich., 1900). On relations with Mexico see Agustín Cue Cánovas, *El Tratado McLane Ocampo: Juárez, los Estados Unidos y Europa* (2nd ed., Mexico City, 1959); Dexter Perkins, *The Monroe Doctrine, 1826–1867* (Baltimore, 1933); James M. Callahan, *American Foreign Policy in Mexican Relations* (New York, 1932); J. Fred Rippy, *The United States and Mexico* (New York, 1926); and Paul N. Garber, *The Gadsden Treaty* (Philadelphia, 1923).

Canadian relations are covered in Keith A. Murray, *The Pig War* (Tacoma, Wash., 1968), which deals with a confrontation on San Juan Island, 1859; Alvin C. Gluck, Jr., *Minnesota and the Manifest Destiny of the Canadian Northwest: A Study in Canadian-American Relations* (Toronto, 1965); Donald F. Warner, *The Idea of Continental Union: Agitation for the Annexation of Canada to the United States, 1849–1893* (Lexington, Ky., 1960), the most thorough treatment of the subject; Donald C. Masters, *The Reciprocity of 1854* (London, 1937); Lester B. Shippee, *Canadian-American Relations, 1849–1874* (New Haven, 1939); Charles C. Tansill, *The Canadian Reciprocity Treaty of 1854* (Baltimore, 1922); and Cephas D. Allin and George M. Jones, *Annexation, Preferential Trade, and Reciprocity: An Outline of the Canadian Annexation Movement of 1849–50* (Toronto, 1911).

On the problems of neutrality, young America, Europe, and Cuba, see Donald M. Spencer, *Louis Kossuth and Young America: A Study of Sectionalism and Foreign Policy, 1848–1852* (Columbia, Mo., 1977); Alan Dowty, *The Limits of American Isolationism: The United States and the Crimean War* (New York, 1971); Alexander DeConde, *Half Bitter, Half Sweet: An Excursion into Italian-American History* (New York, 1971); Andor Klay, *Daring Diplomacy: The Case of the First American Ultimatum* (Minneapolis, 1957), which deals with the Koszta case; Howard R. Marraro, *American Opinion on the Unification of Italy, 1846–1861* (New York, 1932); Marraro, ed., *Diplomatic Relations between the United States and the Kingdom of the Two Sicilies, 1816–1861* (2 vols., New York, 1951); Arthur J. May, *Contemporary American Opinion of the Mid-Century Revolutions in Central Europe* (Philadelphia, 1927); John G. Gazley, *American Opinion of German Unification, 1848–1871* (New York, 1926); Hugh Thomas, *Cuba: The Pursuit of Freedom* (New York, 1971); Lester D. Langley, *The Cuban Policy of the United States: A Brief History* (New York, 1968); Philip S. Foner, *A History of Cuba and Its Relations with the United States* (2 vols., New York, 1962–63); Basil Rauch, *American Interest in Cuba, 1848–1855* (New York, 1948); Amos A. Ettinger, *The Mission to Spain of Pierre Soulé, 1853–1855* (New Haven, 1932); Herminio Portell Vilá, *Narciso López y su Época* (La Habana, 1930); and Robert G. Caldwell, *The López Expeditions to Cuba, 1848–1851* (Princeton, 1915).

On the relationship with China, see Robert A. Hart, *The Eccentric Tradition: American Diplomacy in the Far East* (New York, 1976); Peter W. Fay, *The Opium War, 1840–1842: Barbarians in the Celestial Empire in the Early Part of the Nineteenth Century and the War by Which They Forced Her Gates Ajar* (Chapel Hill, N.C., 1975); John K. Fairbank, ed., *The Missionary Enterprise in China and America* (Cambridge, Mass., 1974); Edward V. Gulick, *Peter Parker and the Opening of China* (Cambridge, Mass., 1973); Warren I. Cohen, *America's Response to China: An Interpretive History of Sino-American Relations* (New York, 1971); Christopher Hibbert, *The Dragon Wakes: China and the West, 1793–1911* (London, 1970); Clifton J. Phillips, *Protestant America and the Pagan World: The First Half Century of the Ameri-*

can Board of Commissioners for Foreign Missions, 1810–1860 (Cambridge, Mass., 1969); Te-kong Tong, United States Diplomacy in China, 1844–1860 (Seattle, 1964); George H. Dunne, Generation of Giants: The Story of the Jesuits in China in the Last Decades of the Ming Dynasty,(Notre Dame, Ind., 1962); Kwang-Ching Liu, Anglo-American Steamship Rivalry in China, 1862–1874 (Cambridge, Mass., 1962); John K. Fairbank, Trade and Diplomacy on the China Coast: The Opening of the Treaty Ports, 1842–1854 (Cambridge, Mass., 1953); Earl Swisher, China's Management of the American Barbarians: A Study of Sino-American Relations, 1841–1861, with Documents (New Haven, 1953); Maurice Collis, Foreign Mud: Being an Account of the Opium Imbroglio at Canton in the 1830s and the Anglo-Chinese War that Followed (New York, 1947); Foster Rhea Dulles, China and America: The Story of Their Relations since 1784 (Princeton, 1946); Dulles, The Old China Trade (Boston, 1930); Paul H. Clyde, ed., United States Policy Toward China: Diplomatic and Public Documents, 1838–1939 (Durham, N.C., 1940); George H. Danton, The Cultural Contacts of the United States and China: The Earliest Sino-American Contacts, 1784–1844 (New York, 1931); Kenneth S. Latourette, The History of Early Relations between the United States and China, 1784–1844 (New Haven, 1917); and Frederick W. Williams, Anson Burlingame and the First Chinese Mission to Foreign Powers (1912; reissued, New York, 1972).

For Japan, see Richard J. Chang, From Prejudice to Tolerance: A Study of the Japanese Image of the West, 1826–1864 (Tokyo, 1970); Oliver Statler, Shimoda Story (New York, 1969), a study from Japanese sources of Townsend Harris's mission; Matthew C. Perry, The Japan Expedition 1852–1854: The Personal Journal of Commodore Matthew C. Perry, Roger Pineau, ed. (Washington, D.C., 1969); Foster Rhea Dulles, Yankees and Samurai: America's Role in the Emergence of Japan, 1791–1900 (New York, 1965); William L. Neumann, America Encounters Japan: From Perry to MacArthur (Baltimore, 1963); Hikomatsu Kamikawa, ed., Japan-American Relations in the Meiji-Taisho Era, Kimura Michiko, trans. (Tokyo, 1958); Robert S. Schwantes, Japanese and Americans: A Century of Cultural Relations (New York, 1955); Lawrence H. Battistini, Japan and America: From Earliest Times to the Present (New York, 1954); Henry F. Graff, Bluejackets with Perry in Japan (New York, 1952); Chitoshi Yanaga, Japan Since Perry (New York, 1949); Arthur Walworth, Black Ships off Japan: The Story of Commodore Perry's Expedition (New York, 1946); Payson J. Treat, Diplomatic Relations between the United States and Japan, 1853–1895 (2 vols., Stanford, Calif., 1932); and Inazo Nitobe, The Intercourse between the United States and Japan: An Historical Sketch (Baltimore, 1891).

Accounts of the thrust into the Pacific and Asia are: James Kirker, Adventures to China: Americans in the Southern Oceans, 1792–1812 (New York, 1970); Richard O'Connor, Pacific Destiny: An Informal History of the U.S. in the Far East, 1776–1968 (Boston, 1969); Lawrence H. Battistini, The Rise of American Influence in Asia and the Pacific (East Lansing, Mich., 1960); Battistini, The United States and Asia (New York, 1955); Eldon Griffin, Clippers and Consuls: American Consular and Commercial Relations with Eastern Asia, 1845–1860 (Ann Arbor, Mich., 1938); Tyler Dennett, Americans in Eastern Asia: A Critical Study of United States' Policy in the Far East in the Nineteenth Century (New York, 1922); and John W. Foster, American Diplomacy in the Orient (Boston, 1903).

Pertinent biographical studies are: Samuel E. Morison, "Old Bruin": Commodore Matthew C. Perry (Boston, 1967); Ivor D. Spencer, The Victor and the Spoils: A Life of William L. Marcy (Providence, R.I., 1959); Roy F. Nichols, Franklin Pierce: Young Hickory of the Granite Hills (2nd ed., Philadelphia, 1958); Michael Catherine Hodgson, Caleb Cushing: Attorney General of the United States, 1853–1857 (Washington, 1955); Carl Crow, He Opened the Door of Japan (New York, 1939), on Townsend Harris; Claude M. Fuess, The Life of Caleb Cushing (2 vols., New York,

1923); and John F. H. Claiborne, *Life and Correspondence of John A. Quitman* (2 vols., New York, 1860).

CHAPTER TEN

A fine scholarly synthesis that places Civil War diplomacy in an international setting is David P. Crook, *The North, the South, and the Powers, 1861–1865* (New York, 1974), abridged as *Diplomacy During the American Civil War* (New York, 1975). See also essays in Harold Hyman, ed., *Heard Round the World: The Impact Abroad of the Civil War* (New York, 1969); Philip Van Doren Stern, *When the Guns Roared: World Aspects of the American Civil War* (Garden City, N.Y., 1965), a popular synthesis; Frank L. Owsley, *King Cotton Diplomacy: Foreign Relations of the Confederate States of America*, rev. by Harriet C. Owsley (2nd ed., Chicago, 1959); Jay Monaghan, *Diplomat in Carpet Shippers: Abraham Lincoln Deals with Foreign Affairs* (Indianapolis, 1945), which covers Union diplomacy; and Donaldson Jordan and Edwin J. Pratt, *Europe and the American Civil War* (Boston, 1931).

Specialized studies that concentrate on Anglo-American relations are: Norman B. Ferris, *The Trent Affair: A Diplomatic Crisis (Knoxville, Tenn., 1977)*; Ferris, *Desperate Diplomacy: William H. Seward's Foreign Policy, 1861* (Knoxville, Tenn., 1976); Richard I. Lester, *Confederate Finance and Purchasing in Great Britain* (Charlottesville, Va., 1975); Brian Jenkins, *Britain and the War for the Union* (Montreal, 1974); Mary L. Ellison, *Support for Secession: Lancashire and the American Civil War* (Chicago, 1972); Stuart L. Bernath, *Squall Across the Atlantic: American Civil War Prize Cases and Diplomacy* (Berkeley, Calif., 1970); Frank J. Merli, *Great Britain and the Confederate Navy, 1861–1865* (Bloomington, Ind., 1970); Wilbur D. Jones, *The Confederate Rams at Birkenhead: A Chapter in Anglo-American Relations* (Tuscaloosa, Ala., 1961); Evan John [E. J. Simpson], *Atlantic Impact, 1861* (London, 1952), which deals with the *Trent* affair; William O. Henderson, *The Lancashire Cotton Famine, 1861–1865* (Manchester, England, 1934); Ephraim D. Adams, *Great Britain and the American Civil War* (2 vols., London, 1925); and Thomas L. Harris, *The Trent Affair* (Indianapolis, 1896).

On relations with France the best scholarly account is Lynn M. Case and Warren F. Spencer, *The United States and France: Civil War Diplomacy* (Philadelphia, 1970). See also Daniel B. Carroll, *Henri Mercier and the American Civil War* (Princeton, 1971); Henry Blumenthal, *France and the United States: Their Diplomatic Relations, 1789–1914* (Chapel Hill, N.C., 1970); Blumenthal, *A Reappraisal of Franco-American Relations, 1830–1871* (Chapel Hill, N.C., 1959); and Serge Gavronsky, *The French Liberal Opposition and the American Civil War* (New York, 1968). Other noteworthy special studies are: Charles P. Cullop, *Confederate Propaganda in Europe, 1861–1865* (Coral Gables, Fla., 1969); Joseph M. Hernon, Jr., *Celts, Catholics and Copperheads: Ireland Views the American Civil War* (Columbus, Ohio, 1968); Raimondo Luraghi, *Storia della guerra civile americana* (Turin, 1966), which places the conflict in the setting of European revolutionary upheaval; John H. Franklin, *The Emancipation Proclamation* (Garden City, N.Y., 1963); A. R. Tyrner-Tyrnauer, *Lincoln and the Emperors* (New York, 1962); Mary P. Trauth, *Italo-American Diplomatic Relations, 1861–1882: The Mission of George Perkins Marsh, First American Minister to the Kingdom of Italy* (Washington, 1958); Albert A. Woldman, *Lincoln and the Russians* (Cleveland, 1952); Thomas A. Bailey, *America Faces Russia: Russian-American Relations from Early Times to Our Day* (Ithaca, N.Y., 1950); George W. Dalzell, *The Flight from the Flag: The Continuing Effect of the Civil War upon the American Carrying Trade* (Chapel Hill, N.C., 1940); Carlton Savage, *Policy of the United States toward Maritime Commerce in War* (Washington,

1934); and James M. Callahan, *The Diplomatic History of the Southern Confederacy* (Baltimore, 1901).

For pertinent biographical studies see John Niven, *Gideon Welles: Lincoln's Secretary of the Navy* (New York, 1973); David Donald, *Charles Sumner and the Rights of Man* (New York, 1970); Glyndon G. Van Deusen, *William Henry Seward* (New York, 1967); Martin B. Duberman, *Charles Francis Adams, 1807–1886* (Boston, 1961); James G. Randall, *Lincoln the President* (4 vols., New York, 1945–55), of which the fourth volume was written mostly by Richard N. Current; Margaret A. Clapp, *Forgotten First Citizen: John Bigelow* (Boston, 1947); Robert D. Meade, *Judah P. Benjamin: Confederate Statesman* (New York, 1943); and Henry Adams, *The Education of Henry Adams* (Boston, 1918).

CHAPTER ELEVEN

Charles S. Campbell, *The Transformation of American Foreign Relations, 1865–1900* (New York, 1976) is a synthesis that attempts to explain expansionism, as does Robert Beisner, *From the Old Diplomacy to the New, 1865–1900* (New York, 1975), in much briefer form. Works that stress continuity in American expansionism provided by economic motivation are: Ernest N. Paolino, *The Foundations of American Empire: William Henry Seward and U.S. Foreign Policy* (Ithaca, N.Y., 1973); Howard B. Schonberger, *Transportation to the Seaboard: The "Communication Revolution" and American Foreign Policy, 1860–1900* (Westport, Conn., 1971); William A. Williams, *The Roots of the Modern American Empire: A Study of the Growth and Shaping of Social Consciousness in a Marketplace Society* (New York, 1969); and Walter La Feber, *The New Empire: An Interpretation of American Expansion, 1860–1898* (Ithaca, N.Y., 1956). For analyses of the same theme, but without the economic stress, see Milton Plesur, *America's Outward Thrust: Approaches to Foreign Affairs, 1865–1890* (De Kalb, Ill., 1971) and Joe Patterson Smith, *The Republican Expansionists of the Early Reconstruction Era* (Chicago, 1933).

On the Spanish and French interventions, Santo Domingo, and Mexico, see Dexter Perkins, *The Monroe Doctrine, 1826–1867* (Baltimore, 1933); Perkins, *The Monroe Doctrine, 1867–1907* (Baltimore, 1937); William C. Davis, *The Last Conquistadores: The Spanish Intervention in Peru and Chile, 1863–1866* (Athens, Ga., 1950); Rayford W. Logan, *The Diplomatic Relations of the United States with Haiti, 1776–1891* (Chapel Hill, N.C., 1941); Ludwell L. Montague, *Haiti and the United States, 1714–1938* (Durham, N.C., 1940); Charles C. Tansill, *The United States and Santo Domingo, 1798–1873: A Chapter in Caribbean History* (Baltimore, 1938); Alfred J. and Kathryn A. Hanna, *Napoleon III and Mexico: American Triumph over Monarchy* (Chapel Hill, N.C., 1971); Carl H. Bock, *Prelude to Tragedy: The Negotiation and Breakdown of the Tripartite Convention of London, October 31, 1861* (Philadelphia, 1966); Agustín Cue Cánovas, *El Tratado McLane-Ocampo: Juarez, los Estados Unidos y Europa* (2nd ed., Mexico City, 1959); Harford M. Hyde, *Mexican Empire: The History of Maximilian and Carlota of Mexico* (London, 1946); Lynn M. Case, ed., *French Opinion on the United States and Mexico, 1860–1867* (New York, 1936); James M. Callahan, *American Foreign Policy in Mexican Relations* (New York, 1932); Frank E. Lally, *French Opposition to the Mexican Policy of the Second Empire* (Baltimore, 1931); Egon C. Corti, *Maximilian and Charlotte of Mexico*, trans. from the German (2 vols., New York, 1928); and Warren R. West, *Contemporary French Opinion of the American Civil War* (Baltimore, 1924).

For the purchase of Alaska and Russian relations, see Ronald J. Jensen, *The Alaska Purchase and Russian-American Relations* (Seattle, 1975); Howard I. Kushner, *Conflict on the Northwest Coast: American-Russian Rivalry in the Pacific Northwest,*

1790–1867 (Westport, Conn., 1975); Archie W. Shiels, *The Purchase of Alaska* (College, Alaska, 1967); Hector Chevigny, *Russian America: The Great Alaskan Venture, 1741–1867* (New York, 1965); Thomas A. Bailey, *America Faces Russia* (Ithaca, N.Y., 1950); Foster Rhea Dulles, *The Road to Teheran* (Princeton, 1944); Victor J. Farrar, *The Annexation of Russian America to the United States* (Washington, 1937); Farrar, *The Purchase of Alaska* (Washington, 1935); and Benjamin P. Thomas, *Russo-American Relations, 1815–1867* (Baltimore, 1930).

On relations with Britain and Canada, see Richard A. Preston, *The Defence of the Undefended Border: Planning for War in North America 1867–1939* (Quebec, 1977); Adrian Cook, *The Alabama Claims: American Politics and Anglo-American Relations, 1865–1872* (Ithaca, N.Y., 1975); Leon Ó Broin, *Fenian Fever: Anglo-American Dilemma* (N.Y., 1971); Brian Jenkins, *Fenians and Anglo-American Relations during Reconstruction* (Ithaca, N.Y., 1969); Mabel G. Walker, *The Fenian Movement* (Colorado Springs, 1969); Kenneth Bourne, *Britain and the Balance of Power in North America, 1815–1908* (Berkeley, Calif., 1967); Sydney F. Wise and Robert C. Brown, *Canada Views the United States: Nineteenth Century Political Attitudes* (Seattle, 1967); Thomas N. Brown, *Irish-American Nationalism, 1870–1890* (Philadelphia, 1966); James O. McCabe, *The San Juan Water Boundary Question* (Toronto, 1964); Donald F. Warner, *The Idea of Continental Union: Agitation for the Annexation of Canada to the United States, 1849–1893* (Lexington, Ky., 1960); Robin W. Winks, *Canada and the United States: The Civil War Years* (Baltimore, 1960); Florence E. Gibson, *The Attitudes of the New York Irish toward State and National Affairs, 1848–1892* (New York, 1951); William D'Arcy, *The Fenian Movement in the United States, 1858–1886* (Washington, 1947); Hunter Miller, *San Juan Archipelago: Study of the Joint Occupation of San Juan Islands* (Bellows Falls, Vt., 1943); Goldwin Smith, *The Treaty of Washington, 1871: A Study in Imperial History* (Ithaca, N.Y., 1941); Lester B. Shippee, *Canadian-American Relations, 1849–1874* (New Haven, 1939); and James M. Callahan, *American Foreign Policy in Canadian Relations* (New York, 1937).

Other pertinent specialized and biographical studies are: Philip S. Foner, *A History of Cuba and Its Relations with the United States* (2 vols., New York, 1962) and French E. Chadwick, *The Relations of the United States with Spain: Diplomacy* (New York, 1909), for the *Virginius* affair; William M. Armstrong, *E. L. Godkin and American Foreign Policy, 1865–1900* (New York, 1957); Allan Nevins, *Hamilton Fish: The Inner History of the Grant Administration* (rev. ed., 2 vols., New York, 1957); Roy F. Nichols, *Advance Agents of American Destiny* (Philadelphia, 1956); Chester L. Barrows, *William M. Evarts: Lawyer, Diplomat, Statesman* (Chapel Hill, N.C., 1941); Brainerd Dyer, *The Public Career of William M. Evarts* (Berkeley, Calif., 1933); and pertinent works cited for previous chapters.

CHAPTER TWELVE

The most useful general studies for the period are: John A. S. Grenville and George B. Young, *Politics, Strategy and American Diplomacy: Studies in Foreign Policy, 1873–1917* (New Haven, 1966); David M. Pletcher, *The Awkward Years: American Foreign Relations under Garfield and Arthur* (Columbia, Mo., 1962); William M. Armstrong, *E. L. Godkin and American Foreign Policy, 1865–1900* (New York, 1957); Edward Younger, *John A. Kasson: Politics and Diplomacy from Lincoln to McKinley* (Iowa City, 1955); Charles C. Tansill, *The Foreign Policy of Thomas F. Bayard, 1885–1897* (New York, 1940); Albert J. Volwiler, *The Correspondence between Benjamin Harrison and James G. Blaine. 1882–1893* (Philadelphia, 1940); Allan Nevins, *Grover Cleveland: A Study in Courage* (New York, 1932); and Alice F.

Tyler, *The Foreign Policy of James G. Blaine* (Minneapolis, 1927). See also Kenneth J. Hagan, *American Gunboat Diplomacy and the Old Navy, 1877–1889* (Westport, Conn., 1973); Peter Karsten, *The Naval Aristocracy: The Golden Age of Annapolis and the Emergence of Modern American Navalism* (New York, 1972); and Walter R. Herrick, Jr., *The American Naval Revolution* (Baton Rouge, La., 1966).

On canal diplomacy and Latin American policy, see Frederick B. Pike, *Chile and the United States, 1880–1962: The Emergence of Chile's Social Crisis and the Challenge to United States Diplomacy* (Notre Dame, Ind., 1963); Daniel Cosío Villegas, *The United States versus Porfirio Díaz,* Nettie Lee Benson, trans. (Lincoln, Nebr., 1963); Thomas F. McGann, *Argentina, the United States, and the Inter-American System, 1880–1914* (Cambridge, Mass., 1957); Herbert Millington, *American Diplomacy and the War of the Pacific* (New York, 1948); Miles P. Du Val, Jr., *Cadiz to Cathay: The Story of the Long Diplomatic Struggle for the Panama Canal* (2nd. ed., Stanford, Calif., 1947); Harold Lindsell, *The Chilean-American Controversy of 1891–1892* (New York, 1943); E. Taylor Parks, *Colombia and the United States, 1765–1934* (Durham, N.C., 1935); Henry C. Evans, Jr., *Chile and Its Relations with the United States* (Durham, N.C., 1927); William R. Sherman, *The Diplomatic and Commercial Relations of the United States and Chile, 1820–1914* (Boston, 1926); and Harold and Margaret Sprout, *The Rise of American Naval Power, 1776–1918* (rev. ed., Princeton, 1946).

For relations with Germany and Italy, see Alexander DeConde, *Half Bitter, Half Sweet: An Excursion into Italian-American History* (New York, 1971); Otto zu Stolberg-Wernigerode, *Germany and the United States of America during the Era of Bismarck,* trans. from the German by Otto E. Lessing (Reading, Pa., 1937); Alfred Vagts, *Deutschland und die Vereinigten Staaten in der Weltpolitik* (2 vols., New York, 1935); John G. Gazley, *American Opinion of German Unification, 1848–1871* (New York, 1926); Clara E. Schieber, *The Transformation of American Sentiment toward Germany, 1870–1914* (Boston, 1923); and Jeannette Keim, *Forty Years of German-American Political Relations* (Philadelphia, 1919).

For China and Chinese immigration, important studies are: Alexander Saxton, *The Indispensable Enemy: Labor and the Anti-Chinese Movement in California* (Berkeley, Calif., 1975); Francis L. K. Hsu, *The Challenge of the American Dream: The Chinese in the United States* (Belmont, Calif., 1971), an anthropological analysis; Stuart C. Miller, *The Unwelcome Immigrant: The American Image of the Chinese, 1785–1882* (Berkeley, Calif., 1969); Gunther Barth, *Bitter Strength: A History of the Chinese in the United States, 1850–1870* (Cambridge, Mass., 1964); Rose Hum Lee, *The Chinese in the United States of America* (Hong Kong, 1960); Elmer C. Sandmeyer, *The Anti-Chinese Movement in California* (Urbana, Ill., 1939); R. D. McKenzie, *Oriental Exclusion* (New York, 1927); Tien Lu Li, *Congressional Policy of Chinese Immigration* (Nashville, Tenn., 1916); and Mary R. Coolidge, *Chinese Immigration* (New York, 1909).

For fisheries, seals, and other problems, see Robert C. Brown, *Canada's National Policy, 1883–1900: A Study in Canadian-American Relations* (Princeton, 1964); John B. Brebner, *North Atlantic Triangle: The Interplay of Canada, the United States, and Great Britain* (New Haven, 1945); and Charles C. Tansill, *Canadian-American Relations, 1975–1911* (New Haven, 1943). See also pertinent references cited for previous chapters.

CHAPTER THIRTEEN

For imperialism and the new manifest destiny, see Rubin F. Weston, *Racism in U.S. Imperialism: The Influence of Racial Assumptions on American Foreign Policy,*

1893–1946 (Columbia, S. C., 1972); David Healy, *U.S. Expansionism: The Imperialist Urge in the 1890s* (Madison, Wis., 1970); William A. Williams, *Roots of the Modern American Empire* (New York, 1969); Ernest R. May, *American Imperialism: A Speculative Essay* (New York, 1968); May, *Imperial Democracy: The Emergence of America as a Great Power* (New York, 1961); Edward M. Burns, *The American Idea of Mission: Concepts of National Purpose and Destiny* (New Brunswick, N.J., 1957); Hans Kohn, *American Nationalism: An Interpretative Essay* (New York, 1957); Walter La Feber, *The New Empire: An Interpretation of American Expansion, 1860–1898* (Ithaca, N.Y., 1956); Richard Hofstadter, *Social Darwinism in American Thought* (rev. ed., Philadelphia, 1955); William E. Livezey, *Mahan on Sea Power* (Norman, Okla., 1947); Ralph H. Gabriel, *The Course of American Democratic Thought* (New York, 1940); Julius W. Pratt, *Expansionists of 1898: The Acquisition of Hawaii and the Spanish Islands* (Baltimore, 1936); William L. Langer, *The Diplomacy of Imperialism, 1890–1902* (2 vols., New York, 1935); Albert K. Weinberg, *Manifest Destiny* (Baltimore, 1935); and Parker T. Moon, *Imperialism and World Politics* (New York, 1926).

Useful surveys or special studies are: Edward P. Crapol, *America for Americans: Economic Nationalism and Anglophobia in the Late Nineteenth Century* (Westport, Conn., 1973); Tom E. Terrill, *The Tariff, Politics, and American Foreign Policy, 1874–1901* (Westport, Conn., 1973); Foster R. Dulles, *Prelude to World Power: American Diplomatic History, 1860–1900* (New York, 1965); Dulles, *The Imperial Years* (New York, 1956); Dulles, *America in the Pacific* (New York, 1932); Doris A. Graber, *Crisis Diplomacy: A History of U.S. Intervention Policies* (Washington, 1959); George R. Dulebohn, *Principles of Foreign Policy under the Cleveland Administrations* (Philadelphia, 1941); William Stull Holt, *Treaties Defeated by the Senate* (Baltimore, 1933); and Alfred L. P. Dennis, *Adventures in American Diplomacy, 1876–1906* (Boston, 1928).

On Samoan diplomacy there is: Paul Kennedy, *The Samoan Tangle: A Study in Anglo-German-American Relations, 1878–1900* (New York, 1974); Edwin P. Hoyt, *The Typhon that Stopped a War* (New York, 1967); Ernest P. Dodge, *New England and the South Seas* (Cambridge, Mass., 1965); Jean I. Brookes, *International Rivalry in the Pacific Islands, 1800–1875* (Berkeley, Calif., 1941); Sylvia Masterman, *The Origins of International Rivalry in Samoa, 1845–1884* (Stanford, Calif., 1934); and George H. Ryden, *The Foreign Policy of the United States in Relation to Samoa* (New Haven, 1933). For rivalry in the Congo see Edward W. Chester, *Clash of Titans: Africa and U.S. Foreign Policy* (Maryland, N.Y., 1974); Clarence C. Clendenen, Robert Collins, and Peter Duignan, *Americans in Africa, 1865–1900* (Stanford, Calif., 1966); David M. Pletcher, *The Awkward Years* (Columbia, Mo., 1962); and Edward Younger, *John A. Kasson* (Iowa City, 1955).

For Hawaii, see Merze Tate, *Hawaii: Reciprocity or Annexation* (East Lansing, Mich., 1968); Tate, *The United States and the Hawaiian Kingdom: A Political History* (New Haven, 1965); Ralph S. Kuykendall, *The Hawaiian Kingdom, 1874–1893: The Kalakua Dynasty* (Honolulu, 1967); Kuykendall, *The Hawaiian Kingdom, 1842–1898* (Honolulu, 1953); Kuykendall, *The Hawaiian Kingdom, 1778–1854* (Honolulu, 1938); William A. Russ, Jr., *The Hawaiian Republic (1894–1898),* (Selinsgrove, Pa., 1961); Russ, Jr., *The Hawaiian Revolution (1893–1894),* (Selinsgrove, Pa., 1959); Theodore Morgan, *Hawaii: A Century of Economic Change, 1778–1876* (Cambridge, Mass., 1948); Sylvester K. Stevens, *American Expansion in Hawaii, 1842–1898* (Harrisburg, Pa., 1945); and Harold W. Bradley, *The American Frontier in Hawaii: The Pioneers, 1789–1848* (Stanford, Calif., 1942). See also John A. Andrew III, *Rebuilding the Christian Commonwealth: New England Congregationalists and Foreign Missions, 1800–1830* (Lexington, Ky., 1976).

For the Venezuela affair and pertinent biographical studies, see Gerald G.

Eggert, *Richard Olney: Evolution of a Statesman* (University Park, Pa., 1974); Bradford Perkins, *The Great Rapprochement: England and the United States, 1895–1914* (New York, 1968); John A. S. Grenville, *Lord Salisbury and Foreign Policy: The Close of the Nineteenth Century* (London, 1964); Alexander E. Campbell, *Great Britain and the United States, 1895–1903* (London, 1960); Howard K. Beale, *Theodore Roosevelt and the Rise of America to World Power* (Baltimore, 1956); Lionel M. Gelber, *The Rise of Anglo-American Friendship* (London, 1938); Dexter Perkins, *The Monroe Doctrine, 1867–1907* (Baltimore, 1937); and Allan Nevins, *Henry White— Thirty Years of American Diplomacy* (New York, 1930). See also pertinent references previously cited.

CHAPTER FOURTEEN

Important accounts of the war and its diplomacy are in: Philip S. Foner, *The Spanish-Cuban-American War and the Birth of American Imperialism, 1895–1902* (2 vols., New York, 1972); Paolo E. Coletta, ed., *Threshold to American Internationalism: Essays on the Foreign Policies of William McKinley* (New York, 1970); John A. S. Grenville and George B. Young, *Politics, Strategy, and American Diplomacy: Studies in Foreign Policy, 1873–1917* (New Haven, 1966); H. Wayne Morgan, *America's Road to Empire: The War with Spain and Overseas Expansion* (New York, 1965); Walter La Feber, *The New Empire: An Interpretation of American Expansion, 1860–1898* (Ithaca, N.Y., 1956); Ernest R. May, *Imperial Democracy: The Emergence of America as a Great Power* (New York, 1961); Margaret Leech, *In the Days of McKinley* (New York, 1959); Howard K. Beale, *Theodore Roosevelt and the Rise of America to World Power* (Baltimore, 1956); Foster R. Dulles, *The Imperial Years;* Frank Freidel, *The Splendid Little War* (Boston, 1958); Wilfrid H. Callcott, *The Caribbean Policy of the United States, 1890–1920* (Baltimore, 1942); Orestes Ferrara, *The Last Spanish War: Revelations in "Diplomacy,"* trans. from the Spanish by William E. Shea (New York, 1937); Julius W. Pratt, *Expansionists of 1898;* Walter Millis, *The Martial Spirit: A Study of Our War with Spain* (New York, 1931); French E. Chadwick, *The Relations of the United States with Spain: The Spanish-American War* (2 vols., New York, 1911); Chadwick, *The Relations of the United States with Spain: Diplomacy* (New York, 1909); Elbert J. Benton, *International Law and Diplomacy of the Spanish-American War* (Baltimore, 1908); Horace E. Flack, *Spanish-American Diplomatic Relations Preceding the War of 1898* (Baltimore, 1906); and Pascual Cervera, ed., *The Spanish-American War* (Washingon, 1899), a collection of Spanish documents.

For specialized studies on military aspects see Hyman G. Rickover, *How the Battleship* Maine *Was Destroyed* (Washington, 1976), which concludes that an internal explosion sank the ship; Richard D. Challener, *Admirals, Generals, and American Foreign Policy, 1898–1914* (Princeton, 1973); Graham A. Cosmas, *An Army for Empire: The United States Army in the Spanish-American War* (Columbia, Mo., 1971); James H. Hitchman, *Leonard Wood and Cuban Independence, 1898–1902* (The Hague, 1971); Jack Cameron, *A Leap to Arms: The Cuban Campaign of 1898* (Philadelphia, 1970); and William R. Braisted, *The United States Navy in the Pacific, 1897–1909* (Austin, Tex., 1958). For public opinion, racial attitudes, and newspapers, see Willard B. Gatewood, Jr., *Black Americans and the White Man's Burden, 1898–1903* (Urbana, Ill., 1975); Gerald F. Linderman, *The Mirror of War: American Society and the Spanish-American War* (Ann Arbor, Mich., 1974); George P. Marks, III, ed., *The Black Press Views American Imperialism (1898–1900),* (New York, 1971); Samuel E. Morison, Frederick Merk, and Frank Freidel, *Dissent in Three American Wars;* Charles H. Brown, *The Correspondents' War:*

Journalists in the Spanish-American War (New York, 1967); Jacob E. Wisan, *The Cuban Crisis as Reflected in the New York Press, 1895–1898* (New York, 1934); and Marcus M. Wilkerson, *Public Opinion and the Spanish-American War: A Study in War Propaganda* (Baton Rouge, La., 1932). For the Philippine War and related aspects, see Peter W. Stanley, *A Nation in the Making: The Philippines and the United States, 1899–1921* (Cambridge, Mass., 1974); John M. Gates, *Schoolbooks and Krags: The United States Army in the Philippines, 1898–1902* (Westport, Conn., 1973); William J. Pomeroy, *American Neo-Colonialism: Its Emergence in the Philippines and Asia* (New York, 1970); Henry F. Graff, ed., *American Imperialism and the Philippine Insurrection* (Boston, 1969); Bonifacio S. Salamanca, *The Filipino Reaction to American Rule, 1901–1913* (Hamden, Conn., 1968); and Leon Wolff, *Little Brown Brother: How the United States Purchased and Pacified the Philippine Islands at the Century's Turn* (New York, 1961).

For anti-imperialism, see Daniel B. Schirmer, *Republic or Empire: American Resistance to the Philippine War* (Cambridge, Mass., 1972); E. Berkeley Tompkins, *Anti-Imperialism in the United States: The Great Debate, 1890–1920* (Philadelphia, 1970); and Robert L. Beisner, *Twelve Against Empire: The Anti-Imperialists, 1898–1900* (New York, 1968). On relations with Britain and other European nations, see Bradford Perkins, *The Great Rapprochement: England and the United States, 1895–1914* (New York, 1968); R. G. Neale, *Great Britain and United States Expansion, 1898–1900* (East Lansing, Mich., 1966); Alexander E. Campbell, *Great Britain and the United States, 1895–1903* (London, 1960); Charles S. Campbell, Jr., *Anglo-American Understanding, 1898–1903* (Baltimore, 1957); Richard H. Heindel, *The American Impact on Great Britain, 1898–1914: A Study of the United States in World History* (Philadelphia, 1940); Lionel M. Gelber, *The Rise of Anglo-American Friendship* (London, 1938); and Bertha A. Reuter, *Anglo-American Relations during the Spanish-American War* (New York, 1924).

For biographical and other specialized studies, see Kenton J. Clymer, *John Hay: The Gentleman as Diplomat* (Ann Arbor, Mich., 1975); H. Wayne Morgan, *William McKinley and His America* (Syracuse, 1963); Whitney T. Perkins, *Denial of Empire: The United States and Its Dependencies* (Leyden, 1962); William H. Harbaugh, *Power and Responsibility: The Life and Times of Theodore Roosevelt* (New York, 1961); W. A. Swanberg, *Citizen Hearst: A Biography of William Randolph Hearst* (New York, 1961); William A. Williams, *The Tragedy of American Diplomacy* (Cleveland, 1959); Louis Halle, *Dream and Reality: Aspects of American Foreign Policy* (New York, 1958); John E. Weems, *The Fate of the Maine* (New York, 1958); Richard W. Leopold, *Elihu Root and the Conservative Tradition* (Boston, 1954); Earl S. Pomeroy, *Pacific Outpost: American Strategy in Guam and Micronesia* (Stanford, Calif., 1951); Julius W. Pratt, *America's Colonial Experiment* (New York, 1950); Tyler Dennett, *John Hay: From Poetry to Politics* (New York, 1938); Merle E. Curti, *Peace or War: The American Struggle, 1636–1936* (New York, 1936); Henry F. Pringle, *Theodore Roosevelt* (New York, 1931); and Alfred L. P. Dennis, *Adventures in American Diplomacy, 1896–1906* (New York, 1928). See also pertinent studies cited earlier.

CHAPTER FIFTEEN

For the Open Door policy and the international politics of Asia, see Delber L. McKee, *Chinese Exclusion versus the Open Door Policy, 1900–1906: Clashes over China Policy in the Roosevelt Era* (Detroit, 1976); Jeffery M. Dorwart, *The Pigtail War: American Involvement in the Sino-Japanese War of 1894–1895* (Amherst, Mass., 1975); John K. Fairbank, ed., *The Missionary Enterprise in China and America*

(Cambridge, Mass., 1974); Michael H. Hunt, *Frontier Defense and the Open Door: Manchuria in Chinese-American Relations, 1895–1911* (New Haven, 1973); Akira Iriye, *Pacific Estrangement: Japanese and American Expansion, 1897–1911* (Cambridge, Mass., 1972); Robert McLellan, *The Heathen Chinese: A Study of American Attitudes toward China, 1890–1905* (Columbus, Ohio, 1971); Yur-Bok Lee, *Diplomatic Relations Between the United States and Korea, 1866–1887* (New York, 1970); Paul A. Varg, *Open Door Diplomat: The Life of W. W. Rockhill* (Urban, Ill., 1952); *The Making of a Myth: The United States and China, 1897–1912* (East Lansing, Mich., 1968); Varg, *Missionaries, Chinese, and Diplomats* (Princeton, 1958); Eugene P. Trani, *The Treaty of Portsmouth: An Adventure in American Diplomacy* (Lexington, Ky., 1969); Stuart C. Miller, *American Ideas of a Special Relationship with China, 1784–1900* (Cambridge, Mass., 1968); Marilyn B. Young, *The Rhetoric of Empire: American China Policy, 1895–1901* (Cambridge, Mass., 1968); Thomas J. McCormick, *China Market: America's Quest for Informal Empire, 1893–1901* (Chicago, 1967); Charles E. Neu, *An Uncertain Friendship: Theodore Roosevelt and Japan, 1906–1909* (Cambridge, Mass., 1967); Raymond A. Esthus, *Theodore Roosevelt and Japan* (Seattle, 1966); Ian H. Nish, *The Anglo-Japanese Alliance: The Diplomacy of Two Island Empires, 1894–1907* (London, 1966); Edmund S. Wehrle, *Britain, China, and the Antimissionary Riots, 1891–1900* (Minneapolis, 1966); Robert A. Hart, *The Great White Fleet: Its Voyage Around the World, 1907–1909* (Boston, 1965); John A. White, *The Diplomacy of the Russo-Japanese War* (Princeton, 1964); Roger Daniels, *The Politics of Prejudice: The Anti-Japanese Movement in California and the Struggle for Japanese Exclusion* (Berkeley, Calif., 1962); Lawrence H. Battistini, *The United States and Asia* (New York, 1955); Charles S. Campbell, Jr., *Special Business Interests and the Open Door Policy* (New Haven, 1951); Garel A. Grunder, *The Philippines and the United States* (Norman, Okla., 1951); George F. Kennan, *American Diplomacy, 1900–1950* (Chicago, 1951); Dutten J. Clinard, *Japan's Influences on American Naval Power, 1897–1917* (Berkeley, Calif., 1947); Foster R. Dulles, *China and America* (Princeton, 1946); Fred H. Harrington, *God, Mammon, and the Japanese: Dr. Horace N. Allen and Korean-American Relations, 1884–1905* (Madison, Wis., 1944); Alfred W. Griswold, *The Far Eastern Policy of the United States* (New York, 1938); Stephen C. Y. Pan, *American Diplomacy Concerning Manchuria* (Providence, R.I., 1938); Payson J. Treat, *Diplomatic Relations Between the United States and Japan, 1895–1905* (Stanford, Calif., 1938); Thomas A. Bailey, *Theodore Roosevelt and the Japanese-American Crises* (Stanford, Calif., 1934); Tyler Dennett, *Roosevelt and the Russo-Japanese War* (Garden City, N.Y., 1925); and Dennett, *Americans in Eastern Asia* (New York, 1922).

On relations with Russia in this period, consult William A. Williams, *American-Russian Relations, 1781–1917* (New York, 1952); Thomas A. Bailey, *America Faces Russia* (Ithaca, N.Y., 1950); Pauline Tompkins, *American-Russian Relations in the Far East* (New York, 1949); and Edward H. Zabriskie, *American-Russian Rivalry in the Far East, 1895–1914* (Philadelphia, 1946).

For canal diplomacy and relations with Latin America, see David G. McCullough, *The Path Between the Seas: The Creation of the Panama Canal, 1870–1914* (New York, 1977); Lawrence O. Ealy, *Yanqui Politics and the Isthmian Canal* (University Park, Pa., 1971); James H. Hitchman, *Leonard Wood and Cuban Independence, 1898–1902* (The Hague, 1971); Wilfrid H. Callcott, *The Western Hemisphere: Its Influence on United States Policies to the End of World War II* (Austin, Tex., 1968); Lester D. Langley, *The Cuban Policy of the United States: A Brief History* (New York, 1968); Allan R. Millet, *The Politics of Intervention: The Military Occupation of Cuba, 1906–1909* (Columbus, Ohio, 1968); Sheldon B. Liss, *The Canal: Aspects of United States-Panamanian Relations* (Notre Dame, Ind., 1967); E. Brandford Burns, *The Unwritten Alliance: Rio Branco and Brazilian-American Relations* (New York, 1966);

Dana G. Munro, *Intervention and Dollar Diplomacy in the Caribbean, 1900–1921* (Princeton, 1964); David F. Healy, *The United States in Cuba, 1898–1902: Generals, Politicians, and the Search for Policy* (Madison, Wis., 1963); Thomas F. McGann, *Argentina, the United States, and the Inter-American System, 1880–1914* (Cambridge, Mass., 1957); Miles P. Du Val, Jr., *Cadiz to Cathay: The Story of the Long Diplomatic Struggle for the Panama Canal,* (2nd ed., Standford, Calif., 1947); Du Val, Jr., *The Mountains Will Move: The Story of the Building of the Panama Canal* (Stanford, Calif., 1947); Gerstle Mack, *The Land Divided* (New York, 1944); Samuel F. Bemis, *The Latin American Policy of the United States* (New York, 1943); Wilfrid H. Callcott, *The Caribbean Policy of the United States, 1890–1920* (Baltimore, 1942); Dwight C. Miner, *The Fight for the Panama Route* (New York, 1940); J. Fred Rippy, *The Caribbean Danger Zone* (New York, 1940); Rippy, *The Capitalists and Colombia* (New York, 1931); David A. Lockmiller, *Magoon in Cuba: A History of the Second Intervention, 1906–1909* (Chapel Hill, N.C., 1938); William D. McCain, *The United States and the Republic of Panama* (Durham, N.C., 1937); E. Taylor Parks, *Colombia and the United States, 1765–1934* (Durham, N.C., 1935); Russell H. Fitzgibbon, *Cuba and the United States, 1900–1935* (Menasha, Wis., 1935); Dana G. Munro, *The United States and the Caribbean Area* (Boston, 1934); and Howard C. Hill, *Roosevelt and the Caribbean* (Chicago, 1927).

Other noteworthy specialized and biographical studies are: Göran Rystand, *Ambiguous Imperialism: American Foreign Policy and Domestic Politics at the Turn of the Century* (Lund, Sweden, 1975); Gabriel Kolko, *Main Currents in Modern American History* (New York, 1976); Richard D. Challener, *Admirals, Generals, and American Foreign Policy, 1898–1914* (Princeton, 1973); Raymond A. Esthus, *Theodore Roosevelt and the International Rivalries* (Waltham, Mass., 1970); Arnold H. Taylor, *American Diplomacy and the Narcotics Traffic, 1900–1839: A Study in International Humanitarian Reform* (Durham, N.C., 1969); David H. Burton, *Theodore Roosevelt: Confident Imperialist* (Philadelphia, 1968); Julius W. Pratt, *Challenge and Rejection, 1900–1921* (New York, 1967); A. L. Tibawi, *American Interests in Syria, 1800–1901* (Oxford, 1966); Howard K. Beale, *Theodore Roosevelt and the Rise of America to World Power* (Baltimore, 1956); Richard W. Leopold, *Elihu Root and the Conservative Tradition* (Boston, 1954); Robert E. Osgood, *Ideals and Self-Interest in America's Foreign Relations: The Great Transformation of the Twentieth Century* (Chicago, 1953); Allan Nevins, *Henry White: Thirty Years of American Diplomacy* (New York, 1930); and Charles C. Tansill, *The Purchase of the Danish West Indies* (Baltimore, 1932). Works pertinent to this period are also cited in preceding chapters.

CHAPTER SIXTEEN

For the Moroccan crisis, see Howard K. Beale, *Theodore Roosevelt and the Rise of America to World Power* (Baltimore, 1956); Eugene N. Anderson, *The First Moroccan Crisis, 1904–1906* (Chicago, 1930); Allan Nevins, *Henry White: Thirty Years of American Diplomacy* (New York, 1930); Alfred L. P. Dennis, *Adventures in American Diplomacy, 1896–1906* (New York, 1928); and a survey, Julius W. Pratt, *Challenge and Rejection, 1900–1921* (New York, 1967).

On Anglo-American problems, see Bradford Perkins, *The Great Rapprochement: England and the United States, 1895–1914* (New York, 1968); Alexander E. Campbell, *Great Britain and the United States, 1895–1903* (London, 1960); Charles S. Campbell, Jr., *Anglo-American Understanding, 1898–1903* (Baltimore, 1957); Harry C. Allen, *Great Britain and the United States: A History of Anglo-American Relations, 1783–1952* (New York, 1955); and Lionel M. Gelber, *The Rise of Anglo-American Friendship* (London, 1938). On special problems, see Norman

Penlington, *The Alaska Boundary Dispute: A Critical Reappraisal* (Toronto, 1972);
Alan J. Ward, *Ireland and Anglo-American Relations, 1899–1921* (London, 1969);
Hugh L. Keenleyside and Gerald S. Brown, *Canada and the United States* (rev. ed.,
New York, 1952); Charles C. Tansill, *Canadian-American Relations, 1875–1911*
(New Haven, 1943); L. Ethan Ellis, *Reciprocity of 1911* (New Haven, 1939); and
John H. Ferguson, *American Diplomacy and the Boer War* (Philadelphia, 1939).
   Details on the Hague conferences, peace movement, and international orga-
nization may be found in David S. Patterson, *Toward a Warless World: The Travail
of the American Peace Movement, 1887–1914* (Bloomington, Ind., 1976); Calvin D.
Davis, *The United States and the Second Hague Peace Conference: American Diplomacy
and International Organization, 1899–1914* (Durham, N.C., 1976); Davis, *The
United States and the First Hague Conference* (Ithaca, N.Y., 1962); Roland Marchand,
The American Peace Movement and Social Reform, 1898–1918 (Princeton, 1973);
Warren F. Kuehl, *Seeking World Order: The United States and International Organiza-
tion to 1920* (Nashville, Tenn., 1969); Merze Tate, *The Disarmament Illusion: The
Movement for a Limitation of Armaments to 1907* (New York, 1942); Merle E. Curti,
Peace or War: The American Struggle, 1636–1936 (New York, 1936); James B.
Scott, *The Hague Peace Conferences of 1899 and 1907* (2 Vols., Baltimore, 1909);
and Frederick W. Holls, *The Peace Conference at the Hague, and Its Bearing on Inter-
national Law and Policy* (New York, 1900).
   For Dollar Diplomacy in Asia, see Michael H. Hunt, *Frontier Defense and the
Open Door: Manchuria in Chinese-American Relations, 1895–1911* (New Haven,
1973); Richard D. Challener, *Admirals, Generals, and American Foreign Policy,
1898–1914* (Princeton, 1973); Jerry Israel, *Progressivism and the Open Door: America
and China, 1905–1921* (Pittsburgh, 1971); Walter V. and Marie V. Scholes, *The
Foreign Policies of the Taft Administration* (Columbia, Mo., 1970); Paul A Varg, *The
Making of a Myth: The United States and China, 1897–1912* (East Lansing, Mich.,
1968); Charles Vevier, *The United States and China, 1906–1913: A Study of Finance
and Diplomacy* (New Brunswick, N.J. 1955); Pauline Tompkins, *American-Russian
Relations in the Far East* (New York, 1949); Edward H. Zabriskie, *American-Russian
Rivalry in the Far East, 1895–1914* (Philadelphia, 1946); A. Whitney Griswold,
The Far Eastern Policy of the United States (New York, 1938); Stephen C.Y. Pan,
American Diplomacy Concerning Manchuria (Providence, R.I., 1938); John G. Reid,
The Manchu Abdication and the Powers, 1908–1912 (Berkeley, Calif., 1935); and
Scott Nearing and Joseph Freeman, *Dollar Diplomacy: A Study in American Imperial-
ism* (New York, 1925).
   For relations with Japan and Wilson's diplomacy in Asia, see Akira Iriye,
Pacific Estrangement: Japanese and American Expansion, 1879–1911 (Cambridge,
Mass., 1972); Iriye, *Across the Pacific: An Inner History of American-East Asian Rela-
tions* (New York, 1967); William R. Braisted, *The United States Navy in the Pacific,
1909–1922* (Austin, Tex., 1970); Madeleine S. Chi, *The Chinese Question During the
First World War* (Cambridge, Mass., 1970); Ian Nish, *The Anglo-Japanese Alliance:
The Diplomacy of Two Island Empires, 1894–1907* (London, 1966); William L.
Neumann, *America Encounters Japan: From Perry to MacArthur* (Baltimore, 1963);
Roger Daniels, *The Politics of Prejudice: The Anti-Japanese Movement in California and
the Struggle for Japanese Exclusion* (Berkeley, Calif., 1962); Burton F. Beers, *Vain
Endeavor: Robert Lansing's Attempt to End the American-Japanese Rivalry* (Durham,
N.C., 1962); Roy W. Curry, *Woodrow Wilson and Far Eastern Policy, 1913–1921*
(New York, 1957); Russell H. Fifield, *Woodrow Wilson and the Far East: The
Diplomacy of the Shantung Question* (New York, 1952); Tien-yi Li, *Woodrow Wilson's
China Policy, 1913–1917* (New York, 1952); and Harley Notter, *The Origins of the
Foreign Policy of Woodrow Wilson* (Baltimore, 1937).
   Noteworthy biographical studies for this period are: Henry F. Pringle, *The*

Life and Times of William Howard Taft (2 vols., New York, 1939); Herbert Croly, *Willard Straight* (New York, 1924); John A. Garraty, *Henry Cabot Lodge: A Biography* (New York, 1953); and Ralph E. Minger, *William Howard Taft and United States Foreign Policy: The Apprenticeship Years, 1900–1908* (Urbana, Ill., 1975). See also pertinent titles cited previously.

CHAPTER SEVENTEEN

Studies that cover various aspects of Dollar Diplomacy in Latin America are: Warren G. Kneer, *Great Britain and the Caribbean, 1901–1913: A Study in Anglo-American Relations* (East Lansing, Mich., 1975); Richard D. Challener, *Admirals, Generals, and American Foreign Policy, 1898–1914* (Princeton, 1973); Walter V. and Marie V. Scholes, *The Foreign Policies of the Taft Administration* (Columbia, Mo., 1970); Wilfrid H. Callcott, *The Western Hemisphere: Its Influence on United States Policies to the End of World War II* (Austin, Tex., 1968) and his *The Caribbean Policy of the United States, 1890–1920* (Baltimore, 1942); Dexter Perkins, *The United States and the Caribbean* (rev. ed., Cambridge, Mass., 1966); Dana G. Munro, *Intervention and Dollar Diplomacy in the Caribbean, 1900–1921* (Princeton, 1964); and his *The United States and the Caribbean Area* (Boston, 1934); Doris A. Graber, *Crisis Diplomacy: A History of U.S. Intervention Policies and Practices* (Washington, 1959); Samuel F. Bemis, *The Latin American Policy of the United States* (New York, 1943); P. Edward Haley, *The Diplomacy of Taft and Wilson with Mexico, 1910–1917* (Cambridge, Mass., 1970); Herbert M. Mason, Jr., *The Great Pursuit* (New York, 1970), dealing with Pershing in Mexico; Kenneth J. Grieb, *The United States and Huerta* (Lincoln, Nebr., 1969); Clarence C. Clendenen, *Blood on the Border: The United States Army and the Mexican Irregulars* (New York, 1969) and his *The United States and Pancho Villa: A Study in Unconventional Diplomacy* (Ithaca, N.Y., 1961); Peter Calvert, *The Mexican Revolution, 1910–1914: The Diplomacy of Anglo-American Conflict* (Cambridge, Mass., 1968); Howard F. Cline, *The United States and Mexico* (rev. ed., Cambridge, Mass., 1963); Robert E. Quirk, *An Affair of Honor: Woodrow Wilson and the Occupation of Veracruz* (Lexington, Ky., 1962) and his *The Mexican Revolution, 1914–1915* (Bloomington, Ind., 1960); Isidro Fabela, *Historia Diplomática de la Revolución Mexicana, 1912–1917* (2 vols., Mexico City, 1958–1959); Frank Tannenbaum, *Mexico: The Struggle for Peace and Bread* (New York, 1950); George M. Stephenson, *John Lind of Minnesota* (Minneapolis, 1935); James M. Callahan and Melvin M. Knight, *The Americans in Santo Domingo* (New York, 1928).

For missionary diplomacy in the Caribbean, see David F. Healy, *Gunboat Diplomacy in the Wilson Era: The U.S. Navy in Haiti, 1915–1916* (Madison, Wis., 1976); Hans Schmidt, *The United States Occupation of Haiti, 1915–1934* (New Brunswick, N.J., 1971); Arthur S. Link, *Woodrow Wilson and the Progressive Era, 1910–1917* (New York, 1954); Ludwell L. Montague, *Haiti and the United States, 1714–1938* (Durham, N.C., 1940); Charles C. Tansill, *The Purchase of the Danish West Indies* (Baltimore, 1932); Arthur C. Millspaugh, *Haiti under American Control, 1915–1930* (Boston, 1931); Isaac J. Cox, *Nicaragua and the United States, 1909–1927* (Boston, 1927); and Carl Kelsey, *The American Intervention in Haiti and the Dominican Republic* (Philadelphia, 1922).

On relations with Mexico, see Jules Davids, *American Political and Economic Penetration of Mexico, 1877–1920* (New York, 1976); Larry D. Hill, *Emissaries to a Revolution: Woodrow Wilson's Executive Agents in Mexico* (Baton Rouge, La., 1973); Charles C. Cumberland, *Mexican Revolution: The Constitutionalist Years* (Austin, Tex., 1972), his *Mexican Revolution: Genesis under Madero* (Austin, Tex., 1952) and his *American Foreign Policy in Mexican Relations* (New York, 1932); Charles W. Hackett, *The Mexican Revolution and the United States, 1910–1926* (Boston, 1926); and J. Fred Rippy, *The United States and Mexico* (New York, 1926).

These studies are also useful: Arthur S. Link, *Wilson* (the first three volumes) (Princeton, 1947–1965); Paolo E. Coletta, *William Jennings Bryan* (3 vols., Lincoln, Nebr., 1964–69); and Harley Notter, *The Origins of the Foreign Policy of Woodrow Wilson* (Baltimore, 1937). See also pertinent titles previous cited.

INDEX